PENGU

SUPERWOM

Shirley Conran was th
Observer Colour Magazine and women's editor of
Daily Mail, where she launched the weekly women's
magazine 'Femail'. She also has great experience as a
textile designer and as a colour consultant and she has
designed her own paint range. She handled the publicity for the Women in Media campaign for legislation against sex discrimination and was on the
selection committee for the Council of Industrial
Design for eight years.

    Superwoman was published in 1975 and was
followed by *The Superwoman Yearbook*.

Shirley Conran

SUPERWOMAN IN ACTION

Penguin Books

Penguin Books Ltd, Harmondsworth, Middlesex, England
Penguin Books, 625 Madison Avenue, New York, New York 10022, U.S.A.
Penguin Books Australia Ltd, Ringwood, Victoria, Australia
Penguin Books Canada Ltd, 2801 John Street, Markham, Ontario, Canada L 3 R 1 B 4
Penguin Books (N.Z.) Ltd, 182–190 Wairau Road, Auckland 10, New Zealand

—

First published by Sidgwick & Jackson as *Superwoman 2* 1977
Published in Penguin Books 1979

—

Copyright © Shirley Conran, 1977
All rights reserved
Original line drawings by Anthony Reid Partnership,
M. Atcherley, M. Ricketts. M. Smythe, A. Sultie

—

Filmset in Great Britain by
Northumberland Press Ltd, Gateshead, Tyne and Wear
Printed and bound by
Richard Clay (The Chaucer Press) Ltd, Bungay, Suffolk
Filmset in Monophoto Times

For my god-daughters:

JESSICA PEARCE

LUCY ATKINS

ORIEL PRIZEMAN.

May they never have a dull moment.

Contents

BOOK ONE · SUPERWOMAN WORKS!

BOOK TWO · HOME MADE

BOOK THREE · SUPERWOMAN TAKES OFF!

x CONTENTS

Acknowledgements

For their enthusiasm, hard work, encouragement and criticism, I am particularly grateful to George Seddon and Mileva Ross, with whom it has been a pleasure to work. I also owe a lot to Mike Ricketts, Sonja Stern, Sonya Mills and Jill Beck of Scripts Limited, who somehow managed to decipher Linear C.

For their valuable assistance, I should also like to thank Celia Brayfield, Dave Hobday, Pauline Horrigan, Derek Dutton, John Prizeman, Gavin Lyall, Andrew Bicknell, Joan Durrant, Rosemary Lewis, Nann du Sautoy, Mary Allen, Kitty Groves, Eileen Totten, Moyra Henning, Philippa Lewis, Nicholas Clayton, Dee Wells, Eileen Sheed, Penny Jeffery, Dinah Wheeler, Ruth Mathews, Arthur Sanderson and Sons and the many other people and organizations who were kind enough to help me.

S. C.

Overture to Beginners

The first *Superwoman* was a book about housework and how to avoid it. The title was ironic because no one person could have done all the work that the traditional housewife was supposed to. Byron might well have written, 'Housework is of man's life a thing apart, 'tis woman's whole existence.'

What *is* a Superwoman? The answer is simple. She is not a woman who can do anything but a woman who avoids trying to do too much. She knows her own limitations and sticks happily within them; she realizes that Life is untidy and so are the children in it.

A Superwoman chickens out. She knows that perfection is Hell to live with and her standards are her own, rather than the idiotically high ones set by TV ads, magazines and other women (interwoman competition can be as cruel and gruelling and unnecessary as any of the traditional competition in a man's world).

Naturally, a Superwoman does as little housework as possible and this can be quite difficult; you have to be well organized to keep it in its place, which, as far as I'm concerned, is firmly underfoot. Good organization doesn't just happen naturally, any more than good sex. You have to learn how to do it and then put in a lot of practice, like the piano.

Another good reason for avoiding housework is in order to have more time for yourself. Because, as well as being the supporting cast of the entire family show, YOU ARE THE ONE AND ONLY STAR OF YOUR OWN LIFE.

So a Superwoman is sensibly selfish. It took me years to acquire the discipline, control and iron will that was necessary in order to stop doing things for other people and start doing things for myself. At first I told myself I didn't have the time. But then even if you work a regulation forty-hour week and sleep eight hours a night, you *still* have seventy-two hours a week left over (which is almost twice as long as a 'working' week) in which to do something that's stimulating or rewarding or at least *something*.

Otherwise, where does that time go? Down the drain, most of it. Life has a habit of slithering away unless you firmly sort out your priorities and put the rewarding things FIRST. Oddly enough, the rest then seems to somehow get done without much effort on your part. (Any executive knows that if you leave your pending tray long enough, you'll find you can throw most of it away.)

Any time you save is either time in which to do nothing (in which case you need no help from me) or time in which to achieve something, which is what this book is about. It is designed to help you make the most of what you've got: a family, a man, perhaps children (the most expensive modern luxury there is), friends, a home, perhaps a job, some free time and the Welfare State.

Superwoman in Action can help you to enjoy being *with* your family, as opposed to servicing them. It can help you get away from them, from time to time, and enjoy a rewarding life of your own, if that's what you need.

Perhaps you want a better home, or a better job (or any job, come to that), or an absorbing interest, or to feel that you are needed in this world? Perhaps you want all of those things or perhaps you want to change your life completely? If so, this is your blueprint.

Getting more out of your life may require a bit more forward thinking than usual, but there's no harm in that, provided that you don't aim too high and you keep things simple. In an increasingly complex, bureaucratic world a Superwoman aims (only aims, you notice) at simplicity. So if you think that some

of the things I suggest are too simple to write down, I disagree: you never know what you don't know.

If, like most of us, you also feel short of money, then you probably don't realize just how much you can get or what you can do for next to nothing. The leisure pursuits I mention generally cost as little as possible – sometimes nothing – and I've detailed the ways in which you can help yourself to some of the terrific Welfare State free-money benefits and the services that you are entitled to and for which you pay taxes. I didn't invent the rules: I'm only showing you how to play the game: *you* are the one who can win it.

BOOK

1

SUPERWOMAN WORKS!

How to Get Out of the House Profitably

If your life is full of happiness, pleasurable pursuits and absorbing work, if your devoted family never gives you any trouble, if your home ticks over effortlessly and there is no washing up waiting at this moment, you are indeed a Superwoman.

But if you feel that you want to get a bit *more* out of life, it's probably easier than you think to help yourself to a bigger, richer slice of the cake.

WHAT DO YOU WANT?

Perhaps you want a new, absorbing interest? Or a new way of life? Perhaps you want to get more money? Perhaps you want more self-confidence and fun? Perhaps you want a job, or a better job, or to train for a completely different sort of job? Perhaps you want to learn more about something,

or to get better qualifications and want some free money while you acquire them? Perhaps you miss children who have grown up and left the nest, or perhaps you want a bit of a rest from the ones that are still in it?

There are a lot of things you can enjoyably do with your time, including nothing at all. And nothing at all is probably what you feel like doing, if you have small children: in this situation, having any spare time is an impressive achievement. But looking after tiny babies can go on and on (it's habit-forming) long after that helpless tiny baby is taller than you.

Children are a joy and you wouldn't want yours any other way, but they can tie you down and exhaust you and leave you with no life of your own or time to think about it. As they grow older, they can nibble away at your self-confidence: a mother's place is in the wrong. Although this insidious eroding drip, drip, drip isn't exactly their fault and it isn't exactly your fault, the fact is that it *does* happen. You suddenly find yourself thinking 'I've got a wonderful family: I'm John's wife and I'm Brian's mother, but apart from that, who am I and what is there to prove it?' Or perhaps you don't even get around to wondering. Perhaps you just feel low or depressed and wonder 'is that all there is? Is that *it*?' This is why it's essential to have an interest of your own which you can keep up and keep apart from the rest of the family activities.

You may want a little more learning because you didn't take advantage of the educational opportunities that you had when you were young. (Very few people do.) Or perhaps you studied the wrong thing. If there is anything you regret not having learnt, why not do it now? It is not difficult to find local courses unless you are living in an isolated area or want to study something really esoteric. Going to courses will give you a chance to oil your possibly rusty brain, to fill in any educational gaps, and to practise working with other people and enjoy it.

You can aim low or high; a few evenings of talks or lectures, or a full-blown Open University course. If you aim low you are more likely to succeed and your first project (an end in itself) could also be the first step towards a more ambitious scheme. You can take day or evening part-time classes (a few colleges have crèches and playgroups, so it's worth checking this point), or

go on one of the very popular summer residential college courses. (The whole family can go to some of them. See Book 3, Superwoman Takes Off!, p. 381.)

Few people realize the enormous range of educational opportunities which are now available for women. (See 'How to get better educated', p. 85.)

There's another reason why this private time off should be an important part of your family life. You may be one of those mothers who find that you are not cut out for an *entirely* domestic life – that you need stimulation of a higher mental level than 'Magic Roundabout'. Or, inconceivable though it may seem when surrounded by your 1.8 golden-haired toddlers (national average), you may later want to take a job. Even if you don't want to work (assuming you have the choice) until your children have left the nest, how do you plan to fill those thirty years between forty-ish and seventyish? Two in three married women over forty are working outside the home and the numbers are increasing.

Perhaps you don't want paid work. Perhaps you just want a fascinating new interest or something *different* to happen. Perhaps you want to pick up a hobby that you abandoned years ago, or pursue the education you feel you missed. But perhaps you feel you haven't the time, the talent, the energy or the money? If so, prepare to be surprised. Because the time to start preparing for this amazing new life of yours is – NOW – and the first step is not to gain something, but to avoid losing it – your self-confidence.

This is the number one problem for women who return to work after having a family. One way to keep your self-confidence and discipline is to pursue a serious, continuing interest outside your family life, preferably where you meet other people and don't discuss measles, cooking, clothes or money. Another way is to listen to current affairs programmes on the radio: how *can* you be cut off when you have that amazing institution of ours, which is unrivalled in this world? Turn the knob and you get Jimmy Young, then turn it a bit further for 'World at One' or 'Woman's Hour'.

While you're enjoying yourself with your family (i.e. tied to your young ones) you're in an enviably good position to plan and prepare the next stage in your career or a completely new job, either part-time or full-time. *Now* is the time to try what you've always wanted to do – and get paid for it. While you're enjoying your happy home life, or counting the days till it's over, you could prepare for a new career. If you can find enough time, you might even sign up for a full- or part-time course in a subject that

really interests you and may eventually provide you with a decent salary.

Perhaps you don't want a job. Perhaps you've always wanted to take a university degree, or learn to type or to embroider altar cloths, with a view to setting up your own little cottage industry at some future date.

If you're feeling jaded or isolated remember that a short course is a good preliminary incubator to get you back into circulation, to jolt your mind into action, to prepare you for going back to work. Because going back to work can be as alarming as the first time you went to school. Self-confidence is confidence in your own, proven abilities plus the nerve, capacity and experience to flannel your way through any situation that you are likely to meet, and the lack of it can often be agonizing and crippling.

Self-confidence can fall suddenly, like a soufflé, for minor reasons, major reasons or none at all that you can see. It's only human to sometimes lack confidence for short or long periods. You may have reason to do so, but you're far more likely to exaggerate the reasons. When you lose confidence, your judgement goes as well. You can't tell the mountains from the molehills.

If you lack confidence it's important to know that you can gain or regain self-confidence. It's also important to know how to. Learn to assess yourself (see p. 41), get out of the home and meet people (see p. 6) and if things get worse, talk to a good friend about it. It's much easier to

assess accurately someone else's mole-hills as such and the very fact of explaining your feelings to someone else often clarifies and pinpoints your problem.

Again and again I have been told that the best way to get yourself out of a rut and recharge your self-confidence is to go to day or evening classes for a couple of hours a week to learn something you will really enjoy, such as squash, yoga or embroidery.

If you really do lack self-confidence, you might consider attending one of the special personal development courses for women who want to get back into the doing of things and feel that their minds are rusty. These courses have cheery, encouraging names, such as 'Fresh Horizon', 'Fresh Start' or 'Second Chance'. (See p. 52 for addresses.) They may be an intensive course for a day, a week, a month, part-time for a term or up to a year. You have to pay minimum college fees (from around £3 a course). Glorious enthusiasm has been shown by women who have been on these courses. They not only help to train your self-confidence but if necessary you can be advised about jobs or have further training arranged for you. If you feel that your self-confidence needs a boost, the government will, in some cases, send you on a charm course (at their expense) to improve your self-confidence and show you how to get a high-powered job (see p. 58 for PER).

One surprising exercise to improve your self-confidence is talking to men, or so I was told by a careers guidance officer who specializes in helping housebound women who feel shy or isolated. She added, 'You mustn't be isolated.' Isolation is bad for self-confidence. Getting outside your own front door and helping other people in a simple sort of way can have an amazing effect: it sounds trite to say that you can improve your life by joining a group but I've seen the changes and they are often dramatic. If you join a group you get responsibility outside the home, outside the family and children, and later you can show an employer that you haven't been a cabbage. It is very important to get involved in things in your community. An awful lot of good part-time jobs are got through personal contacts. If you're known in your community you get on to the grapevine, get to know new people, get to know the local system and know what's going on.

Another suggestion for banishing shyness is to get involved with new people by starting a little bit of community work, perhaps in a tenants' association, a parent/teacher association, a playgroup or a Hospital League of Friends.

There's no shortage of voluntary work which can not only be stimulating but may act as a valuable training for paid work later on. Ask your local library for details of local women's organizations. There may be a local consumers' organization in your area – they constantly need volunteers. Your local church, whether or not you worship there, is probably in touch with many local organizations that need voluntary help.

Telephone your local hospitals and clinics to ask for details of voluntary work programmes. Call your local political party and ask if they need any help fund-raising/canvassing/driving/telephone-answering. You may wind up on the local council or as a JP on the Bench. This is how many such women started.

'Yes, yes' you may say 'but that's not for me: I'm not the do-gooding type and I can't stand committees: I merely want something interesting to happen to me.'

It won't.

You have to make it happen.

HOW TO MEET PEOPLE AND HAVE FUN ON THE CHEAP

What can you do in your spare time that's fun, legal, non-fattening, costs next to nothing and is totally absorbing? Where can you meet new people, perhaps even make some money?

You'll hate me when I tell you. At evening classes.

The image you have of them probably features being squashed under a hacked-about, splintery infant desk which ruins your tights while you're being lectured under naked lights in a dingy classroom by a little cocksure expert who mesmerizes you with boredom while he's squeaking on the blackboard. But evening classes have changed dramatically in concept and content in the last few years and the courses are as good, if not better, than

what's privately available at *ten times the price or more*. You can spend a fortune at private health clubs, yoga sessions, fashion design schools and private language schools, or on tennis and golf lessons. You can probably learn all these subjects from evening, daytime or weekend classes.

In many places there are crèches and playgroups at the adult education institutes so that the children can be looked after while mother learns Italian, paints a landscape or joins a yoga class. There may be family classes on Saturday mornings, organized as workshops for painting and crafts for parents and children to learn together. These can be a great success.

The difference between doing these things mainly at public expense or privately (where you pay) is *the clever sell*. This winkles the money out of your purse with alluring advertisements and glamorous brochures inviting you to go on an 'intensive' course (they mean 'short') to become an expert in six weeks, to drop a stone, to wind your big toe round your neck or to astound your friends by becoming Jimmy Goldsmith overnight, thanks to your dynamic new inside knowledge of the Stock Exchange.

You get evening classes at bargain prices because they're subsidized by your rates and taxes.

In all parts of the country, there is often a special provision for old age pensioners, disabled and other groups (for instance unemployed widows or anyone on social security) or other cases of special hardship.

Anyone who wants to enrol for

part-time day or evening classes can find the addresses of local centres under 'Education' in the telephone directory. Ask them for a list of courses; there is often a staggering variety to choose from (see p. 8).

What's available, of course, depends on where you live (there's a bigger variety in more populated areas) and on the generosity or meanness of the local education authority.

Classes can save you money or help you make it. By learning to do your own home maintenance you could save yourself hundreds of pounds and you might set up your own little business doing other people's maintenance and charging them for it. Teachers say that once they've overcome their early conditioning, which renders them helpless and mutinous at the sight of a screwdriver, women are better at joinery and other handicrafts than men because they listen more carefully. You can learn home decorating, how to paint, plaster, convert old houses, modernize your home, upholster old furniture or even make your own bed (really make it). You can take a plumbing course and unstop your own sink, or put in a new one. You can take a carpentry course and make your own fitted shelves and cupboards. You can take an electronics course and mend your own television or a car maintenance course and free yourself from the tyranny of garages.

The last time I had my sewing machine mended, the man did it in front of me, didn't even clean it and

it cost me £8 for half an hour's work. You can not only learn how to look after your sewing machine or how to maintain your car, but also how to navigate a sailing dinghy, do home nursing or be a playgroup leader.

In some parts of the country you can even take a course in marriage!

So why not learn the tango, or all about beauty culture, or how to look after antiques (all activities which can be learned at local authority day or evening classes in as little as one and a half hours a week)?

It's amazing how quickly you can become a Grade 2 expert (knowing more about a subject than anyone else in your immediate vicinity) and once that's established, you stand a good chance of becoming a Grade 1 expert (getting to know your subject and having the family recognize, respect and be proud of it).

This in turn guarantees you enough time to pursue your activity to the point where it becomes not only enjoyable but profitable (advanced poker, lecturing on the care of antiques, teaching beauty culture), or to hop on to your next activity.

The easy part is planning to put a bit of time aside every week; the difficult part is setting your foot outside the front door.

Here is the Inner London Education Authority list, which offers the biggest choice, but it may give you ideas about what subjects can be available, and you might want to ask for a special class in your area (see later): __

HOW TO BE AN EXPERT

(A few of the things that you can learn for next to nothing)

Animal care and training

Aquaria: tropical fish survival course

Bee-keeping: if you want to make your own honey and sell it

All about *Birds:* just like the Duke of Edinburgh

Dogs and other pets

Horsemastership: just like Princess Anne. Well, somewhat ...

Pigeons: we'll all be needing this course if postal prices continue to soar like a bird: in fact pigeons are already being used to deliver blood samples

Poultry-keeping: no more chicken tasting like fish!

Art and craft

Antiques: learn to spot, buy, brush up and sell

Art Appreciation

Art History: absorbing and gives you something to talk about

Carving and Sculpture: I spent years doing this and could carve my own tombstone. Fun if you don't expect instant results

Costume: riveting information. Useful for all sorts of things, apart from designing film costumes and school plays

Drawing or Painting: among the most popular courses in the country

Enamelling

The History of Furniture

Handwriting

Jewellery: why wait for someone to give you bracelets?

Lithography: mass-produce your own pictures

Modelling and Pottery: easily one of the most popular courses with the right equipment

Mosaics

Photography: blow up your own

All about *Porcelain*

Cookery

General Cookery

Bread and Yeast Cookery

Cakes and Pastry

Chinese Cookery

Continental Cookery

Deep Freeze Cookery

Dinner Party Cookery

Sweetmaking

Vegetarian Cookery: learn all about the basic cheap bean

Dancing

Ballet

Ballroom

Folk/Country/Square

Modern

Morris/Tap

National

Old Time

Stage

Domestic craft

Basketry: very soothing
Children's Wear
Dressmaking: for beginners
Embroidery and needlework
Fabric Design: most agreeable, but not if you want to make money
Flower Arranging
Flower-making: why wait for them to grow?
Home Furnishing and Soft Furnishing: another money saver
Interior Decoration, Painting and Decorating: a real investment
Lace-making
Leatherwork
Lingerie
Millinery: surprisingly popular
Pattern Cutting
Care of *Sewing Machines*
Sewing on a Budget
Tailoring: another top class, even if you only learn how to alter things
Toy-making: most satisfying
Upholstery: a money maker
Weaving, Knitting, Spinning: I very much enjoyed my weaving classes and set up in business afterwards doing contract work for shipping

Drama and films:

a terrific, exciting choice here

Drama and Dramatic Art
Film Appreciation
Making Films
Mime

The following are good self-confidence builders and get very good results:

Conversation
Debates
Effective Speaking
History of Theatre
How to Speak
Public Speaking
Stage Make-up
Stage Technique
Speech Training and Elocution

Languages

Anglo-Saxon: not very popular
Arabic: soaring in popularity and costs a fortune if you learn it privately
Bulgarian
Chinese: for the forward-thinking
Danish
English: vast numbers of classes here
Esperanto
French: the most popular class
German: second most popular class
Greek
Hebrew
Irish: for Devolutionists
Italian: third most popular class
Japanese
Latin
Norwegian
Polish
Portuguese
Romance Linguistics
Russian
Scottish Gaelic: for Devolutionists
Serbo-Croat
Spanish
Swahili: easier than you'd think, but the least popular class
Swedish
Turkish
Welsh

Literary, cultural and historical studies

Anthropology: like Prince Charles
Archaeology: like Prince Charles again
Architecture: like Prince Richard
Astrology: like Patric Walker
Astronomy: like Patrick Moore
Authorship, journalism, writing: good luck to you
Civics: well worthwhile if you want to understand what's happening around you and influencing you
Current affairs
Economics: if this can be taught, why doesn't anyone seem to be learning?
Geography: know where you're at
Heraldry, Genealogy
English History
European History
Local History
London History
World History
Law: dozens of different courses available
Literature
Logic
Maths – Computer, Metric System
Philosophy
Psychology: including human relations, childhood and adolescence
Religion
Science – Biology, Botany, etc.

Sociology and Social Affairs: including personality study. Get out of a rut and join discussion groups.

Music

Appreciation and Theory
Bands and Orchestras
Individual Instruments: guitar/banjo/violin/piano, etc.
Jazz
Opera
Vocal: what you might call 'singing'

Physical education:

Keep fit and enjoy it

Angling
Archery
Badminton: easily the most popular sport
Boxing
Cricket
Cycling
Fencing
Football: Rugby and Soccer
Golf
Gymnastics – circuit training, keep fit
Hockey
Judo/Kendo
Mountaineering
Netball and Basketball
Sailing and Rowing
Skiing
Squash, Fives, Volley Ball: the growth sports of the moment
Swimming
Table Tennis
Tennis: getting more popular
Trampoline
Weight-lifting
Wrestling

Yoga: the fastest growing keep-fit course and rightly so. Book early

Technical crafts

Bookbinding
Electricity: including electricity in the house and car electrics
Flying: an introduction
Horticulture and Gardening
Metalwork
Meteorology
Model Engineering
Motors:
  Cars and Scooters, Maintenance, Advanced Driving. Here's where you save a fortune!
Picture Frame Making
Radio, Television, Tape Recording
Seamanship and Navigation: chart-work, pilotage
Shoe Repairing: there's a thought
Silverwork
Woodwork: Cabinet-making, Boat-building, General. Satisfying, therapeutic and a thoroughly useful investment. Can you get a carpenter, and if so can you afford him?

Other ideas

Beauty Care
Camping: mini-cost holidays for ever with no booking or packing problems
Chess: for any age
Child Care
English for Newcomers
Field Studies
First-Aid and Home Nursing
General Education: English/Maths
Health

Marriage and Housewives Course
Philately
Playgroup Leaders Course: if you haven't got one start one
Poise, Personality, Good Grooming: who doesn't need it?
Preparation for Retirement: a wise step if you're getting on
Special Classes for Deaf and Blind: very popular
Special Classes for Stammerers
Stock Exchange and Investment
Study Techniques: for people returning to study
Travel Talks
Typing: you can also learn other basic office skills such as shorthand and book-keeping
Wine Appreciation: great fun. Yes, you do taste.
Wine-making: what to do creatively with your old potato peel, etc.

When to book: Courses are usually planned at the beginning of the year and by August a full list of programmes should be available from the library. Classes usually begin in late September, and you book a couple of weeks before they start.

Many adult education institutes run one-term courses which may start at any time of the year. There is also a growing demand for short intensive courses of perhaps only two or four sessions on a special topic such as 'House Purchase and Ownership'. There may be a special quick course to get lucky skiers limbered up and fit before going out to the slopes.

Classes such as yoga and squash fill up almost immediately, so book *as early as you can* and be prepared for queues. You usually need to go to the institute to enrol. If the course you want is fully booked ask to go on the waiting list so that you will get a place if someone drops out.

While it is best to join a class at the beginning of the session, it is nearly always worth joining late rather than putting it off for a year. It is also worth checking what new courses start *before* next September, in case you find one alluring.

Dropping out: People drop out of classes for different reasons and they often hate themselves for it afterwards. If you find that your course is too advanced or you're too advanced for the course, tell the teacher or the principal and ask if you can move into another class.

It is often very easy to flag or skip classes after initial enthusiasm fades. There's one big basic psychological reason: the classes are so cheap you won't be losing that much money. So a cold wet winter night or a good television programme can make you weaken. Once you miss the first class you can expect to miss others. So decide at the start that your evening class days are permanently booked: you have an appointment with yourself. Make sure your family knows this and tell them to nag you at the first sign of weakness (children are often genuinely helpful). Don't look at the television programme pages of that day. Write a note at the end of your diary to remind yourself why you wanted to join the class, what you will gain from it, and that you

may have to wait a complete year before you can start again.

How to get a class in a new subject: Adult education is supposed to be readily available to all who want it. If you can't find a class in a subject which interests you, get in touch with the principal of your local institute. If he finds that enough people are interested, a class can often be arranged – but you'll have to convince him that it's needed. So round up several other people who also want to take tap dancing, wine-making or whatever it is. Courses may be planned up to a year ahead, so suggest a new idea as soon as possible and don't expect your new class to appear overnight.

What adult education is – and what it isn't: The idea of adult education is to give you the opportunity to develop interests, leisure activities and encourage your creativity. There are no entry tests and you don't have to have any qualifications to join. However, some courses are planned to teach at different levels – beginners; intermediate; advanced. If in doubt about your grading, start at the lower one and plan to move up fast.

Adult education courses are usually called 'non-vocational', which simply means they won't equip you for a career. But they can still be a good way to add to skills, to brush up rusty ones or to improve your qualifications. They are also a good way to get used to learning again, if you want to do something more ambitious later.

Where to get more academic courses: If you want to get formal qualifications for a job or career (e.g. O and A levels or Higher National Diplomas) there are part-time classes usually run at colleges of further education, polytechnics or other specialist colleges. For more academic courses you may want to attend the extra-mural department of a university or one of the Workers' Educational Association (WEA) courses, with part-time study and tutorials in individual subjects. You do not need formal qualifications to attend these.

If you want to take up full-time study later, it is often much easier to get a college place *and a grant* if you can show proof that you have completed some kind of organized study such as an extra-mural or WEA course.

Your local library should have information on these courses, as well as on local adult education institute classes.

Throughout this book I often suggest that when you need to find out something you go for help to your local library. The public library is not only a place where you borrow books for nothing, it's your local information centre. Here you can find out when the town was founded or what Queen Victoria liked for breakfast. You can discover the name of your MP or the location of your nearest yoga class.

Don't underestimate your library – or your librarian. Librarians have been trained for years to locate information for your benefit and the Library Association affirms that librarians like to be asked questions: it's the lure of the chase they enjoy.

A skilled librarian knows exactly where to go for something that might take you hours to find by yourself. Through computer systems they are in touch with other libraries throughout the land (not only public) and these libraries nearly all have their different specialities and contribute to an interloan scheme.

The library is also used as a centre to announce information (a sort of updated town crier). They keep lists of local organizations, social clubs, sports and playcentres. Provided it's not a busy Saturday morning, the librarian is often happy to help you solve a crossword puzzle, to refer to the library's microfilm copies of *The Times* or back numbers of *Which?*, or to photocopy documents for a small charge. They will help you with local history or guide you through the intricacies of your local council.

You can ask for information on any topic or enquire by telephone or letter. If the answer isn't immediately available in the branch reference material, the librarian can usually get it for you or suggest likely sources. There's often a housebound service so that books and recordings can be delivered to people who can't get to the library.

Libraries are run by the local education authorities: these are the district councils in metropolitan areas and the county councils in non-metropolitan areas.

HOW TO DO WHAT YOU'VE ALWAYS WANTED TO DO AND GET PAID FOR IT

One of the most beguiling, practical and glamorous chances for you to benefit from is the Training Opportunities Scheme, TOPS. This is an amazing government scheme which provides *free* full-time training courses for people who want to make a fresh start, change their job or train for a new one, or are simply unemployed. 'TOPS is for the individual' is their motto. The Training Services Division is really keen to get more women to take a TOPS course.

You choose your course to suit yourself. It must last at least four weeks and not longer than a year and is supposed to result in your getting skills or qualifications likely to get you a job. As well as free training, TOPS trainees get generous free weekly cash payments and allowances which (all at the time of writing) could be worth £4000 a year, including the cost of training.

If you have a husband who's keeping the family you can use your tax-free TOPS allowance (from £25.70 a week, depending on circumstances, plus travel and lunch money, equipment, etc.) to get your children looked after by a live-in mother's help or daily mother's help in your own home, or at kindergarten, while you spend up to a year training to be a plumber or a riding mistress or a secretary.

A single woman without dependants can also get an allowance of from £25.70 a week. There are extra payments if you're supporting your family. You get free midday meals or a meal allowance, free travel if it's over two miles to your course centre, your fees and textbooks paid for if you want to go to college and free lodgings or a lodging allowance if necessary. There are slightly different arrangements for widows or women who are drawing social security. But a widow can start her TOPS training course and draw her TOPS allowance immediately she is widowed.

You could spend that free money on a nanny or a housekeeper to look after things at home while you go out and get a training. And you don't *have* to take a job the minute you've trained.

There are over 600 courses available under the scheme – from bricklaying to postgraduate courses in universities. If you know of some other course that interests you (say, stained glass design), they would consider paying for you to go on it. You can learn to be an electrician or a computer operator, you can learn shorthand and typing, catering or book-keeping. You can study fashion design, floristry, accounting or management.

You can also upgrade a skill that you already have. If you are a secretary you can become a bilingual secretary. If you've been a confidential clerk (confidentially, that's doing the filing) you can take a management course; one of the best of their good offers. If you've been doing something boring in an office, you could take a course in business administration. If you've already done a cookery course you might take a hotel and catering course.

All courses are open equally to men and women – and that is official policy. So if you have the ability to take one of the courses – and you will be assessed on this – then you have a right to take it, though you may have to wait a few months if there isn't a free place. If you want you can be trained for a job that is traditionally thought of as 'man's work', such as heavy vehicle repairing, plumbing, plastering or TV servicing. In fact, they wish more women would take craft training of this kind. Women have been particularly successful in electronics, where job opportunities are expanding.

There are three kinds of TOPS training: in skillcentres, in colleges and on the job.

1 Most of the practical jobs, such as plumbing or electronics, are taught in the government-owned skill-centres. There are about sixty-three skillcentres in the country and more will probably be built. (Northern Ireland has its own scheme.)

2 Alternatively, you can go to courses run at a college of further education (where you can do office courses), art college, polytechnic, technical college or university. (Some are run jointly by TOPS and the college.) There are also special advanced management and professional courses for qualified people over the age of twenty-seven.

3 If you need to learn 'on the job', TOPS arrange training for you with an employer. For example, if you want to qualify as a riding instructor, you will be sent to a British Horse Society riding school for six months at TOPS's expense (and of course you will be paid the TOPS allowances as well). You can train at the school for one of three British Horse Society recognized instructor qualifications: as an assistant, intermediate or full instructor. You are allowed only one course sponsored by TOPS. So if you get your assistant-grade qualification, you can't stay on for another six months to move up to intermediate. But if you already have the intermediate qualification, TOPS will sponsor you so you can get a top-grade qualification.

One course that's helpful for women who want to get back to work or aren't happy in their job is a 'Wider Opportunities' course. You can spend up to twelve weeks trying out different sorts of work, guided by a special instructor, in order to find what suits you before choosing your main TOPS course.

How to get on a TOPS *training course:* Most TOPS training is supposed to be 'vocational', which means that it is aimed to develop your talents and skills in order to fit you for a specific job. You have to be over nineteen and have been away from full-time education for at least three years, show some reasonable talent for what you're about to study, and not have had a government training course in the past five years, although this period may be reduced if you want a higher-level management course. You can't just take course after course.

You must give up your existing job to take a TOPS course. You can't take time off from your job to do one: the TOPS people say that if you need extra skills for your present job that is your present employer's responsibility, and he should pay for it. However, if you leave your job, take a TOPS course and later go back to the company and ask for another better job where you can use your new skills; it is unlikely that you will be pursued by angry TOPS officials.

Contact your nearest jobcentre or employment office (address is in the phone book under Employment Service Division) and ask to see the training officer. It is best to make an appointment first.

If you are an unemployed executive or have worked in management-type jobs you will get special advice on TOPS higher-level management and professional course schemes through a PER (Professional and Executive Recruitment) office.

If you want to attend a college course, it is usually best first to find out about it yourself and see if you will be accepted by the college principal.

Get a letter of acceptance from the college and then take it to the training officer and arrange to be sponsored. If TOPS has already arranged with the college to run a course just for TOPS candidates this may not always be necessary. But the final decision on who is accepted for a college course is made by the principal. TOPS can't order a college to accept anybody.

You can also ask for this leaflet at your local jobcentre or employment office:
Train for a Better Job with TOPS (TSA L79).

See you at the riding school!

PROFILE OF A WORKING MOTHER

Today everybody knows that a woman's place is not necessarily in the home. Sometimes home is where the harpy is, and sometimes she has good cause to be bitchy.

A growing number of women who feel that they're taken for granted, unappreciated or neglected in the home, are starting to find that, be it ever so hectic, there's no place like work. Work outside the home, that is, in a job you enjoy, where you're needed, where you're welcome. Work can be a means of forgetting your troubles, your despair, your loneliness. It can be the basis of self-esteem and fulfilment.

Your home need not suffer if you work provided you're sensible and drop your standards. A recent German study of Common Market housewives proves that we don't save time with our labour-saving gadgets – we raise our standards unnecessarily high and work harder and longer. The moral is that if you're at home then you do more work at home. But if you organize your life so that you haven't got much time to spend on housework, then the housework magically diminishes.

It seems to me that the homes of non-working mothers are seldom any more neat or clean than those of working mothers: it is possible for non-working housewives to be just as lazy housekeepers as those who are working. And some of them are not at home anyway. They may be out socializing, earnestly playing tennis, seriously having coffee mornings or home-fantasizing (matching the candle-holders to the curtains, combing the town for the right-sized pine-cones for the open fireplace, etc.), popping tranquillizers or drinking (a growing problem: there are now over a quarter of a million female British alcoholics, according to Alcoholics Anonymous). You might just as well be doing something mildly constructive and profitable, like a bit of work.

Nowadays, husbands are less likely to prevent their wives from taking a job: some men almost weep with relief at the idea of help with the inexorable mortgage and the household bills (the high cost of Vim and vests, as playwright John Mortimer put it). Nowadays, it can be more worthwhile, under the present crazy tax system, for the wife to earn a little than for the husband to do lots of heavily taxed overtime or get a socking great rise which takes him into a higher tax bracket. However, there is still one major, deep-rooted masculine fear about working women – that they're going to grab men's jobs at cheaper rates. This fear is sometimes too great to express. So, if you come up against a lot of unfocused hostility, that could be the answer.

Since 1967 the number of men in the workforce has fallen at pretty much the same rate as the number of working women has increased. *But they are doing different sorts of work.* Jobs traditionally held by men have declined during this period while women have been going into the service jobs (public and private). Men often disdain this sort of job, such as part-time work in schools, hospitals, catering, shops and local government and other welfare areas. This trend has been happening throughout the world, according to an OECD study.

Roughly one woman in two now goes out to work and the increase has been especially drastic among the over-forty-fives. More jobs are now open to women. There's more social approval of working mothers. Families are now smaller.

It is official state policy (because women are needed for work) to offer retraining schemes, refresher courses, career guidance and even confidence-building courses in order to encourage women to return to work.

What's the catch? There are two dangers, both of which can be avoided. One is exhaustion and the other is guilt, and they are linked. I don't mean physical fatigue, which is remedied by a long night's sleep or a day spent alone and doing nothing, or by spending a weekend with friends. I mean a bone-deep, draggy, never *not* tired feeling. The more guilty you feel because you are working the more you rush around polishing doorknobs and taking the children to the zoo and slaving over a cold deep-freeze, and the more exhausted you get. *Then* you get guilty about feeling exhausted. You can't think how to cope and you're too tired to work out what's gone wrong and who's to blame. You feel inadequate and near to tears. That's when you start to feel resentful. But you're not allowed to show it because you suspect that everyone will triumphantly ask, *'Whose idea was it to go out to work in the first place?'*

Avoid this vicious little circle by making sure it never starts. I'll tell you a secret. Even if household tasks are shared it is generally the woman partner who bears the responsibility for organizing the domestic three-ring circus. This is the exhausting part, not the work. So try and share the responsibility, not only the tasks. And don't think that only mothers with jobs feel inadequate and exhausted. Instead of the working mother's anxiety as to whether she can juggle the whole lot simultaneously, many non-job mothers have a restless feeling that they should want to do more, that they're wasting the best years of their life, with only a clean kitchen floor to show for it.

However, if a job gets to feel too much for you, consider getting a different one, perhaps less demanding and emotionally exhausting, or nearer home.

The second danger is that mothers have been conditioned to feel guilty about taking a job outside the home, especially if they *enjoy* it; but recognizing this and accepting it will take you half-way towards overcoming the problem, as any psychologist will tell you. The generation that *won't* feel guilty is, we hope, the one that we're bringing up right now. Develop a positive attitude to your job and stop trying to compensate for it. Your family is benefiting and so are you, and never let them forget it.

There are obvious disadvantages to a child in having a working mother, but there are less obvious advantages. Seventy per cent of women analysed in a *Family Circle* survey showed that working mothers were happier and more interesting and their children were more self-reliant. Children with working mothers don't suffer from smother-love or over-fussing and they won't be nagged (no time). They learn to be realistic, independent, responsible for their words and deeds and sometimes even stoical – no mean preparation for the toughness of life.

A working woman is not so likely to cling to her children when it's their turn to leave the nest. A working mother has her own interests. Children of working mothers don't have a permanent, in-house punching bag and prayer rail, but they do have a mother who is likely to have a younger outlook, who is more likely to be tolerant and open to new ideas.

A FEW NEW FACTS OF LIFE

Your life: The average female life is now seventy-five years. The trend is towards early marriage. Your child care years could be over at thirty-five. That leaves forty years ahead for Ms Average.

What sort of women work?
Over forty per cent of the British labour force is female (9.3 million women).

Sixty-four per cent of working women are married.

Two million British women with children under sixteen work full-time.

Three and a half million British women with children under sixteen work part-time.

One in four women with children under five work outside the home full- or part-time (not always from choice).

The state of divorce
One in three first marriages ends in divorce.

Of this year's teenage brides, one in three will divorce.

One in five heads of British households are women (breadwinners not always from choice).

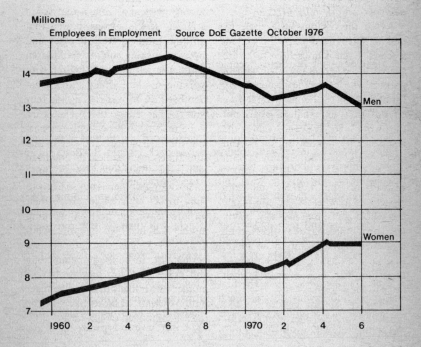

Millions
Employees in Employment   Source DoE Gazette October 1976

HOW TO JUGGLE TWO JOBS (HOME AND WORK)

Where home juggling is concerned I think you can serenely keep two balls in the air simultaneously (job and children: job and mate: children and mate) but three is very difficult.

However, by 1977, for the first time in British history, the steadily rising curve of working wives meant that the *majority* of married women are no longer 'housewives'. This trend, encouraged by the government, means that it's no longer unusual for a woman to juggle two jobs – home and work.

A working mother will, with any luck, get twice as much out of life, but you can't run your house as if you weren't working. A working mother has to work faster and more efficiently in the home (and she has to be *twice* as reliable outside it, because people expect her not to be). But if you have to continue housekeeping with a job you *become* fast and efficient – because you can't manage otherwise. There is no *one* right way of doing things. Nobody can tell you totally how to improve and organize because it depends on who you are, what you like doing, what you want and what you don't. You have to find out what *your* needs are and then make your own private rules to suit yourself and the rest of the family. Here are a few suggestions.

Cut down on housework: The first thing you do is cut out as much as possible of the unnecessary, old-fashioned household clutter and jobs.

You can't have everything, and you certainly can't dust everything. To recall Conran's Law of Housework – it expands to fill the time available plus half an hour: so it is obviously never finished. The important thing is not to do the housework but to decide how much *time* you are going to allow for your housework. What doesn't get done in that time is left undone (perhaps for the next time, perhaps for ever). Keep housework in its place, which, you will remember, is underfoot, and regard it not as a reflection of your worth but as the minimum essential support-work to keep the place functioning as a background to living.

Consider cutting out anything that makes work (e.g. instead of polishing silver, pack it away). But don't cut out the things in life that *sometimes* make it seem gracious.

Use the maximum labour savers but the minimum number of machines (there will then be fewer to break down).

Increase your home help: I don't mean paying for it. Funnily enough, money does not solve the problem of running a home (women who haven't had live-in help never believe this). You just have to organize the help as well as the children. If you're not careful, you can have the help's psychological dramas dumped in your lap just as soon as you get back from the office. If you have living-in older help they often get jealous of you, your job, your sex life and your security, and start sniping at all four. If the help is younger – such as a student au pair – she often isn't sufficiently experienced, interested or responsible (and neither were you at seventeen) and you'll spend half your time worrying about her sex life or maybe turning up the television full blast so that you can't hear it.

No, the people who should help you run the home are the people who are in it. Every member of the family must help with the housework. And on no account must you thank them unless they thank you. If you don't have a Japanese bowing ceremony this is more important than you think. Think of it every time you thank somebody for washing up the meal you didn't eat entirely by yourself or making a bed that you did not unmake entirely by yourself.

Share the work: calculate the time jobs take you and apportion them according to hours. You can't really work out any other way (except by seeing how much you have to pay someone else to do it) whether mending the vacuum cleaner is equivalent to getting breakfast. Most husbands now say that they are willing to share the chores with a working wife, but they don't assume equal hourage: the best you can hope for at the moment is one average husband hour to between two

and five and a half wife hours at housework.

You might decide that you'll both do a blitz on Saturday morning and the rest of the week it can go to hell. If you decide this – stick to it. Or you can do something more ambitious such as sharing out the work on the following lines. Draw up your own schedule according to the work. The whole point is to get away from that guilty feeling that he's *helping* you. Not at all. You both have a job to do.

Schedule

Job	Hours a week	Who does it?
Shopping	....	....
Meals:		
preparation	....	....
cooking	....	....
clearing up	....	....
Clothes:		
cleaning	....	....
mending	....	....
Floor care	....	....
Furniture care	....	....
Cleaning bath- room(s)	....	....
Making beds	....	....
General tidying	....	....
Car care	....	....
Domestic maintenance, boiler and machinery care	....	....
Garden	....	....

Otherwise, the question of whether or however the husband should help around the house can be solved by jointly paying someone else to do it. I don't know about your principles, but so long as males or females want cleaning work, I don't see why there shouldn't be cleaners.

From time to time check whether you are delegating enough of the housework. Think of yourself, not as a cook-general, but as a general. Remember that it is *not* quicker to do it yourself. It's quicker not to do it at all. Accept the fact that your helpers may not do things as well as you, and simply remember (1) that you are not doing them, and (2) to handsomely praise effort (which is what you wish people would do for you).

Cut down on cooking as much as possible: And I *don't* mean buy convenience foods or stand packing a deep-freeze on a Saturday afternoon and then complain about backache. There's plenty of perfectly good, nourishing food which is *really* convenient and involves minimum preparation and shopping, like ham, smoked mackerel, cheese, fruit, tomatoes, yoghurt and bread. So why not simplify food?

A friend of mine who found herself too exhausted to work after work sat down and worked out a way to avoid mid-week cooking in the evening. Her simple plan might inspire you to try one of your own.

1 She cooks three evening casserole/stew-type meals at once on Saturday or Sunday.
2 On Monday she serves one of the casseroles.
3 On Tuesday she serves cold ham and salad.
4 One evening she serves take-away food.
5 One evening she leaves it to her man – and enthusiastically eats whatever turns up.
6 One evening she goes out to the cinema or to a concert or to visit friends (*not* for a meal) instead of eating.

Conserve your energy: Realize that you can't do everything those ladies in the glossy magazines seem to. An action-packed, day-in-the-life-of always starts with Her at dawn, looking immaculate. She bakes a cake, has a face-pack and takes the kids to school before going to the office (meditating on the train) where, serene and relaxed, she goes through a similarly impossible day before returning to give a dinner party in the evening (which she sometimes prepares before breakfast when she isn't being photographed). Don't you believe a word of it.

Sort out your priorities: There are so many choices when a mother's energy has to be simultaneously channelled into two directions (or more), and it's often hard to know which should take priority. At 11.00 in the morning the emergency conference or the sudden workrush take priority over the lamb chops but at 7.00 that evening, when there's nothing for supper, the missing lamb chops achieve greater significance. There's only one way to sort priorities out. Unless one of your family is ill, business life is for business hours (35 hours a week) and family life is for the rest of the week ($168 - 35 = 133$).

Prune your activities: Then you must sort out your social and sporting life. Nobody gets *everything* they want; you must decide what you want *most* and cut out the rest.

Incidentally, I've noticed that at all the really distinguished parties that I go to (not many) the grandest tycoons, the most beautiful women and the cleverest politicians generally drink ginger ale before dinner (*all* of them trying to look as if it's whisky) and they leave by 11.00. Don't let anyone behave as if you're sabotaging their party if you leave before 1.00 in the morning.

Get some time to yourself: It's difficult to arrange if you have small children but it's then even more necessary to get it. For me, when I come home tired, it's twenty minutes spent in the bath, and I pour everything into it. It smells of flowers, it's coloured, it bubbles . . .

Never do anything you hate: It's not too difficult, if you're determined. For instance, I haven't ironed anything for ten years. If anything wants ironing, he who wants it does it.

HOW TO GET THINGS DONE
(the things you *want* to do, as well as the rest)

The most difficult thing for a mother to organize is some private pursuit within her own home. Whether it's studying, doing freelance work or writing poetry on the kitchen table, something always seems to get in the way. This is because there are always interruptions, diversions and seductions. It's really hard to achieve something in the privacy of your own home, whereas in an office or a classroom there's nothing much else to do apart from what you're supposed to be doing. There are too many seductions at home. I don't mean the milkman. I mean that there's *always* some good reason not to start: a couple of cups to wipe, a programme to watch or the telephone ringing.

If you don't have the enforced discipline of going *out* to work, then it's very, very hard to achieve anything constructive. The way to change this is to discover your own priorities in order of their importance to *you* (not to other people). For this you will need a cup of coffee, a comfortable chair, a notebook, and one quiet hour to yourself. Now scribble down a list of everything you *want* to do. I don't mean routine household cleaning. I mean everything *except* that.

List A: What you want to do eventually
  (Go to India on a bus, etc.)

Now make:

List B: What you want to do this week

  These are your short-term objectives, to be realized within six days (e.g., getting the dress finished in time for the Saturday party, or reading last week's Sunday papers).

  Now draw up Action Lists A2 and B2 of what you have to do in order to achieve A and B.

For example:

A2: Get Gran to agree to look after children in Feb.

Raise £120.

How? Possibly sell clothes/silver/picture/stereo/get temp. twilight job.

B2: Get up at 6.00 tomorrow morning or stay up until 2.00 tonight to read Sunday papers.

Pin these four lists up behind the kitchen door, or (if that's already covered with pin-up lists) behind your bedroom door, or (if you want to keep quiet about having Aims) in your underwear drawer. Sometimes I prefer to keep my goals secret so no one except myself knows what I'm aiming at. Sometimes I prefer to state my aim, however ridiculous, out loud to *anyone* who'll listen, because then it's out in the open and I seem to try harder. Also, other people can often help if they *know* what you want.

Now, *for one week only*, write a daily list of what you actually do (take suit to cleaners, dog to vet, etc.). This List 5 is the most important of the lot because you will probably find that most of your day's activities are non-productive, so far as your A and B lists are concerned – and *they* are the things you really want to do. So, in future, check the things on the A2 and B2 lists and *do one first*, before your routine work.

Cautionary tale: When I stopped full-time work and started working from home, I sorted my work out neatly into creative/earning work and system support work (being my own

secretary and doing the housework). I made one big mistake – and I went on doing it for nearly a year until I stopped and analysed what I was doing (using the list method). I used to do the boring support work in the morning and leave the afternoon free for my *real* work, which brought in the money. The drawback was that I never finished the morning's work until 6.00 in the evening. What I had to learn was to reverse my priorities, do my productive work in the morning and the system support work afterwards – if at all – and it was my List 5 that sorted out a situation that now seems glaringly obvious but which wasn't at the time. List 5 will show you why women aren't Beethoven, Shakespeare, Botticelli, etc.

The things on your A and B lists are the things that will make you feel that you have *achieved* something for yourself, instead of merely keeping your head above the daily tidal wave of family maintenance. This is, of course, no small achievement in itself, but somehow it doesn't seem like that.

Check *all* your lists quietly at the end of the week, over another cup of coffee. See what got crossed off and what didn't and ask yourself why certain things didn't get done. Were you not tough enough with yourself? Too easy on other people? Check, too, that you're not striving for perfection. (That way madness lies.)

Don't forget Conran's Second Law of Housekeeping, that *possible* Daily Output is always halved by Unforeseen Interruptions.

One surefire way to reduce your

work is to learn to say NO, and to keep saying it, cheerfully, but firmly, whenever *anyone* asks you to do *anything* that isn't on your lists A, B, A2, B2. The trick here is to say NO as the first word, followed, perhaps, by an explanation, although no explanation is necessary, just a repetition of your first monosyllabic message, or perhaps, 'I'm afraid not' or 'I'm sorry I can't'. Say this charmingly and firmly, then *stop*. (That's the trick.) Then let the other person speak. If you are immediately asked again, immediately repeat the routine. DON'T ALTER IT THE SECOND TIME. No matter how worthy other people's aims and problems are, their lists are not your concern: don't let other people delegate to you.

Learn to protect your time, because your time is what you need first of all, in order to achieve *anything* ... Today's time, that is. The way to stop wishing you'd done more in the past, or thinking in terms of vague daydreams for the future, is to stop and start those lists TODAY. You have nothing to lose, except your life.

WHAT TO DO WITH THE CHILDREN?

The question of what to do with the children is the one that prevents most mothers who would like to do so from returning to work. This is the question that haunts many mothers who have no choice *but* to work. The problem is grim enough when the children are at school, but it is infinitely worse during the school holidays or if the children are under five. The stark fact is that there is an almost total lack of available, affordable, reliable pre-school care and there are far from enough holiday centres in existing schools.

Looking after a family and taking care of children is obviously the most important job in the world. Unfortunately, society only pays lip service to this. It doesn't pay us for doing it and it is not particularly interested in seeing that it gets done: otherwise child care arrangements for working mothers (full- or part-time) would be every government's priority. But, whatever the government says, the government's motto (no matter which lot is in power) seems to be: 'Women and children last.'

Apart from the needs of a young child, a mother probably prefers to be with her baby until it is two years old, or she probably wouldn't have had it to begin with. However, some mothers have no choice. They are obliged to go out to work, often because they are the breadwinners. More than $3\frac{1}{2}$ million British women are breadwinners (i.e. main source of family income). More than $\frac{1}{2}$ million mothers are lone parents of nearly 1 million dependent children. So nearly a million children in this country probably have harassed, overburdened mothers.

And if a new mother *does* have the choice but finds that the bliss of looking after a young child for twenty-four hours a day isn't so fulfilling as she had expected, she can become clinically depressed. (Easy to sniff at but impossible to ignore if you've ever experienced it.)

I personally don't think that young children should be without their mothers. But what I think is beside the point. The facts are what matter. And the facts are these:

A report from the Department of Employment (Manpower Services Commission) in June 1976 said:

Married women are potentially the most important source of extra labour over the next decade ... The first priority for many mothers thinking about employment or training is the care of their children while they are away. If society is to make the fullest use of its human resources and at the same time to provide equal opportunities for women for work and training, the key factor for many women must be the expansion of child care facilities. This is particularly important for the one-parent families, where the lone parent is, in fact, usually a woman ... The TSD [Training Services Division] attaches importance to the expansion of facilities for care of young children and of after school and holiday activities for older children of working mothers.

The Plowden Report on Primary Education (1967) came out strongly in favour of schooling for the under-fives. It called for an expansion programme for nursery schools, so that all parents who wanted their children to attend could have their wish. The Committee estimated that 50 per cent

of three-year-olds and 90 per cent of four-year-olds would attend. Both major political parties support this recommendation.

What, in reality, is the position?

BRITAIN HAS THE WORST RECORD IN EUROPE FOR PRE-SCHOOL FACILITIES. Only 12 per cent of British three- to four-year-olds can go to nursery school, compared to 50 per cent in France, Belgium and Italy. Other countries can do it – and so can we. We did it magnificently and very quickly in the last war when women were needed to work.

Wartime nurseries were rapidly provided for mothers who had to work. They were run on the lines of nursery schools from 7.30 a.m. to 6.30 p.m. They were well equipped with little camp beds and kitchens, and the children were given breakfast, lunch and proper tea. So why not now? Why can't they be organized in exactly the same way as they were thirty-five years ago – *before* the Welfare State?

The position is far worse now than then. Since 1949 the number of local authority nurseries has *fallen by nearly* 50 per cent from 933 to 453 in 1976, and today, in spite of the great demand and long waiting lists, perfectly good nursery schools are threatened with the axe. The position has become unbelievably complicated and confused. You don't know where the buck starts, let alone stops. In the public and private sectors there are basically seven sorts of school which are the responsibility of *either* the Department of Education and Science, and the local education authority, *or* the Department of Health and Social Security and the local social services department (see p. 36). Consequently, nothing is the final responsibility of anyone, so they can all shirk it and do. Lady Britton, Chairwoman of the British Association for Early Childhood Education, told me:

Apart from one or two local authorities, such as Nottingham, there has been no advance in the last few years. And don't believe anything you hear to the contrary, especially from officials. It is very, very difficult to get *true* comparative figures out of them. When money was available (under Margaret Thatcher's 1972 White Paper) many local authorities never took up their allocations and of those that did, some now have the building left empty or they are using them for other purposes (not nurseries).

Lack of public money, nevertheless, is given as the reason for doing nothing. But masses of public money is being spent by the Department of Employment on getting women back to work while the main factor that stops them getting back is shuffled from In tray to In tray.

Under-five schooling and care and instruction are not just of importance to the mother, working or not. They may be good for your child, as well as you, because:

1 Boredom is a two-way process. You haven't got *that much* in common with a three-year-old. It is good for them to spend time with other children of the same age. Dull children will often come to life in kindergarten: clever children are often frustrated without it. Children need constant stimulation from an early age.

2 There is no reluctance later, when they're five, to leave their mother and go to proper school.

3 When children play and learn with other children of the same age they acquire, almost without noticing it, the ability to communicate with others without being self-conscious or shy. They learn more easily and happily when they do go on to primary school. Some primary teachers say that they can spot such children on the very first day that they start school because they're so much more self-possessed and quick to learn. It's also easier to spot difficulties or handicaps such as partial hearing or sight, speech or personality problems. There is then a great deal that can be done to help.

A few factories provide crèches and kindergartens for their women workers. The Civil Service, the biggest British employer of women, did set up one day nursery near Cardiff which was open to the children of both men and women employees. But it has now closed.

But these things are not insurmountably difficult to arrange in other countries. Employers in Italy and Turkey are obliged to provide kindergartens by law if they employ more than a specific number of married women: alternatively, the manufacturer has to pay a levy towards the cost of a state day nursery. Often, several firms join forces to start one nursery available to all their female employees. More than 40 per cent of French firms that employ over 500 people provide child care.

In Britain the TUC has officially stated that it supports kindergarten care, but although the unions have $2\frac{1}{2}$ million women members, few leading trade unionists will go out of their way to get help for women, as opposed to talking about it. Some trade unionists actively oppose crèches attached to factories: they say it might tie a woman to a job, like tied cottages. But look at male-oriented job perks: cars, secretaries, travel, entertaining expenses, trips, cut-price mortgages, low interest loans ... and so on. They are *meant* to tie a man to a job. And one thing is certain. If young children were suddenly made the equal responsibility of the male parent, then kindergartens would pop up overnight everywhere as they did in the Second World War.

But what *is* current official policy about looking after the under-fives? It is to encourage playgroups and amateur child minders. Very commendable, very practical, but just not good enough.

There are a quarter of a million playgroups in Britain, but they are no help to the working mother with a job – having a child at a playgroup *is* a full-time job. Playgroups won't allow most mothers to go out to work; they are often in a chronic state of breathlessness from trundling the child either

to or from the two- or three-hour sessions ... and perhaps doing their stint to help run the playgroup.

As for the child minder herself, some mothers might find it a little difficult to adjust to this sudden official Cinderella-like transformation of that wicked backstreet slut, who chained infants to the bed and fed them on chips and tea, into the saintly saviour of the nation's under-fives. And to make her even *better*, the BBC are now running TV courses and publishing books featuring well-known child minder Jimmy Savile in order to teach child minders about the basic problems of diet, first-aid and hygiene, play and communication and what to do with problem children, apart from leaving them in a pram or playpen all day. Child minders are simply not what the working mother wants – especially if she's tried them.

Another nightmare for the working mother with children of school age is the school holidays, and this may recur three times a year for ten years. In the majority of areas the empty schools are organized as play centres during the holidays. So why could this idea not be developed as a matter of course by *all* local authorities? It's worth finding out where this is done in your area. Your local citizens' advice bureau staff should be able to put you in touch with any such scheme.

Incidentally, who benefits from those three annual school holidays? Not the mother, who has to reorganize her schedule entirely; not the children, who get bored and forget what they've learned, and who aren't needed these days to help bring in the harvest, which was the original idea of the long summer vacation.

I see no reason for more than one week at Christmas, one week at Easter and three weeks in the summer time (staggered so that the whole country is not on holiday at the same time). It would be more in the children's interest to have three months' extra schooling. As for the teachers: we are *all* under stress these days and they ought to be able to organize their lives efficiently so that they don't need over one third of the year off to recuperate from work for which they're supposed to have a vocation.

Most of the critics of nursery schools seem to be fairly old, and emotionally biased. They seem to have rarely known any children in kindergarten or known any mother who was forced to work. They belong to the once privileged, now dusty generation who cannot believe that women work from necessity, which is not always financial. They seem to believe that women who want nursery education are just sloughing off their responsibilities so that they can swan off and earn pin money.

Their emotional attitude to under-five care is, 'How can a mother abandon her children?' The answer is that she is not, and it's good for them. These illogical, blinkered people, who don't want to face the facts of life today, don't get apoplexy at the idea of living-in nannies or unqualified, inexperienced au pairs to look after children. They never minded the unmarried aunts or obliging grannies who traditionally minded working-class children while their mothers were at their jobs. Today, families don't live close to each other. Granny probably lives 200 miles away and is having a wonderful time as a social worker, while Auntie is a trainee computer programmer. Today we're *all* working class and we all have the right to work; and a lot of us don't have the choice.

In the meantime, in the face of apathy or open hostility, what can *you* do about it?

You can start a playgroup or join a playgroup. You can organize a baby-swapping rota, which, as I've said before, is far more liberating than husband-swapping. Advertise in a local newsagent's or local newspaper. You can join with other parents to press your local education authority to open a holiday school near you if there isn't one. But most of all you can start campaigning as soon as your baby is born, or before, for proper kindergarten care.

HOW TO GET WHAT YOU WANT
(how to protest)

This guide to getting publicity can be used for any sort of pressure group, not just one campaigning for kindergartens.

That first thing to do is to *decide what you want*, exactly what your main aim is, and then to add any other less important ones. In this case:

Aim: A rapid increase in maintained public nursery schools and classes for all under-fives

Subsidiary aims:

1 To ensure that there is one co-ordinating body responsible for this – the Department of Education and Science, working with local educational authorities.
2 To demand clear legislation spelling out the obligation of education authorities to provide under-five nursery education, and not simply 'have regard to it', as in the 1944 Education Act, which has allowed so many local authorities to wriggle and prevaricate.
3 To stop kindergartens closing.

Rule 1 is to get a friend – you won't do anything unless you've got a mate to plan, work, encourage, complain to and celebrate with.

Rule 2 is to get several more friends on the pyramid principle of two each.

Rule 3 is to apply a little pressure in the right place, as publicly as possible.

It's *amazingly easy*, involves very little work or money, is quite exciting and a great way to make friends ... and for the first time, perhaps, you will experience that heady exultant feeling of POWER ... WHAM!

The next step is to get informed and keep informed. Read your local paper. Nobody is going to go out of their way to tell you if your local nurseries are going to be closed. They are going to vote it through quietly, then say, 'I'm afraid it's too late' – and this can all happen within a month.

Emergency action

If there is a threat to close the local nurseries swing into action quickly. Contact other parents, the staff of the school and all the local playgroups and organize a march to protest – however small. Get fathers involved.

If you suspect that there may be a move to close schools you can go to the local education committee meetings, which are open to the public. Of course you won't, *but this is the way to save your schools.* Find out when the next meetings are by asking at your library or local newspaper or telephone your county hall.

Find out what is available for full-time under-five care (or not, as the case may be). Contact your local social services department. (You will find them in the phone book – or ask at your local library.)

For further support, encouragement and ammunition (a good, short, simple pamphlet, plus a longer, detailed, back-up information sheet) join the National Campaign for Nursery Education (Chairwoman: Vicky Hurst) at 33 Hugh Street, London SW1 (tel. 01-828 2844). There's no charge to join.

Also get in touch with the British Association for Early Childhood Education (BASE) (Chairwoman: Lady Britton); London office: Montgomery Hall, Kennington Oval, London SE11 5SW (tel. 01-582 8744).

Then you start

The aims of any protest campaigns are to:

1 Show *your* power to the people in power. Show that a lot of people care – and they are voters.
2 Put your case to the public as well as to the people in power. By airing your grievance publicly you will get more support and put your opponents in the hot seat.
3 Force the people in power to change their cosy plans.

How do you do this? The next bit is easy, cheap and boring. You write letters, letting everyone know that you're on the warpath and why; and what you want done.

The shorter the letter is, the more powerful it will be. Use clean paper and decent envelopes (not beige ones – they look as if there's a bill inside).

Get the letters typed. Get duplicates run off by an office service shop on a Xerox or do it yourself at your local library. Always address people by name, so that they know you have nailed them. Never write to 'The Chairman of the Education Committee'; always write to 'Councillor Bloggs', preferably at his home. You get their names by ringing up your county hall and addresses from the *Municipal Yearbook* at your local reference library. Pass round the hat for the cost of letters and postage. On no account allow yourself to be stuck with the bill.

Write to:

1 The editor of your local newspaper. One of the easiest ways to mobilize support is by a short, simple letter *asking* for it in the letters column of your local paper.

Tell them the situation. Ask them if there's anything else they want to know. Then write to the national papers. The pre-school playgroups, which now number over a quarter of a million, were born ten years ago as the result of a letter to *The Guardian* Women's Page. So write to the woman's editor of a paper *as well as* the editor. Make them see that you're not going to give up easily.
2 Find out who your MP is (ask the local library). Write to him and ask him *what he's going to do about it* (write to him at the House of Commons, Westminster, London sw1). Then go and see him at his local surgery (local party headquarters). Don't feel apologetic. He was elected to look after your interests and he's supposed to know and report to his party leader on local public opinion.

Write to your local MP on the following lines. Don't ask what his views are, just ask plainly for what you want:

Dear Mr X,
 I believe that a nursery school provides excellent pre-school training for children by giving them opportunities to be with other children in surroundings

which are safe and interesting. They learn to play and communicate with people outside their immediate family, and to grow in independence, which helps their start in full-time school. My child needs this facility. Please tell me what is being done to provide it.

Don't be fobbed off with a reply that's as woolly as his party's policy and which says – very politely – nothing. Write back to say that if he wants you to vote for him next time, you want to know, on paper, what he's going to do about it.

Next, flex your fingers, pass the hat around for more postage money and write to the most important local people concerned. These are:

The leader of your local council (both district and county);
All your local councillors (both district and county);
The chairman and members of the education committee;
The chairman and members of the education sub-committee;
The director of education for your area (who's the one that gets paid to run the system);
Your ward councillor (he represents you locally on the council).

Write to *all* the women ward councillors (after all, they're working, aren't they?). Find out their names and addresses at your local library.

Write roughly the same letter to all of them: they're not going to compare notes. And if they do you've made your point twice. Have letter-writing parties, and get your friends to write

similar letters, but make them slightly different on different paper and send them at different times.

Your aim is to get all those in authority thinking about it. Be prepared for resounding ignorance when they reply – and don't accept it. Write back and ask them how many children fall into the seven kindergarten categories (by now you probably know, but they may not). If your figures are different, don't assume theirs must be correct. Write back and ask them to check their figures as they don't agree with yours. Remember (as they will): (1) that you voted for them, and even if you didn't, they don't know; (2) they want your support; (3) they don't want you to support anyone else, because they don't want to lose their jobs. Very few people realize how much importance M.Ps and local councillors attach to *every* individual letter they receive.

You're going to put a lot of effort into writing those letters. So make sure that they arrive and *that nobody can deny it*, by sending them by recorded delivery (9p extra, as I write). It's worth it. Carefully file the replies. *Keep the correspondence going* by asking questions and commenting on the replies you receive.

Perhaps your friends are unable to give more help than signing their name on a letter. But a lot of people are prepared to sign a *petition*. Stand at the gates of the school and ask all the mothers to sign; also make sure they give their addresses or nobody will take much notice of the signatures. Ask other signers to take away a copy of your letter and collect signatures themselves. Always offer to collect the signed letter yourself and make a definite appointment to do so.

After letters and a petition, direct action:

The visits

Visit the appropriate department and preferably the appropriate man. Keep him or them constantly informed of your needs and their urgency. Be polite but firm and persistent. Grow a thick hide. *Anyone* can have tenacity, and that's what counts. People often give in just to get rid of you. Take your facts with you. Hand out copies. Remember always that a lot of the decision-making people have no idea what's happening in the real world outside their dusty old age group.

At the moment, nursery education has a pretty low vote-catching electoral priority. But there are $4\frac{1}{4}$ million children in Britain under five, and they must have quite a lot of voting parents whose family life and income are vitally affected by this issue.

Lady Britton advises:

Pinpoint one person. Try and get a group, even if it only consists of three or four people, so that you look representative of other mothers and can't be labelled as a lone eccentric. The people to buttonhole in person are your local education committee. The most susceptible time to get your local councillor enthusiastic about your problem is just before the May elections. It is often when people feel that their own position is in danger that they bother to get things done.

Don't think that no one will notice your efforts. In my own county (Surrey) there was a threat to close all the nursery schools and spontaneously, without any organized protest, the mothers all flocked to the nursery to see what they could do to help keep them open.

Then they organized coaches to go to County Hall on the day that the Education Committee was meeting in order to discuss the closures. The mothers took their children and they buttonholed everybody who went in. And they won in the end. The schools were not closed down after all. The men simply complied immediately.

Let those words spur you on to your next step, which should be:

An event

This might be simply presenting your petition to the Mayor, but there's no reason why you shouldn't present one (however small) to the Prime Minister at No. 10 Downing Street (I have). Telephone beforehand (01-233 3000) to say that you're coming, and they will have a policeman to welcome you.

On no account leave the children at home when you protest. Don't let the councillors or MPs get away with dealing with children in theory. Always face them with the children. Encourage them to bawl (not difficult): Don't be pushed away. Stay put. Don't be frightened off by front hall commissionaires in uniform. *Stay right where you can be seen and photographed and televised.* Try to stage your protest when something is happening – a full council meeting or the meeting of the education committee.

Get the children involved. In the grand committee room of the House of Commons, fathers, mothers, teachers and children have sung nursery songs in protest. MPs were amazed but could not ignore them. Don't forget that what attracts publicity is royalty, babies and dogs, so use whichever is available. Encourage the children to wave balloons or little flags with your message on ('Hands off our school' or similar). Look upon it as an exercise in theatre and you won't feel so self-conscious.

Any mother's protest is newsworthy, especially with prams and particularly if escorted by a policeman, which is amazingly easy to arrange; you should always inform the local police in advance. Telephone to say that you are going to hold a quiet mothers' protest and they will almost certainly provide you with an escort if you ask for one nicely.

Don't forget, also, to inform local newspapers, radio and television, *by letter in advance addressed to the news editor and picture editor*. Include the name, address and *phone number* of the person who is responsible for giving information to the Press. Head your letter with the date, the time, the place, and

Mothers' Protest.

Then say (as quickly as possible) what is going to happen, where, when and (last of all) why.

The day before phone all the news editors; at 3 p.m. for the evening papers and 8 p.m. for the dailies, to remind them of your protest. Phone again next morning before 10 a.m. Do not leave any messages, because they might easily not get passed on. Say you want to speak to the news editor or his deputy. When you've done that, ask to speak to the picture editor or his deputy (on newspapers). Don't be shy, they're a fatherly lot and they should appreciate your giving them such clear, reliable advance information. Just ask if they have received your letter and whether they want any further information. You may easily find that they haven't had it or they've lost it, so be prepared to read it out.

You must decide on one person to deal with the Press, with no other official job, and she should write down her key points beforehand and if she forgets them (highly likely: I nearly always do) she should fish the list out of her pocket and read it. (Just write down what you are doing and why in note form.) She should also take a notebook, a couple of biros and lots of 2p pieces for the telephone (because news editors ask you to phone them back and so you may have to use callboxes near your protest). Don't be aggressive. There's no need. Just be firm. Be determined that you are going to enjoy yourself. And you'll be surprised to find that you will.

Remember:

1 **Every local authority has the power *now* to extend the provision of nursery education.**
2 **The Government has offered real money to every local education authority to finance more nursery education. Sometimes this money is**

not taken up, or it has been quietly used to put up buildings which are used for something else, or (even worse) left empty. Both major governing parties deplore this inefficient and underhand behaviour.

3 A really determined local council can wriggle out of it but they are supposed to provide schooling for all under-fives, and that is the law as laid down in the 1944 Education Act.*

Anybody can wriggle out of anything but you can see that your local councillors don't wriggle out of it unnoticed and unchallenged.

* The 1944 Education Act (Section 8[2] [6]) says: 'A local Education Authority shall in particular have regard to the need for securing that provision is made for pupils who have not attained the age of five years by the provision of nursery schools, or where the authority considers the provision of such schools to be inexpedient, by the provision of nursery classes in other schools.'

A GUIDE TO THE UNDER-FIVES CARE SYSTEM
(if you can call it a system)

When researching this junior spaghetti junction I spoke to one of the Education Minister's top advisers on pre-school care. She is married and looks forward to having children 'and carrying on with her career'. *What are you going to do with the children?'* I asked. 'Oh, they'll be no problem,' she said merrily, 'You see, I know all the dodges.' You, too, may want to start investigating them, so here is your guide.

It's hard to find your way around our pre-school care system for under-fives. This is *not* because your brain isn't big enough to cope with it. It is because it is an inefficient confused system, born of several basically inadequate and confused policies. But as you'll have to find your way around it, there's a guide on the next pages.

Category	Description of kindergarten	Get further information (how to find one, how to get into one) from:
	The Department of Education and Science (DES) and the local education authority are *only* responsible for the following:	
Public	*Nursery Schools.* For 3- to 5-year-olds. The children are taught lessons (full- or part-time).	Your local education office (find where from town hall or local library).
Private	*Nursery Schools.* The same but parents pay fees.	Your local social services department, with whom they have to register.
Public	*Nursery Classes.* For 3- to 5-year-olds in primary school, full- or part-time.	Your local education office.
	The Department of Health and Social Security and your local social services department are responsible for the following:	
Public	*Local Authority Day Nurseries.* For children from 6 months to 5 years in difficult family situations. *More* than full-time. Open 8 to 6 all year round except public holidays. Staffed by nursery nurses, not teachers. These are almost always overbooked and difficult to get into.	Your local social services department (find whereabouts from your doctor, citizens' advice bureau, town hall or local library).
Private	*Day Nurseries and Day Care Centres.* Usually for 2- to 5-year-olds, usually expensive. Staff training standards vary, so watch out!	Your local social services department, with whom they have to register. See *Yellow Pages* under 'Nurseries'.

Category	Description of kindergarten	Get further information (how to find one, how to get into one) from:
Private (continued)	*Crèches* for children of 0 to 3 (often attached to factories and private companies which depend on women). Usually for 6 months to 3 years.	There are over 2500 such crèches in Britain. For details, check with your local employment office or jobcentre.
Private	*Playgroups.* Originally started by parents on a voluntary part-time basis while the nationwide network of nursery schools and day nurseries was being organized ... (ho ho!). This is really supervised play. Children are supervised mainly by voluntary part-time mothers who take it in turns.	
Private	*Child Minders*, who look after children in their own homes. If they are not registered with the local social services department they may be cheaper but dangerously unfitted to look after children.	Your social services department with whom registered ones are registered. Anyone who isn't registered (and there are thousands of them) is operating illegally.
Public	*Supervised Holiday Play Schemes.* These are not often for the under-5s but sometimes you may be lucky.	Your local citizens' advice bureau.
Private	*Nannies and other helps.*	Local jobcentre advertisements in local newspapers. The best place to advertise for a mother's help seems to be *Nursery World.* For any other sort of living-in help the best place seems to be the *Lady.*

A pre-school playgroup is a centre organized by parents in premises such as an empty church hall or community centre which have been approved by the local authority. It takes children aged from three to five for about three hours in either morning or afternoon from two to five times a week. So it's only suitable for mothers with a part-time job, or none at all. Nominal fees pay for heat, light, toys, modelling clay, paints, books and other equipment. The children are taught no formal subjects but learn to get on with other children, to accept authority, to be imaginative and unselfish. It's also a good way for mums to meet other people with the same interests – other mums.

If you haven't a local playgroup, how about starting one near you, on a co-operative basis with other mothers? Get advice from the Pre-School Playgroups Association, Alford House, Aveline Street, London SE11 5DH (tel. 01-582 8871). You'll also find that your local social services department will go out of their way to help you and may even give you a grant to get started. Pre-school playgroups are part of government policy and a quarter of a million other mothers have started them in this country in the last ten years – so it can't be all that difficult.

If you want to start a playgroup you must register with the local social services department and comply with the common-sense conditions drawn up by the Department of Health. The social services department will advise you on the requirements, which are mainly such obvious ones as an outdoor play area, safety catches on windows, adequate light, heat and ventilation and sufficient lavatories (one to every eight children).

MOTHER'S HELP! HELP! HELP!

If you have several children and if you can afford it, I think the best home help is to get a daily mother's help, rather than a nurse or nanny, because children, no matter how young, shouldn't get used to a lot of attention all the time. And you're far more likely to be lucky with people who don't live in, because your setting is then just part of their life; they're not subconsciously fighting with you for centre-stage.

Alternatively, it seems easier to live happily with young foreign girls who know that they're going home within a year and who are here for a reason (to learn the language from your children). There are drawbacks. They simply don't know how to do any housework or cookery; back home, that was all done by *Mutter* or the servants. They are unlikely to be responsible, likely to need supervision. Remember what you felt like at that age? Indifferent to everything (especially children) except make-up, hair and fellas. Why should you suppose that, deep down, Helga is any different?

Most workers have the weekends off and the evenings off and one way to keep Helga happy is to let her have this time off. If you get someone whom your children like and who just covers you for your full-time office hours, then you're either lucky or clever and probably a combination of both. Don't push your luck. When you've got her *never stop checking*. It isn't sneaky. It's only fair to your children. It's only fair to the mother's help. There is no need to trust her until she is proven trustworthy. If you can't hop home unexpectedly at lunchtime get someone else to do so, on a pretext of picking up a book or a letter. This sounds nasty, but they're *your* children and you have a duty to them and you can't take risks.

As in all contracts, what has been arranged should be clearly understood. You should both have a copy of this in writing, dated and signed by both of you. Any later variations should be similarly noted, so that there's proof of what has been agreed.

I have found only one system which works faultlessly: lists behind the kitchen door. A list of emergency telephone numbers and addresses. A timetable for the children. A timetable for the mother's help with time off (*and* time on) clearly marked down in black and white. *You* need to know what *she* has agreed and what *you* have let yourself in for. (You can also point this out to your friends who say that the lists remind them of Eton/ prison/Auschwitz/the Navy.) Have a few trial runs with your emergency list (the house is now on fire, the children haven't returned from the park, the baby has fallen downstairs, the cat is

eating the lunch, what are you going to do about it?).

The simpler the children's meals, the more likely they are to get them as you planned. Fruit, cheese, salads and hot vegetable soups are nutritious and undemanding, and easy to organize. If she is supposed to do any housework, your mother's help should clearly understand that the children come before the home and you just have to accept that this is a golden excuse not to do housework. There should, however, be good evidence that the time has been 'spent' with the children and not watching the television or doing homework (hers, not theirs). Check by simply asking your children (if they're old enough to tell you), 'What did you do today?/What did you make today?/Where did you go today?'

You have to decide whether you want an au pair or a home help. An *au pair* is a part-time helper who will do thirty hours' work a week (i.e. she's only 'on' for thirty hours a week, including evening baby-sitting; the Home Office say she should do a maximum of five hours a day and have one full day off per week when she's not learning English). She is supposed to be treated as a daughter of the house, not given heavy work, not paid much (comparatively) and you don't have to pay National Insurance contributions for her.

Au pair girls from EEC countries don't need a work permit for full- or part-time work for six months. After a stay of six months, they can apply to the Home Office for a resident's permit. Get the form from the Immigration and Nationality Department, Lunar House, Wellesley Road, Croydon CR9 2BY (tel. 01-686 0688). To do this, first get an EC1 form from the local jobcentre; this must be filled in by the employer and sent with two passport photographs, passport and/ or identity card.

No girl under seventeen can come as an au pair and Immigration has to be satisfied that (a) she's an au pair, not a white slave, (b) she gets enough free time and (c) she's really going to learn English. If you don't meet her upon arrival in Great Britain she should have a letter stating who she's coming to work for as an au pair and for how long and where she's going to study.

If you want a foreign *home help*, you either apply to an employment agency for one who's already in this country or you can arrange through an employment agency to import one. If you want to import one, go to a *reliable* agency, and be prepared for a wait, a lot of paperwork and a gigantic bill, including air fare, some of which may be refunded if she walks out soon after arriving; many do. Whoever you hire, ask for at least two references and check carefully on them.

Foreign nationals (anyone other than Commonwealth or EEC) must get a work permit before coming in. You apply to the local employment office (under 'Employment' in the telephone directory). They send the permit to the foreign national, who produces it with her passport when she arrives at Immigration. She may also need a visa, depending on which country she comes from.

Within a few days of arrival she has to register with the local police. She should apply in good time (two months) to renew her permit. Get her medically checked fast (and I don't mean for pregnancy).

What you get for the very high wages is supposedly a professional domestic helper who works forty hours a week, expects a room of her own with a TV, all her food (no mean sum these days) and her National Insurance contributions paid entirely by you.

With any foreign help watch out for incessant telephone calls to the folks back home and the inflated bills. The cost should firmly be provided for in the advance agreement.

With homegrown help the living-in situation is the same, but untrained full-time home helps are often more demanding and more neurotic. If you pay more than the going rate you will not be popular with your neighbouring working mothers, but you will generally find someone who is that bit more responsible. A bonus system can be a good idea, provided you don't pay the bonus before the Christmas or summer holiday, (a) when extra to contract money is regarded a Right, or (b) before visiting their own folk when the temptation to stay with them or continue to sit at the seashore is often too great. But pick your own bonus system, and relate it to achievement. I know someone who employs her evening baby-sitter on a yearly basis, with an end-of-year bonus. She then gets reliability and the children always get the same person. A good idea.

Other forms of help: Escort work seems to be a growing market for old age pensioners and women who have a spare couple of hours a day. This involves their meeting children from school or kindergarten, taking them home and giving them tea. There is therefore no latch key problem. It can often be the ideal solution for mothers who can take their children to school in the morning on their way to work but can't get off early enough in the afternoons to fetch them.

It's a particularly good idea if you can make a similar arrangement with a mother whose children also go to your children's school. She can make a bit of money almost painlessly (a phrase I rarely use) and if you're very lucky you can extend the system in the school holidays. It might even be possible to find a non-working mother to cope throughout the day with your children as well as her own.

A registered child minder can look after your children for up to eight hours daily in her home. Costs vary and are arranged between parent and child minder. There are bad child minders and there are good ones.

As to *evening baby-sitters*, either you can afford them and you can get

them – or you can't. And that's the cost of having children. Raising a modern child can be more expensive than running a Bentley, especially after 6 p.m.

YES, YOU DO HAVE QUALIFICATIONS

Whatever you're doing or thinking of doing at the moment, assessing yourself can be a marvellous, rainy-day boost to morale and it costs nothing.

A lot of women think 'oh no, if I sat down and thought about it I'd feel even worse', but assessment is a great way to face, and nearly always beat, a sagging morale.

A lot of women think it's a great slice of self-indulgence. I'm fervently in favour of self-indulgence but in fact a self-assessment is more like a monthly bank statement – it clearly shows your assets and present position.

Assessing yourself is merely taking a hard, thorough look at your *advantages* and *disadvantages*. You decide:

What you don't want to do.
What you can't do.
What you can do.
What you could probably do.
What you want to do.

It's a bit like playing that old Victorian game of 'Confessions' in which you list your favourite food, favourite flower and your favourite virtue, and so on.

A careers guidance officer told me that you should never underestimate your home job, for job it is, albeit unpaid, and never, *ever* describe yourself as 'just a housewife'. That 'just' is bad for your self-esteem.

Running a home, like running a factory, involves principles of management, judgement and decision as well as other practical skills: you're not only the managing director, you're probably also all the workers, the personnel officer, the canteen staff and the all-important office cleaner. After two to twenty years of looking after a home and being her own boss, a women often doubts her advantages, loses some of her self-confidence and thinks that she's incapable of doing anything else. How wrong she is!

If you have survived motherhood, you have coped with many more pressures, problems and tensions than are met in an office. Dealing with difficult relations (all relations are difficult) may have led you to develop the sort of tolerance and adaptability that no young woman, fresh from school or college, has had the time to acquire; and no one can go to college to learn it. You have served a long and hard apprenticeship and have acquired many skills that you didn't have when you walked down the aisle. And that's what qualifications are – proof of skills and experience. All you have to do with yours is realize this and sort them out to your best advantage.

Sometimes your experience is positively preferable to five O and two A levels. For instance, reliable people with a family background are badly needed in the social services, especially if they have had experience with children. You are qualified for special social work training courses without having the Os and As that are necessary for the young. Some of these courses are especially for non-graduates and geared to women with family responsibilities.

As with sex or yoga, assessing yourself is a pleasant and harmless experience. You can do it alone, with a friend or go to a professional. In order to calculate your blessings, experience and abilities, you can use the self-assessment guide that follows and, having done so, book a *free* appointment with your local occupational guidance unit.

It is always a good idea to write out your lists and if possible get them typed *before* seeking professional advice from a careers guidance expert, if only to get it all sorted out in your own mind.

Don't try to think it out in ten minutes while you're doing the washing up. You really need to concentrate. The secret is to set time aside to do it. If you can't manage it in what's laughingly called the privacy of your own home, make an appointment with yourself and your notebook in your warm, cosy, quiet local library or the nearest park, garden or field, provided the sun is shining.

In order to pinpoint your possibilities list:

What you're good at (your talents): For instance, playing the mouth organ, or driving a bus, or reading poetry aloud.

What other people think you're good at: These are probably virtues that you think are so ordinary that you tend to discount them because you think that everyone is similarly gifted. But if someone else says 'you write such lovely letters' or 'you do pick things up quickly' or 'you're very good with your hands' or 'you're very good at explaining these government forms, dear', do not discount them. These are all highly marketable assets in the business world.

What you're not good at: Such as 'keeping the kitchen tidy', writing letters, getting ready in a hurry or being patient with sick people or simply noise. These traits might cut out some office jobs.

Oddly enough, the easiest way to pare your choices down to what you want is not by picking out what you *think* you really want to do but by eliminating the sort of job you won't or can't do.

Your interests: Eighteenth-century glass, or tennis, or your children.

What doesn't interest you and why: Other people's children, anything in the rain, football, what the southern area reps achieved last month, anything mathematical. (You can spend hours on this list once you get started, getting faster and faster.) When writing out this list, scribble your reasons (that's the catch: you can't just say 'because it's boring' – it isn't to lots of people) and you may learn a lot about yourself.

For instance, anyone with the above dislikes possibly wouldn't make a good saleswoman for Avon cosmetics, probably wouldn't enjoy being matron of a school and is unlikely to shine at the Board of Trade.

Your hobbies: I never know what to put under this heading. My mind goes blank and I am suddenly rendered hobbyless but afterwards, when it isn't necessary, I remember that my hobbies are yoga, swimming and cooking. *Your experience:* Write it all down as an outline autobiography (see the curriculum vitae on p. 63).

List any qualifications. You may not realize that qualifications in one career can often lead to another or are acceptable in another, different area. For instance, nursing, teaching, or secretarial training and management might be useful for social work; so write down *any* qualifications even if it's a twenty-year-old life-saving medal. Don't forget to write down in your life-before-marriage what you were good at or particularly liked doing at school; at college; at work; or on holiday jobs. For instance:

1965–70	Typist in solicitor's office
1970–74	Three experiences of childbirth, subsequently reached O level in patience, tolerance and understanding
1970–76	Found, furnished and ran two flats, one house
1972–74	Made and delivered daily supper to neighbouring, semi-invalid mother-in-law. A level in patience, tolerance and understanding
1973	Put in two mornings a week at local playgroup
1974	Helped to organize charity bazaar for local children's hospital
1976	Joined residents' committee of local estate

This mother has a basic office training and understands administration, can work with other people in a team (*much* more difficult in unpaid voluntary work than in an office), can fit a lot in, has plenty of gumption and has *shown* her interest in helping other people (as opposed to talking about her wish to do so).

Your secret ambition: Out with it, however unlikely it is. To sing Carmen at Covent Garden, to be Bernard Levin, to run a flower shop, to live in the country, or to travel to India/Far East/anywhere from Ruislip.

Now analyse it: Why do you want to be Carmen? Because you want constant praise, or because you want to be in show business or because you want to be the most successful member of the show. You certainly have ambition, even though you think you haven't, and you might investigate a job with your local theatre or with a theatrical agency.

Look again hard at any job that you want to do if you can give no reason, or a weak reason, for not having done it.

After you've drawn up your lists show them to someone who knows you really well and from whom you are willing to accept criticism without bursting into tears or flouncing out. Do not consult your husband. He may be biased (indulgently or otherwise).

Try your mother (who may know you best and may have studied you longest) or a sister or brother (who you can expect to be uncharitably honest with the experience of years behind every devastating remark). Or

consult a close friend, provided you've known her a long time. You're more likely to be your true self with a Her than a Him.

Once you've finished your list (especially the autobiography), check whether any of the following points can be included. All the following activities involve responsibility, experience and judgement (although you may not think this every morning as you slap the Farex into the baby's bowl):

Baby Care	**Child Care**
Adolescent Care	**Care of the Old**
Home Nursing	**Cooking**

All the following abilities are also saleable:

Beauty Care	**Sewing:**
Shopping	Slip-covers
Decorating	Curtains
Driving	Cushions
Gardening	Embroidery
	Lampshades

Any of the following are generally proof of organizing power, which indicates common sense, logical thinking and rationalization:

PTA	**Political Involve-**
Scouts	**ment**
Guides	**Fund Raising**
Brownies	**Church Activities**
Other Community Activities such as conservation, or environmental groups	

So that sums up your qualifications, skills and talents and experience to date. That's what you *can* do and it's probably a lot more than you thought. Yes, you do have qualifications.

Finally, *assess your character*. After all, you can probably do it in ten minutes better than Gypsy Petulengro. *Don't* look it up in the stars, just ask yourself:

Are you an introvert? (happiest alone, work best alone, don't like meeting people, happiest with a few, good friends)

Are you an extrovert? (love crowds and parties, often the life and soul of, feel uneasy alone, are sparked off by other people and spark off other people)

Do you like working alone?

Do you like working with a team? (leading it, following a leader, everyone sharing responsibility – if so I predict that you're in for trouble)

Are you practical? (well, you know if you are or you aren't)

Are you an idealist? (generally relates to previous answer – if no, yes; if yes, no – and age and experience, with which idealism tends to diminish – and with good reason – you then have goals rather than ideals)

Are you creative? (do you like making things, having your own ideas about things to make? Are you inventive? Do you think up new ideas? Do people pump you for ideas? Can you *sell*?)

Are you artistic? (anyone who's gifted would never admit to being artistic – well not after going to art school – because it's the sign of an amateur and is loaded with pretensions)

Can you give orders?

Can you take orders?

Can you give ulcers? (voluntary work is a good guide to this. Do people volunteer to work with you a second time?)

Can you avoid ulcers? (this is the one that sorts out the men from the boys, if you can work under pressure and avoid being pressurized)

To decide what's broadly practical and possible (always a good idea) tick which work pattern you think would suit you:

Do you like regular hours or as long as it takes?

Can you work regular hours or as long as it takes?

Do you want to work full-time?

Do you want to work part-time on a regular basis?

Do you want to work part-time on an irregular basis (school holidays off)?

Do you want to work evenings only?

Next, decide whether you're going to have a job or a career. A job is something with no particular thought of future advancement because you don't *want* to move and are happy in that job (such as being a nursery

school supervisor or a ward clerk in a hospital), or because you want to take your job up or put it down when you feel like it.

If you are interested in a job with career prospects, do you want to learn from your job and gain promotion from experience or from acquiring training? For instance, a factory-assembly-line, unskilled job can often easily lead to a semi-skilled job, which opens the way to a skilled job, and after that, such dizzy posts as supervisor, forewoman and inspector.

Are you prepared to train or study for a job or career? Do you want a structured career with a large company or to take your chances with a small company where you're bound to be noticed and needed?

Do you enjoy the unexpected challenges and emergencies, or do you prefer a steady, comfortable life because then you'll know what's going to happen tomorrow? (*Never* take a job if someone describes it as a challenge. It means there's either something wrong with it or it's too much for one person.)

And finally, have you got a good business sense? If so, what proof of this have you got?

I hope you got back from the park.

I hope they didn't close the library on you.

I hope that back home, they didn't have to sent the police to find you.

I hope you got a pleasant surprise.

GETTING READY FOR A BETTER JOB (whether or not you're in one)

Lots of people know exactly what they can do and what they want to do and trot out and do it. Well, that's wonderful, but if you're not like that, join the club. And as a matter of fact, such clever know-alls might be missing better opportunities that they don't know about. Not being too sure of what you want is a pretty good position to be in, these days. Because never before have there been so many good free schemes to give you advice, practical help, training courses and sometimes even money while you train. You couldn't ask for more positive encouragement to make a new start when you want to.

Most women spend their working life in two periods, maybe more, with a child-care period between. But while you're marking time in one period, you can be preparing for the next, when not wiping noses or running up a fairy dress.

Interestingly, the two-phase career, or the second career is not now confined to women: many men are choosing to make a second start. The accelerating rate of change in our society means that jobs have to change to match new needs. Stockings go out of fashion and factories go bankrupt. The birth rate falls so we need fewer teachers. North Sea Oil has opened up hundreds of new jobs. Consequently there are many schemes and educational courses specifically tailored for the second starter or for people who want to switch jobs to something better or build on the qualifications that they already have.

If you want to know what work training you can get cheaply that will fit in with your home life, there is plenty of free advice. Contact your local occupational guidance unit to discuss training and how to choose your job, or go and see the training officer at your local jobcentre. (Take the 'Superwoman's free job guidance chart' on p. 56 with you so that you can follow their Initialese.)

It is worth finding out direct from your local colleges if they run any training courses that interest you, because you may be able to get TOPS to pay the fees – and pay you to go on it!

If you are interested in a career in social work, you can get details of special courses which will suit women with family responsibilities but no qualifications.

Write direct to the Central Council for Education and Training in Social Work (CCETSW) for leaflets on your local opportunities and training. Write to CCETSW, Derbyshire House, St Chad's Street, London WC1H 8AD (tel. 01-278 2455). Offices also in Bristol, Edinburgh, Leeds and Rugby.

Another free careers advice service is run by the *Daily Telegraph* for its readers. Daily questions should be sent to the Daily Telegraph Careers Information Service, 42 Colebrooke Row, London N1 8AF. Enclose a stamped and addressed envelope.

If you are prepared to spend a few pounds and get to London, you can make an appointment for a consultation with the National Advisory Centre on Careers for Women (NACCW) at 251 Brompton Road, London SW3 2HB (tel. 01-589 9237). They will also give information by letter on request. A fee is charged in either case. Their patron is Queen Elizabeth the Queen Mother, and they were founded in 1933 by representatives of universities, women's societies, schools, colleges, professional organizations and the Fawcett Society. They specialize in returners and have done a great deal of research on their problems. Their booklet *Returners: Some Notes for Those Returning to Employment or Considering Training for a New Career* costs 85p post free from their address. A charming yet businesslike organization, they advise on training and careers but are not an employment agency, although they will put you in touch with one.

Preparing for a future training/job or career is not done in an afternoon. It's a short-term job in itself. But over-investigate rather than under-investigate the possibilities. Find out from more than one source what's available (plenty), and where it leads. Try to meet people who do it. Try to visit one of the places where it's done. Try to make as many contacts as possible. Check out with them the value of what you're about to do. Check which diplomas and certificates are respected in the business world, and which are worthless. Lots of women spend a lot of time and savings on a correspondence course leading to certificates which counts for nothing as a qualification for employment. It's infuriating to find that you have carefully learnt out-of-date methods of computer programming or accountancy.

Be wary of any private, high-fee schools, especially if they're advertised on local radio, and especially if they're for computer, hairdressing or film courses. Trot off and check with your local education offices or through TOPS. You'll almost certainly be able to get a similar course which has to conform to a high standard and will probably be free.

Try a little specific reading, when you've decided what interests you. There are lots of free leaflets and pamphlets (you should see my desk at this moment), and you can get a shopping basket of them at your local jobcentre. Also read any specialist journals, many of what are kept in public libraries – although you may need to ask for them.

Should you decide to train, then throw your mind forward just a bit farther and plan what you will do with that training. I know a photographer's wife with four children who is halfway through a university French course but says that she has never thought what she's going to do with her degree. I hope she doesn't end up like many women I know, who are still, twenty years later, trying to work out why they took a useless arts degree and what they can now do with it. Perhaps you only want to use your training for your personal, private life – enrichment. But, even so, it might be better to get one that would open the way to a good job in case you ever need it.

HOW TO GET THE BEST WITH WHAT YOU'VE GOT

Your attitude to work and getting it

Women whose children no longer need their full-time attention, and who therefore feel an increasing restlessness, often ask me for help in 'finding an interest outside the home' or in 'getting a job'. I find that they often have two problems. One is an understandable lack of self-confidence (a lot to be modest about, as Churchill put it). The other is that they don't want to strive or to work *realistically* towards anything, or to risk anything, or to even use the assets that they have ('no, I want something *different*'). What someone like this wants is a glamorous £10,000-a-year job (no experience needed) where she can meet people and 'express the real *me*'; working hours to be 10 to 4 with all school holidays off. And she doesn't want to apply for the job, she wants it *offered* to her, by some Fairy Prince of Industry.

I have never come across such a job (if I had, I'd have taken it), and it is vital to understand that this sort of job doesn't exist.

However, there are plenty of good, exciting opportunities for *everyone*. There is financial and other help for anyone who wants to start or start again. There are plenty of positively glamorous training and brush-up opportunities for a 'mature student', which is the official description of any female student over the age of twenty-three.

What is often most difficult for a woman is not acquiring the training, or reorganizing her home life in order to let her get away from it for a bit, but facing her own ambivalent attitude. She wants to go out into the world that she's missing, but deep down she doesn't want to leave her protective shell, so she finds masses of excuses not to do so. This can show in an understandable lethargy that she wants to escape from but that actually prevents her from escaping. This problem is very common, and most of us have it. The way to deal with it is by admitting it, facing it and stamping on it. What is difficult but essential is to stop making excuses to yourself (and anyone else who'll listen to you) and to decide coldly that you'll just have to live with whatever it is you might fear – embarrassment and shyness – and risk rejection or ridicule. (Incidentally, these things probably exist nowhere except in your head.) Mumble to yourself the-only-thing-we-have-to-fear-is-fear-itself and get up, go out and DO IT.

And each time you will find it gets easier and more enjoyable. Perhaps you have no choice but to get a paid job. As one *Observer* reader wrote, 'Now, suddenly I must find work because we need the money, and I find it humiliating. After being my own boss for twenty years I cannot see the

liberation in being interviewed and rejected. I cannot see the fulfilment in working...'

The indignation she expresses is echoed by many women who resentfully feel that 'I was never brought up to expect this' and that society has somehow pulled a fast one on them by changing when their backs were turned nursing babies.

But life is a state of flux and only change is constant and Archimedes agreed with me.

And *nobody* has been ideally equipped for life and *nobody* is going to do anything about it and your so-called 'rights' are neither here nor there unless they are enforceable. Life is tough and unfair. It's no use whining about what you *can't* do (because of your lack of drive, geographical circumstances, sheer bad luck or the wrong choice of parents).

There has to come a time when you stop blaming governments, schools, husband, children, women's lib, sex or your gender for what you *haven't* got and decide to do the best with what you have got. Because you can't do better than your best and it's not too difficult to do your best. (I have often found this a consoling thought when waiting to be interviewed or when scared of failure, after a success.)

There is one situation, however, that is more difficult to deal with than most. This is when you have been sacked or made redundant. It doesn't really matter whether it was your 'fault' or not, the sudden loss of a job can be a crippling blow to your self-esteem – or even a paralysing one. You may come to a full stop, you may feel unable to *try* to get a new job. The shock, the shame and the stigma of failure may be magnified (by you alone) out of true perspective. No longer being Mr X's publicity officer can be as devastating as no longer being Mr Y's wife. You may suffer a similar crisis of identity, and feel that you have no standing, you are just out of work, ashamed of it and hating it – and everybody knowing about it. This, of course, means that just when you most need your self-possession in order to get another job to find the money to pay the inexorable bills you are suddenly drained of your self-confidence, drive and energy and filled with anxiety.

Paradoxically, this is the time when you are most likely to refuse all offers of help and withdraw from your normal life like a hurt animal.

You may easily become fairly short-tempered, and disagreeable. Like feeling grief at death these are symptoms of bereavement, only what you are mourning is your lost position.

Again, you must accept that your reaction is normal but know how to overcome it. You should concentrate on regaining your self-confidence.

The Government-backed Professional and Executive Recruitment Agency (PER – see p. 55) is a go-ahead, streamlined, countrywide organization who attempt, among other things, to restore bruised self-confidence and morale to anyone who wants to return to work. They help people who have been made redundant from managerial jobs to get back

on their feet and in a good job again. They also help those who simply want a change after a time with the same company, or those women who had a fairly responsible job before bringing up a family and now want to return to work. They would like to help more women who are still only *planning* to return to work after being at home with a family.

The PER attitude is straight-forward, realistic, down to earth and understanding. 'We try to show people that it can be difficult for *everyone* and that you must be persistent, rather than disillusioned and depressed if something doesn't turn up immediately,' explained the PER official. 'We show that it is important to organize yourself and turn job-hunting into a 9 to 5 job instead of sitting down and feeling sorry for yourself.'

Anyone turning to PER can get practical guidance from experts. They, or the Training Services Division of the Manpower Services Commission, run courses on which you are taught how to write a letter of application and a curriculum vitae, and how to handle different kinds of interview. The cream of the career specialists and professional business consultants give the talks and do the teaching. One of the best and most practical of the schemes is the three day *Self-Presentation Course*, for men *and* women (see p. 58). This is a confidence-building programme, a sort of high-powered charm school that offers expert coaching in the basic skills of how to go after a job and get it, as well as teaching you how to assess the current and future job market. Everything is free, your travel expenses and lunch allowance are paid.

Special Intensive Updating Courses may last from two to four weeks.

There are other, longer courses sponsored by the TSD. Some last from *four weeks to a year*. They are held in polytechnics and colleges of further education.

You can find out more about the Professional and Executive Recruitment scheme from your local job-centre, or by checking in the phone book, or on the list at the end of this chapter for your nearest PER office, or by contacting head office at 4 Grosvenor Place, London sw1 (tel. 01-235 7030). You ask to speak to the Candidate Consultant or Training Consultant and mention your type of work.

When you enrol with PER you have to fill in *only one form* and a candidate consultant will help you fill it in if you wish. This form is important because it puts you on the PER register so as to provide information that will be put through a computer and eventually circulated to prospective employers. There's no need to wait for the consultant to suggest that you might benefit from any of the half- or three-day courses in self-presentation. Don't wait to be asked – *you* say that you *need* one.

Another frequent problem today is the woman who has spent years working for a degree only to find that it's a useless asset when it comes to getting a job. But a degree is an excellent frozen asset – it doesn't date, deteriorate or lose its value, so do not underestimate its future possible value. As well as being tangible proof of a certain level of intelligence, learning, and verbal and written skills, a degree is proof of your ability to use your brain in a disciplined manner. Your degree may not have equipped you for any specific job but it may still provide a short-cut towards training for a speciality. Many professions accept graduates for a shorter period of training than is required for non-graduates. And you can't be accepted for some special management training schemes unless you already have a degree.

If you have a qualification that would be useful when getting a job – but it's been years since you got it – don't overestimate how rusty you are. Details of professional knowledge change but essentials don't. Many professional organizations have schemes to bring members up to date. You can often catch up very quickly.

It's always worth writing to the headquarters of your professional organization to find out what refresher courses are available. You should always *try* to keep in touch by subscribing to your professional journals and don't lose touch with the people you know who are still working in the field. When you're planning to go back, meet them, catch up, ask for their advice and recommendations about recent books and developments.

Whatever your qualifications, if you are thinking of brushing up your knowledge, retraining or training for something quite different, you should use all the free help you can get.

If you're not quite sure what you want to do, make an appointment with the occupational guidance officer of your local careers office (see chart on p. 56), who will help you sort out the possibilities that exist for you and what you're suited for.

Non-residential 'fresh start' courses

No O or A levels required. These colleges are increasingly popular. Much recommended by guidance officers. Courses vary from one day a week for six weeks to one year full-time.

Outside London
Consult your local education authority.

London area
Fresh Horizon courses at The City Lit, Stukeley Street, London WC2B 5LJ. One year full-time study. Alternatively two days or two evenings a week.

Careers Foundation course at Paddington College, Saltram Crescent, London W9 3HW. One year full-time.

Fresh Start course at Richmond Adult College, Kew Road, Richmond-upon-Thames. One and a half days a week: period depends on course.

Second Chance course, Mile End Annexe, Avery Hill College, English Street, London E3. Two days or two evenings a week for two years.

PER (Professional Executive Recruitment) Offices

Aberdeen: 3 Golden Square, Aberdeen AB1 1RD (tel. Aberdeen [0224] 21231)

Birmingham: Fountain Court, Steelhouse Lane, Birmingham B4 6DS (tel. 021-236 6971)

Bradford: Sun Alliance House, Eldon Place, Bradford BD1 3TF (tel. Bradford [0274] 32925)

Brighton: 53 West Street, Brighton BN1 2RL (tel. Brighton [0273] 23431)

Bristol: Minster House, 27–29 Baldwin Street, Bristol BS1 1LY (tel. Bristol [0272] 299854)

Cardiff: 4th Floor, Pearl Assurance House, Greyfriars, Cardiff CF1 3AG (tel. Cardiff [0222] 23286)

Chelmsford: Cater House, 49 High Street, Chelmsford CM1 1DE (tel. Chelmsford [0245] 60235)

Coventry: 6th Floor, Bankfield House, 163 New Union Street, Coventry CV1 2PE (tel. Coventry [0203] 29495)

Edinburgh: 127 George Street, Edinburgh EH2 4JN (tel. 031-225 2736)

Glasgow: 48 St Vincent Street, Glasgow G2 5TS (tel. 041-221 7044)

Gloucester: Grosvenor House, Station Road, Gloucester GL1 1TA (tel. Gloucester [0452] 35525)

Guildford: 66–68 Chertsey Street, Guildford GU1 4JP (tel. Guildford [0483] 35666)

Hull: Brook Chambers, Ferensway, Hull HU2 8LU (tel. Hull [0482] 223671)

Leeds: Westminster House, 29 Bond

Street, Leeds LS1 5BE (tel. Leeds [0532] 445131)

Leicester: Northampton House, 177 Charles Street, Leicester LE1 1LT (tel. Leicester [0533] 536321)

Liverpool: 3rd Floor, Graeme House, Derby Square, Liverpool L2 7SP (tel. 051-227 4111)

London: 4–5 Grosvenor Place, London SW1X 7SB (tel. 01-235 7030)

Luton: 56–62 Park Street, Luton LU1 3JB (tel. Luton [0582] 417562)

Maidstone: London House, 5 London Road, Maidstone ME16 8HR (tel. Maidstone [0622] 54341/677612)

Manchester: Elisabeth House, 16 St Peter's Square, Manchester M2 3DF (tel. 061-236 9401)

Middlesbrough: Sun Alliance House, 16–26 Albert Road, Middlesbrough Cleveland TS1 1PR (tel. Middlesbrough [0642] 244222/247887)

Newcastle: 7–12 Nelson Street, Newcastle upon Tyne NE1 5AZ (tel. Newcastle [0632] 28543)

Norwich: Norfolk Tower, Surrey Street, Norwich NR1 3PA (tel. Norwich [0603] 60068)

Nottingham: Lambert House East, Clarendon Street, Nottingham NG1 5NS (tel. Nottingham [0602] 49781)

Oxford: 105 St Aldates, Oxford OX1 1DD (tel. Oxford [0865] 723216)

Plymouth: National Westminster Bank Chambers, St Andrews Cross, Plymouth PL4 0AA (tel. Plymouth [0752] 69561)

Portsmouth: 54 Arundel Street, Portsmouth PO1 1NL (tel. Portsmouth [0705] 815241)

Preston: Victoria House, Ormskirk Road, Preston PR1 2DX (tel. Preston [0772] 59743)

Reading: Sun Alliance House, Oxford Road, Reading RG1 7LU (tel. Reading [0734] 595666)

Sheffield: Chesham House, Charter Row, Sheffield S1 3EB (tel. Sheffield [0742] 77556)

Southampton: 62–64 High Street, Southampton SO9 2EF (tel. Southampton [0703] 26358)

Stoke-on-Trent: East Precinct, Charles Street, Hanley, Stoke-on-Trent ST1 3AR (tel. Stoke-on-Trent [0782] 262255)

Swansea: Grove House, Grove Place, Swansea SA1 5DH (tel. Swansea [0792] 43481)

Warrington: 75 Sankey Street, Warrington WA1 1SL (tel. Warrington [0925] 52153)

Washington: Derwent House, Washington, Tyne and Wear NE38 7SU (tel. Washington [0632] 466660)

Wrexham: Halkyn House, Rhosddu Road, Wrexham, LL11 1NE (tel. Wrexham [0978] 56575)

CHOOSING A JOB

There are masses and masses of jobs that you can do, and where you're needed; there are some that might not be at all suitable: some might be more suitable than others.

The Government Manpower Services Commission says that the training of women is a priority of special national importance, and as you can see from this book, the opportunities are there if you care to pick them up – and they are especially aimed at mature women who want to return to work.

Today, theoretically, a woman can try her hand at anything. However, there still remain two main limiting factors: they are lack of training and age.

Some areas, such as advertising copywriting, are youth-orientated to the point of panic; some jobs need a high standard of physical fitness; I keep telling you it's too late to be Margot Fonteyn (it's almost too late for *her*) or Chris Evert or a PT instructor.

Some training periods are likely to be too long for granny, who, at her age (forty plus), can now do quite a lot of other things that she couldn't do when she was fresh out of school.

Professional work may mean a long study and training period of up to seven years. If you are not prepared for four to seven years of study and training you cannot be a doctor; accountant; actuary; veterinary surgeon; architect; surveyor; engineer; housing manager; lawyer; journalist; dancer; musician. Nor can you be a Top Dog on the Stock Exchange or in the Diplomatic Corps.

But that still leaves quite a lot of choice, so don't settle for a dead-end job that will eventually bore or depress you.

Manpower says that women should take the opportunities (offered by TOPS among others) to train for jobs that, until now, have tended to be male dominated. They are particularly anxious for more women to train as engineering technicians and in elec-

tronics, where job opportunities are expanding, and there are not enough men to fill them.

Similarly, they would like more women to train for craft-based trades in manufacturing and construction, and such jobs as plumbing and carpentry. An evening plumber or a sewing-machine repairer can earn more per hour than the Prime Minister, and the price of a carpenter is above rubies.

Women are also under-represented in general management, says Manpower (only 2 per cent are women, whereas over 40 per cent of the working force is female). They are very anxious to encourage more women to take TOPS courses that lead to managerial qualifications and say: 'There can be little doubt about the long-term need for talented managers drawn from a wider social cross-section of the population, a need which able women could help to meet … particularly in those industries which employ large numbers of women, such as the clothing industry, hotel and catering, computing and chemicals, banking and insurance.'

SUPERWOMAN'S FREE JOB GUIDANCE CHART

When you need further job training, this is your guide to the best that is available for nothing. And don't think that because it's free, it's mediocre. It's an amazing, highly professional, no-expense-spared service – and your taxes pay for it, so why not use it? The dreary, tiled, governmental labour-exchange image has vanished. There's a new, expensive, streamlined system waiting to be used by you. Here it is. This is how it works:

In 1974 the Government set up the Manpower Services Commission as an independent agency to co-ordinate all employment and training services previously run by the Department of Employment. The ten members on the Commission represent private industry (the Confederation of British Industry), the TUC, local authorities and the Government. Northern Ireland has its own Department of Manpower Services which runs on similar lines.

The Manpower Services Commission runs two agencies. They are:

1 The Employment Service Division (ESD).
2 The Training Services Division (TSD).

The Commission also administers directly the Government's Job Creation Programme.

The Employment Service Division

1 This runs the nationwide network of 900 local *employment offices* (the old employment exchanges) and *Jobcentres*.

It also gives free advice on choosing a job and career guidance through the Occupational Guidance Service (see p. 58). The employment offices and jobcentres (new name for the new-look, smartened up, more welcoming image that the Government wants to give the service) do the job of employment agencies, and help people to find work in manual, clerical and secretarial jobs. Employers notify the offices and jobcentres when they have vacancies.

2 For people with managerial, professional and technical work backgrounds there is the specialist government employment agency, *Professional and Executive Recruitment service* (PER).

PER was set up to provide all the services and expertise of a commercial management consultancy. It is *free*. It also runs *free* special courses to help its candidates land the job they want. It charges fees to employers and has been very successful in finding staff for top jobs. There are thirty-six PER centres in major towns around the country. Contact them directly (see p. 52) or ask for information at your local employment office/jobcentre.

If you fit into the range of jobs PER handle you register directly with them at the PER office. Once registered you can ask to go on one of the special short PER courses for job seekers, or they can give you details of special

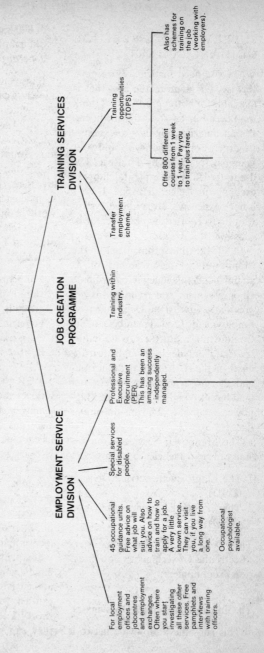

SUPERWOMAN'S FREE JOB GUIDANCE CHART

MANPOWER SERVICES COMMISSION

EMPLOYMENT SERVICE DIVISION

JOB CREATION PROGRAMME

TRAINING SERVICES DIVISION

For local employment offices and jobcentres and employment exchanges. Often where you start investigating all these other services. Free pamphlets and interviews with training officers.

45 occupational guidance units. Free advice on what job will suit you. Also advice on how to train and how to apply for a job. A very little known service. They can visit you, if you live a long way from one.

Occupational psychologist available.

Special services for disabled people.

Professional and Executive Recruitment (PER). This has been an amazing success - independently managed.

Training within industry.

Transfer employment scheme.

Training opportunities (TOPS).

Offer 800 different courses from 1 week to 1 year. Pay you to train plus fares.

Also has schemes for training on the job (working with employers).

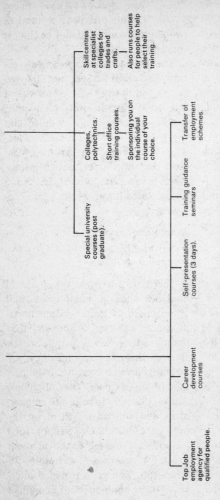

Top Job
employment
agency for
qualified people.

Career
development
courses

Self-presentation
courses (3 days).

Training guidance
seminars

Transfer of
employment
schemes.

Special university
courses (post
graduate).

Colleges,
polytechnics.

Short office
training courses.

Sponsoring you on
the individual
course of your
choice.

Skillcentres
at specialist
colleges for
trades and
crafts.

Also runs courses
for people to help
select their
training.

All services are free, although PER charges a fee to employers for finding top staff

training courses sponsored by the TSD. You needn't be a redundant executive to register with PER or take a course. You may just want a change, you may be thinking of moving jobs or planning to go back to work after being at home for a few years.

What's available through PER?

(a) *Self-Presentation courses* to teach top job seekers how to market themselves, get informed on what's available and acquire the knowledge and self-confidence to go after the job they want. Courses last three days and are *free*.

(b) *Career Development courses* which are *free* and last two weeks, during which you learn the latest management skills. They are for anyone who feels that he or she needs a refresher or wants to catch up on the theory side of management in order to qualify for a better job. They are also useful for anyone who may have been doing the same job for many years and is planning to change it.

(c) *A Training Opportunities Seminar* (also *free*) which lasts a day and is to advise people who want to get extra qualifications for a different job. At the seminar the range of courses specially tailored for managers under the TOPS scheme (see earlier) is introduced and explained.

(d) *Transfer of Employment schemes*. This is a two-week *free* residential course for unemployed executives who want to start a new business life, either on their own or in a company. Its appallingly stodgy title is 'Execu-

tive Career Review Development Course'! You are paid a tax-free training allowance and may be eligible for other *free* money.

The Transfer of Employment section also aims to get unemployed people out of work-starved areas and into good jobs. In order to do this, people are often paid to move and big, give-away money can be involved. This can cover moving expenses, legal costs and also other cash helps towards a new start, possibly including an increased-housing-cost weekly allowance.

3 Another service run by the *Employment Service Division* is *free Occupational Guidance*.

There are forty-five occupational guidance units in major towns and cities staffed by trained occupational guidance officers. Although they mainly advise young people at the start of their working life they will help anyone who wants to find a new kind of job or career. They often help women planning to return to employment and will advise them on the practical aspects of how to apply for a job and feel more self-confident about it. They will also advise on training for a new job. You get a personal interview lasting about an hour and a half – and you can have more than one interview with a trained expert who will assess your potential.

You will discuss your assets, interests, aptitudes, qualifications, experience and family circumstances in order to help you reach a sound decision about your future. The guidance officer can also tell you what training opportunities are available for you – and he can even call in an occupational psychologist to advise you and help you decide what you should do. In fact, this free service could cost you between £20 and £50 if you went to a commercial vocational guidance organization – and probably you wouldn't get a better service. If you live a long way from one of the occupational guidance units, they will send an officer to see you.

Job advice: You can get in touch with an occupational guidance expert through your local jobcentre (look that up in the phone book). It's always best to phone and make an appointment for an interview. Alternatively, you can telephone them directly in the following towns, where they are listed in the phone book under Occupational Guidance Unit: Aberdeen, Birmingham, Belfast, Bournemouth, Bradford, Brighton, Bristol, Cambridge, Cardiff, Chelmsford, Colwyn Bay, Coventry, Derby, Edinburgh, Exeter, Glasgow, Gloucester, Guildford, Hull, Ipswich, Leeds, Leicester, Lincoln, Liverpool, London (four here), Luton, Maidstone, Manchester, Middlesbrough, Newcastle, Nottingham, Oxford, Plymouth, Portsmouth, Preston, Reading, Sheffield, Southampton, Stoke-on-Trent, Sunderland, Swansea, Swindon, Wolverhampton, Wrexham.

Training Services Division (TSD)

This provides free training and refresher courses for people wanting to learn new skills or improve those they already have. The TSD runs the amazing TOPS scheme mentioned earlier, where they pay you a weekly wage to learn the skill of your choice, and the skillcentres, which are specialist colleges where you can learn various trades and crafts. The Division also organizes various special schemes for people who are already employed in industry. Under the general title of Training Within Industry (TWI) these schemes provide additional training in co-ordination with the twenty-two industrial training boards throughout the country.

You can find out about the different training schemes at a jobcentre/employment office, where you can arrange to see a training officer.

HOW TO GET THE JOB YOU WANT

Getting a job is the art of the possible, so settle down on the sofa and plan your campaign. Make a job of getting a job. Do it methodically, for so many hours a day.

First, decide roughly what job you want and if necessary talk to your local occupational guidance officer and check what's going at the jobcentre or PER. You want to get a 'feel' of what the market is, especially if you've been out of it for some time.

Regularly read the ads in the trade magazines, specialist journals, national and local press. You can do this in the peace and warmth of your local library. If you have a profession, union or trade organization or belong to an institution ask whether they run any kind of register of job vacancies. More do than you might think. If you're a graduate, continue to use the university appointments board and they will send you their vacancies list.

Get on the local grapevine by telephoning friends, acquaintances and organizations or people you have worked with before. Tell them that you're looking for a job and ask if they will keep an eye peeled for you.

You might get a good job faster if you get inside a large organization by taking a slightly lower-grade job; being actually on the spot is a recommendation. A lot of the best jobs are never advertised (particularly in large organizations) but promoted from within the firm. The higher up the ladder you get, the more likely this is to happen. There's a lot to say for starting at the top, but it's *not* always possible. There may not be room at the top at the moment, and if you hold out for that you may never start at all. Be prepared to start at a low level of responsibility; get your foot in the door in any way you can. To get my foot in a door I have worked as a waitress, a frying-pan demonstrator, a telephonist and a receptionist, which helped me to get over early shyness and was later

useful when I had to interview people as a journalist. Once you're in, lie low for a bit, absorbing it all, and then decide in which direction you want to move (perhaps sideways before upwards). Wait until you're indispensable, then pounce.

Remember that many public organizations are compelled by regulations to advertise jobs for which they've already picked someone internally, so be prepared for this time-wasting farce, which is supposed to prove impartiality.

Don't neglect private agencies (*you* don't have to pay them) who may test you, give you an idea of what the market's like and tell you what the top going-rate is for the job, which can be very useful indeed. However, don't expect someone else to look after you. Even if an agency is advising you, pursue your own line of research. They are dealing with hundreds of people: *you* are more interested in you than anyone else is likely or able to be. But check with the agency daily, nevertheless.

Don't pursue one job at a time. Pursue them *all*, *all* the time. This approach is a lucky dip.

You might put an advertisement in a newspaper or magazine or in the corner tobacconist's. Don't necessarily choose the job columns; try the personal columns.

Make a list of potential employers, local or otherwise. (Look them up in *KOMPASS*, Volume 2 (a directory of British companies and their executives; find it in the reference section of your library), or the *Yellow Pages*.) A

recent survey has *shown* that the energetic cold-canvass approach (writing out of the blue with an unsolicited application) gets three times as many job offers as answering ads. Address your application to a particular person by name (it's easy to find out: you just telephone and ask the name of the person you're after). Make sure you're applying to the right person in the first place. If in doubt, apply to the managing director by name. He or his secretary will pass your letter on to the correct person and it will have been seen by someone fairly high up and come from his desk so is bound to be read carefully. Check names, spelling, address, telephone numbers. It is irritating to be asked for something by someone who hasn't bothered to get your name right – this indicates sloppiness, right from the start.

Even if there isn't a job going at the time – make a play for one in a way that will be remembered. A friend of mine sent a postcard to the Editor of the *Evening Standard*. It read:

'For Sale: 1945 Celia Brayfield VGC. Only 2 lady-owners. New ideas all round. £2000 p.a. ONO.'

This was for a newspaper job in which wit, ideas and originality would be needed; if you're applying for a computer job don't try that sort of thing. She got a return postcard which read:

'Ageing Editor stunned by shock offer. Wishes to view immediately.'

She went for the interview in turquoise velvet dungarees and a T-shirt smothered in red stars. No hat, no little white gloves. She was interviewed and given the ring-up-in-three-months-in-case-we've-got-something routine. She did so, until three years later she was offered the job of writing the television programme preview page.

Writing a short, witty, memorable message is one thing, but don't try the sort of bright, slick, contrived, flirtatious approach that is used for selling aeroplane seats. For instance: 'I'm Linda, fly me. I'm twenty-two and blonde with a dynamic telephone personality. I love meeting people and I'm looking for an interesting job with opportunities to travel. Why not give me a whirl in your sales force?'

Keep your letter really short. Don't churn out identical letters to different people, because it shows and such letters go straight into the wastepaper basket. Say what you're applying for and why and say that you'll phone for an appointment. Don't leave it for them to reply (they're not in the acknowledgement business) and explain that you are enclosing your curriculum vitae (Latin for a potted autobiography which shows your education, work, experience and job background). Never tell a lie, although you may omit a few facts; everyone does. Give no charming details, no wit, no dynamic attack; cut the poetry and just give the facts with the dates. And make sure it's up to date and beautifully typed. Make lots of photocopies of it because, unlike your application, this should be *im*personal. For an example of a curriculum vitae, see p. 63.

Keep 'description of present job' brief, but include anything that might be relevant to the job you are seeking. Under 'other information' give any evidence of organizational commitments, voluntary work, achievements, languages, sport.

When you have written and reread your CV expect to feel amazement at the brilliance of this creature, followed by furtive guilt. This is because you have, naturally, carefully left out the bad bits (called editing). On no account change your CV at this point: it sounds fine.

Most large firms and public organizations have a standard application form. Do not be alarmed by these. They are basically the same. They want education, work experience, your especial interest, age and previous salary. It's a sort of write-your-CV-to-our-instructions kit. Some are more detailed than others and there's usually half an inch for you to give any other personal details and say why you want the job. Don't be daunted by this gruesome thing and don't be deterred as I once was. I had *trained* for a job for three months but was so appalled by the four-huge-pink-page form I was asked to fill in, that after looking at it for a guilty week I dropped all ideas of applying for the job.

1 Allow plenty of time for the filling-in of the form. They're not only after your details, they're seeing how neat you are and whether you can cram your name into an inch.
2 Read the thing right through first,

making notes on a separate bit of paper.
3 Follow the instructions carefully (referring to your own CV) and fill in *every* blank. Don't expect to fit everything in: everyone doesn't have the same size address or handwriting.
4 If you are asked for references, make sure you ask your referees beforehand if they don't mind doing them.
5 If you can't cram your life into a half inch of buff form (they must have very dreary lives) type a separate sheet of paper, giving the information. This is allowed and it's your *one* chance of making a personal impact in Round 1.

Elimination of unsuitable candidates: Always take a photocopy of the filled-in form, so that you remember what you said. Reread it before going to any interview, which with luck will be the next step. Before the interview you should have informed yourself of a few facts about the company and what it does. Potential bosses tend to be put off if you don't know what they do. You *can't* know too much about that and what the job is that you might fill. You need to know the minimum qualifications they're asking for, whether or not you have them. You should already have found out (by telephoning and asking) fairly full details of what the job is, what work and hours are involved, what the prospects are, what the pay and fringe benefits are.

Curriculum Vitae
_____

Name   Date of Birth
Nationality   Place of Birth
                                          Current Address

                                          Telephone Number

_____
Secondary Education
(Type of School and Name)

Attended from   to
Qualifications obtained

_____
Further Education
(University/College/ Institution)

Attended from   to
Course(s) taken

Qualifications obtained

Any other studies undertaken/qualifications obtained

Professional bodies,etc. to which applicant belongs

_____
Positions Held
From   To   Name of Company and Address   Title

(NB: Employers usually ask for the last three positions held)
_____
Current Position (or if unemployed at present, last position held)

From   To   Name and Address of Company   Title

Description of present job

Other information

_____

What do you say after you've said yes or no?

Make sure you know whether you will be interviewed by a selection board or by a personnel officer or other person. There's no one sure way to handle an interview, because there are too many imponderables, and the worst thing you can do is to run through an exact dialogue in your head: you then risk being thrown by any question that takes you off your prearranged track.

There are two probable problems. You might be n-n-nervous and you might be tongue-tied. You can make it much less of an alarming ordeal by holding a dress rehearsal first. Sit down quietly and imagine the very worst that could happen. You go to the interview, are tongue-tied, immediately contradict yourself, and then start giggling. Now (branded as a nervous liar) you want to go to the lavatory or worse. You suddenly can't remember what you've done before or why you want the job. Etcetera, etcetera, etcetera. Run through this little scene twice and then forget it. Because they can't do anything to you. They can't cut your tongue off or fire you if they haven't hired you. If they upset you, walk out with dignity (I have) and remember that *you* are interviewing *them* as well. The whole point of the interview is to see not only whether you're suitable for the job but whether the job is suitable for you.

And every interview is easier. Comedian Frankie Howerd, consoling me after a disappointing TV show, said:

'You never learn and you never mature until you've got a few failures under your belt. You need that experience and you can't get it any other way than by accepting it and chalking it up afterwards. Every time you get a bum audience you've got to think it's *not* a bum audience, it's *valuable experience* and you've got to get a lot of it before you qualify as a comedian. Or anything else.'

You should also prepare for being questioned. You don't want to unleash a nervous, Joyce Grenfell monologue every time anyone asks you anything (especially when you are asked about your children or why you left your last job) but neither do you want to say 'Yes' (gulp) ... or 'No' (cough) ... followed by a short silence, while they wait for you to expand/expound.

Try to rehearse with a friend. What you want the other person to do is to try and interview in a fairly formal, polite but cold fashion. Get him or her to look at your CV or application form and question you about it. Rehearse any bits that you seem shaky on or worried about : 'Do you really think you'll be up to it?'; 'It's been rather a long time since you worked in an office, hasn't it?'; 'Why do you want this job?'

If you're really nervous, don't rehearse with a spouse, who might make you even *more* nervous by being kind, correct and interested but somewhat brusque. 'Now be your age, you'd better not say anything so damn ridiculous.' It will either end in tears or giggles.

Before you go to the interview, decide that it's not the most important thing in your life – although it is important. Forget that you're shy. Remember that everyone is shy. Remember that if they didn't think you were any good they wouldn't be seeing you.

A careers guidance specialist told me that the most common mistakes made by women being interviewed are:

1 They don't know their market value.
2 They expect to be judged on their personality rather than on their experience and achievement.
3 They are not specific when asked what they're good at. They answer vaguely: 'Other people say I'm quite good at organizing.'

A particularly well-worn cliché is: 'I'd like a job where I can help people; because I'm good at that.' Very laudable but, after all, most jobs help some people in some way. Interviewers often interpret this statement as a sign of not wanting to take a job where achievement (or otherwise) can be measured against someone else's achievement (as with salesmen and sales figures).

Always sell yourself from strength, which means spelling out the things that you are good at, by clearly giving your qualifications, skills and experience and how you have used them. It's no use just bleating that you have a BA in this or that.

Wear comfortable shoes and comfortable clothes. Wearing something new can sometimes make you feel uncomfortably 'on show'. There are exceptions, but on the whole, dress to suit the company you're about to keep.

Get there in good time. It feels much worse to be late and flustered than to be kept waiting – which you probably will be.

You may be interviewed by the person you're hoping to work for or by the company personnel officer, who will be much tougher. You may be interviewed by a series of people, half of whom aren't expecting you and are busy doing something else. Being interviewed by a board can be worst of all. Quite often each person has his self-important role to act out and there may be a certain amount of conflict between the panel members. One may be nice, one throws trick questions, one may be the peacemaker and the quiet one in the corner may be the chief hatchet man in a bad mood. One has probably read a book on psychology (you read it too; it's bound to be *Test Your Own IQ* by H. J. Eysenck [Pelican] or one of the De Bono books). Quite often each person is only really interested in his own questions, so you find yourself running three non-sequitur, Marx Brothers conversations at the same time. Keep cool. Keep calm. Be positive. Don't let anyone provoke you. Humour them.

Never overestimate your shorthand and typing speeds – because they may test you. Never exaggerate the work you're doing at the moment because they're likely to check. Also if they hire you and give you seemingly suitable work you risk being unable to do it.

You must have an answer to everything in your CV that looks odd or a bit shady. If there's a huge gap, you've got to be able to say, 'I had glandular fever and was unable to work for three years: it has now cleared up and I've had no trouble for five years.' If you've been to twenty-seven schools, you've got to be able to say, 'My father was in the army and so we moved around a lot.'

Expect them to throw problems at you which might come up in the course of the job. Never criticize the firm or anyone in it, especially if they ask you what you think is wrong with the organization, or what you would like to see changed. Give them a bit of bland praise and say that you would need more facts to evaluate the position before you could analyse the problem and suggest a solution. Be prepared for questions such as: 'How do you see the role of this organization?'; 'How do you see your role in this organization?'; 'What makes you think you could do this job?'; 'Why did you take/leave *that* job after such a short/long time?' Be careful to avoid any mention of intrigue, unfairness or office politics or union showdowns in your last job and try to avoid criticizing your last boss. Warning bells will ring   TROUBLE MAKER and they won't want to risk your saying the same sort of thing about them.

If you're returning to work and they ask you what your husband thinks (they're not supposed to) smile sweetly and say, 'I'm very fortunate, he's very supportive.' When they ask what arrangements you have made for the children say something like, 'I'm very lucky: I've got a *wonderful* mother.' (Don't mention she's in Scarborough.) Say that you have a home help who's been with you for years and can always take them to the dentist.

Don't say too much. Don't look over-anxious. Don't say how healthy or good or talented your children are. Make it clear that you have long-standing arrangements and you're not worried about them. Swiftly throw in here (because you must cover it) that if, by any chance, your child needed you for a day, you would expect that day to be deducted from your holiday time. Children are still a grave disadvantage to a working woman whereas they're considered an advantage to a working man because they tie him down.

At some point in the interview you will be asked if you have any questions. At this point you have to play it by ear. Don't immediately ask what you're going to get out of it. An employer is interested in what you can do for the firm and the alternative viewpoint is an instant turn-off. So ask what work you'll be doing, to whom you'll be responsible and with whom you'd be working. If you're ambitious, you can definitely make this clear from your astute and intelligent questions about the firm's immediate plans (theirs), aims (theirs), and expansion (theirs). On no account start off by asking about pay (yours), holidays (yours), and pension scheme (yours).

You may be about to be slotted into a predetermined system or you may be about to start bargaining for a bigger water carafe or £1000 more than they are offering, but this point comes towards the end of the interview or even at the next one. If, however, you do reach this point make it clear what your exact expectations are (they may call them demands). Never expect to get *anything* that you haven't asked for and that hasn't been agreed. Always expect to bargain. They're in business, aren't they?

Working Part-time

Of course, it depends how you define 'work'. The majority of British working women have a part-time job. Theoretically, this seems to be getting the best of both worlds – having an outside interest as well as time for the home and family.

TAX ADVANTAGES

As long as you don't earn too much, part-time work can add a lot more to the family income than if your husband does overtime or gets a raise, because there can be tax advantages for a working wife; for instance, the first £985 (at time of writing, but this figure may change) isn't taxed.

Part-time work is defined as taking up less than thirty hours a week. So you might work from 10 to 4, five days a week and be classified as a part-time employee. You might work in the mornings only or in the afternoons only or, if you're doing factory work, on the popular 'twilight' shift in the early evening, or you might do a full day's work for only one, two, three or four days a week.

If you have nursing or secretarial training it's possible to do temp work whenever you feel like it (during the school holidays for instance, or during the summer). You might be lucky enough to get a job (perhaps field work interviewing in market research) where you can fit a certain number of hours into your own schedule, and it doesn't matter when, so long as you do it. You might be held on retainer to be available when somebody needs you for well-paid bursts of impossible-to-schedule work (often called sessional) in supply teaching, helping at a hospital or on a market research project.

Twinning: is also a new way of doing part-time work; two women share and are responsible for one full-time job. If you both have children, twinning can be a particularly rewarding way of getting out and earning, provided you take it in turns for one to work while the other looks after all the children. This idea was pioneered by one of the big high-street banks and has since spread to other companies. It works well and husband and wife can do it, as well as two friends. An advantage to the employer is that if you twin a job, there is always one person in reserve in case of illness, so, in a way, a twinned job is more likely to be reliably womanned. Get your twin before approaching an employer, appear together at the interview, *stress that you have worked together before* (even if unpaid) and explain how you will work together.

A part-time job you can do may not always be available just when you need it. It may be a good idea to take a full-time job and later, when you are experienced, have proven reliable and are valuable to your employer, try to negotiate to work fewer hours on a part-time basis. Conversely, doing a part-time job is also a perfect way to ease yourself back into full-time work and thus adapt gradually at home.

Kay Sykes, who went back to work for three mornings a week as a personal secretary, saw the need for top people to do part-time jobs in business and started her own employment agency, Part Time Careers (10 Golden Square, London W 1 R 3 A F; tel. 01-437 3103). Although there is a certain amount of work for graduates who have specialist skills such as cataloguing, marketing or statistical work, the greatest choices are for high-level executive secretaries. Kay says: 'As labour is very expensive today, many people prefer to pay well for really good part-time assistance, rather than have second-rate full-time people, which is where older, more responsible and experienced women have a good chance.'

Her advice to returners is '*Please* make sure that the skills you had in the past are now up to date again. Otherwise you're only going to exasperate everyone and get a footling job. These days you're unlikely to get a *good* on-going part-time job unless you have a skill.'

If you are rusty you can go to afternoon or evening classes or, again, TOPS will *pay you* to take one of their clerical, secretarial or commercial courses – these are always full-time. Among women who have taken TOPS commercial courses 20 per cent take a part-time job afterwards.

Working from Home

What many women most want to know is 'What can I do in my own home that will earn me money?'

POSSIBILITIES

Most businesses were run from homes and cottages until the Industrial Revolution, and there are still many profitable ventures that can be run from home today, provided that local by-laws allow it. For instance: travel business work; public relations work; estate agent work; design work; fashion work; toy work; craft work; and the many, many other ideas that are suggested in this book.

There are also plenty of other part-time jobs or services that can be run from home, especially if you can organize such things as lectures, temporary nursing, any sort of agency work, painting and decorating, furniture repairs, correspondence courses.

There are many kinds of teaching that can be done in your own home, such as teaching backward children to read (my mother does this), or crafts, or languages, or musical instruments such as the guitar or piano.

You might run gardening services, such as producing for a local nursery or raising indoor plants for sale, or like another friend of mine in her early forties, start your own city window-box business. Another of my neighbours became tired of producing make-believe costumes for the local children (fairy, witch, knight, wizard, Superman, etc.) for free, so she had cards printed, took sample kits to local shops and now works all the year round (with worker assistance) because from her ex-nursery she now runs *Dressing Up Limited*.

I'm sure these ladies won't mind my saying that they're not more unusual or talented than anyone else ... they were just willing to sit down, think of a scheme and then TRY IT.

Perhaps you might try running a service. It seems to me that more initiative might be shown by women who want to work, in servicing the needs of other women (especially those with children) who are already working.

For instance, making a date with the maintenance man is almost impossible for a full-time working girl. So why doesn't some TOPS graduate female plumber or carpenter specialize in evening work at overtime rates? Evening door-to-door salesmen are very successful and many companies are aware of this vital fact: the woman with the fattest purse is most likely to be out during the day and at home in the *evening*. So why not try some job that services the working woman after 6 p.m.?

Or why not set up as the neighbourhood odd-job superwoman, for women who can't receive delivery of the new sofa, get meters read or meet the boiler repair man?

If you've got to look after children (yours) then perhaps you could also do it for other people and get paid for it? Could you be your local Dial-a-Mum? Only another working mother understands the weight of anxiety involved in wondering how-can-I-get-time-off-to-take-him-to-the-dentist. Perhaps you could specialize in baby-sitting, childminding or emergency child care (such as when a mother has to go to hospital). Look around and see where the local weak areas are. Discuss it with the other mothers, decide what you ideally want – and then plan to get it. Find the gap between what's available and what's needed – and then plug it!

Remember that somebody, somewhere needs you, and that there are plenty of ways of meeting up with that person through agencies, advertising in local newspapers, leaving your brand new visiting cards all over town, and telephoning everyone you know in the neighbourhood to tell them (briefly) of your plans.

Don't think that working from home is going to be easy, although one of the advantages is that you're not going to waste time travelling to the office. Apart from the problem of interruptions, there is nothing basically difficult about working from your home – and that's the trouble: the interruptions aren't often big enough to take seriously but they can all add up to a situation that is very difficult indeed, what with the milkman, postman, the odd religious enthusiast, the children and the cat.

If you provide a service working from home:

1 See that you have some *reliable* way of dealing with inquiries. One no-answer is easily enough to put a would-be client off for ever. So is 'Mummyth out thopping, I fink . . .'

2 Don't be a slave to the telephone. Once you've got started, the cheapest way to be efficient is to have two telephones and one answering machine. One telephone for your out calls and the other permanently hitched on to an answering machine with an Elastoplast stuck over the dial so you can check if the Post Office sting you for any calls.

An answering machine is far more reliable than an answering service. (But make sure you don't get let in for a long contract: I use Robophone, on a yearly contract.)

Check your answering machine *without fail*, possibly at 9 a.m. and 3 p.m. Keep your tin-voice message as short as possible (i.e. 'This is Julia Ross. Please leave a message and I'll call you back'). If you use an answering service, you must use it efficiently, otherwise it puts people off immediately.

3 Organize an office area in your home, even if it is only a drawer.

4 *Be reliable*. Don't have an amateur, pin-money attitude to your job. People are going to expect you to be unreliable (and in my experience, part-time women workers *are*, more often than not) which is all the more reason why you shouldn't be.

5 Remember NO EXCUSE IS A GOOD ENOUGH EXCUSE.

What to avoid

Beware of:

1 Any grand title (such as Market Research Agent), that disguises door-step or telephone selling, on commission.

2 Unlicensed employment agencies.

3 Any advertisement involving a registration fee for being put on their list.

4 Small advertisements that promise you amazing results. You are unlikely to make 'hundreds of pounds on the continent without selling' in your spare time. Not unless you're the new Cora Pearl.

Ask yourself – 'Why do you think they picked *you*' to entice? They don't even *know* you. There's no such thing as a fairy godmother, especially not in the small ads.

5 Correspondence courses that offer to turn you into a Top Model or Harold Robbins within months. (I tell you, writing best-sellers isn't all it's cracked up to be.)

6 Retraining at vocational schools (i.e. computers). Make sure that you speak to someone well established in the particular industry you're aiming at, or in the business that you wish to join. Find out if they are hiring people who have retrained at that school.

Speak to other people who have gone to the school and find out if they got their jobs as a result. Ask the school for a few references and check them.

7 Any request for money.

Be very careful when considering home work where the prospective employer, to whom you are looking for money, first wants *you* to buy something (i.e. a knitting machine). Perhaps he's just putting over a smart bit of sales technique to sell his knitting machine, dangling the carrot of your earnings at the other end of the stick. Either you *never* get the work so you *never* get the money or you may be obliged to spend the money you earn in paying off your instalments on the machine with which you earn it.

Also, he may have sold knitting

machines that same evening in the same street to *all* your friends to whom you're hoping to sell your knit-wear or whatever.

8 Any sort of piece-work or commission-based schemes because you will probably have to slave at depressing work and there's no guarantee that you will make any money – you may even *lose* some.

In particular, watch organizations that get women to sell cosmetics and run parties to sell underwear or plastic containers: it can take a lot of expensive driving or telephone organizing to do so. They are exploiting you, your friends and assets, such as your car and telephone, heat, light and food. You're unlikely to realize that so much of your difficult-to-measure, money-and-time outlay is directly benefiting them. You may *seem* to make a bit of money (and it won't be much when you cost it per hour) but the little you make can dribble away in those indirect costs.

So why do it? Most of the time because you're lonely, want to meet people, want a bit of money and feel unqualified to do anything else. But this sort of amateur selling may easily be wasting your resources and *not* enriching your life as promised. There are often easier ways of meeting people and making a bit of money (back to the TOPS schemes).

9 Contracts. Get advice and make sure that you don't sign your name too lightly on things, particularly if you are an older woman who is lonely and likely to respond too easily to a salesman's pitch or Newman-blue eyes.

HOW TO BE AN UNQUALIFIED SUCCESS

(and get an interesting job if you haven't any O levels, A levels, ONCs or any other qualifications)

Ask any millionaire, captain of industry, politician or other impressive pundit how many O levels he needed in order to qualify for his job and he will shoot you a look of pure astonishment.

Qualifications are fine as an indication of your training but they don't mean that you're totally competent to take any job. And lots of jobs need qualities that are not quantifiable by certificate: I know nobody who has an A level in Tact or Bargaining or Ability to Keep his Temper. There's nothing sacred about a certificate and nothing shaming in not having one: employers often demand them when they're not really necessary.

I asked an occupational guidance officer what I should do if I wanted to apply for a job that is advertised for someone with O or A levels. Quick as a flash she replied:

'Ignore it. Don't wait to get to the application form stage, contact the employer yourself directly by phone or letter. You don't have to join the system – you can beat it.

'Alternatively, write direct to organizations or firms in your area that you might like to work for. Just write in and ask if they have a suitable job for you and enclose a few notes about yourself [see p. 63]. I always encourage people to "cold canvass" like this because it so often works successfully. Even if there isn't a vacancy, they often remember you when there is.

'You can find names of all major employers in your area with the help of your local librarian. Look them up in *Kompass* (volume 2), which is a register of British Industry and Commerce [published in Croydon by Kompass Publishers Ltd].

'I always advise anyone looking for a job to try to make personal contact by telephone or *letter*. You get much farther this way and you register more with the employer. You do have to show some initiative like this if you want a job. It is no use just waiting for something to turn up.'

Many employers put down O and A level requirements for a job only because they see that everyone else does. But if the employer thinks you're suitable when he sees you he'll often forget all about Os and As. Don't apologize for not having certificate qualifications: who you are and what you have already done are often much more important to a potential employer. Common sense, energy, cheerfulness, initiative and efficiency may be much more useful to him than an O level in biology that you got twenty years ago.

'If you can't avoid the system and have to fill in an application form, you can still make it more personal. Say something about yourself and

your experience that doesn't seem to fit into any of the questions on the form: write it down on a separate sheet of paper or in a letter attached to the form. Enclose a copy of your autobiography (see p. 63). Never feel you have to keep to the rules of the system. Always try to show some *extra* effort which will make your application stand out from all the other applicants.' This doesn't apply, however, if you want to get into the Civil Service, where forms and qualifications are bureaucratically unavoidable.

If you want to train for a job there are over 700 TOPS courses available for people without O or A levels, and many other courses which normally require them *but* are open to older people who have experience rather than qualifications.

Jobs where you probably don't need O or A levels

You might enjoy *hospital work* as a nursing auxiliary, occupational therapy aide, social work assistant, voluntary service organizer, art or music therapist or instructor for the mentally handicapped. It's also possible to work in hospital catering, domestic, laundry and sewing services. If you're an efficient housekeeper you might feel like running this side of a hospital ward. Apply to your local jobcentre or the superintendent of the nearest large hospital.

Alternatively, there is a trainee scheme for hospital cooks, if you can already do family cooking. Get information about the National Trainee Scheme for Cooks in Hospitals from the Department of Health and Social Security, Alexander Fleming House, Elephant and Castle, London SE1 6BY.

If you feel that *school* or *college* life would suit you and you want the holidays free, then it's possible to get work in the school office or catering department.

There are many opportunities in *local government* and *public services* besides the social work. There are jobs such as assistant to the education officer or in the housing department or the library or parks, or in the recreation departments. Clerical officers and assistants are always wanted by different government departments, ranging from social security to the local crown and county courts.

If you like the atmosphere of a bustling big *office* there are many opportunities, including office machine operator (working Xeroxes, duplicating machines and computers). If you like meeting new faces and feel like working in a *shop* or *store* or *supermarket* it's possible to get a job as a sales assistant in your favourite department. Many big stores give their employees as much as 20 per cent discount on everything they buy in the shop, so you can save on housekeeping. You might work as a fashion assistant in a big store, or in a florist's or a garden shop or centre, or as a receptionist in a gas or electricity showroom or with a doctor or dentist.

There are some good opportunities in *industry*. The dress manufacturers

are sobbing for machinists all over the country and there are also part-time opportunities. Similarly there are many openings in the food preparation industry, which can be quite well paid and obviously enjoyable.

Go to the local jobcentre, to see what they've got. They're not like the dreary old places they used to be, and they're self-service, so you needn't be interviewed if you don't want to be – browse around the jobs, as if in a bookshop.

THE BIGGEST MISTAKES THAT WOMEN MAKE

Careers advisory officers all made surprisingly similar comments on the mistakes that women make when they want to go back to work. Here are fourteen.

Mistake 1: 'She really made her biggest mistake when she stopped work and assumed that, because she was bringing up children, she would never have to get a job again.'

Mistake 2: 'She assumed that she'd never *want* to get a job again.'

Mistake 3: 'Never assume that because you're interested in children when your own are young that you have a universal interest in children that will last for life. It rarely does ... If a mother wants to start a new job working with children I advise her to wait. If she plans to teach four-year-old infants, she should wait until her youngest is at least eight years old – then see if she still feels the same way about four-year-olds.'

Mistake 4: 'She isn't practical about her own abilities ... she isn't realistic about the opportunities available ... she's too romantic.'

Mistake 5: 'The majority of women returners I see underestimate their competence and abilities. A woman needs to be a bit more confident. She needs to make a conscious effort to be positive: she mustn't cop out by saying that she's shy or hasn't any self-confidence. Everyone's shy and nobody has ... The family attitude can make or break a woman in this frame of mind: a condescending or tolerantly amused attitude can be crushing.'

Mistake 6: The Queen of the Hearth syndrome ... the woman who thinks that running a home for a few years automatically equips her to take on anything, without training or experience.

Mistake 7: Again indicative of a Queen of the Hearth. 'She thinks she's always right ... nobody is allowed to contradict her ... She won't fit into other people's established work pattern and wants to do everything in her own way ... This is the hardest thing to get a woman to realize about herself. But you've got to see how the system works before laying down the law to other people ...'

Mistake 8: Especially when there are teenagers in the office – and there generally are: 'If you treat teenagers as children (because they're not much older than your own) then you're in for trouble: this can cause a lot of tension.'

Mistake 9: 'She's so used to being on her own and not working to a set routine that she finds it hard to accept a timetable and stick to it ... I have found that anyone who has been to any kind of afternoon or evening classes always has more realistic ideas about herself when she starts looking for a new career ... I always suggest that a woman go to a class before going back to work: something that she will enjoy. It's not so much what she learns. It's the regular commitment to do something, being with other people, exchanging ideas, having to do set reading and writing in an orderly way that is invaluable.'

Mistake 10: 'When a woman starts work again she tends to underestimate how much time it takes to run her home in the way that she's been doing it. It's often a good idea to have a dummy run for a week or two before you start the job.'

Mistake 11: 'Perhaps the saddest mistake that a woman makes when getting a new job is not giving herself the best chance, taking the first job she's offered, not finding out what job is available or what she's suited for and never taking advantage of the good, free help that's offered in career guidance and training. Over half of the women I see don't really know what they're good at and don't really know what they want.'

Mistake 12: Is made when she goes after the job. 'Few women know how important it is to present themselves properly when they are being interviewed for a job or think in terms of the employer's reason for their meeting ... She can be her own worst enemy if she goes on about wanting to take time off to take the children to the dentist: what an employer is least interested in is when you're *not* going to be there. Wait until you've got the job and have proved how valuable you are, then people are generally prepared to make concessions, within reason.'

Mistake 13: Not doing anything (and whining on about it) because there is no immediate opportunity that is exactly right. This often indicates lack of guts, fear of competition, fear of the world outside the cosy home and fear of being turned down by some of the people some of the time. Everyone who succeeds has risked failure.

Mistake 14: Giving up too easily.

THE TEN FAULTS MOST LIKELY TO SUCCEED

(in exasperating colleagues and bosses)

1 Getting hysterical: Any show of emotion or temper is called 'hysteria' if it comes from a female source. If it comes from a male source it is called being tired and emotional, or not being in a good mood today.

Unlike men, women are not taught from birth to suppress their emotions. Very few men know how to handle people who behave emotionally 'in public' and they are often terrified by the prospect. The threat (brimming eyes) is therefore more powerful than the act (tears or shrieks of rage). As people do not behave logically but are emotionally motivated, women are often specifically hired as a barometer of emotional response (*viz.*, some political secretaries). A useful and highly marketable asset. But if you need an emotionally responsive person, you mustn't be surprised if she responds emotionally (*viz.*, some political secretaries).

2 Dithering: This wet-hennish form of indecision is often a sign of over-anxiety or a stress situation. It can exasperate a whole office at a time as everyone's opinion is sought and nothing gets done. A woman going back to work must be on the watch for this, as it's a common occurrence. Deal with it by recognizing that it's likely to happen. Ask what exactly you're supposed to do and break down the work into a list of separate tasks. Write down anything you're told because you tend to forget if you're told a lot of new things at once. Re-read them later.

YES-NO-YES-NO-YES-NO-

3 Inability to sort out priorities: A major symptom is inflexibly emptying your In-tray on the first-in/first-out principle, with no exceptions. Obviously a sign of fright and lack of imagination. Obviously blocks promotion, except in the Civil Service.

4 Not being prepared to accept discipline (possibly because you've been dishing it out for fifteen years as Queen of the Hearth): This is the I-know-best-no-matter-what-the-company-policy-is syndrome. This sort of woman is the potential office dragon, often over-protective of her boss to the extent that he's never allowed to talk to anyone else.

5 *Inability to delegate:* This can indicate overdeveloped feelings of self-importance, lack of security, jealousy or greed: sometimes all four. Obviously blocks promotion. Sometimes, of course, this attitude shows plain common sense after a few of your projects have been gummed up in the works by colleagues or have taken three times as long to finish as they should have done. (Check yourself if you hear yourself mutter 'quicker to do it myself' or 'the only way to get anything done round here ...', etc.)

You must deal with this situation or you'll end up the office martyr or in a nursing home. If the problem is coming from below make certain that you've instructed people clearly. Talk to each person separately and privately and ask if they have any problems with the work and any suggestions for improving present methods. If the problem is with top management or on your immediate level, try the personal approach again and talk to your boss about it. Be cool, underplay it, and make certain that you have a precise case for complaint. Avoid saying 'Everybody knows that', or 'It's perfectly clear/obvious that ...'

Collect your evidence with times and dates over a long enough period to make a case. It's better to be the office sneak than the office martyr – or thought to be inefficient yourself.

6 *Over-enthusiasm for delegation:* Often involves setting up enormous chains of command to do something quite simple and unimportant. This can be empire building, molehill building or calling wolf ! wolf ! A quick way to ensure non-co-operation and mutiny among colleagues.

7 *Over-attention to detail:* This fault is being unable to see the wood for the trees and is obliquely referred to in remarks such as 'The trouble is, she doesn't know when to stop', or 'Of course she's a perfectionist'. Sufferers can't relax, are inclined to over-complicate the filing and would rather spend time obsessively tidying up than being productive.

8 *Inability to compromise:* Such inflexibility automatically means that you are incapable of negotiation (plain stubborn). You won't make allowances for other people's attitudes or human weaknesses, but you expect other people always to see things your way because you, as usual, are Right.

9 *Dizziness:* This is thought to be good for the office but it's bad for you. Imitation Goldie Hawns (as opposed to the real one) are generally loved and enjoyed but are never to be taken seriously – and they *never* get promoted.

10 *Giggling.*

Of course, lots of men also suffer from the above problems: Avoid them.

YOUR OFFICE PHRASE BOOK

To survive office life, flourish and prosper it's essential to know how to interpret the slings and arrows that may come your way along with the odd bouquet.

A man will often use a compliment in order to keep a woman in her place (taking his dictation) and establish both devotion and control in his office, shop or factory as well as keeping the wage bill down a bit. Compliments to the female staff are often only a way of keeping the natives quiet: they are the glass beads of British industry.

It may be nice to be flattered but try saying the same things back to him and you'll see how pointless they are. The following phrases may be pleasant on the ears but don't overestimate their value.

Well-used office phrases

'You're looking very charming this morning ...' ('If I may say so': optional extra)

'You're looking very pretty this morning ...'

'You're looking very lovely this morning ...'

'You're looking very beautiful this morning ...'

'You're looking very attractive this morning ...'

For office parties only

'You're looking rather adorable this evening, you know.'

'You're looking pretty sexy this evening, you know.'

Sometimes remarks of this type are conducted through a third party, as if you were not present, e.g. '*Isn't* she looking lovely tonight, Tony?' (nudge, wink).

If a man really *relies* on you, he'll say, 'Miss Wilkins/Freda, I don't know *where* I would be without you!' This means that you have an outstanding number of virtues, but are never going to get promoted because you are too valuable. It may be time to think of moving on.

Certain adjectives are considered very, very flattering when used about a man but when used about a woman those very same words can be a tough putdown, a deadly insult that can scythe your self-confidence away in one sentence.

If a man actually admires your toughness when negotiating or when handling your department he may call it something else, such as firmness.

Sometimes a man may in fact say 'tough' when he means tough and likes it, only to have you burst into tears because poor indoctrinated you has interpreted it as a deadly insult.

If a man *really* wants to compliment you he'll tell you that you think like a man. This means that you have many virtues, that you think clearly, logically and unemotionally, that you express yourself in similar fashion and are also very attractive. But quite often a man wants to insult you simply because you've done your job well and he is bloody-minded, jealous, resentful, competitive and out to get you.

In which case, be prepared to be called (behind your back):

A tough	bitch/cow
An unfeminine	,, ,,
A terrifying	,, ,,
A hard-faced	,, ,,
A ruthless	,, ,,
A difficult	,, ,,
A go-getting little	,, ,,

Never underestimate the power of a man, especially if he's feeling a little insecure.

Just so that you know where you stand, and are not vulnerable to verbal hand grenades, here is a list of admirable business qualities and the words in which they are often dressed up:

What they mean	*What they say*
She's firm *or* You know where you are with her.	She's tough.
She doesn't stand any nonsense.	She's ruthless.
She knows what she wants and she'll make damn sure she gets it.	She's assertive/pushy.
She won't let anyone stand in her way.	She's competitive.
She knows where she's going.	She's ambitious.
You don't have to tell her twice *or* She's quick on the uptake.	She's got a mind like a razor.
She certainly gets things done.	She's efficient.
She's determined, all right.	She's purposeful.

The two main insults that fly around the unliberated office are 'aggressive' and 'unfeminine'. These terms are as pointless as 'bitch' or 'cow'; they are so woolly that you don't even know what is meant. So if anyone ever calls you unfeminine (the oldest trick in the book) ask them what *exactly* they mean. You will find that whatever they are actually accusing you of is applicable to men as well as women.

It is *not* unfeminine to decide what you want and pursue it with firmness and clarity.

AMBITION ... FOR BETTER, FOR WORSE?

Lots of women want a vague glow called 'success' but they don't want to be seen to want it and they don't want to work for it. They want success to be dropped in their lap, gift-wrapped in blue ribbon, without any effort on their part. But this is as unrealistic as expecting someone to know, by some mysterious means, what pleases you sexually without actually telling him.

There is no special virtue in ambition if all it means is to be seen to have succeeded or to be married to someone who has succeeded. There is certainly no virtue in using to the full the talents and advantages that the good Lord gave you.

Are women ambitious? Of course they are as ambitious as anyone else. Ambition is not linked to gender. Some women are ferociously ambitious but channel their drive through their children (poor little things) or through their husbands. But such women will never admit that they are ambitious. Oh no, they just want The Best for their loved ones, even if their loved ones don't want it.

It is still socially unacceptable in Britain for a woman to say or show that she's ambitious. It is considered 'unfeminine'. She's sniped at in this way only *before* she's successful; it's permissible to be ambitious once she's a proven success. Because of this women often pretend, especially to themselves, that they're not ambitious, even when they want to be the power behind the throne or Mother in 'The Brothers'.

Some people are ambitious and some aren't, and if you are, don't apologize for it. The Empress Josephine, Jacqueline Kennedy Onassis, Margaret Thatcher, Elizabeth Arden and Barbara Cartland didn't get to the top by accident or by melting into the background. If you've ever wanted to be the prettiest girl at the party, or wanted to Show Them (your family, your office colleagues, your ex-girl friends, your ex); if you've ever gone in for a newspaper or magazine competition or wanted your child to win a school prize, or wanted your husband to get promoted, then there's a strong chance that you are ambitious. In the nicest possible way, of course.

Very few people in later life aim too high: they are more likely to be looking for help because they are stuck in a boring unsatisfying job. One of the quickest ways to improve a career is to *change jobs*.

So why did they stick in the boring job so long? Perhaps because they were nervous of being turned down for a better job. Women don't want to be rejected, women want to be loved (or at least, liked), because until recently their self-esteem depended not on their achievements but on the approval of others. Women tend to be willing to exchange the *real* rewards for fake rewards. They are very susceptible to flattery, and they love compliments. But it's unrealistic to expect constant approval and once you're approval-dependent you're never going to risk the disapproval of the boss you're leaving or the rejection of the boss you're approaching.

The first thing you realize if you're out in the tough, exciting, working world is that you're probably going to make a lot of friends and you're possibly going to make a lot of enemies. You can't win all the battles.

It wasn't until I was over forty that I realized that it was all right to enjoy being ambitious. So I decided to have a career, instead of just hopping from job to job. Just to make sure that I don't disown it again or disguise it as something more swansdown, I have developed a habit of telling people what my ambition is, however unlikely it might sound at the time. Having announced my aim I can't pretend that I don't want it. I quite often don't get what I want, but I quite often do. Knowing what you want is halfway to getting it.

Getting to Know More

HOW TO GET FREE MONEY

There are several ways to get money to pay for your further education, all worth pursuing.

PERSIST, PERSIST, PERSIST. Don't give up at the first financial thumbs-down. There may be other sources you can tap once you've tracked them down. Very often you will find that this money is yours *by right*. It isn't just for kids fresh from school. It's for people who want to be educated. There's no age discrimination, so firmly stand your ground to anyone who suggests that there is.

Be on the watch for subtle put-downs – 'Do you think you can stand the pace?' 'Are you happy about your home arrangements?' (No, never) – 'Do you feel you're strong enough?' – 'How does your husband feel about it?' It's irrelevant; serenely treat it as such. But don't put anyone's back up, even if a snarl is justified.

We all know people who are where they are because they have been able to pull strings – and knew which ones to pull and got other people to pull the ones they couldn't reach. You don't have to be rich or famous or well-connected to do this. You just have to know how the system works and how to operate it to your own benefit. Here's how to do it, whether you want the money to train for a job or for further education or a degree or just for the hell of it (this is called non-vocational study).

String 1: The amazing TOPS scheme (see page 14) pays for up to one year in colleges of technology and further education. You get a tax-free grant ranging from £25.70 a week, free travel, free lunches and a lodging allowance if you have to leave home to train to be a glassblower or a market gardener.

Get the details from your local job-centre, apply for the college course you would like to take, and ask TOPS to sponsor you. You'll almost certainly get the money provided you ful-fil their reasonable requirements.

String 2: If you are ambitious for an academic qualification, act when you *apply* for a place in a college. Im-mediately ask the principal for help in getting a grant, because she or he obviously knows all the ropes and will tell you the right way to go about it. This can be tremendously impor-tant.

String 3: Apply to your local educa-tion authority (LEA). Get the address from your library and write in good time. Apply at the beginning of the year, if possible, for September.

You should apply for any grant to your local authority *before* you have been awarded a place. They are *obliged* to pay the fees and give you a maintenance grant if you have the necessary two A levels and have been offered a place in a university, poly-technic or college of further educa-tion. These are called Mandatory Grants. There is *no upper age limit* for students to get this money. These grants are for approved courses that lead to a first degree or other diplomas which are recognized as degree level and usually require three years' study.

Women who get a place for a degree (or similar) course but who are ac-cepted as 'mature students', and so need not have passed the required O or A levels for entry, are not auto-matically eligible for a mandatory grant. If turned down for this they should apply to their local educational authority for a Discretionary Grant. These discretionary grants are also given to people taking a course below

degree level or to people who have had a full mandatory grant before. Discre-tionary grants aren't given to you automatically: the LEA decides whether you are a worth-while reci-pient of their cash and, if so, how much you should get. If you're a mature student a great deal will depend on where you live. Some LEAs are more sympathetic and generous than others.

String 4: For general information about grants and what you might get, ask your LEA or write for informa-tion to the Department of Education and Science (Awards Branch), Eliza-beth House, York Road, London SE1 7PH.

In *Scotland*, it's the Scottish Educa-tion Department (Awards Branch), 2 South Charlotte Street, Edinburgh EH2 4AP.

In *N. Ireland*, it's the Department of Education for N. Ireland, Rathgael House, Baloo Road, Bangor, County Down BET 192 PR.

All these departments also publish free guides explaining the system. Get *any guides you can*, because the more you know about what's going the more likely you are to get it. If you want to take a first degree or do teacher training get *Grants to Students: A Brief Guide* from the Department of Education or your LEA.

String 5: The National Union of Students (you needn't be a member) can be very helpful. They can tell you how to get grants and help you if you have any problems with your LEA. Among their publications are *Grants:*

Handbook and Survey of LEA Awards, Mature Women's Grants and *Educational Charities*. Write to the NUS at 3 Endsleigh Street, London WC1 0DU.

String 6: To discover other money sources, get the Advisory Centre for Education's *Grants for Higher Education*, compiled by Judith Booth. This gives information about various other organizations which give grants (published for ACE by Barrie and Jenkins: get it from your library).

String 7: You can also get financial information and advice on how to operate the system from the National Institute of Adult Education, 19B De Montfort Street, Leicester LE1 7GH (tel. Leicester [0533] 538977).

String 8: Students accepted for the long-term residential colleges such as Hillcroft College (South Bank, Surbiton, Surrey KT6 6DF) or Ruskin College, Oxford (see p. 87), which only take mature students, are eligible for grants under an Adult Education State Bursary Scheme administered by the Department of Education and Science (DES). For certain specialist courses at these colleges students may be able to get a grant from their LEA. For further information, contact the head office at National Institute of Adult Education (address above), or the Scottish Office at the Scottish Institute of Adult Education, 57 Melville Street, Edinburgh EH3 7HL (tel. 031-226 7200).

String 9: For postgraduate study, once again try TOPS. They offer higher-level courses in universities, business colleges, polytechnics and colleges of further education. You can get details from any jobcentre, employment office or PER office. *If you're over twenty-seven* you can take a TOPS course leading to a higher degree or a recognized postgraduate diploma or certificate. For instance, you can get a diploma in management studies; a postgraduate diploma in marketing; a diploma in personnel management; a diploma in institutional management; an MSc Business Studies; an MSc Industrial Management; an MSc computer science – and TOPS will pay you to do it.

String 10: There are various other sources of finance for postgraduate study. The Department of Education and Science will give State Bursaries in some cases. Read *Grants to Students* and various leaflets from DES, Honeypot Lane, Edgware, Middlesex.

String 11: For postgraduate studies in the social services the Social Sciences Research Council has various award schemes and there are now *no upper age limits* for these grants. Information from Pre-Awards Section, Social Science Research Council, 1 Temple Avenue, London EC4A 0HH.

String 12: For further studies in science and technology, the Science Research Council sometimes gives awards to older applicants who have a good honours degree. Details from the SRC, State House, High Holborn, London WC1R 4TA.

String 13: Information about other organizations that may finance postgraduate study is given in *Grants and*

Awards, produced by the University of London Careers Advisory Service. It is part of the Careers and Graduates Series and available from the University of London Publications Office, 50 Gordon Square, London WC1H 0PJ.

String 14: Another information publication, the *Summary of Higher Education Awards Made by Various Industrial and Professional Organizations and Government Departments* (gets my award for the most tedious title of the year), is published by the Department of Employment and should be available in the reference department of your public library or HMSO bookshops.

HOW TO GET BETTER EDUCATED
(What's available if you're not straight out of school)

Here's a short guide to the ways in which you can advance your education. If you're toying with the idea of starting a course (and many, many women think about it very tentatively at first because they are timid or fear ridicule) then write for leaflets and booklets from local colleges, and discuss possibilities as thoroughly as possible before deciding what suits you. Vocational guidance may not only clear your own mind as to your aptitudes and inclinations; this will also clearly and firmly indicate your intentions to your family, as something to be taken seriously.

Consider taking *evening classes*. That wonderful, early nineteenth-century invention, 'night school', which metamorphosed into 'evening classes' and is now grandly termed 'adult education', can be pursued at an evening institute or adult college or adult education institute (different). (See pp. 6–13.)

Follow *courses by radio*; very good for languages. Ask at your local library for the *Radio Times* 'Look, Listen and Learn' which gives details of all programme courses. Or write for details to the BBC.

Write to the local polytechnic and your local college of education and ask for their prospectuses.

The Workers' Educational Association (WEA) in spite of their dreary name are very good for tutorials and lectures on such wide-ranging subjects as psychology or the history of art. And you don't need any O or A levels to join for part-time study, tutorials, lectures and discussion groups. They're more intellectually orientated than evening classes. Ask for details at your local library. *University Extension courses* are very similar and often linked to WEA. Most universities also have extramural departments which give short lecture courses (get details from your local university). Many museums organize wonderful talks and lectures, often in the lunch hour. The Victoria and Albert Museum, London, is a glowing example of this sort of programme.

You can take a *correspondence course* anywhere in the world. If you want to do a University of London external degree, write for prospectuses to the Secretary for External Students, University of London, Senate House, Malet Street, London WC1E 7HU. Another good series of correspondence courses (where you can get O and A levels, as well as degrees) is offered by the National Extension College (NEC), 8 Shaftesbury Road, Cambridge CB2 2BP.

Short-term residential adult colleges (country-wide) offer weekend and holiday courses in a wide variety of special interests for adults studying for their own pleasure and self-development. Programmes include pottery, musical appreciation and photography (erotic novelist Molly Parkin found a handsome young husband at one of these). Get current programme from the National Institute of Adult Education.

You can take a degree course ...

At *universities* – including Birkbeck College (part of the University of London) which offers evening classes from 6 to 9 p.m. in term time and is still a unique way to get a degree while working full-time.

At *home* – anywhere in the country with a correspondence course as an external student of the University of London, or by going to a local college part-time.

At *polytechnics* – for a Council for National Academic Awards (CNAA)

degree. (See p. 89, 'Everybody's entitled to a certificate'.) To find what's available and help you to choose, consult the *Handbook of Polytechnic Courses* (published by Lund Humphries), or *Compendium of Courses Approved by CNAA*. They should be in your public library.

At the *Open University* – open to anyone without qualifications. There is no time limit to getting a degree, so you can take a break in study for a year or so and then pick up where you left off. You get a BA or BA(Hons.) degree. You can get details from the *Guide to Applicants for Undergraduate Courses*, obtainable from Open University, PO Box 1, Milton Keynes, MK7 6AA. Details of refresher, non-degree courses (if you want to update your knowledge) from Post Experience Student Office, Open University, PO Box 76, Milton Keynes MK7 6AN. Postgraduate degree details are available from the Higher Degrees Office, Open University, PO Box 49, Milton Keynes MK7 6AD.

Taking an Open University degree is a major challenge and many people, understandably, fall by the wayside. Nevertheless, many a homebound wife takes one successfully, then has her photograph in the daily papers, captioned 'Forty-five-year-old mother of six graduates!'

Three years is the minimum time in which you can get a BA degree but it's more realistic to reckon on four to six years. The best part is that you need NO QUALIFICATIONS: no Os, no As. You do most of the work at home (which is lonely and requires great discipline) and it is supplemented by special television and radio programmes. You do written work for a tutor, spend a few hours a month at a study centre and spend one week a year at a residential summer school. (This is enjoyable and vital to your morale.) The fees are fairly low but you're not eligible for a local education authority grant. The older you are, the better your chance of getting in.

Write for details to: Open University, PO Box 48, Milton Keynes MK7 6AB (tel. Milton Keynes [0908] 74066). For Open University you've got to apply in January – a year in advance.

Full-time residential adult colleges: These are particularly for adults who left school early without any formal qualifications. Grants and scholarships are available. Some of the courses lead to qualifications acceptable for entry to university or colleges of education (particularly good for women). No preliminary qualifications necessary.

These colleges offer one- or two-year courses for people who want to make a fresh educational start, a time of training and reassessment, preparing for a career change or going on to higher education just for the pleasure of learning. Colleges are: Hillcroft College, Surbiton, Surrey (women only); Newbattle Abbey College, Dalkeith, Midlothian; Plater College, Boar's Hill, Oxford; Ruskin College, Oxford (the Trade Union College); Coleg Harlech, Gwynedd; Co-operative College, Stanford Hall, Lough-borough, Leicestershire; Northern College, Wentworth Castle, Stainborough, Barnsley, South Yorkshire S75 3ET.

More information from the National Institute of Adult Education, 19B De Montfort Street, Leicester LE1 7GH (tel. Leicester [0533] 538977).

Teacher training: In spite of a surplus of disgruntled teachers and the dropping birthrate there's still a shortage of teachers in certain subjects such as mathematics, music and handicrafts, and some of the colleges of education make special provisions for mature students with family commitments. These include Chorley College of Education, Ethel Wormald College of Education, Liverpool; James Graham College of Education, Leeds; Manchester College of Education; Thomas Huxley College of Education, London.

You can take a ...

New degree course at reorganized colleges of education, formerly teacher training colleges, now upgraded slightly so that you get a degree. You can learn to be a teacher or take a more general degree.

Diploma of Higher Education (two-year courses for would-be teachers) can be taken at polytechnics as well as colleges of education; they may be used as a stepping-stone to a final degree year. *Qualifications for entry* are three O and two A levels (except for open university), but don't worry if you haven't got them. Mature students can often qualify on an interview and their experience, especially if they've taken evening classes or a WEA course.

Three-year Bachelor of Education ordinary degree; four-year B.Ed. honours degree; or, if you already have a degree, *one-year's certificate or diploma course in teaching.* (The Certificate in Education is being phased out.) *Qualifications for entry* are five O levels or equivalent, with an extra two A levels for degree courses. Don't be discouraged. There are special tests for 'unqualified' students in some areas.

For further information on colleges of education, see the *Handbook of Colleges and Departments of Education* (published by Lund Humphries) from your library.

Teachers in further education (teachers who are going to teach in colleges, rather than schools) **can take a ...**

Full-time certificate course: There are four colleges (Bolton, London, Huddersfield and Wolverhampton); the course is one year if you're a graduate, or if you're skilled, e.g. a carpenter who wants to teach carpentry.

Part-time City and Guilds Further Education Teachers' Certificate, available at many centres (usually technical and further education colleges) throughout the country. Again you have to be a graduate or skilled.

Social work courses

Qualification is the Certificate of Qualification in Social Work (CQSW). If you're over thirty you don't need O or A levels. There are two types of course specially for you:

1 A two-year course for non-graduates in polytechnics and colleges, with special arrangements in some cases for students to obtain employment and a form of secondment in the second year.
2 A similar three-year course for non-graduates with family responsibilities. These provide a shorter working day and longer holidays.

There's also a two-year part-time CQWS course for graduates. Apply for details to the University of London Department of Extra-Mural Studies.

Get leaflet 1:3 issued by the Central Council for Education and Training in Social Work (Information Service) which will tell you what's available locally. Write to Derbyshire House, St Chad's Street, London WC1H 8AD.

Certificate in Social Service (CSS): Two- to five-year day-release courses in some colleges of further education for people who are already doing social work. No certificates needed for mature people. A good CSS may be useful when making application for a CQSW course.

Residential social work qualifications: For details get CCETSW leaflet 2:2 (see above).

Probation and after-care service: An information leaflet, PN 10, is obtainable from the Probation and aftercare Department of the Home Office which may sponsor candidates at recognized courses. There are various graduate and non-graduate training courses. Of note are:

1 A two-year non-graduate course open to anyone at polytechnics and some university extra-mural departments.
2 A two-year CQSW course for candidates over twenty-seven: one year full-time study and one year supervised training.

Qualifications for entry: no O or A levels needed for over-forties with suitable experience.

For further information get leaflet PN10 from the Home Office.

Youth and community service

All courses are listed in *Training for Professional Youth and Community Work*, free from the National Youth Bureau, 17–23 Albion Street, Leicester LE1 6GD.

Particularly good two-year courses are offered at Scraptoft College of Education in Leicester, Goldsmiths' College (Department of Adult Studies) in London, Manchester Polytechnic, Liverpool University and N.E. London Polytechnic.

Scotland

The Scottish educational system differs from England and Wales in many respects. For general advice and information you should consult the Scottish Institute of Adult Education, 53 Melville Street, Edinburgh EH3 7HL (tel. 031-226 7200). Useful guidebooks in your local library should

include *Directory of Day Courses* (published by the Scottish Education Department), and *Handbook of the Scottish Central Institutions: Courses, Entry Requirements*, also available *free* from Paisley College of Technology, High Street, Paisley, Strathclyde PA1 2BE.

For information about colleges of education in Scotland get *Memorandum on Entry Requirements and Courses*, published by HMSO. Also the Scottish Universities Council on Entrance publishes a *Compendium of Information*.

EVERYBODY'S ENTITLED TO A CERTIFICATE

(a swift guide)

(A) School education

There are two main British examinations:

1 *GCE* (General Certificate of Education) O (Ordinary) Level is taken at fifteen or sixteen. The courses aren't difficult and you can take them out of school (like most other certificate courses) at part-time day or evening classes. A (Advanced) Level is generally taken two years after O level if you are

aiming for higher education or one of the professions. S (Special or Scholarship) Level is taken by a few university candidates.

2 *CSE* (Certificate of Secondary Education) is a more practical equivalent of GCE O level. There is less emphasis on written work, for the less academic. GCE O and A levels and CSE certificates are obtainable in five grades: A–E and 1–5 respectively. A, B and C of O levels are considered a pass. Grade 1 of CSE is equivalent to an O level pass. Two CSEs may be needed for apprentice jobs; requirements for jobs at technician level are more flexible; two or three As, plus three Os or CSEs at Grade 1, are needed for university entry.

(B) Further education (practical training)

Further education is not *higher* education. There's a huge variety of courses at colleges of further education, ranging from handbag design to hairdressing. They are practical rather than academic and aim to give you a saleable skill.

You can learn subjects to A level at colleges of further education. You stand more chance of getting a grant if you take a 'vocational' course (they mostly are). This doesn't mean that you have to be a nun, but that you actually need the training to earn your living. The courses are practical full-time or part-time classes or part-time study during the day.

School leavers can study in part-time day-release courses (which means that their employer gives them time off to attend one whole day or two half days each week) or block-release (several weeks off, with pay, to attend a course). You can also catch up on O and A levels at an FE college. If the course you want isn't in your area, you can often take it somewhere else.

The qualifications you get at a college of further education are certificates or diplomas generally awarded by the *City and Guilds of London Institute* (better known as City and Guilds) – for craft or technical subjects, ranging from hotel catering to growing trees; and *Royal Society of Arts* certificates and diplomas for office staff. You can get an RSA in shorthand and audio typing, or you can get a package deal certificate called Office Practice. City and Guilds do computer programming training. RSA do most of the rest up to degree level.

Craftsman training: There are no entry qualifications for general courses, which range from carpentry to dressmaking; a general course is needed to qualify for a *Craft Course* (two years' part-time study); *Advanced Craft Course* (a further two years' part-time study), unless you have certain CSE or GCE passes. Certificates are awarded. Get further information from the *Crafts Advisory Committee*, 12 Waterloo Place, London SW1 4AU.

Technician training: A City and Guilds Technician Certificate Course takes two or three years part-time.

You need two or three CSEs or equivalent GCEs or to have done well in the Craft General Course.

Ordinary National Certificate (ONC): These are about A-level standard. They take two years part-time in subjects such as science, business studies, public administration, catering and hotel work.

Ordinary National Diploma (OND): Awarded for more work in the same subjects and takes two years full-time or three years alternating periods at college and at work (with pay). This is known as a sandwich course.

In technical subjects, ONCs and ONDs are not better than City and Guilds Certificates (CGs) . or vice versa. They are more theoretical than CGs but less academic than A levels and lead to a greater choice of careers than CGs.

(C) Higher education

Minimum requirement: one A level before you start. You must be over eighteen. You take higher education courses in universities, polytechnics, some technical colleges and colleges of education. You can study for either a: *Higher National Certificate,* which takes two years' part-time work; or a *Higher National Diploma,* which takes two years' full-time work or three years' sandwich.

An HNC is a bit below degree standard (one degree under ...) and HND is about degree standard. They cover the same subjects as ONC and OND, i.e. public administration,

catering, engineering, business studies, etc.

If you do well in your first year of an HND course you can transfer to a degree course.

(D) Specialist higher education

Professional qualifications (e.g. in accountancy or law) are awarded by the appropriate professional body after an approved course of training and a series of exams often combined with practical experience.

Occupational therapy, physiotherapy, radiography and other subjects which are related to medicine are generally taught in special schools attached to hospitals so that the students can practise while they are being preached to.

Diploma in Art and Design (Dip AD): You need five O levels or equivalent and you need to do a one-year foundation course. This is a very good general course and worth while in itself. You then take either a *Fine Arts Course* (e.g. painting, sculpture) or an *Industrial Design Course* (e.g. graphic, textile, fashion, furniture, product design).

Council for National Academic Awards (CNAA): The only body, apart from universities, which awards degrees. The degrees are of equal standing but more practical, less academic, than university degrees, e.g. in business studies rather than economics. Most CNAA courses, either normal or sandwich, are at the new polytechnics; some are in colleges of further education. CNAA degrees are often a more certain route to getting a job than a university degree.

Universities: Degree courses take three years, sometimes four. There are forty-five universities in Great Britain.

Minimum entry for university is five GCE passes of which two (perhaps three) must be A level. You must get the right mixture of O and A levels for the course you wish to pursue at university. Check entry requirements and available courses in the *Compendium of University Entrance Requirements* at your public library.

Courses in the same subject vary greatly from one university to the next, so look for the most suitable course rather than the smartest university. Check in the publication *Degree Course Guide*, available in your public library.

Depending on the college, you can get an honours degree in one, two, three or four categories or even in between. This is called a Bachelor's Degree. Usually your second degree (after a further course of exams and study) is your Master's Degree. Or you can get it at Oxford or Cambridge after a year, just by paying some money.

The final course (after yet more work) is a PhD or Doctor of Philosophy. Then your friends can call you Doctor, but you need not have studied *any* philosophy. Work includes writing a thesis. This is a long essay or short booklet and it has to be properly typed with as many as eight copies.

WHO'S RESPONSIBLE FOR YOUR EDUCATION?
(a simplification)

In England all education (including the universities, civil science and the arts) is under the Secretary of State for Education and Science. He or she is also ultimately responsible for universities throughout the UK.

In Wales the Secretary of State for Wales is responsible for nursery, primary and secondary education only. Further and higher education comes under the Secretary of State for Education and Science.

Scotland and Northern Ireland each have their own departments of education. The respective Secretaries of State for Scotland and Northern Ireland have full educational responsibility in their countries except for universities.

Who sees you get your education?

The local education authorities (LEAs) who are responsible for the provision of school education and most post-school education outside the universities. They provide grants, including those for university.

The universities administer themselves and get finance from the Government through the University Grants Committee.

However, the *Open University* is financed directly by the Department of Education and Science, not through the University Grants Committee.

LEAs are the elected councils of:

1 The metropolitan district councils (in urban areas).
2 County councils (in non-urban areas).
3 In *London*, the twelve inner boroughs and the tiny city of London come under the Inner London Education Authority (ILEA), which is a powerful, largely autonomous committee of the Greater London Council. There are twenty outer London boroughs in the suburbs whose councils – like the metropolitan district councils – are the education authorities for their administrative areas.

In *Scotland* the nine regional councils are the local education authorities on the mainland. The three island authorities (Orkney, Shetland and the Western Isles) run the education services in their own areas. All twelve are under the Scottish Education Department.

In *Northern Ireland* the local education authorities are the education and library boards, which work with the Northern Ireland Department of Education.

How do they operate?

The elected local council (whichever sort it is) acts as the local education authority, and appoints an education committee. Most members are elected councillors, but they also appoint experts and people interested in education who live or work in the area.

The education committee usually splits up into sub-committees with responsibility for different branches of the service, i.e. schools, staffing, further education, etc. The person who carries out their policies is the chief education officer or the director of education, who is a full-time paid public servant and not elected. Paid council officials run the education services in the area under him. He usually has a deputy and several assistant education officers. The assistants share out different sections of the service, often corresponding to the specialist sub-committees – schools, staffing, further education, etc.

It is worth remembering that the powerful local education authorities are your local councillors. They are elected by you the ratepayer to represent you. They only stay in power if they satisfy the local electorate, and that includes you. So let your LEA members know if you think they aren't carrying out their duties.

To find out who is responsible, look up the *Education Committees Yearbook* at your local library. It will tell you the names of the paid officials as well as members of the education committee and sub-committees.

Education decisions have to be made or rejected finally by the full council. Council and education committee meetings are open to the public. Most sub-committee meetings are *not* public, but it depends on the authority.

A SHORT GUIDE TO A NEW CAREER

What will you be doing in five years' time? What will you be doing in ten years' time? Statistically, there's more than half a chance that you'll be working outside the home. But women tend to drift into jobs rather than plan what they want to do like men.

My definition of a job as opposed to a career has nothing to do with qualifications – it's simply planning ahead in a fairly loose way and having a goal to work towards. It is never too late to start and it's not too late to aim really high. Often women don't do this because it has never occurred to them, or because they're afraid of ambition, or because they don't like to put themselves forward. There are *always* good work opportunities.

Don't be put off by scare stories about teenagers starving in the streets, or that we haven't been in a worse job situation since the Jarrow march, etc. Just look at the pages and pages of Situations Vacant newspaper advertisements; look at the never-ending government advertisements to train or retrain.

Most work falls into one of the ten areas listed below. You may not know much about any of them and you'll certainly underestimate the enormous choice of available jobs within each area. Having decided which area interests you, see which sort of occupation might suit you. If you enjoyed organizing things at school (or since) you might aim for a managerial or administrative job. If you like meeting people you might consider research, selling or office work. If you're good with your hands you might head for a craft occupation or industry or a technical job.

Choice of main areas

Medicine
Education
Catering
Social service
Selling (what women know about from the other end)
Industry (can be much more interesting than women think)
Office
Professional other than above
Crafts
Technical

Which sort of work?

What you need to find out about a new job is the minimum education requirements (which you can often ignore), when to apply for training, duration and cost of training and whether you can get anyone else to pay (a) your fees, (b) your living costs. Go for the most intensive, shortest course; it's often simply not necessary to take a long course which goes on for years.

At this point you decide whether or not you want to train. Some of the jobs described below don't even need O or A levels (for a longer list see p. 97), and some of them have special short-cut training schemes for older people, where nobody asks for Os and As because they're much more interested in people with experience in life.

Civil Service apart, don't worry about lack of qualifications unless you want to be a brain surgeon. Quite often people ask for them only because

ESSENTIAL ATTRIBUTES

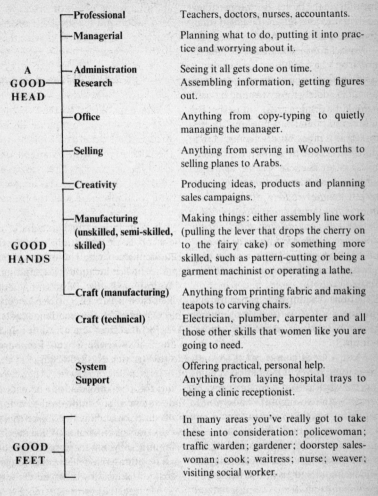

A GOOD HEAD	**Professional**	Teachers, doctors, nurses, accountants.
	Managerial	Planning what to do, putting it into practice and worrying about it.
	Administration	Seeing it all gets done on time.
	Research	Assembling information, getting figures out.
	Office	Anything from copy-typing to quietly managing the manager.
	Selling	Anything from serving in Woolworths to selling planes to Arabs.
	Creativity	Producing ideas, products and planning sales campaigns.
GOOD HANDS	**Manufacturing (unskilled, semi-skilled, skilled)**	Making things: either assembly line work (pulling the lever that drops the cherry on to the fairy cake) or something more skilled, such as pattern-cutting or being a garment machinist or operating a lathe.
	Craft (manufacturing)	Anything from printing fabric and making teapots to carving chairs.
	Craft (technical)	Electrician, plumber, carpenter and all those other skills that women like you are going to need.
	System	Offering practical, personal help.
	Support	Anything from laying hospital trays to being a clinic receptionist.
GOOD FEET		In many areas you've really got to take these into consideration: policewoman; traffic warden; gardener; doorstep saleswoman; cook; waitress; nurse; weaver; visiting social worker.

everybody else does. What they mainly go on is the personal interview. In fact, a careers guidance officer advised me to ignore O and A minimums, even if specified in advertisements. 'You don't have to join the system, you can beat it,' she said.

Some of the following training sounds depressingly long. (I can't think beyond a year, myself.) But there are often short-cuts and the best of these is probably offered by TOPS; no TOPS course takes longer than a year. *Always check whether a TOPS course is available* (*visit, telephone or write to the training officer at your jobcentre*) *because you'll be trained at no cost and paid to do it. TOPS training is available for jobs in all the main areas in group 1, all the sorts of work in group 2, and many of the following specific jobs.*

Career training can involve training before a job (full-time) or on the job (evening classes, day- or block-release).

You will, of course, want to know how long the training period is going to be, whether you have any previous qualifications which will allow you to train, or whether you can train if you have *no* previous qualifications.

I have listed some suitable and interesting jobs that you may not know about and also jobs that mature women often want to do without realizing the difficulties, qualifications and/or time which may be involved. When I list 'Qualifications', they are qualifications needed to *train* you for the job, not qualifications to *do* the job.

The best sources of advice about what a particular type of job involves are usually the union or professional association and the specialist or trade journals – so you should read them. If the professional organization you want isn't given in the text or listed here, look it up in *Trade Association and Professional Bodies in the United Kingdom*, published by the Pergamon Press. It will be in your public library. Find out all details of courses from the college you wish to attend (and also whether they're likely to accept you) and then pursue the matter at your local jobcentre with the training officer or at PER.

If you want further advice on general adult education, contact the head office of the National Institute of Adult Education (England and Wales), 19B De Montfort Street, Leicester LE1 7GH (tel. Leicester [0533] 538977). For Scotland, contact the Scottish Institute of Adult Education, 57 Melville Street, Edinburgh EH3 7HL (tel. 031-226 7200).

It is polite and wise, when writing for free information, to enclose a stamped, self-addressed envelope which is large enough to take (hopefully) lots of brochures. When making inquiries, if you want to be certain that your letter arrives, I would suggest that you send it by recorded delivery.

At present, as I write, there's a great shortage of the following, which are traditionally women's jobs.

If you are a nurse or a secretary, the English-speaking world is still your oyster. There's also a shortage of dieticians, librarians, occupational therapists, radiographers and veter-inary assistants. There are good op-portunities for women in the service industries (shops, hospitals, local government work) and in education and catering, clerical and office work and the Health Service.

There are also shortages of sys-tems analysts, computer program-mers, office machine operators (xeroxing, etc.), chefs and cooks, waiters and waitresses.

The officially-tagged 'male' job areas are short of accountants, electri-cal and electronic engineers, engineer-ing draughtsmen (nice job, that), postmen, toolmakers, tool fitters, bus and coach drivers.

Most of the professions which are traditionally male-dominated have continuing shortages: these include accountancy, banking, insurance, en-gineering, research chemistry, den-tistry, medicine and librarianship.

CAREERS THAT WOMEN ASK ABOUT

Accountancy

Training period: Course of four to five years (three years for graduates).

Qualifications needed: Three O levels and two A levels including maths.

Late entry prospects: The Associa-tion of Certified Accountants pub-lishes an annual list of employers who may be willing to accept mature trainees: it's difficult after thirty-five.

Read: Accountancy Age, Account-ancy, the *Accountant.*

Information from: The Association of Certified Accountants, 29 Lincoln's Inn Fields, London WC2A 3EE; The Institute of Chartered Accountants in England and Wales, Chartered Ac-countants' Hall, Moorgate Place, London EC2R 6EQ; (Scotland) In-stitute of Chartered Accountants, 27 Queen Street, Edinburgh EH2 1LA; (Ireland) Institute of Chartered Ac-countants, 7 Fitzwilliam Place, Dub-lin 2.

Advertising

Training period: Training is mostly on the job.

Qualification needed: Four O levels and one A level; any specific training in another field may be useful.

Late entry prospects: Creative, not good; market research, good. Adver-tising is a ridiculously youth-oriented profession dominated by insecure, ageing, would-be trendy, creative directors.

Read: the journal *Campaign.*

Information from: The Communi-cation, Advertising and Marketing Education Foundation Ltd, 1 Bell Yard, London WC2A 2JX.

Agriculture and Horticulture

Training period: TOPS course; one-year basic course; alternative three-year sandwich course.

Qualifications needed: Range from four O levels.

Late entry prospects: Good for full-timers, but not part-timers. Good seasonal work prospects: freelance gardening is a growing industry.

WARNING: Make sure you can stand a lot of physical work.

Read: *Farmers' Weekly.*

Information from: the Women's Farm and Garden Association, Courthold House, Byng Place, London WC1E 7JH; National Farmers' Union, Agriculture House, Knightsbridge, London SW1; Horticulture Training Adviser, Agriculture Training Board, Bourne House, 32 Beckenham Road, Beckenham, Kent BR3 4PB.

Ambulance Driver

Training period: Up to six weeks' full-time training (including medical).

Qualifications needed: British driving licence. There's also a driving test. Apart from that, exact requirements vary from county to county but you must be strong, fit and not squeamish. Shift work, generally 7 a.m. to 3 p.m.; 3 p.m. to 11 p.m.; 11 p.m. to 7 a.m.

Late entry prospects: Good up to the age of forty-five.

Information from: your local hospital or area health authority.

Animal Nursing Auxiliaries (who do responsible work supervised by a vet)

Training period: Two years: a mixture of employment and part-time courses.

Qualifications: Three O levels.

Late entry prospects: No upper age limit for training, which is given on the job. Depends on getting a suitable apprenticeship. Good prospects for full- and part-time work, depending on local demand.

Read: *Veterinary Record.*

Information from: The Royal College of Veterinary Surgeons, 32 Belgrave Square, London WC1X 8QP.

Architecture

Training period: Seven years (two in employment).

Qualifications: Three O levels and two A levels (maths plus a science essential).

Late entry prospects: Fairly good in theory, but there's not much work in fact, and even if you do make it, dealing with the building industry could drive you mad.

Read: *Architects' Journal.*

Information from: the Royal Institute of British Architects, 66 Portland Place, London W1.

Archive Work

These are the record keepers of history. They catalogue it, index it, microfilm it. Mainly employed by local authorities, government offices, universities and libraries. Repairers and photographers also needed.

Training period: One year full-time for graduates.

Qualifications needed: Degree necessary, most appropriate in History. Latin and French are useful, also Law.

Late entry prospects: Good for full-time; limited part-time work.

Read: *The Times Literary Supplement.*

Information from: The Hon. Secretary, The Society of Archivists, County Records Office, County Hall, Hertford, Hertfordshire. For *Archives, Repairing* from: The Camberwell School of Art and Crafts, Peckham Road, London SE5.

Banking

Training period: On the job, or TOPS specific courses available.

Qualifications needed: Good general education.

Late entry prospects: Good. Not only behind those bars but also as machine operators, clerical and secretarial staff. Opportunities also in branch banking; executor and trustee work; foreign business and income tax. Excellent perks including that great incentive, the low-interest mortgage, sometimes as low as 5 per cent or lower. Don't ask about it too quickly at the interview.

Information from: The Institute of Bankers, 10 Lombard Street, London EC3; (Scotland) The Institute of Bankers, 20 Rutland Square, Edinburgh 1.

Beauty Therapy

Training period: TOPS course; if you want to be a manicurist the nail products firms offer short courses. Write to their head office for details.

Qualifications needed: Good general education.

Late entry prospects: Very good indeed, if your talents lie in this direction. But beware expensive courses advertised in glossy magazines.

Information from: The Confederation of Beauty Therapy and Cosmetology, c/o The Secretary, 12 Ravensbury Road, St Paul's Cray, Orpington, Kent.

Elementary **Book-keeping**

Training period: Depends. Often included in secretarial training at a college of further education or technical college. TOPS course.

Qualifications needed: None, except general GCE, including maths.

Late entry prospects: Very good indeed, both full- and part-time as a receptionist/book-keeper, especially in schools, hotels, with doctors, dentists.

Information from: The Institute of Administrative Accounting, 418 Strand, London WC2R OPW.

Career Services

Training period: TOPS course available, one year.

Qualifications needed: Simply working experience up to a degree.

Late entry prospects: Very promising. Older, more responsible people welcomed.

Read: *The Times Educational Supplement* and *Education.*

Information from: The Institute of Careers Officers, 2nd Floor, Old Board Chambers, 37A High Street, Stourbridge DY8 1TA.

Catering and Institutional Management

Training period: TOPS course. Special abridged course of one year for mature students.

Qualifications needed: None, but for two-year OND course, four O levels.

Late entry prospects: Good. This is the course that you take if you want to get a school-food job, leaving your holidays free.

Read: The *Caterer* and *Hotel Keeper.*

Information from: The Hotel, Catering and Institutional Management Association, 191 Trinity Road, London SW17 7HN.

Chiropody

Training period: TOPS course; or three years.

Qualifications needed: Five O levels.

Late entry prospects: Very good full-time and part-time.

Read: The *Chiropodist.*

Information from: The Society of Chiropodists, 8 Wimpole Street, London W1M 8PX.

Church Work

This depends on what sort and it's always best to consult your local minister.

Qualifications needed: Good recommendation from your local minister and general education.

Late entry prospects: Each person is considered individually and almost all work experience is valuable. A woman can't be a priest yet.

Information from: The headquarters of your denomination. The address will be in the Annual Careers Guide (get it from your library); The Advisory Council for the Church's Ministry, Church House, Dean's Yard, London SW1P 3NZ; The Church Army Headquarters, 185 Marylebone Road, London NW1 5QO.

Citizens' Advice

Training period: Provided locally.

Qualifications needed: Reasonable experience, intelligence and patience.

Late entry prospects: Good, but the work is voluntary (i.e. unpaid) although some bureaux (especially in cities) have paid staff, generally trained social workers.

Information from: Your local citizens' advice bureau, or centrally at the National Council of Social Service, 26 Bedford Square, London WC1 3HU.

Civil Service

Runs the country. It co-ordinates the various departments of the government and helps to form their policy. Many people think that the Civil Service is a fuddy-duddy, impersonal organization. This is not necessarily so; the service is divided into different departments and each is subdivided. The system is based on team work and co-operation, so if you like to work alone, don't do it.

Read: *Government Departments and Their Work* to find out what's available in the Civil Service, which has over fifty departments (get it from the Civil service Commission – address below – or your library).

The great job advantages are that you have security (once in, carried out feet first), that amazing pension scheme, regular pay increases, good pay, generous holiday allowances and special consideration for women such as flexible working hours and training schemes for returners. There are countrywide opportunities for em-ployment and promotion; a move needn't dislocate your career because you can often transfer to a similar job in your area.

Late entry prospects: Very good: the Civil Service has always welcomed women.

There are all sorts of jobs available from filing clerks to architects. Jobs are available in Social Security, Inland Revenue, Customs and Excise, Department of the Environment, Department of Overseas Trade, Crown and County Courts, Ministry of Agriculture, Fisheries and Food, Central Office of Information, Forestry Commission, Home Office, etc.

Information about all Civil Service jobs can be obtained from the Civil Service Commission, Brook House, Alencon Link, Basingstoke, Hampshire RG21 1JB. They also have many leaflets on *local* job opportunities, so you could write and ask what's available in your own area.

Company Secretary

Training period: About three years full-time or five years part-time. Study for exams of the Institute of Chartered Secretaries and Administrators (study period may be less for graduates and HND holders).

Qualifications needed: Experience in business law, accountancy, taxation and administration. Other work experience useful in personnel, banking, insurance. Two O levels and two A levels or four O levels and one A level or ONC/OND Business Studies or Public Administration.

Late entry prospects: Very encouraging for people up to ages forty to forty-five.

Read: *Professional Administration.*

Information from: The Institute of Chartered Secretaries and Administrators, 16 Park Crescent, London w1.

Computers

Training period: It depends what you want to do. TOPS courses available for computer operators and programmers and data preparation clerks. ONC/HNC and OND/HND courses offered in computer studies.

Qualifications needed: A level maths.

Late entry prospects: Good up to thirty-five. Poor part-time possibilities. Beware of crummy commercial computer programming courses, which *sound* as though a job is provided at the end of your training. Beware of out-of-date private training. It's essential to take an up-to-date course.

Read: *Computing* and *Computer Weekly.*

Information from: The British Computer Society, 29 Portland Place, London w1n 4hu; (Scotland) The Scottish Business Education Council, 22 Great King Street, Edinburgh eh3 6qh.

Dental Auxiliary

These are the people who work with dentists in schools and hospitals helping with dental treatment for children.

Training period: Two years full-time.

Qualifications needed: Four O levels including English, biology and another science subject.

Late entry prospects: Very good indeed, both full- and part-time.

Information from: The General Dental Council, 37 Wimpole Street, London w1m 8dq.

Dental Hygienist

Works with dentist.

Training period: Nine months in hospital in a big town.

Qualifications needed: Four O levels, including one science subject.

Late entry prospects: Very good indeed. Full- or part-time work.

Information from: The British Dental Hygienists' Association, c/o Eastman Dental Hospital, Gray's Inn Road, London wc1x 8ld.

Dental Surgery Assistant

The ones who mix the fillings and pop the pink fizzy pill in the water.

Training period: One year in dental hospital or technical college.

Qualifications needed: None, apart from a good educational background and intelligence.

Late entry prospects: Good for full- and part-time.

Read: *Dental Practice, Dental Health* and the *British Dental Journal.*

Information from: The Association of British Dental Surgery Assistants, Bank Chambers, 3 Market Place, Poulton, Blackpool.

Dietician

Training period: Eighteen months to four years depending on qualifications (SRNs, catering managers, biochemists and home economics teachers qualify for eighteen-month course).

Qualifications needed: Start with four O levels including English, chemistry and maths.

Late entry prospects: Pretty good.
Read: *Nutrition.*

Information from: The British Dietetic Association, 305 Daimler House, Paradise Street, Birmingham B1 2BJ.

Driver

If you can drive, you can drive a minicab, a delivery van or a Rolls-Royce (they offer a two-week special course) or learn to drive a bus, or a heavy goods vehicle (TOPS training available).

Driving Instructor

Training period: From two weeks, depending on school and your ability.

Qualifications needed: Full driving licence for four years out of last six. Some knowledge of car mechanics necessary. A local driving school may train you to train other people, otherwise the Motor Schools Association (12 Tilton Street, London SW6) have a two-week full-time course costing about £120.

Late entry prospects: Good.

Engineering

The money here can be marvellous. There's an enormous variety of jobs with many different TOPS courses available.

Training period: Depends on what you want to do: from under a year on a TOPS practical training course to six years (three years for a degree, plus three years on-the-job practical training) to become a chartered engineer.

Qualifications needed: Depends how high you want to go. For a degree you need A-level maths and physics. O-level chemistry also useful.

Engineering Technician

Training period: On the job with day-release or pre-entry course. Since 1976 training has been much more flexible to make it easier for women to qualify.

Qualifications needed: 4 O levels, including maths.

Late entry prospects: Good. Female technicians are always needed in engineering offices.

Information from: The Women's

Engineering Society, 25 Foubert's Place, London w1v 2al, or the Council of Engineering Institutions, 2 Little Smith Street, London sw1p 3dl.

Floristry

Training period: One year or behind the counter in your local florist. Full-time, day-release or evening classes available at some technical colleges.

Qualifications needed: General good education, i.e. none. Secretarial or sales experience useful.

Late entry prospects: Very good indeed for full- and part-time work.

Information from: The British Flower Industry Association, 281 Flower Market, New Covent Garden Market, London sw8 5nb.

Hairdressing

Training period: Three-year apprenticeship with day-release classes. Alternatively one- or two-year technical college course. Be wary of expensive private schools of hairdressing.

Qualifications needed: None.

Late entry prospects: Depends on employer. Plenty of full- and part-time work.

Read: *Hairdressers' Journal.*

Information from: The British Hairdressing Apprenticeship Council, 11 Goldington Road, Bedford, or the Hairdressing Council, 17 Spring Street, London w2.

Health Visitor

A Health Visitor acts as a link between people and their GP, clinics, hospitals and social services.

Training period: From one year for SRNs to three to four years if no previous training. Special extended courses for people with family commitments. TOPS training.

Qualifications needed: Five O levels.

Late entry prospects: Good.

Information from: The Council for the Education and Training of Health Visitors, Clifton House, Euston Road, London nw1.

Home Economics

High-powered housekeeping (formerly known as domestic science). Work available in industry, large companies, social and public services, welfare, teaching, new food product development, public relations, advertising, consumer advice centres, demonstrating, small residential or non-residential schools, nursing homes, hospitals, homes for the old and the handicapped.

Training period: From one year shortened course for mature students).

Qualifications: Vary according to course, from four O levels.

Late entry prospects: Good.

Read: *Home Economics.*

Information from: The National Council for Home Economics Education, 214 Middle Lane, London N8, and the Association of Home Economists of Great Britain, 307 Uxbridge Road, London W3 9QU; the Association of Teachers of Domestic Science, Hamilton House, Mabledon Place, London WC1.

Home-help Organizers

Running the home-help service is an increasingly important part of the social services. You liaise with doctors and social workers who allocate home helps to people who need them.

Qualifications needed: Good general education, i.e. none. Tact, persuasiveness and good organizing ability needed.

Training period: Training on the job, by correspondence course or day release.

Late entry prospects: Excellent.

Further information: From your local social services department.

Hospital Administration

Some good jobs going here and lots of local opportunities. Many posts with training schemes provided.

Training period: Varies and depends on the job and any previous useful experience, degree or professional qualifications.

Qualifications needed: Depends on the job and training you want. From minimum of four O levels.

Late entry prospects: Very good indeed. Full- or part-time.

Read: *Health and Social Services Journal* or *Hospital and Health Services Review.*

Get leaflets on training schemes from the National Staff Committee for Administrative and Clerical Staff, Friar's House, 157 Blackfriars Road, London SE1 8EU. *Information* about prospects and training from the Institute of Health Service Administrators, 75 Portland Place, London W1M 4AN. *Further information* about vacancies in your area from the personnel officer of your regional health authority (ask your local hospital, doctor or library for the address).

Hotels and Catering

Training period: Varies from one year to four, depending on work you want to do. There's a wide range of very good TOPS courses including hotel reception, general catering, cooking and institutional management (there's a specially abridged course for mature students).

Qualifications needed: Apart from TOPS courses, from four O levels.

Late entry prospects: Good in all areas (everyone needs to eat).

Read: The *Caterer* and *Hotel Keeper*.

Information from: The Hotel, Catering and Institutional Management Association, 191 Trinity Road, London SW17 7HN; also the Hotel and Catering Industry Training Board, PO Box 18, Ramsay House, Central Square, Wembley, Middlesex HA9 7AP.

Housing Management

Working in local government or housing associations.

Training period: Some jobs, such as housing visitors, need no previous training. Otherwise on the job, plus day or block release. Full-time courses from eighteen months for graduates or three-year course plus one year practical experience.

Qualifications needed: Three O levels and two A levels; can be less if you're over thirty-five and taking institute exams.

Late entry prospects: Very good because there is also work for supporting staff which is non-qualified work and can be done on a part-time basis.

Read: *Housing, Municipal Journal, Local Government Chronicle.*

Information from: The Institute of Housing Managers, Victoria House, Southampton Row, London WC1B 4EB.

Insurance

You can be anything from a city broker to the local part-time representative of the Pru, cycling round on your bike for weekly premiums. There are a lot of jobs (including selling, clerical, secretarial, statistical and computers) in areas such as general, life, marine, motor, property and aviation.

Training period: Three years of part-time study while working on the job for your Chartered Insurance Institute exam.

Qualifications needed: From two O levels and two A levels or equivalents.

Late entry prospects: Reasonably good for full- or part-time work. Good working conditions.

Information from: The Chartered Insurance Institute, 20 Aldermanbury Square, London EC2V 7HY.

Interior Design

There are two ten-week courses available on block release. Two O levels needed. This leads to licenciateship of the Institute of British Decorators and Designers. As this is an extremely competitive field, mistakes can be very expensive. It is extremely difficult to get work done these days to the essential standards and having done it, I DO NOT RECOMMEND IT for anyone, let alone a returner. Don't think that because you've got good taste and creative ideas and are artistic that this sort of work is quick to learn. If you're thinking of setting up on your own you could easily and quickly end up in tears and broke. It's safer to work in a furnishing store or for a manufacturer but don't be surprised to get drudge work and low pay, especially if you're working for one of the glamour names.

Training period: One of the few private courses that I would recommend is run by the Inchbald School of Design, 7 Eaton Gate, London s w 1 a o 1 (tel. 01-730 5508). They offer a ten-week course in basic design and decoration (for £500) and a one-year course for £1600. Otherwise TOPS may sponsor you on a one-year college course in art and design and pay you a salary as well as the fees. If you really want to qualify, a DipAD in interior design takes four years.

Qualifications needed: Three O levels and two A levels.

Late entry prospects: Bad at all ages.

Information from: Your local college or school of art or from the National Council for Diplomas in Art and Design, 344 Gray's Inn Road, London EC4.

Journalism (see also Radio and Television)

Newspapers are hardest of all. It's difficult to enter, whatever your age. It helps if you have shorthand, typing and other qualifications.

Training period: Some big newspaper groups have their own training schemes, nearly all for young entrants and recent graduates. The classic start is a job as a trainee with a local weekly or daily newspaper and they may send you on a day-release course. There are one-year full-time courses sponsored by the newspaper industry and controlled by the National Council for the Training of Journalists. After this you get a job – where you can serve a three-year apprenticeship (two years for graduates).

Qualifications needed (apart from thick skin, colossal cheek and persistance): Five O levels, including English language.

Late entry prospects: Difficult, except in specialist areas. If you have expert knowledge in some field there may be opportunities in trade or professional journals. The other way to start is simply to pick up a pen, start writing and see how it sells to your local newspaper. Submit everything clean and typed, double spaced; cut out the poetry and stick to the facts (well, that's what they told me).

Read: *UK Press Gazette* and *Campaign.*

Information from: The National Council for the Training of Journalists, Harp House, 179 High Street, Epping, Essex CM16 4BG.

Landscape Designers

Needed in parks, in towns, in new developments, in factory areas.

Training period: TOPS course in environmental horticulture, otherwise for graduates or mature students. The Institute of Landscape Architects examinations require one-year full-time to three to four years part-time training. There's also a full-time four-year polytechnic course for non-graduates.

Qualifications needed: Three O levels and two A levels, a strong backbone and plenty of stamina.

Late entry prospects: Good full- and part-time, but there's lots of competition for training.

Information from: The Institute of Landscape Architects, Nash House, 12 Carlton House Terrace, London sw1.

Languages

Don't think that because you can speak a language fluently you can translate or interpret it professionally. Most translating work involves highly specialized material, either scientific, technological, legal or commercial. There's hardly any work in literary translation and, if there is, it usually goes to a writer who already has a literary reputation.

Training period: You can learn a language at evening classes or a college of further education, and there are TOPS courses for secretarial linguists. Full-time one-year courses for graduates in interpreting and translating are available at Bath and Bradford Universities and the Central London Polytechnic.

Late entry prospects: Very good with growing Common Market opportunities.

Information from: The Institute of Linguists, 91 Newington Causeway, London SE1 6BN.

Law (Legal Executives, Solicitors, Barristers)

It is the solicitor's responsibility to assemble all the facts, and prepare the case. A barrister is often called on to advise on legal points before the case starts. (In which case it may never start.) What the barrister does is summarize the case and present it in court. In Scotland the equivalent of barristers is advocates, but solicitors apply for both legal systems.

Legal Executives
This is often specialized administrative work in one of the following areas:
  Conveyancing (dealing with land sales)
  Accountancy (money business)
  Preparing for litigation (assembling the evidence)
  Probate (tidying up everything on behalf of the dead)
  Training period: By way of part day-release, full day-release, evening classes or even correspondence courses. Three years working in a solicitor's office before the final examinations.

Qualifications needed: English O level.

Late entry prospects: Good for returners, especially with secretarial experience.

Information from: The Institute of Legal Executives, Ilex House, Barr Hill Road, London SW2 4RW.

Solicitors
The study of law is usually taken in two parts: (1) a study period followed by an exam and then (2) practical experience followed by an exam.

Training period (for non-graduates): Non-graduates take a year's course and then serve four years of articles (apprenticeships in Scotland) as a solicitor's clerk before taking Part 2. In all it takes five years to qualify from scratch.

Qualifications needed (for non-graduates): Three O and two A levels or one O and three A levels.

Law graduates are usually exempt from Part 1 exams. They may take a full-time one-year course at a college of law or certain polytechnics in preparation for Part 2 either before or after being articled for two years.

Graduates in other subjects can take a one-year full-time course for Part 1 and then the articles for two years before Part 2. Alternatively, you can go straight into articles for two and a half years and take Part 1 exams while you're working. You can then take Part 2.

Late entry prospects: The older, wiser and more experienced you get the more they increase. The difficulty is getting someone to take you on to begin with.

Information from: (England and Wales) The Law Society, 113 Chancery Lane, London WC2A 1PL; (Scotland) Law Society of Scotland, 26 Drumsheugh Gardens, Edinburgh EH3 7HR; (N. Ireland) Incorporated Law Society of Northern Ireland, Royal Courts of Justice, Belfast BT1 3JE.

Barrister
Training period (to complete the Bar examinations): Maximum two years.

Qualifications needed: Graduate entry only except for occasional mature students. You have to join one of the Inns of Court and attend three dinners for eight terms (two years) and pass the Bar examinations. You then have to complete a year's apprenticeship under an experienced barrister. (Don't underestimate those dinners.)

Late entry prospects: Always difficult. Fierce competition. Nice work if you're good and lucky: the problem may be getting taken into chambers.

Read: Choose from the *Legal Executive, Law Society Gazette, Solicitors' Journal, Justice.*

Information from: (England and Wales) The Council of Legal Education, Inns of Court School of Law, Gray's Inn Place, London WC1R 5DX; (Scotland) Faculty of Advocates, Clerk of Faculty, Advocates' Library, Parliament House, Edinburgh EH1 1RF; (N. Ireland) Under-Treasurer, Inn of Court of Northern Ireland, Royal Courts of Justice, Chichester Street, Belfast BT1 3JE.

Librarian

Steady job prospects here, well paid: if you enjoy a lively, questing atmosphere this could be the job for you.

Training period: Two years full-time for graduates: three to four year course for non-graduates.

Qualifications needed: Two A and three O levels, including English language.

Late entry prospects: Not bad.

Read: *The Times Literary Supplement* and the *Library Association Record.*

Information from: The Library Association, 7 Ridgmount Street, London WC1 7AE.

Local Authority work

This is what your rates are spent on (and some taxes). It's local housekeeping on an enormous scale. It's keeping the community running and improving it (hopefully) and helping and improving the lives of the people in it. It's paid community work. There are almost as many different available jobs and good opportunities for late entry as there are in the civil service; it's impossible even to list them because there are so many.

Local authorities employ two million people who range from teachers and architects to drivers and dustmen. The main areas include clerical, educational, rating and valuation, housing and town planning, transport, consumer protection and social services (including home-help organizers (see p. 105) who do immensely important work for people who are really in need). Local government has a very good record for training and encouraging women. Good opportunities for late starters, depending on

what you want to do and previous experience.

Training: In some areas, for some jobs, it is deliberate policy to recruit mature staff who are most likely to understand other people's needs and problems. They are especially welcome in the departments with deal direct with the public such as housing and working with children or old people.

Qualifications needed: O and A levels are not always necessary and lack of them may not prevent promotion. Many local governments offer traineeships and are very generous in giving staff opportunities to qualify professionally.

Further information from: Your local council direct. For district council enquiries write to the chief executive (formerly known as the town clerk) of your district or borough council. For county council inquiries write to the chief executive (personnel services) at your county council office (county hall). Get the address from your telephone book or local library.

Manufacturing

On the whole, women haven't had much practical experience of working in industry. It is still thought of as primarily a man's world run by feeble-minded megalomaniacs with red Jaguars, bossy mothers and extraordinarily complicated sex lives. Say 'factory work' and you will still conjure up a mental picture of greyness and dirt, or workers relentlessly on strike or quietly going mad on an assembly line while watched by men in white coats with stopwatches.

In fact, there are many good opportunities in industry. It's often well paid from the start; you don't always need formal qualifications; there are many TOPS training courses, so that you can acquire any necessary skills; it's easy to enter, and it can be easy to get promotion to such jobs as supervisor, foreman, inspector or progress chaser (this last is a co-ordinating job, checking that the right materials have been ordered, orders have been started on time, packed and delivered). There are three basic categories: unskilled, semi-skilled and skilled. It's not difficult to move from unskilled work to semi-skilled with better pay, and you don't have to work on production.

Industry jobs also include timekeeping, personnel and office staff work, marketing and merchandising (seeing that retail outlets have regular stocks of your goods) and 'sales reps' (otherwise called commercial travellers) who sell goods to the stores.

To find what jobs are available visit your local jobcentre and read the situations vacant columns in local newspapers, or contact the companies direct: write to the personnel officer.

Training: By day-release, evening class or postal course. If you have a job in the *costings* department you can register as a student for examinations with the Institute of Cost and Management Accountants, 63 Portland Place, London W 1 N 4 AB. *Buyers* can study on the job for the examination of the Institute of Purchasing and Supply, York House, Westminster Bridge Road, London SE 1. *Training period* depends on the course.

Qualifications needed: Three O levels and two A levels or an ONC or OND in Business Studies.

Late entry prospects: Can be good, depending on individual and background (see also Purchasing and Stock Control, p. 120).

Market Research

This is the science of investigating public opinion and then assessing what it all means. It is finding out what the mass of people like and dislike; what they want and – more tricky – what they *might* want (for example, a new kind of baked bean); and what their habits are (which can range from watching 'Coronation Street' to baking wholemeal bread and supporting the Liberals). Many large firms have their own market research departments and there are also market research companies which do surveys on commission for organizations and businesses.

Qualifications needed: There are four main types of market research work:

(a) Interviewing, for which you need no qualifications except an easy manner, physical stamina and a pair of stout boots;

(b) Analysis staff, for which you need a reasonable education;

(c) Research assistant, for which you need two A levels.

(d) Trainee Research Executive, for which you need the relevant degree (economics, statistics, psychology or sociology) followed by a year of practical experience, after which you can expect to reach executive level.

Late entry prospects: Very good, including part-time. The interviewing or 'field work' jobs are often available for a particular project which lasts a few weeks so you can arrange your work around school holidays or fit it into your own timetable. You can often get promotion from part-time interviewing to full-time supervisory jobs. The B B C also employs part-time interviewers all over the country to question people about their viewing and listening habits for its audience surveys (see p. 121).

Read: Campaign.

Information from: The Market Research Society, 15 Belgrave Square, London SW 1 X 8 PF.

Medical Laboratory Scientists and Technicians

This involves carrying out tests on tissue samples and other specimens so that doctors can diagnose illnesses and treat them. There is also research work, investigating diseases and their cures. Medical laboratory staff in hospitals don't spend all their time in the lab, they also see patients in the wards to collect samples. Other medical technicians may be involved in medical work such as cardiac and pulmonary tests, electro-physiological and radio therapy.

Training period: For routine non-professional jobs training combines practical experience working in a hospital with day-release classes and lectures. Otherwise it depends on what you've already done, and how high you hope to climb.

Qualifications needed: Normally four O levels; training up to State Registration takes four years. It takes two years less if you have two suitable A levels, or only 1 year for a graduate with the relevant degree.

Late entry prospects: Very good indeed if you have a tidy, accurate mind with scientific bent and pay attention to detail.

Read: the *Journal of Clinical Pathology, Medical Technologist, Laboratory News.*

Information from: The Institute of Medical Laboratory Technology, 12 Queen Anne Street, London W 1 M OAU and the Institute of Science Technology, 345 Gray's Inn Road, London WC 1 X8P.

Medical Records Work

This is keeping hospital, medical and health records as well as having librarian and administrative duties (organizing the patients). There's also a lot of work interpreting statistical data which can be very interesting and rewarding. Plenty of job opportunities.

Training period: Usually in-service training combined with study. There's a correspondence course from NALGO Correspondence Institute, 8 Harewood Row, London N W 1.

Qualifications needed: Two O levels for the Certificate; five O levels for the Diploma. Secretarial training very useful, especially if you've done medical work.

Information from: The Association of Medical Records Offices, 16 Beacon Hill, Dormansland, Lingfield, Surrey RH7 6RH.

Midwifery

Training period: If SRN with appropriate obstetric training – ten months. If other SRN or sick children's nurse – one year. Other categories of nurse and State Enrolled Nurse – eighteen months. No nursing training – two years, training full-time.

Qualifications needed: Minimum two O levels. You also have to be an SRN or sick children's nurse or pass the Central Midwife's Board Education tests.

Late entry prospects: Age limit of fifty and mothers obviously have one outstanding qualification for delivering other people's babies – they know what it feels like. A marvellously rewarding job.

Read: *Nursing Times, Nursing Mirror, Midwife's Chronicle, Midwife and Health Visitor.*

Information from: The Royal College of Midwives, 15 Mansfield Street, London W1M OBE; (N. Ireland) Council for Nurses and Midwives, 216 Belmont Road, Belfast BT4 2AT.

Museum Work

Training period: This interesting work varies according to post and is a job plus individual studies. Two years' experience necessary before taking final examinations and for diploma; this can be cut to eighteen months for graduates.

Qualifications needed: Four O levels for a museum assistant; three O and two A levels for a more responsible post which leads to the diploma examination; and honours degree for senior posts.

Late entry prospects: Very good indeed. Openings for women in all types of museums (university, private, local and national) and in all fields of study.

Read: *Museums Bulletin.*

Information from: The Education Officer, Museums Association, 87 Charlotte Street, London W1P 2BX.

Restoring

Can be absorbing work if you're good with your hands.

Training period: Depends upon whether you're conserving or mending pictures, archives, books or furniture, dress or model making or repairing dinosaurs. TOPS courses are available.

Qualifications needed: Again, these vary, but any craft experience a definite advantage.

Late entry prospects: Age unimportant if you have the necessary qualifications and experience.

Information from: The Education Officer, Museums Association, 87 Charlotte Street, London W1P 2BX.

Nursing

There is always a demand anywhere in the world for a British SRN. The training makes a useful background for looking after a family. The pay can be good and part-time work is available. Nursing qualifications can also lead to lots of other interesting jobs: nurse tutor, health visitor, industrial nurse and school nurse (very handy for mothers) as well as all the senior jobs in nursing administration.

Nursing Auxiliaries

Look after patients supervised by nurses.

Training period: On the job, in hospitals. Sometimes the hospital provides an introductory three-day course.

Qualifications needed: Two O levels, common sense and good health. You had better not be squeamish, but as writer Katharine Whitehorn has pointed out, few women *really* faint at the sight of blood, for obvious monthly reasons.

State Enrolled Nurse

Bedside care, administering drugs, operating theatre work. Particularly useful for someone starting late be-

cause the training is shorter and less academic than for SRN.

Training period: Two years, or part-time courses up to three years available for women with home responsibilities.

Qualifications needed: Good general education. No O levels on the whole.

Late entry prospects: Great.

State Registered Nurse (SRN)

Good feet needed, good health and ability to digest hospital food.

Training period: Generally three years full-time; two years for graduates. You get paid while you're training.

Qualifications needed: Minimum two O levels but most hospitals will ask for more and teaching hospitals are very fussy.

Late entry prospects: Good general prospects.

Read: *Nursing Mirror, Nursing Times.*

Information from: The Nursing and Hospital Careers Information Centre, 121 Edgware Road, London w2, or ask your local hospital or any health authority; The General Nursing Council for England and Wales, 23 Portland Place, London w1a 1ba; (Scotland) The General Nursing Council for Scotland, 5 Darnaway Street, Edinburgh eh3 6dp; (N. Ireland) Council for Nurses and Midwives, 216 Belmont Road, Belfast bt4 2at.

Nursery Nursing

Involves looking after babies and

young children in nurseries, in homes for children and hospitals. Huge demand, but not many training vacancies.

Training period: You need to take the National Nursery Examination Board Exam or the Royal Society of Health Diploma for Nursery Nurses. Motherhood is actually a *qualification* which cuts a year off your training. Training can be on the job in a nursery plus attendance two days a week at a technical college or college of further education. This kind of training may be sponsored by your local council social services or education department. Some local colleges offer a one-year full-time special course for mature students with experience of children. You can also train at one of the recognized fee-paying colleges which *must* be affiliated to the Associated College of Nursery Training (long, long waiting lists; apply two years in advance). Training lasts eighteen months to two years. No upper age limit.

Qualifications needed: Two or three O levels minimum.

Late entry prospects: Good.

Read: *Nursery World.*

Information from: The National Nursery Examination Board, The Royal Society of Health, the Association of Nursery Training Colleges (expensive private training). They're all at 13 Grosvenor Place, London SW1X 7EN; (Scotland) The Scottish Nursery Examination Board, 38 Queen Street, Glasgow C1 3DY. Or write to the Social Services or Education Department of your local council.

Occupational Therapy

Helps people who have been disabled by illness or accidents to readjust their bodies or their minds through work or craft. Very rewarding work.

Training period: Three years at a School of Occupational Therapy. Two years if a graduate in relevant subjects.

Qualifications needed: Five O levels; having an A level helps.

Late entry prospects: Good opportunities for full- and part-time work.

Read: *British Journal of Occupational Therapy.*

Information from: The British Association of Occupational Therapists, 20 Rede Place, London W2 4TU; (Scotland) The Association of Occupational Therapists, 77 George Street, Edinburgh 2.

Optical Work

There are two main professions: ophthalmic and dispensing opticians; or orthoptists.

Ophthalmic Optician

This involves the examination of eyes, correcting visual defects with spectacles, contact lenses and special exercises. You need neat hands, a clear mind and accuracy.

Training period: Three years' university training (four years in Scotland) and one year supervised practical work before registration.

Qualifications needed: Minimum five GCEs of which 2 must be at A level – one in mathematics, another in English.

Late entry prospects: Good. Part-time or sessional work fairly readily available.

You can often get a loan on favourable terms to help you to buy an established practice or partnership. Details from the British Optical Association, 65 Brook Street, London w1y 2dt, or the Scottish Association of Opticians, 116 West Regent Street, Glasgow c3.

Dispensing Optician
They fit spectacles or other visual aids.

Training period: Two-year full-time course or three-year day-release or three-year correspondence course taken while in suitable employment plus one month yearly full-time study. This is followed by a year's paid employment before registration.

Qualifications needed: Four O levels including mathematics.

Late entry prospects: Good.

Information from: The Association of Dispensing Opticians Ltd, 22 Nottingham Place, London w1n 4at.

Orthoptists
An orthoptist works under an opthalmic surgeon. She diagnoses and treats squints and other eye problems, and generally assists the surgeon.

Training period: Three-year full-time course, at an Orthoptic Training School.

Qualifications needed: Four O levels, one A level. A lot of the work is with very young children and needs unending patience and accuracy.

Information from: The British Orthoptic Association, 35 Lincoln's Inn Fields, London wc2.

Personnel Management

This is *not* a job you wander into because you're 'good with people' or 'good at organizing'. For this job you will need to be properly qualified and prepared for lots of study. You need contradictory abilities: a tidy, orderly mind, efficiency, and an ability to get on with people. Posts are few and it is difficult to start after you're forty. But different sorts of experience come in useful so it's worth considering if you really want to do it.

Training period: Can vary from fifteen months for graduates and older people with suitable commercial experience to four years part-time at polytechnics and technical colleges to take the Institute of Personnel Management (IPM) examinations. TOPS advanced course available for diploma.

Qualifications needed: Three O levels and two A levels or experience in a personnel department.

Read: *Personnel Management* and *IPM Digest.*

Information from: The Institute of Personnel Management, Central House, Upper Woburn Place, London wc1h 0hx.

Pharmacy

Trained pharmacists are always needed for work in hospitals or pharmacies or in industry, developing new drugs. Training can be absorbing and rewards can be high.

Training period: Three years for degree, followed by one year pre-registration experience.

Qualifications needed: At least three A levels in chemistry/physics or maths/biology or botany/zoology.

Read: *Pharmaceutical Journal* and the *Chemist and Druggist.*

Information from: The Pharmaceutical Society of Great Britain, 1 Lambeth High Street, London SE 1.

Pharmacy Technician/Assistant

You dispense medicines of all kinds and run pharmacy departments: accuracy and reliability are essential as you ladle out the phenobarbitone to doctors who will leave it in their cars.

Training period: During employment: three years part-time if unqualified; two years if you have three O levels including a science.

Qualifications needed: Either none or three O levels.

Late entry prospects: Good.

Information from: The Pharmacy Assistants' Training Board, 321 Chase Road, London N 14.

Photography

You're not going to be Sarah Moon overnight but there are lots of regional opportunities (all those wedding photographs), and developing work can be very soothing, undemanding, part-time and fairly well paid. There's also a demand for scientific, record, museum, industrial and illustrative handbook photography.

Training period: Two to three years full-time or sandwich or part-time course.

Qualifications needed: Four O levels or four O levels and one A level.

Photographer's Assistant

This is the best way to learn to be a photographer. You can study for exams by day-release or evening classes. It is necessary to be orderly and methodical. You must be prepared for low pay to start with, to be sworn at, to transport the heavy gear, to be able to wire up the lights, get impossible props and generally act like a very intelligent odd-job man. A basic knowledge of photography and film is required (ability to point a Polaroid is not enough).

Late entry prospects: Difficult, often depending on luck and opportunity.

Read: the *Photographer* or the *British Journal of Photography.*

Information from: The Institute of Incorporated Photographers, Amwell End, Ware, Hertfordshire SG 12 9HN.

Physiotherapy

Involves helping patients to recover from sickness or accident with remedial exercises, massage or electrical treatment. It can be physically strenuous work. You meet all kinds of people and there's something wrong with all of them. It can be very rewarding to help put it right. *Note:* There are lots of part-time jobs for the untrained as assistants to occupational therapists and physiotherapists. They are called paramedical aides.

Training period: Three years full-time in a recognized training school.

Qualifications needed: Four O levels and one A level. Good health, strength and sporty outlook.

Late entry prospects: Very good for full- and part-time so long as you're prepared to be on call and do weekend work. Unless you've had previous PT or dancing experience it's difficult to train if you're over thirty-five to forty because of the physical strength needed.

Read: *Physiotherapy.*

Information from: The Chartered Society of Physiotherapy, 14 Bedford Row, London WC1R 4ED.

Police

Prospects for women have really opened up here in the last few years and there are opportunities in detective work, and as heads of departments.

Training period: Two to three years as constable, then an exam.

Qualifications needed: British nationality, no previous convictions and reasonably good education.

Late entry prospects: Top recruiting age usually thirty-five. No part-time jobs.

Information from: Your local Chief Constable; graduates write to the Police Graduate Liaison Officer, F Division, Home Office, Horseferry House, Dean Ryle Street, London SW1P 2AW; (Scotland) Police Recruiting Department, Scottish Home and Health Department, 44 York Place, Edinburgh EH1 3JT; (N. Ireland) Recruiting Branch, Royal Ulster Constabulary Headquarters, Brooklyn, Knock Road, Belfast BT5 6LE.

Political Work

You need tact, organizing ability and (preferably) devotion to the cause. Try some hard-slog voluntary work in the local outfit before you decide to wade into a political life. Opportunities are clerical/secretarial/MP's research/ MP's agent. Can be an exciting and absorbing life: can even lead to being an MP.

Training period: Conservative and Labour Parties have their own training schemes and examinations.

Late entry prospects: Not particularly good, but personality a decisive factor.

Qualifications needed: No set qualifications but above average intelligence and education necessary before you're accepted for training. Any relevant experience (e.g. in research) can also be useful.

Information from: party headquarters: LABOUR: General Secretary's Department, The Labour Party, Transport House, Smith Square, London SW1.

LIBERAL: The Liberal Party Organization, National Liberal Club, Whitehall Place, London SW1.

CONSERVATIVE: The Conservative Central Office, 32 Smith Square, London SW1.

Prison Psychiatric Work (see Social Work)

Prison Service

If you fancy yourself as Googie Withers, calmly sorting out everyone's horrific problems in one full-colour hour, I have to tell you that a lively interest in social problems is *not* all that's needed.

Training period: Five-week course at a prison or, borstal followed by another eight-week course at the Officers' Training School, Yorkshire. The work isn't necessarily residential, but it is shift work. Fast promotion.

Qualifications needed: General education. A degree is useful, particularly in social science.

Late entry prospects: They recruit up to fifty, if you're fit. No part-time jobs. Paid as you learn.

Information from: The Establishment Officer, The Home Office, Portland House, Stag Place, London SW1E 5BX; (Scotland) Director of Scottish Prison Service, Scottish Home and Health Department, Broomhouse Drive, Edinburgh EH11 3UY.

Probation and After-care (see Social Work)

Psychology

Training period: Depends on job required, can be none but can be in-service training or postgraduate course (one to two years).

Qualifications needed: Degree in psychology.

Late entry prospects: Good. We are all getting battier.

Information from: The Society of Analytical Psychology, 30 Devonshire Place, London W1; British Psychological Society, 18 Albemarle Street, London W1X 4DN.

Public Health Inspector

Great tact needed as you examine and condemn dustbins, restaurant kitchens, factories, etc.

Training period: University degree – four years; sandwich course – three years or day-release four-year course.

Qualifications needed: Three O levels and two A levels (or OND or ONC).

Late entry prospects: Good.

Information from: The Public Health Inspectors' Education Board, 13 Grosvenor Place, London SW1; (Scotland) the Sanitary Inspectors' Association of Scotland, 20 Woodmill Terrace, Dunfermline KI11 4SR.

Public Relations

This work might be in a specialist firm, government departments or local government or in industry, charities or political work. You're the contact between the organization for which you work and the staff and/or the public. You might have to get information, dish out information, doctor it or suppress it, write speeches or organize parties, receptions or Press tours. You might have to launch new products or new people.

Qualifications needed: Basically you should be a fast and efficient worker, quick on the uptake, a clear thinker with a pleasant telephone voice. Apart from that you're going to get this job on personality (positive to pushy, not mouse-like) and previous experience (journalism, secretarial, voluntary or organizational work can all help).

You have to be able to write a straight statement and present it in an interesting way so that it won't end up in the wastepaper basket (where most of them do).

Late entry prospects: Very good providing you have the basic attributes.

Press Officer

To be successful you need to know about what you're publicizing (much rarer than you'd think), to be efficient and to understand how the media work technically (*very* rare).

Training period: No full-time training. It's best to learn on the job and take a correspondence course before taking the Communication, Advertising and Marketing examination in PR.

Information from: The Institute of Public Relations, 1 Great James Street, London WC1 3DA, or Communication, Advertising and Marketing Education Foundation, 1 Bell Yard, London WC2A 2JX.

Publishing

Publishing is a competitive, commercial business.

Training period: None.

Qualifications needed: Secretarial and accounting skills are useful in those areas. In any other area competition is fierce. What counts is experience, a sound knowledge of language (although a degree isn't necessary), business and literary flair (i.e. the ability to spot a hot prospect).

Late entry prospects: Not good

without previous experience or some special skill to offer: freelance and part-time work opportunities for experienced people in indexing, picture research, illustration, cartography, copy editing, proof reading, typography. In general only people who have already established themselves in publishing are given the job of reading manuscripts.

Read: (for background information) that charming classic work (written in 1976) *The Truth About Publishing* by Stanley Unwin (published by George Allen and Unwin); *The Times Literary Supplement* and the *Bookseller*.

Purchasing and Stock Control

Again, housekeeping on a vast scale. There are two different functions in this area. Buying is the grander job and keeping account of stock is another function. Buyers might buy anything in any quantity from toilet rolls to a whole oil refinery.

Buying

Training period: Depends on previous work experience. A purchasing diploma takes three years part-time (evening school) or day release (company sponsored). Basically, get a job first, perhaps as a buying clerk and certainly in a buying office.

Qualifications needed: Five O levels or equivalent work experience in any of above fields.

Late entry prospects: Very good. No upper age limit, older people welcome, but you must be prepared to travel around the country a lot.

Stock Control
Training period: One year part-time (evening school) or day release.

Qualifications needed: None.

Late entry prospects: No problem.

Read: *Procurement Weekly* or *Purchasing and Supply Management.*

Information from: The Institute of Purchasing and Supply, York House, Westminster Bridge Road, London SE1 7UT.

Radio and Television

There are thousands of jobs that aren't Angela Rippon. They need administrators, accountants, market researchers (one of the best jobs, especially part-time and available all over the country), librarians, advertising, sales, secretarial and clerical staff as well as specialist researchers, editors, producers, directors, carpenters, camera men, graphic designers, tea ladies and lighting experts. Secretaries do sometimes get promotion into programme production and even, in local radio, get a chance to broadcast. A good way to learn about radio

is to do voluntary work for your local hospital broadcasting service.

Read: *UK Press Gazette, Campaign, Broadcast* and the *Listener.*

Late entry prospects: Practically no commercial radio or TV training schemes. Very few BBC schemes and difficult to get on unless you're already working for them. *Not* difficult to get your toe in the door on small local radio stations because everyone's doing sixteen jobs at once and it's terrific fun; so consider taking anything to get in and learn.

Information from: The BBC Appointments Department, Broadcasting House, London W1A 1AA; Independent Radio and Television Companies are listed in the *ITV Yearbook,* published by the Independent Broadcasting Authority and available at your library.

Radiography

Taking diagnostic X-ray photographs in hospitals and clinics.

Training period: Two years full-time.

Qualifications needed: Five O-levels including a science.

Late entry prospects: Good for both full- and part-time.

Read: *Radiography.*

Information from: The Society of Radiographers, 14 Upper Wimpole Street, London W1M 8BN.

Reception Work

For doctors, dentists, hotels.

Training period: Secretarial course

with book-keeping. TOPS course
available.

Qualifications needed: None, but a
pleasant voice and appearance, a calm
courteous manner and a liking for
arithmetic all help.

Late entry prospects: Very good
indeed.

Retail Trade

This is such a vast area that obviously
training, qualifications and late entry
prospects differ according to the shop
or store. There's a huge range of opportunity and choice from window
dressing and display (best to learn as
an assistant) to stock control. You can
choose the sort of shop or department that interests you: mother-care,
beauty-care, books, records, gardening, clothes, food or whatever has to
be bought. You need a strong backbone and a pair of feet to match, as
well as selling ability and patience.
You'll meet lots of people, many of
them uninteresting. You can have as
much responsibility as you care to
take, and a selling job can lead to
management or buying. If you're any
good, you're generally spotted quite
quickly as promotion-worthy. Part-
time work is often available, especially
in holiday periods or at weekends
(which is, of course, just when you
don't want it), or doing the midday
shift (12–4 p.m.).

If you want to make a career of it,
then you'd do best to head for one of
the big department or chain stores
such as the John Lewis Partnership or
Marks and Spencer. They have a

positively motherly attitude to their
employees as well as generous staff
discounts and medical schemes. Other
interesting stores are British Home
Stores, the Lewis Group, the Deben-
ham Group, Woolworth, House of
Fraser, Dolcis, Mothercare, Finefare,
Tesco, Aerated Bread Company
(ABC) and W. H. Smith. To find out
about jobs and training schemes apply
to the personnel manager of the shop
that you would like to work in or else
write to their head office (get their
address from the local branch) and
address your inquiry to the personnel
manager. Ask for career pamphlets
and opportunities in your area and
enclose your autobiography (see p.
43). The careers literature will probably be for the wrong people (school
leavers) but it will give you a lot of
useful background information about
the firm's policies and training facilities.

The John Lewis Partnership has a
particularly good outlook. They employ lots of part-timers, give a good
training to improve career prospects
and they don't care much about the
age of the applicant so long as she is in
good health and likes people. W. H.
Smith are equally modern in their
outlook and will cheerfully accept
women returners up to the age of fifty-
five. Jobs are at two levels: non-
development (including part-timers
and full-timers) and development – for
people who are interested in promotion to supervisor. Full-time staff can
take the group's own training course.

Riding Instructor

Good prospects here if you're fit and agile and can ride.

Training period: Depends on ability. You can get the correct training only in an approved BHS (British Horse Society) riding school. TOPS course available.

Qualifications needed: Riding instructors need two O levels and an Adult First Aid Certificate (get this via St John's Ambulance Brigade). Stable managers don't need these.

Read: *Horse and Hound.*

Late entry prospects: Depends on individual and part of country.

Information from: The British Horse Society, National Equestrian Centre, Kenilworth, Warwickshire CV8 2LR.

Secretarial

There are many different kinds of secretary and they're all in demand, especially bilingual and specialist secretaries, such as legal, medical, executive. Being a secretary can mean audio or shorthand typing, it can mean running an office or being a PA (personal assistant is one interpreta-

tion) to the person who actually runs the firm (apart from any specialist knowledge needed, this is one of the best ways to learn how to run a firm). Too many people (men as well as women) avoid secretarial courses because they think they will get trapped behind a typewriter. This is not so. What keeps a woman behind a typewriter, when she knows that she merits a higher paid job in the firm, is simply the inability to give in her notice. After all, she can always get another secretarial job but if she's *that* good, and states in writing to the correct person (and it's often better if this isn't her dependent boss) that her reason for moving on is lack of promotion possibilities, then they won't want to lose her.

Women who can do part-time secretarial work have their pick of flexible jobs at home or outside it, one, two, three, four or five days a week, mornings only or afternoons only. Schools often employ part-time secretaries who work only in term time.

Training period: Depends on course; six months to two years. TOPS courses available for general secretarial, advanced secretarial and all the specialist courses.

Qualifications needed: Good general education.

Late entry prospects: Very good, full- or part-time. Offices often prefer an older, responsible, reliable woman.

Information from: TOPS. There are many expensive private colleges but why bother if you can go on a TOPS course and be paid to go to a local college of further education?

The **Services (WRNS/WRAC/ WRAF)**

The work is in four main areas: technical (i.e. electrical and mechanical), clerical, domestic and miscellaneous (physical trainer, musician or kennel-maid are examples in this category). This obviously isn't going to interest women who have heavy family interests but I mention it for those who haven't, or who are divorced.

Training period: They give you training in all sorts of special trades and jobs which can be very useful when you come out. Once you've done eighteen months' service, you can, at any point, give eighteen months' notice to leave the service. Training is on the job.

Qualifications needed: These differ, depending on whether or not you want to be an officer and if so in what sort of work. There are also direct entry schemes from civilian life for those who are qualified and want to change their job.

Late entry prospects: Can be good up to mid-thirties; afterwards depending on experience.

Information from: Your local recruiting office. Look it up in the telephone book.

WRNS: Ministry of Defence, Old Admiralty Building, Spring Gardens, London SW1 A2BE.

WRAC: Ministry of Defence, Lansdowne House, Berkeley Square, London W1X 6AA.

WRAF: Ministry of Defence, DDWAF, Adastral House, Theobald's Road, London WC1X 8RU.

Social Work

Covers a huge field (see p. 88) including child care, care of old people, educational care, welfare, residential care, and working for the social services departments. Mature women with a working knowledge of life are particularly welcomed. There are several special courses for them, including a course for those with home responsibilities where you don't need O or A levels. Work is available if you have *no* qualifications.

Training period: Eighteen months to four years, depending on what work you take and what you want to specialize in. TOPS schemes available.

Qualifications needed: A good education and some relevant experience.

Read: *New Society* or *Social Work Today* or *Health and Social Services Journal*. Get all the leaflets from the Central Council for Education and Training in Social Work (advice on careers, education and training), Derbyshire House, St Chad's Street, London WC1H 8AD; (Scotland) 9 South St David Street, Edinburgh EH2 2BY; (N. Ireland) 52 Ballyversal Road, Clyfin, Coleraine, Co. Londonderry BT52 2ND.

Information about all kinds of social work from Social Work Advisory Service, Derbyshire House, 26 Bloomsbury Way, London WC1A 2SR. Inquiries about probation and aftercare to Probation and After-care Department, Home Office, Romney House, 446 Marsham Street, London SW1P 3DY.

Speech Therapy

Very useful work, especially with children.

Training period: Three-year course.

Qualifications needed: Three O levels and two A levels (sometimes waived for older applicants).

Late entry prospects: Mature students welcome; plenty of opportunities for full- or part-time.

Information from: College of Speech Therapists, 47 St John's Wood High Street, London NW8 7NJ.

Statistics

The science which is increasingly running our lives in this computer age. Statistical assistants, who are accurate at maths and *not* qualified, collect the figures: the qualified statisticians interpret them. The Civil Service is (unsurprisingly) the biggest employer of statisticians. There's probably more opportunity for the older woman in private industry, especially if she has some business or management experience.

Training period: Few courses are available in statistics *per se:* they're generally part of a degree course in subjects such as maths, economics or sociology. You can take a three- to four-year part-time course at a technical college.

Qualifications needed: Two O levels (one in maths) for assistants. University entrance standard for a degree course.

Late entry prospects: Fair.

Read: The *Economist* and the Royal Statistical Society's *News and Notes.*

Information from: The Institute of Statisticians, St Edmund's House, Lower Baxton, Bury St Edmunds, Suffolk IP33 1LP (the Institute will supply a list of firms which have statistical departments).

Teaching

It's a pity that this work, which is so suitable for the mothers of school children, is now in short supply because we have a surplus of teachers – except for under-fives of course.

Training period: Three years, usually at a College of Education (see p. 87) for non-graduates to get a Certificate of Education. One year for graduates. There are still good opportunities for teachers of maths and science, and graduates in maths and science don't have to take a teacher's training course. If you graduated before 1970 you can teach in primary schools and if you graduated before 1974 you can teach in secondary schools, without having to do this extra teacher's training course.

There are special further courses to teach the blind or the deaf. Teaching mentally handicapped children needs no further qualification, although there are courses of up to one year for those who wish to do so.

Qualifications needed: Five O levels and one to three A levels depending on course.

Late entry prospects: Terrific for anyone wanting to teach maths or science. Otherwise there are fewer opportunities. But they are still going to need *some* teachers, so it is worth trying if this is your real ambition. There are now special schemes for teachers who wish to switch to maths, as well as refresher courses.

Read: *The Times Educational Supplement, The Times Higher Educational Supplement,* The *Teacher.*

Information from: The Department of Education and Science, Elizabeth House, 39 York Road, London SE1 7PH; (Scotland) General Teaching Council, 5 Royal Terrace, Edinburgh EH7 5AF; (N. Ireland) Department of Education for Northern Ireland, Rathgael House, Balloo Road, Bangor, Co. Down BT19 2PR.

Travel and Tourism

Languages are useful but not necessary. Much of the work is dealing with the tourist traffic *to* this country (which is increasing) and it's not nearly so glamorous a job as it sounds.

Training period: Can be from nothing to five years, which sounds a little over-qualified, but it's when you learn all the mysteries of air fare struc-

ture, etc. You can also prepare by part-time study or by a correspondence course for the examination of the British Institute of Travel Agents.

Qualifications needed: Four O levels minimum.

Read: *Travel Trade Gazette.*

Information from: The Institute of Travel Agents, 158 High Street, Staines, Middlesex.

For airline work: Recruitment Service Officer, British Airways, European Division, Douglas House, S. Ruislip, Middlesex, or contact head offices of other airlines.

Youth Work

Unqualified workers with suitable experience are employed full-time by some authorities. This work needs patience, tact and good administrative abilities.

Training period: Two years (or three years part-time).

Qualifications needed: Five O levels.

Late entry prospects: Many, many

opportunities, for really useful work. No O levels or A levels needed necessarily for older candidates to be accepted for training courses.

Read: *New Society*.

Information from: The Information Section, Department of Education and Science, Elizabeth House, 39 York Road, London SE1 7PH; (Scotland) Scottish Education Department, New St Andrew's House, St James' Centre, Edinburgh EH1 3DB; The National Association of Youth Clubs, 30 Devonshire Street, London W1; The National Youth Bureau, 17 Albion Street, Leicester LE1 6GD.

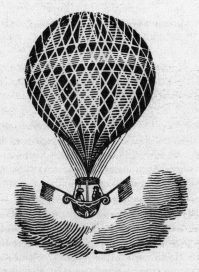

Getting away from it all

If you want to leave your cares behind you (and acquire a whole new set) there are many interesting jobs beyond these shores, which can be learned and practised here before going abroad. Many of the qualifications suggested above will also enable you to take a job abroad, perhaps working for a large international company and not only in English-speaking countries. There are always jobs abroad for bilingual secretaries, nannies, nurses and trained bilingual teachers, as well as teachers of English.

Ships need assistant pursers (secretarial skills necessary), nursing sisters and children's hostesses (nursing experience needed), cabin stewardesses, hairdressers, manicurists and lecturers to entertain or instruct the passengers.

There's also the possibility of being a *courier* on package tours. Everyone I've known to do this has enjoyed it, including one headmistress who was passed over for promotion. She gave in her notice, had a marvellous time travelling to and from Turkey for a year and was then asked back to run a very large school.

You can help others through the British Volunteer Programme, for which you must be professionally or technically qualified and fit because the idea is to help underdeveloped countries to stand on their own feet – so you've got to be capable of standing on yours.

There is also *missionary work* for Christians Abroad. The training period and qualifications depend on the applicant, but you will undoubtedly be expected to do more than read the Gospel. The greatest need is in the developing countries for skilled people with teaching and/or technical qualifications, such as graduate teachers, doctors, nurses or other medical staff : agricultural experts are also needed. Special post-professional training is available at residential missionary colleges. The language of the country is usually learnt in the field (or bush or forest or desert).

Information from your local church (you'll probably need a recommendation from them) or Christians Abroad, 38 King Street, London WC2E 8JT.

Apart from the joy of being abroad, there are great tax advantages when working for international organizations such as United Nations agencies or the Common Market Secretariat in Brussels or the British Council (which is an overseas operation dedicated to spreading our culture abroad). Jobs are secretarial, clerical, administrative, scientific and professional.

Information about the European Economic Community (fierce competition) from the Recruitment Division of the Commission of the European Communities, 200 rue de la Loi, 1049 Brussels; otherwise try the British Council, 65 Davies Street, London W1Y 2AA; Ministry of Overseas Development (for doctors, nurses, teachers and UNO jobs), Eland House, Stag Place, London SW1E 5DH; or the British Volunteer Programme, 26 Bedford Square, London WC1B 3HU. For short-term and holiday jobs abroad write to the Central Bureau for Educational Visits and Exchanges, 43 Dorset Street, London W1H 3FN.

Starting Your Own Business

There are more small businesses in Britain than you might think – they make up one fifth of the private sector. There are 1.25 million companies that employ four people or fewer – and lots of these businesses are owned by women.

Sheila Hamilton, manager of the Small Firms Information Centre (South-East England) told me:

The women who come to us when they're starting their own business are generally interested in setting up a part-time business at home. It's often in hairdressing, baby-sitting, knitting, local specialist cookery, such as making cream puffs for a restaurant in Sevenoaks, or starting their own boutiques. There's also lots of interest in making children's clothes and toys.

There's no reason why you shouldn't be one of these women, and if you are thinking of starting your own business, the most practical way to go about it is simply to *start doing it*.

Like Gaul, any business can be divided into three parts:

1 Thinking of the idea.
2 Checking out the idea and putting it into practice.
3 Running and developing it.

Number 2 is the rock on which most schemes founder. So once you've decided what to do ... DO IT NOW, WHATEVER IT IS.

HOW TO DECIDE WHAT TO DO

Do something you know about and are good at, and stick to it. Try to talk to other people in the same field, to learn to avoid the pitfalls they can tell you about. If you have a special skill – typing, translating, accountancy – advertise it in places where the people who might employ you will see your ad. Stick to an area you know. For instance, if you were trained as a secretary, you might start a home typing agency. The multi-millionairess Marjorie Hurst started Brook Street Secretarial Bureau from her flat in Portsmouth when her husband left her and their two babies. Now her business has spread all over the world.

You might start a business in your kitchen. Advertise in local papers offering to cater for parties or business lunches. You might organize them at so much an hour or sell them at so much a head, doing all the cooking in your home and delivering it in a van, or taking over someone else's office or home kitchen. Lots of women do this happily and profitably, including the Queen's cousin, Lady Elizabeth Anson, who ended up doing Prince Charles's twenty-first birthday; nepotism it may have been but she wouldn't have got the order if she hadn't made herself famous for her original food and organization. Among women who have made a fortune out of cooking can be numbered Janet Keiller (marmalade) and Elizabeth Shaw (mint chocolates). If you have a speciality food product try and sell it via the local health shops or the local privately-owned grocers. Or you can sell your home-grown or home-made produce at the local Women's Institute market. You don't have to belong to the WI; you simply apply to become a shareholder in their market scheme – if you are accepted, this will cost you 5p. Send a large stamped, addressed envelope to Market Adviser, NFWI, 39 Eccleston Street,

London SW1W 9NC, asking for a list of markets.

You might start a home industry in your bedroom. If you have a hairdrier, set hair: if you have a sewing machine or typewriter, start using it for profit. You might try something artistic, in a rarely-used room, such as printing personal bookplates, or making dolls or parsnip wine. I have seen many simple starts such as these lead directly to astounding success: David Hicks in a basement, Mary Quant in a bedsitter, Vidal Sassoon with only two hair-driers.

You might sew cushion covers or do knitting (with or without a machine) or crochet work. The most expensive dresses in Britain seem to be handknitted or crocheted. Look in *Vogue* to see who makes them and apply direct for sub-contracting work.

There are many other people that you don't hear about who enjoy themselves and make money from large stores such as Liberty, Heal's, Harrods and the General Trading Company, as well as local craft shops, by supplying them with dolls and their wardrobes, soft toys, lithographs, painted flowers, pottery, jewellery, bedspreads, quilts, children's clothes and other homemade products.

You don't always need a room to start in. I know a woman whose husband left her unexpectedly and penniless so she took a stall for £2 on a Saturday morning at a near-by market and started selling the family junk. She now has six stalls and an antique shop. What writer Katharine Whitehorn has described as the patent, seventies, non-stick, vanishing husband may provide an (unwelcome) incentive for the family woman to start a business, but the husband who is present and more or less correct can be either a blessing to your business or the kiss of death – depending simply on his attitude. Sheila Hamilton says that the two most important points for a woman who wants to start a successful business are (1) being prepared to stick at the job after the initial enthusiasm wears off and (2) having the support of her partner.

How, I asked her, do women deal with that second important point? She said:

Before you start, make quite sure that your husband approves of the idea. Don't just *think* he does: make sure that he approves and make sure that he comes out and says so. His attitude can mean success or sabotage: you don't want to find yourself with a good business and a bad marriage. The biggest hurdle for a woman starting a business is first to sell the idea to her mate and get him enthusiastic, and the next problem is to *keep* him enthusiastic. The most successful way to do this is to get him involved. Get him to be responsible for something, however small. Don't let this be your direct idea ('Will you keep the books, please, darling?'). Instead ask him if you can count on his help, then ask him what he would like to do. He's undoubtedly got some expertise that can be used: if it isn't the skill he uses in his normal job, then maybe he can offer his strength (to pack) or his skills in some other area (driving, for instance). Don't be nervous of asking him. You'd do the same for him, wouldn't you? And he isn't much of a husband if he just sits back and either won't help at all or is passively destructive.

HOW TO FIND OUT WHAT MIGHT SELL

If you are thinking on more ambitious lines or, having started a small business from the kitchen table, you now wish to expand, test your market before doing so. Make sure there's a demand for your product before getting seriously involved in producing and selling it in quantity.

When you think there's a gap in the market for apricot suede hacking jackets or individual egg cosies, ask yourself *why* there's a gap in the market: there could be a sinister reason.

Has anyone else tried selling them and, if so, why aren't they doing it now? Did they go bust? Or is there a limited supply of apricot-coloured antelopes? Is it almost impossible to get apricot dye? Are people allergic to apricot suede or was it such a big hit last year that everybody's now tired of it?

Don't think there's a market for something merely because you and your friends would like to buy the joss sticks or lacquer boxes imported from wherever you saw them on your last foreign holiday. You and your friends are not typical customers: you and your friends are not a very *large* market, so always *check the market for your product*. You can do this in several ways.

Show a sample to a store buyer. Don't just try shops like Heal's and Liberty. They are for the same sort of customer. Try something more expensive, such as The White House (for the Sheikh market), and then try cheaper shops, including your local ones. You don't want to produce the right product but see it fail in the wrong market.

Telephone the shop owner or store buyer and ask what time the buyers see sales representatives (you). You're unlikely to get an appointment. You trot along and may perhaps have to wait and wait; if so, *don't* feel you're being humiliated: it's the only way the buyers can try to see everybody who wants to sell to them, and still get on with their job. You may have to hang around for up to an hour, perhaps in a draughty dark corridor. And when the buyer sees you he may seem to dismiss your months of work in five minutes and two sentences, one of them being something like, 'I might buy it in red for Christmas, if you left the ears off and it was a pound cheaper.'

Don't be discouraged. This is exactly what you want to hear and what you need to know. That buyer is highly experienced, which is why he's got the job and why he can sum up your work in five minutes, *so far as his market is concerned*. Your reply should be, 'How many do you want and what sort of red and when would you want me to deliver for Christmas?' Because you might be able to bring the price down if you bought the fabric in bulk, wholesale, instead of over John Lewis's counter, and subcontracted the work. (Advertise in local papers for out-workers.)

If he turns you down, ask him if he can suggest some other store who

might prefer your green gnome egg cosies with the ears as they are. He might say, 'Well, it's not our trade, but you could try Heal's.' Never be discouraged by just one buyer or just one turn-down. There's nothing personal in it. You are not being rejected. What you are doing is *testing their opinion*. You are putting your toe in the water and testing the market for a new product, just like Cadbury's or ICI do before they launch a new product.

You can't win without risking a failure. It is simply IMPOSSIBLE for you to walk out of your front door and be an overnight success with everybody. Every time you get turned down (if you find out *why*), it should guide you a bit further along the correct path.

You can do more of your own market research directly with potential consumers, to find out if there's any need for your goods or service. There are three ways of doing this and common sense is vital when looking at the results. Remember that nobody knows what they like until it exists: if you ask people if they like technicolor custard, they won't be able to say yes or no with certainty until after they have tried it (although some undoubtedly will). If they could tell in advance, then everybody would write best-seller books and nobody would ever make a loss on custard or anything else.

Some needs are easier to assess than others. If you are thinking of offering a service (such as starting a nursery school) you might draw up a questionnaire and pop it through letter boxes, along with everybody else's junk mail; make sure it's in a classy envelope, so that yours gets opened.

Alternatively, you can talk to people you know (but remember they may be over-enthusiastic) or interview strangers after knocking on their doors. Buy a clipboard and a notebook and ask their opinion of your product. Stand in the local high street and stop passers-by (but not on Friday or Saturday when they're busy with weekend shopping) and ask their *opinion*. Never ask for their help. Ask them why they think they might like your product or why they think they wouldn't like it; if they would buy it or if they wouldn't. Ask why they don't use one now and whether they'd perhaps give it as a present. Ask them what they think it costs (offer a selection of three prices).

Your questions won't be as subtle as those of a trained researcher, but should help if you're just trying to find if there's a local market for your pâté or quiche or marmalade (please will *somebody* reading this book start marketing a reasonable home-made marmalade? I would be happy to provide a recipe). If possible, set up a little bridge table and offer a little taste of your product, if you're thinking of selling a food. That's all they do at the Ideal Home Exhibition and I've seen several food successes take off there (including a famous farmhouse flavoured yoghurt firm), mainly from one bowl of the stuff and a lot of little throw-away ice-cream spoons.

In this second stage of your business, when bits of apricot suede litter the whole home or the demand for your marmalade is driving the entire family crazy and even the cat smells of oranges, you may wish to expand further. You've now got a bit of money but no time to do your own market research. But you've obviously got to do *something*, and you've got no time to think of anything, because you're so busy churning it all out and doing sixteen things at once.

Professional research can be very important at this point, before you sink real money into a business. You don't have to spend thousands to consult a professional market research company. They can give you the benefit of their experience by organizing a small, simple pilot research scheme for you. It's called a *qualitative research project*. They set up a typical customer target group (with perhaps two or three meetings with two or three groups) and investigate consumer attitudes towards the proposed product. The researchers will not ask anything so crude and obvious as 'Do you like this?' or 'Would you buy this?' but they will be able to give an informed guess as to what the market reaction will be to cider marmalade or apricot suede hacking jackets, and they will give you the probable reasons for it.

This sort of scheme costs from about £500 – which could be a lot of money not lost on apricot suede and might make you a fortune in apricot denim. For further information, write to the Market Research Society, 15 Belgrave Square, London sw1 8pf (tel. 01-235 4709), who will recommend suitable firms.

To note possible retail stores and buyers and to discover what the competition is producing you should also read *all* the relevant trade magazines (*Gifts and Fancy Goods*, etc.) and, when the time comes, go to the trade fairs, where you can *see* the competition and *meet* the buyers. You might even exhibit if the stall space is small and cheap enough. A little money is generally well spent on keeping in touch with your trade.

YOUR LONG-TERM AIMS

Some people simply find themselves in business because there's such a steadily growing demand for their chocolate layer cakes that they start charging for them. More people wade in tentatively from the shallow end and learn as they go. What is important, if you're successful, is that you don't get pushed or rushed into going too fast, or you will end up out of your depth and perhaps in a sea of money troubles.

So decide early on when you're going to stop and have a reassessment. This could be when sales reach a certain point or after a certain period of time. Don't make it too soon: you simply must not expect success to drop into your lap and you must be deeply suspicious of it if it does, in case you turn out to be a nine-day wonder.

Another thing to decide on, while you still have some perspective and

energy, is exactly what you want to do. Do you *want* to be running red velvet, earless gnome egg-cover shops all over Europe? Do you want to build up the business, then flog it to Hamley's (or someone else) as a going concern, with you retained at a fat fee as gnome consultant? Do you want to be the famous gnome designer (fame can't pay the grocery bills) or do you just want an interest that won't interfere too much with your life and that leaves you free to enjoy that little cottage in the country that years of blood, sweat and gnomes have paid for?

With this in mind clearly define your long-term aim and the short-term, not-too-rigid, stepping-stone goals by which you will achieve it. Write them down and pin them up where you can see them. Check on your progress regularly. Write a report sheet to yourself every month, with a column for good-news items and a column for bad-news items. Ponder over the bad-news items, to decide why you went wrong (not exactly, just generally) and how you can avoid it in future. Mistakes are what is called Experience; so comfort yourself with the fact that Experience is always Expensive.

Ponder over your good-news column as well and analyse the reasons for it: there may be a growing gnome market in Saudi Arabia or you may find that everybody's starting to use gnome egg-covers to keep something else warm, in which case you might need to change your market target.

YOUR BUSINESS DECISIONS

As soon as your business becomes bigger than a simple situation where you alone do some work, hand it over and immediately get paid for it, you should calculate your business risk.

Much more important than working out how much money you might make is calculating, in terms of time and money, how much you can afford to lose. This is one of your most important business decisions and it is unrealistic to say 'nothing'. But don't be optimistic at this point.

As far as you're concerned 'loss' is the dirtiest four-letter word, and 'break even' isn't much better. You must, nevertheless, fact the fact that few businesses break even in the first year or even in the first few years. You are unlikely to make a profit immediately. You may have to plough it all back into the business for years. You may work your guts out and lose your money, instead of making it. And in the meantime, you have to keep up appearances because, remember, you have to exude calm confidence. You also have to keep up any family financial commitments that you have, such as feeding them or paying the insurance or HP payments.

At this point (if not before) you should consult an accountant (see p. 153). Your bank manager might recommend one; on no account get the friend of a friend who'll do it for you in the evenings when he's got the time. You can't afford to economize in this unbusinesslike way and you don't want any favours, because there's often no comeback. You need sound professional advice at the going rate and you want to know in advance how much it's going to cost you.

Whether it's a bank manager, accountant or lawyer, listen only to expert advice. And if you have very little money you can afford only the *best* advice, from the best, and probably most expensive, experts. Don't necessarily take it. Don't be intimidated by experts. It is their job to explain to and advise you in their specialist areas but you must make your *own* decisions in your *own* business.

Don't try to use big-business language, it isn't necessary. A business is just a good idea, attention to detail, common sense and arithmetic. If you don't understand what your experts are talking about, make them explain everything they say in ordinary, everyday language until you do understand it. What you are discussing is your business and it should be talked about in your language. And don't forget that you are paying them to advise you. Don't let them brainwash you, perhaps unintentionally, into thinking that as you don't understand something you had better let them decide what to do. This is the biggest business fault that women have: *don't* delegate your responsibility for *your* business. If you're tempted to do dutifully what someone else tells you to do, first check that he's rich and successful, and secondly, discover his motives. Thirdly, check other alternatives.

Female intuition is a reality (now

they tell us), according to researchers at Harvard and Johns Hopkins University. Women are more visually attentive to other people and their skill and sensitivity in non-verbal communication is far greater than men's. Women swiftly interpret the meaning behind facial expressions, tone of voice, body movement and other sorts of wordless communication that men don't believe in because they can't see or hear them. Hence such apparently illogical remarks as 'I don't trust that man, people with eyes like that are never reliable and he reminds me of your Uncle Alfred.'

If you can't decide which of two decisions to take, either do nothing or else stop and reassess. Don't ever make a decision just for the sake of it (especially if you 'don't feel happy about it') unless a decision is unavoidable. Trust your intuition: try to fish it to the front of your mind, especially if it's anything that worries you – however foolish it might seem. Your most valuable asset is your common sense and your experience and intuition is often experience in disguise and in shorthand. If in doubt – don't. The reason why might become apparent later.

YOUR BUSINESS ATTITUDE

To succeed in business you need a fine mixture of optimism (which keeps you going) combined with pessimism, in order to guess shrewdly and realistically, and recognize and check on the risk. If you know what *could* go wrong then it may well never happen.

From now on my advice may seem gloomy, but only because I've seen many a good idea and a good start wrecked by something that could easily have been avoided, given a little experience. Experience is knowing what went wrong before, what might go wrong again and how to avoid it.

You can pick up this business attitude, as well as a lot of second-hand experience, by talking to people in business *about* business, instead of recognized sociable subjects such as petunias and the weather and the ages of their children. Ask them what their job is, and how they started. Ask them what the problems were. Wait, before telling them yours. Never let the phrase 'Can I pick your brains?' pass your lips. Anyone with brains to pick will instantly stiffen and resent your trying to get for nothing what he sells for a living. What you should say is, 'I wonder if you could *advise* me on a small point.' Everyone, but everyone, likes dishing out advice. But don't talk endlessly about your business out of office hours: other people don't.

During office hours

Be straightforward and businesslike: do not be kittenish, vampish, girlish, helpless-little-womanish, etc. Make sure that you are efficient, neat, professional and reliable. No coffee stains on invoices or letters unposted because your husband put them in his pocket and they stayed there for two weeks. Allow no home-life intrusions of any sort.

Keep your private life out of the business. OUT. There are other men in other places. Isn't your business life complicated enough?

Brief yourself properly for meetings and always draw up an agenda which is a list of what you want to discuss and decisions to be made. Do not be late: you are not Marilyn Monroe, so aim to be fifteen minutes early for meetings. You can then gather your thoughts well in advance and decide on the three main points to pursue. It's unrealistic to aim to keep more than three in your head. At the end of a meeting, try to summarize the three most important things that have been decided.

Whatever the state of your business you must look and act calmly confident. You can't expect anyone else to believe in you if you don't seem to have confidence in yourself. So be confident and positive, *especially* if you don't feel it. Keep setbacks to yourself, keep quiet about failures, and cheerfully broadcast your triumphs. Nothing succeeds like success, and success attracts success.

When things go wrong

Keep your head, together with your credibility and other people's confidence, and *keep quiet*. Look what happens to a nation's currency as a result of loss of confidence – the value plummets.

When things go right

Don't be ruined by success! Don't believe that you have a golden touch, that you can never fail. Keep cautious. Treat each venture as if it were your first.

Don't make the mistake of thinking that being your own boss is easy. When you're working for yourself you're working for the toughest possible boss. Any woman who *seems* to be an Overnight Success will confirm that starting a business is sheer hard slog, needing self-discipline, nerves of steel, bulldog stamina and endless hard work. You will have to take the decisions, keep the books, beat up the business, churn out the publicity, cope with the customers and deliver the goods, as well as producing the products. Be prepared to work all the hours you're awake at all the necessary jobs, including those that you couldn't ask anyone else to do (scrubbing filthy warehouse floors, etc.).

If your day is jam-packed and you have to sort out a lengthy specific problem, there is only one way I know of doing it. Decide that it will take x hours, then get up x hours earlier. Be prepared for more discipline, longer hours, far more responsibility and self-control than you've ever been used to.

And be prepared to find that, strangely enough, having your own little business is far more satisfying and rewarding than anything you've done to date.

I asked a friend of mine, who runs two successful boutiques what she got out of it:

The enjoyment of course [she said]. I used to buy for a big London store but it was very demanding and I had to give it up when I got pregnant, then I found that I couldn't get to the smart shops because of the kids and I didn't like the clothes that were selling locally. So I thought, I'll try opening on my own. I suppose that now my children are grown up I could go back to being a head buyer. But I prefer my own happy little scene, with nobody yelling at me and no one able to sack me. It is now my cosy way of life. I like the independence, the freedom (although I didn't get much to begin with) and above all the self-expression. This is what I *do* and it's what I *am*, like someone else is a painter or a writer or Mine Host at a country pub.

YOUR EXPANDING BUSINESS

There's no obligation to think big, or plan on expanding – it's easier to have a small turnover and a high profit margin than the reverse. However, if your business is going to stay successfully small or successfully expand you may have to prepare to think bigger.

From now on you must take regular time off. Being ill or exhausted is bad for business. Of course, there will be patches of overwork, but flap and exhaustion as a way of life are plain foolishness and sometimes an odd sign of self-indulgence and self-importance.

Don't try to carry on your normal life as if you weren't starting a business. Cut non-business, non-family obligations and pleasures to the minimum until you are *smoothly* in business. First, see whether your domestic arrangements could be improved, now that you have a little more money coming in. If you have children, money spent on a home help might be more profitable than, for instance, getting a manager, so get sufficient home help as soon as you can afford it. Whether or not it is tax-deductible, it's part of your cost of running a business.

Be wary of getting a non-productive manager. Be wary of hiring anybody who exists only to liaise or give orders to other people. Instead, as your business begins to expand, in order to simplify your organization and accounting try to sub-contract as much work as you can. Taking on permanent staff is a responsibility. You have to keep them profitably occupied, which is often difficult: being busy doesn't necessarily mean that you're profitable.

Although it might *seem* at first to be a bit more expensive, if you sub-contract for a fixed fee, you know roughly what you're getting, when you're getting it and how much it will cost – and you are taking on no long-term obligations: you are keeping your options open. When ordering, always give your order number *and the agreed expected delivery date*. No use having boxes of red velvet egg-covers turn up two months too late for the Christmas trade and then being stuck with the stuff. Try to avoid paying in advance for anything or anyone, however plausible the reason; think of a more plausible reason not to.

Try not to rely on anyone. This is difficult, but if you rely on someone, then you're vulnerable. They have their own lives to lead and understandably put theirs before yours. Don't *expect* anyone else to be as enthusiastic about your business as you are. If they are, well, that's wonderful, but expect no loyalty, devotion, etc. Only expect what you're paying for and you risk less disappointment. Don't *expect* anyone to understand or be interested in your difficulties.

If you continue to work from home and start employing more than a secretary you had better find out from the town hall whether you're tangling with by-laws. You can't start a scent factory in your garage. You can't employ sixteen pizza-makers in your own kitchen. I know a girl who *did* start selling pizzas out of her kitchen window to the factory workers across the road. Then she hired a cook: but then she had to move her business out of her kitchen because of local laws governing safety and hygiene.

Check that your lease (or freehold) has no restrictions such as on the number of people who can work at your place of business. Leases vary, so check with the lease or the landlord or your local authority, and expect your rates to go up once they know.

YOUR BASIC OFFICE SYSTEM

Keep your organization simple and you're more likely to keep it in order. The organization is merely keeping track of what's happened to everything. The important thing is that you should understand it and your accountant should understand it, when you get one.

Before you send anything out goods, or cheques, or invoices) write it down in a book. When you receive a cheque write it down in a book. The one office rule I stick to is that cheques are dealt with immediately. They are never put down. They are checked off, checked out and put in the envelope to go to the bank at the end of the week.

Send any valuable documents or difficult-to-duplicate documents by recorded delivery (or registered post, if it's abroad). There are three reasons for this. First, the letter may arrive faster. Everyone I know has this touching faith in the Post Office and goes around saying, 'but I don't understand, I sent it first-class mail on Monday; it *must* have arrived by Friday.' Secondly, the letter is more likely to arrive. The Post Office once mislaid over 200 of my letters, which they later found and returned with an apology, and since then I have always, as a matter of course, sent letters to lawyers, banks, agents and accountants by recorded delivery. Thirdly, people can't pretend not to have received your letter if it is sent recorded delivery and clearly marked as such underneath your signature on the letter.

Your office organization might consist simply of: an inexpensive electronic calculator (always do a mental rough check on it); the cheapest, reconditioned, secondhand typewriter you can find; and a secondhand filing cabinet.

YOUR FILING SYSTEM

Ruthlessly cut down on filing. (One way of doing this is to do it yourself, even when you can afford not to). Although both are important, filing no more shows a profit than housekeeping does. The first, top and nearest file in your filing system should be an account of the system. A simple file is kept in date order with the most recent letters on top or towards the front of the file. If the file is subdivided, then this is done in alphabetical order. Never leave clips or pins in filing.

The theory of filing is that of drawing up a family tree. There's the main subject, then subsidiary branches, then perhaps twigs on each branch. Your main subjects might, for instance, be:

Accountant/general correspondence
Accountant/system
Accountant/notes for
Agents
Bills

Correspondence, specific for people and firms with whom you regularly deal (keep in alphabetical order)
Design/job costings
Design/design correspondence
Design/ideas
Export/orders
Export/correspondence
Insurance/policies
Insurance/correspondence
Invoices (yours to other people)
Lawyer
Miscellaneous correspondence (date order)
Money/bank statements
Money/order book C (see p. 141)
Money/account book B and cheque book (see p. 141)
Money/paying-in book D and account book A (see p. 141)
Money/bank correspondence
Office administration
Orders/from you
Orders/to you (never accept an order unless it's written, dated and numbered)
Petty cash vouchers

It doesn't matter how simple and scruffy your system is so long as you bother to invest a couple of hours in setting it up: you don't even need a filing cabinet. I still do my filing in a couple of grocer's cardboard boxes.

MONEY, MONEY, MONEY

Your basic book-keeping

'Women tend to think that they're weaker in finance than men – but they're very often better', says the

Small Firms Information Centre. Whatever your ability, or seeming lack of it, don't try to ignore the book-keeping side of the business: it is particularly important at the beginning, when you haven't any time for it. And it never gets less important.

In particular, don't write accounts down on the back of envelopes. A lot of small firms fall down on this. Many an accountant turns up yearly to inspect the books, only to find that there aren't any – just this towering pile of old envelopes and scribbled bits. Sorting it out can be very expensive. On the other hand, avoid an elaborate accounting system that you don't use because you have to *think* about it. Better a simple system where you fling everything into the right place because you understand it and it's easier than having it on the kitchen table.

Until you need an accountant you can keep track of sales and spending, debts and payments by doing two simple things:

To avoid confusing your business with personal finances, open a separate business bank account.

Buy the minimum number of account books, the fewer the better. They could be two payment books (A and B). It's worth getting two proper (different coloured) account books, with columns.

Book A is for entering money that is paid *to* you.
Book B is for entering money that is paid *by* you.

Also get two biggish *duplicate* books (C and D).

Book C is for your orders *to* other people.
Book D is a paying-in book for the bank. I ignore the bank's paying-in books and keep this duplicate book which suits me better. I write down details only once and tear off the top copy to send (recorded delivery) to the bank.

When a cheque comes in, enter it in Book A, then Book D, then shove it off quickly to the bank before it gets lost, and to cut down on interest charges. When you pay a cheque enter the details in Book B, then on your cheque stub, and only then write the cheque. Always check that your payments reach your account. So get your bank statement sent monthly. When your bank statement comes in, tick off your cheques on the statement (make sure they return them to you) and tick off the payments made into your account after checking them, then folding in half the checked pages in your duplicate book. Anything that hasn't reached your account is instantly visible. I have twice in one year had sums of over £700 go astray, so don't think that you needn't check on your bank. Money is hard enough to make: make sure you keep it.

Shove your bank statements and your empty chequebooks in a file.

Shove receipts each month in a separate big plastic sandwich bag and stick them in a file.

Keep a little book for petty cash. Scribble down £5 in it when you draw out the money. When you next reach for £5, first scribble down what you spent the last fiver on. You can remember £5-worth of petty cash at a time without difficulty. But try to avoid paying for things with petty cash because you often don't have a record of it. Make it as difficult as possible for yourself to get and to dip into the petty cash, otherwise it can be a constant little money leak.

Keep a diary: it's often useful later for checking your expenses or what you did on a certain date.

Getting paid

When you send someone an invoice or bill, it is an exact account of what they owe you money for. If you don't send an invoice, their accounts department won't know that they owe you money. The invoice should be sent at the same time as the goods, unless you have made other arrangements.

A short summary or statement giving the overall sum owed should be sent at the end of the month. Business theory says that bills are paid at the end of the month after the first statement has been sent. By invoicing on the 29th, rather than the 1st of the next month, you should theoretically get paid a month earlier.

Established businesses with great big accounts departments pay as slowly as they can. But you can often get the buyer you're dealing with in a big store to make special arrangements for payments to you within the month. They understand that as a small supplier you can't afford to hang around waiting for your money for four months or longer because it would cripple you, you'd go out of business and then they would no longer be able to get your red velvet wonder egg-covers.

You may have sensibly made arrangements that the goods be paid for *before* delivery (*pro forma*), in which case you just bill in advance and don't hand the goods over until payment is made. Don't sell goods on a sale or return basis – 'on spec'. Your goods are gone, and the shop hasn't invested in them, so it might be less keen on selling them than some other product in which the shop's money is tied up, and responsibility for possible dirt or damage can be tricky. Never allow credit for more than two months, for any reason whatsoever. Whatever the story you're offered, try to turn up *without warning* at the place of business of the person concerned and stand there and ask for your money or your goods. Be prepared to wait all day and make a (loud) nuisance of yourself. Embarrass it out of them as a last resort, and if that doesn't work – nothing will.

YOUR BUDGET

A budget is there to help you keep your eye on where the money is supposed to go and where in fact it went. It should be regularly checked to see if it is accurate (which it won't be) and if you can cut it (especially the tiny things: all those tiny things mount up to a big sum).

Anything you buy that isn't in the budget is *over* budget, so the money that pays for it comes *off your profit.* Anything which costs more than you guessed in your budget (such as your telephone bill) is over budget and comes *off your profit.* You'll probably have to revise your budget regularly to begin with (perhaps every month) but eventually you can have a yearly budget. Remember that there's nothing sacred and unalterable about a budget just because you wrote it down on paper. A budget is a statement of intention at the time you wrote it.

Just as important as your budget are your *costings.* This is your estimate of what each product costs to produce. If you undercalculate this sum (a classic beginner's mistake) the amount that you have left out will come *off your profit.* Include in your costings a percentage for overheads, whether or not you pay them. This covers light, heat, power and rent of the back bedroom or wherever it is that you are assembling your Wondergnomes. Someone has to pay for them, so the eventual consumer should.

Distinguish between variable and fixed costs. *Fixed costs* are those that you know won't alter, such as your rent and rates. You will have to pay them whether you produce 1 or 4000 items in the place. *Variable costs* depend on the things you are making and are such things as materials, outworkers and packing, advertising and telephone bills. Don't forget to include your own salary in your costings, and if you don't take a salary then *imagine* one at £X a week and add your time into the costing.

Don't forget (whether you're paying it or not) that what your working money (capital) costs is the amount of interest that it would earn in a building society or, if you've borrowed it, what the bank is charging to lend it to you. So include bank interest on capital in your costings at base bank rate plus at least 3 per cent, or whatever fiendish sum your bank charges you. (If your bank won't reduce their charge to 3 per cent over base, try getting another bank.)

When costing it is vital to make an allowance for contingencies: these are mistakes and things you never thought of. Perhaps your sewing machine or calculator breaks down and you have to hire or buy another one. Perhaps somebody *else* goes bankrupt, owing you money. THERE ARE ALWAYS CONTINGENCIES AND THEY NEVER MAKE MONEY FOR YOU; YOU ALWAYS HAVE TO SHELL OUT MORE.

Now for that *profit margin:* decide this in advance, and at first check it monthly. Yes, I know you're up to your eyebrows in vital work, but if you don't show a profit you probably won't have a business pretty soon, so discipline yourself to check this.

Your profit margin might be a reasonable 8 per cent, or as much as the market can stand, such as 200 per cent. You might be charging for the genius of your idea as well as producing the gnomes.

YOUR BALANCE SHEET

A balance sheet is the last thing you have to worry about in the early days of a business. When the time comes, if you don't already know, ask someone (such as your accountant) to show you how to read a balance sheet. They can look alarming if you don't understand them – but don't pretend that you do if you don't; you'll make it worse for yourself in the long run. A balance sheet is a sort of bird's eye view of a business, and to produce it is a job for a qualified accountant. It shows your financial position at a given date (often the end of your trading year) and gives a summary of your assets and liabilities, your capital, profit and loss.

Whatever and however sketchy your accounting system don't get behind with it. If you've had no book-keeping or office experience you might

go to evening classes or get help from your Small Firms Information Centre (see pp. 147–8).

THE BASIC BANK MANAGER

The Small Firms Information Centre say that one of the main problems they encounter is that people who are starting a business don't know how to approach a bank manager and 'sell him on the idea', thus persuading him to lend money for the venture. 'And many people make the mistake of *demanding* money as if it was theirs by right.' This unrealistic attitude is, of course, fatal.

As soon as you are seriously in business (if not before) go and see your bank manager. From now on, you don't keep your money in the nearest bank but in the most useful one, and this depends a great deal on the manager. You may have to move from the local branch bank to the nearest City branch, where everybody is borrowing vast sums. Better to be the smallest borrower in the big pool than to spend half your time arguing for a loan with someone who's not really there to subsidize a business (which is one big way that banks make their money) but to stop Mrs Smith from overdrawing £10. It pays to shop around for a bank manager. If you have a timid, tedious, small-town-minded bank manager – move. When you find a business-like one stick with him, even if it means moving to another branch when he's promoted.

To establish a good relationship with your bank manager you must be straightforward and businesslike, without pretending to be anything that you are not. Certainly don't kowtow to him in any way. Explain your plans precisely. This is a very useful exercise, because you have to clarify your ideas in order to explain them to someone else. He's a good person to bounce ideas off, but don't expect him to have creative ideas. If he did, he wouldn't be where he is. Keep these plans as short and accurate as possible. Say 'I plan to do £*X* turnover this year: I have the following firm orders in hand and I expect the following orders which have not yet been confirmed. I need to borrow *Y* in order to buy my materials and pay workers, and my accountant has drawn up this repayment plan that I'd like you to comment on.'

I am a great, great fan of bank managers because they are realists, by definition and experience. Over the years I have always explained to them roughly what I wanted to do, and why and by when and how I intended to do it. I have always found that if they advised me not to do something, that there was generally a good reason for it, which they were happy to explain: a 'no' invariably turned out to be for my own good. I always keep them informed and if I have to change my plans (i.e. can't repay them) I always discuss it with them. ('Well, Mr Bolton, what do we do *now*?')

Have a regular short appointment with your bank manager, perhaps every three months. Don't just go and see him when you want money. Don't dread that telephone call or letter when you're overdrawn. Don't go into overdraft without asking his permission. Don't have an ostrich-in-the-sand attitude and hope he won't notice. They *always* notice and they write it on their little pink cards in your file. You don't want to be tagged as unreliable, in however small a way.

A good rule with banks is to *arrange* to borrow 10 per cent *more* than you think you need. (You needn't borrow it if you don't need it.) It may also be prudent to arrange repayment 10 per cent slower than you think you can. Honest people are generally anxious to repay and therefore overestimate their ability to do so.

Having got your bank manager you can now work out how to get the money you need to finance your business. If you have enough cash for the moment, that's wonderful, but before doing anything to expand your business from the spare room or the kitchen table into the outside world, check your assets and your financial responsibilities, present and probable.

Even if you have enough cash to be called capital (thanks to poor Gran) then you should still discuss future plans with your bank manager. Also realize that you are now in the dangerous position of spending money simply because you have it, just like down at the supermarket. Don't forget that it's the *second* stage of the business that needs money (see later), so start cautiously, with secondhand equipment wherever possible.

If you are immediately successful

and euphoric and immediately need a cash injection, don't do anything drastic such as mortgaging the old home or cashing your insurance policy (better to borrow on it, anyway) to solve a temporary money problem. Money problems are generally thought to be temporary, and there are generally more to come.

If you want to raise a loan, *on no account* go to a bucket shop loan company: do business only with a reputable bank. Tot up your assets (if any) before discussing a loan with the manager and decide what collateral you can offer to secure your loan, and how you're going to pay that inexorable interest. You won't be able to get a loan without any collateral.

You will find that a British woman starting a new business has very little credibility. Everyone is polite but they don't altogether take you seriously and there is good reason for this. Too many women have started a business frivolously, for pin money. They started it on a whim and they dropped it on a whim when they got bored or when the going became difficult or they realized that they would have to forego their holiday in order to look after the boutique.

Be tolerant of this masculine attitude: it is not based on sexism but experience. It's up to you not to whine that it's not fair, but to *show* them that you are to be taken seriously.

YOUR BUSINESS ADVISERS

Everyone who's in business would like someone who doesn't cost a fortune to advise her how to operate more efficiently, economically and profitably. You may be amazed to hear that the Department of Industry has set up a special FREE round-the-clock service to do just that – to help small businesses to get started and grow profitably. To help you help yourself (and cultivate *real* national enterprise) you can also take a terrific FREE course, paid for by the government, for people who are about to start, or have just started, their own business. These private courses are held at residential private business schools, such as the Sundridge Park Management Centre Ltd, at Bromley, Kent. The two-week courses give intensive tuition in modern business techniques and methods, creative thinking, profitably, brainstorming, cash flow exercises, invoicing and stock checking. There is also a self-presentation course to boost your confidence and show you how to put your best foot forward for bank managers and their ilk.

You can get further details about this course from Professional Executive Recruitment, either through your local P E R office (see list on pp. 52–3) or the head office at 4 Grosvenor Place, London s w 1 (tel. 01-235 7030).

To help you provide yourself with a thorough background of the information you need, the Government also offers a FREE mini-library of interesting, clearly written FREE little books that virtually constitute a How to Start Your Own Business Kit. There are twenty of these slim paperbacks, including *Starting in Business, Start-*

ing a Retail Business, Entering the Hotel and Catering Industry, Obtaining a Franchise (you need less capital for this, you have training and open with the benefit of a name behind you), Marketing (a particularly good one), Raising Finance (the big question), Starting a Manufacturing Business, How to Start Exporting and Employing Staff.

A book on really simple accounting for small firms is also due. This set of give-away free books is only one of the amazing offers made by the Small Firms Information Centres. The people who work in them with whom I've talked have all been sensible, quick, cost-conscious, to the point and fun to talk with. They are not a grey bunch of civil servants and, understandably, they tend to stress this.

They give information or factual advice on any of the problems you're likely to meet, whether financial, technical or managerial. Anyone can use the centres, so help for you might be just a telephone call away, as they say. If you have a special problem they will recommend a special adviser for whatever you want to know. This might be how to stop shoplifters or whether you need permission to put up an advertising sign or whether there's anything to stop you from employing workers in your home. Just phone them and ask. Everything is confidential and you can quickly be put in touch with the company or source you need; they have an introductory service to local authorities, chambers of trade or commerce and export experts. They can virtually

launch you socially, like a debutante, in your local commercial social world.

But the best and newest service they offer is a team of fairy godfathers – experienced counsellors who are expert, successful retired businessmen. They can advise on your accounts system, look at any management problems or suggest a marketing or purchasing system. They do not merely solve existing problems but also advise on expansion and future policy. The first visit is free and subsequent ones may be as cheap as £5 a day. This Small Firms Counselling Service is extending all over the country after a wildly successful start in the South West of England.

If you live in a rural area and want to keep bees or start some other cottage industry there's another special government-financed organization called the Council for Small Industries in Rural Areas (35 Camp Road, Wimbledon Common, London SW19 4UW). They not only give you advice, but can also advance a loan ranging from £100 to a maximum of £25,000. Similar facilities are provided in Scotland by the Scottish Development Agency, Small Business Division (102 Telford Road, Edinburgh EH4 2NP), and in the crofting countries and islands by the Highlands and Islands Development Board (Bridge House, Bank Street, Inverness, Scotland).

Addresses of Small Firms Information Centres

Scotland: 57 Bothwell Street, Glasgow G2 6TU (tel. 041-248 6014)

Wales: 16 St David's House, Wood Street, Cardiff CF1 1ER (tel. Cardiff [0222] 396116)

Northern Region: 22 Newgate Shopping Centre, Newcastle upon Tyne NE1 5RH (tel. Newcastle [0632] 25353)

North Western Region: Peter House, Oxford Street, Manchester M1 5AN (tel. 061-832 5282)

Yorkshire and Humberside Region: 1 Park Row, City Square, Leeds LS1 5NR (tel. Leeds [0532] 445151)

East Midlands Region: 48–50 Maid Marian Way, Nottingham NG1 6GF (tel. Nottingham [0602] 49791)

West Midlands Region: 53 Stephenson Street, Birmingham B2 4DH (tel. 021-643 3344)

Eastern Region: 35 Wellington Street, Luton LU1 2SB (tel. Luton [0582] 29215)

London and South Eastern Region: 65 Buckingham Palace Road, London SW1 0QX (tel. 01-828 2384)

South Western Region: Colston Centre, Colston Avenue, Bristol BS1 4UB (tel. Bristol [0272] 294546)

A similar service is provided in N. Ireland by the Department of Commerce.

Head Office: Small Firms Division, Department of Industry, Abell House, John Islip St, London SW1P 4LN. (tel. 01-211 5245).

YOUR CASH FLOW CRISIS

Your capital rarely seems an acute problem at the beginning but, ironically, it gets more painful and chronic as you become more successful. That is when you need to find the money to pay those outworkers and to buy the thousands of yards of red velvet that you need to produce the Wonder-gnomes.

Theoretically, you pay for the production of the item and sell it to someone who pays you a bit more and this is your profit margin. You want prompt payment so you offer a hefty discount for payment within fourteen days. (Ask your accountant what you can afford.) Always try to take and give discounts: always buy everything wholesale, even stationery. Whatever your price is, it had better be competitive (discover what the competition charges) and one that people are prepared to pay.

As soon as possible, get an accountant to help you with your costings and then keep your eye open for ways in which profit might trickle away. I once ran a small textile business and when profit started dropping I traced the leak back to the warehouse and found that the bales of fabric were being carelessly measured and held loosely as they were measured, so what was paid for as a metre was in fact about 1 metre plus 5 cm. As my 10 per cent profit on each metre was 10 cm that extra 5 cm neatly halved my profit.

Your little profit may be swallowed up by bank interest, and meanwhile you need *more* ready cash to finance *more* red velvet and outworkers because export orders are now pouring in from all over the world – Saks, Fifth Avenue, Galeries Lafayette in Paris and Harrods in Buenos Aires. This period in your life is called a cash flow crisis and it is at this point that the amazingly famous new lady tycoon finds herself living on macaroni for months on end.

Because however many orders and ideas you have, you won't be able to put them into practice without sufficient cash.

Try to avoid being too successful too fast. Try to grow steadily and learn to crawl before you leap. Avoid expanding your business too fast, so that your capital is insufficient. Because people want to buy your goods, don't order more of them than you know you can pay for.

Keep checking your budget, your costings and your cash flow. Try to avoid spending on anything that is non-productive, no matter how good the reason. Don't delegate looking-after-the-money. Don't let anyone else get their hands on the tiller or the till.

Having written that, I'm amazed that anyone ever starts a business. But the more amazing thing is that you learn all this quickly once you start. And, apart perhaps from having a baby, there is no greater feeling of satisfaction than running your own business, which is why so many people do it and so many people want to do it.

THE VATMAN COMETH

VAT is value added tax – the tax that makes small people give up their business in despair, gives them ulcers or nervous breakdowns, ensures that no accountant will ever be out of work and guarantees the phenomenal success of the pocket calculator. This is the tax that makes you spend a vast amount of time doing sums on behalf of the government. However, this is the system and you can't avoid registering for VAT if you have a business with a *turnover* (not profit) of £10,000 a year or more.

Briefly, VAT is a tax that is collected on almost anything you buy or sell, do or have done to you. It is collected at each stage of the manufacture and distribution of most goods and services: so when you sell goods or services to your customers, you have to charge them VAT on top of your price (if you are VAT registered). However, you can also claim back VAT that you have paid on goods and services supplied to *you* for your business (telephone, petrol, equipment, machinery, raw materials, etc.).

So every three months you add up the VAT you've charged your customers – this amount is called the output tax. You also add up the amount of VAT that has been charged to you – this is called the input tax. It will have been invoiced to you by your suppliers of telephone, petrol, equipment, etc. You then pay Customs and Excise the amount you have charged (output) after deducting the amount you have been charged (input).

Sometimes, input is bigger than output, in which case you get a repayment from Customs and Excise. This happens when you have paid more VAT for goods and services received than you have charged to your customers for goods or services that you have sold them. The only person who can't claim back VAT is the eventual consumer (Mrs Muggins).

If you are not registered, you must report to your VAT office if your turnover after three months is £3500; after six months, £6000; after nine months £8500; or after a year, £10,000.

It is very important to get your record system working correctly from the very beginning because three months can pass very fast and it can seem that no sooner have you dealt with one lot of VAT than the next one is inexorably settling round your shoulders.

You must keep an *exact* record of (1) all the VAT you have paid on everything that contributes to your business, and (2) all the VAT you have collected from the customers to whom you sold your goods and services.

A simple way of keeping track of payments you have made is by never letting anyone have their bill back. When you write the cheque to pay it,

scribble on the cheque 'To pay your invoice 0027' and chuck the bill into your receipts file. It is not a receipt, but as far as you're concerned, the matter is settled. Don't let the bank get away with not returning your cheques. Insist.

Your invoices and business stationery must state your registered VAT number. The bills you send out and the bills you pay must all have the VAT clearly separated from the basic cost.

In order to do this you have to keep your Purchases book and your Sales book in three damned columns instead of one. They are:

Basic Cost   VAT   Total Cost

VAT rates go up and down, depending on the whims of the Chancellor of the Exchequer. Currently, VAT is charged at a rate of 8 per cent except for certain items that don't attract VAT (see below) and at $12\frac{1}{2}$ per cent for what are considered luxury goods. These include most domestic electric appliances (including washing machines), petrol (as if it wasn't expensive enough), furs, jewellery and boats. I can't help feeling that if the Chancellor of the Exchequer had to wash the family's smalls for a week he would not consider a washing machine a luxury.

Some goods and services pay no VAT. If so, they are either 'zero rated' or VAT exempt. When *zero rated*, manufacturers and traders can reclaim VAT that they have paid out to suppliers.

Zero rated: Zero rated are: most

food (except in a restaurant, which is why take-away meals are such good value), books, magazines and newspapers, children's clothes, public transport and housing construction.

Exempt from VAT: Certain trades don't charge VAT and are *not* entitled to claim VAT relief. They include: education, insurance, health, postal services, land, rent, burial or cremation and betting.

If you want to know more about VAT, you can get two books, numbers 700 and 701 from VAT offices. Together they total 300 pages and are merely a general guide. There are also books that cover specialist areas such as export, import and catering. You get these (and any information you need) from your local VAT office, which is in your telephone directory under Customs and Excise. They say that if anyone is worried about how to keep VAT records an inspector can come round and help, or you can ring them or make an appointment to go and see them.

You're supposed to pay your VAT money when you send in your quarterly return. If not, you will get 'chaser' letters. You can expect three months' leeway if you get in a muddle and can't pay, and after that, the penalties can be very severe. 'If someone is badly in arrears they risk having a distraint put on their goods,' I was told. This might easily mean bailiffs knocking on the door and a pantechnicon outside to take your furniture away.

THE SIMPLE GIRL'S GUIDE TO INFLATION ACCOUNTING

Whoever you are, whatever the size of your business, you need to understand Inflation Accounting (or Current Cost Accounting or CCA), otherwise you may unintentionally find yourself running down your capital and counting on profits that are not really there.

Basically, to work out the CCA profit of a business, the charge against income for stocks and fixed assets is based on the current replacement cost and not on the out-of-date price you paid.

There are *two* simple main points. They're even simpler and more obvious if you have no preconditioned idea of how to draw up accounts.

1 *It's essential that assets sold show a profit of total sale cost, less current replacement cost of the asset.* You have £70 and you start a floor cushion-making company on 1 January. Say that your company immediately buys ten cushions at £5 each and puts pretty and original covers on them which cost £2 each. Each cushion may now cost £7 and you sell them at £14 each by 1 March. The traditional profit (now called 'historical') is £7 each, making a total of £70, which is 100 per cent profit on your investment.

But if the price of cushions has risen by £1 and the price of cushion covers by £1 between 1 January and 1 March your profit is the sale cost less the *replacement cost* of cushion (now £6) and the cushion cover (now £3), which now totals £9. So your CCA profit on each cushion is £14 (sale price) less £9 (replacement price), which is £5. This is more like an overall profit of £50 or 70 per cent.

In CCA, the profit is the difference between the sale price and value to the business of stock sold. In this example it is £50. The other £20 which the company gained from the sale is money needed simply to stand still; it's called a *holding gain*.

Sale price of £140 is therefore accounted for as follows:

Original cost of ten cushions and ten covers	...	...	£70
Holding profit	...	...	£20
Real profit	...	...	£50
Total	...	...	£140

2 Fixed assets such as machinery – say the sewing machine that ran up the cushion covers – wear out eventually, so some charge (called depreciation) must be made against the profit figure to go towards providing the eventual replacement of the machine. To calculate depreciation cost, it's unrealistic to set aside a proportion of what the sewing machine *originally* cost; you must set aside a portion of its *current* cost.

In CCA accounting the profit and loss column looks similar to traditional accounting, but there is a new extra statement called the appropriation account. This shows the CCA-calculated profit and the asset revalua-

tion (what your assets are worth *now*, if you had to replace them). Dividends are also shown, as is the amount that is thought necessary to hold over against future needs (generally a wild guess).

YOUR BUSINESS BRAINS

If you're going into business you do it in one of three ways: as a *sole trader*, as a *partnership*, or as a *limited liability company*. You can trade under your own name without any special permission, but if you want to create a business name by using anything other than your name *alone* you have to apply to the Registrar of Business Names at Companies House, 55 City Road, London EC1Y 1BB (tel. 01-253 9393). It costs £1 to register and they'll send you free leaflets.

A *sole trader* is a private person working by herself who bears the entire ultimate responsibility, no matter how many people she employs. She gets all the profits but if the business collapses she's liable for all the debts and her personal possessions can be sold to pay them.

If you go into *partnership* you have no more protection than a sole trader. If your business goes bust you're actually worse off, because you're liable for the debts of the partnership as a whole and not merely for your part of it. So you may forfeit not only the money you have invested but (if the other partner or partners can't stump up their share) your earnings and personal possessions can be seized to pay the entire partnership debts.

If you want to go into partnership it's vital to have the relevant documents drawn up by a lawyer who is married to neither of you. These should state how much money you're going to invest and when; how much work you're both going to put in and when; what your mutual responsibilities are; who will sign the cheques (both of you, preferably); who will make the decisions and whether or not they are to be jointly agreed upon before any action is taken.

You should also state how you should each be reimbursed and who will get what if you decide to split. If you've ever been involved in a divorce, you'll know how easily misunderstandings can occur between two people who once knew and trusted each other. You'll then see how necessary it is in a partnership to get things straightened out before you start.

To limit the risk of your investment (so *you* can't go bankrupt) you can form a *limited company*: company debts can be paid only by company money and your personal money and belongings are not at risk. A limited company may not give you the best tax advantages, but it does protect you from losing everything and having the house sold over your head. But

you have to take on certain obligations (imposed by the Companies Act) and produce properly audited yearly accounts.

It will cost you about £50 to set up a company and your accountant can do it.

At this stage you will definitely need an accountant and you may need a lawyer. Solicitors must by law be professionally qualified but *anyone may practise as an accountant*. So be very, very careful. Whoever you choose, check that he is a member of one of the professional bodies, such as the Institute of Chartered Accountants. Write to them at Chartered Accountants Hall, Moorgate Place, London EC2R 6EQ. It's a good idea to ask other people who do your sort of work who their accountant is, because specialist knowledge and experience can save so much time as well as money.

It's worth belonging to your local chamber of commerce. I know a girl who was left with £30 and a one-week-old baby. Five years later she had a world-wide soft toy business. She lived in a country town in Leicester and says that the key to her success was joining the local chamber of commerce (ask at your local library where they are). While still making her toys by hand she met other small business people, bank managers, insurance agents, solicitors and accountants and was able to discuss her problems and get personal professional recommendations. Other owner-managers understand what it's like to have no one to share your problems with and how isolated and worried you can sometimes feel.

Such an organization is a good place to ask around for a recommendation for an accountant or lawyer. Draw up a list of possibles, then visit everyone on the list. These two professional advisers are going to be very, very important in your life, so don't rush into it. Make sure your sort of business will suit them: try to get to a partnership rather than an individual: two will have more experience than one and one at least should always be available.

List your probable expenses before you go to the accountant, and be prepared for him to think of a lot more that hadn't crossed your mind. For instance:

Cost of premises, including rent, rates, heating, decorating, light, cleaning.

Cost of equipment: furniture, floor coverings, desks, delivery vehicle, machinery.

Cost of telephone and postage: stationery, photostatting, etc.

Cost of accountant, solicitor, insurance: Don't forget to insure for loss of profits in case of fire, flood or theft, which could hold up your business. Also insure premises, stock, equipment, employer's liability. Ask your insurance agent's advice about insurance.

Staff salaries.

Cost of stock.

Promotional cost: cards, catalogues, photographs, brochures, direct mail, advertising and public relations if you have to entertain (and I see no reason why you should).

Tax: VAT and otherwise. Also National Insurance stamps.

Remember that those seductive 'justifiable expenses' *are still paid for you out of your money*, not by the Inland Revenue. If you pay for something that is a tax-deductible expense, IT DOESN'T COST YOU NOTHING: you're *still* paying with your money: but you don't pay tax on that money.

Do not necessarily do everything your accountant tells you. You hire *him*. He probably sees everything from a minimizing tax viewpoint. You may have other criteria. You may not want to run a Rolls-Royce, simply because you can justify it as a tax deduction.

You don't want too small a firm of accountants, but you don't need Price Waterhouse either, because there's a great danger in a small person going to a big company. You risk being handed to the most junior possible person and your bill is going to reflect their overheads. They don't want you, they don't need you, and you probably can't afford them anyway.

Similarly with solicitors. Make sure your solicitor *is* a solicitor; check with the Law Society, 113 Chancery Lane, London WC2 1PL (tel. 01-242 1222).

In legal matters, be prepared to negotiate. Women are notoriously bad in this area, say lawyers, accountants and insurance advisers. They say that women see a situation as 'right' or 'wrong' and not in terms of being resolvable as quickly, cheaply and painlessly as possible. Remember that 100 per cent of people who litigate think that they are going to win, and 50 per cent of them are wrong. And nothing, neither emeralds nor plumbers, is as expensive as lawyers.

Be particularly careful not to waste time and money on lawyers over a matter that really boils down to your hurt pride or indignation. (Watch when you hear yourself saying, 'I'm doing it for the principle.') Judge Maude, when he retired, was asked what advice he would give to someone about to take a case to court. He just gave a vulture-like smile and said 'Don't.' And as that well-known business philosopher Zsa Zsa Gabor once rightly said to me (when I asked why she'd stopped suing someone who said she'd had a facelift), 'Who the hell has time for a lawsuit?'

BOOK

2

HOME MADE

Setting Up Home

HOW TO BE YOUR OWN DESIGNER

As space gets more valuable and you have less of it, you have to be more ingenious in planning. You may have just one room in which to eat, pay bills, watch television, sew on buttons, sit, drink and entertain. A designer will make amazing lists of all the activities your room is used for (i.e. recreational area ... drinking space ...) and then divide it up accordingly, but you can't divide what isn't enough in the first place.

Whether you're thinking of cheering up a bedsitter or planning a complete conversion, home design needs careful planning and involves four major practical decisions. What you would *like*: what *must* be done: how much you can do yourself: how much you can afford to have done.

Start by making a list of what you hope to do and a secret list of what you think are other people's mistakes. Plan to spend only 60 per cent of your money, leaving 20 per cent for 'contingencies', which translated mean mistakes or things you forgot to include. The other 20 per cent should be retained for things that turn out to be far, far more expensive than you ever expected. In ten years spent with a design firm, I never saw one job finished under budget. If your original decorating budget covers your final finished work, I'll happily buy *your* book.

If you are a muddler, plan the minimum furniture, never save souvenirs, and keep no newspapers or magazines. Be lavish with your budget when it comes to storage space; in order to keep sane and tidy you need lots of drawers, shelves or bags to shove things into.

To plan get some graph paper and decide on a scale, whatever suits you best. 1–20 (metric) or ½ inch = 1 foot is relatively easy to handle. Make plans relatively easy to handle. Make plans of your rooms, each to scale: then measure your furniture and draw that to scale. Write the name on each piece of it, e.g. 'grandmother's rocker', and cut out the pieces. You can now juggle the furniture around the plans of the rooms. You need far more space than you think (for instance, allow 75 cm (2 feet 6 inches) depth of chair space round a dining table, because you have to pull the chairs out in order to sit on them). Even when a plan looks perfect you will find that the room, once filled with furniture, looks far smaller than you imagined and *different* from the way you imagined it. The more you take out of a room the bigger it looks. There is no exception to this rule.

Work out a colour plan. The less ambitious you are with colour, pattern and texture, the more likely you are to be successful. Stick to one basic colour scheme, i.e. beiges, browns and creams, or black, greys and white – then everything will flow into everything else. To get the colours right when choosing fabrics and carpets see them under natural as well as artificial light.

When you go shopping take a list of the items you need and *buy only those*, no matter how many fantastic bargains you see on your rounds.

Your financial order of preference should be warmth, light, comfort, decoration.

Your decorative planning sequence should be heating, lighting, flooring, built-in furniture, paintwork, curtaining, furniture, accessories.

If you live in a furnished flat try to avoid spending money on fixtures that you can't take with you.

If your home is big you need more furniture to fill it or it may feel self-consciously empty. If your home is small, keep it uncluttered. Have plain, light-coloured walls with matching curtains, wall-to-wall carpets, where you can afford them, and mirrors.

Living-room can mean three separate rooms, or a kitchen/dining-room, plus sitting-room, or an open-plan kitchen/dining-/sitting-room. This last arrangement can be rather beat-up or very grand, but it's the least exhausting plan for a woman with no home help.

Many couples start with two small rooms and prefer to knock down the dividing wall and turn them into one big room. But unless you have a ridiculously narrow house, never knock the hall passageway wall down as well or you will suffer from draughts, dirt and a lack of privacy, while the sofa will always be strewn with raincoats if not satchels.

The Golden Rule for all small living-rooms is, the more space in the middle of the room the better. Channel the traffic of comings and goings and site a telephone where it won't disturb the general conversation. Put the TV where you don't have to shift the furniture round when you want to watch it, or else have it on a trolley wagon. Have small furniture that looks light and is easy to move, but don't buy a small two-seater sofa because invariably only one person sits on it: it may be better and cheaper to have easy chairs and no sofa. Circular dining tables save space.

Try to buy everything to stack: stacking stools, stacking chairs, stacking side tables, stacking bookshelves and stacking china.

If a table is also used as an office desk, buy an office cabinet on castors which can tuck away under the table when needed as a desk-drawer unit, or be used as a bedside table or telephone table. Also buy versatile furniture such as flap-up, fold-down or otherwise expanding tables, a kitchen stool which converts to a small step-ladder, and children's beds of different heights on castors which slide under each other during the day. Buy dual-purpose furniture such as convertible sofas or beds with drawers beneath or beds with more beds beneath. Use built-in furniture where suitable.

Avoid sliding doors on cupboards in kitchen and bedroom unless you're desperately short of space and money. They tend to be the cheapest to make but the doors often jam and it's always difficult to get to the middle of the cupboard.

Shallow drawers are easy to keep neat. Keep deep drawers tidy by sub-dividing them with knife boxes, shoe boxes, cheap trays, deep plastic cat-litter trays or seed boxes. These are good for make-up, bottles, jewellery, sewing kit and all kitchen storage because you can pull them out to get at the back items. They are also good for keeping underwear, children's clothes and small toys.

Use the backs of wardrobe doors to hang compartmented shoe bags for belts, scarves, gloves, handbags, ties, tights and shoe-cleaning equipment. It may even be possible to construct a 5-cm (2-inch) deep wooden frame for the back of the wardrobe door and fix hardboard trays across it to hold small items. Stick a hanger through your laundry bag and hang it on the back of the bathroom door.

If you're chronically untidy (or if he is) you need not only a place for everything, but also an extra, empty space in which to fling what's left when you are caught on the hop. Keep an empty drawer or cupboard or buy a big laundry basket for a quick temporary tidy-up.

Housing the family sound equipment is a simple, practical problem liable to be complicated by unpredictable human elements such as the chooser of the sound system – who tends to be male, fussy, blind to decorative considerations and immune to reason. Of course, the sound system should be part of the rest of the room, and not a walnut-veneered blot on a Philip Johnson landscape, but you'll never convince the serious stereo enthusiast of this unless you can also provide the essential environment his equipment needs. It should be:

1 on a level, solid base, not attached to the floor, because slamming doors, stamping feet and mass bopping tend to create bad vibes for hi-fi;
2 in a draught- and dust-free atmosphere;

3 easy to get at;
4 provided with proper storage for records, cassettes, cartridges, tape or any other audio-visual extravagances.

Always stack records upright. I know a pop concert impresario who stacks them between full Coca Cola cans.

HOW DO YOU MEASURE UP?

How deep is the ocean? How high is the sky? It doesn't really matter to you; what matters is whether you can hang your coat in the wardrobe or get the right number of knees under the dining table.

What follows is a summary of standard measurements. Remember that nobody is standard, so make allowances if you are an exquisite miniature and your husband is a giant, or vice versa.

Furniture

Dining and desk chairs: Allow 60 cm (2 feet) width per person and 75 cm (2 feet 6 inches) depth to allow for pulling chairs back from table before standing. A dining chair should be 45 cm (18 inches) from floor to seat for eating at a table 75 cm (2 feet 6 inches) high.

Dining table and office desk height: 71 cm (28 inches) is average table height. Narrowest width for dining table to seat people on both sides without unavoidable knee-brushing, 60 cm (2 feet). You may want an extending, folding table, but see that the legs and cross-bracing allow room for human beings. A round table saves space, saves knee-knocks and is the best shape for general conversation. However, if the room is long and narrow it may be better to choose a rectangular table.

Bookshelves: Allow minimum 30 cm (1 foot) height per shelf (bigger for art books or LPs) and 30 cm (1 foot) depth.

Bookshelves should be supported by brackets or uprights every 60 cm (2 feet) or they will sag under the weight of books. Shelves can be supported on a frame system or on metal adjustable brackets slotted into narrow, upright, metal strips which are fixed to the wall.

Wardrobes: Never build or buy a clothes cupboard less than 60 cm (2 feet) deep. Average masculine shoulders are 45 cm (18 inches) wide and hangers need breathing space to avoid bunching up.

A Swedish designer calculated that the average man needs 105 cm (3 feet 6 inches) minimum width for clothes hanging space, but I prefer to put my trust in the American designer who calculated that the average well-dressed man needs 190 cm (6 feet 4 inches) of well-designed closet, but that the average well-dressed woman needs almost twice that amount of space – 360 cm (12 feet) – to keep well organized. That includes drawer space and out-of-season clothes space. He didn't define what he meant by 'well-dressed'. As far as I'm concerned that's Widow Onassis' level but it's useful to quote to a man when you're sharing out the personal storage space.

Bathroom: You need about 950 × 950 mm (3 × 3 feet) for a shower, approximately 1700 × 700 mm (5 feet × 2 feet 4 inches) for a bath, 700 × 800 mm (2 feet 4 inches × 2 feet 8 inches) for a basin, 700 × 800 mm (2 feet 4 inches × 2 feet 8 inches) for lavatory or bidet.

Bed, sheet and blanket sizes for armchair and other shoppers

Bed width:

75 cm (2 feet 6 inches) is too narrow for real comfort.

90 cm (3 feet) is minimum comfort for one.

135 cm (4 feet 6 inches) is standard for two people; 120 cm (4 feet) width is too narrow.

150 cm (5 feet) or Queen size is more comfortable.

180 cm (6 feet) or King size allows for the occasional non-communicating night.

Bed length:

200 cm (6 feet 6 inches) for anyone under 180 cm (6 feet).

215 cm (7 feet) would perhaps have to be specially made for anyone taller.

Bed width:	Sheet size
75 cm	175 × 275 cm
(2 feet 6 inches)	(70 × 108 inches)
90 cm	200 × 275 cm
(3 feet)	(90 × 108 inches)
105 cm	200 × 275 cm
(3 feet 6 inches)	(90 × 108 inches)
120 cm	200 × 275 cm
(4 feet)	(90 × 108 inches)
135 cm	250 × 275 cm
(4 feet 6 inches)	(100 × 108 inches)
150 cm	250 × 275 cm
(5 feet)	(100 × 108 inches)
180 cm	275 × 275 cm
(6 feet)	(108 × 108 inches)

Blankets should be the same width as sheets, but can be shorter.

Continental quilts: Don't buy too small! (Everyone does, the first time.) Minimum quilt width for one adult is 135 cm (approximately 54 inches) and for two adults 180 cm (approximately 72 inches). Buy small double-size for a child in a 90-cm (3-foot) width bed: the overhang is too small on the recommended size. Buy the largest possible size for a double bed to avoid overhang disputes or cold bottoms.

NOT MUCH MONEY, EVEN LESS SPACE

The minimum living equipment is less and cheaper than you imagine. You can do without almost anything new, except for divan beds and window blinds. Carpet, chairs, tables, storage items, all can be acquired cheaply secondhand.

There's no problem if you are living alone in one room – provided you have no belongings. This means, in fact, that there's *always* a storage problem. Solve it with a storage wall of shelves and stacking bins. John Lewis have terrific, inexpensive, folding, stacking, white-painted bookcases in their whitewood departments. Dexion maxi-bins – sometimes found in hardware shops – come in various sizes and bright colours and can hold anything. So can rows of plastic shopping bags or shiny black plastic dustbin liners (don't overweight them).

You could economize and use industrial shelving, or make instant shelves (for books, tennis balls or cornflakes) with planks of wood supported on bricks piled up in double rows, i.e. two to each column. Expect to support your planks every 90 cm (3 feet). This also works (with broader planks) for fast mass seating.

Window blinds are probably cheapest, but curtains need not be permanent or lined. Use white sheeting (later to be used for sheets) or coloured towelling (later to be used as towels).

Scrub, scrape, strip, paint or polish the floorboards; cover the centre with cheap Indian cream rugs (small ones: big ones are very hard to clean, something you don't realize until you've tried to heave a large, wet Indian rug out of the bath). Use lino paint to cover nasty-coloured linoleum.

You can get furniture cheaply if you know where to look, in junk shops, builders' yards, street markets and furniture marts, but you have to be prepared to wait. You'll never find what you want if you're in a hurry. Don't advertise for furniture or answer advertisements for furniture. You can waste a lot of time and money. Instead, haunt the auction rooms.

For new furniture that doesn't cost a fortune, QA (quick assembly), KD (knock down) and Demountable are all furniture kits which you assemble yourself. Sofas, desks, wardrobes, chairs, tables, dressers and even beds are available. Most pieces are designed to be put together with nothing more than a hammer, screwdriver or wrench; some come with a specially designed 'key' to tighten bolts or recessed screws. If buying on the spot, always ask a salesperson to demonstrate the assembly method because some of them would tax Einstein's brain.

Beware of over-elaborate KD or QA furniture. I once bought two screw-it-to-the-wall bookshelf-with-built-in-desk units for my sons. I actually assembled one and screwed it to the wall, an invitation for a boy to *prove* that it wasn't *properly* screwed-to-the-wall. After it had been torn out of the wall three times, I gave the other kit to the postman and *he* hasn't done anything about it yet except sigh heavily when I ask.

Wicker furniture is a good buy, and it's light to move around, has a pleasant summery look to it and is unlikely to disintegrate unless used outside. But it's unstable, it often squeaks, snags your tights and can be ripped apart by cats. Men don't like it because they can't throw themselves into it comfortably.

Perspex furniture is durable, light-weight and easy to clean, and comes in attractive colours that are added when the plastic is in liquid form, so it cannot fade or peel. There are two disadvantages, however. When you dust it, a static charge builds up and this makes dust cling, so pale Perspex furniture can tend to look grubby. The other drawback is that it scratches very easily – and stays scratched; you can't rub it down with half a Brillo pad. It doesn't mellow with age, like wood. You can sometimes file it down and oil it, but that can leave a nasty blob instead of a scratch.

Whitewood furniture is generally the best buy; sturdiest furniture that's the least trouble. You can always paint it. It needs a coat of primer to seal the porous wood; don't try to skimp this or the result will be blotchy and rough. On the other hand, it needs only one coat of clear varnish, or use Ronseal's pine-wood shade poly-urethane varnish, to make it look like smart pine furniture: I've seen a whole whitewood kitchen successfully treated in this way.

There are only two things to say about junk. First, never buy it if there's a suspicion of *living* wood-worm. You can tell by the minute pinhead holes (scattered like grape-shot) and the tiny piles of wood dust underneath (each pile about the size of $\frac{1}{2}$p). Lots of lovely furniture has been successfully treated for woodworm, but if in doubt – don't buy it.

My second point is that most junk-shop owners are well behind current trends. You have only to look at the cut of their jeans to know that they don't spend their evenings with their noses in *Vogue*. It's therefore not difficult to buy just a little ahead of the trend and pick up really pretty things cheaply, as well as enjoying the thrill of the chase and the restoration. (To get the idea see collections on p. 192.)

With aged upholstery learn not to be put off by the guts spilling out of sofas, large burnt areas or a profusion of stains. Instead, look at the basic shape and remember that *anything* can be cleaned, re-covered or repaired; but always check for moth and wood-worm and split frames. Buy up-holsterer's rubber webbing (from branches of John Lewis) to replace any springs which have gone ping. After removing the springs tack the webbing across the frame: north to south, then east to west, or vice versa. If you're buying new upholstery, measure the space before you visit the shop or open the catalogue in order to make sure that there's room to get a four-seater sofa through the door and up the stairs and round the corner.

This is one problem that you don't have if you buy unit furniture. I personally find unit seating uncomfortable because the units tend to push apart and leave you sinking floor-wards. But there's a lot to be said for it. The whole idea of unit seating is that you buy a piece at a time as you can afford it, and once you have enough you can always reassemble it in different ways, different rooms or different houses. Always buy units with removable covers, or the new ones will make the old ones look shabby. Always choose a big, established manufacturer who doesn't look as if he's going to go bankrupt next week (in which case you'll never get the end of your sofa) and always choose solid, heavy furniture that doesn't skid about.

Be imaginative: if you want a huge coffee table you could cut the legs off a cheap kitchen table and possibly cover it to floor level with a felt throwover cloth. I discovered this trick after letting my flat to a nice American journalist who sawed down the legs on my kitchen table, *then* told me and said that he hoped I didn't mind. I was speechless, but when I saw that instead of a cheap-looking white kitchen table I had a sumptuous coffee table, I forgave him.

A good example of luxury one-room living on a next-to-nothing budget is an attic which belongs to a panther-like creature who works for the Jamaican Government. Her priorities were a telephone, two good locks on the door plus bolt, chain and peephole, all of which she fixed in place herself. The fitted, dark-brown carpet was another top priority, because she loves walking barefoot, because everyone she knows sits on the floor against big cushions (which she made from foam offcuts) and because the floor was in such bad condition that it had to be covered with something.

'I spent all my money on the carpet,

the cushions, paint and a tool kit,' she told me. 'If you have a good tool kit you can do most small carpentry jobs yourself, and anyway you darn well have to these days, you just can't find any odd-job men, they've died out like pterodactyls. I covered almost the whole of one wall with an instant mural – a huge tree-against-the-blue-sky poster which was an advertisement for a bank; I wrote to them and asked for one, then cut their name off the bottom.'

Some modern designers say who needs furniture anyway, even if you have the money to buy it? Why not a foam pad or old mattress (covered along with the floor by a deep-pile carpet) on which you doss down at night in a sleeping bag? A foam pad platform with a shaggy carpet over it and bright cushions can make a casual recliner or bed or provide seats for a crowd, for the girl who collects the whole football team.

You might have a series of slab cushions which you, or any teenagers you try to look after, can use for sitting or sleeping on or building up to suit the purpose of the moment. The occasional visitor can be seated on these fabric-covered, semi-rigid foam pads, which can be used as individual low lollers, piled up for seating at a low table, or laid out, side by side, for overnight guests. Storage boxes can be used as side tables or else can have foam-padded tops when used as occasional seats. It's a thought, especially for the young and supple-kneed.

MAKING AN ENTRANCE

First impressions always count, so yours had better be good. The smaller your hall, the easier and cheaper it is to get it looking great. The problem is that it's generally too small and uncomfortable or boring to take seriously. And think of all the necessary junk that it might have to house, for instance:

Checklist: Mat / dog leashes / rubbers / boots / scarves / skates / gloves / briefcases / hats / telephone / chair / writing pad with pencil / umbrellas / newspapers / mail / magazines / coats / messages. To this I would add a wastepaper basket; where else can you shove all that unsolicited junk dropped into your mailbox?

If your hall needs a facelift, first decide whether you want it to be functional or an amazing surprise, or both. If it is cramped or dark or faces north, paint it a brilliant, rich burnt orange or tomato juice or some colour with warmth and impact. Avoid pale, cold colours, such as pale blue or lavender, which tend to look dull, anaemic and chilly.

The hall is one place where you can have a bold wallpaper without getting sick to death of it, because you are generally passing through instead of sitting in it. However, being blessed with filthy children, I prefer to paint my hall rather than paper it. A small hall takes such a lot of hard wear and it's easier to repaint than to repaper (and the children might do it themselves).

All hall junk is divisible into that which hangs, that which stands and that which simply sits. Use hooks for the first and a tall bookshelf for the rest. All you then need is a mirror.

A hall may be a good place for a stop-in-your-tracks bulletin board to show off a collection. I know a girl who used to hang her collection of antique keys in the hall and another who used a long, 90-cm (3-foot) wide passage as an art gallery for her etchings.

No floor will get dirtier than that in your hall, so avoid plain, pale shades. If you're using carpet go for something dirt-coloured (such as earth brown); remember that no doormat is ever too big, and Lord Roberts's Workshops for the Blind will make special sizes for you. But never leave it to the mat to say welcome.

KITCHEN SENSE

The farther and more separate the kitchen is from the sitting-room, the farther the cook is from (a) conversation, (b) help and (c) television. Do you want your kitchen just for preparing food or as a sociable place where the whole family will tend to assemble? Or even as a place to enter-

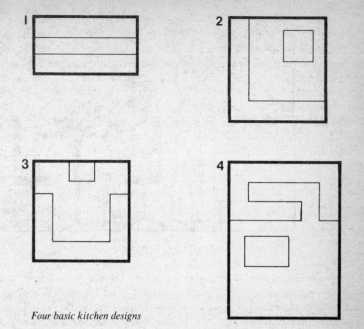

Four basic kitchen designs

tain – as more and more people are doing these days. Whichever it is, it's a factory capable of producing up to 1000 meals a year, so, if you're starting from scratch, plan it with factory efficiency before adding the indoor plant in copper saucepan.

You can often improve your kitchen efficiency without spending a penny, simply by checking on your basic plan as follows, to avoid unnecessary walking or doubling back on your tracks.

1 The *layout* order for a kitchen is food storage/refrigerator/preparation counter / sink / preparation counter / stove / oven / serving area.
2 The best *storage grouping* is as follows:

food: near preparation counter or table;
coffee and tea: near kettle;
seasonings and saucepans: near stove;
work table: within reach of sink and stove;
china and glass: near eating area (and sink if possible).

Four basic, owner-driver kitchen designs are:

1 Galley, lined on two sides with working units. The minimum useful size for cooking family meals is 4×2.60 m (13 feet × 8 feet 6 inches) wide. A one-sided galley kitchen shouldn't be narrower than 1.60 m (5 feet 3 inches).

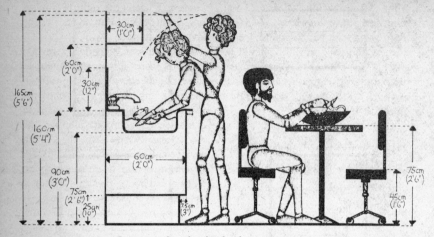

Correct working heights for the average woman

2 L-shaped working area, with units on two touching sides of the room and table in the remaining corner, which can be used for eating.
3 U-shaped plan on three touching walls (this provides more storage and working space). Doors and any table for eating should be on the remaining wall.
4 Room divided for cooking and eating by a waist-high peninsular unit. A peninsular kitchen is a good idea for a mother with young children, especially if divided by a half door to keep the children out of the work area.

Many accidents and illnesses are caused by awkward working heights and badly placed storage areas: your kitchen is probably the most accident-prone area of your home.
Correct working heights for the average woman, who is 1.60 m (5 feet

3 inches) tall are given below. Either subtract or add to them according to whether you're smaller or taller, and you'll have a tailor-made kitchen.

To obtain the *one vital measurement* stand up straight against the wall in the shoes you usually wear in the kitchen. Get someone to mark the distance from the floor to the flat of your hand when, with arms straight at your sides, you hold your hand parallel to the floor. This measurement is the height that the *bottom* of your sink should be if you want to avoid stooping over it.

To calculate the height the counter top should be add 15 cm (6 inches) – approximate depth of sink – to the palm-of-hand measurement. You will then be able to stand at the worktop without the slight stoop which is the worst posture, resulting in tension, backache or a slipped disc.

If you are the average woman and

your extended palm is 75 cm (2 feet 6 inches) above floor level, your sink *bottom* should be 75 cm (2 feet 6 inches) and your worktop should be 90 cm (3 feet). Builders generally make both too low – I can only assume that such men are midgets, or that they don't do much cooking.

Other general measurements are:

(a) 175 cm (5 feet 10 inches): height for top shelf in unobstructed wall unit;
(b) 165 cm (5 feet 6 inches): height for top shelf set back over worktop;
(c) 90 cm (3 feet): height for standing at a worktop;
(d) 75 cm (2 feet 6 inches): table or sit-down counter top height for eating or working when sitting on standard chairs;
(e) 45 cm (1 foot 6 inches): height for chairs and benches;
(f) 25 cm (10 inches): height for lowest storage shelf;
(g) 7.5 × 7.5 cm (3 × 3 inches): toe recess necessary. Add 7.5 cm (3 inches) to counter top if there isn't a toe recess;
(h) 60 cm (2 feet): depth for general storage;
(i) 30 cm (1 foot): depth for china storage;
(j) 30 cm (1 foot): minimum height for splashback behind counter and sink.

I sometimes work with the international architect and kitchen designer, John Prizeman. We argue a great deal because the main thing I have learned from him over the years is that *there is no such thing as a perfect kitchen*. What is the right layout for one kind of situation is the wrong layout for another.

Prizeman says, 'There is a certain tendency, especially in magazines, to treat a kitchen as a gallery for attractive junk. But however pretty it may be to imagine that one is really in a nineteenth-century farmhouse, the basic necessity is to make the kitchen as efficient as possible for cooking. Afterwards, add decorations to an efficient kitchen, rather than efficiency to a culinary museum.'

If you really have got a country kitchen, plan for a kitchen that is a sociable meeting and eating place. When choosing a floor, remember that dogs and children have muddy feet. Make sure that the working part of the kitchen is planned so that it cannot become a general circulation area. Protection from the outside climate and dirt is vital; if possible arrange to enter the kitchen through an outside lobby or 'mud room' for stripping off coats and boots.

Standard or specially made units? There are two ways to fit out a new kitchen: either choose the standard range of equipment that is nearest to your needs, or go to a specialist who can custom-tailor a kitchen exactly to your requirements. The cost may well be about the same and the harassment should be about equal (non-delivery of standard units versus non-appearance of carpenter). The best standard units have one clear advantage: the overall design is likely to be better than the average carpenter or cabinetmaker can produce unaided.

As all kitchen units and equipment are made in different heights and depths, a group from different manufacturers can look a real mess. You can almost always easily adjust the depth of the units to stand in one neat line by getting a carpenter (or doing it yourself) and building a narrow 10–15-cm (4–6-inch) counter shelf to be fitted at worktop height behind your units. Where you have a very deep bit of equipment, you simply saw a bit out of your shelf to accommodate it neatly.

You can use a similar principle to line up units of different heights, standing them on plinths, painted to match floor, wall or cabinets (this is a job for an experienced carpenter).

It's sensible to seek an experienced, independent designer's help, and he should at least save his fee in ensuring that the plan is economical and that you choose the best equipment. BIG BONUS: You can order the equipment through him at maximum discounts, which may well cancel out his fee.

Alternatively, many kitchen-unit firms have their own design service, which is often amazingly cheap and provided with no obligation to buy the firm's units.

The kitchen *floor* should be tough, washable, non-slippery and non-noisy (you're going to make enough clatter with the pans) and not too hard on the feet. Good materials are linoleum or vinyl (see 'Resilient floors', p. 188). A carpeted kitchen is, in my view, impractical, insanitary and insane.

Kitchen *walls* might be tongue-and-groove boarding, possibly stained a

brilliant colour. Walls can also be covered with paint, steam- and condensation-proof vinyl, or plastic-coated wallpaper.

There's no material that's suitable for all *worktops*. Formica is standard, with wood chopping blocks or a chopping area. All sink and worktop splashbacks should be at least 30 cm (1 foot) high and must be proof against water, grease and detergent. Any of the materials suitable for floors or worktops can be used. Use ceramic tile, treated wood, linoleum or Formica plastic panels.

Ventilation is doubly important if you plan a sociable kitchen. Ideally every kitchen should have a good-sized exhaust fan; a cooker can put out as much as 100 kg (200 lb) of grease-laden moisture a year. In old houses a ducted hood can sometimes be led into the chimney. It is much cheaper to buy and install a *ductless* hood, which does not expel the air but recirculates it. The grease and odour filters trap a lot of kitchen smog but, of course, do not cool the atmosphere.

Electrical work: A fully-equipped kitchen needs a lot more electrical outlets than you would think, but never as many as designers tell you. Six socket outlets is a comfortable minimum, ten is luxury. One cooker outlet is needed, or two if split-level units are used at some distance from each other. Waste-disposal units need a separate outlet and should be earthed for safety.

Lighting: Working areas, sink and stove need to be especially well lit. Use spotlights or fluorescent lighting over working areas; I prefer spotlights as they are more flattering – I am at my least glamorous in the kitchen and need all the help I can get. Lighting circuits may also have to allow for ceiling, worktop and cupboard lights. If you can't afford to buy all the electrical equipment needed in one shopping swoop, spare capacity should optimistically be left.

Sinks: A double sink with two drainers is, to my mind, almost the equivalent of a dishwasher, and uses far less energy. Most sinks are stainless steel (noisy but wears well and doesn't rust), vitreous enamelled (can scratch and start rusting) or earthenware (can chip and is now hard to get, but to my mind is nicest). You can get a Perspex sink specially made in wonderful colours: it won't chip but scratches easily. Ideally there should be draining surface on both sides of the sink, grooved to drain into the sink: otherwise have one on the left if you are righthanded, or vice versa.

Dishwasher: The best place for a dishwasher is probably under the sink. Don't get too small a dishwasher. Buy a reputable make (*not* British) and one that isn't too complicated to operate.

Chair: If you want to relax in a big kitchen while someone takes your photograph, there's nothing to beat a rocking chair, but for ironing and sewing, cooking and chopping, writing shopping lists or just flopping into, the best kitchen chair is the adjustable, secretarial typing chair. It's on wheels, the seat goes up or down to fit you, the back automatically adjusts to yours: get one with an easily cleaned fabric or plastic seat. Then sit *well back* in it. (I didn't write that last sentence: the typing agency added it.)

Designing an efficient and low-cost kitchen is only a matter of deciding what can be dispensed with if you aren't going to get it anyway. Everyone's priorities are different, but in my opinion the minimum essential kitchen consists of a cold tap, a double sink, a cooker, a refrigerator and two tall bookshelves (one for china and pots, one for food in packs or tins) or one outsized odd bit of furniture – what the French call an *armoire* and the British call a wardrobe. The fashion designer Jean Muir bought, for next to nothing, a huge, ugly, carved-everywhere Indian *armoire* and painted it white: it has the look of an elegant frosted cake and holds *everything* she needs for the kitchen.

A classic micro-kitchen kit is simply a wallful of wooden shelves which gives suitable storage for everything, keeps clean through constant use and cuts out the expense of doors and drawers, etc. The shelf at waist height should be deeper than the others (to act as a counter) and be given a waterproof varnish (from hardware stores). A small, round, stainless-steel sink can be let into it and a garbage pail can stand near by or underneath the waist-height shelf. I find this system works very neatly in a small, basic, country kitchen.

How to design your own kitchen

1 *Decide how much you're going to*

spend, remembering that labour-saving equipment is the working woman's first investment. *Check measurements of the room*, including diagonals and ceiling heights. Mark position of existing drainage, gas, water and electricity fixtures. *Decide equipment* and subtract cost from original budget sum.

2 *Draw sketch designs* at a scale of 1 to 20 (metric) or $\frac{1}{2}$ inch = 1 foot. Use tracing paper over graph paper, it's easiest.

3 *Consider* where things are to go. For instance, do you want your sink in front of the window so that you can look out, or against a wall so that you can have storage space over it? If possible, allow for the following worktop space: 90 cm (3 feet) for preparation and dirty dishes; 75 cm (2 feet 6 inches) for clean dishes before storing; 60 cm (2 feet) for serving from oven and burners; 45 cm (1 foot 6 inches) for counter top near refrigerator.

4 *Check* that each work area has adequate related storage space.

5 *Check* that you have allowed at least 120 cm (4 feet) for a person to pass between standing equipment.

6 Then, if possible, mark with chalk where each piece of furniture will be placed on the actual floor of the new kitchen and play-act cooking, serving and clearing up a meal to see whether it works.

7 *Check* easy access to related rooms such as dining-room, laundry, children's areas.

8 *Check* the place for food delivery (where you dump the shopping bags when you stagger in with them).

9 *Check* that any pets have somewhere to be fed where you won't put your foot in the cat's milk or fall over the dog.

10 Choose materials and colours. Remember that anything on display and not in constant use will get greasy.

11 Remember that you'll probably never get it perfect: a kitchen just isn't a factory assembly line, thank Heaven.

SUPERBATH

A bathroom is the last bastion of privacy in today's intrusive world. Provided you have no children, it's possible for your bathroom, however small, to be a little sybaritic paradise with scented water and soft music (only your transistor), soothing and regenerating in every way.

If you share it with three children it's more likely to be a sleazy mess of squashed ducks, submarines and a sagging towel rail. Forget all dreams of elegance, and hope only to keep it ship-shape. Have somewhere near the bath to store those damned ducks, even if it's only a cheerful plastic play

bucket. Have one big toothpaste for everybody, otherwise the floor will be covered in tube tops. Fix lots of plastic-covered cup hooks to hold tooth mugs or towels. If there's room for shelves put them up wherever you can.

If you are designing or redesigning a bathroom and have plenty of room and plenty of money you have no problem. You trot along to Godfrey Bonsack (the pop star's ablutions consultant and supplier of gold taps to sheikhs), and have your fantasy bath: circular, sunken, double or twin. Most people's problems are more likely to be lack of space and money combined – with conspicuous presence of damp, draughts and unflattering plastic bath-caps.

Always make a list of your requirements, whether you're buying £5 worth of face-lift or a complete new bathroom. Even a small amount of money goes farther in brightening up a bathroom than in any other room in the house. Buy pictures (prints or reproduction line drawings), try to co-ordinate your towels (dye them all dark purple or chocolate or maroon) and choose one or two indoor plants that thrive in the damp.

If you are creating an entirely new bathroom, either a first or a second, plan it as near as possible to the water supply and drains in order to save money on plumbing. For the same reason two bathrooms are best placed side by side or on top of each other, or next to the kitchen, or on top of it. But there are many other possible places: in part of a hall or landing, in the empty well over a staircase, over a porch or garage. I've made a bathroom (with shower, not bath) from a 60 × 180-cm (2 × 6-foot) niche on the stairs and my present bathroom was converted from a coal cellar (pale blue, it is, with tiled floor and silvery spotlight, like an Italian trattoria). I've also had a bedroom in which the bath and basin were behind louvred doors, flush with the louvred wardrobe (WC was separate). This is a really good, space-saving, private bath idea if your bedroom is big enough. Or you might add a bathroom with one of the very good, do-it-yourself home extensions, but this is more expensive. Wherever you put it, you will be clobbered for extra rates.

Building regulations lay down that a lavatory, or bathroom that contains a lavatory, must *not* open directly into a kitchen, workroom or living-room; you need a lobby or a passage in between. The exception to this rule is when a bathroom opens off a bedroom or dressing-room, provided that the lavatory isn't the only one in the home. If you haven't an opening window or skylight you must have a mechanical extractor fan wired to the light switch to avoid condensation and smells.

Overflows from baths and cisterns can now be plumbed back into their own waste pipes, thus avoiding soaking brickwork. The only other thing you need know about plumbing is that you should always be able to get at your water tanks, stopcocks and pipes.

A bathroom should ideally contain

a bath, WC, possibly a bidet, hand-basin, possibly a dirty linen receptacle, chair, storage cupboard for towels, plenty of cupboard space for make-up and other supplies, plenty of counter space to stand things on and possibly display shelves for one or two decorative objects. Having decided what you want, decide where you want to put it in the bathroom, so draw up a scale plan.

The *floor* should be waterproof; do make sure that your flooring is stuck down with the correct adhesive. Use padfelt lining under a foam- or rubber-backed nylon carpet for the bathroom; any other sort of carpet rots very fast, probably within two years.

Walls may be tiled or painted with emulsion or silk vinyl, which is more durable. If you have wallpaper, back the bath and basin with sheet Perspex. If you have a very small bathroom, you can get an extremely pretty effect by covering walls, ceiling and any fitted cupboards with flowered wall-paper (the smaller the flowers, the prettier it will look). But only buy a waterproof paper (try Sanderson's American papers or Cole's French and Portuguese ones) and don't mess about trying to varnish one yourself.

Pine panelling is also very effective and cosy in a small area. With the current price of wood and carpenters it might be cheaper to use gold leaf, but if you have walls in bad surface condition it's a quick way to hide them and simultaneously cut down the condensation.

You need efficient *light* for morning make-up and shaving and I like another soft light for a relaxed evening bath (see ' Spreading the light ', p. 180). Make sure that you can *heat* the room up quickly. Have a single-bar electric radiant heater fitted over the door (it must have permanent wiring and a pull-cord switch).

Install *baths* 30 cm (1 foot) out from the wall if there's room so that you have a convenient surrounding counter at bather's level. A bath should also have generous elbow-room and side-fitting taps (two children can then bath at one time), and mixer taps if you can afford them. Fix safety handgrips for the very old or very pregnant, screwed into the wall at an angle at two different heights to help people to hoist themselves in and out. Have a non-slip tread mat to stick to the bath bottom. Glass fibre baths are cheaper, not cold to touch, often have non-slip bottoms, are impossible to chip, and have more exciting colours than traditional ones. They also scratch easily. A dark-coloured bath can look downright sleazy, and it never looks clean.

Basins should have a flat top with recessed draining areas for soap, and there should be at least one mirror over the basin. Since children swing on a basin and workmen stand on it, get a pedestal basin, not wall-fixed, so that it can stand up for itself and can't be pulled out of a wall. The plumbing should be hidden in the pedestal. There are now some very, very tiny basins for you in your small corner (try Ideal Standard or Adamsez) and there are also showers which fold flat against the walls.

You can get small fitted *shower* cabinets made especially for tiny rooms; I have one 50 cm (20 inches) wide.

Hot and cold water should reach the shower at the same pressure, so make sure that the plumber doesn't tap the cold in straight from the mains (a favourite trick) because you'll have a lot of trouble getting water at the right temperature and flow. Have a thermo-statically controlled mixer valve, which cuts down danger of accidental scalding. Always have a shower cur-tain (get fixtures from John Lewis shops) or you risk soaking the carpet, which soaks the floorboards, which can rot then without your noticing. Keep the curtain tucked into the bath or shower tray or the water will run down the curtain to the floor. Get the biggest shower tray available in metal, plastic (warm to naked feet) or ceramic.

WCs should be as near silent as possible. Low-level siphonic suites are quieter than the traditional type.

If you're fitting a *bidet* (which is intended for washing the bottom but can be used for anything, such as giving the hydrangeas a good soak), you don't need the sort with a foun-tain in the middle; plumbers tend to look furtive when discussing 'biddies'. Make sure that your plumber knows how to fit one. I have seen a bidet fitted with the fountain connected to the cold tap only, which could give you a nasty surprise. I have also seen a bidet fitted flush to the wall, as if for one-legged ladies.

If you have the space it's a good idea to keep the washing machine out of the busy, messy kitchen and have it in the bathroom instead. But keep the medicine cabinet *out* of the bathroom, so that no tiny tot can lock itself in with the aspirin.

HOW TO ENJOY BEING IN BED

The ideal adult bedroom should be designed like a living-room, but with a bed and bedside storage. It should be warm, restful, seductive and cheerful to wake up in and sunny in the morning. (Try Chinese Yellow walls or window blinds if you face north.) It should have adequate storage, a socket outlight by the bed; and, if possible, a desk and chair.

Above all, a bedroom is a place for quiet, privacy and fantasy. You may see yourself in a froth of frills and lace, luxurious furs or old-fashioned black leather with witty punk hand-cuffs. Your getaway image may be that of a demure Victorian maiden, a luscious Colette overblown rose, the sultan's favourite or Modesty Blaise. Whatever your fantasy, your bedroom is where you can happily indulge it. There are just one or two practical considerations to bear in mind.

To allow for any easy change of fantasy, try to keep the background neutral. Don't use a small, patterned wallpaper over ceiling and walls unless it's a small room and you're going for a cosy look. Don't use a large pat-terned wallpaper at all. Use a mid-tone background colour for a carpet.

To switch your moods as inexpensively as possible use different bedspreads, cushions, loose covers on chairs and change the pictures when you feel like it.

Incidentally, if you have a guest bedroom you should sleep in it yourself for two or three nights to check that its standard of comfort is similar to that of your own. You may be amazed to find how much it lacks.

Bedheads: The point of a bedhead is for decoration and comfort and it's no use having the first without the second. I once bought an exquisitely carved Jacobean fireplace covered with peacocks for a friend's bedhead. She was delighted until she found that she couldn't sit up in bed without the carved wood digging into her spine. Your fantasies may be more practical but the logic of a bedhead is to have something to lean against when you sit up in bed: a sort of fixed cushion. This might be one of those pale pink padded creations (incidentally grease marks from hair accumulate on these in no time and ruin the Mae West sexy image) or a 10-cm (4-inch) thick slab of synthetic rubber cushion which measures the width of the bed and has an unzippable cover for cleaning. It can be hooked to matching fabric loops suspended from a brass/chrome or wooden strip fixed at a suitable height above the bed.

Electric blankets: In old, cold houses without central heating there's nothing to beat the luxury of an electric underblanket, except perhaps an electric overblanket. Double-bed models have individual temperature controls so, should you wish, you can swelter while he merely smoulders. Electric blankets are safe; the nervous can reassure themselves with the thought that no reputable firm wants to be sued by a lot of sizzled corpses, and anyway a low-voltage blanket wouldn't have the strength to kill you. BUT make sure that the electric blanket that you buy complies with *British Standard regulations*, and get it serviced yearly by the firm that manufactured it. (Try to avoid the Electricity Board. I have found them to be unreliable and liable to charge a fortune.) The only drawback to an electric blanket is that it involves yet another electric flex to trip you up as you stagger into your bed.

Mirrors: These can add sparkle, glitter, depth and interest to a bedroom. Moreover, every woman needs a full-length mirror in her bedroom in which to take a severely appraising look at herself when dressed, and an even more severe look at herself when undressed.

Mirrors are now made in metric sizes only. The imperial sizes, which they have replaced, are shown in brackets:

760 × 440 mm (30 × 18 inches)
1200 × 600 mm (48 × 24 inches)
1200 × 360 mm (48 × 15 inches)
1520 × 440 mm (60 × 18 inches)

Lighting: As well as general lighting, there should be adjustable lighting at the dressing table and on each side of a double bed, where suitable shades should shelter the insomniac's light from the eyes of a sleeping companion.

Although lined and interlined curtains are generally an unnecessary extravagance, bedroom curtains should be heavy enough, or lined, to cut out all light so that a light sleeper doesn't inevitably wake up at dawn.

Storage: Bedside tables should be bedside chests. What's romantic about the nosedrops, box of tissues, notepad or whatever is your necessary bedside comfort?

It's not always necessary to keep your clothes in your bedroom, particularly if it's small. This does not imply a dressing-room, but room for a wardrobe in the hall or a cheap dress rack wheeled into a nearby walk-in cupboard.

If you have room for them, there are plenty of modular, built-in storage units available in all price brackets from whitewood to teak, for assembling yourself. Louvred doors are a good idea because the ventilation allows perspiration smells to disperse. Ideally, the built-in doors should open to reveal shelves, drawers, hanging space, dressing table and washbasin, but this tends only to happen in colour advertisements.

Unless your bedroom is very small, avoid sliding doors to built-in wardrobe units as you risk catching your fingers and the item you want is always in the unattainable middle section.

Ideally, a dressing table should be in the bathroom (by the washbasin) and the mirror should be surrounded by bulbs like that in an actress's dressing-room – and for the same reason. If your dressing table is in your bedroom and you can't afford a built-in unit, try fixing a flat wooden panel over two whitewood chests with space beneath in which to tuck a stool or chair. This can then also act as a desk.

However you plan to house make-up, it always ends up looking a mess. If you're having a swish built-in dressing unit (in bedroom or bathroom), flap-up counter tops are useful for storing deep bottles that fall about when you open drawers. Allow 35 cm (14 inches) depth, which will house the deepest hairspray.

Have a line of containers, whether they're silver christening mugs or jam jars, to hold cotton wool, make-up brushes and tubes of make-up, combs, manicure sticks and buffer. Use plastic knife boxes to sub-divide drawers.

I apply my make-up in front of the kitchen sink (I've fitted a mirror over it) and keep the jars in an eye-level cupboard: this is because during the early-morning rush *nobody* ever wants to jostle me out of the way of the kitchen sink.

CHILDPROOFING THE HOME

Planning the children's quarters in a family home is the most important problem if Dad is to remain a civilized, even-tempered adult and Mum is to enjoy being a mother without becoming a slave.

Respect your children's need for

privacy and you may teach them to respect yours. If it is possible to have one, a child's room is not a luxury, it is a necessity so that a mother can retain her individuality and sanity. In many houses where the dining-room is seldom used it might be better employed as a children's sitting-room.

If your space is very small it's best to remember that if you can't beat 'em, join 'em. Make up your mind to live in a cheerful litter and, until the last one is twelve, don't expect to be civilized before bedtime when lots of storage space is the answer to tidying up. Luckily, children like shabby, worn rooms with bright colours and chipped paint in which they can run amok, within reason. This is by far the easiest sort of room to let them have, so don't waste money on children's furniture: buy junk furniture, paint it the mad colours of their choice and don't worry about the damage.

It is unfair to children to have fragile, valuable articles in rooms which they use. If you must have delicate things about, keep them 122 cm (4 feet) above the floor, but as children tend to throw things they will probably get broken anyway. Whether it's curtain fabric or a doll, don't buy anything for a child's room

that you would mind seeing wrecked.

Walls: Plain painted walls show every mark of every starfish hand. Assume the walls are there to be drawn on. I don't believe in carefully painting one portion of the children's room with blackboard paint. It will be the one area guaranteed never to inspire a *natural* child (as opposed to a designer's child) to pick up a crayon in creative malice. A pinboard is essential for sticking their paintings and photographs on and their heroes. Make it as large as possible and paint it the colour of the walls.

Floors: You need a swabbable floor covering which cuts out carpet but not short-pile rugs (for older children only, as young ones sometimes slip). Avoid wooden boards with splinters unless they are well sealed. Cork is comfortable, feels warm to little bare feet, but is expensive. I like linoleum in a not-too-light, not-too-dark shade (ideal background surface for crayon drawings) and I never bother to polish it, as it has to be mopped so often, and little children might slip on it.

Furniture: There's plenty of nursery furniture on the market. I naturally believe in prams that can convert into beds or carry-cots, old-fashioned high chairs that convert into low chair and table, and playpens, but, apart from these items for under-twos, I believe in buying sturdy, kickable, grown-up furniture for children. They grow out of their clothes at a depressingly expensive rate: curb your maternal instincts and don't buy kiddy-size furniture that they will also grow out of. Buy sturdy child-proof furniture.

Pick zipped, upholstered furniture that is easily cleaned, on a strong metal frame.

Bunk beds certainly save space and children love crawling and fighting over them. I scrapped ours because I couldn't bear standing on tiptoe to make the top bed and crawling round on hands and knees to make the bottom one, but continental quilts make things easier. Incidentally, it's very difficult to make a room look smart with bunk beds, unless it is designed on the lines of a ship's cabin (which isn't a bad idea for a tiny room to be shared by two boys in a small modern house). I prefer two proper single beds, in two different heights which slide under each other during the day, leaving the maximum play space (made by John Allen, Parkway, London NW1).

Storage: I have tried drawers, cupboards, toy boxes, wardrobes and specially designed kiddies' storage units and I find that the easiest way to keep children's junk tidy, whether it be Teddy-bears, books or pocket calculators, is on adjustable open shelves built across one wall of the room. If you have the space to run adjustable shelves for toys and books right along one wall, make one shelf 60 cm (2 feet) deep, which will provide a practical desk or play bench for puzzles and constructional work and perhaps cut out the necessity for a space-consuming table. Tiny toys on which you break your neck or collections of such dangers as marbles can be kept in plastic washing-up bowls or cat trays. I keep them in two nine-drawer, cheap

wooden office filing units which measure 45 cm (18 inches) high × 45 cm (18 inches) deep × 90 cm (3 feet) wide and also act as seats and low table tops, as well as Apollo 8 or the North Pole.

When the toys get too much for the shelves to hold, I make children sort out for themselves what they want to throw or give away (after all, you expect them to respect *your* possessions).

I don't believe you can ever expect a young child to tidy up its own mess unless you supervise, which means that clearing up takes twice as much of your time as if you had done it yourself in the first place. But they'll never learn unless you do. And as I've said before, the one rule they learn to respect is 'if you leave anything on the floor you must expect it to be trodden on by grown-ups'.

Safety: Never leave a young child alone in the bath and always test the water temperature with your elbow before popping him in it. Never let a baby have a pillow in case he accidentally smothers himself. Never leave a hot water-bottle in a small child's bed in case it leaks or he opens it and scalds himself. Don't give small, swallowable toys to small children. Never let young children get within reach of matches, razor blades, hot drinks or soap. Don't use a tablecloth which they can pull over on themselves. Never leave the kitchen if anything is cooking in a pan of deep fat and *always turn saucepan handles so that they don't protrude beyond the stove.* Keep the first-aid kit in the kitchen, not the bathroom, where a child might lock himself in with it. You're supposed to keep it locked, but who can ever find a key in an emergency? I prefer to keep it in a high cupboard. Don't keep poisonous cleaners under the sink, where a child could sip the Teepol or the turps – put them, too, in a high cupboard and keep your china under the sink.

If you have any glass doors that a child could run into, criss-cross coloured tape across them (it looks horrible, but then so does the gash in a child's forehead). Make sure that doorways, stairwells, passages and landings are properly lit with light switches at the top and bottom of the stairs. If you have a crawler, fix a safety gate at the top and bottom of the stairs and at entrances to the kitchen. Lock up the garden shed. And if you don't put *anything* on a mantelpiece (or a mirror above it) then a child won't be tempted to reach or climb near a fire to get it.

SPREADING THE LIGHT

Except for designers, photographers and lighting experts, no one believes that lighting can make a bad interior look good and a good interior look bad. But it's true.

The best lighting system is the one that you don't notice as a lighting system. You don't notice cords coming down from the ceiling, you don't trip over spaghetti junctions on the floor and you don't notice ugly shadows as in early Ealing films.

Some light fittings can be really beautiful. Tiffany shades, Art Nouveau flower petal designs or bluebells on stalks and almost anything in Christopher Wray's Chelsea emporium. If you're more of a purist you may prefer an Italian plastic mushroom or a twenty-two-bulb snake fitting, luminous rocks or one of those dinosaur's head instant-concussion numbers, as seen (too late) in smart furniture shops.

Lighting is either general and diffused (overall), or specific, to illuminate a certain area. Specific light is needed for precision work, writing, sewing, eating, and needs concentrated lighting from one source, which can be an adjustable spotlight or one of the many Anglepoise models. When you left home for a bedsitter, your first investment for life should have been an adjustable table lamp, and every student should have one.

Basically your light source can be suspended from the ceiling, attached to the walls or stood up by itself on floor or table.

A *ceiling light* might be a spotlight fixed in the central rose, a ceiling pendant or a classic globular paper Japanese Noguchi lantern; or one of those thirties-style inverted umbrellas of pearlized glass. But the average ceiling light is neither unobtrusive nor good-looking and there's a lot to be said for converting a central fitting into a ceiling track (which is a relatively simple wiring job), for more, and more versatile, lighting. This system can be very useful in a kitchen, if the areas where you need light (preparation – cooker – sink) are near each other. If they are not, then use wall-mounted spotlights.

Spotlights suspended from overhead, or from a wall-fixed track are a good method of illuminating a row of pictures or display shelving. In an office, they are a neat way of providing specific light from the same power source for more than one person. In a nursery they are out of the reach of everyone except you.

Indeed, a series of spotlights can be a cheap and easy way to solve most lighting problems for a whole home. Don't expect them to provide an even, overall level of light because their purpose is the reverse; never place a spotlight so that it shines directly into someone's face, because the light is too glaring. Bounce it off the ceiling or the wall or an especially beautiful object such as your brass Buddha, a vase of daffodils or a dramatic scarlet wall.

Spotlights multiply the effect of a room's highlights and conceal its deficiencies. This is why the dress you saw last night from the bus looked better in the shop window than it does on you. A few pools of light in a room can make a tranquil atmosphere in which to soak, as though you were in a bath, at the end of the day, while your mind unravels. In fact, I always have spotlights in the bathroom. Most spotlights are of the Edison screw variety, not the push-in-and-wiggle sort that have bayonet fixings. Some miniature bulbs have different diameter fittings. For simple shopping, always use one size of bulb with one sort of fixture.

Shop around for cheap fixtures (then go back to John Lewis who are never knowingly undersold). For instance, you can get almost everything electrical (flexes, bulbs, switches, as well as major appliances) at a trade discount from British Distributing Company, 594 Green Lanes, London N8 (tel. 01-800 1245). However, it's not a place to browse. You have to know exactly what you want.

The most flattering and relaxing light for a dining table is candlelight: not really very expensive or much bother. Otherwise, I like diffused wall lighting and I detest pendant lights over a dining table. In order to avoid headaches and glare they have to be pulled to below eye-level; this big, black shape looms between you and the person across the table and every time you pass the salt you risk hitting it.

Wall-fixed or ceiling-fixed diffused lighting can be provided by a simple circular translucent plastic shade, as plain as possible. There are special outdoor models to welcome mosquitoes to the patio or illuminate the Jehovah's Witness at your front door. You can also get outdoor spotlights, as well as indoor ones, to floodlight the syringa.

Concealed lighting is flattering and looks expensive, although it needn't be. Try fitting a bulb in a shop fitter's cheap light cradle (like a fencer's mask). Stand it on aluminium cooking foil for extra safety and put it on the back of a high cupboard, armoire or other high furniture, or behind a stereo speaker, where the light can't be seen. You get a 10-

megawatt luxury impression. Lighting that comes from below-knee level also looks positively exotic and amazing. Glamour is further achieved by using a dimmer switch, which enables you to increase or dim the light according to your mood, as in cinemas. It's not much more complicated or expensive than an on-off switch.

If you intend to make up and/or shave in the bathroom, fix a strip light on either side of the mirror, rather than above it (depressingly, it will underline every line on your face). Always make up in daylight for daylight; it's really being cruel to be kind to yourself.

The bulb you use in your fitting controls the brightness and quality of the light you get; clear glass gives a brighter light, pearl glass gives a softer effect and silvered reflector bulbs are both bright and soft. The higher the wattage the brighter the bulb and the more electricity it consumes.

A night light (called a nursery bulb) is dimmest of all at 5 watts. Miniature bulbs for old-fashioned lights are 25 watts. Unless they are the major light source in a room, table lamps take 40- or 60-watt bulbs. Working lights and principal sources of light should take 100- to 150-watt bulbs, depending on your requirements, and some central lights take an even higher wattage. The most popular bulbs are 60 or 100 watts. If using fluorescent tubes, look for tubes marked 'colour 27 de luxe warm white'. Don't fall for anything merely labelled 'natural' or 'daylight' or 'warm white', because you will look greenish or bluish.

If you are wiring a house for the first time, or rewiring, check:

1 That you have enough socket outlets in the right place. (You always need more than you think; perfection is a pair per wall.)

2 That the switches are where you need them – by the door, by the bed and at the top and bottom of stairs and long passages. Two-way switches are essential for the last two.

3 That wall and ceiling fixings are in the ideal position, too high for children, low enough to change the bulb easily (with step-ladder, if necessary) and to avoid glare. Remember to allow for tall men, if you've got any.

How to buy a classic table lamp or standard lamp and shade

1 Try to buy both together, from the department manager or an assistant who knows what he's talking about. The John Lewis group have excellent lighting departments.

2 Buy the carrier at the same time as the shade.

3 Take the base with you when you go shopping, no matter how difficult it is to carry back in the bus.

4 Don't buy too small a base, which will look tiddly. Don't buy too small a shade for the base. Don't buy too big a shade for the base. It's very difficult to judge these proportions and the wrong choice can *easily* look faintly ridiculous, which is why you may need an expert second opinion.

5 Buy a shade that you can easily clean yourself.

QUICK CONSUMER'S GUIDE TO FLOOR COVERINGS

Flooring is a big investment. If you're one of those people who move house every few years, putting in costly flooring or wall-to-wall carpeting is apt to be a rotten investment. You can't take either with you, and the next owner of your home may not share your taste so he won't want to pay for it. Another warning: a scramble of pets in your house can make a few hundred pounds' worth of wall-to-wall carpeting look, to put it politely, like a dog's breakfast in only a few months. (I've known a kitten wreck a fitted carpet before I'd even had the bill for it.) If you want to keep a decent fitted floor covering, as well as pets, use any other kind of surface. Coco matting is not a bad idea, so long as it's fitted like carpet, but it looks sleazy if it curls at the edges.

Don't have white or very pale floors of any sort – paint, carpet, rugs, linoleum, tiles – unless you're prepared for cleaning headaches.

Wood

There are two sorts of wood floor; hardwood, such as parquet or tiles, and softwood, such as pine. If you have an old house with wooden floors, you're lucky. Minor disadvantages are that wood scratches when heavy furniture is moved or children with metal tips on their shoes run across the floor, but it does resist ordinary wear and can be quickly cleaned with a damp mop.

If you have an old, heavily varnished, dingy, wooden floor, you can either strip it and revarnish or repaint it with yacht paint. I love the look of a well-sanded pine floor sealed with polyurethane. This is a tough, long-wearing, plastic surface coating that eliminates the need for waxing. You can sand and seal a floor yourself, with a hired sander, but if you can afford it, have it done professionally since sanding is exhausting work and sealing needs a long drying time. *Two polyurethane coats are needed* (don't economize here).

My husband and I once laid a 9×6-m (30×20-foot) floor of pale birch squares, and although we did it in a fairly sloppy manner (it was our first attempt) it really looked terrific. The polyurethane finish was great; the floor wasn't waxed once in ten years. However, we did it in the evenings after office work and the effort nearly killed me. I'd never do it again.

A wood-tiled or parquet floor with a varnish seal and a wax finish should never be washed with water (although you can damp-mop it occasionally). The frequency of waxing depends on wear as well as on your time and enthusiasm. Don't think you can get away without waxing. In time it will crumble like shredded wheat.

Carpeting

Rugs or carpets add warmth to a

room, protect the floors, muffle sound – which can be more important in a flat than in a house. You'll get a good, spacious effect with wall-to-wall carpeting and it is easy to maintain. All you need to keep it clean is good vacuum cleaning and a professional shampoo every two years (amazing clean-ups are possible). Make sure that wall-to-wall is professionally laid, on good underlay, otherwise floorboards may show and seams come apart; also you may lay the pile the wrong way.

If you have halfway good-looking wooden floors you might use rugs, but even if they're rubber backed they tend to slip and old ladies tend to break their legs on them. An almost room-sized piece of broadloom can be cheaper than a big rug.

Solid-colour carpeting shows more stains than the tweedy or patterned kinds, but looks more luxurious. Theoretically, a medium-intensity colour shows less dirt than a *very* light colour or a *very* dark one: but from my ten years' experience as a designer the colours which least show the dirt are dark green or dark brown. Most carpet stains seem to be in various shades of brown. So if you start off with a brown carpet they are least likely to show up. Other dark carpets show up every cat hair, speck of dust and thread of white cotton.

Stair carpets: Carpet which is the full width of the stairs and continues round the stair turns looks best, but is extraordinarily extravagant as it will wear on the edge of the treads and you will not be able to move it up a bit because it won't fit the turns – so it will wear out about *six times faster*. Keep your stair carpet as wide as possible (for good looks) but the same width throughout. Then allow an extra 45 cm (18 inches) rolled under at the bottom and the top of the stairs so that you can move it up or down as it starts to wear. Use the best contract quality that you can afford and have it professionally laid if you can. After a liftetime spent trying to skimp on stair carpet, I promise you that money saved here is money fast wasted. It's the only carpeted surface in the house on which you shouldn't economize. If you can't carpet your stairs sensibly and expensively, don't do it at all. Cover them with matting or stain the treads, which will then be very noisy.

There are five basic carpet textures: cut pile velours (which looks like velvet), cord and twist pile, shag (which looks shaggy like a sheepdog), and carved (which has a textural, 3D pattern and is otherwise the same as velours). There's also Saxony, which is somewhere between velours and shag and is very popular in America. (Broadloom just means broad and is so called because it is woven on a broad loom.)

Velours looks grandest but shows footprints and traffic patterns.

Cord is easy to clean, robust and comparatively cheap. It wears best because of its relatively flat surface but doesn't feel luxurious or bouncy underfoot.

Shag can look floppy, can flatten in patches if the tufts are too long, and high heels can snag in it. Otherwise it looks good. I find it very difficult to clean but, because of this, it's also easy to disguise stains. A tufted construction is traditional, but nowadays there is often a latex backing to stop it stretching and give it a good 'lay'. Bonded carpets are not looped under the basic weave; instead the fibres are bonded into place. This can save up to 30 per cent of the fibre, but they won't last so long. However, they're fine for bedrooms and other light-traffic areas.

Why do you need carpet underlay? For quiet, for extra underfoot bounce and resilience and to make the carpet last longer, which it certainly does (sometimes, in my experience, up to twice as long). Always buy good underlay – it's a good investment, and it'll certainly last far longer than the carpet. It should be laid over an extra paper lining (called padfelt in the trade). There are three basic carpet underlays:

Old-fashioned felt, which can stretch and shred and isn't very clean.

Foam rubber, which gives a good 'bounce' and is often attached to the back of the carpet at the factory.

Waffle sponge rubber, which comes in different thicknesses. Don't pick an excessive, anklebreaking thickness.

Carpet fibres are:

Wool: The Old Reliable wears on like an old soldier, is easy to clean, resilient, comfortable, warm, resistant to abrasion. What more can you ask? Alas, at present wool is very expensive, but some of the synthetics are just as serviceable and attractive, especially if blended with a percentage of wool. But you can't home-dye synthetics, as a rule.

Acrylic: Resembles wool, is far cheaper, resistant to soiling, is durable, resilient, can't mildew or be attacked by moths. Various acrylic fibres have trade names like Acrilan or Courtelle. Be wary of getting it in pale colours.

Polyesters: Fibres such as Dacron can have the weight and luxury of wool, but are shinier and less resilient, with poor stain resistance. Good for bedrooms. Shag construction can wilt unless ends are tightly twisted.

Nylon: This is the best-wearing of the man-made yarns. It is tough, resistant to soiling, cleans easily and is reasonably priced. It has one problem, static electricity. This means that you can get little electric shocks off metal furniture or even other people. Some manufacturers now incorporate anti-static in the fibre, which eliminates the problem.

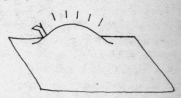

You need the best quality carpet where it gets the hardest wear (hall and stairs). You can get away with cheaper carpet in the bedroom. Check whether your carpet is mothproof or fireproof, what it's made of and how to clean it.

CAUTION! Carpet sellers can be as slippery, devious and downright

A QUICK CONSUMER'S GUIDE TO FLOORING

Relative cost guide on 1–10 scale	Material	Suitable for	Possible advantages	Possible disadvantages
1–2	Brick	Ruggedly brutal interiors; workmanlike areas	Hard to hurt, porous	Wears and chips quicker than you'd expect
3–10	Carpet, wall-to-wall*	Everywhere except kitchen and play room	Warm, sumptuous, sound-absorbent	Easily stained; don't lay it yourself, if possible
3–10	Carpet, square	Everywhere except kitchen and play room	Easy to lay, moves with you	Easily stained
2–5	Ceramic tiles*	Mainly kitchen/bathroom	Easy to clean, hygienic	Hard on feet for long periods of standing, cold, noisy
2–4	Clay tiles*			
5–8	Cork tiles (vinyl treated)	Everywhere, but mainly kitchen/nursery/bathroom	Warm, easy to clean, yielding, sound-absorbing; get it pre-sealed	Dirt shows easily on darker surface; choose caramel!
1–3	Linoleum tiles	Everywhere, except over uneven floorboards, because it will crack and split	Cheap, easy to lay, wide variety of finish	Only moderate wear unless it's inlaid
1–2	Linoleum sheet			
8–10	Marble slabs*	Everywhere except kitchen	Sumptuous, easy to clean, durable	Hard on feet for long periods of standing, cold, noisy

Type	Price	Suitable for	Advantages	Disadvantages
Quarry tiles*	6–8	Mainly kitchen	Easy to clean, durable	Hard on feet for long periods of standing
Rubber tiles / Rubber sheet	3–7	Heavy-duty areas where you're standing, i.e. kitchen	Resilient, warm, sound-absorbent	Slippery when wet: not much choice of pattern
Slate slabs* / Terrazzo*	6	Everywhere except kitchen (too hard on feet)	Durable, sumptuous, easy to clean	Hard on feet for long periods of standing, cold, noisy, can crack if you drop a really heavy object on it
Vinyl tiles / Vinyl sheet / Vinyl asbestos tiles (more brittle, less flexible but much cheaper)	3–7 / 3–7 / 1–3	Everywhere / Avoid greasy areas such as kitchen; avoid using vinyl asbestos tiles over uneven floorboards because they may crack or split	Easy to clean, relatively cheap, wide variety of finish; tiles easy to lay	Easily marked by indentations and abrasions unless vinyl throughout
Woodstrip* / Wood block (parquet)	2–4 / 4–10	Everywhere except damp areas such as bathroom, kitchen, conservatory, utility rooms	Can look elegant, soothing, traditional; good with antiques, long life	Expensive; not suitable for rooms with water

* moderately expensive to install.

crooked as they're traditionally supposed to be. If you can wait, some of the best department stores in the country have money-saving carpet sales that come close to matching the fringe operators' prices. Be wary of 'warehouse' stores (although there are reliable firms, such as Sapphire). Be wary of the relics of warehouse fires, which appear in the ad columns with a relentless monotony that should alarm fire brigades and insurance firms. Be sceptical of 'factory-to-you' advertising. For carpeting, as with any other important invest-ment – I can't emphasize this enough – go to a reputable dealer who will stand by his product, and *haggle* with the man who runs the shop. (I never thought I had the nerve until I didn't have the money.) Tell him that you can afford £x a square yard, choose a carpet (which may be twice as much) and keep saying that you want that colour and quality, only cheaper, to fit your budget. You may have to walk out and come back a couple of days later.

There's a lot to be said for carpet tiles. They're easy to lay (millionaire author Frederick Forsyth laid them himself to take his mind off writing *Day of the Jackal*) and easy to trim, and you can shift the worn ones around and rip out the unsavoury ones. You can replace them cheaply. The only thing to be said against them is that they look institutional and dreary, although the quality and

colours are improving, and I've seen some really terrific David Hicks-type geometric designs.

Resilient floors

If you really want an easy-to-care-for floor, cover it with a water-resistant material which can be washed with a mop and detergent and water. Some need waxing to maintain a shine, but Moses didn't come down from the Mount saying that a shine was ab-solutely essential. In any case, resilient floors can most practically be used in kitchens, bathrooms, dens, play-rooms, nurseries, utility rooms, base-ments and halls. Some of the hand-some, new, textured vinyl floors look good in any room. I have found those cream or white, pockmarked vinyl tiles surprisingly effective and sur-prisingly easy to keep clean (in spite of my earlier warning against light floor-ing).

Resilient surfaces include linoleum, vinyl, cork and rubber tile. A pattern shows less dirt than a solid colour, but dirt can collect in embossed or textured patterns.

Linoleum is comparatively inex-pensive and will last several years, depending on the quality chosen and wear given; it is grease-resistant and easy to lay; it needs to be waxed to protect the surface. *Inlaid linoleum* is somewhat more expensive, but wears very well. 'Inlaid' indicates that the pattern goes through to the backing, while in ordinary linoleum the pattern has been printed on the surface and *is likely to wear out*. Inlaid linoleum needs polish. It is grease-resistant but can be damaged by cleaning products which contain alkalis, so use only the recommended cleaner. It is made in various thicknesses; light duty (1.1 mm) for general use, heavy duty (3.2 mm) for playrooms, kitchens or downstairs passages.

Vinyls in sheet or tiles make the most resilient floor coverings. Vinyl surfaces are resistant to wear, grease, alkali and dirt. They are easy to wash. Scuff marks can be removed with Flash; black heel marks or cigarette burns can be buffed off with fine steel wool (half a Brillo pad); then repolish the area.

Sheet vinyl is generally produced in rolls of 1–2-m width (3–6-foot) × 2 mm quality for domestic use. It is easily marked by indentations and abrasions. You have a wide choice of patterns and colours, in a durable but moderately quiet material. Sheet vinyl with a cushioned backing is an effective sound-absorber and very soft for walking, so it is good for kitchens. Some vinyls are finished with a high gloss and require no polish, but probably after a period of wear you may want to shine them up a bit. Otherwise, sponge-mop with a mild detergent and rinse off.

Vinyl tile is more practical. It is uniform in composition throughout, is the most expensive resilient flooring, the most attractive and easy to maintain. There is a wide range of good designs, textures and colours. It is easier to lay tiles than large sheets, particularly if you buy the self-adhesive (peel-and-stick) type. As with carpet tiles, a badly scarred or stained section can be easily, and invisibly, replaced. Vinyl tile comes in 23- or 30-cm (9- or 12-inch) squares. Get thickness of 1.1 mm for general domestic purposes and 2 mm for heavy duty.

Much less expensive than pure vinyl is *vinyl asbestos composition tile*. This tile can be bought with self-sticking backing and you can lay it yourself without much difficulty. It is more brittle than pure vinyl and requires more care. Vinyl asbestos tile is a blend of asbestos fibres, vinyls, plasticizers, colour pigments and fillers and comes in the same sizes as vinyl tile. Leading manufacturers offer patterns textured to simulate wood, marble, quarry tile or brick.

Rubber tile is made of synthetic or natural rubber. There's a narrow range of colours and patterns, mainly marble. The tile (standard sizes) is resilient, has a high resistance to indentation but is softened by petroleum products so don't try to get marks off with nail varnish remover or drycleaning fluid. Waxing and buffing are necessary. The surface becomes slippery when wet, so it is not now used often in the home.

Cork tile is soft and warm underfoot and sound-absorbent. It makes a handsome floor but is broken down by heavy traffic, grease and alkalis, so considered unsuitable for kitchens by purists, although many people have it. The best tile has a clear film of vinyl applied to it to improve durability, water resistance and ease of maintenance. It's available in strips or squares of varying size and varying thicknesses from 4.5 mm (general domestic purpose) to 6 mm (heavy duty).

Non-resilient flooring

This includes brick, ceramic and clay tile, quarry tile, stone, slate, marble and terrazzo. These are all expensive and difficult to install but are good-looking and should last longer than you. Ceramic and clay are used mainly in bathrooms and kitchens because, if properly laid, they are waterproof, easy to wash and hard to stain or dent, and can be easily disinfected. Most non-resilient flooring is laid in mortar. It's a good solution for terraces, garden or patio, even kitchens, though it is hard on dropped glassware and does feel rather unyielding. I dreamed I dwelt in marble halls and they were terribly hard on the feet.

Happy House Rules

TWELVE THINGS NO HOME SHOULD BE WITHOUT

- A comfortable bed.
- An alarm clock.
- A comfortable chair.
- A good, big, sensible, sturdy table.
- A trolley (for everything except serving meals; for washing up, TV set, bathroom table, and an extra surface on which to pile work).
- An adjustable, efficient reading light (for bedside or table).
- A safe place for household documents.
- A good lock and chain on the front door (and peephole, if necessary).
- A full-length mirror.
- Enough coathooks on the way in.
- Power cover for fuel strikes: bottled-gas camping stove, or electric hot plate; Tilley paraffin camping lamp for heat and light.
- Basic sewing kit for emergencies.

TWENTY WAYS TO MAKE YOUR LIVING-ROOM LOOK MORE EXPENSIVE...

The basic recipe is a warm, clean, tidy, calm atmosphere to which (if possible) you add fresh flowers, soft Scarlatti-type music, masses of books which don't look as though they were bought in bulk, and (if possible) a crackling log fire. To this add several of the following:

- One big exuberant plant. Put all your money into size and durability.
- A weekly change of fresh flowers, however few.
- A heaped dish or wicker basket of lemons or oranges.
- A table with several neat piles of shiny magazines.
- Slabs of mirror.
- Fur. Fling an exotic rug across a sofa or try fake tiger skin cushions.

- Masses of cushions. Knit or needle-point or patchwork one or two covers if you're feeling creative.
- Plain wall-to-wall carpet.
- Anything leather, *so long as it smells*.
- Anything that looks heavy or weighty; a real, genuine, solid something or other, whether it's an armchair or brass lamp.
- Pretty candlesticks with fresh candles.
- Low pools of lighting in a darkish room. You don't necessarily need those spotlights. In Finland they use candles in warm, dark rooms, then add Sibelius with a howling wolf and wind outside: as warm as a hug.
- One dark colour over walls and woodwork: especially good in small rooms. Suitable sombre colours include sludge green, maroon and the perennial bitter chocolate.
- Alternatively, cream woodwork, which looks softer and classier than white, especially when used with white walls. This is lucky because white woodwork yellows so fast (even if they claim it's non-yellowing).
- Curtains are more opulent than blinds: don't use those pronged hooks for French pleats, because they tend to fall out and are difficult to get back and may easily look wobbly and not rich at all.
- One very large picture or properly mounted poster or print or photograph.
- Lots and lots of prints, and I don't mean that popular Chinese lady

with the green face. The best place to shop is in big museums because their reproduction is superior. I have a lovely little Elizabethan portrait reproduction from the Victoria and Albert Museum: she has beautifully embroidered strawberry flowers on her white satin sleeves, is mounted on hardboard so that she doesn't need a frame, and cost £1.
- Alternatively, a row of Indian miniatures (reproduction is fine). Again from museums or from your local trendy art or bookshop.
- Genuine old prints of flowers, hunting scenes, Victorian fashions or local views. They're surprisingly cheap if you find them in antiquarian bookshops before the books are ripped apart and the plates sold separately and exorbitantly.
- A Collection displayed on table or shelf. There are four things you can collect free: big beautiful shells, sculpture driftwood, big pebbles (which you should either varnish or keep in water) and dried flowers, thorns, teazles and grasses, which can look elegant in simple glass cylinders. If you have a little money to spend (say 50p a week) you can collect old tins.

Other collectors' items might be:
Old clockwork toys (especially cars and trains)
Teapots; jardinières; Victorian riding crops; thirties china, glass and Bakelite (never mind if it's a bit chipped), pink or blue and white china (non-

matching); inlaid papiermâché trays
Old bottles (standing in a row against the light), soda siphons and stone ginger beer bottles
Regimental brass buttons
Old flatirons, trivets and other cast-iron household ware, curling tongs, old scissors, glove and boot stretchers, great big old iron keys
Old lace (pin it on thick coloured card)
Old postcards or new postcards
Wooden printing blocks
Anything Rupert, anything Brumas, anything Popeye
Early Action Men
Sixties teenage annuals or fan books

Memorabilia:
Churchilliana
Anything from the Festival of Britain (especially Eric Ravillious mugs)
Coronation mugs
Beatles souvenirs
Silver Jubilee tat

These are, of course, the antiques of the future.

... AND FOURTEEN WAYS TO AVOID MAKING IT LOOK CHEAPER

Avoid:
- A light floor, especially a white floor unless it's real marble, because the upkeep is beyond reasonable toil and it will quickly look grubby.
- Sisal matting.
- Rush matting, unless it's immaculate and properly fitted, wall to wall.

- Anything hessian.
- Anything Swedish checked.
- Greasy upholstery (especially on satin-padded bed headboard).
- Knock-down furniture that's falling apart or never stood up straight in the first place.
- Painted furniture that is chipped.
- Tin mugs.
- Dying plants.
- Pink gladioli (unless it's one stem in a cylindrical glass).
- Half-burnt, witty candles.
- Fluorescent lights.
- Using your stereo or television as an auxiliary coffee table.

HOW TO BE A RICH AND CLEVER ART COLLECTOR

It's not acquiring a number of pictures, but making your *own* unique collection that counts. The prints can cost anything from a few pounds to a few hundred pounds. You might want to collect posters, lithographs, woodcuts, engravings, etchings, screen prints or rare photographs. What matters is that you decide on a style or a theme and stick to it.

There's nothing new about prints. Dürer and Rembrandt made great prints, so did Toulouse-Lautrec, Matisse and Picasso. Some of today's

top names are Oldenburgh, Raus-
chenberg, Stella, Dine, Hamilton,
Hockney, Paolozzi – just a few of the
many artists who started experiment-
ing with print-making in the sixties,
working closely with the craftsmen
who make the prints. New photographic tricks were mated with old
screen-printing techniques, much ex-
perimenting took place, much mixing
of techniques, and a whole new movement started.

For the collector with next to no
money this sort of print offers a way
of getting good, genuine art cheaply
(I have a *real* Picasso on my wall, and
so can you if you can afford this
book). This sort of art is genuine
because *a print is not a reproduction*, to
be rolled off by the thousand. A print
is not a copy of a picture: a print has
been designed as a print, whereas a
reproduction is a copy. (See the
Recognition Course that follows for
what different sorts of prints there are
and how you tell the difference.)

Whatever your reasons for starting
to collect prints you had better accept
the fact that you're not immediately
going to outsmart the market and
make a fortune. Remember, too, that
art can *decrease* in value, but if
you buy your art for love it will not
disappoint you, although it may
eventually bore you, but then that's
love.

Depending on your likes, there are
prints at all price levels, although the
price will depend whether you pick a
winner at the start of his career, or
whether you spend more money but
take less risk, by purchasing someone

who is safely established. (I recommend the latter course if you're beginning.)

When buying graphics the quality
of printing work is all-important: even
the paper can matter. You can learn
this only by studying it from experience – you can't learn it out of a
book. You are going to make mistakes, just as you do in clothes, just as
you do in interior decoration. However, art mistakes are not irretrievable
losses like those see-through harem
trousers. The gallery that sold you
something that you tire of will generally resell it for you – it was their
choice as well as yours. Visit your
nearest small gallery and talk to the
owner. Gallery owners know a lot
themselves and are usually both kind
and keen to start a beginner off on a
path that they so much enjoy. They can
also suggest reputable dealers in the
sort of art which interests you.

Many libraries have a lend/buy
service or can direct you to one. If you
feel uncertain to begin with, you can
often rent a picture, and see how you
like living with it.

What to collect

The best-value, cheapest art buys are
posters, which are, in effect, un-
limited-edition prints, often done by
an artist for museum or gallery exhibitions. If you've got a large empty room
and a small budget I suggest that you
get such posters for immediate, spectacular effect.

Photographs are gaining increasing
value as art, especially old photo-

graphs, or modern photographs by well-established names. Write to the Photographers' Gallery (6 Great Newport Street, London wc2) – or better still, pay them a visit. Rarity as well as beauty affects the price of photographs. Some dealers now destroy a negative, in the same way that a print-maker destroys a plate when a certain predetermined number of prints have been made, to ensure that no more can be made (this is what is known as a 'limited edition').

When buying photographs accept only monochrome prints that have been *processed to last*; otherwise your investment might literally fade away. Glass sweats and may rot a framed photograph. Use sheet Perspex offcuts from shops such as Paperchase, 216 Tottenham Court Road, London w1 (tel. 01-637 1121).

Why are reproductions cheaper than prints? David Hockney was once criticized for producing a book (*Grimm's Fairy Tales*) that originally cost £500. He said, 'I made the book as a set of etchings. If you want to make good etchings, very beautifully and carefully by hand, with lots of talented, highly-trained people working on it, then it costs a fantastic amount.

'You're not making it for the masses, you're making it for the connoisseur. You're paying for the love and care and time that's been lavished on it by the artist, the craftsmen, the printers and the publisher, that's what the limited edition offers. You're buying a beautiful, integrated *original*.'

What sort of limited print edition should you buy? A print in a large

edition is comparatively cheap, but will never have the scarcity value of a print in a small edition. So, if you're not particularly interested in resale value, choose from the large editions to get the best money's worth. A limited edition print may have two numbers on it: the lower one is the total number of prints in the series, while the upper one is the serial number of that particular print; e.g. 7/200 would mean it was the seventh printed of 200 prints. The smaller the first number the higher the value, because the first prints are the sharper ones.

Is a signed print more valuable? The print is what you're buying. All original prints are now numbered and signed because the artist is signing his approval of that print. Not every print is good enough: I should think that Richard Hamilton rejects as many as he approves. For the artist to sign a reproduction is, to my mind, merely a marketing device: some might call it a confidence trick. What you are buying is merely an autograph.

How to look after your art: Never wash gilt picture frames with soap and water or the gilt will come off. Clean them with a soft 50-mm (2-inch) paintbrush, or a soft badger shaving brush, if Grandad had one. Don't clean frames with any product that contains varnish or wax or you may damage the edges of the painting.

Never try to clean or repair the work of art itself, unless you really know what you're doing, because you stand to ruin it. Ask your gallery to name a restorer, if you don't know one. Never wipe paintings with a damp cloth (especially not water colours) and never dust them with a feather duster, because the feathers tend to catch on paint particles and pull them off.

Avoid hanging paintings in any place that is very hot, very cold, very humid or very dry. Don't *ever* hang valuable art in bathrooms, kitchens, beach houses or near swimming pools. Keep good pictures away from radiators and air conditioners.

How to spot a print:

A quick recognition course
Take a deep breath and don't try to remember this, but just refer to it. It's easy to spot the difference in print techniques when you actually see them, but it's impossible beforehand.

A mass-produced colour print taken from a colour photograph of a painting is called a *reproduction*. However skilfully printed, it is not worth more than the paper it's printed on, although often a pleasant reminder of the original painting, or a pleasant picture in itself.

Traditionally, artist's prints have been made by one of four basic methods:

The relief method: as in *woodcuts* and *linocuts* (or potato cuts, come to that) where portions of the flat surface are gouged out and the printing surface is left upstanding.

The intaglio method: this includes *engraving* (scratching the design direct on to metal) and *etching* (scratching the picture on to a metal plate thinly covered with wax, which is then etched out in an acid bath). The printing area is then recessed in the metal plate. The recesses are filled with ink, the plate is wiped clean and the print is made under great pressure. If you run your thumb over an engraving, whether it's a Rembrandt or somebody's calling card, you can feel the raised surface of the printed areas.

The surface method: as in *lithographs*, a stone slab or special plate is covered with a greasy image which accepts ink, while the rest of the surface is treated to reject ink. This method produces exquisitely delicate colours.

Screen printing: this is done with a sort of stencil screen – you might have used one at school. A Terylene screen is stretched over a frame, the non-printing areas of the design are sealed with gelatine and the colour is forced through the non-gelatinous areas of the screen under pressure. If it is a hand screen print then the pressure is somebody's hands on a squeegee board and there is no great merit in the fact that it's hand printed. Screen printing produces wonderful, clear, glowing colours and can make a print look almost like a painting.

Mixed media prints are produced when two or more of these methods are used to produce the final print, which may also include direct photographic processes.

Who publishes what

Avant-garde etchings and silk screens:

Editions Alecto, 27 Kelso Place, London w8 (tel. 01-937 6611).

Contemporary: Curwen Gallery, 1 Colville Place, Charlotte Street, London w1 (tel. 01-636 1459).

Expensive contemporary: Marlborough Fine Art Ltd, 6 Albemarle Street, London w1 (tel. 01-629 5161).

Established contemporary: Petersburg Press, 59A Portobello Road, London w11 (tel. 01-229 8791). Original graphics and deluxe quality prints by American and English artists. Viewing by appointment only.

Established contemporary: Observer Art, 2 Motcomb Street, London sw1 (tel. 01-235 0934).

Contemporary prints: Christie's Contemporary Art, 8 King Street, St James's, London sw1 (tel. 01-839 9060).

Comtemporary prints: Waddington and Tooth Graphics, 31 Cork Street, London w1 (tel. 01-439 1866).

Inexpensive posters: Camden Graphics, 43 Camden Passage, London n1 (tel. 01-226 2061) produce an adequate (just) leaflet. Predictable but good-value selection includes Pre-Raphaelites, Mucha and Arthur Rackham. Also good charts for children including picture maps, flowers of the world, historical maps of England, Wales and USA, clan map of Scotland, as well as the history of space travel, sailing or steam railway engines.

For instant-decor *reproductions*, standard but good, try Athena International, Head Office: PO Box 13, Bishop's Stortford, Hertfordshire (Bishop's Stortford 56627). Pick your own Picasso, Botticelli, Renoir or Klimt. Block mounted (very nice) or framed. Also good, cheap, assemble-yourself clip frames for pictures and photographs. Available from Athena shops, or by mail order. 1978–9 catalogue, 60p.

ARMCHAIR SHOPPING
(with catalogue address book)

All men think that all women love shopping: how wrong they are! It's depressing to see prices shoot up weekly, it's depressing to queue (perhaps in your lunch hour), to be served by harassed, overworked assistants, and it's exhausting to heave it all home. That is why mail order shopping is here to stay. It accounts for around 4 per cent of all retail sales in Britain, only slightly less than department store sales. One in every four parcels posted in Britain is mail order.

Snobs used to turn their noses up at the big mail order catalogues – today only the ignorant do so. You can safely buy almost anything you will ever need, and a whole lot you won't, from the *pick of the postal catalogues* listed below. If you have ever hung around a hot, stuffy store waiting to be served, or been bullied by a surly assistant when he/she finally turns to tell you that they're out of stock, or been chivvied by your bored children before buying what your husband later turned out to hate, you are a *candidate for the catalogues.*

If you hate putting pen to paper it can be tedious to write off for a few catalogues in the first place, but not if you steel yourself and spend one whole evening doing it. Then, when you want to order, you have to do a little more work. You have to list item numbers, description of item, preferable shades, second choices, quantity and price. But whatever the effort, it may be nothing compared to the agony of genuine modern shopping.

You can return mail order goods if you're dissatisfied but apart from Mail Order Protection schemes (see further on) there are few regulations covering mail order. Check how long is the period allowed for returning unwanted goods – it varies. If a firm sends you goods by mail order which you haven't ordered, the firm has six months to collect them. If they don't do so you can keep them. Alternatively, you can write (send the letter recorded delivery and keep a copy yourself) any time within five months of receiving the goods, saying that you didn't order them and giving them your name and the address where they can be collected. If the firm doesn't collect the goods within thirty days of receiving your letter, you can keep them.

Mail order goods can be cheaper than store-bought ones because the savings on expensive retail operations

(all those indolent assistants with insolent eyelashes, and high rents in expensive city centres) can be passed on to the customer.

Although the sum of the weekly instalments is the same as the cash price, the cost of the credit is obviously built into the price, so, if possible (in inflationary times), buying on the never-never is the cheapest way to buy mail order.

Another way to cut the price is by becoming a spare-time agent. They get around 10–12 per cent commission on what they sell and often on their own purchases.

It can be difficult to judge from a photograph what the goods really look like and whether the quality is up to standard. The best mail order firms try to deliver merchandise which is *better* than it looks in the catalogue, rightly reckoning that they'll have a delighted customer who'll come back for more, rather than a disappointed one who won't. (I've worked as a selector for a mail order catalogue and know this can be so.)

Admittedly, if the goods fail to give satisfaction it's a great bother for you to repack them and send them back. If goods are returned there could be a delay in returning your money if the company is not a reputable one, so *choose your company with care.*

It may be difficult, if not impossible, to get your money back from a mail order firm that goes bankrupt. Because of the seventies scandals, a *mail order protection scheme* was set up by various publishing organizations, including the Newspaper Publishers'

Association (which covers all national newspapers), the Periodical Publishers' Association and provincial newspapers and magazines. Under the scheme readers can be reimbursed if they have sent money for goods to an advertiser who goes bankrupt before they receive the goods.

So if you send money for goods in response to a mail order advertisement and they don't arrive after, say, about four weeks, you should first telephone, and if that doesn't work, try and contact the trader by recorded delivery letter. If unsuccessful, or if you are dissatisfied, *write to the advertising manager of the publication in which you saw the advertisement*, giving details of the order; cheque or postal order number of money sent; and copies of any correspondence you have had with the trader. You must make the claim within two months of the appearance of the advertisement. *The scheme does not cover small classified advertisements or mail order catalogues* – so these are still risky unless you're dealing with a reputable firm.

Women's magazine offers, which are chosen by the editor and not by advertisers, are terrific value (the fashion editors really put a lot of care and work into their offers). Look out for the fashion offers in *Cosmopolitan, Woman, Woman's Own, Over 21, The Times*, the *Sunday Times* and the *Observer*. And remember that the most satisfactory mail order buying might not be from mail order houses but from big city stores advertising in newspapers, usually at sale times. Sheets, linen and towels are safe

travelling bets – but you've got to wait for the sales.

Don't imagine that Direct Mail is always cheapest; discount houses will usually give you the best bargains – especially with electrical goods.

The best big mail order firms

The two heavyweight catalogue firms are Littlewoods and Great Universal Stores, both of which put out six catalogues; some of them are similar but with different names and covers:

Littlewoods' catalogues are:
Janet Frazer, Peter Craig, Burlington, John Moores, Littlewoods and Brian Mills.
Great Universal Stores' catalogues are:
Kays, Trafford Warehouses, Marshall Ward (two editions of this one – one for agents and one for non-agents), Great Universal, John Noble and John England.
Other big catalogues include:
Freemans, Empire Stores, Grattan and Worldwide.

All these mail order firms are members of the Mail Order Traders' Association of Great Britain, 507 Corn Exchange Buildings, Fenwick Street, Liverpool L27RA (tel. 051-236 7581), who will take up complaints.

At first glance there's too much choice in the catalogues and looking at them can overwhelm, but like eating peanuts, you just can't stop once you've started. Some of the designs are crude and garish – many overblown rose patterns – but there's a lot of basic good stuff. Many of the household durables are brand-name items (and not necessarily from the cheap end of the market). There's a big range of kitchen equipment, gardening equipment, sleeping bags, brand-name furniture, cameras, watches, hair driers, irons, washing machines, DIY furniture, bedding, curtains, bathroom equipment, hosiery, bicycles and so on.

The range of clothes is fairly limited, to say the least, but some are excellent value – the baby clothes, toddlers' clothes and school clothes. Simple summer cotton dresses for all ages are good value – but watch out for what looks like denim but turns out to be a cheap denim-coloured cotton. Don't expect Fiorucci fashion and a perfect fit at catalogue prices. (Lulu doesn't *always* wear clothes straight out of the catalogue.)

Personally, I wouldn't risk buying underwear without trying it on, but then I'm an odd shape (isn't everyone?). But you can send it back if it doesn't fit and there's an amazing array of underwear ranging from the kinky (black frilly corset accessorized with matching G-string) to the antique (where else can you get men's cavalry corselets, coms and liberty bodices?), as well as an incredible range of armour-plated corsets (all from J. D. Williams).

The Janet Frazer catalogue, supposedly one of the top up-market catalogues, has stylish luggage, good watches, Dorma Mary Quant-designed sheets, Hygena kitchens, Austinsuite storage walls, electrical goods

and lots of whiteware (fridges, washing machines, freezers, etc.). However, you might get them cheaper at a discount store or warehouse.

Here are the addresses to write to for the leading mail order catalogues. Nearly all operate the FREEPOST scheme, so there's no need to stamp your letter, if you include the word Freepost in the address:

Empire Stores: Bradford, West Yorkshire B99 4XB

Freemans: London SW9 0YX

Grattan: Bradford, West Yorkshire BD99 2XG

J. D. Williams: PO Box 285, The Dale Street Warehouses, Manchester M60 6ES

Janet Frazer: Leigh, Lancashire WN7 1BR

Peter Craig: PO Box 121, Bolton BL3 5HQ

Littlewoods: PO Box 31, Bolton BL3 5HF

John Moores: PO Box 80, Bolton BL3 5YX

Brian Mills: PO Box 45, Bolton BL3 5YY

Burlington: PO Box 3, Bolton BL3 5YN

Kays: Worcester WR1 1JF

Trafford; *Great Universal*; *John England* and *John Noble:* Central New Appointments, Devonshire Street, Manchester M60 6EL

Marshall Ward: Bridgewater Place, Manchester M60 6AP

The pick of the specialist mail order firms:

Bedding

Aeonics Ltd, 92 Church Road, Mitcham, Surrey CR4 3TD (tel. 01-640 9231). Specialize in good-value *continental quilts* and have a selection of pleasant plain covers, as well as patterned ones. Check that your quilt, if filled with duck down, conforms to the new BS 5335 standard, or, if synthetic, is Green Label quality Terylene P3, which can go in a washing machine. A continental quilt gives you light, angel-wing warmth and is the equivalent of three heavy blankets. Buy the biggest size you can afford, and buy adult-size ones for children (they grow, don't they?). Don't buy stuff-it-yourself duvets – it takes for ever and you have to do it in the street or garden because the stuff flies everywhere.

Helios Home Supplies, Marlborough Hill, Macclesfield, Cheshire (tel. Macclesfield [0625] 25460). For the sort of linen cupboard with everything in graded colours that you only see in glossy magazines, buy from Helios. You'll get beautiful and unusual co-ordinated designs by Yves St Laurent and Mary Quant for Osman and Dorma in *towels, bedwear and curtains*. Particularly good lace bedspreads by Moonweave, Candlewick by Diana Coupe, Old Bleach tablecloths and Old Hall cutlery. Real style and a change from everyone else's Habitat.

Limericks, 110 Hamlet Court Road, Westcliff-on-Sea, Essex SS0 7ET (tel. Southend [0702] 43486). An old-fashioned firm selling *everything that everyone else has stopped selling*. You can buy protective, heat-resistant table felt; quilted overlay mattress covers; Sleepskin (better for you, they say, than electric blankets); sleeping bags which unzip to make double-bed size quilts; green table felt (mend that bridge table!); butter muslin; hessian; duster cloth; towelling and white sheeting by the yard. Exceedingly cheap white cotton sheets, bolsters, bolster cases, stretchable bunk sheets, pillows and wonderful-value feather-filled cushion pads.

Plumbs (Mail Order) *Ltd*, Salmon Street, Preston PR1 6NY, Lancashire (tel. Preston [0772] 50811). For continental quilts and covers, conventional bedding in fashionable designs at low prices. Stretch covers for any style of furniture. Three-piece suites with removable cleanable upholstery. Catalogues available for all products.

Books

Hatchards, 187 Piccadilly, London W1 (tel. 01-734 3201). Books are the easiest presents to wrap and there's always something for everyone on your Christmas list. Apart from their catalogue, if you want to order a book, telephone them or write to their mail order department.

John Smith and Son, 57–61 St Vincent Street, Glasgow (tel. 041-221 7472). Another bookshop I've found to be very efficient and prepared to take a lot of trouble to deal with your order. Excellent Christmas catalogue.

Children's clothes

Lewes Design Workshop, 24 High Street, Lewes, Sussex (tel. Lewes [079 16] 3487). Clever *cutout clothes kits.* The design and the pattern are printed on fabric like a rag doll, so you just cut along the lines and sew together. Fun clothes for babies, children (and adults). Mostly simple cottons, trousers, skirts and peasant dresses in bright colours and stylized designs.

Mothercare-by-post, Cherry Tree Road, Watford, Hertfordshire WD2 5SH (tel. Watford [0923] 33577). Mothercare are the biggest and the most practical suppliers of *everything for babies, children and mothers-to-be.*

Their catalogue rounds up a big selection of almost everything from the Mothercare stores. For new mothers there are nursing bras, slips, nightdresses and a good-value basic layette for the new baby. There's a big range of baby-stretch garments in many designs (including some really practical dark colours). Also good

nursery safety equipment such as cooker guards, safety chests and play-pens to safely imprison them. Everything a baby could want to sit, stand, crawl or dribble in. Mothercare promise to exchange or refund your money if you return any unwanted goods within two weeks and promise no questions asked.

Pollyanna, 660 Fulham Road, London SW6 (tel. 01-731 0673). The classic, chic mail order firm for *children's clothes.* The great thing is that they're *wearable* and look just as charming when crumpled as when fresh.

Rosie Nice, 12 Clifton Road, London W9 1SS (tel. 01-580 6500). Imaginative knitting with bright colours and patterns; *chunky sweaters* a speciality. For two- to five-year-olds.

Tuppence Coloured, Brookside Cottage, Stour Provost, nr Gillingham, Dorset (tel. South Petherton 40347). Beautiful Liberty fabrics and *quilted clothes*, for three- to five-year-olds, girls and boys. Very, very bright primary colours or subdued prints. Great style – only Sally Tuffin could have done it.

The White House, 51–52 New Bond Street, London W1Y 0BY (tel. 01-629 3521). This is where princesses buy their *embroidered baby clothes*, sheikhs their bed linen (£120 for one double sheet and two pillow-cases), and queens their handkerchiefs (lace-trimmed French ones around £3 each – worth it for grandmother perhaps?). Great towelling bathrobes, carefully cut (like the ones taken off in French films).

Classy clothes

Angela Gore, 1 Hardwick Street, London EC1R 4RB (tel. 01-278 4165). Angela Gore designs for the Hunt Ball set. Her inexpensive, simple, easy-to-follow catalogue contains samples of all her fabrics. Her clothes are country evening dresses covering up the likely-to-be-chilled areas, and long skirts for when people say 'don't dress' but you're obviously supposed to make a bit of an effort.

Bernat Klein Design, Waukrigg Mill, Galashiels, Scotland TD1 1QD (tel. Galashiels [0896] 2764). Really beautiful fabrics, gorgeous silk tweeds and the famous vibrant-coloured mohairs. It's top of the market – proof that mail order fashion is not drab and dreary. Clothes choice is kept small and simple, including lawn cotton shifts, hand-knitted classic sweaters, mohair jackets and long skirts, evening dresses in pure silk as well as plain and printed polyester. They will send you samples of cloths and colours if you ask, and you can buy all clothes fabrics by the yard as well. Catalogue 20p.

Janet Reger, 2 Beauchamp Place, London SW3 (tel. 01-584 9360) and 12 New Bond Street, London W1 (tel. 01-493 8357). Janet Reger's wicked underwear is very expensive but worth it if you haven't got much of a bosom. My voluptuous friends tell me that her clothes tend to be on the small side. Heave-ho bras to give that buxom wench look, waist-nipping waspies and ravishing little suspender belts and slips. Catalogue about £2.

DIY drink

Southern Vineyards Nizells Avenue, Hove, Sussex BN3 1PS (tel. Brighton [0273] 779971). Many people are disappointed in their early attempts at home *wine-making* because of insufficient instructions. If you want cheap, good-tasting wines made from grape-juice concentrates, send for this firm's appetizing (and free) catalogue, which is also an instruction book. It tells you all you're likely to want to know, from how to make the stuff to what sort of glass to serve it in, and also contains an excellent cookery section.

Herbalist

Culpeper, 21 Bruton Street, London W1X 7DA (tel. 01-629 4559). Enormous selection of *herbs and spices*, herbal remedies, hair and bath preparations. Also good ranges of honey, vinegar and herbal teas, soaps, bath essences and pot pourris. Their skin ointment works overnight miracles on troublesome spots – it's expensive but lasts for years.

Household goods

Charterhouse Products 18–21 Charterhouse Square, London EC1M 6AJ (tel. 01-253 7421). You can even buy *chandeliers* by post (together with the funny lightbulbs they need and chains from which to suspend them). Choose from many styles – the inverted water-fall underneath which Josephine flirted, or those as swung on by Errol Flynn. The catalogue is expensive but your money will be refunded if you return it.

Habitat, Hithercroft Road, Walling-ford, Oxfordshire (tel. Wallingford [049 13] 5000). Standard, safe, so-called good taste, as bought by newly-weds in the sixties. Prices can be high, but they offer useful things such as front door mats. If you're buying it in the stores you should check quality carefully. Most goods can be ordered by mail but can take up to a month to arrive. Reasonably priced, excellent catalogue priced 50p.

Reliant Blinds, Asheridge Road, Chesham, Buckinghamshire (tel. Chesham [024 05] 75014). Curtaining costs a fortune but you can cut your bills by either using *blinds* alone at the windows (which can look a bit bleak), or by using blinds with 'fake' curtains – just a length of hemmed fabric hung permanently on either side of the window, never to be pulled. Mary Quant is design adviser to Reliant Blinds, so their patterns are as good as you would expect. There's also an excellent plain range – try golden sand for a cheerful morning glow, whether or not the sun is out: try chocolate or white for stark chic.

Rooksmoor Mills, Bath Road, nr Stroud, Gloucestershire GL5 5ND (tel. Amberley [045 387] 2577). Everybody adores them. Rooksmoor claim to be

the country's leading suppliers of *rush and maize matting*. It's sold made up to cover any size or shape area from a closet to a bathroom. Also supply their own beds with mattresses covered in real striped ticking, and a big range of *cane furniture* for indoors and outdoors. Selection of *carpeting* including their own Magic Carpet which, they say, is almost stainproof and everlasting.

Scotcade, 33–34 High Street, Bridg-north, Salop WV16 4HG (tel. Bridg-north [074 62] 61431). Has a small range of upmarket items, specializing in *discounted brand-name small elec-trical goods* such as Tower electric casseroles, pocket calculators, digital clocks – also gold and silver jewellery and cutlery. A lot of the discount is lost through the high added postage charges, but you can pay by Access or Barclaycard.

Kitchen specialists

Divertimenti, 68–72 Marylebone Lane, London W1M 5FF (tel. 01-935 0689). The best of British and continental *kitchen utensils*, cookware and table-ware, including a large selection of knives, saucepans, earthenware cook-ing pots, bottling and preserving equipment. Also stock the incredible Magimix machine. Useful section at the back of the catalogue on how to look after knives, pots and pans. Beautifully produced catalogue.

David Mellor, 4 Sloane Square, London SW1W 8EE (tel. 01-730 4259). Lovely seventy-page catalogue which is really a good cook's kitchen guide. Contains over 700 items of *kitchen equipment*, most of which are illustrated with beautifully drawn, clear pictures. Large selection of stainless steel and carbon steel knives, unusual shaped moulds, stewpots, preserving equipment and English and French pottery.

The General Trading Company, 144 Sloane Street, London s w 1 x 9 b l (tel. 01-730 0411). Shop here like the Royal Family do, for really exquisite *china*, *fine glass* and beautiful *cutlery* (silverplated classic knives with pistol-grip handles) as well as the most impeccable picnic baskets.

Lakeland Plastics, Alexandra Road, Windermere, Cumbria (tel. Windermere [096 62] 2255). Here you'll find everything you need for *home freezing*. Polythene bags and wrappings, rigid and foil containers, colour coding and labelling accessories (devise your own system), freezer baskets, knives and thermometers. They also run a free advisory service on freezing and have a good selection of books on the subject.

Presents

Global Village Crafts, South Petherton, Somerset (tel. South Petherton 40194). The sort of catalogue that's recommended by the *Guardian*. Wholesome, woven straw, handblocked Indian things, goodies from Peru, bamboo nutmeg graters from China and a whole host of other things that

you can do without, but are definitely fascinating and make good original *ethnic presents*. Possibly a good present for husbands-of-dieters to buy is the heavy cotton wrapover skirt from Rajashtan, which expands and contracts to fit all sizes (why not get it right for once?). Catalogue £1.

Sports and government surplus

Black and Edgington, 53 Rathbone Place, London w 1 p 1 a n (tel. 01-636 6645). For the best, toughest *sports equipment*, from sneaker shoelaces to tents. Specialists in family camping equipment, hill-walking clothing, rucksacks and backpacks. Sleeping bags also a speciality.

Laurence Corner, 62 Hampstead Road, London n w 1 (tel. 01-387 6134). The main store for government-surplus *camping, outdoor and protective wear*. For really cheap, chic, meaningful hats (solar topees, etc.), landgirl's breeches, nurses' capes and massed uniforms. Also cheap, down-to-earth (ho ho!) camping equipment and really good, cheap chunky sweaters.

Scout Shops, Churchill Industrial Estate, Lancing, Sussex b n 15 8 u g (tel. Lancing [09063] 5352). Are owned by the Scout Association. This is where you get the penknife with the thing for getting stones out of horses' hooves. Also tents, rucksacks, climbing boots, compasses, barbecues, emergency kits, axes and tin plates, etc.

Toys

Barnums Carnival Novelties, 67 Hammersmith Road, London w14 8uy (tel. 01-602 1211–4). If you want animal masks, crackers, Father Christmases, horror face masks, a mask for Hallowe'en or 1000 balloons with 'Happy Birthday Harry' on them; if you're running a fête, fair or fundraising event and need anything from bingo booklets to hoopla rings and carnival queen crowns; if you want to hire a marquee or a gold and white stall for indoor or outdoor fêtes. Genuine old street pianos for hire. An excellent catalogue for £1.25 (including postage). £1 is refunded to you if you return it within twelve months. Customers holding a catalogue receive a new price list twice a year and information about new items.

Galt Toys, Brookfield Road, Cheadle, Cheshire (tel. 061-428 8511). Galt are very serious about play. Specialists in good design, sturdy wood and tough materials, they believe that these 'tools of play' should help to develop and stimulate all abilities. Catalogue suggests toys most suitable for all age groups starting from three months (this year aunts needn't get it wrong). There are small wooden trains, trikes, rag dolls, old-fashioned brick sets, huge jig-saws, painting and printing materials. Also a large range of sturdy equipment for garden play, ranging from a climbing frame (expensive), see-saw and swings, to window-saving, bounce-back nets for cricket and tennis practice.

Hamleys, 200–202 Regent Street, London w1r 6bt (tel. 01-734 3161). The biggest toy shop of all. All the expensive adult-fantasy stuff that the childless believe every child wants. picture-filled catalogue helpfully divided up into department sections can even save Londoners from battling through the maddening Christmas crowds and hours of on-the-spot indecision. Good games, garden play equipment, dressing-up gear and what is known as party novelties. Free catalogue available in September: Christmas orders should be in by mid November.

Department store catalogues

I once had a baby on 12 December and did all my Christmas shopping by telephoning one store for twenty minutes. Until then I never realized how painless Christmas could be.

Unfortunately, many stores are cutting down on costs and catalogues seem to be disappearing. However, the following stores produce their catalogues in autumn and it is a wonderfully easy way to do your shopping if you can afford it (and you can if you buy small presents or books). You pick your choice from the catalogues and some firms will even do all the wrapping and posting for you. The only thing you have to do is pay the bill, with your order, by cheque or postal order, if you're not an account customer.

Try:

Harrods, Knightsbridge, London sw1
    (tel. 01-730 1234);

Fortnum and Mason, 181 Piccadilly, London w1 (tel. 01-734 8040) (gift ideas leaflet);

Robert Jackson, 172 Piccadilly, London w1 (tel. 01-493 1033) (gourmet foods, hampers and stocking fillers).

You can also get some ideas for Christmas presents by looking through the advertising pages of *The Times*, the *Sunday Times* and the *Observer*.

There are many firms offering food presents such as smoked salmon, whole York hams, whole cheeses, clotted cream, honey, as well as stocking fillers and so on.

Exchange & Mart advertise some really useful (and weird) things – also good for buying presents for collectors, such as old, unusual books, 78 records, medals, coins, toy soldiers, etc.

How to Convert

WHAT TO DO

Only those who have tried converting a house will know that I speak the truth when I say that a conversion is absolute hell, and that every conversion is a different sort of hell. Debutante converters don't want to hear this: instead they turn to those case histories in the glossies, which invariably end 'and six months later, we were holding our first candlelit dinner party'. In fact, it is far more likely that six months later you will have a nervous breakdown, because the builders are still on site, settling in for the winter and showing no sign of nervous strain.

Nevertheless, converting can be exciting and creative and rewarding, so don't be put off by what follows. But forewarned is forearmed: you're much more likely to be having that candlelit dinner party to schedule if you are prepared for the worst.

Improving your home is one of the few ways left to increase your capital assets without being taxed.

How you start depends whether you want to improve the place you live in now or whether you are thinking of buying a place and then improving it. If you're buying, you are now allowed to see the building society surveyor's report; formerly they wouldn't let you do this even though you had to pay for it. Pay enormous respect to it and study it with the utmost pessimism. A report on an old building is necessarily somewhat vague; it is often not possible to find out exactly what condition the building is in without almost tearing it apart.

Ideally, you should experience your building in all weathers before making decisions (this should take about a week in Britain). This is the time to change your mind, because later it will become very expensive.

Before you start, decide roughly what you want. It's important to distinguish between an improvement, which adds value to your house, and an indulgence, which doesn't, no matter what it costs. Don't decide to turn the house back to front just for the hell of it. The last occupant probably lived there quite efficiently and happily in its present condition.

WHAT TO AVOID

Victorian houses, with rooms on many levels, bay windows and thick walls, can be very difficult to convert. Georgian terrace houses are comparatively easy, because the windows are regular, the floors on one level and internal partitions are of light construction. Often the main reason for change is that there are only two rooms to a floor. This can probably be altered to three rooms a floor by building a small extension on the back to make kitchen and bathrooms.

Don't finally decide what you are going to do before showing your lists to your builder or architect, and hearing what he has to say about the expense and complexity of the work involved. Anything structural is going to involve a lot of money, and plumbing seems to cost more than emeralds. So don't set your heart on installing an extra lavatory as far away as possible from the present plumbing arrangements just because *you* find that this is the most convenient place for it. Some items, however, only *seem* to be as permanent as the foundations: it is often possible to move the stairs and the kitchen if you have some good reason for doing so.

WHAT TO SPEND

Having decided how much you can afford, you should consider whether you are justified in spending it – as an investment: whether, should you want to sell later, your house will fetch the price you paid for it, plus the cost of conversion. If not, you may still decide to go ahead, but you should again consider whether you really want to rip out the walls, go for a substantial open-plan scheme, knock two floors into one and build a 15-foot high cage for tropical birds in the middle (as Vanessa Redgrave did), because you might then end up with a property that would make an estate agent wince. On the other hand, you don't want to lose confidence and do something dull. In order that you don't spend more money on your home than you would recoup with a sale, before starting building work, find out the going rate and maximum prices for houses like yours in your area. Ask a local estate agent for a rough price.

Your first spending priority should be to protect your investment rather than improve it (you don't want your home to *lose* value). Get a surveyor to check that the house is watertight and has a sound roof, chimneys, guttering, pipes and drains, and to look for damaged brickwork, rising damp, rotting door or window frames. Get several estimates and a written guarantee if you're installing a damp course or removing dry rot.

WHAT ADDS TO THE VALUE OF YOUR HOUSE

Modernizing it altogether.
Modernizing the plumbing.
Modernizing the bathroom.
A second bathroom.
A second lavatory.
Modernizing the kitchen (but don't regard more than £1000 spent on this as adding to the value of your house).
Rewiring, if your electrical system is over thirty years old.
Making another bedroom by enlarging the attic or by adding a room on top of a garage, or with a prefabricated back extension (but it may not add to the investment value if you spend more than 20 per cent of the present value of your house).
Repainting.

Possibly a good investment, depending on how it's done
Building a wall to make one large bedroom into two small ones.
Knocking down a wall to reorganize the living space.
Moving the stairs.

What improvements may NOT add to the value of your house
Spending a lot on the kitchen.
Adding a sunroom, conservatory, garage or carport.
Knocking down the hall wall so you walk straight into the living-room.
Knocking two rooms into one.
Don't plan too small a new bathroom. Just as newly-marrieds always buy their first refrigerator a couple of sizes too small, they are also blissfully unaware of the amount of space that is needed for a baby, folding bath, baby chest and duck collection.

Personally, I'm against building-in all cupboard space, because doing so often destroys the proportions of a small room and leaves no space to move furniture around, and what woman doesn't like to do that occasionally? However, if you build wall-to-wall storage units, an important point to watch for is to add a polystyrene ceiling moulding (cove) along the top, to match the rest of the room. It costs little and avoids that ugly sawn-in-two look.

What not to do yourself, because it's dangerous and you need a skilled expert: any major job involving roof, walls, damp course, plumbing, loft floors, central heating boilers, gas or electrical appliances, dry rot or woodworm, bricklaying, plastering or drains.

A major conversion is not much cheaper (it may cost even more) than a new home. Generally speaking, the shell represents one third of the cost of a new house; finishes, services and equipment account for the other two thirds.

GETTING EXTRA ROOM

If you can get more room by building an extension, I would do this any time: moving is more expensive and more unsettling than you ever allow for, and the money involved is money down the drain, whereas a well-planned extension (and there are several really good prefabricated systems available) can be a sound investment. Choose between a *package deal* and a *standard extension*.

A package deal is the design and construction of a tailor-made extension which provides one or two extra rooms in the attic or at ground level at the back of the house. It might be to enlarge your kitchen or add a WC, bathroom, granny apartment, or an extra bedroom. A package-deal system should do all the work for you, involving initial consultancy (free), design, survey, drawings, liaising with the local authority, plumbing, and electrical work. They sometimes offer finance (which, as I write, qualifies for tax relief as a house improvement loan) and are well, well worth it if you proceed cautiously with an experienced firm.

A standard extension is not tailor-made but there's a choice of good lightweight, prefabricated construction systems. You are responsible for providing the concrete base slab on which to erect the walls and roof. Pay particular attention to the insulation.

GETTING THE MONEY TO PAY FOR IT

1 Try asking your building society for an additional mortgage. Tax relief is normally allowed on mortgages of up to £25,000 (this must be for a main or only residence).
2 Tax relief is also allowed on a bank loan for home improvement (so make sure that your loan is so labelled), but not on money lent for home repairs or general maintenance.
3 Ask your local council for a loan at mortgage rates.

Can you get any free money?

You can get up to £2500 free money to help improve an old house, if you go about it in the right way and comply with council conditions. Thoroughly investigate the possibilities of a grant: be persistent and don't be put off by having to swim through bureaucratic treacle.

You can almost certainly get a grant if your house has no proper drainage, damp course, bathroom or kitchen. Grants are not supposed to help you to improve a modern house or add on extra bedrooms but to improve and extend the life of old housing. You can't get a grant for a building that was built or converted after 1961. If the rateable value is over £400 in London or £225 anywhere else you won't be eligible for an improvement grant, but you may get a different grant.

There are four types of grant. An *improvement grant* is yours *as a right* to improve old houses, provided you comply with certain conditions. Normally this is to help meet expenses of up to £5000 for a house and up to £5800 for a house of more than three storeys that's being converted into more than one dwelling.

An *intermediate grant* is to provide

a house with standard amenities for the first time, including replacements or essential repairs, such as installing a hot or cold water supply or a sink or a bath. This is *also your right*, and the grant will help to meet up to £1200 for new amenities or £1500 for repair or replacement work.

A *special grant* is a discretionary grant for landlords to improve bed-sitter accommodation or a house shared by people not in the same family. You get this only if you are *not* converting the building into flats.

A *repair grant* is a discretionary grant for houses within a Housing Action or General Improvement area and the maximum eligible expense is £1500.

Find out about grants at the home improvement office of your town hall or through your architect (one who knows the local ropes can be of great help here). My local builder advises you to telephone the grant application office at the town hall. Allow four to five telephone calls daily over two weeks to get the permissions. Fifty telephone calls isn't much for £2500 tax free. Here's what you have to do to get it.

1 Prove your ownership at the Land Registry Office.
2 Get permission from your building society.
3 Get agreement from any sitting tenant.
4 Get planning permission from the local authority; this involves simple before-and-after plans, not necessarily architect's plans.
5 Get permission from the sewage department.
6 Comply with fire prevention regulations if the building is to be sub-divided.

The drawbacks

1 The great drawback to obtaining a grant is the time it takes to get a decision. After you have all those proofs and permissions, and have applied for a grant, it may be six weeks before an official comes to inspect your place and another six to eight weeks to process your application. And if you've already moved in, you won't want to hang around with three children and no lavatory for three months. Don't book a builder until you have a grant, because he won't want to hang around waiting for a 'yes' or 'no' from the council. When you do get a 'yes' you may then have to wait for the builder. *On no account* go ahead with putting in the damp course, or whatever, in a reasonable manner, before you have a decision. You may not get your grant. Bureaucracy discourages efficiency. Most local authorities will give you permission to go ahead after their initial inspection, but at your own risk and in no way committing themselves to giving any grant.
2 Once you have a grant you can expect regular inspections to make sure you're complying with building regulations. That's reasonable.
3 The grant will usually cover only up to *half the total cost* of the work,

although some local authorities will lend you the other half on mortgage terms. In the case of houses within a Housing Action or General Improvement area, the half may be increased to 75 per cent and 60 per cent respectively.

4 Generally the grant won't be paid until the work has been completed to the authority's satisfaction, so you may still have to organize a bridging bank loan to cover payment of work until it has been completed.

CHOOSING YOUR EXPERT

(Surveyor, architect, builder, direct labour)

If only for an initial consultation you should invest in a professional adviser and I can't stress this too strongly. Never ask a friend for professional advice, if only because you haven't a legal leg to stand on if things go wrong. Moreover, professionals generally resent giving free advice, and paying for it can be cheaper than losing a friend.

A surveyor can advise you if you're thinking of doing work yourself (for instance, you want to know which walls are load-bearing, if you're thinking of knocking any down). Generally you should ask for a full structural survey, which will include structure, timber, main fittings and approximate cost of any recommended repairs. But don't ask for a valuation unless you need it, because this is expensive.

You will have to ask and pay extra for a report on drains, electrical wiring and central heating; get a heating engineer to check on that.

A surveyor's report is a document of doom that makes you feel as if the house is about to crumble around your ears. Treat it calmly but with respect. Perhaps you can use it to beat down the price of the house by deducting from the asking price the amount that will be needed for repairs, according to this survey. One man I spoke to complained because the drains cost him an extra unscheduled £850. His surveyor's report had said, 'Drains not tested and do not look satisfactory', but he crossed his fingers and hoped for the best. The best is not going to happen in your conversion, either. You can't be too pessimistic.

There is no set survey fee, so make sure you start out your conversion career by agreeing one. Currently, it should cost from £50 to £100 for a full structural survey for a three- to five-bedroom house. Get a qualified surveyor from a local reputable estate agent or the Royal Institute of Chartered Surveyors (RICS).

At a later stage a surveyor can also draw plans to get local authority consent, write the specification, get tenders from builders and supervise site work. He won't do this work for nothing, so check how much it's going to cost you. Don't consult an interior designer if any structural work is involved. He may not have had the necessary training and experience, he may not be insured and you won't have the twelve-year comeback that one has against architects. The more complicated your job, the more essential it is that you consult an expert.

Never convert for the first time without consulting a good, experienced architect. A consultation to discuss the problem on site will cost only a few pounds. He should be able to recognize the full potential of the building for your needs. You may think that you can do this unaided, but a good architect can (because of his training and experience) usually suggest better ideas, and also ways to save money. He doesn't impose his taste on yours: he translates *your* taste.

Architects' fees should be paid according to the standard scale in the RIBA's Conditions of Engagement. Get a copy from RIBA Publications Ltd, Finsbury Mission, Moreland Street, London EC1V 8VB (tel. 01-251 0791).

The cost will vary according to the service you want – preliminary advice; plans; a scheme design with plans, outline specifications and estimated cost (expect a charge of around 5 per cent of the estimated total cost); or a full architectural service.

The full fee for conversion work is about $12\frac{1}{2}$ per cent of the total cost of the job. If you don't want the architect to supervise you can knock 3 per cent off that but in my opinion it would be sheer folly to do so. The supervision work is the part that makes strong women weep and marriages split. The full service consists of analysis of your requirements; relating these to the

existing structure; drawing the designs; getting planning approval and building regulations approval; drawing up the specification of work to be done; putting the job out to tender to different builders and choosing the best quotation; drawing up the building contract; checking that the work is done and up to standard.

The difficulty of finding a good architect to handle a conversion is that most good architects don't want to do this sort of work. It is not considered creative, the client's personality and furnishings are bound to be dominant, the budget is always tight, and there is a vast amount of supervisory work and site visits involved for a very small creative and financial return.

Many architects prefer not to work for friends or agree to suspend the friendship for the duration of the contract; the chances that you will never be friends again are high. Things can go badly wrong through no fault of yours or his, but any bitterness can persist as long and as sourly as between the divorced. If the work is disastrous, or never gets completed, you won't like to sue a friend. But it is accepted as part of the deal that you can sue your architect and he is, as a matter of course, insured against this possibility. Remember that architects remain legally responsible for their work for twelve years afterwards.

If you have a friend who is an architect the best thing to do is to ask him for a recommendation. He should both understand and respect this attitude. Alternatively, find a satisfied client. If an architectural practice is recommended, make sure that you are going to deal with the same partner. Or you can write and ask for a list of qualified architects in your area from the Client Advisory Service of the Royal Institute of British Architects (RIBA), 66 Portland Place, London W1N 4AD (tel. 01-580 5533). Make it clear what sort of work is to be done and how much you are thinking of spending. If you merely want an extra bathroom you won't want an architect who specializes in running up blocks of flats. It isn't absolutely necessary to use a local architect, but a local architect probably knows the capabilities (or otherwise) of local builders, electricians and carpenters.

A newly-qualified architect will probably be brimming over with ideas, and will put in hours of love and care on the detail drawings, but my attitude is that I can't afford to train a new architect on my job. It's too expensive, and the men on the site will probably be able to run circles round a novice.

If the architect needs any specialist advice, perhaps from a structural engineer or quantity surveyor, he chooses them and you pay them.

Tell the architect your *real* budget. Do this in writing and make it clear that you can't get your mitts on one more pound. Do not go back on this. An architect once asked me despairingly why it is always so difficult to get a client to say how much he wants to spend. One of the reasons for the caginess of the client may be that he believes architects to be artistic chaps who are vague about money, so he wants to keep a little something in reserve. This is bad practice, because one of the architect's professional responsibilities is to stick to the mutually agreed budget, and he can be legally held to this, and made to pay up for any extra incurred by him without your written approval.

There are three major causes of extra expense:

Mistakes, such as measuring up a room 10 cm (4 inches) short, so that a new set of panelling has to be bought. The firm who makes the mistake should pay the extra cost.

Changes of mind on the part of the client. Such as deciding to install central heating when seven eighths of the work has been completed. The client pays for this and the extra redecorating and making-good involved.

Nasty surprises – known as contingencies. Even after the best surveys unexpected snags are apt to come to light as hidden faults in the old structure are exposed. Allow 15 per cent for contingencies alone. As some builders tend to find extras up to the contingency sum allowed, put 10 per cent in the contract and be prepared to go 5 per cent over the top. This is a secret between the architect and the client that the builder should not know about.

The contract, which is drawn up between the builder and the architect, can settle on a fixed price, although this naturally does not cover changes of mind, or extras.

A lawyer who has been through it all asked me particularly to add that it cannot be taken for granted that an agreement exists between architect and builder. In conversion work, or, indeed, in any work costing not more than, say, £5000, there is often an appalling lack of the kind of specification that anybody could understand and rely upon (or indeed any specification at all). It cannot be stressed enough how vital it is that the builder is made to explain, in much greater detail than he is willing to, what exactly will be provided. And the same applies to an architect. It is also vital that the architect's drawings should be discussed and *fully understood by the client*, and that elementary questions (such as whether there is sufficient fall in the land to allow for a sewage pipe) have been considered by him before he devises his plans.

YOUR BRIEF, THE SPECIFICATION, AND THE PLANS

The next job is to discuss with the architect what you want. Make sure that well in advance of this meeting you and your mate have *thoroughly* discussed (a) what you want and (b) how much you can spend. Arguments in front of the architect are expensive for you and bewildering for him. Decide which of you is to deal with the architect. *Don't both of you do it.* And don't appeal to him as umpire to decide whether a dishwasher is more important than a second lava-

tory (as always in conversions, the answer is 'it depends'), or whether pink would be best although Fred prefers beige.

Crystallize your ideas by collecting a folder of scraps and ideas, including other people's conversions, cut out of magazines or technical journals. This will probably amount to ten different styles, but at least it's a talking point from which to narrow down to one brief. Get what you want down on paper. You might start by writing three little lists.

Phase 1: Necessities; these might be to reroof or to straighten out Dickensian plumbing.

Phase 2: Subsequent priorities; these might be changing a window into glass doors or refitting the kitchen.

Phase 3: What you'd like to do if or when you can afford it; might be fitting a sauna bath in the cellar.

You will be truly astounded by the architect's estimate of the cost, but it is likely to be a fairly accurate one. You then scrap Phase 3 and the architect prepares his brief. This is a summary of what you want the finished scheme to look like and provide. It will probably be illustrated by simple diagrams and perhaps drawings. Keep a copy of everything for checking against what actually gets done.

Once you've approved this, the architect draws up a *specification* which he puts out to tender; to get prices for the work from different building firms. You then scrap Phase 2, having got a clear idea of what you can't afford. You then decide on a builder and go through the specification again in an effort to make savings on his price.

You and your mate slash it savagely. The architect then does an even more vicious hatchet job. You then revise the specification after considerable argument and a few tears over essentials which have been demoted to luxuries, such as the cleaning cupboard. You now realize that a lot of your necessities are, in fact, luxuries. You may even decide that the architect and the building firm are luxuries and say good-bye to them. You will, of course, have to pay the architect for his services so far.

It is important to realize that an architect can be legally entitled to be paid his full fee (i.e. a percentage of the total building costs) whether or not the building actually takes place, and whether or not he does any useful supervision. Do not take the latter for granted. Make sure you get it in writing.

Your sketch plan

You need some sort of a sketch plan of the floor layout to help you sort out your ideas, discuss them with builder and architect and, perhaps, to get planning permission. It helps if you can get copies of the house plans either from your deeds or from plans that may already be in the possession of your local authority. If not, a builder, surveyor or architect's assistant can produce them quickly and fairly cheaply. Don't try to do *accurate* plans yourself. It will take ages and you risk inaccuracy.

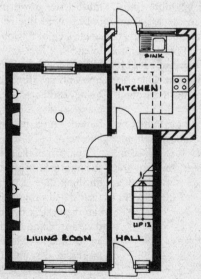

When looking at the plans remember that:

The top of the page is north (unless otherwise stated).

The thick black lines are the walls.

New brickwork has a diagonal line pattern.

Dotted lines are walls that may be demolished.

Two thin parallel lines are windows, the cheese wedge is a door and the stripes are stairs.

A little ○- or ▽ shows individual power and lighting points.

All people over-estimate the amount of room in a sketch plan, and the finished rooms are always smaller than they envisaged. There is always less room to move among the furniture than there seemed on paper. This is because they forgot to allow for their own size. You take up more room than you think. You are at least 45 cm (18 inches) wide and need another 30 cm (12 inches) to allow for elbow room. To get a better idea, cut out a bit of paper the size of an armchair (on plan), label it 'self' and push it around the drawing.

Whether for plans or anything else on your job, never use student labour. This is *not* cheaper. It may seem cheaper before you start but you are far more likely to get slower work and mistakes: he is *not* qualified or experienced.

HOW TO HANDLE A BUILDER

If you haven't a local architect or surveyor the best way to choose a builder is by recommendation from someone who's employed one (recently). Otherwise, look in the *Yellow Pages* (*always* follow up references) or get suggestions (without responsibility) from the National Federation of Building Trade Employers (NFBTE). A small builder is generally far cheaper and easier to deal with than a large builder because you deal with the productive people at only one remove and there are rarely any unproductive people.

Never ask a builder to estimate without a written specification. If you have to arrange this without professional help, write 'For total work and materials involved' after each item. That 'total' is all-important. Never leave *anything* to the discretion of the builder: this is asking for trouble. You must write down in clear language (which need not be technical) every single step of the job, from beginning to end.

Type four copies of your specification and get three firms (at least) to quote. Estimates are always free. You may be surprised to find that one builder's price may be double that of another.

Apart from the price the vital thing to confirm is your builder's start and finishing date. I also like to ask for their dated progress plan so that you can then check by how much (not if) they are falling behind – not for any legal, binding reason but because it means, at least, that the builder has to give some thought to advance planning, instead of plucking a date out of the air. The time to ask for this plan, which they won't want to give you, is just before signing the contract – your maximum moment of power. It's reasonable to ask for it – you merely want to know the date and work progress calculations that the builder made in order to arrive at the final finishing date. If you don't get this time plan before the contract is signed, you are unlikely to get it afterwards.

Dates of payment should also be arranged in advance. A small job lasting only a few weeks is generally paid upon completion. Anything bigger generally involves stage payment in monthly arrears. Arrange that this is done in accordance with a 'time-and-work-completed schedule'. I don't suppose that you will mind paying them earlier if the work is completed faster than anticipated: I doubt if you will be called upon to do so.

You or (more likely) your architect may be able to arrange a penalty clause if the work isn't finished on time. I have had such an arrangement: the penalty sum wasn't very big but I suspect that had the arrangement not existed I would still be without door-knobs, locks, window panes, etc.

An architect should also be responsible for approving interim payments. He issues the builder with a certificate of work inspected and approved (check that he has inspected it). The builder gives you the certificate and you pay up, by pre-agreement.

A small part of the payment should always be withheld until the job has been completed to your satisfaction, say 10 per cent for six weeks after

both sides agree that the job is finished, or $2\frac{1}{2}$ per cent for six months. This means that you have more chance of getting those tedious, little, time-consuming finishing touches completed and anything broken along the way mended.

Once chosen, your builder should write a formal letter on the firm's writing paper, giving his total price for the job *and* materials excluding extras, which are to be accepted by him only on a written, signed and dated order from the client, Mrs X or Mr X (but not two people). Get the builder to also write his price on the final page of two copies of the specification, together with his name, the name of his firm, the date and their stamp.

It's reasonable for a builder to cover himself in a quotation by stipulating that it doesn't allow for decayed timber, defective brickwork and other – literally – unforeseeable items. Do not regard these as an added expense. Allow for them in your budget as an unforeseeable expense. Always get the cost of any such extra work agreed in writing before the work is put in hand.

Once you have accepted your builder, *always* try to cut down on his estimate before finally accepting it. (Again, this is far easier if you have an architect or surveyor.) In order to do this you will have to know what each item costs, which means that the builder will have to price it, which he won't like doing at all. But, again, you can sweetly point out that he must know what each item costs, in order to arrive at the finished price. Once you have a detailed, itemized list you can always cut things out or cut to cheaper finishes, and you will be in an even better position when it comes to arguing about extras at the end. (It always comes to arguing about extras in the end.)

One woman, a home editor married to a brilliant international designer, told me that the conversion point at which she nearly tottered into a nursing home was when she saw the bill for extras. 'You have to argue about things that seem insane, such as whether the price of a central heating system described as "all inclusive" should include the flue,' she said. 'Builders have an amazing capacity to leave things out of a voluminous specification and then invoice you for them afterwards, as if they had planned the extras right from the beginning.' *Moral:* Check the specification not only for what's on it but for what might have been left out. Professional advice can be invaluable at this point.

Never pay a builder in advance for anything, ever. If he can't run his business so that he has enough money to pay for a few bricks and other advance materials, then you don't want to entrust your money to this fellow. If you have to pay for special fittings then pay the firm that supplies them *direct*. Get the invoice sent to you and *see* the fitting before paying it. The building trade is notorious for bankruptcies.

Before signing the contract ask your builder to confirm on his firm's headed writing paper (dated and signed) that the firm is properly insured for third party liability, otherwise you might be responsible if the scaffolding collapses on the plumber or a carpenter is electrocuted. You should also tell your own insurers (recorded delivery) that you are indulging in building work and make sure that your existing policy covers fire damage to work in progress and is perhaps increased to cover the new value of your building.

Agree with the builder who will be responsible for your work and to whom all instruction, queries and criticism can be directed. In other words, who's the foreman. Specify in your contract that a working foreman should be on site during *all* normal working hours, and that any extra or different work is only to be done if signed and dated instructions are given by one of you to this foreman.

Never change your mind or add one single extra after building work has started, unless some major error becomes apparent. Such changes are not only very, very expensive (because you're at their mercy, and have to agree to their price) but – much more important – they will mean that the work will take longer and this will give the builder a perfect excuse for not sticking to his time plan. Not sticking to the time plan is what is most likely to drive you to depression/drink/despair.

DEALING WITH DIRECT LABOUR

I don't think you can do this, as a

matter of course, if you have a full-time job outside the home. I *have* done it (and in another country at that) with no problems, but I'm still amazed, and it can be attributed to luck. In general it is as likely to happen as the Duke of Edinburgh dropping in to help with the bricklaying.

However, if you are available and can be called on at any time, if you are prepared to regard dealing with direct time labour as a proper part-time job, if you have had previous experience (preferably bad) of a conversion job, if you can discipline yourself into having the necessary firm, tough, untrusting nature and are prepared to forget the words 'kind' and 'reasonable', I don't see why you shouldn't run your own contract. This might save up to 40 per cent of the basic cost of the job, which is what the building firms slap on for overheads.

It is possible to use a small builder for the foundations, concrete, brickwork and plaster work, and *then* directly employ electricians, plumbers, central heating engineers and installers, carpenters and decorators (generally in that order). Hire them to specification and get that dated, signed, and a written price for it. You should also get these specialist subcontractors to buy any necessary materials at wholesale or discount prices. See the goods on site and the (dated) bill before paying it.

But don't make a major move without having a survey, a specification, a set of plans and a price in advance from your direct labour which is clearly stated on paper. If you decide

to use direct labour, let your surveyor or architect know this before he writes the specification; he can then separate it into a separate specification for each subcontractor.

With the exception of British plumbers, with whom I've had dreadful, dramatic and expensive experiences dating back over the last twenty years, I like dealing with labour direct. You make payments in stages, they submit bills for materials, you check that the materials have been used (count the doorknobs) and generally keep track of what you promise them and what and when you pay them, writing it in one simple exercise book, *always* dating the entries and getting them to sign for money you have paid. All you need is this one book, in which everything, but *everything*, is written down.

The only difficult part, of course, is organizing them all to come at the right time and, believe me, this can be more difficult than organizing a debutante ball. Again, a consultant architect or surveyor can be a great help in planning this timing sequence. Always contact them to check several days before they are due to start and *never* behave well if they don't.

Once your workmen have started the job, don't you be understanding or stiff-upper-lipped or anything but tough and straight. Certainly if you're in charge of the job don't threaten to tell your husband. They don't care a bit and it weakens your position for ever.

Before they all appear on site, decide:

Where they are going to put their equipment (ladders, concrete mixer, masses of dusty dust sheets, etc.).

Where they are going to have their meals and make their tea and get any water.

What the lavatory and washing situation is.

No two buildings are the same and it's obviously not possible to encapsulate all the sequences of building work in one paragraph (which is what I'm about to do), but you might use the following sequence as a guide. Discuss it first with your architect, surveyor, building inspector or local planning department. Although the latter can be a bit of a pain, they can also be very, very helpful.

Demolition, foundation digging, prepare for sewage, damp-proofing or dry rot treatment, brickwork, laying solid floors, walls and structural repairs, roofing and guttering, internal walls, plumbing, heating, electrical (remember telephone), plastering, glasswork, painting and decorating.

This list isn't all-inclusive and it probably isn't in the right order for your job, but at some point you've got to work out that the sewage obviously has to go in at the same time as the foundations and before the solid floor, and all the other operations must be similarly planned. Use a critical path method (see further on) to co-ordinate the right sequence of events for your job, whether it be new work, an addition or a conversion.

MEN AT WORK???

Make two resolutions when you are ready for the workmen to move in. Do not go away while the work is in progress, and don't make plans for after it is finished. I have known some builders drink the cellar dry, use a new sofa as a carpenter's bench (a favourite trick, this) and wreck a newly-finished kitchen (newly finished by them). Try to get your job done in summer. Of course, everyone else is trying, but it is so much more endurable to be un-expectedly without heat, light, water or lavatories for long periods in the summer.

Be prepared for broken promises, poor workmanship, non-appearance of such star performers as the electrician, new goods that arrive damaged or are quickly damaged, new goods that are immediately installed in the wrong place or the wrong way. Always discreetly check on work done *after* the builders have left for the night and always bring up any queries with the foreman the very next morning, before work starts again.

YOUR CRITICAL PATH

This is a sort of time plan on one

sheet, like a school timetable. Buy a piece of cardboard, about 50 × 75 cm (20 × 30 inches), tough enough to withstand constant handling for several months, and mark it off in squares. Divide it vertically into weeks and horizontally into the people you are about to be served by, or possibly do battle with: *Architect, Plumber, Electrician* and so on, right down through the list of subcontractors. Fill in the dates when these people say that they will be arriving to do something at your place and when they say they will have left, having done it. These people can be fey and elusive. You may find it extremely difficult to pin any of them down to a given month, let alone day, but it is very important that you do this before work starts. (If you have an architect, he should do it anyway, but you can still be checking.)

Pin this board in front of your telephone (or somewhere central, if you haven't got one) and attach a diary to it, to use as a log-book for making notes. Record in the log-book all instructions and dates of arrival of important materials and fittings. If you suspect that the men aren't turning up as arranged, jot down the number of men that turn up daily – if this tends to be only from 11 to 12.30 a.m. you can argue with your builder from a strong position (although be prepared for him to imply that this log-book of yours is sheer fantasy, a cunning attempt on your part to force him to doubt his own sanity, like Ingrid Bergman in *Gaslight*). This book will also be useful if you have to resort to law (and if you have to,

don't threaten – do it). However, the more you prepare for trouble the less likely it is to happen, because the builder realizes right from the beginning that you are a force to be reckoned with.

The plan and diary log-book will not only help you to keep track of what isn't happening, it will also somehow absorb your spleen and keep you sane. It is also useful if you finally get on to the solicitor, because he will be impressed by your accuracy, so long as you sound forty degrees cooler than you feel.

Buy a large office duplicate book in which to scrawl all relevant letters, then you automatically have a date-order filing system. *And* confirm all site conference decisions in it. Keep every scrap of paper relating to the job, even notes made by the electrician on the back of a dirty envelope.

When dealing with workmen you must be polite, controlled, relentless, pessimistic and trust to your own powers of reasoning, however inadequate these may be considered. If you don't understand what it is they're asking your permission to do, don't *ever* tell them to do what they think is best. Make them keep on explaining until you understand the logic of it – or lack of logic. You may feel embarrassed at first when insisting on one-syllable explanations, but remember who is footing the bill. And if they can't explain it, the odds are that it isn't logical.

Be prepared for men who come to mend one thing to break another before leaving. One woman I know who spent £6000 on a conversion had to have double glazing panels replaced three times. Carpenters hammered a nail through the same water pipe three times in succession. The vinyl tile floor, laid by experts, oozed bitumen for weeks afterwards. All the towel rails fell off the walls. None of the locks locked. The men who came to treat the woodworm knocked a can of dark brown, smelly, ineradicable liquid over the newly-tiled hall floor. Also mice ate through the PVC cable and fused all the lighting, but I count this an Act of God.

Be tough, but keep calm at all times, because temper will get you nowhere when commenting on non-co-ordination of deliveries ordered months beforehand. Contractors have a habit of ordering things a week before they need them, when the items are on a three- or four-month delivery. Check this doesn't happen in your case. Check, and be seen to check, the delivery date quoted on all items, and put the delivery notes on your critical path.

HOW YOU CAN HELP THEM

Finally, which of *your* actions most madden those to whom you have entrusted your conversion?

Architects don't like those who have no idea of the true cost of building work and who stagger back, disbelievingly, clutching their breasts when informed of the true facts.

Instructions should come from either husband or wife, but not both. You and your husband should act with the builders and architect rather as you should in front of the children. Keep a calm, united front and always back each other. Do not argue in front of the workmen. Bottle it up until they've gone home. Nobody likes changes of plan once work is in progress, even if you are willing to pay for it.

No one can stand a client living on the job or moving in on the date that the job was supposed to be finished, even when she has had to move out of her previous home on that date. However, my own view is that if you don't move in, they will never move out.

HOW TO CONVERT AND STAY SANE

Of course, there *are* wonderful workmen, who finish the job on time and are a positive pleasure to have around the house, singing as they go, like Snow White's seven dwarfs. If that's the sort of artisan you have, he won't mind a progress check: 'Ho ho, we're two days ahead of schedule,' he will chuckle, peering indulgently at your Critical Path, as he makes you a cup of tea. But you can't rely on it, so remember the boy scout's motto and BE PREPARED – for THE WORST!

In many conversion jobs there comes a point at which women start to break down, and marriages start to break up. So be quiet but firm, *right from the beginning*. No fluttering hands, no pretty little wails of, 'Oh, but it *must* be finished by the 27th because ...' This simply doesn't work. They don't *care*. Furthermore, they see through this old-fashioned, female 'charm-the-artisan' gambit.

The 'British worker' is an optimist, especially when it comes to work. He always undercalculates the time it will take. Before he starts your job he has arranged to take on another one six weeks later with another lady who is going to feel exactly the same as you do about getting the job finished. And there's another poor soul waiting after that one. So he works hard on the start of your job, but then mysteriously disappears, then turns up for two hours, or for a quick cup of tea, then dashes back to his other job. Then he's off to Mrs No. 3, like a sort of Latin lover, awash with tea. And remember, there was another woman *before* you who is probably still waiting for him.

On the whole, British workmen seem to think that a woman's time is less valuable than theirs. They will not make exact appointments. They are *really surprised* if you reproach them for not turning up on the day that they said they would; they expect *you* to take time off from your work (perhaps losing money by doing so) or hang around the place the whole week just in case they turn up a few days after they said they would.

Abroad, this attitude is called the British Disease. Prepare for it with your log-book and your very visible, pinned-up-on-the-wall Critical Path

(do a copy before you start, in case the first mysteriously gets destroyed) which you will use efficiently to keep track of their inefficiency.

Your chart will not *cause* any trouble unless some artisan tries to use it as a magic scapegoat. It will not *prevent* any trouble. It is merely an accurate record of what was arranged, what has happened and what has not happened, and without it you will be *sunk*, with not a leg to stand on (which is why some artisans take exception to it).

Inefficient people do not like having their lies and broken promises calmly recorded. It makes them uneasy. Be prepared for a little male chauvinist flak, because it is very important that you recognize it as such, or you may start to doubt your sanity. Your husband will probably side with the builder, architect, designer or whoever it is because he is an *expert* and you are not.

Don't assume that the professionals are the good guys; the architect or that chap from the builder in the decent suit. The architect may be gullible and the foreman just tell you a different, up-market brand of lie. The situation may easily deteriorate into a difficult-to-pin-down situation, when they gang up on you. You are 'difficult' if you expect things to happen as arranged: they prefer not to visit your place, they explain to their boss as if you had chicken pox. No, they never say why, but this idea may *also* get subtly put across to your husband. He may even tell you to stop being 'difficult'. If so, what you should do is have a look at your Critical Path and give the following thought a try out: *You are not crazy: they are!* You are chief victim and star witness. This is important, because this is the point at which you are (understandably) likely to get 'hysterical'.

This is the point at which you start to feel there *is* no point. You wish you'd never thought of it, you can't think how you got into it and you want to get out of it and never see the builder again. At this point, DON'T sack your builder and hand the job over to your husband, or you will probably be in a *worse* situation. Better the builder you know than the builder you don't know. The next lot will be just as bad; nobody likes finishing someone else's job, and if they do they have a marvellous built-in excuse for getting it wrong.

Your husband may at this point feel impelled to take over. I don't know your husband but what I do know is that:

1 If he had been 'in charge' of the job whatever has just happened would probably have happened anyway.
2 If he is able to handle contractors efficiently he would probably have done so in the first place.
3 If this job somehow got delegated to you in the first place he will probably to some degree resent taking it over, and resent it even more if he can't get better results than you. His tedious male machismo is then at risk.

The inefficient resent the efficient.

In particular, men who are lazy in the head (which is the most common cause of inefficiency) resent an efficient woman. But efficiency is your *only* form of self-protection, when your money and sanity are involved, on a conversion job. There are three things to remember if chaos is (perhaps) to be avoided. The first is (1), as I've said earlier, to write into the contract an on-site, supervising foreman *at all times*. (2) Don't avoid your first showdown. Remember, right from the beginning, that the first showdown will probably occur and prepare for it: don't get familiar with them. Be pleasant and polite but keep your log-book and your distance: it's much more difficult to have a five-star row with a man you've been charming deliberately. You *must* be taken seriously and they are not used to taking women seriously and, sad to say, if you're on your own, with no back-up feller, then you will be taken even less seriously. Your first show-down is an important stage in your conversion programme. Like teaching puppies not to wet the carpet, never let them get away with it the first time. Give them an inch and they'll take a liberty. Make the biggest, showy, all-star fuss you can: this is the first battle and if you win it hands down things will be much easier in future. (3) Your weapon is the only thing that you've got and they want – money. So hang on to the money. They'll come whining to you when the payment is due but the work has not been done. Refuse it. Therefore never arrange payments on a date alone, but for work completed by that date. And never pay in advance or your workmen may simply disappear.

There is only one way to *try* and get the job finished. That is by keeping the same builder, keeping cool, keeping informed, keeping track of what happens and (most important) keeping as much money as possible in *your* hands until it is ALL FINISHED.

WHERE TO GET AN EXPERT

If you don't know where to start looking for an expert you can get in touch with your local house maintenance improvers and repairers through the following professional bodies:

Royal Institute of British Architects, 66 Portland Place, London W1N 4AD (tel. 01-580 5533)

Royal Institution of Chartered Surveyors, 12 Great George Street, London SW1P 3AD (tel. 01-930 5322)

National Federation of Roofing Contractors, 18 Holborn Viaduct, London WC1V 6SP (tel. 01-248 6893)

National Federation of Building Trade Employers, 82 New Cavendish Street, London W1M 8AD (tel. 01-580 4041)

National Association of Plumbing, Heating and Mechanical Services Contractors, 6 Gate Street, London WC2 (tel. 01-405 2678)

Institute of Plumbing, North Street, Hornchurch, Essex RM11 1RU (tel. Hornchurch [040 24] 45199)

Electrical Contractors Association, 55 Catherine Place, Westminster, London SW1 (tel. 01-828 2932)

National Inspection Council for Electrical Installation Contracting, 93 Albert Embankment, London SE1 (tel. 01-582 7746)

British Wood Preserving Association, Suite 71, 62 Oxford Street, London W1N 9WD (tel. 01-580 3185)

There is no professional body that deals with *house deterioration*. Get advice from your local town hall or a chartered surveyor. Get quotations from firms such as Rentokil for damp proofing, dry rot, pest control and insulation.

ADVICE AND CONSENT

Building regulations and local by-laws can be complicated and they differ from place to place.

Never start altering, improving or building anything extra without first checking whether any permission to do so is needed. If it is, then get it. Otherwise you may be forced to demolish the work you have just done.

Ask your town hall to advise you (ask for the building control office). Allow at least six weeks for getting permission.

Planning permission is not concerned with interior work unless you are changing the use of a building or dividing it into flats. It is concerned with the way land is developed and the juxtaposition of buildings – generally speaking the look, amenities and population density of the area. Once given planning permission is valid for five years. You don't need planning permission for an extension which doesn't increase the size by volume (as it was in 1948 or when built) of your building by more than one tenth, or 115 cubic metres, which should be big enough for most extensions.

Building regulations deal with safety and hygiene. They don't affect certain outbuildings such as a garden shed, a porch or greenhouse of the approved size. Once given, approval is valid for three years. Approval is needed for:

alterations to structural work;
alterations to walls or ceiling;
new or extended rooms;
new or altered stairways;
new or altered drainage or flue pipes;
a new lavatory.

Make sure the builder has obtained any necessary consents if you've arranged for him to do this, if you haven't an architect, because it's *your* responsibility to comply with local regulations.

You may have other private restrictions, so *check the deeds*. They may prevent you from having a window that overlooks a neighbour's or from building in the garden. *Check the mortgage conditions*.

If you are making any alterations in the *plumbing*, you will need permission from your local public health department, which will also check your drains, if you have any doubts about them. The local authority is generally very helpful about advising

you on any plumbing or draining problems.

All new *electricity, gas and water systems* should be checked by the appropriate local board. The local electricity board should be able to advise you on electrical appliances, wiring and rewiring. If you're not satisfied that they're doing this job properly, write direct to ask for action to the Marketing Department of the Electricity Council, 30 Millbank, London sw1 (tel. 01-834 2333).

THE CONVERTER'S CREED

(to summarize ...)

Our motto: Extras are always extra expensive

1 Always get a recommendation in writing from the professional or trade organization of the fellow you're about to hire. This includes *everyone* from the architect to the subcontractors. Make sure they're not being recommended by their mother or sister: speak to the recommenders, rather than write.
2 Always get the price for *anything or anyone* in advance, *in writing*, dated.
3 Always get a guarantee where applicable.
4 Always try to deal with experienced, well-established firms or people. You can't afford to train people on your job.
5 Never pay anything in advance.
6 Never arrange the payments on a

date basis; insist on work progress payments related to time.

7 Never pay up totally until a few months after the job has been completed.

8 Never trust anyone to do what has been arranged when it has been arranged. Check immediately beforehand *and afterwards*.

Some Like It Hot

(All you hope you need to know about central heating)

HOW TO FIND EXPERT SHORT CUTS

There are lies, damned lies and statistics and you will be confronted with all three when you go shopping for central heating. In moments of bewilderment and depression remember what *Which?* started because two people wanted to find the cheapest way to heat a house. *Which?* still cannot say. It is as impossible to say what is the best sort of central heating for everyone as it is to decide the best shape, cut and size of cloth for the average man's ideal suit. This is why you need specific help! Don't try to work it out by yourself. Your calculations won't be any cheaper and will probably be wrong.

What the average woman wants to know about central heating is which sort is cheapest, which fuel is cheapest, can you get it on hire purchase, how much does it cost to run, how can you tell if an installer is overcharging, how do you know if they've installed it properly, how long does it take to install, do you have a separate water heater and if not what happens in summer, will it make a mess, will all the plants die and the furniture burst at the seams and how can you stop it ruining your complexion?

To answer most of these questions you needn't bother about the science or the language of central heating. What you need to know is: how to get a qualified impartial consultant, who will recommend a good installer, so that between them you will be kept warm in winter (and especially warm when it's especially cold) and provided with enough hot water, all as cheaply as possible.

Be prepared to make about six telephone calls; don't skimp them. First get advice from a heating engineer who is a member of the Heating and Ventilating Contractors' Association, ESCA House, 34 Palace Court, London w2 4JG (tel. 01-229 5543). Its customer inquiry service will give you names of qualified heating engineer members in your area. HVCA members guarantee their materials and workmanship for one year after installation and this guarantee is underwritten by the Association. It's not always easy to find an HVCA member when you want him, but it is well worth waiting. HVCA members are supposed to give impartial advice and, without charge, they will visit your home, design a system and prepare an estimate.

To find out what *installation costs* have a specification given by a qualified, recognized engineer in accordance with the HVCA *Small-Bore Domestic Heating: Guide to Good Practice*. There is a British Standards Institution standard for ensuring that boilers are safe to operate, but unfortunately, there is no BSI check on installation.

You can also ask a heating engineer for an estimate of *running costs*. Fairly accurate calculations are possible if the heating engineer visits the house itself, and you can hold a firm to a running cost quotation which is made in writing.

Registered members of the Institute of Plumbing are qualified to *install* central heating, but the Institute doesn't operate a guarantee scheme, although many members do so. Only contract your heating scheme to someone who will guarantee it for one year and who, you are pretty sure, is likely to be around that long. A member of a trade association is a good bet. You can also get central heating installed by members of the National Association of Plumbing, Heating and Mechanical Services Contracts, 6 Gate Street, London wc2 (tel. 01-405 2678), and the Scottish Plumbing and Mechanical Services Federation, 2 Walker Street, Edinburgh EH3 7LB (tel. 031-225 2255).

All the heating fuel head offices have a list of recommended installers in your area, but of course the fuel suppliers will not guarantee their work. You must expect the installer to be biased in favour of the fuel marketed by the people who recommended him. Similarly, if your installer is an 'approved installer' of, for instance, the Billings Betterbuilt boiler, guess which boiler he is going to recommend?

There are training schools for installers. Oil companies and the Coal Utilisation Council run practical courses, at the end of which there is an examination and a certificate; understandably, however, they do not accept responsibility for their approved installers. Most installers tend to be too busy to attend school and learn how to run their business; they take on too much work and will cheerfully agree to tackle something that

they do not fully understand. But
there are good, efficient, responsible,
small plumbing firms. Here is how to
make sure you end up with one of
them:

1 Draw up a heating plan for your
  own home; decide how much
  warmth you want, where and when,
  in each room and passage, and how
  much hot water. Write it down.
2 Pick an installer with a good local
  reputation, preferably a member
  of some recognized organization.
  Make sure he knows that you are
  going to check on him by asking
  him for references from previous
  customers.
3 Discuss your heating plan with him
  in your home and even if you con-
  verse in kindergarten language
  make sure you understand what he
  is talking about. (If this makes you
  feel foolish, remember who is paying the bill.)
4 Check on him. Plenty of men are
  being struck off the approved lists
  put out by the various authorities.
  So if your installer waves a piece of
  paper under your nose to prove
  he is approved, telephone the
  authority concerned to check
  whether he is *still* approved, because
  anyone can call himself an installer.
  I could put a notice outside my front
  door saying 'Shirley Conran: Heating and Ventilating Engineer', and
  nobody could stop me. Check your
  installer with the firm supplying the
  boiler and the organization behind
  the fuel which you intend to use,
  because both have a vested interest

in ensuring that you get a good
installation.

  Incidentally – there is no such
thing as an independent heating
installer: straightforward commission is not a dirty word but is
recognized business practice. The
installer who buys six boilers at a
time because he has sold one to a
customer will get a larger commission on each of the six than if he
buys only one – but he will then
have to sell the other five boilers. He
would indeed be unbiased if he did
not earnestly recommend that same
boiler to the next customer he visits.
5 Check on the installer's estimate by
  getting two other estimates.
6 Get the specification signed by both
  you and the installer. Date it. Both
  of you should sign any alterations.

What's the cheapest way to pay?
Many installers will give discounts on
a heating system that is installed in the
spring, because this is the period – or
at any rate has been to date – when
work is in short supply. The cheapest
way to pay for equipment is undoubtedly in cash. The cheapest way
to borrow the money is probably from
your bank, so try that first. (Ask for
a home loan.) Alternatively, you can
buy equipment on hire purchase for all
four types of central heating system.
Repayments vary up to ten years and
hire purchase incentives seem to vary
from year to year.

  Do not pay all the bills until you
are sure that your central heating does
what you were told it would. Put a
withholding clause in the contract,

stipulating 90 per cent payment on completion and the 10 per cent remainder after three months. Remember that he who pays the piper calls the tune, and can first make sure that the pipes are in working order. If your first quarter's bill wildly disagrees with the forecast get on to the installer and the manufacturer and make them investigate the reason.

A word of warning: your first quarter's fuel bill will probably be the biggest – console yourself with that thought when you receive it. The reasons are that (a) you will have kept the house radiators too hot; (b) you will have been warming up the fabric of your house; and (c) you will have been fiddling with the thermostat and showing it off to your friends. When the first quarter's bill arrives Dad always 'hits the insulated ceiling and *always switches off the central heating*. Because, no matter how cheap your central heating is, it is always more expensive than *no* central heating.

I think it's very important that you overestimate rather than underestimate the temperatures you stipulate to your heating consultant – and do so in writing. After all, you can always turn it down, but you can't turn it higher than your calculated requirements if a Siberian winter hits us against all expectations, or if you're ill in the bedroom, or just like to lie in on a Sunday morning, or if the consultant gets the damn thing just a tiny bit wrong. I've had four personal installations and three of them had to be reorganized after installation because they wouldn't provide what I

regarded (and had requested) as adequate heat.

Similarly, not every expert specifies large enough hot water storage tanks. 'You bath more than you said you did,' cry husbands. 'I wash up more than you think I do,' retort their wives. In my last two conversions the hot water tank was wildly underestimated by the architect (I had an architect because I was working, so couldn't do it myself) and, until we had them expensively exchanged, we all bathed in 5 inches of water, like Buckingham Palace in wartime. So make sure you make a fuss about this right from the beginning. You won't pay unnecessary running costs if you get the sort of tank where, when the children are away, you flick a switch and only half of it operates. Better to overestimate in this way, in my opinion.

WHAT IT COSTS

The cost of central heating depends on where you live because fuel prices vary from place to place. It depends on whether you live in a draughty old house or a new bungalow. It depends on your insulation. It depends on your life style; a couple out at work all day will have a lower bill than a family with small children.

The Department of Energy, who are impartial advisers (their job being to save fuel, not sell it), publish a good little free booklet called *Compare Your Home Heating Costs*. (Get it from the DoE, Thames House South, Millbank, London SW1P 4QJ.) There are different editions for each region and they are frequently revised. It compares different average costs and running costs for particular situations and is for people who want to know whether they can save money by switching fuels or who want to improve their old heating or buy a new system.

A few final points

Spend money on insulation before spending more on heating. You have to pay for insulation only once, but once it's done properly you will save visibly on every future heating bill.

Spend money on a yearly maintenance check. If your system is overhauled regularly (like a car) it will run and run most economically.

Spend money on controls, efficient thermostats and time switches, especially if you are out all day. Set the timer to switch on half an hour before you get up and switch off half an hour before you leave; and half an hour before you get in and half an hour before your usual bedtime.

Consider having a heat-as-you-use water system (it's all improved since Granny's dribbling geyser), either permanently or for summer, if you have a solid-fuel central-heating system. This is now possible with electricity as well as gas, although only in small quantities as yet for sinks and showers but not for baths.

Consider spending money on a boiler one size larger than your heating engineer calculates that you need. Then you have the reserve power

in case you find that it isn't as hot as you want, in case you want to install more radiators or an extension at a later date.

Don't switch fuel systems, without taking into account the real cost of installation payments on new equipment, spreading payment and quarterly bills.

Shop around because costs of equipment and installation vary a great deal and so does cost and availability of H P and loan finance. Get several different firm written estimates before deciding what to install.

THE ROCK-BOTTOM BASIC PRINCIPLES OF CENTRAL HEATING

There are two sorts of heat: *radiant heat*, which directly warms anything in its path, such as your mottled legs in front of the plump, pale blue, hissing comfort of an open gas fire. You have to sit near a radiant heat source in order to be warmed by it: your fore will be toasted but your aft may be frozen, but they don't make your head stuffy, like convector heaters, can. Open wood or coal fires and electric bar heaters are also radiant heaters.

Convected heat is air that is warmed and then circulated. Some convector

heaters have a fan to help the circulation. The fan is what causes the nasty background whine in a tangential heater, but convection is nevertheless the fastest way to heat a room.

It is important to know precisely what heating you are talking about, particularly if you are talking to an estate agent.

Full central heating implies a quickly adjustable system which warms the whole house and also has a reserve capacity to cope with unusually cold periods.

Background central heating merely takes the chill off the air. Money is better spent on keeping one room properly warm.

Partial central heating means either central or background central heating but only in one part of the house.

Selective central heating means that you can have full central heating in one part of the house at a time but not in all the house at the same time.

Ducted warm air: Air heated in a furnace is wafted through a house by hidden ducts above the ceiling and under the floor. The air enters the room through one inconspicuous grille and exits through another; it may then be recirculated after passing through a dust and dirt filter.

Nomadic heating is any useful form of heating that you can take with you when you move. If you're still in a bedsitter, or on the move, buy heating appliances that can travel with you but can still be a useful part of a heating system later on. These are electric, plug-in tangential heaters (warm up fastest but are noisy) and

convector heaters (both fuggy), oil-filled radiators and radiant heaters (keep the reflector clean and polished because it makes a great difference to the heat), and portable paraffin stoves, which should not smell if you use good fuel and keep the wick clean; but you need somewhere to keep the fuel and you have to keep filling up.

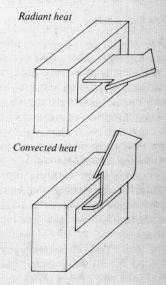

Radiant heat

Convected heat

There are four practical choices of fuel for central heating: electricity, gas and coal (vulnerable to strikes), and oil or paraffin (vulnerable to Arab price rises). Solar heating is not yet practical.

Gas is still the best all-round value for central heating, and that's what HM the Queen has at Buckingham Palace. Gas is clean, efficient and needs no storage. A gas boiler needs a flue, which incorporates two pipes; one is to bring in the necessary air for combustion and the other is to take the waste gases away. A flue measures about $60 \times 60 \times 15$ cm $(24 \times 24 \times 6$ inches) deep and must be fitted from the boiler through the outside wall, which means the boiler must be placed against an outside wall or in front of an existing chimney. If you haven't a mains gas supply you can buy bottled gas such as Calorgas, Butagaz or Butane.

Electricity is clean, efficient (you just switch it on and it works), needs no fuel storage, doesn't need a boiler or a flue. It is also easily the most expensive fuel, right up in the Widow Onassis price range for whole-house heating. Electric radiators are oil-filled and you never change the oil. They are not a permanent fixture and your rating assessment will not be increased, as it will with gas, oil or solid-fuel central heating. Underfloor heating seems to make my legs swell and ceiling heating may give you headaches.

Oil needs a tank, by no means goldfish-sized. You'll want storage space for at least 600 gallons (2700 litres) which can be housed in a smallish cellar. It costs more to install than other systems. An oil-fired burner can smell slightly, it can be a bit noisy and you have to remember to re-order the oil.

Solid fuel (coal) is comparatively cheap but comparatively filthy. As a central heating system, it is not automatic, it is semi-automatic. The coal has to be heaved from the coal cellar to the boiler. There are self-feeding hoppers, which cut the need for hand stoking, but do not eliminate it. Coal is heavy, dirty and makes dust. It needs storage space and the boiler needs a flue. It is still relatively cheap but we are as much at the mercy of the miners as of the Arabs.

Central heating designs

A *central heating system* is one where the heat originates from one source (the boiler) and is then piped out through the house either as hot air or hot water. It's difficult to install a hot-air heating system in an existing house, but in a new house it is both practical and enjoyable.

In a hot-water system the water heated by the boiler is pumped through small copper pipes. Depending on the diameter of the pipes, the system is called small bore (12–22 mm diameter) or micro bore (6–10 mm). One pipe takes the hot water from the boiler and another returns the luke-warm water to be reheated. The pipes can be fitted under the floor surface or unobtrusively against skirtings.

You can have *single-* or *double-panel* radiators. Single panels are more efficient than double, so if you have enough wall space choose a long single radiator. You can get them low to fit under windows and curved to fit round bay windows or oval ballrooms. The installation engineer will want to place your radiators under the window, to counteract the cold air coming in. However, look at the heat-loss chart and consider installing them not against exterior walls or under windows, which are the points at which heat escapes, but against interior walls. Elaborate louvred panels and radiator covers can prevent up to 25 per cent of the heat from reaching the room.

An alternative to panel radiators, *skirting heaters* are about the height of skirting boards but they are cumbersome and sometimes stain the walls above them.

The water in pipes and radiators is separate from that in the hot water part which supplies your water taps.

The water is pumped round the pipes by an electric pump. This is usually switched on and off automatically by a room *thermostat* in order to maintain an even indoor temperature. You set your thermostat to the temperature you want and then it automatically switches the boiler and pump on when the heat drops below that temperature or off when the heat rises above it. The thermostat should not be placed in a particularly warm place (e.g. the kitchen) or a cold one (e.g. a draughty part of the hall). A good place to site a thermostat is in the living-room, but away from windows and away from a radiator or fire. If you go away in winter, you can turn your thermostat down very low, so that the heating system operates only to prevent freezing.

If you have a *time clock* (a *programmer* is a sophisticated time clock) you set it, like a cooking timer, for the times you want the heating system to operate and the thermostat to control it. Two-programme timers are advisable, because they can switch on and off in the morning and then again

in the evening: you get a lot more control for only a few pounds extra. The time clock can be installed next to the boiler or the thermostat or wherever you please.

A simple form of control is the on/off valve on your radiators. By turning these you can stop the supply of hot water to the radiators in a room that isn't being used.

Don't believe that a boiler doesn't give out heat without meaning to. The room with the boiler in is the one room where you will be over-radiatored. Don't have a boiler in a room you want to keep cool in summer.

I do not agree with the cold-blooded *recommended temperatures* as laid down in standard practice. They are:

Living-rooms	21–22°C (70–72°F)
Bathrooms	22°C (72°F)
Lavatories	20°C (68°F)
Kitchen, hall and landing	18°C (64°F)
Bedrooms	13–18°C (55–64°F)

But are you more likely to be naked and shivering in the bedroom or in the living-room? A vicar once wrote to me to say that he could find no one willing to instruct him as to what temperature it would be reasonable to keep his wife at. I thought that he should work on 19°C (66°F) for passages, 20°C (68°F) for lavatories and bathrooms (the hot water quickly warms the room if you're bathing), 21°C (70°F) for living-rooms, and allow her to creep up to 21°C (70°F) in the bedroom.

It's vital to remember – and record in the specification – that the temperatures must be maintained inside when the outside temperature is below freezing. *This is when your heating is a necessity.* I have found that heating installations tend to be underpowered when it comes to fact as opposed to theory, so be generous: up your boiler size rather than the reverse.

Noise: It's vital to make sure that your system operates noiselessly. Make it clear to your installer in writing that you won't pay the bill if the heating system doesn't operate silently. A boiler, a circulating pump and anything that is fan assisted can be maddeningly noisy, quite apart from unexpected vibrations, whirrs and bangs, like a pop group warming up.

Anything that incorporates a fan makes an inexorable little noise that might easily drive you berserk. Thermostatically operated heaters and boilers can also be noisy and when they hover around the required temperature the clicking on and off can get you to that tense point where you're waiting for the other boot to drop.

Don't believe anyone who tells you that some boiler operates noiselessly. They mean 'without much noise', and you had better remember this if you think of putting the boiler in the dining-room or next to the bed. When it's been installed it will be too late to argue.

To cut down pipe noises, fix pipes to floors and walls with padded and foam clips.

Central heating may bring you problems of too little or too much moisture in the air, especially if your insulation is relentlessly efficient. Lack of moisture can irritate eyes and nose and dries out the skin like the Sahara. It can make antiques split, paintings crack and wood panelling shrink. A humidifier which adds moisture to dry air should always be built into a warm-air heating system. For a hot-water system you can get simple radiator-mounted humidifiers or electric ones.

On the other hand, your trouble may be *condensation*, moisture always present as droplets on cold surfaces, especially on windows or cold walls of the bathroom or kitchen. It is dispersed by good ventilation to get steam out of the house quickly (this might be as simple as opening the window), sufficient background heat to take the chill off, and the use of surfaces which stop the moisture-laden air from condensing. Avoid gloss paints, papers and tiles; absorbent materials such as cork or tongued-and-grooved boarding absorb condensation and release it gently back into the room later.

If you have an internal kitchen or bathroom, fit an electric extractor fan and make sure that you get a powerful enough model, or it will be a waste of money. Install it as near as possible to the bath or cooker or whatever the source of the steam is. Don't install one of those cheap, inefficient, little scruffy, grubby circular fans in your window. Don't install those expensive glass doors and windows with glass louvres at the top; it's simpler to open a window.

Double glazing prevents condensation, because the warm steam never comes into contact with the cold outer glass, and this is, for me, its only realistic advantage.

Central heating maintenance

Maintain *gas* or *oil* boilers in early summer by arrangement with the fuel company. Clean flues and chimneys of *solid fuel* boilers in early summer. (Get a sweep from the *Yellow Pages*.)

If the tops of your radiators stay stubbornly cold they need bleeding (that'll show 'em). You will have been handed a bleeder key, which looks like the key to a clockwork train. You release the trapped air (which is causing the trouble) by turning the valve at one end with the bleeder key and holding a pudding basin beneath to catch the drops of water that fall when the air hisses out.

If central heating was already installed in the house when you bought it, better have it checked by a qualified heating engineer. You don't want the boiler to pack up in midwinter, only to find that the manufacturers have gone bankrupt and no spare parts are available, etc. You want to prepare for this sort of gruesome discovery before it happens and find out well in advance where alternative spare parts can be obtained.

Hot water

Domestic hot water is provided with oil and gas central heating systems and in summer you can set the programmer so that you get the hot water without the space heating. With solid fuel you generally need a separate electric immersion heater to provide (more expensively) your summer hot water. With electrical heating you will need a separate heater. If you have an immersion water heater, always have a time switch. Ignore the theory that it's cheaper to keep the water simmering for twenty-four hours than to heat it up when you need it.

For supplementing water from a central heating system or in the absence of central heating I would, in fact, choose an *instant water heating system* (like an Ascot) for supplying water for sink or bath. You get what you pay for – a continuous, slow flow of hot water (about 2 litres or $\frac{1}{2}$ gallon a minute at 65 C/149 F) for as long as the tap is turned on. It can be gas or electric powered, but the electrical ones are small, only for basins and showers and not suitable for baths.

For small houses or heating only one part of a house

There is one form of heating that's halfway between a room heater and full central heating system. This is a room heater with a *high-capacity back boiler* that acts a bit like an old-fashioned kitchen boiler. It warms the room and from the back boiler as well as domestic hot water you can either run about five radiators properly or take the chill off a large house. During the summer it can be used just to heat the water. You can't get an electric heater with back boiler, but there are plenty of solid fuel and gas hearth heaters of this sort. There's also a *big oil stove* that operates like a solid fuel or gas heater with back boiler. The fuel is supplied from an oil tank, in the same way as an oil-fired central heating system. As well as the hearth fire, a little central heating and hot water is provided. Thermostats and time clocks can be fitted to these models.

A modern open grate can be fitted with a solid fuel back boiler, but for maximum output and control the alternative is an enclosed room heater with a little glass window in the front, through which you can see the cosy glow. They run on comparatively cheap coal, such as Housewarm, which can be burnt on enclosed fires even in smoke-controlled areas.

HOW TO SAVE MONEY AND ENERGY
(your checklist)

Energy-saving ideas can be divided into:

A Simple actions that quickly and easily become a habit, such as shutting doors and using the poker less aggressively.

B Some quick, easy, inexpensive insulation that you can do yourself.
C Some investments that should be considered *before* you buy central heating and where experts may be needed (for cavity wall insulation, for instance).

To save heat

1 Use the poker sparingly and gently if you have an open fire; a long, thin poker is best to clear ash between the grate bars without losing unburned fuel.
2 Keep an open fire grate filled with a 75–100-mm (3–4-inch) layer of fuel. Regulate the burning rate by using the air control at the front; this helps maintain a low burning rate without letting the fire die out.
3 Limit full heating to one room.
4 Close curtains at night.
5 Use false side curtains and a blind over radiators; not long curtains.
6 Use Milium curtain lining, which is aluminium-backed so that when the curtains are drawn the heat is bounced back into the room.
7 Use heavy curtains.
8 Make sure that radiators are not hemmed in by sofas, armchairs or other furniture.
9 Fix aluminium foil on insulation boards behind radiators on outer walls; this reduces heat loss to the outside. Difficult to fix, but worth it.
10 Fit individual radiator thermostats to control the temperature in each room.
11 Experiment with a little less heat

where possible (e.g. set time clocks or switches on central heating systems to come on later in the morning and go off earlier at night or when the house is unoccupied during the day).

12 Keep doors shut in unused rooms.

13 In living-rooms you do use (if you have children) fit a cheap, automatic door shutter, which shuts the door as noiselessly as a butler and just as creepily. Try the Gibraltar model and get it from big stores, DIY or hardware shops.

14 Replace worn parts as soon as possible (e.g. broken radiants on gas fires).

15 Consider replacing very old appliances with more efficient new ones.

16 Arrange servicing of your central heating system by a regular service contract so that it stays at top efficiency. Get it done in summer, not in September when everyone else is howling to be serviced.

To heat water more cheaply

17 Lag the hot water tank – a jacket made from 75-mm (3-inch) thick insulation material is best. Standard size jackets fit most tanks.

18 Lag hot water pipes in roof spaces (cold ones too, to prevent freeze-ups and subsequent burst pipes when it thaws).

19 Switch off the immersion heater when not in use or install a time switch. Ours is on only from 5 to 7 nightly. It's not unduly inconvenient now that we've got used

to it. We can still have more luxurious hot baths than Marie Antoinette. The saving was immediately obvious on the bill.

20 Turn down the thermostat on the hot water system a few degrees: 55°C (130°F) is adequate.

21 Repair any dripping hot water taps.

22 Make sure hot water taps are always fully turned off.

23 Do not wash up under constant running hot water; use a bowl, or the sink.

24 Install or use a shower instead of a bath; you will automatically use far less hot water. A good, powerful shower can also be noticeably more refreshing and more invigorating.

25 Wait until you have a full load before using the washing machine or dishwasher.

26 Use only cold water for rinses when washing by hand, or for twin-tubs or wringer machine rinses.

27 Arrange for regular servicing of your appliances, where necessary (your supplier or manufacturer will advise).

To keep heat in and draughts out

28 Insulate roof spaces by lining your loft with a 75-mm (3-inch) layer of glass or mineral fibre. (Do not insulate *underneath* water tanks and don't conceal ceiling joists or someone may fall through the ceiling.) If you use granular insulation material (e.g. expanded poly-

styrene) 100 mm (4 inches) is worth while.

29 There are two basic ways of preventing heat loss through walls. With 230-mm (9-inch) solid and rendered walls the room interiors have to be lined with insulating material. Check with a qualified surveyor or architect for advice on the dry lining of solid walls to reduce heat loss.

30 If you have cavity walls (most houses built since the 1920s do) you can have the walls injected with insulating foam or treated mineral wool.

The insulation material is injected into your wall through small holes drilled on the outside. There's no damage to the wall, no disturbance inside the home and the job usually takes less than a day. Don't be hoodwinked by phoney operators who inject detergent instead of urea formaldehyde foam. Use only contractors on the approved list who are covered by an Agrément Certificate. (This means that they are competent to give expert advice on the suitability of your walls for insulation and will carry out the work satisfactorily.) Contact the Agrément Board to get (or check on) your installer, and make sure he gives you a long-term guarantee and that he looks solid enough to keep it. The Agrément Board list costs 35p from the Agrément Board, PO Box 195, Bucknalls Lane, Garston, Watford WD27NG. New home owners have to wait about

eighteen months while the house dries out, before cavity injection wall treatment, but rock wool can be used straight away. Rentokil Ltd, 16 Dover Street, London W1X 4DJ (tel. 01-499 4324), will give you a free survey for cavity filling and also roof insulation. You have no obligation to buy anything. I have found Rentokil far from cheap; so be sure to get other quotes, but getting a survey is a useful way to start.

31 Install plastic foam or metal draught excluder strip round external doors and windows. (Metal is more expensive but it lasts and doesn't peel off.) Do-it-yourself with Chamberlin draught excluder or Metal Weatherstrip or Durastrip. This also cuts down outside dirt and noise.

32 Consider fitting double glazing. It can noticeably reduce draughts, condensation and noise, but it is an expensive and cumbersome way of saving energy and last on my priority list.

33 Check floorboards and skirtings for gaps and fill in with old newspapers. Use hardboard to cover floors with uneven floorboards or small gaps.

34 Fill skirting gaps by wedging thin slivers of wood in the big gaps or with plastic wood compound in the small ones.

35 Quadrant moulding (which looks like a broom handle split lengthways) can be nailed round really draughty skirting: it may even look quite smart. Fix it to the

floor, not to the skirting board, so that it moves with the floor.

36 Put down carpet underlay. (A few sheets of newspaper under the carpet will also stop draughts.)

37 Cover solid concrete floors with cork tiles or carpet and underlay.

38 Block off unused fireplaces. Stop heat loss through disused chimney flues by using a sheet of asbestos or hardboard to block off the fire opening. Don't wedge it up the chimney (more dirty and difficult and you risk soot accumulating behind it). It is vital to install an air brick or grille to keep the chimney free from condensation.

39 Fit open fireplaces in occasional use with a throat restrictor in the flue immediately above the fire (reduces cold draughts and saves heat).

WORD OF WARNING. Be wary of fitting draught excluders in kitchen or bathroom because you need some ventilation to prevent condensation and mould growth. All fuel-burning appliances need air to breathe and insufficient ventilation can be dangerous if you have an oil, gas, or solid fuel system.

40 Get further energy-saving advice from your local solid fuel, gas or electricity showroom or your local HVCA member.

Get *free* energy-saving booklets from the Information Division, Department of Energy, Thames House South, Millbank, London SW1P 4QJ.

Get double glazing advice from the Insulation Glazing Association, 6 Mount Row, London W1.

For oil-fired heating get *The BP Heat Handbook* from BP Heat (PO Box 101, London E1 9BR).

For specific problems the Department of the Environment publishes the following leaflets, obtainable from HMSO, Atlantic House, Holborn Viaduct, London EC1 (tel. 01-583 9870): No. 45, *Warmth without Waste*; No. 54, *Thermal Insulators*; No. 44, *Smoky Chimneys*; No. 10, *Dry Rot and Wet Rot*; No. 3, *Lagging Water Systems*; No. 61, *Condensation*.

Other helpful organizations are:

Humidifier Advisory and Consultancy Service, 31 Napier Road, Bromley, Kent BR2 9JA.

Insulation Glazing Association, 6 Mount Row, London W1 (tel. 01-629 8334), who provide a free leaflet and list of members.

Pilkington Double Glazing (MDA), PO Box 8, Nottingham, will supply free leaflets on DIY double glazing.

HOW TO KEEP HEAT WHEN YOU'VE GOT IT
(insulation)

Only since the energy crisis has insulation been taken seriously. The Department of Energy claims that if your home isn't insulated properly 40p of every £1 you spend on heat is wasted on heating the air outside your home. The Department reckons that insulation costs can generally be covered by visible savings on your fuel bill within three to five years.

Insulation claims tend to exaggerate possible savings, so when you look at average heat loss figures don't think you can eliminate all the loss. But you can cut it down considerably and when you insulated properly you won't even have to look at the bills to tell the difference – you can feel it. The places to make the biggest savings are in the roof and the walls. The easiest, cheapest saving is to insulate the hot water tank.

The only insulation that I'm dubious about is double glazing, which professionally done may cost from £250 to more than £1000. The window heat loss is small compared with that lost through the walls and the investment is far, far higher than all the rest put together.

WHERE TO FIND THE EXPERTS
(address book)

Heating and Ventilating Contractors' Association, ESCA House, 34 Palace Court, London w2 4JG (tel. 01-229 5543)

National Association of Plumbing, Heating and Mechanical Services Contractors, 6 Gate Street, London WC2A 3HX (tel. 01-405 2678)

National Federation of Builders' and Plumbers' Merchants, 15 Soho Square, London w1 (tel. 01-439

Where your heat goes:
through the-

	%
Roof	25
Walls	35
Windows	10
Ground	15
Draughts	15

Where your fuel goes:

Space heating	64
Water heating	22
Cooking	10
TV, Lighting, etc.	4

1753), for lists of merchants in your area specializing in central heating.

Consumer Association, 14 Buckingham Street, London wc2 (tel. 01-839 1222). They publish *Which?*, which advises on heat and heaters.

British Gas, 59 Bryanston Street, London w1 (tel. 01-723 7030) or your local regional showroom.

Solid Fuel Advisory Service, The National Coal Board, Hobart House, Grosvenor Place, London sw1 (tel. 01-235 2020) for recommending solid fuel system installers in your area or dealing with any solid fuel problem.

Electricity Board (to recommend installers in your area or your local central showroom): head office; 46 New Broad Street, London EC2 (tel. 01-588 1280)

Electrical Contractors' Association, 33 Palace Court, London w2 (tel. 01-229 1266) for a list of members in your area.

For recommending oil-fired central heating in your area:

BP Heat, PO Box 101, London E1 9BR (postal inquiries only)

Shell-Mex Ltd, Shell-Mex House, Strand, London WC2R 0DX (tel. 01-836 1234)

Esso Petroleum Co. Ltd, Victoria Street, London sw1 (tel. 01-834 6677)

Some loft converters

Attica, 600 Kingston Road, Raynes Park, London sw20 (tel. 01-540 0808)

Crescourt Loft Conversions Ltd, 4/54 Roebuck Lane, West Bromwich, West Midlands (tel. 021-553 4131)

Elite Loft Conversions Southern Ltd, Hooten Lane, Leigh, Lancashire (tel. Leigh [05235] 677815)

Some room extenders

Banbury Buildings Ltd, Ironstone Works, Adderbury, Nr Banbury (tel. Banbury [0295] 52500)

BeeJay Home Extensions Ltd, The Croft, Nugent's Park, Pinner, Middlesex (twenty-four-hour answering service on 01-428 9511)

Blacknell Buildings Ltd, Westmead, Farnborough, Hampshire (tel. Farnborough (0252) 44333)

Halls Ltd (Show Centre and offices), 1 Bath Road, Heathrow, Hounslow, Middlesex (tel. 01-759 9137)

Marley Buildings Ltd, Peasmarsh, Guildford, Surrey (tel. Guildford [0483] 69922)

Speciality Shopping: A Designer's Address Book

Apart from the ordinary, everyday frustrations of decorating a room ('we don't do that colour any more') you often find that you want to get something essential to your glossy magazine mind's eye design – but have no idea where to get it. It may be the answer to a simple query (where to get floor paint or who makes brass doorknobs), or it may be an unusual finish (a slate slab for a fireplace or how to get a quilt to match your curtains).

This basic Designer's Address Book gives you some idea of what's available and where to find it. The firms included will generally send you *free* leaflets, catalogues and specific samples. With this list, your local stores and the *Yellow Pages*, you should be able to cope as competently as any smart decorator.

Whether you're decorating and furnishing a room or a house there are three ways of setting about it:

1 Make the best of what's available, nearest and cheapest NOW. This isn't impossible, so long as you aren't too ambitious.

2 Back your own individual taste and judgement and take more time and trouble (but not necessarily money) to get exactly what you want and what reflects your style.

3 A combination of 1 and 2 but only taking trouble over a few key items.

Once I had to furnish a home in a hurry and didn't have time to trot around the town comparing samples; I decided (on a variation of the Henry Ford principle) to buy nothing unless it was blue or white. I did all the shopping by catalogue, except for a special visit to a ceramic factory to choose the traditional blue and white tiles. The scheme ended up as a mixture of pale blue, periwinkle, mid-blues and French navy with willow-plate type patterns and traditional tiles. It looked far better co-ordinated than many a more ambitious scheme that I may have worked on for months.

I know someone who has similarly furnished a flat in a scheme of browns and cream using Marie biscuit beige, sherry, ginger, cowboy browns and bitter chocolate. (If you pay someone to do it, this is called a tone-on-tone scheme.)

Whichever way you operate, if you're starting from scratch try to get as much free advice as you need; start by visiting one of the Design Centres. People tend to be irritated because it's not possible to buy anything except souvenirs on show direct from the Design Centre, but it's an invaluable starting point and well worth a trip for seeing what's available and for getting ideas. They will tell you where you can buy the items.

The Design Council (which runs the Centres) publishes a series of paperback books on basic home decorating and planning. They cost under £2 each (at present, but prices change) and you can buy them by mail if you write to the Mail Order Section, Design Centre, 28 Haymarket, London SW1Y 4SU. Ask for the booklist which includes a large range of design publications that are sold in the Design Centre bookshop. All these too can be bought by mail order.

Design Centres: 28 Haymarket, London SW1Y 4SU (tel. 01-839 8000); Scotland: 72 St Vincent Street, Glasgow G2 5TN (tel. 041-221 6121).

Design Council Showroom: Pearl Assurance House, Greyfriars Road, Cardiff CF1 3JU (Cardiff [0222] 395811).

Your nearest John Lewis store is the closest you will get to a retail Design Council: they keep a careful and responsible eye on quality and price. Their reputation 'we are never knowingly undersold' is carefully upheld, as I know through experience as a fabric supplier to John Lewis, not just as a customer (although that too).

British Standards Institution, 2 Park Street, London W1A 2BS (tel. 01-629 9000). Manufacturers submit their products and if they satisfy the appropriate British Standard they are awarded the Kitemark. The Institution will only deal with consumer problems concerning a product which has been given such an award.

Citizens' Advice Bureaux: If you have a faulty product and the retailer is unhelpful, go to your local branch of the citizens' advice bureaux. They will give you advice and may refer you to the local inspector of weights and measures or the relevant government department. You may also write to the manufacturer, who, in many cases, is prompt in sorting out any such problems.

Consumers' Association, 14 Buckingham Street, London WC2N 6DS (tel. 01-839 1222). The Association carries out comparative tests on products and services, the results of which are published for members in the *Which?* magazine. (Look up back numbers in your local library before buying expensive machinery.) They also publish authoritative paperbacks. They do not, however, operate an advice or

information service direct to the general public.

Electrical Association for Women, 25 Foubert's Place, London w1v 2al (tel. 01-437 5212). An independent voluntary organization that gives information and advice on most kinds of electrical equipment but especially BEAB-approved appliances. They also run one-day courses that include almost anything from how to change a plug to how to save energy. Cost is around £2 which includes a snack lunch. For further details write to the Services Administrator at the above address.

Bathrooms

Armitage Shanks Ltd, Northumberland House, 303–306 High Holborn, London wc1 (tel. 01-405 9663). All sanitary ware – basins, WCs, bidets and showers. Acrylic baths and accessories in white, pastels or strong, bright colours.

Bonsack Baths Ltd, 14 Mount Street, London w1 (tel. 01-629 9981). For the Total Bathroom. Pop star lavish at pop star prices. Where oil sheikhs buy their solid gold swan taps: circular baths, double baths: total fantasy

land. You can also buy a toothmug here, from the sumptuous bathroom accessories. Design department will design Your Fantasy Bathroom.

Carron Company, Baths and Plastics Division, Falkirk (tel. Falkirk [0324] 24999). Perspex baths and washbasins in many colours.

Edward Curran Engineering Ltd, Sinks and Baths Division, PO Box 23, Hurman Street, Cardiff (tel. Cardiff [0222] 33644). Steel baths in vitreous enamel finish in white and other colours. Baths may be ordered with a slip-resistant finish.

Evered Supplies, 18 North Audley Street, London w1 (tel. 01-499 1845). Luxury baths and soaking tubs as used by glossy magazine photographers. French decorated porcelain baths and basins and the inevitable gold-plated taps.

Glynwed Baths Ltd, Bilston Works, Bilston, West Midlands (tel. Bilston [0902] 43121). Baths and basins in cast-iron with porcelain enamel finish. Showroom at 28 Brook Street, London w1.

Humphersons, Beaufort House, Holman Road, London sw11 (tel. 01-228 8811), 62 Church Road, Barnes, sw13 and at 55 Heath Road, Twickenham, Middlesex. Bathroom and kitchen specialists. Vast range of bathroom fixtures on display in the Holman Road and Twickenham showrooms, kitchen showroom at the Barnes office.

Ideal-Standard Ltd, PO Box 60, Kingston-upon-Hull (tel. Hull [0482] 46461). A really forward-looking efficient firm with beautifully simple designs. Excellent value. They use all the top designers and have a very good design service. Worth writing to if you have any bathroom problems. Specially designed basins and baths for tiny bathrooms. (Good bathroom showroom in Heals, Tottenham Court Road, London).

Nicholls & Clarke Ltd, Niclar House, 3–10 Shoreditch High Street, London E1 (tel. 01-247 5432). Sanitary ware with simple, clean lines in many colours. Showroom at the above address.

Renubath, 596 Chiswick High Road, London W4 (tel. 01-995 5252). They will resurface or change the colour of your boring or worn old bath as long as it's vitreous enamel, not plastic.

Twyfords, PO Box 23, Stoke-on-Trent, Staffordshire (tel. Stoke-on-Trent [0782] 29531). Washbasins which fit into counter tops as well as other fittings. Showroom at Shelton New Road, Cliffdale, Stoke-on-Trent and 204 Great Portland Street, London W1.

Bathroom fittings

J. T. Ellis & Company Ltd, Crown Works, Wakesfield Road, Huddersfield, Yorkshire (tel. Huddersfield [0484] 39521). Vanitory units with Formica tops. Decorative moulded doors, louvred or plain, in many colours.

English Rose Kitchens Ltd, Wharf Street, Warwick. Laminated cupboards and sanitary units.

Humphersons, Beaufort House, Holman Road, London SW11 (tel. 01-228 8811). Lots of bathroom taps, tiles and other fittings.

Johnson Brothers, Trent Sanitary Works, Stoke-on-Trent, Staffordshire (tel. Stoke-on-Trent [0782] 29581). Modern ceramic basins and bathroom accessories.

John Lewis, Oxford Street, London W1 (tel. 01-637 3434) and branches. Good, reasonably priced bathroom accessories.

Pilkington Tiles Ltd, PO Box 4, Clifton Junction, Manchester (tel. 061-794 2024). Accessories to match any standard tile colour as well as stock range.

Blinds

Eaton Bag Company, 16 Manette Street, London W1 (tel. 01-437 9391). Beautiful split bamboo roller blinds.

Faber Blinds (Great Britain) Ltd, Viking House, Kangley Bridge Road, London SE26 (tel. 01-659 2126). Venetian blinds available in twenty-seven colours (including black and white). These can be made to fit in between double-glazed windows. Also large range of vertical louvres.

G. Hall & Co., (Sunstor Blinds), Fitzherbert Road, Farlington, Portsmouth, Hampshire (tel. Cosham [07018] 73411). Venetian and vertical blinds and a large selection of plain and patterned fabric roller blinds.

Living Daylights, 119 Regents Park Road, London NW1 (tel. 01-586 3911). Do handpainted and printed blinds to customers' designs.

Sundecor Blind Company Ltd, 28 Abbey Manufacturing Estate, Mount Pleasant, Wembley, Middlesex (tel. 01-903 6868). All sorts of blinds, including reeded vinyl in white and pastels, paper-fibre, roller blinds and vinyl spring roller blinds which you can cut to fit your windows. Selection of prints including Boussac and Liberty.

Sunway, 240 Bath Road, Slough, Berkshire (tel. Slough [0753] 26611). Several ranges including two-tone venetians (one side coloured, one side white). Lots of fabric roller blinds, some of which match Sanderson fabrics.

William O'Hanlon & Co. Ltd, 49 Dale Street, Manchester (tel. 061-236 3223). Venetian blinds in various colours. Also Sunlover roller blinds and a

selection of plain and patterned curtain fabrics.

Carpets

Afia Carpets, 81 Baker Street, London W1M 1AJ (tel. 01-935 0414). Possibly the best service in London. Quick, helpful, knowledgeable.

Brintons Ltd, PO Box 16, Kidderminster, Hereford and Worcester (tel. Kidderminster [0562] 3444). Good range of reasonably priced plain, textured and geometrically patterned Axminsters. Their showroom is at The British Carpet Centre, 99 Kensington High Street, London W8 5TB. An introduction from your retailer is needed.

Byzantium, 1 Goodge Street, London W1 (tel. 01-636 6465). Inexpensive Greek, Indian and Moroccan rugs and bedspreads in wool and mixtures.

Carpets International, 14–15 Berners Street, London W1 (tel. 01-580 8776). Offers a really wide range including CMC, Crossley, Kossett, Gilt Edge, Harington, Illingworth and Debron. They also give advice on fitting and laying techniques and maintenance.

J. Crossley & Sons Ltd, Dean Clough Mills, Halifax (tel. Halifax [0422]

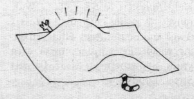

65789). Good range of carpeting which includes Keltic (tweed); plain, including York Wilson and Broadacres, which is a shaggy carpet in a soft white/beige colour; also haircord carpet and pre-shrunk, self-adhesive carpet tiles. Showroom at 14–15 Berners Street, London w1 (tel. 01-580 8672).

Cutlers of Houndsditch Ltd, 113 Houndsditch, London EC3 (tel. 01-283 3681). They offer discounts to companies, groups, societies, etc. Many branded carpet samples, some in stock.

Dodson Bull Carpet Co. Ltd, Barbican Trade Centre, Aldersgate Street, London EC2Y8AE (tel. 01-628 7020). Thirteen showrooms throughout Britain; stock a comprehensive range of all types of carpets and carpet tiles. They'll lay them for you.

Frederick Lawrence Ltd, John Evans House, Russell Parade, Golders Green Road, London NW11 (tel. 01-455 0101). Discount available on quality furniture and carpets. Extra discount offered if carpets bought from stock. Also fabrics, wallpapers and furniture discount offers.

Gilt Edge Carpets, Mill Street, Kidderminster, Hereford and Worcester (tel. Kidderminster [0562] 3466). Wide range of plains including Wessex Twist and Endura heavy-duty carpeting, which carries a guarantee of seven years. Showroom at 14–15 Berners Street, London w1.

Heals, 196 Tottenham Court Road,

London w1 (tel. 01-636 1666). Large range of carpeting in popular fashion shades. Also Italian rugs.

Healy Stone Ltd, 4 Snow Hill, London EC1 (tel. 01-236 4433). New and old oriental carpets and rugs. Reasonably priced.

John Lewis, Oxford Street, London w1 (tel. 01-637 3434) and branches throughout Britain; and *Peter Jones*, Sloane Square, London sw1 (tel. 01-730 3434). Carry their own brand of Wilton carpets in four qualities: Jonelle Firm Twist, Jonelle Super Twist, Jonelle Sloane, Jonelle Cavendish. Also a design-award-winning range called Good Companions by Broadloom Carpets. Can't recommend too highly, but they don't carry that much stock.

Kosset Carpets Ltd, PO Box 10, Brookfoot, Brighouse, Yorkshire (tel. Brighouse [0484] 15555). Many plain and patterned carpets available. Carpets for medium domestic use including nylon, foam-backed carpet and plain wool carpeting. Showroom at 14–15 Berners Street, London w1.

Liberty, Regent Street, London w1 (tel. 01-734 1234). This way for mouth-watering, magic carpets. Stock modern and traditional carpets from Turkey, China, Rumania, India, Portugal, Morocco, Pakistan, Belgium, Albania and Tibet.

Hugh McKay & Co. Ltd, PO Box 1, Freemans Place, Durham City (tel. Durham [0385] 64444). Oh the joy of it. A designer's paradise. Over 1000 modern and traditional Wilton designs which can be woven to customers' own colour. Showroom at Roman House, Wood Street, London EC2. Retailer's introduction needed.

Persian and Oriental Carpet Centre, 63 South Audley Street, London W1 (tel. 01-629 9670). Wide selection of really lovely old and new rugs, carpets and kilims. They have access to the only custom-bonded warehouse in Mayfair. They will also clean and repair carpets.

Royal School of Needlework, 25 Prince's Gate, London SW7 (tel. 01-589 0077). Customers may discuss the design and period of carpet they would like made up. Artists' work on display.

Thompson Shepherd (Carpets) Ltd, Seafield Works, Dundee, Angus (tel. Dundee [0382] 645111). Moresque luxury-class 100 per cent wool Wilton in undyed wool has won three design awards. (Available in ten designs.) Penthouse Axminsters in high and low pile giving 3D effect. Superhostess is their tufted, heavy domestic carpet in twenty plain colours. Showrooms at 112 High Holborn, London WC1 and in Manchester and Glasgow.

Tintawn Ltd, Richfield Avenue, Reading, Berkshire (tel. Reading [0734] 56321). Several ranges of wool carpet. Soft-cord, woven carpet with high-density foam backing; Tintawn Thatcher available with or without foam backing and flat, woven-textured carpets. Good value.

Weaver's Shop (Royal Wilton Carpet Factory Ltd), Wilton, Nr Salisbury, Wiltshire (tel. Wilton [0722 74] 2441). Sells seconds, remnants and off-cuts from the whole Wilton Royal range, including Axminsters, tufted and Wilton. Showroom at 26 Conduit Street, London W1. Retailer's introduction necessary.

Youghal Carpets, County Cork, Ireland (tel. Irish Republic 024-2159). Plain, plushy pile carpet in three qualities. Showroom at The Colonade, Porchester Road, London W2 (tel. 01-229 3674).

Ceramic tiles

Kenneth Clark Pottery, 10A Dryden Street, London WC2 (tel. 01-836 1660). Hand decorated, very individual tiles and wall panels. Beautiful work.

Designer's Guild, 277 Kings Road, London SW3 (tel. 01-351 1271). Four designs available produced by Designer's Guild. To order only; minimum order of 4 square yards or metres.

Domus, 260 Brompton Road, London SW3 (tel. 01-589 9457). Big, beautiful range of plain-coloured tiles; Provençal and range of Italian hand-painted tiles. Frostproof tiles for

outdoor use. Also handmade terra-cotta tiles and slabs.

Fired Earth Ltd, 102 Portland Road, London w 11 (tel. 01-727 4321). Traditional and abstract Spanish tiles, also Provençal. They will produce a customer's own specific design.

Heal & Son Ltd, 196 Tottenham Court Road, London w 1 (tel. 01-636 1666). French and Italian range of tiles.

H. & R. Johnson Ceramic Tiles Ltd, 303–306 High Holborn, London w c 1 (tel. 01-242 0564). A famous firm and rightly so. Big range of glazed and unglazed slip-resistant tiles (plain and patterned) and also special tiles for swimming pools. Large selection of tiles for kitchens and bathrooms.

Pilkington Tiles Ltd, PO Box 4, Clifton Junction, Manchester M 27 2 L P (tel. 061-794 2024). Plain and classic tiles. Showrooms both at Manchester and at Poole.

Reed Harris Ltd, Riverside House, Carnwath Road, London s w 6 (tel. 01-736 7511). German, Italian and Spanish tiles and Mosaics.

Rye Tiles, 12 Connaught Street, London w 2 (tel. 01-723 7278) and also at The Old Brewery Wishward, Rye, Sussex. Printed, hand-painted and plain tiles.

Mr Stone's Flooring & Tiling Shop, 90 Muswell Hill Broadway, London N 10 (tel. 01-883 8879). Good selection of tiles. Courteous service.

Tile Mart, 151 Great Portland Street, London w 1 (tel. 01-580 3814); also at 135 Notting Hill Gate, London w 11 and 107 Pimlico Road, London s w 1. Very good selection of tiles from Holland, France, Italy and Britain. In embossed and printed designs, unusual shapes and sizes.

Curtain fittings

W. A. Hudson Ltd, 115–125 Curtain Road, London E C 2 (tel. 01-739 3211). Big range of tracks and curtain accessories including traditional wood and brass poles, ends and rings. Many of these fittings are also available through John Lewis stores.

'Luxaflex' of *Hunter Douglas Ltd*, Bellsize Close, Walsall Road, Norton Canes, Cannock, Staffordshire (tel. Heath Hayes [0543] 75757). Plastic and aluminium curtain tracks which are easy to fit. Also exciting range of decorative tracks and wooden poles.

Silent Gliss, Star Line, Margate, Kent (tel. Thanet [0843] 63571). Range of aluminium anodized tracks which are wall or ceiling mounted. Accessories, hooks, etc. Shower railings and electric automatically operated curtain railing. Also an attractive range of sliding screens.

Sunway, 240 Bath Road, Slough, Berkshire (tel. Slough [0753] 26611). Range of curtain poles in standard lengths. Corded track in gold, silver and white.

Swish Products Ltd, Tamworth, Staffordshire (tel. Tamworth [0827] 3811). Slim tracks suitable for pencil pleats, pinch pleats or gathered headings; also for pelmets and valances. All tracks come in white PVC and some can be fitted with gold or white finials. Valance rails, cording sets, overlap fittings and brackets for hanging net curtains also available.

Doors

Albion Crystalcut Ltd, Simon House, Middlefield Industrial Estate, Sunderland Road, Sandy, Bedfordshire (tel. Sandy [0767] 80330). All kinds of door furniture in crystal, Perspex – clear or smoke.

J. D. Beardmore & Co., 3–5 Percy Street, London w 1 (tel. 01-637 7041). Interior and exterior door furniture in eleven different brass designs. They also do a range in china and black iron. Specialize in period designs. This is the place for the best brass doorknobs. Mail order for orders over £2

and orders over £60 post free (not to be sneezed at, their stuff can be heavy).

Crosby & Co. Ltd, Craven House, West Street, Farnham, Surrey (tel. Farnham [02513] 23123). Specialize in plastic laminated doors which are timber-framed and faced with wipe-clean Warerite. Special sizes and colours to order.

Dryad Metalworks, Sanvey Gate, Leicester (tel. Leicester [0533] 27457). Range of modern door fittings designed by Robert Welch in satin anodized aluminium. Really beautiful.

Eperon-York Ltd, 36 Barbican Road, York (tel. York [0904] 27555). Craftsman-made range of indoor woodwork in modern and traditional designs.

Everest Double Glazing, Everest House, Sopers Road, Potters Bar, Hertfordshire. Sliding double-glazed patio doors, up to 640×250 cm (21 feet $\times$ 8 feet 2 inches). Also entrance doors in anodized aluminium which is weather-proof. They will install them for you. *Freefone* service no. 2044 (through your operator).

Heatherly Fine China Ltd, Unit 3, Ferry Lane, Brentford, Middlesex (tel. 01-568 7963). Specialists in decorated porcelain door furniture and ceramic bathroom accessories.

P. C. Henderson Ltd, Harold Hill, Romford, Essex (tel. Romford [0708] 45555). Wide range of folding door units available, in two- or four-door versions.

Knobs and Knockers, 61–65 Judd Street, London wc1 (tel. 01-387 0091). Very wide range of interior and exterior doors, including Elizabethan, bow-fronted Georgian, Victorian and Western Saloon swing doors. Excellent range of door furniture including traditional brass, glass, china and black iron. Also louvred doors. Branches throughout the country.

Walter Lawrence (Trading) Ltd, Sheering Mill Lane, Sawbridgeworth, Hertfordshire (tel. Bishop's Stortford [0279] 722171). Ready-to-paint Georgian doors, panelled and flush doors. Also fire-proof doors.

Lenscrete Ltd, Queens Circus, London sw8 (tel. 01-622 1063). Wooden sliding, folding partition doors.

W. H. Newson & Sons, 61 Pimlico Road, London sw1 (tel. 01-730 6262) or 49 Battersea Park Road, London sw11 4NH (tel. 01-223 4411). Folding doors and room dividers in various woods; louvred doors; shutters and panels. Reproduction Georgian front doors in Canadian cedarwood. Period door furniture in lacquered and polished brass. Useful catalogue. If you want nails, tiles, DIY tools, trellis, garden sheds, skirtings, picture rails, mouldings, dados (you thought they were dead, didn't you?), bow windows, ordinary windows, sliding walls of glass, pine-louvred doors (I buy mine here), classy Georgian-type front doors, showers, saunas, plaster board, hardboard, polystyrene and rather vulgar toilet roll holders, send for Newson's free catalogue. It's also very useful for checking any prices that your builder quotes to you.

Pilkington Brothers Ltd, St Helens, Merseyside (tel. St Helens [0744] 28882). That famous glass firm. Good for glass doors. Available in six designs in toughened glass. Non-standard doors to order. Also do a wide range of door furniture.

Edwin Showell & Sons Ltd, Josia Park, Union Works, Gowerd Street, Willenhall, West Midlands (tel. Willenhall [0902] 66931). Best known by their trademark UNION – manufacturer of locks, handles, fingerplates and other door furniture. Very wide range.

Town & Country Aluminium Ltd, Reflection House, Cheshire Street, London e2 (tel. 01-247 5691). Sliding glass doors up to 2.5 m (8 feet 8 inches) high and 6 m (twenty feet) wide. Free delivery if within 100-mile radius of London.

Yale Security Products Division, Wood Street, Willenhall, West Midlands (tel. Willenhall [0902] 66911). The lock specialists. Kelvin range of door fittings in satin anodized aluminium.

Fabrics

Armitage & Rhodes Ltd, Calder Vale Mills, Ravensthorpe, Dewsbury,

Yorkshire (tel. Dewsbury [0924] 466221). Upholstery fabric only, but a good range.

Laura Ashley, 40 Sloane Street, London sw1 (tel. 01-235 9728). Exquisitely pretty prints in lightweight and heavier cottons. Also cotton sateen. For curtains and upholstery.

Boussac, 299 Oxford Street, London w1 (tel. 01-493 8719). French and Persian designs available in two widths for curtaining. Range of geometric prints for domestic and contract use. Comparatively cheap and superlatively good. (Sundecor do matching blinds.)

Cole & Son (Wallpapers) Ltd, 18 Mortimer Street, London w1 (tel. 01-580 1066). Beautiful curtain fabric which matches their beautiful wallpapers and paints.

Curtain Galleries, 319 Regents Park Road, London N3 (tel. 01-346 4324). Plain silks, continental curtaining and upholstery fabric to order. They will make up curtains, roller blinds and bedspreads.

Designers' Guild, 277 Kings Road, London sw3 (tel. 01-351 1271). Indian-inspired designs, some of which have matching wallpapers. Linen union upholstery fabrics and good selection of fringes and braids.

Distinctive Trimmings, 17D Kensington Church Street, London w8 (tel. 01-937 6174) and 11 Marylebone Lane, London w1 (tel. 01-486 6456). Hundreds of different braids, trimmings, tassels, cords, etc. Send a fabric

cutting together with an s.a.e. and they will send you samples. Well worth trying.

Felt & Hessian Shop, 34 Greville Street, London EC1 (tel. 01-405 6215). Felts available in seventy-seven colours and hessians in sixty-five. Price lists available.

Form International, Whittington House, 19–30 Alfred Place, London WC1E 7EA (tel. 01-580 2080). Sheer curtaining and lots of co-ordinating upholstery fabric.

Goddard & Jenkins Midland Ltd, Opus One, Suffolk Street, Birmingham (tel. 021-643 5956). For their furnishing fabrics contact Dodson Bull Furnishing Co. Ltd, Barbican Trade Centre, 100 Aldersgate Street, London EC2Y 8AE (tel. 01-628 3456). Large display of fabrics (and carpets). Discount available if payment made within four days.

Habitat, 206–222 Kings Road, London sw3 (tel. 01-351 1211); 156–158 Tottenham Court Road, London w1 (tel. 01-388 1721). Bright, bold prints for upholstery and curtaining. A few Liberty prints and William Morris designs. Also fabric for blinds (as well as a blind service).

Heal & Son Ltd, 196 Tottenham Court Road, London w1 (tel. 01-636 1666). A large fabric department with many classical and modern prints. Over a thousand plain colour fabrics besides.

Hull Traders, Pave Shed, Trawden, Nr Colne, Lancashire (tel. Colne [0282] 86445). Bold, modern prints designed by award-winning Shirley Craven. Some curtaining and upholstery fabrics.

Landau Sekers Ltd, 300 Regent Street, London w1 (tel. 01-636 2612). Wide range of curtaining; some upholstery. Ready-made curtains. Plain textureds in huge choice of colours. Really beautiful, subtle, silky shades.

John Lewis, Oxford Street, London w1 (tel. 01-637 3434). Excellent fabric departments in all their branches combine good taste and quality and a huge selection.

Liberty & Co., Regent Street, London w1 (tel. 01-734 1234). Beautiful prints and traditional and William Morris designs in cotton or linen/cotton printed union. Some of the prettiest fabrics in the world.

Lister & Co. Ltd, 11 Harley Street, London w1 (tel. 01-580 6474). Velvet specialists with a wide range of colours – really good value, some good colours. Also linings and upholstery fabrics. Showroom at Manningham Mills, Bradford. Yorkshire (tel. Bradford [0274] 4222).

Plus Two, 79 Walton Street, London sw3 (tel. 01-589 4118). There are many imported fabrics, many to order. Plus Two are design consultants and have samples of tiles, carpets and wall-coverings.

Ramm Son & Crocker, 20 Newman Street, London w1 (tel. 01-636 6111). Cotton chintzes, traditional fabrics, pretty prints. Traditionally a historic British firm.

Russell & Chapple Ltd, 23 Monmouth Street, London wc2 (tel. 01-836 7521). Jute, twill, hessians, cotton duck, canvas and cottons.

Sanderson, 52 Berners Street, London w1 (tel. 01-636 2800). Many, many, many fabrics and matching wallpapers. Cotton chintzes, velvets, linen union loose-cover fabrics.

Fireplaces

Baxi Heating, Brownedge Road, Bamber Bridge, Preston, Lancashire (tel. Preston [0772] 36201). For solid-fuel, underfloor draught fires in different sizes. Fire fronts in copper, pewter or stainless steel.

A. Bell & Co. Ltd, Kingsthorpe, Northampton (tel. Northampton [0604] 712505). Selection of fireplaces including hole-in-the-wall and reproduction Georgian. Available in slate, tile, stone, marble, wood and stainless steel. Fireplaces can be made to order.

Bolehill Quarries Ltd, Wingerworth, Chesterfield (tel. Chesterfield [0246] 70244), and St Giles Road, Lightcliffe, Nr Halifax (tel. Halifax [0422] 202683). Range of do-it-yourself fireplace kits in natural stone. They supply kits to customer's require-

ments. Large showroom and Cash and Carry warehouses at each address.

Edwin Bradley & Sons Ltd, Okus Road, Swindon, Wiltshire (tel. Swindon [0793] 28131). Supply kits to make your own fireplace in Bradstone Cotswold stone. You can order kits to your own specifications.

Ceramic Fireplace Tile Council, Federation House, Stoke-on-Trent, Staffordshire (tel. Stoke-on-Trent [0782] 45147). Write to them for free colour brochure of tiled fireplaces.

J. Crotty & Son Ltd, 74 New Kings Road, London s w 6 (tel. 01-385 1789). Genuine period marble and wooden fireplaces. Old fenders and firebaskets, etc.

T. Crowther & Son Ltd, 282 North End Road, London s w 6 (tel. 01-385 1375). Genuine period marble and wooden fireplaces. Old grates, firebaskets, etc.

Hart of Knightsbridge, 3 Beauchamp Place, London s w 3 (tel. 01-584 5770). Antique marble mantels. Reproduction period fireplaces. Carved recess and corner cupboards in natural wood or white finish.

Wade Lewis Ltd, 117 Windmill Road, Sunbury-on-Thames (tel. Sunbury-on-Thames [09327] 86522). Two designs of Pither stoves finished in black enamel with brass trimmings or stainless steel with nickel trimmings. Both come with or without back boilers. Also a wedge wall-hung fire in stainless steel.

Flooring

Alliance Flooring Company Ltd, 36 Maxwell Road, London s w 6 (tel. 01-736 3811). Wood, mosaic, cork, vinyl flooring. They also have a fitting service and hire out sanding machines and dance floors.

Amtico, 17 George Street, London w 1 (tel. 01-629 6258). Vinyl tiling with good textured and printed simulations of pebbles, brick, stone, marble. Provençal tiles, traditional Spanish and Portuguese-type designs. Also plain and irregularly shaped tiles.

Armstrong Cork Company Ltd, Armstrong House, Chequers Square, Uxbridge, Middlesex (tel. Uxbridge [89] 51122). Cushioned vinyl floor coverings in sheets. Also do-it-yourself tiles (self-adhesive).

Art Marbles Stone & Mosaic Company Ltd, Dawson Road, Kingston-upon-Thames, Surrey (tel. 01-546 2023). Over ninety kinds of marble. Also slate and granite.

Dunlop Semtex Ltd, Retail Product Division, Chester Road, Erdington, Birmingham B 35 7 A L (tel. 021-373 8101). Three types of tiles: two plain marbled and one printed (which is self-adhesive). Various types of sheet flooring and two cushioned vinyls in various designs. Three qualities of carpet tiles which are rubber-backed and loose-lay.

Flooring Factors & Tile Company, 23 Leslie Park Road, Croydon, Surrey (tel. 01-654 8584). Pre-finished cork tiles and Cork-O-Plast tiles for heavier kitchen-wear. A-B Cork sanded and ready for sealing, HD 75 Cork already sealed. Do-it-yourself parquet floors. Parquetiles in walnut, mahogany or oak. Vinylwood strip floor.

GAF (*Great Britain*), PO Box 70, Blackthorne Road, Colnbrook, Slough, Buckinghamshire (tel. Colnbrook [028-12] 4567). Sheet vinyl flooring in four qualities and over seventy designs, including parquet, brick, ceramic tiles and marble.

Gerland Ltd, 90 Crawford Street, London w1 (tel. 01-723 6601 or 262 2016). (Retail and contract.) Interlocking tiles of vaguely Eastern shape. Simulated slate tiles. Cushioned vinyl floor sheeting in several qualities. Vinyl flexible tiles (in various thicknesses) which can be laid straight on to floor. Also rubber studded tiles.

The Great Metropolitan Flooring Company Ltd, 73 Kinnerton Street, London sw1 (tel. 01-235 1161). (Contractors and suppliers only.) Fitting service for Home Counties and London. All types of wooden flooring including parquet, rubber flooring, carpeting, vinyls, ceramic tiles. Will also sand down and seal your wooden floors.

James Halstead Ltd, PO Box 3, Radcliffe New Road, Whitefield, Manchester (tel. 061-766 3781). Self-adhesive vinyl tiles in three qualities in over forty different colourways.

Vinyl sheet flooring in twenty-four colourways. Wide range of cushioned-back sheet vinyl. Tiles in plain marble.

Marley Retail Supplies Ltd, London Road, Riverhead, Sevenoaks, Kent TN13 2DS (tel. Sevenoaks [0732] 55255). Big selection of cushion flooring. Sheet vinyl (hard-back) and 'Softstep', felt-backed vinyl sheeting. Tiles range from heavy florals to a quite nice marble effect and simulated woodblock.

Nairn Floors Ltd, PO Box 1, Victoria Road, Kirkcaldy, Fife (tel. Kirkcaldy [0592] 61111). Cushion floor sheeting in three qualities. Sheet linoleum and vinyl. Tiles come in two types, one flexible. Two ranges of carpet tiles in twenty-two plain colours. A really good value firm.

Robinson Brothers Cork Tiles Ltd, 8 Bowater Road, Woolwich SE18 5TF (tel. 01-317 8192). Patterned cork tiles in untreated, pre-waxed or polyurethane finish. Also PVC-coated cork floor tiles available in nine designs.

Rooksmoor Mills, Stroud, Gloucestershire (tel. Stroud [045-36] 2577). Rush matting squares and maize matting – both types made up into any shape or size. Also sisal and other cheap carpeting.

Warehouse, 39 Neal Street, Covent Garden, London wc2 (tel. 01-240 0931). Coconut matting tiles in natural colours. Stair carpet and assorted coconut mats and woollen druggets, cotton dhurries and doormats.

Weyroc Ltd, Weybridge, Surrey (tel.

Weybridge [0932] 45599). You can buy tongue-and-grooved flooring chipboard, in ready-to-lay boards. Finished with clear polyurethane. Available through builders' merchants.

Wicanders Ltd, 26 Store Street, London WC1 (tel. 01-636 5959). For all sorts of vinyl-sealed cork. Warmly recommended: expensive but worth it.

Wincilate Ltd, The Town Hall, Bow Road, London E3 (tel. 01-980 2203) and Victoria Docks, Caernarvon, N. Wales. Blue-grey slate for flooring. Will cut to customers' specifications.

Glass and mirrors

Glass and Glazing Federation, 6 Mount Row, London W1 (tel. 01-629 8334). Will give advice on flat glass and mirrors. Free leaflets available.

Pearson Mirrorlite Ltd, Northpoint, Meadowhall Road, Sheffield S9 1FA (tel. Sheffield [0742] 443333). Plastic mirror which is lightweight and shatter-proof and comes in standard sizes. Different colours available and colour chart sent upon request.

Pilkington Brothers Ltd, St Helens, Lancashire (tel. St Helens [0744] 28882). Decorated glass and almost every kind of glass you can think of.

Sander Mirror Company, Sander House, Elmore Street, London N1 (tel. 01-226 8881). Eighty-five different mirror finishes from the palest pastels to very bright, brilliant colours.

Kitchen units

Choosing kitchen units really involves making a choice between different boxes with doors, in wood, white or coloured laminates. Bathrooms can also be beautifully and efficiently furnished with carefully chosen kitchen units.

Most of the following manufacturers offer some interesting accessories including special storage platforms for heavy kitchen appliances such as mixers; swivel corner cupboard shelves; built-in vegetable racks, bottle racks, spice racks, chopping boards, telescopic towel rails, swing-out waste buckets and so on. There is also a wide range of sink units.

Self-assembly units are usually cheaper than ready-assembled units, but tend to come in more limited numbers of sizes and colours (which helps to keep the cost down).

I've chosen the following manufacturers for good design and quality: they've been graded into three cate-

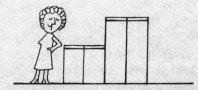

gories – luxury, good value and budget. Free design services are offered by English Rose, Marley, Multiflex, Solar 60 and (best of all) Wrighton. Many other firms offer a design service where you pay a small token charge, which is often refunded when you place an order. Most firms have showrooms throughout the country so if possible go along and see them before making your final decision.

Budget kitchen units

You can buy whitewood units and make them look really good by staining them or using a natural or coloured varnish. Manufacturers who make whitewood kitchen furniture include:

Kuvo Whitewood, Robert Airey & Son Ltd, Kuvo Works, King's Bridge Road, Huddersfield (tel. Huddersfield [0484] 25376).

Liden, Liden Products (Whitewood) Ltd, 227 Lea Bridge Road, London E10 (tel. 01-539 5500).

Adjustable shelving systems can also be successfully used for kitchen storage; manufacturers of suitable systems include:

Click Systems, Low Moor Road, Kirkby-in-Ashfield, Nottinghamshire

(tel. Mansfield [0623] 754012) or through branches of Habitat.

Spur Systems, Otterspool Way, Watford, Hertfordshire (tel. Watford [0923] 34528).

Tebrax Ltd, 63 Borough High Street, London SE1 (tel. 01-407 4367).

Good value kitchen units

Alno, 164–166 King Street, London W6 (tel. 01-748 0671). Eleven different ranges with over 400 different types of cupboards. Many accessories. Planning service.

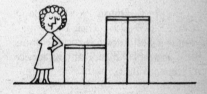

Beekay, 6 Priorswood Place, East Pimbo, Skelmersdale, Lancashire (tel. Skelmersdale [0695] 21331). They will put you in touch with the name of your nearest dealer, who will plan your kitchen for you. There's a small charge but this is refunded if an order is placed. Various kitchen styles.

Eastham, 76 Holmes Road, Thornton, Blackpool FY5 2SQ (tel. Cleveleys [03914] 6771). Really good value ranges including many self-assembly units. Their E-line range includes units in natural teak or oak. Planning service.

English Rose, Avon Works, Warwick (tel. Warwick [0926] 45411). Modern and traditional designs in wood, wood veneers and laminates. *Free* planning service.

Gower Furniture, Holmfield Industrial Estate, Halifax, Yorkshire (tel. Halifax [0422] 46201). Good self-assembly range and extensive colour range of laminate finishes. All usual accessories.

Greencraft, Tom Green (Joinery) Ltd, Ingatestone, Essex (tel. Ingatestone [02775] 4141). Pine-fronted kitchen units. Also 'leather-look' range. *Free* planning service. Self-assembly range in white only.

Grovewood, Tipton, West Midlands (tel. 021-557 3955). Their Daintymaid range is best known. Lots of colours. Self-assembly range. Planning service. Excellent value.

Hygena, P O Box 18, Kirkby Industrial Estate, Liverpool L33 7SH (tel. 051-548 3505). Well known for their QA range. Well-designed brochure shows colour ranges and finishes. Good choice of work tops. Planning service.

Ideal Kitchens, Ideal Timber Products Ltd, Broadmeadow Estate, Dumbarton, Scotland (tel. Dumbarton [0389] 63284). Self-assembly units in plastic laminate finish. Also available in wood veneer.

Kandya, Program Kandya Kitchens, Dunhams Lane, Letchworth, Hertfordshire (tel. Letchworth [04626] 2381). Excellent value – particularly the Kandya KF900 units in their contract range; very simple in plain

white with a beech trim. *Range includes designs for the disabled.* Also self-assembly. Their retailers can provide a planning service.

Magnet, Magnet Southerns Ltd, Royd Ings Avenue, Keighley, Yorkshire (tel. Keighley [0535] 61133). Magnet's ready-assembled units are some of the best value around, with a choice of either polar white or planked teak on doors and drawers.

Manhattan Furniture, Dennis & Robinson Ltd, Churchill Industrial Estate, Lancing, Sussex (tel. Lancing [09063] 5321). The Cassette range is either assembled or self-assembly (which is slightly cheaper). Restricted colour range but good selection of sizes.

Marley, Marley Luxury Furniture, Peasmarsh, Guildford, Surrey (tel. Guildford [0483] 69922). Self-assembly units available in a Formica finish, wood laminate and the following woodgrains: planked pine, hickory and teak. Colours include olive, blue, mandarin white and an off-white. Rigid units in Tropical Cherry wood veneer in wide range of sizes. *Free* planning service.

Qualcast, Charlton Road, Edmonton, London N9 (tel. 01-804 5051). Very reasonably priced and well-designed ranges of kitchen fittings.

Salvarini, Derek Dixon, Salvarini Southern Sales, The Granary, Camley Street, London NW1 OP11 (tel. 01-388 2007). Continental ranges of units, well designed and good value. Fairly restricted colour choice.

Schreiber, Edinburgh Way, Harlow, Essex (tel. Harlow [0279] 26881). Fitted kitchens with furniture to match. Self-assembly units as well.

Solarbo, PO Box 5, Commerce Way, Lancing, Sussex (tel. Lancing [09063] 63451). Thirty-five units available. Lots of accessories include pine tables and shelves. Choice of louvred or plain doors in their pine range. Their brochure includes a planning chart to help you design your kitchen. Also *free* advisory service.

UBM, UBM Group, Avon Works, Winterstoke Road, Bristol (tel. Bristol [0272] 664611). Make ready-assembled and self-assembly units. Mainly laminate finish but some with a simulated woodgrain, timber veneers or solid pine. Various colours available. One range in light oak available from stock.

Wrighton, Billet Road, London E 17 (tel. 01-527 5521). Wrighton won the Design Council award in 1976 for their Waltham range. Good choice of colours and finishes, plus all accessories. *Free* planning service. Strongly recommended.

Luxury kitchen units
Beckermann Kitchens, 40 High Street, Sunningdale, Berkshire (tel. Ascot [0990] 24869). Continental ranges of

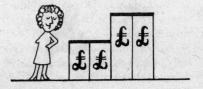

units in wood or laminate finish. Quick delivery service.

Bosch, 47 Market Street, Watford, Hertfordshire (tel. Watford [0923] 26697). Oak, mahogany, pine and laminate finishes. Also selection of the seemingly indestructible Bosch appliances – cookers, freezers, dishwashers and washing machines. Design service.

Elizabeth Ann Woodcraft Ltd, Rhyl, North Wales (tel. Rhyl [0745] 2341). Snowdon range of louvred units in teak or white. Various hi-gloss polyester finishes in pastels. Woodgrains such as oak, elm and walnut can be supplied in matt or hi-gloss. I don't think it's possible to improve on their finish. To my mind, the Rolls-Royce of kitchen cabinets.

Miele, Park House, 207–211 The Vale, London w 3 (tel. 01-749 2463). Miele admit in their advertisements that they're expensive. Lots of accessories, peninsular units and, of course, appliances: washing machines, cookers, hobs, refrigerators, dishwashers, cooker hoods and so on. Planning service.

Poggenpohl, King's Avenue House, King's Avenue, New Malden, Surrey (tel. 01-949 2459). Well-designed kitchens with lots of finishes in coloured woods and laminates. Real space-age stuff.

SieMatic, 11–17 Fowler Road, Hainault, Ilford, Essex (tel. 01-501 2216). A range of designs with many unit variations and accessories from laminate to solid wood front timber. Write to the above address for further information.

Other kitchen equipment
Carron Company, Stainless Steel Division, Carron, Falkirk (tel. Falkirk [0324] 24999). Modern stainless steel sinks to fit into counter tops.

Glynwed Bathroom and Kitchen Products Ltd, Meadow Lane, Long Eaton, Nottingham (tel. Long Eaton [06076] 4141). Specialize in stainless steel and vitreous enamel sinks. Showroom at 28 Brook Street, London w1.

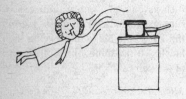

Hamer & Scroggs Ltd, Boultons Road, Kingswood, Bristol (tel. Bristol [0272] 673286). Combined drainer and worktops. Stainless steel sinks and surfaces in formica.

Harrods, Knightsbridge, London sw1 (tel. 01-730 1234). Very limited selection of kitchens – four ranges displayed, both English and Continental.

Heals, 196 Tottenham Court Road, London w1 has an extensive kitchen department, featuring the best of British and European designs.

Jay Kitchen Consultants Ltd, 54 Meadway, London N14 (tel. 01-886 1850). Run by Roma Jay, a specialist kitchen consultant and designer.

Room For Living, 40 Wigmore Street, London w1 (tel. 01-486 3351); 70–80 High Road, Bushey Heath, Hertfordshire (01-950 6945); 113–115 New Zealand Avenue, Walton-on-Thames (tel. Walton-on-Thames [09322] 41438). Wide range of kitchen units, including Nieburg from Germany.

W. & G. Sissons Ltd, Calver Mill, Calver Bridge, Sheffield s30 1xa (tel. Hope Valley [0433] 30791). Stainless steel sinks, some with built-in tidies. Choice of round, square or rectangular bowls.

John Strand Kitchens, 152–156 Kentish Town Road, London NW1 (tel. 01-267 2051). Room sets of units from cheap to middle price range. Planning advice available.

Thorn Kitchen Advisory Centre, Thorn House, Upper St Martin's Lane, London wc2 (tel. 01-836 2444). Permanent display of kitchen equipment and cabinets. They have little models of the range so you can see how your finished kitchen will look and they give you a photograph of it.

Lighting

British Home Stores, 252–258 Oxford Street, London w1 (tel. 01-629 2011) and branches. Undoubtedly the cheapest and best source of versatile

and modern lighting. Track, spot, table and rise and fall lamps available.

Concord Lighting International, Rotaflex House, 241 City Road, London EC1 (tel. 01-253 1200). Large showroom which carries many different types of lighting including spot, track, recessed. Advice is available, customers cannot buy the products from this wholesale showroom, but will be put in contact with their nearest stockist.

Conelight Ltd, Longmead Industrial Estate, Shaftesbury, Dorset (tel. Shaftesbury [0747] 3377). They make a wide range of modern style light fittings, table and floor lamps, wall lights and pendants. Advice and leaflets freely available from their showroom, which is at the above address.

Habitat, 206–222 Kings Road, London SW3 (tel. 01-351 1211); 156–158 Tottenham Court Road, London W1 (tel. 01-388 1721) and branches. Many different types of light fittings including spot lamps, rise and fall (plastic) pine lampshades, brushed aluminium lamps (expensive but well designed), enamelled metal and pretty, cheap paper lampshades.

Lumitron Ltd, Chandos Road, London NW10 (tel. 01-965 0211). Mainly do contract work for architects and designers. (They're the people who light the palaces in the Middle East.) Manufacture every conceivable type of fluorescent lighting and tungsten fitting, a range of acrylic lighting designed by Robert Welsh and also the Global range which won a design award in 1976. Free advice and leaflets at showroom.

WARNING: their main interest lies in commercial rather than domestic lighting and in situations where the lighting is an integral part of the overall design. But you can get lots of good ideas on how to achieve the best effects from your lighting scheme.

Merchant Adventurers Ltd, Hampton Road, West, Feltham, Middlesex (tel. 01-894 5522). Again, mainly geared to commercial lighting but with many ranges suitable for the home. All types of track lighting. Extensive range of spot lighting including a very cheap one made from polycarbonate. All types of tungsten fittings including one called tungsten halogen which gives a very brilliant light without using a higher voltage. Pendant and rise and fall units. Range of crystal glass ceiling lights, globe lights, coloured glass and exterior lighting. Showroom at the above address and also at 37 East Road (off City Road), London N1 (tel. 01-251 4071). Free advice and leaflets and you can buy on the spot.

Philips Electrical (*Lighting Division*), City House, London Road, Croydon, Surrey (tel. 01-689 2166). Small, good range of lighting fittings suitable for domestic use, including spot and fluorescent fittings. A few fittings for exterior lighting.

Christopher Wray's Lighting Emporium, 600–602 Kings Road, London SW6 (tel. 01-736 8434); *Christopher*

Wray Contract Lighting, 604 Kings Road; *Christopher Wray's Workshop*, 613–615 Kings Road; and *Christopher Wray's Tiffany Shop*, 593 Kings Road. Originator of the Tiffany lamp in London. *The* specialists in lighting of the 1880s. Genuine Edwardian and Victorian fittings. In the Workshop you can buy every conceivable spare part for oil lamps. Well worth a visit.

Paints

Berger Paints, Freshwater Road, Dagenham, Essex (tel. 01-590 6030). Berger Colorizer 420 available in 420 colours in vinyl matt, vinyl silk, high-gloss and undercoat. Magicote in gloss, emulsion and vinyl gloss. Colour design scheme service available (costs about £2.50) where the customer marks the physical characteristics of her room on a grid and Berger return it with a suggested colour scheme including matching curtains and wallpapers, together with samples. There is also a technical advisory service at their branch in Bristol.

J. W. Bollom & Co. Ltd, 107 Longacre, London wc2 (tel. 01-836 3728). Emulsion, gloss, eggshell and flat oil paints. Stoving and enamel and metallic paints to order. All paints are flame retardant.

Cole & Son Wallpapers Ltd, 18 Mortimer Street, London w1 (tel. 01-580 1066). Gloss, matt and emulsion paints, many of them historical. Wonderful French wallpapers and matching fabrics. Where top traditional designers shop.

Crown Paints Division, PO Box 37, Crown House, Hollins Road, Darwen, Lancashire BB3 0BG (tel. Darwen [0254] 74951). Crown Plus 2 gloss (non-drip) in matt vinyl or silk vinyl, full gloss or satin gloss. Extensive colour range.

Dane & Co. Ltd, Sugar House Lane, London E15 (tel. 01-534 2213). Eleven brilliant shades in Day-Glo fluorescent paint.

Habitat, 206–222 Kings Road, London sw3 (tel. 01-351 1211); 156–158 Tottenham Court Road, London w1 (tel. 01-388 1721) and branches. Range of about sixteen designers' colours in various finishes (gloss, emulsion and matt). Mail order service from PO Box 25, Hithercroft Road, Wallingford, Berkshire.

ICI Paints Division, Wexham Road, Slough, Buckinghamshire (tel. Slough [0753] 31151). Dulux Matchmaker paints in 400 colours and sixty-three BS colours. Ready-mix range colours. Specialist paints such as enamel and a rust preventative are only available through professional decorators.

International Paint, Connaught Road, Silvertown. London E16 (tel. 01-476 1441). Liquid Lino floor paint for cement and wood. A polyurethane protective covering for wooden floors and furniture. Lacquer for metal and wood. Radiator enamel. Also Darkaline wood stain which arrests woodworm. Write for further information.

Manders Paints Ltd, PO Box 9, Mander House, Wolverhampton (tel. Wolverhampton [0902] 20601). All BS colours in enamels, eggshell and emulsion. Also specialist paints including Gard water-resistant paint. Good for stone or brick fireplaces. Water-repellent for bricks and wood. Effective for about ten years.

Turnbridge Ltd, 72 Langley Road, London SW17 (tel. 01-672 6581). Quick-drying bath enamel available in white only.

U-Spray Paint, Humbrol Consumer Products (Division of Borden Ltd), Marfleet, Hull HU9 5NE (tel. Hull [0482] 701191). Paints in aerosol cans available in gloss (fourteen colours) – suitable for spraying refrigerators, furniture, etc., matt or gloss (black and white). Also available: wood primer, zinc antirust primer and clear polyurethane varnish.

F. W. Woolworth Ltd (all branches). For information ring 01-262 1222. Emulsion; wet-look polyurethane non-drip; also super-hard gloss in various colours.

Showers

The Bathroom & Shower Centre, 204 Great Portland Street, London W1 (tel. 01-388 7631). This showroom has eleven complete bathroom settings, ranges of wall and floor tiles and a good selection of the latest showers and shower cubicles. Good design service where they use scale models so you can see exactly how your bathroom might look. Also a Technical Advice Centre.

Conseal Ltd, Bond Avenue, Bletchley, Milton Keynes MK1 1JJ (tel. Milton Keynes [0908] 76998). Foldaway shower which looks like a wall panel and unfolds into a full-size shower – and really works. Comes with necessary pipe-work.

Doulton Sanitary Potteries Ltd, Westwood Works, PO Box 9, Berry Hill, Stoke-on-Trent, Staffordshire (tel. Stoke-on-Trent [0782] 47001). Shower trays in white and pastels.

Meynell Valves Ltd, Bushbury, Wolverhampton (tel. Wolverhampton [0982] 28621). Two special shower fittings designed for safety, can be gold plated.

Walls and wallcoverings

Allcork Insulation, 20 Dalston Gardens, Stanmore, Middlesex (tel. 01-204 7201). Cork slabs suitable for wall insulation. Dark colours.

C. F. Anderson & Son Ltd, 7–9 Islington Green, London N1 (tel. 01-226 1212). V-jointed timber for wall panelling (tongue and grooved) available in Californian Redwood, Panama Pine, Hemlock, South American Mahogany, Douglas Fir, Knotty Pine and Western Red Cedar. Needs sanding and application of protective finish.

Laura Ashley, 40 Sloane Street, London SW1 (tel. 01-235 9728). Mouthwatering pretty floral fabrics and papers which are very reasonably priced.

Bolehill Quarries Ltd, Wingerworth, Chesterfield, Derbyshire (tel. Chesterfield [0246] 70244); St Giles Road, Lightcliffe, Nr Halifax; and Lower Penpethy, Nr Tintagel, Cornwall. Range of natural stone and slate cladding suitable for interior and exterior walls; includes sandstone, gritstone and Cornish rustic slate. The latter may be used as flooring where there is a solid concrete bed.

J. W. Bollom & Co. Ltd, 107 Longacre, London WC2 (tel. 01-836 3728). Very large range of felts all of which match their paints. Also a selection of good hessians.

Cole & Son (Wallpapers) Ltd, 18 Mortimer Street, London W1 (tel. 01-580 1066). Hand-printed period wallpapers and borders. Excellent range of wallcoverings including suede, felt, hessian, silks and moires.

Crown Wallcoverings Division, Belgrave Mills, Belgrave Road, Darwen, Lancashire BB3 9RR (tel. Darwen [0254] 74951). Ready-pasted easy-strip vinyl and ready-pasted paper.

Designers Guild, 277 Kings Road, London SW3 (tel. 01-351 1271). Patterned papers inspired by leaves, shells and flowers. Some have matching fabrics. Some very pretty things.

Formica Ltd, De La Rue House, 84–86 Regent Street, London W1 (tel. 01-734 8020), and at Coast Road, West Chirton, North Shields, Tyne and Wear (tel. North Shields [08945] 75566). Laminate panelling in over 140 colours and patterns. Panels may be bought in stock sizes, ready-cut or to order.

Hill & Knowles, 1 Bridge Street, Richmond, Surrey (tel. 01-948 4010). Large range of papers, paper borders and wallcoverings, including ceramic tiles. Send 25p for brochure.

Hodkin & Jones Ltd, 515 Queens Road, Sheffield (tel. Sheffield [0742] 56121). Wall niches (with glass shelves); ceiling centres; plaster cornices; panel mouldings and arches, etc.

Home Decorating (Wallpapers) Ltd, 83 Walton Street, London SW3 (tel. 01-584 6111). Hundreds of wallpapers in stock including many continental ones.

G. Jackson & Sons, Rathbone Works, Rainville Road, London w6 9HD (tel. 01-385 6616). Good range of classical cornices, niches and ceiling centres. The majority of the designs are taken from the Adam Brothers' original moulds. They will also do carving and modelling.

Laconite Ltd, Walton Bridge, Shepperton, Middlesex (tel. Walton-on-Thames [09322] 28944). Hardboard panels with simulated 'woodgrain' finish or simulating plain or printed tiles.

Nairn Coated Products Ltd, Lune Mills, Lancaster Lancashire (tel. Lancaster [0524] 65222). Flocked vinyls in traditional designs and other vinyls in floral, abstract and tile designs.

John S. Oliver Ltd, 33 Pembridge Road, London w11 (tel. 01-727 3735). Good range of wallpapers in various colour combinations – some with matching paints. Also carry hessians and felts.

Osborne & Little, 352 Kings Road, London sw3 (tel. 01–352 1456). Printed hessians; Swedish machine printed and hand printed papers, some with matching fabrics.

Robinson's Cork Tiles, Vigers Stephens & Adams Ltd, Leadale Works, Craven Walk, London n16 6BY (tel. 01-800 1290). Various designer of cork wall panels in 12-inch squares.

Sanderson, 52 Berners Street, London w1 (tel. 01-636 7800). The sumptuous showroom is well worth a visit because it's full of room settings and you can get all the samples of paint, wallpaper and fabric from one counter. Many wallpapers include William Morris designs and flocks; the Triad range and also wallpapers by Shand Kydd. Silks, Japanese grasscloths, cork papers and ready-pasted vinyls also available.

Mr Stone's Paint & Wallpaper Shop, 175 Muswell Hill Broadway, London n10 (tel. 01-444 9562). British and foreign wallpapers and wallcoverings including exotic hessians, grasspapers, felts, etc. Also carries a small range of wallpapers by young British designers. Good service.

Storey Brothers & Co. Ltd, White Cross, Lancaster (tel. Lancaster [0524] 65288). Wide range of decorative self-adhesive vinyl wallcoverings.

Tektura, 74 Upper Street, London n1 (tel. 01-226 3034). Over 17,000 different wallcoverings, including felt, cork, vinyl, wool, foil, linen, etc. Advice service available and will undertake contracts. A remarkable business.

The Trade and Hyde Decor Centre, Church Street, Hyde, Cheshire (tel. Hyde [061368] 5111). For unusual wallpapers – Thai silk and grasscloth. Hundreds of well-known papers and vinyl wallcoverings and paints; also hessians.

Windows

P. G. Allday & Co. Ltd, 117 Northwood Street, Birmingham (tel. 021-236 1071). Selection of sliding windows and doors.

J. D. Beardmore & Co. Ltd, 3–5 Percy Street, London w1 (tel. 01-637 7041). Window fittings available for sliding sash and casement windows and also fanlights.

Crittall-Windows Ltd, Manor Works, Braintree, Essex CM7 6DF (tel. Braintree [0376] 24106). Plastic ancillary components (subframes etc.). Very wide range of steel and aluminium frames in standard and non-standard sizes. Window centres at Sevenoaks (Kent), Bristol, Leicester, Glasgow and Manchester; London showroom at 210 High Holborn, London wc1. Distributors throughout the country.

Glass and Glazing Federation, 6 Mount Row, London w1 (tel. 01-629 8334). This is a trade organization incorporating all the top UK double-glazing companies. They have an advisory service on glass and will send you leaflets, give general information and answer queries.

W. H. Newson & Sons Ltd, 61 Pimlico Road, London sw1 (tel. 01-730 6262). Bow windows. Particularly good if you're converting a house or a cottage. Showroom at 192 Ebury Street, London sw1 (tel. 01-730 6141).

Town & Country Aluminium Ltd, Reflection House, Cheshire Street, London e2 (tel. 01-247 5691). For sliding windows and double glazing.

Velux Company Ltd, Gunnels Wood Road, Stevenage, Hertfordshire (tel. Stevenage [0438] 2570). Roof windows, ideal if you're converting lofts into living accommodation.

Yale Security Products Division, Willenhall, West Midlands (tel. Willenhall [0902] 66911). Kelvin range of window fittings.

Yes, You Can Do It Yourself

Our motto: Yes, I would *much* rather somebody else did it, but who is there and who can afford to pay them, anyway?

The secret of DIY is an infinite capacity for taking pains. If you are naturally neat and careful, you will *probably* do just as good a job as your local odd-job man who probably isn't neat and careful, just better at sending a bill.

Don't start with too ambitious a job just because you want it done. Everyone starts repapering the living-room instead of painting the lavatory, but even a *little* experience is valuable.

Don't start by overspending on things you can spoil, such as William Morris wallpaper. On the other hand don't economize where it's foolish to do so. Buy good tools and good quality materials. Only buy equipment as you need it for the job, and think of that power drill not as an extravagance but as an even better investment than your Carmen rollers. The first job that you do with it (fixing shelves?) will probably pay for it. And if you can operate a sewing machine you can operate a power drill, which is much easier.

The way to start a DIY job is to put your feet up on the sofa and make a shopping list of the things you will need and make sure that you buy enough of them. (Not ordering enough is a classic beginner's mistake.) Then you can just put this list in the sales-

272   BOOK 2: HOME MADE

man's hand and stand back while he stacks it up on the counter.

It is worth walking a little further to find a sympathetic DIY shop instead of one that treats you as if you're cheating their other customers out of a living. Try to avoid that frightful machismo-in-overalls that makes you feel clumsy and half-witted in those shops that smell of linseed oil and hemp and can offer you a thousand different screws but no satisfaction.

Before buying anything read the label to make sure it's exactly what you want. And if it's paint or adhesive, find out how to get it off before you put it on. And keep these getters-offers well away from children and pets because they are poisonous.

Before paying for it, and while still in the shop, read the instructions right through, in case there are any qualifying clauses or crafty caveats, such as 'not recommended for use with ...' followed by a list of practically everything.

You needn't always follow the instructions. There *are* short-cuts but instructions always aim at a perfect job because the manufacturer doesn't want any comeback if you don't do it properly. So make sure that you know what you're doing if you *don't* intend to follow the instructions.

You don't necessarily need a mate but it's a good idea to cultivate a nearby twin soul on the understanding that she will help you fix your curtain rails if you help her put her shelving straight. Reciprocal work is rarely fairly shared, so try to work out some

system of fair recompense, because one usually does more than the other, in the natural course of events. *Il y a toujours* one who hammers and one who holds the nails. However friendly you get, don't indulge in any tool swapping. Don't pretend you haven't got it: pretend you've already lent it to someone else or it's broken. This is difficult and unfair because you often want to borrow tools. If you *are* foolish enough to lend your tools, don't hand them over before you have arranged when you can collect them. Don't wait for someone else to bring them back, as is right and proper.

You keep track of them and lend them for as short a period as possible, otherwise *you* might forget to reclaim them.

Particularly avoid lending paintbrushes or chisels or any electrical equipment, whether it's a drill or a sawing machine. They always seem to have a nervous collapse or play Iago once they are in someone else's hands. Never allow children to play with your tools. Lock them up (the tools, I mean) because they're both precious and dangerous.

If your first few jobs go well and you rightly get carried away with your own success, invest in the *Reader's Digest* Do-It-Yourself book and let it guide you through more ambitious projects.

You can also take short day or evening education classes in DIY for very little charge. They include decorating, plumbing, electrical work, carpentry and car maintenance.

Another good investment in self-sufficiency is a one-day course run by the Electrical Association for Women on wiring, insulation and all those other little things that make so many of us artisan-dependent. Lunch is included in the small charge. Write to the Services Administrator, The Electrical Association for Women, 25 Foubert's Place, London W1V 2AL (tel. 01-437 5212).

HOW TO INSULATE YOUR HOT WATER TANK AND LOFT

How to lag a hot water tank

Tools needed: a tape measure.
Materials: a 75-mm (3-inch) insulating jacket.

An unlagged hot water tank can cost you up to £52 a year in wasted heat. You can cut your water heating bills by up to 75 per cent if you fit a thick 75-mm (3-inch) insulating jacket (cost around £5).

If you already have a jacket and it doesn't feel 3 inches thick and it does feel warm and it doesn't encase the tank – get a new 3-inch jacket. It looks a bit like a baby's life jacket: you just fit it round the boiler snugly and tie it on with a couple of belts. It's not more difficult than putting on some baby garments I've struggled with and at least the boiler isn't going to be sick over your ear.

This is as easy as putting on a coat with a belt.

1 With a tape-measure measure the vertical height to the top of the dome and the diameter of the tank.
2 Buy 75-mm (3-inch) thick insulating jacket from your local hardware, DIY or electrical shop or a large store such as Selfridges.
3 Instructions come with the jacket. Smooth the jacket down over the tank. Lightly tie one belt near the top of the tank and the other near the base. Make sure there are no gaps between the jacket sections, through which heat could escape.

How to insulate a loft

Tools needed: a pair of rubber gloves; possibly a pair of sharp scissors; kneeling plank.
Materials: insulating material.

To insulate an average three-bedroom semi-detached house shouldn't take longer than a morning.

Lofts can be insulated with loose-fill granules, a bit like popcorn, which you pour to a depth of 10 cm (4 inches) between the wooden joists.

Or you can buy rolls of glass fibre such as Supawrap, or mineral wool, which is 75 mm (3 inches) thick, not less, when unrolled. Check the width between the joists, and buy rolls a bit wider (they come in different widths) so that when you roll out the wool it pushes up a bit at the sides of the joists and leaves no gaps. A loft 6 × 9 m/54 sq m (20 × 30 ft/600 sq ft) would need fourteen rolls of Supawrap.

Kneel on a plank laid over the joists (so that you don't fall through the ceiling) and start unrolling from the outside walls towards the centre of the loft. Cut the roll at the centre with sharp scissors. When you've unrolled one side, turn round and do the other. Push the ends together in the centre to cover the whole area and work so that you will end up near the loft trapdoor.

It's hard on the knees (but not for long) and you must wear rubber gloves if handling glass fibre, because of the scratching and irritation it can cause.

Insulate the loft trapdoor, but *don't* insulate under the cold water tank, so that a little warmth rises through the ceiling from the room below and prevents freezing.

YOUR ELECTRICAL APPLIANCE FAULT-FINDER
(use it before calling costly electricians)

Tools needed: small screwdriver; fuse wire; possibly a new cartridge fuse; possibly a torch.

When an electrical appliance is switched on and nothing happens the fault may mean a job for the electrician or it may be something simple that you can attend to. As it must be in one of the areas shown in the diagram, investigate them one by one. To find out which is giving trouble, follow this simple fault-finding procedure.

1 The very first thing to do is to plug the appliance into another socket. If it works now the original socket is probably faulty – and this *is* an electrician's job.

However, before calling an electrician, you should check the fuse box to make sure that the trouble really is *in* the socket and not at the fuse box (see Point 4).

If you're having the house rewired, instead of fuses ask for circuit-breakers, which *never have to be mended*. They are switches that turn off when overloaded by current. If you overload one area, a button pops out. Then you simply unplug a few appliances – because you are overloading your power source – and push it back again to reset it.

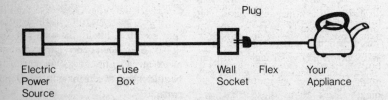

Electric Power Source   Fuse Box   Wall Socket   Flex   Plug   Your Appliance

Possible Sources of Electrical Trouble

If the appliance doesn't work plugged into any socket the fault could be any of the following:

2 A loose wire, or wires, in the plug. Take the cover off the plug by undoing the large screw in the middle and check that all wire-ends are securely connected to their respective pins by the little screws. If the wires are all OK check for ...

3 A dead fuse in the plug. Every modern flat-pin plug has its own internal fuse, held in by clips. A 13-amp plug has a brown one, a 3-amp plug a blue one. Replace the fuse with a new one of the same colour; if this doesn't make the appliance work the old fuse is probably all right and the fault to be found elsewhere, and it may be ...

4 A blown fuse in the fuse box. If this is the case a few other things are probably not working. Switch off the power for the whole house at the main switch, then unplug or switch off a couple of appliances, in case the 'blow' is due to overloading. Then take out one fuse after another until you find one in which the fuse wire stretched between the two terminals is broken. Replace the broken wire with a new piece of the same amperage (fuse holder and fuse wire card are both marked to show whether it's 5 amp, 10 amp or 30 amp; never fit bigger sizes than those that are marked on the fuse carrier).

If the fuse blows again find out which appliance is causing it (probably the one you've just started to

use) and have the appliance repaired. If your wiring is old, this should be Point 2, not Point 4.

5 Power failure is another possibility. If all lights and appliances in the house are dead there may have been a local power cut. (Check on whether a neighbour's power is also gone.) Or the fault may lie only with your supply – for instance, if the cable has been cut.

If your electrical wiring has a circuit-breaker, it may have switched itself off because of a power surge, in which case you merely have to switch it on again at the 'trip switch' on the fuse board. If it keeps cutting out there is a faulty appliance in the house or a fault has developed in the wiring, and in either case it's a job for the electrician. The same is true if you have a fuse box and a fuse keeps blowing.

6 Check the flex. It's not likely that your trouble lies here and if it does, then you can probably see it. But frayed flexes are potentially *dangerous*. If it's frayed near the middle, you'll probably need a new length of flex. If it's frayed at the plug end you may be able to cut off the frayed bit and reconnect the plug. Otherwise take it to an electrical shop.

7 Non-electrical causes. Very often an electrical appliance will perform badly, or not at all, for non-electrical reasons.

For example, vacuum cleaners may suffer from an over-full dust bag or a blockage in the tube or hose. You can clear a blocked hose by attaching it to the 'blow' hole and switching on. Stand clear when you do this! If this fails the hose may be gently cleared with a length of coat-hanger wire, bent into a small loop at the end to protect the hose. Reduced suction because of a split hose can be cured by binding the split with adhesive tape. A loose or clogged felt filter under the dust bag will also cause bad suction. The upright type of vacuum cleaner can fail because of a string getting wound round the impeller blades. It can also lose efficiency through worn brushes or drive belt.

An electric kettle that is slow to boil probably has a lime scale built up on the element. There are plenty of proprietary kettle cleaners for this job, such as Calgon.

When a refrigerator motor keeps starting up too frequently the fridge needs defrosting. If the motor becomes unusually noisy check that the fridge is standing firm and level.

Any trouble with a washing machine or a spin drier is likely to be a job for the dealer. But unusually noisy ones may be unevenly loaded with clothes or may have clothes caught between the drum and the jacket. If a tumble drier is faulty, check whether the lint bag is full. (You should clean it out at least once a week or it clogs up and then the motor may burn out.)

AWFUL WARNING! Whatever the appliance and whatever the symptoms, never in any circumstances do *anything* before disconnecting – not merely switching off.

8 If sockets, plugs, flex, fuses and power supply are all in order the fault lies within the appliance itself, and there's usually little you can do but take it to the repairman or call him in if it is a large machine. Modern electrical appliances are not designed for amateur tinkering. Do not try it. Do not let anyone else try it.

How to mend an electric kettle

An exception to this rule is the electric kettle, which is really a simple device. It's easy (and economical) to fit a new element if you have checked all the other possibilities and decided that the element has 'died'.

First, unplug the kettle. Secondly, unscrew the metal or plastic 'shroud' at the back where the flex plugs in. The shroud is actually a retaining nut for the element, and when it is unscrewed the old element can be lifted out through the kettle top. You'll have to manoeuvre it a little but remember that if *they* got it in, *you* can get it out.

Take the old element to the electrical shop and buy one of the same type (be sure that's what you get). With it you'll get two washers, one of fibre and one of rubber. Push the rubber one (which is water-sealing) on to the base of the thread on the element before inserting it in the kettle; then push the fibre one as far on to the thread as it will go when the thread is projecting out of the back of the kettle. Now screw the shroud on and tighten it up. Be sure that the new element is put in right way up, with its flat pin on top. Some elements are marked 'top'.

Mending door bells and chimes

Tools needed: small screwdriver; small sharp knife.

Materials: glasspaper or steel wool.

A doorbell or chime which has stopped working can be checked out by means of the above fault-finding system. Bells may be powered by batteries or by mains voltage through a transformer which reduces the power to the low voltage needed. Don't bother to understand that bit: just remember it. If your unit is mains-operated you must switch off the power at the mains before attempting any kind of maintenance.

All bells look entirely different inside but the basic operational theory is the same. You press a button which makes an electric connection which activates a plunger which makes the bell ring. If it doesn't, then the trouble is either that there is no power source (possibly because the battery is dead) or that some electric connection is not taking place (either at the bell itself or at the bell-push).

1 Test the battery first, if there is one. If it will light a torch bulb it is not dead, so the fault must be elsewhere. Best way to test the battery is to bare the ends of a short piece of bell wire or flex, wind one end round the threaded end of the torch bulb (remove bulb first, of course), then hold the metal base of the bulb against one of the battery's contacts and the other end of the wire against the other contact. If the battery is dead replace it with a new one.

2 Alternatively, the bell-push itself could be faulty. Check that the button moves easily to and fro and is returned properly by its spring when it is released. Also check the bell-push contacts. They should be free of rust (if not, clean by rubbing with steel wool or glasspaper) and should come firmly together when the push is pressed and spring apart when it is released. These contacts sometimes get flattened through long use; they can be bent back to their proper shape. As the bell-push is outside the house it may become so damaged by damp that it must be replaced.

3 Next check all electrical connections – those springy bits of metal on the unit. They should be clean. They will look dirty or green if they are damp. If they are dirty, clean them with steel wool or glasspaper. Check that the ends are making proper contact.

4 Look at the bell spring and the plunger (which strikes the bell or chime). Remove any dirt from either and make sure that the plunger is moving freely.

5 Next check the bell wire leads. One end is screwed into the bell-push, the other screwed into the bell. They operate on the same principle as an electric plug. If one of the bell wire leads has pulled away from its terminal, strip off plastic to expose enough bare wire to

attach firmly to terminal again. The possibility of damaged leads should be checked both at the bell end and at the bell-push end.

The same points should be checked on mains-operated bell or chime units with an additional check on the connections to the transformer. But – to repeat – nothing should be done to any mains appliance before the power has been turned off at the mains.

THE PAINTED ROOM

The one area in home maintenance where you can't fail to save *lots* of money and perhaps even do a better job than the little man round the corner (if he exists) is in painting your own place.

The way to make the job easy is to choose the right kind of paint and the right tools for your work, and to do adequate preparation.

Tools: steady step-ladder with top platform for your bucket or paint tray; stripping knife; wire brush for stripping washable paper; filling knife; sanding block; wire brush attachment and power tool for metal windows; old chisel or bottle-opener; stirring stick; paint roller and tray; brushes; screwdriver; razor blade and holder; paper plates on which to put the brushes or dripping tins.

Materials: paint for ceiling, walls and woodwork; primer and undercoat if necessary; white spirit or brush cleaner (Polyclens) if necessary; dust sheets or polythene sheet; newspaper;

proprietary wallpaper stripper or wall-washing powder; cellulose filler; plastic wood where necessary; fine, medium and coarse abrasive paper, plus 'wet-or-dry'; masking tape.

Buying paint

For WALLS and CEILINGS there is nothing to beat *vinyl emulsion* paint, which goes on easily and covers well. It is much cheaper than wallpaper, takes less skill to apply and lasts better as it allows dirt to be washed or even scrubbed off. It comes in a wide range of standard colours, and if you don't fancy any of those some shops (including John Lewis stores) have mixing machines which offer a choice of hundreds of shades. The finish can be *matt* (flat) or *silk* (slightly shiny), and while the silk is good on new smooth walls the matt will disguise imperfections in elderly ones.

Always make sure that new plaster dries out for *at least six months* before painting it, or it will sweat.

No paint will hide all the bumps in a really bad wall, however carefully prepared. In such cases, you need to hang lining paper or woodchip paper before painting. These cheap papers are easy to hang, being soft and supple, and there's no pattern matching.

On WOODWORK use the newly-developed gloss paints such as Dulux Silthane, which allow brushes to be cleaned in hot water and detergent. These cut out all the messing about with white spirit or turpentine that's necessary after brushes have been used with traditional oil-based gloss paints. The new paints are also easier to brush on, not so sticky, and you don't get brush marks. They are available under various brand names and can be identified by the words 'easy brush clean' on the can. There is a choice of *full gloss* (very shiny) or *satin gloss* (not so shiny). Some paints are of the non-drip jelly type (which is a bit stiff to use); others are the ordinary, flowing kind of paint. What you choose is a matter of taste, though the non-drip ones are good for one-coat work.

You can also buy *vinyl gloss* or *acrylic emulsions* for woodwork. These are very quick-drying, ideal for a high-speed job, and they also allow brushes to be simply rinsed under the tap. They give a finish somewhere between silk emulsion and satin gloss, but they don't come in so many colours as the new gloss paints and their covering power is less good. I'd use these any day, especially in white.

Primer is for sealing new wood so that the paint doesn't soak into the grain: it is essential on untreated surfaces. *Undercoat* is the first layer of colour; it's cheaper, easier to apply and dries more quickly than the final coat.

How much paint will you need? Paint went metric some time ago, and the 250 ml tin replaces the half pint, 500 ml the pint, 1 litre the quart, 2.5 litres the half gallon, 5 litres the gallon. The way to work out the amount required in square metres is to multiply the height of the room by the length of each of the walls and to add together the figures.

Emulsion: 1 litre covers 13–16 square metres approximately. (Cheap emulsion paints have a high percentage of filler, which results in low covering power. You have to put on more coats to get the same effect as a smaller quantity of good quality paint.)

Eggshell: 1 litre covers 16 square metres approximately.

Gloss: 1 litre covers 18 square metres approximately. (The average door needs 250 ml of paint for each coat. Use this as a guide for your windows. There is no such thing as the average window. If in doubt, buy a 500 ml tin and get on with it.)

One coat or two? If you're painting over the same colour one might be enough, but two are always preferable because they'll ensure a full depth of colour, with no patchiness or missed bits.

Preparation for painting

This is the hard, boring and important part. (Check your transistor batteries before you start.) Once it's out of the way the painting itself is quite a pleasant and satisfying job. How much preparation you indulge in is a matter of temperament, time and circumstance, but the more you do, the more it will show in the finished job. The surface should be clean, dry and grease- and rust-free. There should be no powdery surface or loose, flaking material.

A perfectionist with plenty of time might wash down the ceilings, then strip off all the old wallpaper and paint, or burn off gloss-painted wood-work. But in most cases all this work is unnecessary. Unless the ceiling is whitewashed or very dirty – as in a kitchen – brushing or dusting over is quite enough. Old whitewash *must* be washed off; emulsion painted on over it will peel away. You can identify whitewash if it turns grey when touched with a wet fingertip; sponge it off with lashings of hot water.

Prepare the room by removing every bit of furniture; if this is impossible stack it in the centre under dust-sheets or polythene (from D I Y shops or gardening shops). Take down curtains, lampshades and anything screwed to the walls. Cover the floor with several layers of newspaper. Carpet should be removed unless it's professionally fitted. If it is professionally fitted, tape dust sheets or polythene to the skirting board and when you paint *that* do it with a bit of masking cardboard. Dig it down between the carpet and the wall and pull it towards you as you paint. Warn the family of a picnic diet while decorating is in progress and forget your usual housework routine.

You can't paint over dirt and dust, so dust or vacuum-clean all surfaces.

To strip or not to strip: If the hideous wallpaper in your lovely new home is relatively new and firmly stuck on there's no point in removing it: it makes a good foundation for emulsion paint if brushed clean and if any grease marks are removed with a hot iron through blotting paper (though remember it is very difficult to remove later if it has been over-painted). Important exceptions are

strong patterns and wallpaper with gold in it, which may surface through the paint, eventually if not immediately. If old wallpaper is impregnated with dirt, and so loose in places that the new wet paint raises it in ugly bubbles, it must be stripped off (see below).

Unless paint on woodwork is badly flaking or blistered there's no point in stripping it off. However hideous the colour, well rubbed down it will form your undercoat. (I've changed from black to white with three coats only.) Or you can strip just one or two key places such as window ledges, which are often badly flaked, or chipped doors, which are very noticeable.

Another consideration is how long you're likely to live in the house. If you will be redecorating over the years thorough preparation now will pay off in the future. If you're just a short-term tenant all you want is an acceptable appearance now.

Washing down: On *walls* and *ceilings* that need a thorough clean use hot water and a sponge, with either a floor-type detergent such as Flash or a proprietary wall-washing powder such as Polywash. Rinse off with clean water and leave to dry thoroughly before continuing.

For stripping wallpaper use a proprietary stripper such as Polypeel in plenty of hot water. Soak the paper thoroughly, then peel it away with a stripping knife. A shiny washable paper (or one that's been overpainted) should be scratched with a steel wire brush to let the water through the surface. Vinyl wallpaper is stripped dry by peeling away the decorative plastic surface and leaving the paper backing behind. This acts as a lining paper for you to paint on.

Most *woodwork* probably needs only wiping over with a damp cloth or paint cleaner such as Polywash but be sure to get dirt out of crevices and any greasy finger-marks off doors.

Filling and smoothing: Holes or cracks in the surfaces will show up black unless they are filled before painting. Really tiny ones will get filled with paint, but anything larger than a hairline crack or drawing pin hole should be filled beforehand with white cellulose filler (Polyfilla). The powder kind is best for large jobs. Put a small mound of it on a piece of hardboard or thick card, form a hollow in the centre, pour water into the hollow and mix a stiff paste, adding a little water or powder as you go to adjust the consistency. A hardboard 'palette' like this is better than a saucer or dish as you can scrape off every bit with your filling knife and use it without waste. For small jobs ready-mixed filler in a tub is convenient, but it costs even more.

Apply filler with a filling knife, not to be confused with the stripping knife, which is less flexible. Press filler into the hole or crack with the knife and scrape off excess. Leave it to dry, then sand it smooth. On old dark paintwork fill all the easily-seen holes and cracks, then do a second round after applying the first coat of paint, when many smaller ones will become visible for the first time.

Patches of old flaky paint on walls may need sanding down. Use medium grade abrasive paper wrapped round a wood or cork block. If the roughness is extensive it's easier to keep sanding to a minimum and hang a thick lining paper instead.

Painted woodwork in reasonable condition needs only light sanding to give a 'grip' for the new paint. Silicon carbide paper ('wet-or-dry') is good for rubbing down; used when wetted you get a very good finish. Paintwork in very bad condition should be stripped off as in furniture stripping (described on page 297); you will then have to apply primer (sealer) and undercoat before the finishing coat of paint.

Rusty metal windows should be wire-brushed, preferably using a power tool with a brush attachment, and bare patches touched in with *metal primer* such as Dulux metal primer before painting.

Painting

To open tins of paint, especially large ones, you need a wide, strong blade such as an *old* chisel or the wrong end of a beer can opener. Work the blade all round the lid, not just in one place, so as not to damage the lid and make it fit badly. Stir the paint if instructions say so (jelly paints must not be stirred). Emulsion and other plastic paints don't need much stirring, but it's important with conventional gloss, primer or undercoat in order to mix in the oil. Always transfer some to a painting tray, bucket or can to work with: it's then not a major disaster if the paint gets knocked over, and it's much easier to handle than the full, new paint can.

Paint the *ceiling* first, then the woodwork, then the walls. Always carry a rag, damped with water or white spirit as appropriate, to wipe off drips or splashes *as soon as they occur*. Always clean brushes and rollers as instructed on the can immediately on stopping work for the day. Always stop painting before you're too exhausted to clear up: at least half an hour before you planned. For a short break stand brushes in a jar of water – or white spirit – and rough-dry them before using them again. Don't leave brushes standing on their ends in anything or they will splay.

Walls and ceilings: You will need a bath cap to protect your hair, even if you're using a roller: grey hair will come to you soon enough without help.

For these big areas a paint roller and tray are better than a brush and bucket. The roller is much less messy and tiring, and it gives a better finish more quickly. Lambswool or mohair rollers are better than foam ones but more expensive. Use the roller with criss-cross strokes, covering just as much of the area as you can reach *comfortably*. Stretching too far leads to overbalancing and cricks in the neck, and is tiring. If the paint feels a little sticky and thick, add some water and stir it in, but not too much or the paint will drip off the roller and won't cover well.

The roller won't reach right into corners. Paint the strips between walls and ceiling with a 25-mm (1-inch) brush. To paint neatly round *light switches*, *ceiling roses* and *power sockets* switch the electricity off at the mains and unscrew their cover plates just enough to get the brush behind them.

For walls and ceilings you must, of course, have a step-ladder, and it must be the type with a platform for your paint to stand on.

I know a designer who, for a bet, got an 18-inch-wide roller and painted a 30 × 15-foot basement in one hour: twenty-five minutes with a 5-inch brush for skirtings and corners, thirty-five minutes with the roller and a plastic baby bath.

Woodwork: Always paint in daylight if possible. By artificial light you may miss runs, sags and the odd brush hairs in the paint which can be dealt with easily while the paint is wet but are irritating and difficult to remove afterwards.

Useful brush sizes for woodwork are 12-mm, 25-mm and 50-mm ($\frac{1}{2}$-inch, 1-inch and 2-inch): anything bigger takes ages to clean. A square painting pad is very good for skirting boards: you dab it in a tray and then smooth it on.

Never dip the brush more than halfway into the paint; this way it will be less likely to drip and will be easier to clean. Work on a small area at a time, brushing the paint up and down and then across until it is smooth. There's one exception: jelly paint should not be 'brushed out' but laid on rather thick.

Large areas such as *doors* should be painted quickly so that no one section dries before another: unscrew handles and other fittings before starting. With flush doors begin at the top and work down in sections.

An ordinary traditional panelled door should be painted in this order: mouldings; panels; centre vertical, top, middle and bottom horizontals; outer verticals.

Remove excess paint which runs down and collects in corners with a dry brush. Don't forget the back and front edges of a door. Leave the door ajar for a day or two while the paint hardens.

When painting a *casement* (*hinged*) *window* follow the same principle, painting its component parts individually, starting with the least accessible parts at the top end and the back and working downwards.

With *sash windows* never paint anything that has not already been painted and don't paint the sashcords. In order to avoid getting in a situation where you have to push upward and therefore mark the part that you've just painted, the procedure is: push the top frame halfway down and the bottom frame all the way up; paint the lower part of the top frame; push the bottom frame down again and the

top one nearly up and finish the top frame. Then paint the bottom frame. Never let windows dry fully shut *or they will stick*.

Not getting paint on the glass is a matter of cultivating a steady hand, using a small well-worn brush and cardboard L-shaped guide, or a window-brush (cut diagonally at the tip). Do not overload the brush with paint. Stand at a comfortable angle to work. Paint that does get on the panes can be scraped off when dry with a razor blade in a holder: this is irritatingly time-consuming and should be avoided at all costs. Use masking tape until your hand is steady and keep off the hard stuff. Remove the tape within a day or so or you may never get the adhesive off.

While painting skirting boards a strip of masking tape on the floor against the board is also a good idea to stop the brush picking up dirt.

After painting woodwork *ban everyone from the room* so that the paint can dry without dust settling on it. Drying is speeded up if the room is warm and well ventilated.

Remember that although fresh paint may appear dry the following day it will not be really hard, so avoid knocks when moving furniture back.

Always save a jam or honey jar of paint for emergency touch-ups in every room you paint – and label the jar.

Some painting mistakes and how to correct them

Faults which don't involve damp can

generally be corrected if you rub the surface down, carefully reseal and then repaint with undercoat and top coat. They can be:

Crazing, which may mean that the top coat was applied too soon after undercoat, before it was hard and dry.

Drips or an uneven, frilly effect, which suggests too heavy a coat of paint, unevenly applied.

Flaking, peeling paint may mean that the paint was applied to a damp surface or a powdery surface. To correct it, strip paint, dry surface, rub down and repaint.

Blisters can mean damp. The occasional small one can be rubbed down and the area repainted; larger areas should be stripped, then allow woodwork to dry out, and carefully seal and start again.

A scrunchy, crystalline effect means that the plaster, cement or brick base hasn't yet dried out. Strip paint and leave until there has been no similar disturbance for at least two weeks, then start again.

THE PERFECT WALL

How to hang wallpaper

Tools: a light, folding 180-cm × 60-cm (6-foot × 2-foot) decorator's table (don't economize, it's a good investment) or a kitchen table; a plumb line; a soft pencil; metric tape; 30-cm (12-inch) wallpaper scissors; a sponge and rags; stripping knife for trimming; roller; a 15-cm (6-inch) brush for paste; a hanging brush for smoothing paper on wall; a paste bucket.

Materials: wallpaper (to begin with, I strongly recommend a no-pattern paper, and avoid stripes, however good you are. Get a medium-quality paper; thin ones stretch and tear, thick ones or embossed papers are more cumbersome to handle. Avoid papers which need a long paste soak, because they stretch); glue size; sandpaper.

Adhesive: Some papers come ready-pasted; different papers need different adhesives. Ask what's needed when you buy the paper.

Hints before starting: DON'T PAPER NEW PLASTER FOR AT LEAST SIX MONTHS, or it won't have dried out. You can emulsion paint it as a temporary measure and wait until it is dry.

Always apply a coat of glue size to walls before papering and lightly rub down with sandpaper. This seals the surface, stops paste soaking in and makes paper easier to hang.

Tie a piece of string across centre of bucket so that the brush leans against it and doesn't fall in (very good tip this).

Prepare walls as for painting.

Don't try to paper a distempered wall, because the paper may simply come off. Remove distemper by scrubbing with warm water. Don't paper damp walls or you'll get the paper bulging, blistering and peeling off.

Line the walls with lining paper (this is only necessary if you're a perfectionist, or the walls are in bad nick, or your wallpaper is very special).

Method: Start wallpapering from the centre of a chimney breast, if there

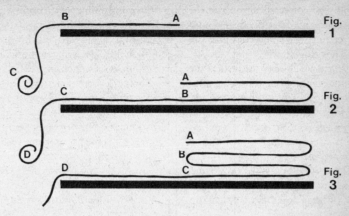

Pasting and folding wallpaper

is one, and if the pattern is a large one. Otherwise, start from the window. On a window wall, always work *away* from the window.

Drop a plumb line to give a true vertical and pencil it on the wall.

Cut the lengths of paper to size plus 10 cm (4 inches) *each* for trimming (allow for pattern matching, if there is any). Mark top 'top' on the *right* side.

Don't overlap paper joins: make them meet (butt your joins).

Look at the diagrams at the top of this page.

Lay one end of the wallpaper on *half* the table, in good light. Brush paste on from centre towards edges, covering all paper on the table **(Fig. 1)**. Fold pasted section in half and move along **(Fig. 2)**. Then paste and fold the next section **(Fig. 3)**. Also concertina the paper like this for lining paper and ceiling paper.

Hold the two top corners and

place on wall alongside your pencilled plumb line (to get it straight) with half the 10-cm (4-inch) overlap at the top (see diagram on p. 286).

Take hanging brush and brush from the middle out to either side (to smooth out air bubbles).

Trim by running the back of the scissors along ceiling join. (This makes a mark on the paper.) Repeat this at the bottom. Pull paper back and cut along the mark, then press to wall again firmly with brush. Use seam roller (or fist) to secure seams but not on embossed paper.

Rough-cut paper to fit round doors and windows, then trim on the wall.

To make a hole for a *light switch* or *ceiling rose*, roughly mark the paper, then cut a hot-cross-bun sized cross (not too big, i.e. not to size) so that you can paper over, then mark with pencil and trim to size with the Stanley knife. Better still, unscrew them before papering (switch off at mains first),

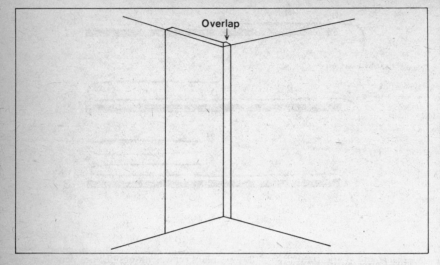

which makes for a much neater job.

Corners: don't try to turn a corner with a full width of paper; cut it down first to fit the gap, allowing 2-cm (¾-inch) overlap on to the bare wall. Hang this, then hang the remainder so it overlaps; use a plumb line to make sure it's vertical. The slight pattern mismatch won't be noticeable.

Wallpaper

When buying wallpaper check that all rolls are from the same batch, otherwise there will probably be colour variations. This is done simply by checking that the letters after the design number are the same.

Check the direction of the pattern, so you don't hang the paper upside down. To avoid this, always mark the top with a pencil when you cut it. The average design repeat is 48 cm (19 inches) and it is usually printed on the back of each page in the sample book. Allow extra rolls if you choose a larger pattern repeat.

Note: Where floor-to-ceiling windows, doors, or built-in wall units replace a large wall area, reduce measurement accordingly.

WALLPAPER AND CEILING PAPER CALCULATION TABLE

This table is a guide to the number of rolls required; it relates to rooms with normal window and door openings. Additional rolls are needed when large pattern repeats require unusual cutting to waste.

For standard rolls 10.05 m (11 yards) long by approximately 52 cm (20–21 inches) wide. Each roll contains approximately 5.2 square metres (55 square feet).

Rollage Calculation Chart

WALLS Height from skirting		Measurement round walls, including doors and windows											
feet	metres	feet	30	34	38	42	46	50	54	58	62	66	70	74	78
		metres	9.1	10.4	11.6	12.8	14.0	15.2	16.5	17.7	18.9	20.1	21.3	22.6	23.8
7–7½	2.15–2.30		4	5	5	6	6	7	7	8	8	9	9	10	10
7½–8	2.30–2.45		5	5	6	6	7	7	8	8	9	9	10	10	11
8–8½	2.45–2.60		5	5	6	7	7	8	9	9	10	10	11	12	12
8½–9	2.60–2.75		5	5	6	7	7	8	9	9	10	10	11	12	12
9–9½	2.75–2.90		6	6	7	7	8	9	9	10	10	11	12	12	13
9½–10	2.90–3.05		6	6	7	8	8	9	10	10	11	12	12	13	14
10–10½	3.05–3.20		6	7	8	8	9	10	10	11	12	13	13	14	15
CEILINGS			2	2	2	3	3	4	4	4	5	5	6	7	7

How to use this wallpaper chart

1 Underline the height of the room in pencil (so you can rub it out for next time).
2 Underline the *total* distance around your room.
3 The point at which the two underlined figures intersect is the number of wallpaper rolls you need.

Paste

Don't underestimate the paste quantities. A standard 100-g (4-oz) pack will make 4.5 litres (1 gallon) which is sufficient for six to eight rolls. For hanging heavyweight, embossed, hessian and washable wallpaper, use a standard packet of Polycell Plus, which will make 4.5 litres (1 gallon), for five to six rolls.

For paper-backed or fabric-backed vinyls use fungicidal heavy duty paste. One standard packet makes 2.25 litres (4 pints), which is sufficient for two to three rolls. Keep paste away from children and animals as it may be poisonous.

HOW TO MAKE FAIRLY QUICK CURTAINS

There are many different and confusing ways to make curtains so I'm only going to recommend one method, which is simple and smart enough to make the effort really worth while.

Use Rufflette Regis pencil pleat curtain heading tape. It's easiest to use and the heading is reinforced so that it stays crisp. Also, the hooks are less likely to fall out than with French pleating prongs (a real swine to get back after cleaning). When buying fabric you *must* allow two and a half times the width of area to be covered,

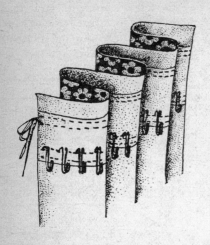

How much fabric do you need? Unless you use the Rufflette Regis system, allow ideally about double the width of the window area to be covered. If you can't afford that, buy ample cheaper fabric or get blinds: skimped curtains look mean.

QUICK CALCULATOR FOR PLAIN CURTAINING
(based on average furnishing width fabric: 122–127 cm/48 inches)

Pencil and pinch pleat headings
(but not Rufflette Regis, which takes more fabric)

Rail width in metres	No. of pairs of curtains required	No. of widths required in each curtain
Up to 1.00	1	1
1.00–1.50	1	$1\frac{1}{2}$
1.50–2.00	1	2
2.00–2.50	1	$2\frac{1}{2}$
2.50–3.00	1	3
3.00–3.50	1	$3\frac{1}{2}$
3.50–4.00	1	4
4.00–4.75	1	$4\frac{1}{2}$

Random gathered headings (where you don't have a regular, measured heading, it's easy to cover up small errors)

Rail width in metres	No. of pairs of curtains required	No. of widths required in each curtain
Up to 1.70	1	1
1.50–2.50	1	$1\frac{1}{2}$
2.50–3.25	1	2
3.00–4.00	1	$2\frac{1}{2}$
4.00–4.75	1	3

otherwise the system doesn't work.

If you prefer to use standard drawstring tape, then you may want to hide your random gathered headings with a pelmet.

If you're going to wash your curtains you risk the drapes and lining shrinking at different rates, so wash material and lining before you start to cut.

There's a delicious selection of fabrics from which to choose your drapes. All you need is money before making a selection from tweeds, silk, satin, velvet, cheap cotton twill, linen, mixtures of all these, or all their synthetic and semi-synthetic, sometimes cheaper and more practical, equivalents.

Whether you like it or not, whether or not you are used to the metric system, it's much easier to use a metric tape measure, otherwise you will find yourself bogged down in a sea of mathematics at some point.

Decide whether you want wall-to-wall, floor-to-ceiling curtaining (which looks most luxurious), or whether you want your curtains to fall to the window-sill or below. Beginners should avoid patterned fabric, and make sure that velvet pile runs in the same direction. Once you have decided on your length and width, check the width of 122–7-cm (48-inch) fabric you need on the quick calculator chart and, for hem and headings, add 25 cm (10 inches) to each cut of the length you want.

Length: Measure drop of curtain (measurement from bottom of runner or base of curtain track to wherever you want your curtain to hang).

DEDUCT 3–5 cm (1–2 inches) if you're about to fit wall-to-wall carpet. You don't want the curtains to touch the floor and get grubby at the hems.

Remember that the weight of heavy curtains will make them drop, particularly if you have used heavy material, which is why you should wait a couple of weeks after hanging them before hemming. I leave hems pinned for a month and then hand-hem them on the spot. I have known ladies to pin the hems up and leave them that way for years.

Grand decorators like curtains to drag a few inches on the floor in order to keep the draught out: so, if yours do, console yourself with that thought.

ADD extra length for headings – 6 cm (2½ inches) – and for hems; allow at least 12 cm (5 inches) for a doubled 6-cm (2½-inch) hem; doubled hems hang better and take no more effort. I allow 25 cm (10 inches) for hems in case I move and the next place has bigger windows. There's nothing more irritating than hems 6 cm (2½ inches) too short. Then, *unless the shop can swear that the fabric is pre-shrunk*, if you're buying a fabric to be laundered, allow 10 per cent extra for shrinkage, and launder the fabric before making the curtains.

To calculate how much plain fabric to buy

1 Measure the length of the gaps to be curtained and add the extra lengths you need for heading and hemming. This is the *length of your cut* (L), if using a plain material.
2 Next, find how many *widths* you need. The first mistake that a beginner makes is to forget that the curtains, when drawn back, must not cover the window space.

The full width of the gap to be covered by the curtains is the width of the window plus a little on both sides. Allow at least 25 cm (10 inches).

Measure the gap to be covered.

Multiply this number by the fullness you need: for double fullness, multiply by two (a little less doesn't matter); for Rufflette Regis tape, multiply by two and a half.

DIVIDE this number by the width of the fabric. The answer is the number of cuts you need to make your curtain.

Width of gap × 2 (or 2½ if using Rufflette Regis tape)

Width of fabric

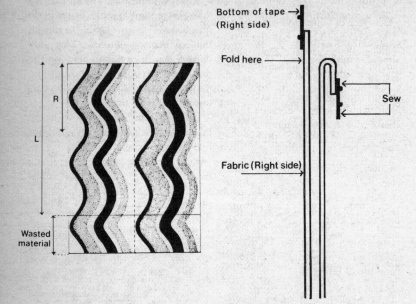

The answer is W = Number of fabric widths needed.

3 Multiply L by W. This is the amount of material you have to buy.

To calculate how much patterned fabric to buy

Matching patterns may be trickier than you think. However clever you are, take your measurements along to whoever you are buying your fabric from and get *him* to double-check your arithmetic, which should be as follows:

1 Calculate as for plain material to find L.

2 Then measure the pattern repeat (R) if the repeat doesn't divide into the length exactly (which it won't).

3 Add to the length of your cut the size of one repeat.

4 So your curtain cuts will be L + R. Use this figure as in Step 3 for plain fabric (above).

Net curtains

You can probably buy these ready-made from large stores. If you make your own curtains, sew double hems and headings to prevent raw edges showing against the light.

How to make quick, unlined curtains

1 Trim off selvedges to avoid puckering of seams and corners.
2 Cut curtains to size. Lay the first cut length next to the remaining material (pattern upwards), to check that the pattern matches before you make the next cut.
3 Join widths where necessary and make side hems, by hand if you want them to hang beautifully.
4 Tack the tape to the top of material, right side to right side (see the diagram above). Then fold it over to leave a 2-cm ($\frac{3}{4}$-inch) (or bigger if you want) doubled heading. Tack bottom of tape to curtain (to get it straight), then sew by hand or machine, at bottom and top of tape.
5 If you are using a tape which has hook pockets, not loops, make sure that you sew the tape so that it ends up with the open ends of the hook pockets nearest the bottom of the curtain.
6 Allow an 8-cm (3-inch) double hem and pin or tack in place.
7 From either end of the tape pull out 4 cm ($1\frac{1}{2}$ inches) of cord and knot the ends.
8 Draw the curtain cord to the required width.
9 Insert hooks.
10 Hang curtains.
11 Allow two weeks to let them fall out, then hem on the spot, by hand.

How to make lined curtains

Making curtains isn't difficult. Making a big curtain isn't more difficult than making a small curtain, it just takes longer, and it looks better to do it by hand. You *aren't* going to ruin all that expensive material. The only danger lies in not matching up the pattern – so, I repeat – don't use patterned fabric if you're making curtains for the first time.

Don't try this method with heavy fabric, because making heavy curtains really is a professional job.

Buy the same amount of lining fabric as for curtains but don't allow for pattern or heading.

Method
1 Trim off selvedges on lining and curtain fabric to avoid puckering seams.
2 Cut curtains to size. Tack all widths together. Stitch vertical seams and press open.
3 Cut lining fabric to size: *it should be 5 cm (2 inches) less all round than curtains.* Tack all widths together. Stitch vertical seams and press open. Hem the lining at top and sides.
4 Lay the curtain wrong side upwards on the floor again. Turn the top and the two sides in 4 cm ($1\frac{1}{2}$ inches) and mitre the corners.
5 Place the lining wrong side downwards, on to the wrong side of the curtain, 2 cm ($\frac{3}{4}$ inch) below the top edge. Centre it (most important) and pin into position. By hand, slipstitch the top and side hems of the lining to the curtain, leaving both hems free.
6 Now pin and sew the heading tape

to the back of the curtain, by
machine if possible. Pull out 4 cm
(1½ inches) of cord at either end and
knot. Draw curtain cord to required
width. Insert hooks and hang curtains.

WELL DONE!

PUTTING UP CURTAIN RAILS

The track: You can get trim white
plastic Trimtrack (Rufflette make it),
which is neat, unobtrusive and needs
no pelmet: it can be bent round a
bay and is very flexible. It can be
ceiling or wall fitted and is not difficult
to assemble. It can be used with
extension brackets to take a secondary
track behind it for net curtain. It takes
a cording set (although only big curtains need this, and I no longer bother
as it's just one more thing to break
down: what's wrong with clean hands
except for stately homes?).

To fix track: Proceed as below but
if it has to be fixed to brick or masonry
screw a thin timber batten up first and
mount the track on it.

Tools: small hacksaw; bradawl or
meat skewer; screwdriver; steady
step-ladder.

Materials: branded curtain rail
complete with fittings.

If you can climb up a step-ladder
you can fix ordinary plastic curtain
rail, as sold in Woolworth's and DIY
shops, provided you have a timber
frame round the window to which you
can fix and don't have to make fixings
into the wall or ceiling.

The first step is to find the length
of rail required. Unless the curtains
are to hang in a recess allow an extra
bit on each side so they can be drawn
well clear of the glass. I allow at least
25 cm (10 inches). Round this
measurement *up* to the nearest 30 cm
(1 foot). When you buy this length you
will automatically get the correct
number of fittings to go with it:
brackets, end stops, gliders and
hooks; but always buy a few more
hooks and gliders in case you need
extra or lose a few. It's maddening to
get your track up and then find
that you haven't enough runners,
especially if you're fitting wall-to-wall
track.

If you want the curtains to overlap
in the middle (and who doesn't?) ask
for an overlap bracket. Check whether
this means cutting the rail in two and
overlapping it in the centre; usually it
doesn't because most systems have a
cheap, ingenious bracket which rides
along and carries one curtain a hand-
span in front of the other.

Cut the rail to length if necessary,
using a hacksaw. If the window is a
bay you can bend the rail into a gentle
curve to follow its shape. Don't bend
it too sharply or the curtain won't ride
round the bend.

Next, fix the support brackets to the
top of the window frame. They must
be properly lined up with each other,
otherwise the rail won't fit on. Normally you can do this by lining them
all up with the top of the window
frame. The brackets should be evenly
spaced about 30 cm (1 foot) apart,
with one about 25 mm (1 inch) from

each end. If there are curves put a bracket on each side of the bend; this may require two extra brackets.

Mark through the hole in the bracket with a bradawl (spike on a handle) or meat skewer. Then push and twist it to make a pilot hole in the wood which will give the screw a start and enable it to be driven home with firm pressure on the screwdriver.

Fit one of the end stops on the rail, then the gliders, then the other stop. Now attach the rail to the brackets. According to its design it may clip on or screw on or both. Some gliders and hooks are combined; fit these to the curtain first, then snap the whole thing on to the rail. Then fit the other end stop.

If you're fitting rail in an alcove or from wall-to-wall, remember to fit *more* than enough hooks (rather than too few) because you can't add any once you've fitted your track without taking the whole thing down again.

Net curtains: I use a simple Woolworth's expanding metal rod for small net curtains.

Don't use flimsy plastic hooks – even for net curtains – because they may not be tough enough. Never wash curtains with plastic hooks still in or they may melt and then be difficult to extract.

WINDOW BLINDS

One of the problems with blinds is their austere look when they're all rolled up ... cylindrical wodges of metal, string and wrong-side-out material that don't do much to enhance any decorative scheme. But if you have small windows, they are better than curtains, which – however well pulled back – seem to cut out light.

You can get blinds beautifully made by mail order, and they're not much more expensive than making your own, but if you prefer to make – or remake – your own with a blind kit, here's how.

When making your own shades you can use a non-fraying material such as linen or heavy cotton, bookbinding cloth, plasticized cotton or felt (which you can't clean, although you can brush it). Heavy, non-fraying materials have two advantages: they require minimum sewing, and you can easily cut out scallops or castle-like crenellations on the bottom edge to make your blinds look decorative – even when rolled up.

Unless you're re-covering one, buy a blind kit and follow the kit instructions for measuring, sewing and fixing.

Having screwed the brackets to the window frame, check that the roller fits.

You'll need 50 cm (20 inches) extra length of material to allow for a roll-over at the top, a pocket for the flat rod at the bottom and for the scallops or whatever at the bottom edge.

Cut material to width, using a sharp pair of shears. You can align sheets of newspaper along and across the fabric to act as a sort of T-square to check straightness.

Turn material wrong-side-out. About 12 cm (5 inches) from the bottom take up a 4-cm (1½-inch) hem straight across the width of the fabric. Into this pocket slip the flat rod provided in your kit.

To make a fancy bottom, find the exact centre of the pocket and run a chalk line from this to the bottom of the material.

Cut a paper or card pattern for the size of the scallops you want. For castle-like crenellations you can make a guide to cut round from a cigarette pack.

Centre your guide exactly on the chalked line and chalk in your outline from the middle to both sides (*don't* start at one side and hope that it will even out) and then cut it out.

Centre your cord holder on that chalked line on the pocket and screw it through the material into the rod. Tack top of shade to roller, exactly as kit instructs. Roll up finished shade so that the 'right' side is inside.

To adjust: wind blind on roller, fit it in place, pull it down and let it up again. If it does not return fully, pull it halfway down, take it off, roll cloth again and replace blind without releasing spring.

FAST LOOSE COVERS (for easy chairs and sofas)

Tools: sewing machine; needles; pins; chalk; upholsterers' hooks and eyes; scissors; newspaper (not tabloid).

Materials: upholstery fabric; draw-string; thread; dark cord or flat braid.

These are not what I'd call simple, but they're easier than making a dress and as the current price of sofa loose covers suggests that they are being made by St Laurent, you might as well try to make them yourself as not have them.

Piping is not difficult and smartly covers up wobbly seams. Buy dark coloured piping cord or flat braid.

1 *Choice of material:* Choose a plain, washable, *pre-shrunk*, close-weave, heavy *upholstery* fabric from a reliable store. Try a cotton repp in a darkish colour, which will hide any wobbly seaming.

2 *How much material to buy?* Measure the height of the back of the armchair to the floor and multiply it by five: add 1 extra metre. This will give you the length needed of 1.2-m (old standard 48-inch) material.

Vary this method for sofas, depending on the length.

3 *Make a pattern:* Take *The Times* for a day or two and keep it to cut the pattern from. It's big and good quality newsprint and it doesn't crumple easily. (Sellotape two pages together for big areas like the back of the chair.)

To make your pattern, pin news-paper sheets to the chair and cut to fit allowing for 5-cm (2-inch) seams (by cutting 5 cm (2 inches) bigger all round). Allow a *further* 5-cm (2-inch) turn-under round the bottom of the chair while still pinned to the chair. Name each pattern piece (e.g. 'outside left arm') and mark with an arrow the direction in which the grain of the fabric is to run.

At this stage it looks impossible, but as soon as you have the fabric on the chair it will all look magically simple.

4 *Cutting out:* Place the patterns on the wrong side of the material. Check grain direction. Draw round the pattern with chalk.

Then cut off the 5-cm (2-inch) seam allowance on the pattern and chalk round the smaller pattern again. Don't take it off the material; put a couple of pins in the middle. This gives you a chalk guideline for stitching. Now cut out the fabric along the first chalk line. Now discard the paper pattern.

5 *Making up:* Pin and tack the cover together on the chair itself, making any necessary tucks and pleats as you go and stitching along the inner chalk line. See the illustrations below.

Start with the back of the chair. Pin the back (of the back) to the chair (see Z). Then pin the front (of the back) to it (see Y). Then attach the seat (see W). Then attach the arms (see X). Illustration 2 shows the chair at this point. Then the front of the seat and the front of the arms (this may be cut in one piece; see P).

The fabric is *still* wrong side outside. Remove from chair and machine seams.

Remember that 5-cm (2-inch) turn-under you allowed for the bottom? That's still hanging loose. Look at the

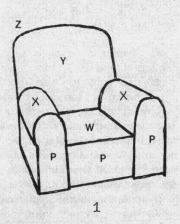

1

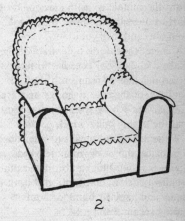

2

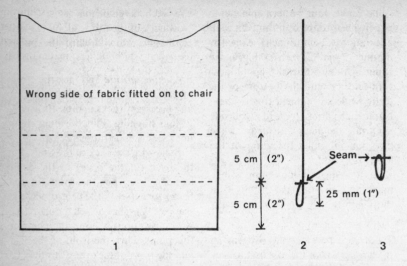

Wrong side of fabric fitted on to chair

5 cm (2″)

5 cm (2″)

Seam →

25 mm (1″)

1   2   3

illustration above before reading on. Tack a 25-mm (1-inch) hem all round the bottom (tack it upwards, because the cover is still inside out).

Fold it up again and tack to provide a channel for the drawstring which will pull the bottom taut.

Fit the turn-under around the chair legs by leaving the corner seams open so the channel is in four sections and the drawstring tape will go inside the legs.

Remove cover *very carefully*, because it's hanging together with tacks, and machine all seams.

If you need to fit hooks and eyes instead of sewing a seam you will discover at this point which of the back vertical seams you have to leave open (then fit with hooks and eyes) because you may not be able to get the chair cover off. It's the chairs with winged tops that need this. Squat, fat, cosy ones are rarely a problem.

Sew all hems and seams on the machine. Turn right side out. Thread drawstring through pockets.

Pull cover over chair, push chair on its back and pull drawstring taut, then knot it.

Stand chair upright and sit in it.

INSTANT UPHOLSTERY
(fast fixed covers)

Tools: a staple gun and staples; Copydex; scissors; pins.

Materials: upholstery fabric; braid.

The principle of this method is to use staples instead of upholstery tacks. You must use strong fabric for furniture that is going to be sat upon. Don't use curtain fabric. Only use mattress ticking or upholstery fabric which is the correct quality.

If you turn a piece of upholstered, modern furniture upside down, you'll find it's all done with a staple gun.

Buy a proper upholsterer's staple gun (they're a cheap investment) from John Lewis. Don't think you can manage with a secretary's staple gun. Don't get one that feels too heavy for you to use.

1 Hold the material up to the part to be covered. Put a pin or two in to hold it and roughly cut.
2 Pin the material on to the chair or sofa.

Staple the fabric straight into the frame of whatever you're upholstering, trying to pick areas that don't show; before you staple, turn material under so it won't fray.

Use the same principle that canvas stretchers use: work round one corner, then pull hard to the opposite corner. Then a third corner, then the opposite, fourth corner, pulling taut as you go.

Then stick braid along the staples with Copydex.

This method is especially good for dining chairs – you can cover half a dozen in an afternoon.

PATCHING A CARPET

The golden rule is always to work from the back.

Tools: a Stanley knife; a bit of hessian; Copydex; newspaper.

Materials: the replacement bit of carpet.

1 Cut out the damaged bit of carpet with a Stanley knife and remove it. It's easiest if you cut a square.

2 Cut a square of the same size from the extra $\frac{1}{2}$ m ($\frac{1}{2}$ yard) of carpet which you thoughtfully ordered when you bought it, matching pattern and pile.
3 Cut a small square of hessian, a little larger all round than the carpet square.
4 Stick the new carpet centrally on the hessian square and leave to dry for five minutes. Use a latex adhesive (Copydex) because it won't soak through.
5 Now cover the surrounding hessian with Copydex, lift the fitted carpet square with a finger or a knife blade and slide the square into place (get it the right way round).
6 Then put a newspaper on top and sit on it for five minutes. The patch may look newer than the rest of the carpet, because, of course, it is. You could try rubbing a little dirt around to blur the joins.

To touch up worn staircarpet (or wall-to-wall): dab on indelible ink of the same colour. It's better than a bald, beige patch, although nothing ever really matches.

HOW TO STRIP FURNITURE

Tools: rubber gloves; paint scraper; cork sanding block; small wood scraper or shave hook; blowlamp or electric iron; power tool with disc sanding attachment; orbital sanding attachment (can be hired).

Materials: branded chemical paint stripper such as Polystrippa or Nitromors; abrasive paper; sanding discs and strips; steel wool; plastic wood filler such as Rawlplastic or Brummer stopping.

Paint or clear varnish can transform an old piece of furniture into something utterly seductive with a new lease of life, but there's often some hard work to be done before that pleasurable stage.

All old paint or varnish must be removed before new paint is applied if a good smart finish is to be achieved.

There are four ways of stripping off old paint: chemical stripping (with Polystrippa), burning off, sanding and scraping. For most furniture you'll probably need to use a combination of these. Chemical stripper will deal effectively with a coat or two of varnish, but if there are several coats of paint it will lift only one or two at a time, so the job can become both tedious and expensive. It's hard to beat a blowlamp for removing thick paint, but this can also be done with a disc sanding attachment on an electric power tool. The snag is that the abrasive discs quickly get clogged with the paint and correspondingly less abrasive, so this method is advisable only if the area to be cleaned is not too big; and it must be flat. Hand sanding is gentle and best for the final finish. Scrapers can be used for getting paint off ledges and curves.

Chemical paint strippers are sold under various brand names and differ in their composition, but they all work in much the same way: you paint the stuff on and wait a few minutes for it to start working; when the paint or varnish goes bubbly it can be scraped

off with a stripping knife. If the item is at all delicate, and especially if it is veneered, use steel wool instead of the knife. Wear rubber gloves throughout to protect your hands.

If the treatment doesn't work completely the first time, repeat it. Any splashes of stripper on skin or clothes should be washed off immediately with cold water, and don't leave the bottle where children can reach it!

After stripping, the piece must be washed clean, usually with water but sometimes with methylated or white spirit (if the stripper isn't water-based), and left to dry. At this stage you may find that though the paint has been removed the wood is still dingy with staining where the pigment in the original paint has sunk in. This may come out with sanding; otherwise the piece needs bleaching with wood bleach such as Rustin's wood bleach, which you can buy at a DIY shop and use according to the manufacturer's instructions.

Burning paint off sounds rather alarming, but is quick and easy and deliciously destructive once you've practised a little with a blowlamp. (Hire one via your DIY shop.) You play the flame over the paint with one hand just long enough to melt a patch of it without singeing the wood beneath, at the same time lifting melted paint off with a stripping knife in the other hand (your hand is 15 cm/ 6 inches away from the flame). To guard against fire it's essential to work well away from inflammable materials and to stand the piece of furniture on something which will not be harmed by hot paint dropping on it, ideally a piece of tin. Try and do it in the garden, unless it's so windy that it will douse the blowlamp. On no account work in a garage if petrol or paraffin is kept there. When you put the blowlamp down make sure that the flame is not pointing towards something inflammable but rather into open space. Blowlamps are fuelled by paraffin, methylated spirit or butane gas; probably the butane lamp is the easiest to use, because you just buy a cartridge and plug it in, on the same principle as a soda siphon. You don't have to fiddle around with liquid fuel and pump priming.

It is possible to strip paint from a flat surface (such as a table or chest of drawers) very effectively with an ordinary electric iron. Put a sheet of kitchen foil between the iron and the paint and leave it, set for maximum heat, on one spot for about thirty seconds, then move it to a new spot while you strip the first one with a knife and so on. The foil is to protect your iron from melting paint.

Removing paint with a disc sander is a relatively crude operation; you can't do corners or curves. It's as well to practise a bit first because the sander has an incredibly fast action and in unskilled hands the fast-rotating disc can bite too far into the wood and leave permanent marks. It's best to tilt the tool so that you sand mainly with the outer area of the disc, and work in a sweeping motion from left to right. (DO keep your fingers well away from the disc while it is revolving.)

The abrasive discs are available at DIY shops and are used with a rubber backing disc that fits into the jaws of the power tool. Choose coarse-grade ones for stripping off paint; medium for cleaning up after chemical stripping, fine for near-final sanding.

For a really good finish sanding by hand cannot be beaten. For delicate work there is no better tool than the hand. The abrasive paper should be wrapped round a bit of rectangular cork, called a cork sanding block, which you buy from a DIY shop. For the best results use it to and fro *along* the direction of the wood grain; if the wood is sanded across the grain or in circles it will get scratched. Take care not to round off any edges and corners. Coarse-grade paper is not necessary at this stage. Start with medium and then go on to fine.

To sand chair legs or rungs, or other cylindrical or twiddly bits, it's best to use the abrasive paper by itself in your hands. Fold it into strips and hold the ends to work round the leg or rung; fold it double and use the crease to work into crevices. To get thick paint off you can also use a small wood scraper (try the Skarsten), while a curved tool called a shave hook is handy for cleaning mouldings.

Final sanding can be done with an orbital sander attachment for a power tool. This is a relatively gentle attachment; it works with a small circular motion and should leave no marks. It is used with special strips of aluminium oxide paper, sold at DIY shops in three grades. You need only hold the tool steady and guide it over the surface, rather like ironing clothes.

Once the wood has been stripped you may find that it needs some filling, particularly if you plan a clear-varnish finish. Use matching plastic wood such as Rawlplastic or Brummer stopping. Pack it firmly and use too much rather than too little as the plastic wood tends to shrink. Any excess can be sanded off.

Don't use Polyfilla cellulose filler if you're finally going to clear-varnish your bit of furniture, because the plugs will show up white. Old filler which shows up white can be picked out and replaced with plastic wood.

If you want to strip a floor you'll need to hire a floor sanding machine – find a local hirer through the *Yellow Pages.* These machines have a bag to catch the sanding dust, but it is still quite a dirty, strenuous job.

Prepare the floor as described under 'How to lay floor coverings' (below). Carefully remove all protruding nails as they may damage the machine. If the floor is heavily painted or varnished round the perimeter, scrape the worst of this off first with a broad Skarsten scraper, otherwise it will clog up the abrasive paper on the machine. Sweep up all the debris from this operation and continue sweeping *as you work*, because the machine will grind loose dirt or grit into the boards and scratch them.

Sand in three stages, starting with coarse abrasive paper and progressing to medium and fine. Buy abrasive paper when you hire the machine and get the hirer to explain how to fit it on to the drum. Once the paper is fitted don't push the machine over the floor – it should be carried, if necessary, using the handle provided.

When starting tilt the drum up slightly before switching on, and lower it gradually so it gets a gentle start and doesn't bite viciously into the floor. The machine will try to bolt away from you; hold it back so that it only moves slowly.

Start the first, coarse sanding in one corner and work diagonally across the floor; sand each strip twice, once forward and once back. Overlap each strip by about 7.5 cm (3 inches).

If necessary repeat in the opposite diagonal direction.

Follow up with medium and fine abrasive paper, in the same fashion but working in the direction of the floorboards. The machine won't reach right to the edges; do these with a disc sander or by hand.

When the floor is smooth and even coloured, sweep or preferably vacuum up every speck of dust. Allow to settle and apply two or three coats of poly-urethane varnish. This gives a clear glossy finish which is non-slip and never needs polishing. It will show scratches in time, but can easily be recoated.

HOW TO LAY FLOOR COVERINGS

Tools: pincers; tack lifter; chalk; hammer; housemaid's rubber kneeler; steel measuring tape; large scissors; trimming knife; work gloves (not rubber washing-up gloves because you'll probably ruin them when a nail catches in them; get household gloves or gardening gloves; John Lewis stores sell them).

Materials: floor brads or oval wire nails; hardboard; hardboard pins; vinyl tiles, carpet tiles or sheet vinyl; flooring adhesive. (Consult the 'Quick consumer's guide to floor coverings', pp. 183–90.)

When deciding whether to lay a floor covering yourself consider three aspects: the cost of the covering involved, its weight and the underlay (only beginners skimp on underlay, which is nearly always necessary).

Don't even consider 'lay-it-yourself' if it's a new Wilton; it's too pricey to risk making any mistakes, and in any case professional laying is usually included in the cost of the more expensive floor coverings. Do it yourself and it will probably wrinkle.

But with a little help you could well re-lay an old fitted carpet. Any fitted carpet should be laid on underlay, either hair or rubber (Dunlopillo make various grades) and money invested in underlay is *well spent*. I know, I've tried getting round it without success for twenty years. Not only do you get a more luxurious, bouncy 'feel' but the carpet will wear better and not go into ridges where the lines

of your floorboards are. Always lay underlay on top of newspaper to keep the dust down under the floorboards.

Help is needed, too, in laying sheet vinyl; the rolls are heavy. But what you can lay alone and unaided are vinyl tiles and carpet tiles.

The first step is to prepare the floor, which will probably be a boarded one, in which case it needs sweeping or vacuuming thoroughly. Remove all old tacks and nails from previous coverings. Use your work gloves, a housemaid's kneeler, a pair of pincers, a tack lifter and a hammer. Scour the whole area: any nails that you can't pull out must be hammered right in.

If you find any loose floorboards hammer down nails which have worked loose and replace missing ones. These should be floor brads, which have square, flat heads that sink in flush with the wood, though oval wire nails about 5 cm (2 inches) long will do. Watch where you bang them in, because they'll do no good unless they go through the joist underneath which supports the boards: you can see where the joists run from the lines of existing nails across the floor. Unless you are going to put down a hardboard underlay fill any gaps more than about 6 mm ($\frac{1}{4}$ inch) wide between the boards by taking a hammer and tapping in strips of wood (which you bought from your DIY shop).

Whether a hardboard underlay is necessary depends on the condition of the floorboards and the type of floor covering to be laid. In newish houses, where the boards are smooth, close-fitting and well nailed down, no underlay should be necessary except possibly under vinyl tiles, which can break up in time if there is too much movement beneath them. In older houses, where floorboards are uneven, gappy and loosely nailed, an underlay is nearly always necessary, though with carpet tiles and sheet vinyl the worst that happens if you don't have underlay is that marks appear through the covering following the joins between the boards. A thick paper underlay can prevent this to some extent.

A hardboard underlay will definitely prevent it. It should be cut (or bought cut) into 60- or 120-cm (2- or 4-foot) squares for easy handling and nailed down, rough side up, with hardboard pins. Tap the pins in at about 23-cm (9-inch) intervals all over the board, not just round the edges. Don't bother to damp the back of the hardboard, like they'll tell you, unless your floor is damp, which it shouldn't be. If it is, check the reason immediately with a qualified surveyor.

Preparation of a concrete or stone floor should mean a *thorough* cleaning to get rid of dirt and concrete dust, which would prevent adhesive from gripping. Any holes should be filled with cement. You won't need a hardboard underlay because the floor surface is already flat and unyielding, like the worst sort of heroine.

Vinyl and carpet tiles

Choose a brand of vinyl tile which is self-adhesive, so that all you have to do is peel off the backing sheet to lay them, without messing about with adhesive. They are usually 23-cm (9-inch) square and are sold loose or in packs of sixteen which cover a square yard, or scant square metre. Carpet tiles are even more trouble-free as they are simply laid dry. They are usually 30-cm (1-foot) square and are sold loose or in packs of nine, to cover a square yard (or scant square metre). Most carpet tiles are cheap-quality plain-coloured and good value for the money because of the laying time they save you and the fact that you can quickly fit in a replacement if you get worn areas, burns or irrevocable stains.

The pack should carry full instructions for laying but the basic principles are the same, whether you are laying vinyl tiles, with adhesive, or carpet tiles, dry. The tiles should be laid parallel to the walls but, of course, the walls are never parallel. So *don't* start in one corner and think that you can just work along in rows. All beginners make this fatal error.

Diagram 1 (see p. 303): Find the halfway points along two facing walls and tap small nails into the floor at these points. Rub chalk into a length of string and tie the string tautly between the nails. Lift the string an inch or two somewhere near its middle and then let it go ping! so that it strikes the floor. It will leave a straight chalk line across the room between the nails. (Don't try to chalk your own straight line across the floor. That's much harder than it sounds and my way is infallible.) Remove the string, then find the halfway point on the chalk line and mark it. From the chalk line lay out a row of tiles to one wall, lining up the first tile at right angles to the line and the centre mark.

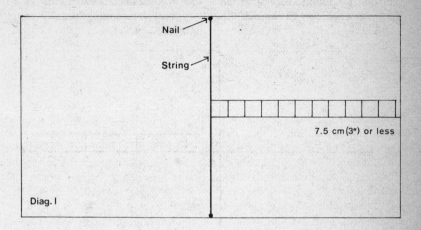

Diagram 2 (see below): If the space from the last tile to the wall is 7.5 cm (3 inches) or less (as in Diagram 1) move the whole row half a tile-width back from the wall, then mark a new chalk line, as before, in line with the edge of the first tile in its new position.

Now lay another row of tiles at right angles to the first, along the chalk line to a wall following the string (as in Diagram 1).

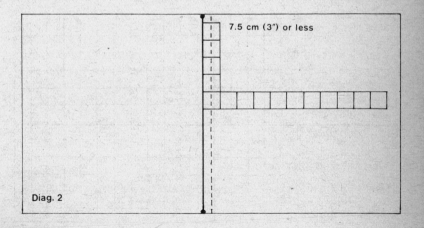

Diagram 3 (see below): Here, again, if the gap between the last tile and the wall is 7.5 cm (3 inches) or less move the whole row back a half tile-width.

You now have to move the entire first row of tiles the same amount to keep the alignment. Now 'snap' another chalk line running flush with the second row of tiles.

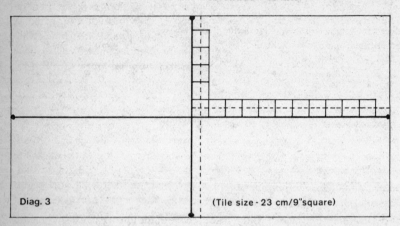

Diag. 3

(Tile size - 23 cm/9"square)

Diagram 4 (see below): Start aligning the tiles permanently, beginning with four in the angles where the two lines cross and working out in all four directions until no more whole tiles can be laid. *Note:* vinyl tiles should be laid with the white fleck 'grain' of each running at right angles to the grain of its neighbours. Again, I learnt this by obstinately doing it the other way first.

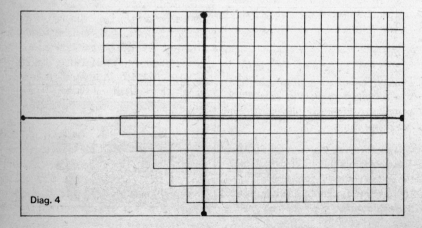

Diag. 4

How to make your tiles fit round the edges: As few rooms are perfect rectangles the spaces between the last whole tiles and the walls are probably off-square, and you will have to make some sloping cuts to get the partial tiles to fit. Take a whole tile, turn it upside down and hold one edge against the skirting board so that two of the sides cross the corners of tiles already laid. Get a thick felt pen and mark the points where the two tiles meet, transfer them to the upper side, join them with a pencil line and cut either with large scissors or with a trimming knife against a steel rule. One of the pieces will fit the space exactly. Don't try to work it out – just try it.

For corners use the same principle but in both directions, to fit the tile to both walls. Or else cut yourself a newspaper pattern.

To cut a complicated outline to fit round the bottom of a door frame make a pattern from a sheet of newspaper. Place a tile on the paper and cut round it with a sharp knife to produce a paper square the same size as the tile, then position it as if it were a tile. Where it comes against the door frame make 12-mm ($\frac{1}{2}$-inch) scissor cuts, fringing the paper all along the edge so that it bends up, then press the paper into place round the moulding with a soft pencil. This will give you an exact outline to cut out. Trace this pattern on the face of the tile and cut it out with scissors.

Sheet vinyl

Sheet vinyl floor covering, either the thin or the cushioned variety, is quite easy to cut and lay provided you have some help in manoeuvring it, as it comes in rolls up to 1.8 m (6 feet) wide.

Before measuring up decide which way the joins should run to reduce waste, according to whether the rolls are 0.9 m, 1.2 m or 1.8 m (3 feet, 4 feet or 6 feet). Avoid joins at doorways.

Alternatively, draw a plan of the floor with all measurements marked on it, take it to the shop and let them work it out for you. Work out, too, according to the pattern you choose, whether any extra vinyl is needed for matching length to length. On no account choose a regular pattern for your first effort.

Leave the vinyl in a warm room overnight; this makes it suppler and easier to handle. Meanwhile clean and prepare the floor as for other floor coverings.

Cushioned vinyl should be stuck down with flooring adhesive. Use the brand recommended by the flooring manufacturer and apply it to the floor in a 7.5-cm (3-inch) wide band round all sheet edges and a 15-cm (6-inch) wide band where the joins will be. Cut off a length about 5 cm (2 inches) longer than the strip of floor it is to cover and lay it down pushed tightly against the skirting board. Trim the ends to fit against the skirting board with scissors or a trimming knife. Fold back half the length and spread a band of adhesive on the clean floor where the edges of the vinyl will lie (widths of adhesive bands as above), then unfold the vinyl and press it firmly into place. Now repeat the procedure with the other half, and go ahead with the other lengths, tightly pushing the lengths of vinyl edge to edge.

Ordinary uncushioned vinyl sheet is laid without adhesive, allowing a little extra all round *because it shrinks when it is down*, so the joins overlap initially.

Cut as before but leave 5 cm (2 inches) extra all round the room – 12 mm ($\frac{1}{2}$ inch) extra at each join – for trimming/shrinkage.

Let the vinyl lie for a week at normal room temperature before trimming it. Now trim overlapping joins by cutting through both layers at once 6 mm ($\frac{1}{4}$ inch) from the outer edge of the top piece, using a trimming knife against a long, straight, flat piece of wood such as a yardstick, which you can buy in DIY shops.

HOW TO FIX CERAMIC TILES

Tools: spirit level or polythene tube; length of wood; plastic spreader; tile-cutter; steel rule; pincers; file; sponge; grouting stick.
Materials: Polyfilla; tiles; adhesive; grout.

The only hard part of ceramic tiling is cutting the tiles. Even the professionals allow themselves one tile in twenty as a margin for failures! So it's best to start with a simple tiling job in which little or no cutting is entailed – a row along the top of a kitchen unit,

a splashback behind a sink, wash-basin or cooker, or a tiled table or window-sill.

Standard ceramic tiles measure 108 mm ($4\frac{1}{4}$ inches) square, though you can also get 152-mm (6-inch) ones. The white ones are the cheapest, the hand-painted designs very expensive; in between come plenty of lovely mass-produced colours, patterns and textures.

Most commercially-made tiles have tiny bumps – 'spacing lugs' – on each side which make them easier to work with than those without. Small spaces have to be left between tiles when they are placed, and no lugs means fiddling about with bits of card as spacers (see below). So try to buy the sort with spacing lugs.

The basic tiles with plain edges all round are called field tiles. For the end of a run of tiles that does not fit against anything you need some 'RE tiles', which have one rounded edge, and for corners you need 'REX tiles', with two adjacent rounded edges.

Tiles are fixed in place with an adhesive rather like soft white butter which is spread on the wall with a notched plastic spreader (buy it when you buy the tiles). The notches leave ridges in the adhesive which improve the stickability. When the tiles are in place and the adhesive has dried the job is finished with 'grout', a white powder that is mixed with water to make a paste and rubbed into the spaces between the tiles. The grout dries hard and turns the tiles into a *solid, waterproof surface*.

Prepare the wall by stripping off

any wallpaper and making sure the surface is clean, dry and free of crumbly plaster. Any holes or depressions should be filled with Polyfilla, for the surface must be quite flat if the tiles are to line up properly.

The key to successful tiling is to get the first row absolutely level; subsequent rows automatically line up on the first one. If you are simply tiling behind a wash-basin or sink unit it will probably be level – but you should nonetheless check with a spirit level. If you haven't a spirit level use a length of clear polythene tube, from a DIY or wine-making shop, almost filled with cold tea. The liquid level is always exactly the same at both ends

and can be used in marking a wall to get a level line (see the diagram below). Any small gap below one end of the tiling can be filled with grout.

Plan the positioning of the tiles to avoid cutting if possible. For a wash-basin or cooker splashback start with the bottom row of tiles. Start in the middle of the area to be covered, just above the cooker or basin or whatever, and work out left and right, one row at a time.

If there must be cutting it is best to arrange the tiles so that there is a cut tile at each end, though not if both pieces are going to be very small; in such a case start at one end and cut only the other end tile. On a window-

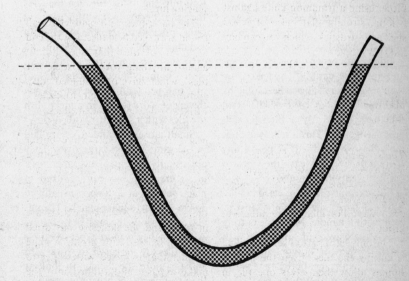

Polythene tube 'spirit level' with cold tea or coffee for visibility. However the tube is held, the two fluid surfaces remain exactly level. You hold up the tube and get someone else to mark the wall beside each end of tea or coffee, then draw a straight line through the points for a perfect horizontal.

sill arrange to have the cut tiles at the back (i.e. nearest the window) and ends.

Where tiles cannot be levelled against an existing feature pencil a bottom starting line on the wall, using a long, straight-edged piece of wood and a spirit level (or polythene tube) to ensure a perfect horizontal. Try not to drop the tubeful of cold tea. If the tiles are to go up more than a few rows, fix a double check for straightness by finding the halfway point on the horizontal line and drawing a straight, vertical line upward.

Spread adhesive on the wall about 2 mm ($\frac{1}{16}$ inch) thick and press the tiles gently into place. To your amazement, they will stay there, though they can be lifted and repositioned if necessary: make sure they are all correctly aligned corner-to-corner.

Edge and corner tiles have no lugs and must be carefully spaced from their neighbours. This is best done by inserting strips of card of the right thickness (generally a bit of cardboard, edge-on). This is removed after the adhesive has dried. Wipe off any spare adhesive and leave the work to dry for twenty-four hours.

For cutting tiles you need a tile-cutter, a hard, sharp-pointed instrument with a handle. Mark the cutting line on the glazed side of the tile with a felt-tip pen or crayon and score along it with the cutter against a straight edge; a steel rule is best.

Do this several times to ensure that you have scored through the glaze, then place the tile on a flat surface

with a matchstick under and along the scored line and press down on both edges. The tile *should* break along the line, but you'll need a bit of practice. Often a tile that butts against an adjacent corner wall will have to be cut at a slight angle. For this follow the procedure described in 'How to lay floor coverings' (see p. 300). Very small pieces or curved shapes to fit round pipes can be 'nibbled' away with pincers: you take a bit off at a time and keep nibbling away at it; surprisingly, it's easier than cutting a straight tile. Smooth the edges with a file.

To grout the tiles mix the paste up as directed and wipe it over the whole tiled surface with a sponge, rubbing it well into the joints between tiles. As the grout begins to dry (this happens quite quickly) rub off the excess with a damp cloth. To give the joints an extra smooth finish run along them with a blunt-pointed stick or the cap of a ball pen (still on the pen). When the grout is dry (allow an hour) polish the tiles with a soft, dry cloth.

Small mosaic ceramic tiles are laid in the same way as large ones. They are usually mounted on paper or a mesh material and can be fixed in place several at a time – usually in 30-cm (1-foot) square panels. The unglazed ones look the most devastating. Although they're more expensive these small tiles are *far* easier to work with and far more spectacular to look at than standard tiles because instead of cutting you need only slice off a row. If this leaves a small gap at the edge it can be filled with grout.

HOW TO DEAL WITH BADLY FITTING DOORS AND WINDOWS

Tools: screwdriver; plane; chisel; bradawl (a spike with a handle); wooden wedges; hammer.

Materials: plastic wood; draught-excluders; rubber wedges; Brighton pattern sash fasteners; L-shaped metal repair plates.

Ill-fitting doors and windows are not just irritating; they let cold air in and expensively-warmed air out. Here are a few ways of fixing them.

Doors

A door that won't shut properly may have warped, but a more likely cause is that the hinges (especially the top one) have pulled away from the frame, through the weight of the door. Get someone to lift the door upwards while you tighten all the screws. This alone may do the trick. If screws won't tighten take them out *one at a time* and plug the holes with wood; a few matchsticks will do, pushed or tapped in tightly, then broken off flush (i.e. flat with the surrounding surface). Replace the screws, which should now tighten up.

Sometimes the trouble is that the hinges have worn, particularly the top one, in which case they will have to be replaced. You'll need help again as it means taking the door off; unscrew the hinges from door frame and door. Replace with new hinges *of the same size*. Rehang the door.

A door will not shut properly if

there is a 'hinge gap' on the hinge side caused by the hinges not being recessed sufficiently into the frame or the screws not being driven fully home. If the hinges are not recessed enough the door will have to come off and the recesses be cut deeper with a sharp chisel.

Alternatively, a door may be 'hinge-bound', fitting too close to the hinge jamb and leaving a gap at the opposite side. Take the screws out of the top hinge and fit a piece of thick card behind the hinge before replacing them; then do the same to the bottom one.

If none of these things makes the door close properly the door is probably distorted and you will have to plane a little off the edge on the handle side and/or the bottom edge. Here again you'll have to take the door off.

When a door rattles in its frame, the door has probably shrunk so that the latch part of the door handle isn't engaging tightly with the latch plate on the door frame. You can remedy this by unscrewing the plate and moving it back slightly, then gouging out the central holes in the wood (see the illustration on p. 310).

Close door and push hard against it, make a pencil line on the frame, with the pencil against the door edge at the height of the plate. Unscrew the plate and with a chisel enlarge the recess it sits in up to the pencil line. Hold the plate in its new position, mark where to chisel new apertures for the latch and lock, then cut these to the same depth as the old ones. Replace the plate in its new position and fill the

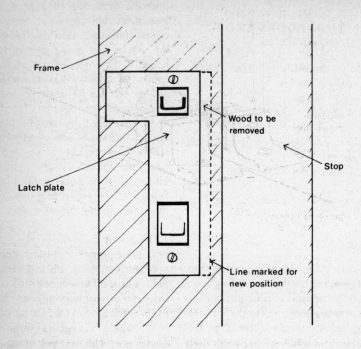

Frame

Wood to be removed

Stop

Latch plate

Line marked for new position

gap at the front with plastic wood.

When you can see daylight all round an exterior door fit a draught-excluder of plastic foam or strip round the top and sides of the frame and a plastic or wood-and-rubber flap across the bottom of the door. Make sure to first clean the frame *thoroughly* or the foam won't stick on. It doesn't last long, but it's a cheap, quick method and it certainly works while it lasts. The plastic strip is nailed on and is much more durable than the plastic foam. You will be surprised to find that draught-excluding noticeably cuts down dirt and noise.

Windows

Foam draught-excluder can also stop casement windows rattling. Stick the self-adhesive material round the frame so that the window closes on it. At the same time check that all catches and stays (those bottom bars with the little holes in) are screwed home securely.

A rattling sash window can be cured by inserting rubber wedges (from hardware and DIY shops) between the two frames, one on each side. For a more permanent job fit the 'Brighton pattern' type of sash

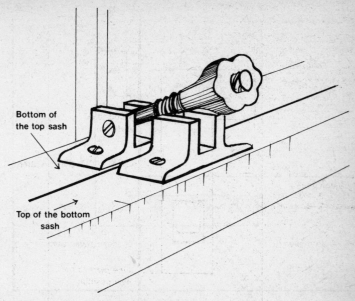

Sash fastener, Brighton pattern

fastener, in which a hinged bolt fixed on one frame lies in a lug on the other and is tightened up with a knob. (When you buy it, get the salesman to identify these bits.) This type of sash fastener draws the two frames together when it is tightened. It is also more burglar-proof than the common lever type of fastener.

Both casement and sash windows can become difficult or impossible to close because corner joints of the window frame work loose. These can be pulled back into shape and held there by L-shaped repair plates (see the illustration on p. 312). In the case of hinged windows close the window and hammer a wedge into the gap between window and frame at the

handle side. This will pull the loose joint together and you can position the plates over the joints, marking screw-holes with a bradawl and fitting.

For a sash window you'll need four wedges (if all corner joints are loose). Lower the top sash to a midway position, then tap in wedges between sash and frame on each side, top and bottom, moving the lower sash up and down as needed to get access. Now fit the plates over the joints as with the hinged window, then knock out the wedges and do the lower sash too if necessary.

Repair plates should ideally be fitted on the outside, which means working from outside the house with perhaps a step-ladder, or, if the win-

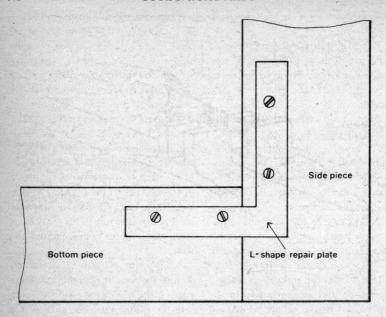

Side piece

Bottom piece   L-shape repair plate

dow is an upstairs one, working from inside as when cleaning a window. If they are fitted on the outside, they should then be painted with metal primer to prevent rusting, then gloss paint.

HOW TO MEND A WINDOW PANE

Tools: hammer; old chisel; pincers; wire brush; steel tape; putty knife; tack hammer; work gloves (not rubber).

Materials: window glass; putty; glazing sprigs or panel pins (all bought from a DIY shop).

It really pays to replace your own broken window panes (or to get him

who broke it to repair it, if he's over ten). Professional labour is expensive and difficult to arrange, yet the operation is quite simple for ground-floor windows which can easily be reached from outside. First job is to don work gloves and remove all the old glass and putty from the frame. Knock the big pieces out with a hammer, making sure that none fall dangerously unnoticed, then take out the glass edges

and old putty (best tool for this is an old chisel).

Buried in the old putty you will find a few small nails, partly tapped into the frame. They were to hold the glass in place until the putty set. Remove these with pincers.

The outside ledge of the frame, into which the glass fits (called the rebate), must next be thoroughly cleaned, right down to the wood; the smallest obstruction can prevent the new glass fitting properly. A stiff wire brush is best for this.

Now measure up for a new pane. Care is vital, for glass is intractable and cannot be stretched or trimmed. So measure accurately from side to side and from top to bottom, using a steel tape and measuring from the inner sides of the rebate which will meet the edges of the glass. Now measure again to check. An old carpenters' saying is measure twice, cut once: measure once, cut twice. *Then deduct 3 mm ($\frac{1}{8}$ inch) from each measurement*. The deduction allows for slight irregularities in the window frame or for its being slightly off square. The shop where you buy the glass will cut it *exactly* to your measurements.

There are many different types and weights of glass, so make it clear that you want window glass. Incidentally, if the window you are repairing is a particularly vulnerable one – a playroom window, for example – you may think that buying a slightly heavier grade of glass is worth the extra cost, because it is less likely to shatter again.

You will also need some putty and a few 'sprigs' (small headless nails used by glaziers). If you cannot get sprigs, small panel pins will do; 20 mm ($\frac{3}{4}$ inch) is a good size. The best putty is the kind that you buy ready-packed in a polythene sachet. It retains its oil and stays supple.

The next stage of the job is to take a putty knife or an old table knife and spread a fairly thin layer of putty right round the rebate on the outside of the window against which the inside of the glass is to lie. (There's a little ledge that you can't see until the putty has been gouged out.) This putty layer is to cushion the glass against the wood.

Now fit the glass in the frame by resting its bottom edge on the lower edge of the frame and swinging it up into the frame. Push the glass firmly against the putty, pressing close to the edges – *not* in the middle of the pane. Some putty will squeeze out on the inside of the glass. It can be cleaned off later.

Now fix the glass in the frame by tapping sprigs or panel pins into the wood close against the glass and leaving them to stick out about 6 mm ($\frac{1}{4}$ inch) so that they hold the glass in place. If you use proper sprigs tap them in with their broader sides against the glass. Use a small hammer for this part of the job, gently tapping the nails and resting the side of the hammer head against the glass during the stroke. (If you don't do this you may break the glass.) You need only a couple of nails for each side of the frame, i.e. eight nails per window pane.

Now, using a putty knife, spread putty into the recess between frame and glass, right round the frame, and trim it to a neat edge. (See how it's done on your unbroken windows.) You really do need a putty knife for this; and it's also useful to have a jar of hot water handy: if you keep dipping the knife into it the hot knife will make the putty easier to manipulate, as well as giving an extra-smooth professional finish.

Leave the putty to dry for at least a week before painting it, then give the frame two coats of gloss.

All this relates to wooden window frames. If your windows are metal-framed there are three small differences of technique.

1 You must use metal casement putty; the ordinary sort will not stick to metal.

2 You will not need sprigs or panel pins, but you will need some glazing clips; these are small spring clips with one arm that goes into a hole in the frame and one that clamps against the glass. You'll see how they work when you remove the old ones along with the old putty.

3 After cleaning out the old glass and putty you should treat the bare metal of the frame with a rust-inhibitor such as Galvafroid before reglazing.

BOOK

3

SUPERWOMAN
TAKES OFF!

Happy Family Outings

(whether it's an afternoon off or a fortnight away)

Around 11½ million foreign visitors came here in 1977 for *their* precious holiday, and we actually live in a tourist paradise without realizing it.

There's more to do in a day in Britain than there is almost anywhere else in the world: a simple list of what's available takes up whole books. (See p. 358 for a Guide to the Best Guides, many of which will be in your local library.) A lot of fun is *free* and a lot of it costs very little ... a day at the sea, rural rides and walks over amazingly varied country, expeditions to ancient historical towns, and the most beautiful gardens in the world.

The once dreary barn-like museums and bleak art galleries have become lively, warm and wonderful places where you can actually *enjoy* a rainy day. There are hundreds of famous castles and homes of the famous, where, for instance, you can see Jane Austen's armchair, read Dr Johnson's notes, potter round Charlotte Brontë's bedroom, read Nelson's love letters and open Churchill's cigar box.

There are lots of other answers to the eternal questions: 'Where can I take them in the holidays?' and 'What can we do *now*?' Bloodthirsty children can visit battlefields such as Marston Moor and Bannockburn. Small boys can chug along in steam railways and imaginative swots can browse among prehistoric temples, Roman villas or archaeological rarities.

Holidays for longer than a day include ideas for children going on their own, holiday exchanges (including abroad), adventure holidays for the whole family (including pony-trekking), working holidays (both voluntary and paid ones) and study holidays for them and you.

HAVE A WONDERFUL TIME IN BRITAIN.

PRICES

All prices and details given were correct at the time of going to press, but **check** with your travel agent, or the organization or company concerned, before booking any holiday or expedition.

OPENING TIMES

These are so varied that it's best to avoid disappointment by checking first, if possible, although not everywhere you may want to visit has a telephone (Stonehenge? Where possible, telephone numbers have been given in the text). Exasperatingly, museums are generally shut tight on public holidays, whereas the big-league stately homes and safari parks usually bust a gut to get as many visitors as possible on these days (so be prepared for a crush). They are generally open from around 10 a.m. to dusk.

Smaller stately homes tend to have infuriatingly erratic opening hours, such as the third Thursday of each month. The owners still tend to find too many reasons (such as cost and lack of staff) for suiting themselves rather than the visitors they need to keep themselves solvent. Which is why many historic homes are shut on Saturday or Sunday, just when you might want to visit them.

The standard opening hours for historic sites and ancient monuments operated by the Department of the Environment are:

	Weekdays	*Sundays**
March April October	0930–1730	1400–1730
May to September	0930–1900	1400–1900
November to February	0930–1600	1400–1600

Scottish opening hours:

	Weekdays	*Sundays**
October to March	0930–1600	1400–1600
April to September	0930–1900	1400–1900

Some monuments are closed for lunch, 1300–1400.

Museums and art galleries are usually open at least six days a week and on Sunday afternoons, if operated by local authorities. Private museums, such as those at universities, will have their own hours of admission, so check before visiting.

* Many monuments are also open on Sunday mornings in the summer but they are all closed for Christmas Eve, Christmas Day, Boxing Day and New Year's Day.

MAP OF COUNTIES OF BRITAIN

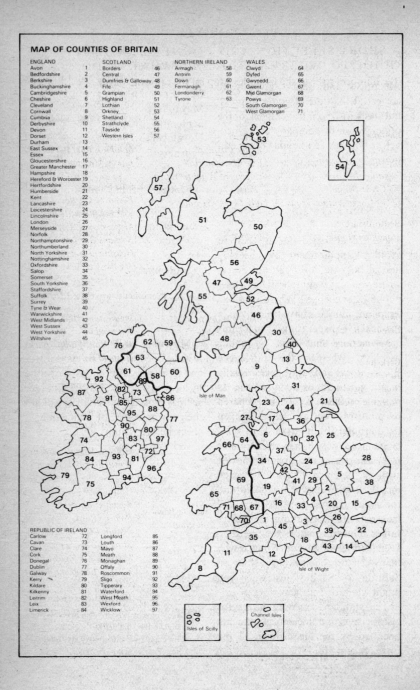

ENGLAND
Avon	1
Bedfordshire	2
Berkshire	3
Buckinghamshire	4
Cambridgeshire	5
Cheshire	6
Cleveland	7
Cornwall	8
Cumbria	9
Derbyshire	10
Devon	11
Dorset	12
Durham	13
East Sussex	14
Essex	15
Gloucestershire	16
Greater Manchester	17
Hampshire	18
Hereford & Worcester	19
Hertfordshire	20
Humberside	21
Kent	22
Lancashire	23
Leicestershire	24
Lincolnshire	25
London	26
Merseyside	27
Norfolk	28
Northamptonshire	29
Northumberland	30
North Yorkshire	31
Nottinghamshire	32
Oxfordshire	33
Salop	34
Somerset	35
South Yorkshire	36
Staffordshire	37
Suffolk	38
Surrey	39
Tyne & Wear	40
Warwickshire	41
West Midlands	42
West Sussex	43
West Yorkshire	44
Wiltshire	45

SCOTLAND
Borders	46
Central	47
Dumfries & Galloway	48
Fife	49
Grampian	50
Highland	51
Lothian	52
Orkney	53
Shetland	54
Strathclyde	55
Tayside	56
Western Isles	57

NORTHERN IRELAND
Armagh	58
Antrim	59
Down	60
Fermanagh	61
Londonderry	62
Tyrone	63

WALES
Clwyd	64
Dyfed	65
Gwynedd	66
Gwent	67
Mid Glamorgan	68
Powys	69
South Glamorgan	70
West Glamorgan	71

Isle of Man

REPUBLIC OF IRELAND
Carlow	72	Longford	85
Cavan	73	Louth	86
Clare	74	Mayo	87
Cork	75	Meath	88
Donegal	76	Monaghan	89
Dublin	77	Offaly	90
Galway	78	Roscommon	91
Kerry	79	Sligo	92
Kildare	80	Tipperary	93
Kilkenny	81	Waterford	94
Leitrim	82	West Meath	95
Leix	83	Wexford	96
Limerick	84	Wicklow	97

Isle of Wight

Isles of Scilly

Channel Isles

A SHORT SELECTION AND COUNTY-BY-COUNTY GUIDE TO 'WHERE TO GO' AND 'WHAT TO DO'

(the numbers refer to the Counties Map on the opposite page)

England

Avon   1
Wildlife Park and British
  Nature Centre
SS Great Britain
Ebbor Gorge Nature Trails

Bedfordshire   2
Houghton House
Luton Hoo
Wrest Park
Whipsnade Park Zoo
Woburn Wild Animal
  Kingdom
Shuttleworth Collection
Leighton Buzzard
  Narrow Gauge Railway

Berkshire   3
Royal Windsor Safari Park
Stanley Spencer Gallery
Snelsmore Common
Savill Gardens

Buckinghamshire   4
Waddesdon Manor
Hughenden Manor

Cambridgeshire   5
Thorney Wildlife Park
Cromwell Museum
Cambridge and County
  Folk Museum
Fitzwilliam Museum
Kettle's Yard
Scott Polar Research
  Institute Museum
University Museum of
  Archaeology and
  Ethnology
Whipple Museum of the
  History of Science

Cheshire   6
Chester Castle
Little Moreton Hall
Bridgemere Wildlife
  Park
Lady Lever Art Gallery

Cornwall   8
Cotehele
Pendennis Castle
Restormel Castle
Tintagel Castle

Cumbria   9
Piel Castle
Lowther Wildlife
  Country Park
Dove Cottage and the
  Wordsworth Museum
Hill Top
Carlisle Museum
Ravenglass and Eskdale
  Railway

Derbyshire   10
Chatsworth
Haddon Hall
Bolsover Castle
Hardwick Hall
Kedleston Hall
Rider Castle Wildlife Park
Donnington Collection
Tramway Museum
Dinting Railway Centre

Devon   11
Dartmoor Wildlife Park
Dart Valley Railway
Torbay Steam Railway

Dorset   12
Maiden Castle
Cloud's Hill

Durham   13
Lambton Lion Park
Bowes Museum

East Sussex   14
Pevensey Castle
The Royal Pavilion
Museum and Art Gallery
Nymans Gardens
Heathfield Wildlife and
  Country Park
Toy Museum

Essex   15
Ingatestone Hall
Tilbury Fort
Mole Hall Wildlife Park
Hatfield Forest

Gloucestershire   16
Chedworth
Dodington House
Sudeley Castle
Hailes Abbey
Hidcote Manor Gardens
Westonbirt Arboretum

Hampshire   18
Beaulieu Abbey
Palace House
Beaulieu Motor Museum
Maritime Museum
Marwell Zoological Park
Weyhill European Wildlife
  Park
Jane Austen's House
Museum of Ancient
  Farming
Royal Naval Museum
  and HMS Victory

DISTANCE IN MILES BETWEEN SELECTED TOWNS

The distance between any two towns listed here can be found in the box formed at the junction of the vertical and horizontal rows reading from the names of the towns.

Aberdeen
427 Aberystwyth
175 309 Avr
403 114 285 Birmingham
480 121 362 88 Bristol
484 100 366 102 44 Cardiff
208 219 90 195 272 276 Carlisle
417 132 299 18 91 114 209 Coventry
384 138 266 40 127 142 176 40 Derby
552 284 455 181 187 226 365 163 197 Dover
115 312 73 288 365 369 93 303 263 436 Edinburgh
555 196 437 163 75 119 347 167 203 243 440 Exeter
142 313 33 289 366 370 94 303 243 270 459 44 441 Glasgow
448 107 330 53 35 56 240 57 93 176 333 110 334 Gloucester
509 271 413 159 188 228 323 141 163 112 393 242 417 172 Harwich
423 108 305 149 208 193 215 167 157 330 308 283 309 181 308 Holyhead
337 214 240 123 224 150 111 88 232 222 278 245 168 185 214 Hull
104 468 198 444 521 525 249 459 419 593 156 596 169 550 464 378 Inverness
306 166 206 109 194 206 110 70 253 191 269 210 159 211 163 55 347 Leeds
412 153 295 39 116 137 205 24 28 169 280 191 299 81 135 178 87 436 96 Leicester
327 100 295 90 159 164 118 107 81 268 211 235 213 128 241 97 128 368 73 107 Liverpool
326 126 208 80 159 172 118 94 59 255 211 236 212 126 221 123 93 367 40 87 35 Manchester
221 254 144 201 285 299 57 202 161 338 106 360 143 250 295 250 117 262 92 181 154 129 Newcastle-upon-Tyne
471 270 374 156 208 236 384 138 139 153 356 277 378 179 66 296 143 512 173 118 215 184 257 Norwich
370 154 272 50 138 153 182 48 16 193 255 213 276 103 151 172 73 411 67 25 97 70 156 124 Nottingham
663 304 545 271 184 227 455 275 311 355 548 112 549 218 354 391 386 704 378 299 343 344 468 389 322 Penzance
81 353 94 330 406 411 135 345 305 478 42 482 61 375 436 350 264 115 233 322 253 252 148 397 297 590 Perth
597 238 479 205 118 161 389 209 245 285 482 42 483 152 284 325 320 638 312 233 277 278 402 319 256 79 524 Plymouth
543 211 425 141 92 136 335 127 167 125 426 123 429 104 144 282 233 583 237 146 228 219 327 183 171 234 468 163 Portsmouth
338 154 235 77 164 179 145 92 136 37 225 223 240 130 183 158 61 379 33 62 73 38 124 145 37 348 265 282 204 Sheffield
528 195 412 128 75 118 322 114 154 78 412 37 413 105 149 269 220 569 224 133 216 207 314 189 158 455 307 146 18 192 Southampton
362 109 244 43 124 138 154 57 34 219 247 199 248 89 190 123 107 403 73 55 51 37 164 173 50 288 297 307 314 158 217 Stoke-on-Trent
226 320 51 296 373 377 101 310 277 466 123 448 84 341 424 316 251 249 306 219 155 395 283 556 145 490 436 246 423 556 282 455 Stranraer
299 190 203 127 215 229 113 126 88 260 184 290 207 180 217 187 38 340 24 103 97 64 80 179 78 398 226 332 251 52 236 99 214 York
488 212 390 110 116 154 300 92 123 72 373 170 394 105 259 168 527 190 98 197 184 274 111 123 281 415 211 72 160 77 147 401 196 LONDON

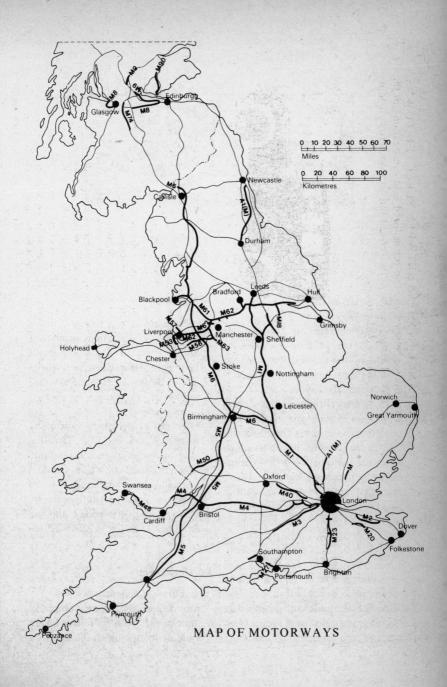

MAP OF MOTORWAYS

Days Out

THE WAY WE LIVED

It's always interesting to visit the castles, abbeys and houses which were lived in by the mighty, the mad, the rich and the promiscuous – the Beautiful People of History.

Here's a careful choice that covers the best of British architecture and shows the whole range of architectural styles in this country, while trying to avoid the obvious. It's an encapsulated architectural education. Don't forget that on the whole when visiting ruins the older the building is the less there may be of it.

Antrim

Carrickfergus – *Carrickfergus Castle*.
Romantic, strongly-fortified Norman castle built on a peninsula jutting into Belfast Lough. Contains a terrific regimental museum.

Bedfordshire

Ampthill – *Houghton House*.
Remains of Jacobean mansion built about 1615 for the Countess of Pembroke. Believed to be the original of Bunyan's 'House Beautiful' in *Pilgrim's Progress*.
Luton – *Luton Hoo*.
Elizabeth II slept here. Started by Robert Adam but with Victorian interior rebuilt after a terrible fire. Magnificent art collection. Includes mementos belonging to the Russian Imperial Family with jewels by Fabergé, English porcelain and fine paintings. (Tel. Luton [0582] 22955)

Buckinghamshire

Aylesbury – *Waddesdon Manor*.
Florid, somewhat vulgar mansion built in the 1880s by Baron Ferdinand de Rothschild in the style of a

French Renaissance château. Collection includes elaborate eighteenth-century French furniture (as good as anything in France), carpets, clocks and porcelain. (Tel. Waddesdon [029 665] 211 or 282)

Cheshire

Chester – *Chester Castle*.
Dating from 1069, one tower contains a vaulted chapel and museum of the Cheshire Regiment, with sinister swords and sad standards.
Congleton – *Little Moreton Hall*.
Perfect example of fifteenth-century 'black and white' architecture. Remarkable wood carving, decorative plasterwork and collection of sixteenth-century furniture and pewter. (Tel. Congleton [026 02] 2018)

Clwyd

Chirk – *Chirk Castle*.
Offa's Dyke, built by the Mercian King Offa in 774, runs through the garden. This castle, lived in for the past 660 years, was built in the reign of Edward II as part of the defence system of the Welsh border (the Welsh wanted to devolve). Previous occupants include Sir Thomas Seymour, who married Catherine Parr, one of Henry VIII's widows (he had six wives but only two widows). Sir Thomas flirted, Lolita-fashion, with the teenage Princess Elizabeth and is thought by some to have put her off marriage.
Rhuddlan – *Rhuddlan Castle*.
Castle, built by Edward I as his

Welsh headquarters, commands the anchorage in the Clywd estuary and the moat is fed by the sea. Clobbered by Roundheads in 1646.

Cornwall

Calstock – *Cotehele*
Exquisitely preserved, late-medieval manor house at the head of a valley, with beautiful terraced garden and many pools below. Fascinating furniture, armour, tapestries, needlework and one of the oldest clocks in working order. (Tel. St Dominick [0579] 50434)
Falmouth – *Pendennis Castle*.
Well-preserved castle erected by Henry VIII as part of his system of coastal defences. Exhibition of Tudor coastal defences, which were as important as south coast airfields in 1940.
Lostwithiel – *Restormel Castle*.
Large Norman castle on picturesque site.
Trevena – *Tintagel Castle*.
Remains of a wild and romantic medieval castle on rocky, towering cliffs. Legend (and Tennyson) says that in the fifth century King Arthur led the native Celts against the invading Saxons. Celtic fifth-century monastery stands on a nearby headland. Wonderful place for a picnic.

Cumbria

Barrow-in-Furness – *Piel Castle*.
On Piel Island; the ruins of a fourteenth-century castle of the abbots of Furness.

Derbyshire

Bakewell – *Chatsworth House*.
One of the grandest houses in England, rebuilt by the Duke of Devonshire at the end of the seventeenth century. It contains a superb collection of drawings, paintings and furniture and the gardens display three different styles of design: early eighteenth-century formal, mid eighteenth-century landscaped, and mid Victorian, designed by Joseph Paxton, architect of the Crystal Palace. (Tel. Baslow [024 688] 2204)

Bakewell – *Haddon Hall*.
Belongs to the Duke of Rutland. The best example of an English medieval manor, incredibly pretty gardens with masses of roses. (Tel. Bakewell [062 981] 2855)

Bolsover – *Bolsover Castle*.
First built by William the Conqueror, but repeatedly rebuilt, so it's now mainly seventeenth-century classic.

Chesterfield. Stately Home country with a full range of architectural styles. Visit medieval *Haddon*; sixteenth-century *Hardwick*; Baroque *Chatsworth*; Neo-classical Kedleston Hall; Victorian *Newstead*. *Hardwick Hall* is a fine example of Elizabethan architecture, built by the formidable Elizabeth, Countess of Shrewsbury, known as Bess of Hardwick. She was a tough adventuress, a tough business woman and an excellent embroiderer.

Quarndon – *Kedleston Hall*.
For over 800 years the home of the Curzon family (amazing – everyone now moves once every eight years on average). The original house was rebuilt by Robert Adam and is probably his best job. The marble hall, staterooms, furniture and pictures are world famous. There's also a museum of silver, ivories and other art which was liberated by Lord C., when Viceroy of India.

Dorset

Dorchester – *Maiden Castle*.
Finest example of a prehistoric fortress in the country, with enormous earthwork fortifications and complex entrance defences.

Down

Downpatrick – *Castle Ward*.
Impressive, mid Georgian country house in 600 acres of exquisite park.

Dumfries and Galloway

Castle Douglas – *Threave Castle*.
Built by Archibald the Grim, this mighty tower of the fighting 'Black Douglas' stands on an islet in the River Dee. Superb gardens and bird sanctuary.

Dyfed

Llandulo – *Carreg Cennen Castle*.
Grim courtyard surrounded by curtain wall and towers; crowns a cliff above the River Cennen, and has secret passage to a cave deep under the castle.

East Sussex

Brighton – *The Royal Pavilion*.
Extravagant home of the Prince Regent and his favourite mistress, Mrs Fitzherbert. This is an architectural extravaganza in the Moghul style, without, and Chinese style within. Even the kitchens have cast-iron palm trees. Lavish! *Museum and Art Gallery*. Mouthwatering display of Art Nouveau and Art Deco furniture, china figurines, glass and materials. (Tel. Brighton [0273] 63005)
Pevensey – *Pevensey Castle*.
Extensive remains of large Roman fortress, with a Norman castle built at the east end. But the sea receded, so it was useless for coastal defence.

Essex

Ingatestone – *Ingatestone Hall*.
Built in 1540. Besides the impressive permanent display, each year there is a special exhibition of some aspect of the history of Essex.
Tilbury – *Tilbury Fort*.
Originally one of Henry VIII's coastal blockhouses, but remodelled and extended by Charles II during the Dutch wars.

Fermanagh

Enniskillen – *Castlecoole*.
Late Georgian house; the interior, designed by architect James Wyatt, is extravagantly decorated with ornate plasterwork.

Gloucestershire

Chedworth – *Chedworth*.
Fine Roman villa, carefully excavated to show the layout of the rooms with excellent mosaic.
Chipping Sodbury – *Dodington House*.
One of England's great family homes, this eighteenth-century house stands in a vast, exquisite park designed by 'Capability' Brown. Masses to look at: delightful carriage museum with horses and ponies, model soldier exhibition, garden centre, tropical fish aquarium, narrow-gauge railway and adventure playground in which to dump your children. (Tel. Chipping Sodbury [0454] 8608)
Winchcombe – *Sudeley Castle*.
Home of royalty for centuries. Henry VIII's sixth queen, Catherine Parr, lived there (and died there in childbirth), as did Elizabeth I. It was the headquarters of Charles I during the Civil War and the scene of two famous sieges. On display is an impressive collection of furniture, tapestries, needlework and porcelain, with paintings by Constable, Rubens and Van Dyck. Stunning Elizabethan gardens, children's play park, picnic areas and many historical exhibitions. (Tel. Winchcombe [0242] 602308)
Winchcombe – *Hailes Abbey*.
Ruins of monastic buildings and a thirteenth-century Cistercian house. Chaucer's Pardoner swore an oath by 'the blood of Christ that is in Hailes', referring to the

Abbey's famous relic, a crystal phial of Christ's blood, now lost.

Grampian

Cockbridge – *Corgarff Castle*.
Sixteenth-century tower house where poor Margaret Forbes and her family were burned by the Gordons in 1571.
Dufftown – *Balvenie Castle*.
One of the largest and best preserved castles in the north of Scotland. Worth a special visit.
Kildrummy – *Kildrummy Castle*.
Most complete thirteenth-century building in Scotland, which doesn't amount to very much.

Gwent

Newport – *Caerleon*.
A Roman legionary fortress and amphitheatre. The only one in Britain to have been completely excavated.
Raglan – *Raglan Castle*.
Much of the fifteenth-century castle still stands. Much of it doesn't.

Gwynedd

Anglesey – *Beaumaris Castle*.
Fine, concentric, moated castle, on the shores of the Menai Strait. Built by King Edward I.
Harlech – *Harlech Castle*.
Built on a precipitous crag between 1283 and 1290 by Edward I (who was very fond of building). During the Wars of the Roses it was besieged by Yorkists for eight years

and inspired That Song ('Men of ...').
Llithfaen – *Tre'r Ceiri*.
Iron Age hill town, with dozens of stone huts, superbly preserved, and standing 1500 feet up on an exposed peak. An awesome sight.

Hampshire

Beaulieu – *Beaulieu Abbey*.
Beside the peaceful Beaulieu River; a ruined thirteenth-century Cistercian abbey which was founded in 1204 by King John. The refectory is now the parish church.
Palace House. Home of Lord Montagu, originally the great gatehouse to the abbey.
Beaulieu Motor Museum. Well-publicized history of motor transport, with rare examples of earliest cars, best of the 1920s and 1930s, and motorcycles and bicycles. (Tel. Beaulieu [0590] 612345)
Maritime Museum. An old inn in riverside village of Buckler's Hard charts the local history and contains relics of Nelson's ships.

Highland

Fort George – *Fort George*.
Fort built as a defence against the Jacobites in the traditional eighteenth-century manner.
Museum of the Seaforth Highlanders, the Queen's Own Highlanders and the Queen's Own Cameron Highlanders with pictures, uniforms, medals, silver and weapons. (Tel Ardersier [066 76] 274)

Humberside

Burton Agnes – *Norman Manor House*.
Wonderful Elizabethan Yorkshire treasure house with fabulous collection of French Impressionists, Elizabethan ceilings, antique ceilings and oriental china.

Isle of Wight

Newport – *Carisbrooke Castle*.
Where Charles I was imprisoned by Cromwell, before having his head cut off. Fascinating relics of local history.

Kent

Deal – *Deal Castle*.
Built by Henry VIII to defend south and east coasts against the wicked French.
Walmer Castle. One of Henry VIII's coastal forts and the residence of the Warden of the Cinque Ports. The Duke of Wellington spent his last days here, and his furniture and belongings have been preserved. Gardens were laid out by that indomitable explorer, Lady Hester Stanhope.
Dover – *Dover Castle*.
Largest and strongest in England, containing within its walls a Roman lighthouse and Saxon church. Magnificent view.
Tunbridge Wells – *Penshurst Place*.
Home of the Sidney family since 1552 and the birthplace of the Elizabethan courtier-poet Sir Philip Sidney. Fine furniture, family portraits, famous gardens and jolly toy museum.

Kildare

Celbridge – *Castletown*.
Of all the beautiful and famous Irish Georgian architecture, this is the first and largest country house in the Palladian style. More magnificent plasterwork, wonderful furniture and pictures. Three cheers for the Irish Georgian Society, who restored it to its original glory.

Leicestershire

Kirby Muxloe – *Kirkby Muxloe Castle*.
Ruined fifteenth-century brick-built fortified house surrounded by a moat.

Lincolnshire

Stamford – *Burghley House*.
England's largest and grandest Elizabethan mansion, built by Queen Elizabeth I's chief minister, William Cecil. For 400 years it has been the home of the Cecils, one of the most important power-making dynasties of Britain. Silver fireplaces, more than 700 tapestries and pictures, Heaven Room and Hell Room painted by Verrio.
The three-day event horse trials take place in the park: well-known trysting place for horsey courting couples.

Lothian

Edinburgh – *Edinburgh Castle*.
Dominates the city like an eagle on
a black crag. Masses to see, including crown jewels of Scotland.

Mid-Glamorgan

Caerphilly – *Caerphilly Castle*.
Largest fortress in Wales with
deadly military catapults and intri-
cate water defences. A splendid
example of thirteenth-century military architecture.

Norfolk

Castle Acre – *Castle Acre*.
Ruins of fine eleventh-century
castle with a stone shell keep at one
end of the village and extensive remains of a Cluniac priory at the
other end.
King's Lynn – *Castle Rising*.
Huge earthen bank surrounds an
almost complete keep.

Northamptonshire

Gretton – *Kirby Hall*.
Partly ruined but outstanding Elizabethan brick mansion built around
a courtyard with seventeenth-
century gardens.

Northumberland

Bamburgh – *Bamburgh Castle*.
Dramatically set on the rocks above
the seashore. Original Norman
keep and authentic castle atmosphere has been used by film and
television producers.

Berwick – *Norham Castle*.
Strong border castle, built about
1160 by Bishop Hugh Puiset of
Durham. Endlessly painted by amateur watercolourists and a few professionals such as Turner.

Holy Island – *Lindisfarne Priory* and
St Cuthbert's.
Cradle of English Christianity in the
north, founded in A.D. 635 by St
Aidan, and sacked by the Danes in
875. In 1802 the monastery was re-
established as part of the Benedic-
tine abbey of Durham. Accessible
at low tide across a causeway.

North Yorkshire

Thirsk – *Helmsley Castle*.
Twelfth-century keep, curtain walls
and towers, and sixteenth-century
block of domestic buildings. (See
also the hyper-romantic ruins at
near-by *Rievaulx*.)

Ripon – *Fountains Abbey*.
In the Middle Ages this was the
richest and most powerful Cistercian house in England. Now a picturesque ruin on the River Skell.

Nottinghamshire

Nottingham – *Newstead Abbey*.
Home of Lord Byron's family until
it was sold off to pay his debts
(drinking, gambling, travelling and

women). Originally a twelfth-century priory, the house was reconstructed by later owners in the Victorian Gothic style. Very Ivor Novello.

Orkney

Skara Brae.
Neolithic village miraculously preserved because it was buried under sand. The houses have rooms with stone box beds, dressers, cupboards and tanks for live fish (the winter larder). Awe-inspiring and a bit eerie.

Oxfordshire

Woodstock – *Blenheim Palace.*
Tangible gift of a grateful nation to the first Duke of Marlborough for his victories in Europe. His wife, Sarah, had interminable quarrels with the architect, Vanbrugh. Sir Winston Churchill was born there. Set in beautiful grounds with formal garden, park and lake. (Tel. Woodstock [0993] 811325)

Powys

Crickhowell – *Courtand Castle.*
Remains of thirteenth-century castle with cylindrical keep and curtain wall in grounds of *Tretower Court*, the finest fortified medieval house in Wales.

Salop

Wern – *Moreton Corbet Castle.*
Castle with a small rectangular keep and ruins of fine Elizabethan house. One of the buildings Cromwell knocked about a bit in 1664.

South Glamorgan

Cardiff – *Castell Coch.*
Fairy-tale castle in beautiful woods, rebuilt and lavishly redecorated in 1875.

Strathclyde

Maybole – *Culzean Castle.*
On a spectacular site overlooking the sea. Home farm buildings, also by Robert Adam, and now a centre for *Culzean Country Park*, with exhibitions and information provided by Ranger Naturalists. (Tel. Kirkoswald [065 56] 240)
Firth of Clyde – *Dumbarton Rock.*
Fortified in the fifth century, with many seventeenth- and eighteenth-century defensive works added.
Oban – *Dunstaffnage Castle.*
Ruined castle built on a rock with a ruined chapel nearby. Home of the Scottish kings and prison of Flora Macdonald.
Strathclyde – *Rothesay Castle.*
Substantial remains of the fine moated castle, much as it was when captured by Norsemen in 1230. Still belongs to the Royal Family.

Suffolk

Bury St Edmunds – *Ickworth.*
Spectacular Palladian house with central rotunda and semi-elliptical wings. Built by the eccentric traveller and friend of Emma Hamilton, the fourth Earl of Bristol (hence all those Hotels Bristol) to hold his collection of paintings and sculpture.

Orford – *Orford Castle.*
Henry II's favourite castle remains as a magnificent twelfth-century keep, fully roofed and floored, with earthworks around it.

Tayside

Angus, Near Monikie – *Affleck Castle.*
Romantic, turreted, fifteenth-century tower house still in good condition.

Doune – *Doune Castle.*
This medieval castle on the banks of the River Teith recreates the life of a Scottish laird in the late Middle Ages. Bonnie Prince Charlie kept his prisoners here after the battle of Falkirk. *Doune Park Gardens.* Laid out in the nineteenth century with walled garden, wooded walks alongside a burn and rare trees. While you're there, visit the *Doune Motor Museum* in the park. (Tel. Doune [078 684] 203)

Glamis – *Glamis Castle.*
Scottish, fairy-tale, turreted castle with legendary secret chamber and many royal connections: both the Queen Mother and Princess Margaret were born here; Mary Queen of Scots stayed here, so did the Old Pretender during the Jacobite rising of 1715. Traditionally, the scene of the murder of Duncan in *Macbeth*.

Kinross – *Loch Leven Castle.*
On an island in the romantic loch, reached by ferry. William Douglas helped Mary Queen of Scots to escape from it in 1568.

Warwickshire

Kenilworth – *Kenilworth Castle.*
One of the finest and biggest British castles, with fascinating and informative exhibition of its history. There was a great siege of Kenilworth in the thirteenth century and an amazing water show was staged when Elizabeth I slept here.

Wiltshire

Mere – *Stourhead.*
A double treat: the house is Palladian with fine Chippendale furniture, while the gardens are stunning examples of eighteenth-century romantic landscaping. The river leads into a series of lakes; along the banks stand temples, grottoes and rustic cottages, and the gardens are filled with ornamental trees and flowering shrubs. Especially beautiful when the rhododendrons and azaleas are in flower.

Westbury – *Bratton Camp and White Horse.*
Large prehistoric hill fort on the edge of the downs above Westbury. The eighteenth-century massive white horse is cut in turf below the camp and can be seen for miles.

SOME GRAND GARDENS

The English invented the landscape garden, thus proving that we definitely have a romantic soul. Our ideal garden seems to be a pretty, picturesque and romantic setting for an impossibly idyllic home; whereas the French planned gardens as if they were ornamental outdoor carpets: one feels that Le Nôtre would have been far happier with plastic flowers.

There are many, many opportunities to visit beautiful British gardens. Some are open most of the year, hundreds more are opened occasionally for charity. They may be modest cottage gardens or even Royal Gardens. A visit can often give you good ideas for your own garden and sometimes you can actually buy plants and eat a delicious country tea (see p. 359). Here are the pick of the bunch.

Bedfordshire

Silsoe – *Wrest Park*.
  Extensive, splendid gardens laid out for the Duke of Kent in the early eighteenth century and later extended by 'Capability' Brown.

Berkshire

Windsor Great Park – *Savill Gardens*.
  Thirty-five acres of beautifully kept woodland garden with a wide range of plants. Unforgettable on a sunny day.

East Sussex

Handcross – *Nymans Gardens*.
  Created in the early part of this century, these are very elegant gardens with fine flower-linked walks, topiary, walled garden and rare conifers.

Fife

Falkland – *Falkland Palace*.
  Hunting lodge of the medieval Stuart kings, with gardens carefully restored to their seventeenth-century plan. (Tel. Falkland 397)

Gloucestershire

Chipping Camden – *Hidcote Manor Gardens*.
  Built from scratch by one man over a forty-year span, these gardens were given to the National Trust in 1948. Include a series of small gardens each devoted to one family of plants and surrounded by hedges of many different varieties.
Tetbury – *Westonbirt Arboretum*.
  Famous collection of trees and shrubs begun in 1829 and added to ever since, with specimens from all over the world. The arboretum looks particularly beautiful when the spring-flowering shrubs are out and in autumn when the maples turn brilliant yellows, reds, oranges and browns.

Gwynedd

Conway – *Bodnant Garden*.

In beautiful position overlooking a valley towards Snowdonia. Formal terrace gardens (including fine camellias and lily ponds); the Dell, a wild garden with superb rhododendrons, magnolias and azaleas; a pinetum and two rock gardens.

Highland

Poolewe – *Inverewe Gardens*.

Begun in the 1860s on barren and rocky moorland on the shores of Loch Ewe, and famed for its huge variety of trees and plants from all over the world. It is protected from Atlantic gales by a belt of pines and by the Gulf Stream, so many delicate sub-tropical plants survive.

Kent

Sissinghurst – *Sissinghurst Castle*.

Famous garden lovingly created by Vita Sackville-West and Harold Nicolson. The best-known feature is probably the 'white garden', using only white flowers and grey-leaved plants. Much atmosphere and extraordinary style.

Norfolk

Sandringham – *Sandringham Gardens*.

Except when the Royal Family is in residence, you can visit their gardens (and the House) and picnic in the grounds throughout the summer. (April, May and September:

Tuesday, Wednesday and Thursday; June, July and August: Tuesday, Wednesday, Thursday, Friday, and Sunday; plus all Bank Holidays and Mondays.)

Oxfordshire

Oxford – *College Gardens*.

Although not large, these are exceptionally beautiful and peaceful, set among fine college buildings. The following colleges open their gardens: Balliol, Brasenose, Corpus Christi, Exeter, New College, Pembroke, Queen's, St Edmund Hall, St John's, Trinity, University College, Wadham and Worcester. A must if you're in the area.

Scilly Isles

Tresco Abbey Gardens.

The Gulf Stream gives the Scilly Isles a warm, frost-free climate, hence those early spring narcissi and daffodils. A large and beautiful collection of sub-tropical plants native to South Africa, the Mediterranean, Australia and Mexico, as well as less exotic British blooms.

Surrey

Esher – *Claremont Landscape Garden*.

Originally begun by Vanbrugh, the architect, and Charles Bridgeman, the landscape gardener, before 1720. There is a lake with an island, a grotto, a turf amphitheatre and avenues.

Ripley – *Wisley Gardens.*
Textbook gardening in the famous gardens of the Royal Horticultural Society. In spring the rhododendrons, azaleas and rock gardens are particularly fine. This is where you go to get excited about gardening, to learn, to look and to buy.

Wicklow

Enniskerry – *Powerscourt.*
These gardens, some of the most beautiful in the world, include flowered eighteenth-century terraces, a romantic waterfall, Japanese garden and deer park. The background is the lovely Wicklow Mountains.

SAFARI PARKS AND *VERY* STATELY HOMES

Nowhere else in the world can equal the British historical *fun parks* which are installed in such lavishly beautiful settings as Woburn and Beaulieu. A day's outing can include a visit to the new zoos without bars, grand homes, beautiful gardens and jolly traditional funfairs (not foul-smelling candy-floss gyp joints) together with exquisite paintings and intriguingly eccentric souvenirs, such as those in the Nazi museum at Longleat. They *really* are a family outing with something for everyone. The animals have been listed in detail so that there are no wailings on the way home: 'But you *said* that there'd be gorillas!'

Most of the safari parks have restaurants, cafeterias, car parks, picnic areas, souvenir and gift shops. Many offer pony, donkey or camel rides, merry-go-rounds, pleasure-boat trips and Noah's arks. Opening hours are generally from around 10 a.m. to sunset, from Easter to October. Understandably, dogs are not always allowed in.

Avon

Westbury-on-Trym, Bristol – *Wildlife Park and British Nature Centre.*
Specializing in British wild fauna; many species including foxes, badgers, deer, otters and squirrels. (Tel. Bristol [0272] 625112)

Bedfordshire

Whipsnade, Dunstable – *Whipsnade Park Zoo*.
Houses some 2000 animals from all over the world in its 500 acres. You can see white rhinos, gnus, blesbok, chimpanzees, wolves, hippopotami, cheetahs, European bison, moose, wallabies and dolphins. (Tel. Whipsnade [0582] 872171)

Woburn – *Woburn Wild Animal Kingdom*.
One of Europe's largest and most glamorous drive-through game reserves. Giraffes, tigers, lions, white rhinos, elephants, monkeys, antelope, zebras, hippopotami, bears, wildebeest, eland, ostriches, chimpanzees, sea lions, dolphins. Guaranteed to exhaust the most lively child. (Tel. Woburn [052 525] 246)

Berkshire

Windsor – *Royal Windsor Safari Park*.
Most of the animals are free-roaming over 150 acres and can be observed either from the safety of your own car or from safari buses. Lions, tigers, cheetahs, baboons, giraffes, white rhinos, llamas, ostriches, zebras, elephants, crocodiles, pythons, dragon iguanas, performing killer whales, dolphins, sea lions, penguins, flamingoes, black and white swans, macaws and monkeys. (Tel. Windsor [075 35] 69841)

Cambridgeshire

Thorney, nr Peterborough – *Thorney Wildlife Park*.
A twenty-five-acre wildlife park with lions, tigers, leopards, pumas, panthers, polar bears, giraffes, llamas, elephants, monkeys, and many birds. (Tel. Thorney [073 18] 221 or Oundle [083 22] 2514)

Cheshire

Nantwich – *Bridgemere Wildlife Park*.
This thirty-acre park contains over ninety different species of European animals and birds: rare species of deer, otters, foxes, wolves, water fowl, birds of prey and foreign birds. (Tel. Bridgemere [093 65] 223)

Cumbria

Hackthorpe, Penrith – *Lowther Wildlife Country Park*.
Many species of animals and birds including red and fallow deer, Japanese and Formosan Sika deer, Chinese water deer, Longhorn, Highland and Ankole cattle, Scottish wildcats, otters, wild boar, polecats, badgers, waterfowl. (Tel. Hackthorpe [093 12] 392)

Derbyshire

Matlock – *Riber Castle Wildlife Park*.
Some rarer species of European animals such as pine marten, polecats, wild bear and lynx live in twenty-acre park. (Tel. Matlock [0629] 2073)

Devon

Sparkwell, nr Plymouth – *Dartmoor Wildlife Park*.
Romantically, on the edge of Dartmoor, birds kept in near natural conditions, deer, badgers, foxes, squirrels, wildcats, wolves, ornamental pheasants, peafowl and birds of prey (for Vulture vultures). (Tel. Cornwood [075 537] 209)

Durham

Chester-le-Street – *Lambton Lion Park*.
Two hundred and ten acres of free-roaming African and European animals and birds: giraffes, elephants, zebras, camels, eland, wildebeest, rhinos, hippopotami, lions, baboons, ostriches, a pets' corner and aviary. (Tel. Fence Houses [038 579] 3311/2)

East Sussex

Hailsham Park, Heathfield – *Heathfield Wildlife and Country Park*.
Some animals are caged and some roam free: chimps, camels, deer, bison, llama, racoons, monkeys, zebras and many birds. (Tel. Heathfield [043 52] 4656, 4748 and 4919)

Essex

Widdington, nr Saffron Walden – *Mole Hall Wildlife Park*.
You can spot woolly monkeys, Canadian and Indian otters, Arctic and red foxes, racoons, red deer and Japanese Sika deer. There are also a penguin pool, a collection of waterfowl, aviaries, and areas with cranes, pheasants, peafowl and smaller tropical birds. (Tel. Saffron Walden [0799] 40400)

Hampshire

Golden Common, Winchester – *Marwell Zoological Park*.
Some of the world's rarest, most beautiful and deadly animals are here. You can see Siberian and Sumatran tigers, scimitar horned oryx, zebras, antelope, cheetahs, leopards, jaguars, lynx and European bison. (Tel. Owslebury [096 274] 206)
Weyhill, nr Andover – *Weyhill European Wildlife Park*.
This park specializes in European wildlife and its growing collection includes fallow, red and roe deer, Arctic and red foxes, wild boar, badgers, stoats, polecats, bears, monkeys and wolves. (Tel. Weyhill [026 477] 2252)

Hereford and Worcester

Spring Grove, Bewdley – *West Midland Safari Park*.
Set in beautiful countryside with hills, woods and three natural lakes (so there's a safari boat). Exhibits include lions, tigers, giraffes, antelope, zebras, white rhinos, baboons, wolves, bears, monkeys and sea lions. (Tel. Bewdley [0299] 2114)

Isle of Man

Ballaugh – *Curraghs Wildlife Park*.
The only place on the Isle of Man where you can see llamas, deer, wallabies, otters, South American tapirs, sea lions, waterfowl and birds. (Tel. Sulby [062 489] 323)

Kent

Bekesbourne, nr Canterbury – *Howletts Zoo Park*.
Caged and free-roaming animals include the first bred honey badger and clouded leopard in the world, the largest collection of tigers, the first bred Siberian tiger in Great Britain and the largest collection of gorillas in Great Britain including four youngsters bred in captivity. John Aspinall (the owner, not an exhibit) and the keeper 'play' with the tigers and gorillas daily. Dogs not allowed. A must if you can make it. (Tel. Littlebourne [022 778] 440)

Leicestershire

Stapleford Park, nr Melton Mowbray – *Stapleford Lion and Game Reserve*.
Established as a breeding place for African lions, this fifty-acre reserve also offer crocodiles, bears, leopards, monkeys, wapiti. (Tel. Wymondham [057 284] 657)

Merseyside

Prescot – *Knowsley Safari Park*.
For lions, cheetahs, elephants, giraffes, antelope, white rhinos and a good dolphinarium. (Tel. 051-426 2176/2259)

Norfolk

Great Witchingham, nr Norwich – *Norfolk Wildlife Park and Pheasant Trust*.
Claims to have the largest collection in Britain of British and European mammals and birds; European bison, wolves, reindeer, wild boar, otters, waterfowl and birds of prey. (Tel. Great Witchingham [060 544] 274)

Kilverstone, nr Thetford – *Kilverstone 'New World' Wildlife Park*.
A forty-five-acre wildlife park with birds and mammals mainly from North and South America: bison, deer, skunks, guanaco, coatimundi, collared peccary, chipmunks, prairie dogs, monkeys, quaker parakeets, parrots and waterfowl. (Tel. Thetford [0842] 5369)

Oxfordshire

Burford – *Cotswold Wildlife Park*.
Small, charming wildlife park with white rhinos, zebras, gazelle, red pandas, leopards, otters, reptiliary and tropical house. (Tel. Burford [099 382] 3006)

Somerset

nr Chard – *West Country Wildlife Park*.
Pretty, idyllic 1000-acre estate in one of England's most beautiful

valleys. Many rare waterfowl, flamingoes, storks and other exotic birds along a chain of nine lakes and waterfalls. Deer, wapitis, camels and elephants in paddocks, and smaller enclosures in the two-acre walled garden contain leopards, pumas, lynx, monkeys and racoons. (Tel. Winsham [046 030] 396)

Staffordshire

nr Tamworth – *Drayton Manor Park and Zoo.*
About fifteen acres set in 160 acres of wooded parkland, with lions, leopards, pumas, bears, sea lions, llamas, wallabies, penguins and pelicans. (Tel. Tamworth [0827] 68481/2)

Suffolk

Grove Farm, Kessingland, nr Lowestoft – *Suffolk Wildlife and Country Park.*
Wooded parkland with river and lake. Exhibits include lions, tigers, puma, civet cats, timber wolves, dingoes, llamas, racoons, coati, porcupines, crocodiles, boa-constrictors, parrots, toucans and vultures. (Tel. Kessingland [050 274] 291)

Wiltshire

Longleat, Warminster – *Lions of Longleat.*
The first safari park! Three hundred acres of woods and rolling grassland ('Capability' Brown at his best) contain hundreds of free-roaming wild animals, among which are those incredible lions, zebras, giraffes, hippopotami, Ankole cattle, chimpanzees and sea lions. You feed the sea lions from a big pleasure boat. (Tel. Maiden Bradley [098 53] 328)

HOW *THEY* LIVED (museums of the famous)

There's a certain wicked thrill about snooping round the houses of the famous, especially when the interiors have been cleverly left as they were; you half expect Sir Walter Scott or Charles Darwin or Ellen Terry to potter through the doorway at any moment. Try these.

Buckinghamshire

High Wycombe – *Hughenden Manor*.
Bought by Benjamin Disraeli in 1849, when he felt that it would befit a potential leader of the Conservatives to have an estate. He used to pick primroses daily to send to Queen Victoria (cunning fox). Paintings of friends and family, letters, furniture and mementos of his political life. (Tel. High Wycombe [0494] 28051)

Cambridgeshire

Huntingdon – *Cromwell Museum*.
Both Oliver Cromwell and Samuel Pepys were pupils in this medieval grammar school. Portraits and documents of the Cromwell family as well as other seventeenth-century household effects. (Tel. Huntingdon [0480] 52181)

Cumbria

Grasmere – *Dove Cottage and the Wordsworth Museum*.
In the midst of the Lake District, which William Wordsworth loved and wrote about, is Dove Cottage, which he shared with his sister Dorothy. At the cottage and museum are their beloved possessions and manuscripts, and at the museum an exhibition illustrating rural life during Wordsworth's lifetime. His grave is in the churchyard.

Sawrey – *Hill Top*.
You might say that Peter Rabbit was born here. This is the house in which Beatrix Potter lived and worked and grew her lettuces.

Dorset

Bovington Camp, Wareham – *Cloud's Hill*.
The last home of T. E. Lawrence, 'Lawrence of Arabia' and author of

The Seven Pillars of Wisdom. Some of his dreary personal belongings and mementos of his extraordinary life.

Hampshire

Chawton – *Jane Austen's House.*
Pretty village house, such as some of her characters might have lived in. Collection of needlework, books, music and watercolours that belonged to her and her family – reminders of the accomplishments of a woman in Jane Austen's time. (Tel. Alton [0420] 83262)

Kent

Downe, nr Orpington – *Downe House.*
Charles Darwin, the great naturalist, lived here for over forty years and it was here that he wrote *The Origin of Species.* Besides his study and drawing room there is an exhibition on the history of evolution. Really worth a visit. (Tel. Farnborough [0689] 59119)
Tenterden – *Ellen Terry Memorial, Smallhythe Place.*
Late fifteenth-century half-timbered house where Ellen Terry lived from the height of her fame until her death. Personal possessions, pictures, playbills, props, memorabilia and theatrical costumes. Also the theatrical collections of other famous actors: Sir Henry Irving, Mrs Siddons, David Garrick and Edmund Kean. (Tel. Tenterden [058 06] 2943)

Westerham – *Chartwell.*
Sir Winston Churchill's home from 1922 until his death, when the house was taken over by the National Trust. Much remains as it was when he lived there: cigar box, busts of Napoleon and Nelson, his desk cluttered with family photographs (when I see desks like this I can't help wondering where the work got done). You can also see his library and rose garden, his paintings and the brick wall he built himself – possibly the most publicized brick wall in Britain.

North Yorkshire

Haworth – *Brontë Parsonage Museum.*
Bleak, isolated house on the Yorkshire Moors where the Brontë sisters, Emily, Anne and Charlotte, lived with their unfortunate, unstable, drunken brother, Bramwell. Here they wrote the novels and the poems that stemmed from their powerful imagination. The Parsonage still contains many personal belongings, including clothes and manuscripts. (Tel. Haworth [0535] 42323)

Oxfordshire

Lechlade – *Kelmscott Manor.*
Hardly a *typical* artist/craftsman's home, this is where William Morris lived in the summer. Many of his arty-crafty friends also stayed in the beautiful Cotswold manor and contributed to the furnishings of the

house, so making it one of the most complete (I won't say perfect) interiors of the Arts and Crafts movement. You can see work by Rossetti, Burne-Jones, William de Morgan, Philip Webb and Walter Crane. (Tel. Lechlade [036 75] 486)

Roxburgh

Melrose – *Abbotsford House*.
  Sir Walter Scott built this mansion on the River Tweed and then sat down and wrote those pop historicals in order to pay for it. The house contains many Scott relics, including his weapon collection. Many of the trees around the house were planted by him. (All authors have little therapeutic tasks for when they get stuck over the plot.)

Strathclyde

Alloway – *Burns Cottage and Museum*.
  Built, stone by stone, by Robert Burns's father, it was the humble birthplace of Scotland's most popular poet. You can see personal relics, manuscripts of poems and songs, including *Auld Lang Syne*.

One poem was originally engraved by Burns on the window-pane of an inn at Dumfries. (Tel. Alloway [0292] 41321).
  Not far away at Kirkoswald is *Souter Johnnie's Cottage*, the home of John Davidson, the village cobbler in 'Tam O'Shanter'.

Blantyre, Glasgow – *David Living-Stone Memorial*
  The whole building is now a museum devoted to the great explorer, but the single tenement room in which the Livingstone family lived has been re-created. Much material on his exploration and missionary work, including his African notebooks, packed with sketches and observations.

Suffolk

Sudbury – *Gainsborough's House*.
  Landscapes, portraits, sketches, notes and letters. If you follow the River Stour down towards the sea, you come to *Dedham Vale*, *East Bergholt* and *Flatford Mill* – the well-documented, picturesque haunts of another great English painter, John Constable. (Tel. Sudbury [078 73] 2958)

TRIPS THROUGH TIME
(unusual museums)

There's a museum in almost any town, large or small, and often an interesting art gallery as well. Here are some of the *special* and most imaginative ones, chosen because they have unique themes, collections or particularly exciting displays.

Avon

Bristol – *S S Great Britain*.
One of the great revolutionary steamships designed by the Victorian engineer Isambard Kingdom Brunel, now being restored to her original grandeur. You can walk round the ship (lots of imagination still needed) and also visit an exhibition (with a ship's biscuit on display). The *Clifton Suspension Bridge*, another of Brunel's engineering feats, is still used to cross the River Avon.

Bedfordshire

Biggleswade – *Shuttleworth Collection*, Old Warden Aerodrome.
Unique collection of historic prejet aeroplanes from Sopwith Camels to Spitfires, maintained in flying condition. On certain Sundays there are flying displays. Also beautiful old horse-drawn carriages, fire engines, motorcycles and cars. (Tel. Biggleswade [0767] 27288)

Berkshire

Cookham – *Stanley Spencer Gallery*.
A small gallery devoted to the work of this fascinating, lewd twentieth-century artist, in the village where he lived and painted. In the church hangs his painting of the Last Supper. (Tel. Bourne End [062 85] 23533)

Cambridgeshire

Cambridge. The ancient university town contains many outstanding museums:
Cambridge and County Folk Museum.
Formerly an inn, full of exhibits which show life and work around Cambridgeshire from the seventeenth century to modern times. (Tel. Cambridge [0223] 55159)
Fitzwilliam Museum.
Top-quality collections of paintings, drawings, china and pottery, tapestries, suits of armour and classical antiquities. (Tel. Cambridge [0223] 50023)
Kettle's Yard.
Private collection of drawings, paintings and sculpture, mainly of British twentieth-century artists, including Ben Nicholson, David Jones, Christopher Wood and Paul Nash. Also exhibitions of modern pottery. (Tel. Cambridge [0223] 52124)
Scott Polar Research Institute Museum.
All aspects of exploration in the Arctic and Antarctic, including relics from Scott's ill-fated expedi-

tion to the South Pole. (Tel. Cambridge [0223] 66499)

University Museum of Archaeology and Ethnology.

Here you're in Tribal Eye territory: masks, tools, carvings and pottery from the primitive peoples of Africa, the Americas, Asia, Australia and Oceania, plus archaeological objects from all periods. (Tel. Cambridge [0223] 59714).

Whipple Museum of the History of Science.

Early scientific instruments, apparatus and books from the sixteenth to the twentieth centuries. Fascinating. (Tel. Cambridge [0223] 54481)

Cheshire

Port Sunlight – *Lady Lever Art Gallery.* Built in the 1890s in the model village which housed the industrious, non-union workers of the Lever Brothers' factory. The adjoining gallery shows a collection of eighteenth- and nineteenth-century English paintings, particularly the sentimental work of the Pre-Raphaelites and of Lord Leighton. (Tel. 051-645 3623).

Cumbria

Carlisle – *Carlisle Museum.*

The keep, probably built in the reign of Henry III, contains the Regimental Museum of the Border Regiment. (Tel. Carlisle [0228] 21275)

Derbyshire

Castle Donnington – *Donnington Collection.*

Racing cars from the earliest models to present day: more for the boys. (Tel. Derby [0332] 810048)

Crich, nr Matlock – *Tramway Museum.*

Collection of horse, steam and electric tram-cars for small boys of any age.

Durham

Barnard Castle – *Bowes Museum.*

One of the most surprising museums in England: huge Victorian mansion in the style of a French château, with a fine collection of paintings and decorative arts of a quality rarely seen outside major city museums. (Tel. Barnard Castle [083 33] 2139).

Stanley – *Beamish North of England Open Air Museum.*

A museum showing the everyday life of people who lived and worked in the North East late last century. At this time the region was in the forefront of British industrial development, and many of its old buildings are being brought together and rebuilt here – and brought to life. Among other things, you can see bread being baked in a coal-fired oven; proggy mat-making; have a swing on the old shuggy boats; visit an exhibition of old everyday things in stately Beamish Hall. (Tel. [0207] 33580 and 33586)

Fife

Anstruther – *Museum of Fishing*.
Displays and reconstructions illustrating the East Coast fisheries and their brave fishermen through the ages.

Gloucestershire

Guiting Power, nr Cheltenham – *Cotswold Farm Park*.
Rare breeds of farm animals that have been neglected because they do not meet modern demands of productivity. This is a *living* museum.

Gwynedd

Portmeirion Village.
Amazingly odd and popular seaside village designed by the controversial architect Clough Williams-Ellis. It looks like an Italian fishing village film set – with a Neapolitan ice-cream colour scheme. (Tel. Penrhyndeudraeth [076 674] 228 or 339)

Hampshire

Buster Hill – *Museum of Ancient Farming*.
Prehistoric farming methods, breeds of animals and species of crops are preserved for experiment in the setting of a reconstructed Iron Age farmstead.
Portsmouth – *Royal Naval Museum and HMS Victory*.

Nelson's flagship and the ship on which he died, HMS *Victory*, is moored in the docks opposite the Naval Museum, which houses prints, paintings, figureheads, ship models and belongings of eighteenth-century sailors. Special collection of Nelsonia. (Tel. Portsmouth [0705] 22351).

Hereford and Worcester

Stoke Heath, nr Bromsgrove – *Avoncroft Museum*.
Imaginative collection of cleverly reconstructed buildings of all periods from the Bronze Age to the Middle Ages. Most ingenious.

London and Surrounding Area

Bethnal Green – *Museum of Childhood*.
Dolls' houses, toys and costumes. There is often a good special exhibition in this small, sunny museum which is a specialist section of the Victoria and Albert Museum. (Tel. 01-980 3204)
Brentford – *National Piano Museum*.
All types of keyboard instruments and mechanical instruments such as self-playing violins, nickelodeons, barrel organs and pianolas. (Tel. 01-560 8108)
Buckingham Palace – *Queen's Gallery*.
The Queen owns one of the largest art collections in the world and you don't have to see it only on television. This gallery was opened in the 1960s to show selections from

her collections to the public – always beautifully displayed. (No telephone number listed.)

Buckingham Palace – *Royal Mews.*

(You go in on the left-hand side.) The famous royal coaches, including the Gold State Coach, used at every coronation since it was built in 1772, driving carriages, the horse-drawn sleighs (never see them in those) and early motor cars. The famous Windsor Grey and Cleveland Bay Horses can be seen too. (Tel. 01-930 4832)

Chelsea – *National Army Museum.*

A new museum with particularly good displays illustrating the history of the British Army in chronological sequence up until 1914. Recordings of soldiers' songs of various periods. (Tel. 01-730 0717)

Chiswick – *Chiswick House.*

Beautiful small house built by the Earl of Burlington to his own Palladian design in the early eighteenth century, and originally planned as a summer banqueting house.

The City – *Guildhall.*

Two collections: the *Clockmakers' Company Museum*, clocks and watches; and *Guildhall Art Gallery*, paintings of London's past. (Tel. 01-606 3030)

The City – *Museum of London.*

Brand new, imaginative, modern museum in the windy, soulless Barbican. Combines collections of the old Guildhall Museum and the former London Museum at Kensington Palace. All aspects of London life from earliest times. (Tel. 01-600 3699)

Forest Hill – *Horniman Museum.*

Man and his environment is the theme, with contributions from all over the world, including a famous collection of musical instruments. Egyptian medicines, Aztec pottery, primitive African weapons and late Chinese exhibits. (Tel. 01-699 1872)

Greenwich – *National Maritime Museum.*

This is where Greenwich Mean Time was calculated. Lovely Queen's House designed by Inigo Jones for Anne of Denmark, James I's queen. One of the finest maritime collections in the world, containing ships and boats from all periods, paintings, drawings, models, charts, maps and instruments. A short distance away, moored on the banks of the Thames, is the *Cutty Sark*, the fastest tea clipper of them all. It is possible to go aboard. (Tel. 01-858 4422).

Ham – *Ham House.*

Originally built in the early seventeenth century and enlarged and flamboyantly redecorated by the Duke of Lauderdale in the 1670s. Many original furnishings, carefully restored by the Victoria and Albert Museum. (No telephone number listed.)

Hendon – *Royal Air Force Museum.*

If you watched 'Wings' on television, you'll enjoy this collection which tells the story of the RAF and its forerunner, the Royal Flying Corps. Flying equipment, uniforms, medals, paintings and drawings – and about forty aeroplanes. (Tel. 01-205 2266)

Kew – *Royal Botanical Gardens.*
Plants and trees gathered by botanists from all over the world. The cheapest day out in London – only 1p. Special attractions include the Palm House, Fern House, Orangery, the eighteenth-century Chinese Pagoda and the seventeenth-century Dutch House. (Other botanic gardens are at Cambridge, Oxford and Edinburgh.) (Tel. 01-940 1171)

Shoreditch – *Geffrye Museum.*
Fine eighteenth-century building, originally used as almshouses. Room settings from the Elizabethan period to 1939 – a good instant guide to changing interior decoration. (Tel. 01-739 8368)

Syon Park, Brentford – *London Transport Collection.*
Buses, trolley buses, tram cars and horse-drawn vehicles. (Tel. 01-560 0881)

Tower Pier – *H M S Belfast.*
Cruiser from the Second World War moored midstream on the Thames. All the guts of a warship can be seen and you can see a free film show, 'Operation Overlord'. (Tel. 01-407 6434)

Lothian

Edinburgh – *Palace of Holyrood House.*
Queen's official Scottish residence, a very regal building in beautiful grounds, first started by James I V in 1501, when Scotland stood on its own. Magnificent Throne Room and impressive State Apartments.

Museum of Childhood.
In an atmospheric old town house there are several floors packed with toys, games, models, pictures and books which belonged to children throughout the ages. (Tel. 031-556 5447)

National Museum of Antiquities of Scotland.
Scottish history from the Stone Age to present day; Anglo-Saxon treasures, country crafts, fearsome Highland weapons and yet more relics of Mary Queen of Scots. (Tel. 031-556 8921)

Canongate Tolbooth.
Charming, intimate museum in an old courthouse. Riveting collection of Highland dress and tartans. (Tel. 031-556 5813)

Braidwood and Rushbrook Museum.
Esoteric collection which covers the history of firefighting all over the world, including old fire-engines, photographs and equipment.

Norfolk

Diss – *Bressingham Stream Museum.*
Six acres of informal gardens with, near by, a large steam museum: forty engines, both rail and road, as well as fairground galloping horses and steam organ merry-go-rounds. Mostly summer openings. (Tel. Diss [0379] 88386)

Northamptonshire

Stoke Bruerne – *Waterways Museum.*
Originally the village mill beside the

Grand Union Canal, now houses a merry collection of the art of barge people – everyday objects painted brightly with flowers and castles. (Tel. Northampton [0604] 862229)

Oxfordshire

Oxford – *Pitt Rivers Museum and the University Museum.*
In superb Victorian building, with carved interior columns, window frames and doorways. The Pitt Rivers ethnographical collection illustrates the Ascent of Man, with extraordinary objects from all parts of the world, including the collection made by Captain Cook on his second voyage of discovery. (Tel. Oxford [0865] 5497)

Christ Church Art Gallery.
Magnificent collection of drawings belonging to one of Oxford's richest colleges. Most famous drawings are by Michelangelo, Raphael and Leonardo da Vinci. (Tel. Oxford [0865] 42102)

Merton College Library.
Probably the oldest surviving library in Britain, founded in the 1370s. Some of the books are a reminder of the time when Spinoza only had ten books in his whole library and books were immensely rare and expensive. (Tel. Oxford [0865] 49651)

Witney – *High Cogges.*
Museum of agricultural history; sturdy instruments and well-documented information realistically displayed in an old farm.

Salop

Ironbridge, Coalbrookdale and Blist's Hill.
This area, now rural, was one of the original dark, satanic, smoky centres of the eighteenth-century Industrial Revolution and so contains some outstanding examples of architecture and machinery. *The Ironbridge*, spanning the River Severn, was the first bridge (1779) to be built of iron. A mile away *The Museum of Ironfounding* at Coalbrookdale commemorates the work of the bridge-builder Abraham Darby and his father, also called Abraham, who revolutionized iron-smelting methods. *Blist's Hill Open Air Museum* is in the same area and specializes in the industrial archaeology of the region. (Tel. Telford [0952] 585820)

Somerset

Bath – *American Museum in Britain, Claverton Manor.*
In a Regency House in the hills above Bath, this fascinating and sumptuous museum is the only place of its kind outside America. Realistic room-settings range from early Colonial to lush nineteenth-century New Orleans. It also covers American maritime history, Red Indian and American folk art, including a large and beautiful collection of patchwork quilts (you get lots of ideas). Delicious American cookies are handed out freely and all the cakes are home-baked (try

George Washington's fruitcake). (Tel. Bath [0225] 28411)

Museum of Costume.

Largest and most detailed costume museum in the world, covering clothing from the seventeenth century to the present day. Interesting and alluring underwear, with a fine range of wicked-looking corsets. (Tel. Bath [0225] 28411)

Street – *Street Shoe Museum.*

Shoes from Roman times to stiletto. (Tel. Street [045 84] 3131)

Wookey Hole, nr Wells.

Dramatic limestone caves, an old paper mill that is being restored and *Lady Bangor's Famous Fairground Collection*, great fun with roundabouts, spinners, bioscope shows, scenic railways and carousels. (Tel. Wells [0749] 72243 or 73258)

South Glamorgan

St Fagan's, Cardiff – *Welsh Folk Museum.*

Very Welsh museum (more Welsh than English spoken), consisting of St Fagan's Castle and an Elizabethan house built within the ruins of the medieval castle. This is filled with furniture, mainly from the seventeenth century. Also a new museum block which illustrates the history of Welsh agriculture, cooking, costume, folklore, sports, games and education. In the grounds is a collection of re-erected buildings: farmhouse, cottage, mill, smithy, chapel and toll house – all furnished correctly. Full marks for

a wonderfully imaginative project. (Tel. Cardiff [0222] 561357)

Staffordshire

Barlaston, Stoke-on-Trent – *Wedgwood Museum.*

For pottery and porcelain freaks – here are the best examples of Wedgwood going back to 1769, as well as fascinating old pattern books and documents. Free pottery demonstrations show how pots are thrown on the wheel – the same method used by Josiah Wedgwood to make his 'First Day' vases on the day that the Etruria factory opened. (Sorry. No children under ten allowed in.) (Tel. Barlaston [078 139] 2141)

Hanley – *Stoke-on-Trent City Museum and Art Gallery.*

Fine collection of ceramics, many of the objects made in the surrounding Potteries and some of them very weird indeed (and wonderful). (Tel. Stoke-on-Trent [0782] 22714)

Longton, Stoke-on-Trent – *Gladstone Pottery.*

Recently-restored Victorian pottery factory, now turned into a working museum.

Sussex

Rottingdean – *Toy Museum.*

At the Grange, has an absorbing collection of more than 20,000 toys and playthings. Child-boggling. (Tel. Brighton [0273] 31004)

Warwickshire

Stratford-on-Avon – *Royal Shake-speare Memorial Gallery*.
Within the Festival Theatre, a not-to-be-missed collection of paintings from the eighteenth century illustrating performances of W. S. plays with famous Shakespearean actors and actresses. When it's not crowded (in the high tourist season) the town is beautiful. You visit Anne Hathaway's Cottage, Hall Croft, Mary Arden's House and the Bard's birthplace. (Tel. Stratford-on-Avon [0789] 3693)

West Midlands

Birmingham – *Museum of Science and Industry*.
Working exhibits and many examples of engineering, for which the city is famous. Early machine tools, steam engines (they run on some days), electrical generators, etc. Also a good transport section, and charming collections of musical boxes, mechanical organs and gramophones. (Tel. 021-236 1022)

West Sussex

Fishbourne, nr Chichester.
Fascinating remains of a great Roman palace thought to have been built by Cogidubnus, one of the few chic Romans not to appear in *I, Claudius*. An excellent museum is attached, as good as anything I've seen on the Continent.

Yorkshire

York – *Castle Museum*.
A must!!! The debtors' and women's prisons within the bailey of the old castle have been converted to create a 'folk' museum, with two reconstructed streets complete with nineteenth-century shops, pub, post office and carriage yard. Also Yorkshire military costumes, arms and armour. (Tel. York [0904] 53611)
National Railway Museum.
New, super, rail museum has taken over those famous old ones – the British Transport Museum at Clapham, London and the York Railway Museum. Exhibits on everything associated with the amazing history of the railways, dating from the time when everyone could afford to travel on them. (Tel. York [0904] 21261)

SOME OF THE BEST BATTLEFIELDS

Not for small children, who are often disappointed that there aren't any bloody, left-over, rusting lances in sight. But it's often awesome to look at a spot which has been the scene of such violence and has changed the course of history in this land.

The following battlefields are those that are not buried under housing estates, but are still visible and visitable.

Central Scotland

Bannockburn.

The National Trust for Scotland has an exhibition at the monument to the *Battle of Bannockburn* where Edward II with 20,000 men lost to Robert the Bruce, who had about 10,000 troops, so it was two to one fighting in 1314. Also a model of the battlefield and an audio-visual account of the fighting. ☛ Just off the Glasgow Road (A80).

East Sussex

Hastings – *Battle of Hastings*.

In 1066, William of Normandy won and King Harold got the arrow in the eye. The English were lined up where the Abbey now stands, and the Normans, Bretons and Franco-Flemish were facing them from below. ☛ Battle is six miles north-west of Hastings.

Gloucestershire

Tewkesbury.

Where the heaviest fighting took place at the *Battle of Tewkesbury* in 1471. A Wars of the Roses engagement which was won by Edward IV, batting for York, and was the final defeat of Henry VI, whose heart was never really in the king business. The teenage Edward, Prince of Wales, was killed here, with other relatives. The museum in Tewkesbury has an interesting model of the battlefield. ☛ The battlefield itself is west of the A38 on the Gloucester road, half a mile south of Tewkesbury Abbey.

Highland

Fort Augustus – *Glenshiel*.

Where the first Jacobite rebellion ended when General Wightman with just over 1000 men, defeated 1800 Jacobites in a narrow pass in 1719. ☛ Twenty miles west of Fort Augustus, the A87 runs through Glenshiel.

Leicestershire

Market Bosworth.

Site of the *Battle of Bosworth Field*, another in the Wars of the Roses. Here, on 22 August 1485, Yorkist Richard III lost his horse, his life and the battle to Lancastrian/Tudor Henry VII. ☛ Visit the spectacular exhibition centre at Ambion Hill Farm which is the focus of a network of marked paths around the battlefield.

Louth

Drogheda – *Battle of the Boyne*.
  In 1690 William of Orange met and defeated the Catholic forces of James Stuart, ex-King of England (hence the 'Orangemen'). ☛ Go four miles west of Drogheda on the north bank of the River Boyne.

Perthshire

Dunblane – *Sheriffmuir*.
  Here on 13 November 1715 the Jacobite forces led by the Earl of Mar were defeated by the Hanoverian army under Argyll. ☛ The battlefield lies between the two minor roads from Dunblane and Bridge of Allan to Blackford.

Warwickshire

Kineton – *Battle of Edgehill*.
  Cavalier Epic in 1642. The Royalists were drawn up with their backs to the hill. The three-hour battle was indecisive. ☛ Edgehill is a long ridge seven miles north-west of Banbury. From the escarpment near Radway the whole battlefield can be seen below, although it cannot be visited for the Alice-in-Wonderland reason that it belongs to the Ministry of Defence.

Yorkshire

Long Marston.
  The *Battle of Marston Moor* in 1644 was a major battle of the Civil War. Parliament won and about 3000 Cavaliers were killed. ☛ The site and memorial stone lie about one mile west of Long Marston.
Tadcaster.
  During the Wars of the Roses the *Battle of Towton* was fought between Yorkist and Lancastrian armies in 1461. The battle took place about half a mile south of Towton on nearby 'Bloody Meadow', where 20,000 to 30,000 men were killed (mostly Lancastrians). ☛ Two and a half miles south of Tadcaster.

ROMANTIC (STEAM) RAIL-WAYS

Steam railways seem to be a growing nostalgic national passion. There is certainly something fascinating about the puff-puffs, the chuffing, the diddley-dum, the whooshing whistle, the steam and the glowing coals, and the gallant little red engine is part of our nursery bedtime lore. Anyway, they make a good outing for children and you can generally ride on them. The opening times of railways which are not open all the year round are given below, since you can't always telephone to check. Fuller details can be obtained from the annual *Guide to Steam Trains in the British Isles*, issued free by the Association of Railway Preservation Societies, Sheringham Station, Norfolk. Write, enclosing stamped, addressed envelope, or telephone 0263 822045.

Antrim

Whitehead – *Railway Preservation Society of Ireland.*
The only place in Ireland where steam still hauls trains on mainline journeys. The society runs tours all over the country. Also train rides at Whitehead on Sunday afternoons in July and August.

Bedfordshire

Leighton Buzzard – Leighton Buzzard Narrow Gauge Railway.
Three-mile trip, Page's Park to Stonehenge (not *that* Stonehenge).

Open Sundays in summer and Bank Holidays.

Clwyd

Sylfaen – *Welshpool and Llanfair Light Railway.*
Five miles from Sylfaen to Llanfair Caereinion.

Cumbria

Ravenglass – *Ravenglass and Eskdale Railway.*
Daily service from Ravenglass to Dalegarth, seven miles away, from March to October. Reduced service in winter.

Derbyshire

Glossop – *Dinting Railway Centre.*
Ten acres and large exhibition hall with mainline steam engines and smaller shunting engines. Engines are in steam on Sundays and Bank Holidays, March to October.

Devon

Buckfastleigh – *Dart Valley Railway.*
Round trip from Staverton Bridge. Large collection of rolling stock.
Paignton – *Torbay Steam Railway.*
Runs between Paignton and Kingswear.

Dyfed

Aberystwyth – *Vale of Rheidol Railway.*
From Aberystwyth to Devil's

Bridge. The *last* British Rail steam service. Runs daily from Easter to October.

Fife

St Andrews – *Lochty Private Railway.*
Three steam locos run passengers two miles to Knightsward on Sunday afternoons, mid-June to September.

Gwynedd

Fairbourne – *Fairbourne Railway.*
For two miles from Fairbourne to Barmouth Ferry. Seaside railway runs over sand dunes. Daily from May to September.

Llanberis – *Snowdon Mountain Railway.*
Only rack railway in Britain, four and three quarter miles from Llanberis to summit. Open April to October.

Llanuwchllyn – *Bala Lake Railway.*
Steam service along the lakeside.

Portmadoc – *Ffestiniog Light Railway.*
Nine and a half miles of scenic railway from Portmadoc. Daily March to November, weekends in winter.

Tywyn – *Talyllyn Railway.*
Seven miles of railway, and Narrow Gauge Museum, open daily April to September.

Highland

Aviemore – *Strathspey Railway.*
Runs between Aviemore and Boat of Garten, along the River Spey.

Display of engines and rolling stock at the Boat of Garten station.

Isle of Man

Ballasalla – *Isle of Man Railway.*
Seven miles from Douglas to Port Erin, with five locomotives dating from 1873 to 1910. Large railway museum at Port Erin.

Kent

Tenterden – *Kent and East Sussex Railway.*
The railway runs from Tenterden to Newmill Bridge, three miles away. Collection of locomotives at both termini.

Romney – *Romney, Hythe and Dymchurch Railway.*
Runs thirteen miles from Romney to Dungeness daily from Easter to the end of September, then Sundays to the end of November.

Sittingbourne – *Sittingbourne and Kemsley Light Railway.*
Two-mile round trip, open weekends and Bank Holidays, April to October, and Tuesdays, Wednesdays and Thursdays in August.

Lancashire

Carnforth – *Steamtown Railway Museum.*
Twenty-seven steam locos (most working) from UK, France and Germany, seen in old steam loco sheds. Engines are in steam on Sundays, March to October, and

excursions run to York, Grange-over-Sands and Ravenglass.

Lincolnshire

Grimsby – *Lincolnshire Coast Light Railway*.
New railway service for holiday-makers, steam on weekends only. Runs daily late May to October.

Norfolk

Sheringham – *North Norfolk Railway*.
Runs along the coast for two and three quarter miles to Weybourne. Seven steam engines.

North Yorkshire

Pickering.
Steam service between Pickering station and Gorsmont Junction, eighteen miles.

Salop

Bridgnorth – *Severn Valley Railway*
Twelve miles of railway from Bridgnorth to Bewdley, with thirty steam locos. Open every weekend and Bank Holidays, March to October and daily in full season.

Staffordshire

Brownhills – *Chasewater Light Railway*.
Chasewater Pleasure Park. Two-mile trip around the lake in the park on summer weekends.

Sussex

Uckfield – the famous *Bluebell Railway*.
Five miles of railway running to Horsted Keynes.

West Yorkshire

Haworth – *Worth Valley Railway*.
Five-mile run from Keighley to Oxenhope, weekends all year and daily in July and August.

BACK TO NATURE

Because the British countryside is so varied, you can find a surprising selection of scenery. On comparatively short walks you can stomp through ferny woodland, salty marshes, chalky uplands, weird moonlike landscapes (in Dorset). You can climb invigorating crags, hills, cliffs and mini-mountains. You can wander along beaches or tumbling rivers, sleepy canals and romantic lakes. What is more you can see – still – an amazing variety of wild flowers (*don't* pick), magnificent trees, birds and woodland animals.

Country parks: Country parks are often based on a grand house or its remains. There are usually picnic places and the family might spend a whole day in the grounds and viewing livestock, house and gardens.

National parks: The National Parks of Britain often organize 'guided walks' or 'walks and talks' so you can learn as you go from experts about the flora and fauna, or about the local rocks. The best ones are in the Lake District, in the Peak District of Derbyshire and on Exmoor.

Nature trails: Teach nature on the job, not in the classroom with somebody yelling at you, and with flowers instead of blackboards. Nature trails are carefully planned, and it's well worth going a little out of your way to find one. Even if you don't get a guided tour trees and plants are generally labelled (unobtrusively). There are also about fourteen *farm trails* in England and Wales. On a farm you are guided round the farm land and buildings, learn about crops and livestock or even how to milk a cow (poor cow). The farm staff explain to visitors how a modern farm works. Admission is cheap – about 10p, with a small extra charge for a written guide.

For details of country parks, national parks, nature trails and farm trails, write to the Countryside Commission, John Dower House, Crescent Place, Cheltenham, Gloucestershire G150 3RA.

The following nature walks are particularly popular:

Avon

Wells – *Ebbor Gorge Nature Trails.*
Two walks of half to one and a half miles, through woodland and valley meadows – opportunity to see buzzards and sparrowhawks.

Berkshire

Newbury – *Snelsmore Common*.
   Nature trail with plants of woodland, marsh and chalk.

Essex

Bishops Stortford – *Hatfield Forest*.
   Nature trail laid through a medieval wood. Fallow deer, and sometimes nightingales can be seen.

Fermanagh

Belleek – *Castlecaldwell Forest*.
   Guided tours round mixed woodland, plus an ecological display.

Gwynedd

Llanidloer – *Llyn Clywedog*.
   Scenic nature trail by reservoir and a wildlife sanctuary.

Hereford and Worcester

Brockhampton Woodland Walk.
   Two miles east of Bromyard. Two walks, each of about a mile, through woodland and by waterside.

Leicestershire

Lutterworth – *Stanford Hall*.
   Two-mile nature trail through

parkland, wood and riverbank, designed specifically for young people.

Lincolnshire

Skegness – *Gibraltar Point*.
   Nature trail through a reserve of salt marsh and sand dunes. Seals may often be seen.

Norfolk

Hoveton – *Great Broad Nature Trail*.
   Marked trail through ferny woodland and by open water. Reached by boat from Wroxham or Horning.

Strathclyde

Dumbarton – *Loch Lomond*.
   Romantic nature trail round Inchcailloch by boat or on foot. Embark at Balmaha boatyard.

Tyrone

Cookstown – *Drum Manor Forest*.
   Nature trails by the lake and woodlands with a heronry and red squirrels.

GUIDE TO THE BEST GUIDES AND INFORMATION CENTRES

The best holiday investments you can make this year are a guide to Britain (with, perhaps, one or two pamphlets on areas of special interest), membership of the National Trust, and one or two specialist books, although you should be able to borrow most of them from your local library.

The *National Trust* is a charity which owns and opens to the public more than 200 buildings of architectural or historic importance, many of them with their contents – pictures, furniture, porcelain. It also owns a lot of beautiful open countryside – including woods, moorland, lakes, hills, 2000 farms and more than 360 miles of unspoilt coastline. The Trust has many fine gardens and some of the most splendid examples of English landscape design; nature reserves, including islands and fens; prehistoric and Roman antiquities; lengths of canal, wind- and water-mills, bridges and other industrial monuments; even whole villages. These are all listed in the booklet *Properties of the National Trust* which is sent *free* to members. The Trust maintains these places for your enjoyment and *members are admitted free to all those properties the public pays to visit*. (Membership costs £7 (£3 if you're under twenty-three) plus an additional £3.50 for each family member at the same address.) Apply to: National Trust Membership Department, PO Box 30, Beckenham, Kent BR3 4TL (tel. 01-650 7263).

The best guides to homes and gardens

AA Guide to Stately Homes, Castles and Gardens. Contains over 2000 places to visit. Around £2.

Historic Houses, Castles and Gardens in Great Britain and Ireland (ABC Historic Publications). Very good value with lots of passport-size photographs (so you can pick which one you'd like to live in and turn up your nose at others). Gives details of opening times and how to get there by coach, rail, bus and road. Costs less than £1.

Treasures of Britain and Treasures of Ireland (Drive Publications). This is much more expensive, but a wonderfully illustrated guide with descriptions and good road maps.

Museums and Art Galleries in Great Britain and Ireland (ABC Historic Publications) is an invaluable companion if this is the area that interests you.

Guides to gardens

If you're keen to visit gardens, check beforehand which are open when. Do so with:

Gardens of England and Wales Open to the Public (published by the National Gardens Scheme, 57 Lower Belgrave Street, London SW1W OLR). The money raised from garden openings through this scheme goes mainly to elderly and retired district nurses. The guide concentrates on the many charming gardens open for one or two days a year, as well as the Royal Gardens and the rest of the big league. I have it as a bedside book.

Scotland's Gardens (from Scotland's Garden Scheme, 26 Castle Terrace, Edinburgh EH1 2EL).

Ulster Gardens Scheme (from the Regional Information Officer, The National Trust, Rowallane, Saintfield, Co. Down).

Countryside guides

National Parks: Information on each park, with details of the geology, plant and wildlife and facilities for outdoor activities (fishing, climbing, caving, planned walks, pony-trekking, etc.) is available from the Countryside Commission, John Dower House, Crescent Place, Cheltenham, Gloucestershire GLO 3RA.

Forestry Commission: Most of the Commission's natural and planted woods are open to the public and have marked nature trails, picnic sites, educational displays and, in some cases, camp sites. General information from the Forestry Commission. Priestly Road, Basingstoke, Hampshire. The following forests have their own information centres: Thetford Forest, Suffolk; Forest of Dean, Gloucestershire; Grizedale Forest, Cumbria; Kielder Forest, Northumberland; Mortimer Forest, Salop; New Forest, Hampshire; Delamere Forest, Cheshire; Cannock Forest, Staffordshire; Dalby Forest, North Yorkshire.

There's a wonderful selection of walks, coupled with maps and descriptions of what to look for in *No Through Road,* which is pricey, but a good investment for free leisure activities (Drive Publications with *Reader's Digest;* about £8). The three sections of the book are planned to provide a complete 'escape kit' (there's even a compass included) for exploring the countryside on foot. More than 100 walks along country footpaths are featured and you may be surprised how close you are to one.

The Inspectorate of Ancient Monuments: A part of the Department of the Environment, the Inspectorate publishes a general guide to all sites and monuments in its care. There are also illustrated guide books for each region (Scotland, Wales, Northern England, Midlands and East Anglia, and Southern England) plus special guides to each site. All available from HMSO Bookshops, or at the sites for under £1.

Holiday guides (all should be under £1)

Study Holidays, Sport and Adventure Holidays, Working Holidays, School Travel and Exchange (Central Bureau for Educational Visits and Exchanges)

Outdoor Activity and Sports Holidays in England, Special Interest and Hobby Holidays in England (English Tourist Board)

Voluntary Service Opportunities Register (free from National Youth Bureau, 17-23 Albion Street, Leicester LE1 6GD)

London guides

You can get *free* basic information leaflets on London from the London Tourist Board, 26 Grosvenor Gardens, London SW1W 0DU (tel. 01-730 0791). For up-to-date information on daily special events there is a recorded phone service (operating from 9 a.m. to 6 p.m., called Teletourist (01-246 8041) and the Board also runs a booking and reservation service for hotels

and budget accommodation. Good guides are: *London, Your Sightseeing Guide*, with Underground map and fold-out, easy-to-follow street map; and *Where to Stay in London 1979* from the London or English Tourist Boards.

Nicholson's *Parents' Guide to Children's London* is a directory filled with practical information, such as where to see anything from dinosaurs to speedway racing, and how to get there. Also a very useful list of public lavatories and – most important – when you can expect to find them closed. From bookshops or London Tourist Board.

There is a special twenty-four-hour information phone service for children which gives details of exhibitions and events of special interest to children, plus information on how to get there, opening times and cost. For Children's London Information Service dial 01-246 8007.

Where to get a real welcome

Holidays can be more difficult to arrange for some people than for others. Not everyone loves children and pets while, sadly, very few cater for the handicapped.

Holidays for the Physically Handicapped is an annually published guide book containing general information about holidays at home and abroad. It lists and categorizes accessible hotels, guest houses, holiday camps, self-catering flats, chalets and adapted caravans, and gives information about activity holidays. Addresses of voluntary organizations, holiday organizers and other sources of information are also given. Available from branches of W. H. Smith Ltd, cost 75p, or from The Royal Association for Disability and Rehabilitation, 25 Mortimer Street, London W1N 8AB, cost £1.50 (including postage).

You can also get *Care in the Air* free from the Civil Aviation Authority, PO Box 41, Cheltenham, Gloucestershire. The introduction is by Douglas Bader, who says that it has been meticulously prepared to cover the problems which can affect the dis-abled, the sick, elderly passengers or anyone who finds walking difficult. It tells how to arrange free wheelchairs, ambulances, special food, special leg room or a seat near the lavatory. It also covers rebate claims. A disabled person can claim as much as 50 per cent rebate, for example, on UK domestic air routes, while a blind passenger and his escort can travel together for *one* adult fare. It is most important *always to inform the travel agent or airline reservation department at the time of booking* about any special situation.

PACKAGED PICNICS

The best outdoor meals are those you take yourself, as they do at Ascot (all those Fortnum's hampers) or at Glyndebourne, where you risk dreadful indigestion galloping through three courses in the eating interval. Don't waste half a sunny day preparing them in the kitchen. Picnics should be impromptu and uncluttered, with no elaborate preparations which will be ruined by the first drop of rain.

If you are driving, decide *who* is to decide where to picnic. *Don't* keep on driving in the hope of finding a better spot because the place you have in your mind's eye is probably 100 leagues in the opposite direction and the grass is always greener fifty yards back.

Some people think that it's unsporting to buy your picnic en route at a perfectly ordinary grocery store. But the British do this all over the Continent, so why not at home? Take a pre-cut tart – either sweet (apple) or savoury (egg and bacon). Or take the minimum of simple food (nothing sticky or liable to melt) and prepare it when you get there.

A simple family menu might include variations on:

1 Hard-boiled eggs, salami, cold sausages, ham, a dismembered fowl – everyone loves eating with their fingers, Henry VIII style.
2 Fresh bread (with knife to cut it), rolls or crisp breads.
3 Green salad to be dressed on site with vinaigrette dressing (in screw-top bottle). Don't forget a salad bowl.
4 Fresh, hard fruit or soft fruit in a box, cheese.
5 Sweet biscuits, but not chocolate ones, which melt and stick together.

If you prefer sandwiches those made on the spot don't need two slices of bread. Danish open sandwiches are delicious, but remember to include one moist ingredient and stick to the Contran Successful Sandwich Formula (halve the bread and double the filling). Starting with a lettuce leaf base, add: (1) slice of cold fried bacon and plenty of fresh ground black pepper, or (2) slice of peeled apple on cream cheese, or (3) chopped radish on liver sausage, or (4) a crisp ring of raw onion on sliced cucumber and anchovies, or (5) cold scrambled egg and capers, or (6) a slice of tomato and black olive on cream cheese.

If it's windy or you insist on swimming, take a vacuum flask of something hot, or a hip flask of something warming. Don't take coffee or tea for midday meal because it always tastes of the vacuum flask. Take hot soup (which doesn't), cold milk or cold drinks that don't taste unpleasant when warm (this rules out Coca-Cola). Try barley water (the Queen's favourite) or unfrozen orange juice with a squeeze of lemon, or red wine – not white, which needs chilling. If you want something mildly exciting for children, try cold milk with a dash of Ribena and a couple of strawberries floating on top.

Don't take chocolate because it melts over everything; take boiled sweets. Never take mayonnaise (it curdles) or butter (it melts). Don't try to cook anything, it's too much trouble.

Take:

Plenty of paper cups and plates. *Real* cutlery (count it before you set out and as you re-pack). *Real*, cheap, thick glasses if you're going to drink wine, because paper cups spoil the taste. (There's nothing gracious about plastic toothmugs and they fall over constantly.)

A kitchen roll to mop everyone up afterwards (paper napkins are unnecessarily expensive). A bottle or plastic container for water, in case there isn't a wayside stream to act as a fingerbowl.

Salt, a corkscrew, a bottle and tin opener (Lewis's department stores do a cheap three-in-one, known as the Bachelor's Companion).

At least three empty plastic bags for any damp towels and bathing suits, and carrying your litter home.

And if you're really feeling like making a meal of it – take cushions and a snowy white tablecloth, and carry the whole feast in a wicker basket, as if you were straight out of *The Wind in the Willows*. And don't forget a couple of rugs and the umbrella.

TRAVELLING GAMES

Children tend to bicker when they're bored on long journeys. Don't let them read, because that's one of the things that makes them sick and gives them headaches. Instead, invent games with small prizes for all, if possible: cheat, not when judging but when setting the game; you're less likely to be found out.

Some games work with some families and not with others and the old favourites never seem to wear out, except on those days when they all prefer to sit at the back of the bus endlessly droning 'Ten Green Bottles' or 'Onward Christian So . . . hohohol . . . . jers'.

Games to play

1 *The Most:* Who can spot the most specified objects – boats, ponds, windmills, hens, etc. – within a time limit of say fifteen minutes or half an hour, depending on age of children. On turgid stretches of motorway you can substitute red cars, lorries or open sports cars for these idyllic rural foci. Don't try anything as esoteric as unusual car numbers, makes of car or foreign registrations because the secret of travelling games is that you have to be able to notch up points quickly and simply.

2 The never-fail classic is *I-Spy*. Choose objects from inside or outside the car and give the first letter of the name it starts with. As with poker there are variations: one is to give the colour, another is to describe the object, but not mention the colour.

3 *Never-ending Stories* (with any luck): Where each person carries on

the story from crisis-point to crisis-point, like *The Perils of Pauline*, only with Piggy Wiggy and what *he* did next. Don't play to a time limit or small children dry-up.

4 *Memory Games:* Like 'Little Tommy went to market and bought a pig, some eggs, a basket to put them in, a Christmas Tree, writing paper', etc. Those who can't remember the sequence are 'out'. The two dangers are that those who are 'out' get bored and the game can madden the car driver.

5 You can also play *What to Take on a Desert Island*, not with discs, but naming six favourite foods, drinks, animals, books, bits of equipment, people. Children never get farther than food.

Paper and pencil games
(for train journeys)

Don't sneer at all the obvious games such as noughts and crosses, boxes, hangman, draw a maze. Older children make alphabet lists of cities, countries, rivers, trees, girls' or boys' names, flowers, all starting with the same letter. And what will *guarantee* a happy and contented silence is drawing up a list of *Things I Hate Most*.

Happy Family Holidays

DAYS OUT WITH THE CHILDREN
(where to take them in the holidays)

If you have nothing better to do than enjoy your children's holidays with them, *every single day*, well, that's wonderful. If you have more than enough work and nobody's giving *you* a holiday, you might consider how much harassment a bit of pre-planning could save you.

Try sharing the load with one or two (not more) parents of the friends of your children (who are almost never *your* friends), who may also be interested in having happier holidays *outside* the home. Read *How to Survive Children* by Katharine Whitehorn (published by Methuen), not only for ideas but for succinct information.

Many local *libraries* run FREE holiday story and activity sessions (much less boring than they sound) at least once a week, at least during the summer holidays.

Modern museums: No longer dusty,

gloomy and guaranteeing boredom, they now spend a fortune on organizing special children's events, tours, lectures, quizzes and other holiday activities. Some even have theatre consultants to make sure that the children feel involved and can *do* things, instead of mutinously trudging past dusty glass cases of relics.

Daytime holiday courses for children: Some community and arts centres (such as the Midlands Art Centre, Cannon Hill Park, Birmingham) run daytime courses for children throughout the school holidays. These include drama, crafts, music, photography, painting and music.

Before the holidays start ask your local librarian for details of sessions in your area.

Holiday play schemes are run at some local schools and by voluntary organizations. Younger children can play, paint, go on outings; older children and parents can help.

For summer holidays, the parent's Bible is the *Reigister of Holiday Play*

Schemes in England and Wales. It shows what's planned in your own and neighbouring areas and is produced by the National Playing Fields Association. The President is well-known parent Prince Philip. Information on play schemes in a particular area is available free on receipt of a large stamped addressed envelope. The complete Register for England and Wales is normally ready by the end of June and costs about £1.50 from the National Playing Fields Association, 25 Ovington Square, London sw3 1 LQ. If you're running a play scheme they'd like to know. If you want to start one, they'll advise you.

INGREDIENTS FOR A RAINY DAY
(whether it's to ward off home or boarding-house blues)

Stand-by ingredients for a wet day

These items will also come in useful while travelling, before bedtime, and might, you hope, keep them occupied while you're having a lie-in in the mornings. Ideally each child should have its own plastic or waterproof shopping bag or case for carrying: felt pens and crayons/scissors/drawing paper/colouring book and/or notepad/transfers/sticky shapes/pencils and rubber.

You can assemble an amusement box which might contain: a scrapbook each (for sticking in postcards, photographs, holiday souvenirs, or for pressing wild flowers, grasses, leaves, etc.); family games pack of cards/a dice and counters/*extra* dice and counters; plenty of scrap paper/old magazines (for cutting up) and Sellotape or Cowgum (which doesn't show through paper, can be rubbed off with your fingers and is dissolved with lighter fuel or dry cleaning fluid, but only by an adult).

Take plenty of paperback reading and for younger children an exciting and lengthy bedtime story, so you can read a chapter a night.

If you're at home

Younger children can make leaf prints; collect, press and label wild flowers and grasses in a scrapbook; make their own pastry; make a pretend inside garden in a bowl, with twigs, cones, pebbles collected from hedge, park or garden; collect shells for decorations or shell pictures and varnish them with colourless nail varnish.

Older children can keep a holiday scrapbook just like the *Sunday Times* colour supplement – with theatre tickets, postcards, their own photographs and drawings and other souvenirs of the holidays. They can draw up a family tree, write a family history with interviews and photographs of all the members, or write, rehearse and stage their own play, with as much miming and as few words as possible. Or write a notebook novel – try Punch and Judy, detective stories, James Bond – anything but love stories. They could also start a collection – stamps, coins, bottles, post-cards, matchboxes – or start a *real* miniature garden in a pot.

If it rains, paint a stone

Young children can be far more difficult to amuse than Queen Victoria, so, if noses are glumly pressed to dripping windowpanes, why not suggest painting stones? For some reason children seem to enjoy painting stones when they're sick of painting on sheets of paper or each other. And stones are cheap, so nip out to the beach, back garden, park or common and collect a few round, fairly smooth stones to keep in reserve. They must be at least as large as an egg. If possible, wash, dry and paint in advance with real undercoat. Otherwise: wash stones, dry them and hand out one per child round the table. Use poster paints, finger paints or, even better, watercolours mixed with poster white. The stones can be painted with pictures of the missing sun, a kitten or anything the shape suggests. Abstracts are, of course, easiest and even the littlest ones can paint them.

All finished stones make useful paperweights or door props, or simply artistic objects for any grown-up's birthday, except yours.

Whether or not it's Easter, children also enjoy doing a bit of artwork on hardboiled 'Fabergé' eggs. Pencil in the design, stand egg in a steady egg-cup and start on the top half. Use watercolour paint, acrylics, felt pens (especially effective), sequins, ribbons, lace and wool for hair if they're painting funny faces.

Seed pictures

This idea might make you blanch, but if older children take to it, it can keep them quiet for days. And you've probably got most of the ingredients in your kitchen. You need a piece of stiff, unbendable card. It's best to wire it for hanging before you start; if you do it afterwards you'll probably have to patch up your finished collage.

Measure a border in pencil all round the card for a clean-cut 'framed' look. Pencil design on to card. Geometric, natural forms, or fantastic flowers seem to come out best. Don't be too ambitious: no edible Guernicas.

Check your store cupboard for what's left of your last, crazy splurge on health food and any local Indian shops for the colours and textures you want, from cream to dark brown, with some soft green and claret colours.

WORD OF WARNING! Use any strong, clear-drying adhesive, such as Araldite, but if you think you'll want to varnish the seed picture for a shiny sea-pebble effect, use a PVA-based glue such as Dunlop's Wood Worker No. 8. This will combine with your plastic sealer without killing you or making you high.

Crease a few pieces of paper down the middle and then put your seeds on to them (for easy pouring).

Analyse your own taste

For idle, quiet fantasy, older children like playing that old Victorian game 'Confession', perhaps relabelled as below:

My ideal virtue...

My idea of beauty in nature...

My idea of beauty in art...

My favourite study ....

My favourite flower ....

My favourite colour..

My favourite qualities in man ....

My favourite qualities in woman ....

My greatest happiness..

My greatest misery...

My favourite amusement ....

My favourite residence...

My favourite authors..

My favourite poets..

My favourite musical composer and instrument...

My favourite heroes in real life ....

My favourite heroines in real life ....

My favourite actors and plays ....

My favourite animal ....

My favourite names ....

My favourite quotation ....

My favourite scent ....

My favourite thing to wear ....

My favourite food...

My favourite drink ....

My present state of mind ....

My motto...

My signature...

Thinly spread the adhesive on to the first small area or band you want to fill and pour suitable seeds into that section. Push lightly into place with the back of a spoon, or with fingers, into one even layer: use tweezers to position the fiddly bits. Work on one small section at a time and be sure to clean spoon, fingers and tweezers between sections or you'll end up with yellow peas split among the green mungs.

The finished picture should dry flat for about a day, then gingerly ease it into a vertical position. Inevitably, some of the beans will fall off; glue these pieces individually and put them back into place with tweezers (this is the fiddly part.) Then hang it.

For the more ambitious there's *Things to Do*, an excellent Puffin book by Hazel Evans that's full of ideas, from practising home-made magic and designing a puppet to making your own telephone or xylophone.

CHILDREN ON THEIR OWN

In America almost every child goes to summer camp as an important part of their growing up process and education from the age of eight until they're sixteen, when they can become a camp counsellor, which brings responsibility as well as money. (See p. 376 if you want to travel free to America and be paid to be a counsellor yourself.) In camp they learn to get along without family support and have lots of healthy outdoor fun. Some camps have specialities such as tennis, painting or slimming. (Yes, for children: it's the new growth area.)

On this side of the Atlantic we're slowly getting used to the idea, and seeing the many advantages, for them as well as you. Most children can enjoy a holiday away from parents, and with other children, although it's best to make the first holiday on their own a short one. Some organizations take children on their own as young as six, but it may be wiser to wait until your child is eight or nine.

Many organizations run activity and adventure holidays for children, but standards vary, so find out beforehand what kind of supervision the children receive and how well qualified the instructors are. Take up references, preferably from a child, or the parent of a child, who's been before, but – best of all – *visit it yourself*. Here are some possibilities:

The Youth Hostels Association offers many adventure holidays for children aged eleven upwards. For example, they can trek, cycle, ride, canoe, stay in youth hostels. Costs vary from about £45 a week, which includes food and accommodation.

Eleven- to fifteen-year-olds who would like something less strenuous and belong to the Young Ornithologists' Club (membership around £2) can go on YHA bird-watching holidays. Details from Mr R. A. Bucknell, YHA Adventure Holidays, 8 St Stephens Hill, St Albans, Hertfordshire (tel. St Albans 55215).

The Scottish Youth Hostels Associa-

tion (7 Glebe Crescent, Stirling FK8 2JA) offers Breakaway holidays in Scotland for children aged fourteen and over. Very active activities including skiing, pony-trekking, angling, sailing. Costs vary according to activity. If you live in Northern Ireland, the *Youth Hostel Association of Northern Ireland* (93 Dublin Road, Belfast BT27) can inform you about the hundreds of youth hostels all over Britain.

The Royal Society for the Protection of Birds (The Lodge, Sandy, Bedfordshire) also runs holidays for young people through the Young Ornithologists' Club. Activities include birdwatching and drawing and painting birds, and these specialist pursuits may also be combined with sailing or pony-trekking on some holidays. Costs from £25 for about five days: a real bargain.

Lake District Leisure Pursuits (Fallbarrow Hall, Windermere LA 233DL) run Students' Adventure Holidays for eight- to fifteen-year-olds.

PGL Adventure Ltd (327 Station Street, Ross-on-Wye HR9 7AH) is a good example of an experienced, commercial organization offering holidays for children on their own. Expert instruction is provided in all kinds of sports, including canoeing and pony-trekking. Children may sometimes try two or three different sports in a week. Hire of equipment and necessary clothing is included in the cost of PGL holidays, as is usual with these activity holidays for children.

The Outward Bound Trust (Avon House, 360 Oxford Street, London W1; tel. 01-491 1355) provides a wide range of challenging courses and expeditions for young and old, the athletic, otherwise, and handicapped. Designed to encourage self-reliance, initiative and endurance, with the ultimate aim of developing a responsible and positive approach to life. Courses (between seven and twenty-six days) include canoeing, sailing, rock-climbing, rescue training, first aid, community care, etc. Centres throughout the country and overseas. Write for full details.

For *riding holidays* contact Ponies of Britain, Brookside Farm, Ascot, Berkshire, for a list of all approved trekking centres for 50p.

The Royal Yachting Association has a list of recognized sailing schools. It costs about 30p from the RYA, Victoria Way, Woking, Surrey.

The British Canoe Union, 70 Brompton Road, London SW3 1DT, produce a list of recognized canoe schools.

Enjoy Britain (21 Old Brompton Road, London SW7 3HZ) offers a range of holidays for young people (many of whom come from abroad). Age groups are twelve to sixteen and sixteen to thirty, and it's more expensive than average. Most centres have swimming pools and tennis courts. Social programmes and special excursions are organized.

The Countrywide Holidays Association (Birch Heys, Cromwell Range, Manchester M14 6HU) organizes youth party holidays, which include special interests such as drama, music and painting.

Colony Holidays (Linden Manor, Upper Colwall, Malvern, Hereford and Worcester WR13 6PP) offers properly supervised and excitingly run community-type holidays for children from eight to fifteen. With a strong educational base these include indoor and outdoor pursuits and games, tracking games, swimming, exploring the country, drama, poetry, handicrafts, music, dancing, storytelling and reading. The holidays take place at New Year, Easter and during the summer holidays and cost from £49 for 7 days: there are also 9-day and 12-day colonies. Price includes supervised travel on coaches from home to destination, and back again.

Forest School Camps (3 Pine View, Fairmile Park, Cobham, Surrey KT11 2PG) run fairly tough holidays for children from six and a half to 17 years. All holidays are under canvas and in deliberately 'primitive' and challenging conditions. Activities for younger children include campcraft and hiking; older ones may go night-orienteering, pot-holing, sailing, canoeing and climbing. Sites include Wales, the Lake District, Scotland, the Border Country.

New Horizon Camps (71 St Albans Road, Cheam, Sutton SM1 2JH) offer rather more restful, very good value two-week camps in Devon, Cornwall, Wales, Derbyshire, at Easter and in the summer. Activities include fossil-hunting and canoeing. Children should be between seven and seventeen, and escorted travel is available from London.

Other ideas: Holiday camps are run by schools, youth clubs, Guides and Scouts and also by *The Woodcraft Folk* (13 Ritherdon Road, London SW17), a co-educational alternative to scouting or guiding. Pity they had to choose such a twee name for a good idea.

Further information

For older children and younger parents, two activity holiday books are produced by the English Tourist Board, who want to encourage this sort of family holiday. The books describe the kind of holiday you can expect, give details of when and where it takes place, plus the type of accommodation and full cost. From dozens of activity holidays you can choose between the traditional (riding, sailing, walking), the extraordinary (shark fishing, grass skiing, orienteering), or special-interest holidays (drama courses, antique-hunting holidays, brass-rubbing weekends). Accommodation ranges from hotels, guest houses or hostels to tents, caravans and self-catering units. Information on relevant associations and any necessary clothing or equipment is also given. The books are:

Outdoor Activity and Sport Holidays in England; Special Interest and Hobby Holidays in England.

Get them from the English Tourist Board (4 Grosvenor Gardens, London SW1 0DU; tel. 01-730 9842); in Scotland the same area is covered in *Tir Nen Og* (Land of the Ever Young), available *free* from the Scottish Tourist Board (23 Ravelston Terrace,

Edinburgh EH4 3EU); similar local information is in *Wales 1979, free* from the Wales Tourist Board (Brunel House, 2 Fitzalan Road, Cardiff CF1 2UY); there is also useful information of this sort in *Sport and Adventure Holidays* (85p plus 15p postage) from the Central Bureau for Educational Visits and Exchanges (43 Dorset Street, London W1H 3FN).

HOLIDAY EXCHANGES FOR OLDER CHILDREN

Unless your children go to friends abroad that you know, holiday exchanges are generally arranged through their school. Many schools now twin with schools in France, Germany, Italy, Spain, etc. – and a part of the reciprocal arrangement is to exchange visits. This will involve your child in spending some time as a guest of the foreign family – and then your repaying that hospitality in Britain. The two children are generally together in both places so you need room for a guest. If your child's school does not operate one of these schemes, strongly suggest that it does so and get a couple of other parents to prod the school into action.

If you are not in a position to entertain a foreign student there are French *centres de vacances* (a sort of glamorous junior holiday camp where they can learn the language among the locals). There are also German and Austrian equivalents and holiday jobs

are available abroad at these holiday colonies for the young (see below, p. 374).

Individual families or children can also stay abroad with specially selected hosts. Contact one of the organizations in this country or abroad which deal with exchanges and home-stays. Details of most of these are given in *School Travel and Exchange*, (price 85p plus 15p postage) from the Central Bureau for Educational Visits and Exchanges (see p. 374). Organizations include:

Accueil Amical (21 rue Saint-Augustin, 75002 Paris), which arranges family stays for people aged twelve to twenty-three, during the school year and in the holidays. Excursions are arranged and permanent contact is maintained throughout the stay.

Anglo-French Exchanges (288A High Street, Croydon, Surrey CRO 1NG) finds exchange students all over France for thirteen- to eighteen-year-olds who wish to exchange for three weeks at Easter or in the summer. Escorted group travel to Paris, Lyons and Marseilles.

The Educational Interchange Council (43 Russell Square, London WC1B 5DC) offers a similar service, also with escorted travel between London and Paris. The cost is, as I write, around £35. Escorted travel to German centres is around £45.

The Euro-Exchange Travel Service (56 St Thomas Drive, Pinner, Middlesex HA5 4SS) finds partners in Europe who want to exchange with children here, ages twelve to eighteen. Three weeks at Easter or in the summer currently costs about £40 with escorted travel from London.

The German Student Travel Service (Terminal house, Lower Belgrave Street, London SW 1 W0NP) arranges visits (not exchanges) to families in Munich, Bonn, etc., for two weeks or more for those over sixteen. Current cost is around £80, including full board and insurance. Travel is extra, so it's expensive.

For paid holiday jobs abroad, read on.

Working Holidays

(for older students and younger parents)

PAID HOLIDAY JOBS ABROAD

You can still see the world, even if you haven't much money, if you're prepared to work your way around it. There's a lot of seasonal work: farm work and fruit-picking in the country, hotel work in the town and down at the beaches, or up in the mountains. There's also plenty of work for helpers in children's camps in Europe and the United States, and don't think that they only want students, all that's specified is over seventeen.

There are some jobs abroad in Europe for older teenagers as au pairs and helpers at *centres de vacances* and other holiday camps; pocket money is paid, board and lodging are included. Organizations which can help in placing young people abroad in these kinds of job include the following:

The Central Bureau for Educational Visits and Exchanges (43 Dorset Street, London W1H 3FN) places monitors in French *centres de vacances*, German children's holiday camps, and in other camps of this type abroad. Applicants must be eighteen and able to work for at least a month, and generally need A level in the language required, or an equivalent qualification or fluency. Pocket money and full board are provided. Closing date for applications is 1 April and applicants are needed in July.

Accueil Familial des Jeunes Étrangers (23 rue de Cherche-Midi, 75006 Paris) needs au pairs aged eighteen or over for one to three months from June to September. Most will stay with French families in their holiday homes. Around £40 a month as pocket money for approximately six hours' work a day (and *don't* expect less work). Get this in writing, give your young one a copy to take with him or her and make sure they have a return ticket before they set off.

Vacation Work (9 Park End Street, Oxford OX1 1HJ) also has details of summer jobs in Europe, as au pairs, in camps, in catering, etc. Its publication, *Summer Jobs Abroad,* which gives information on paid and voluntary work (farm work, hotel work, etc.) available in Western Europe, Scandinavia, North Africa and Ghana, costs £2.25 from W. H. Smith or direct from Vacation Work.

There are also many *International Summer Work Camps* in Britain and Europe. The brochure says that volunteers work, eat and sleep with other young people of many different nationalities (I'll bet they do). Work includes looking after the physically or mentally handicapped, cleaning up and preserving the countryside. Usually all you need is your fare. Board and bed are provided in hostels and tents. Get an information booklet from the Central Bureau for Educational Visits and Exchanges, 43 Dorset Street, London W1H 3FN, called *Volunteer Work Abroad* (30p, post free).

Many people, not necessarily Jewish, are spending their holidays on *kibbutzim* in Israel. You pay your own fare and spend a minimum of one month (but may stay longer) and are expected to work about eight hours a day for five days a week, with one working day off as well as *shabbat* (midday Friday to Sunday morning). Most volunteers accumulate their days off so that they may spend time touring. Many kibbutzim arrange sightseeing tours for the volunteers.

Work ranges from driving a tractor to gathering in crops, from washing dishes to milking cows. In return, you receive free food, free accommodation and pocket money, free cigarettes, laundry, etc. and medical care. You get plenty of sun and stimulating, young companionship. It certainly seems to help young people sort out their uncertainties as to who they are and what they should be doing with amazing speed and in the kibbutzim there is a strong bond of togetherness which is getting very rare in life. If you are feeling like dropping out of the capitalist society it is a good way to check what life is like in a *properly organized commune.* (Minimum age seventeen.)

There is also a scheme which involves working on *archaeological digs in Israel* (minimum age eighteen). Find your own Dead Sea Scrolls in your summer holiday. There are two age groups. For students from eighteen to twenty-six, the all-in price is from £149 for two weeks in Gamala. For people over twenty-six and not full-time students prices range from £188.

For further details of both these projects, write to *Project 67,* 21 Little Russell Street, Bloomsbury, London WC1, or *Hosts Student Travel Service,* 161 Great Portland Street, London W1.

If you don't fancy Israel, the

Archaeology Abroad Service publishes details of excavations and field work taking place abroad. Contact them at The Institute of Archaeology, 31–34 Gordon Square, London WC1 (tel. 01-387 6052). Alternatively for excavations in Britain contact the Archaeological Council of Great Britain, 112 Kennington Road, London SE11 6RE (tel. 01-582 0494).

Perhaps you'd rather spend your holidays digging ditches in Mexico or somewhere similarly far-flung? Short- or long-term working holidays are available for students or young people on farms or in work camps, community service, domestic work or teaching. Sometimes high pay, sometimes low pay, sometimes no pay. For information get an up-to-date copy of *Working Holidays* (£1 including postage and packing) from the Central Bureau for Educational visits and Exchanges, Dept. PE/4, 43 Dorset Street, London W1H 3FN.

You can arrange to work in an American summer camp through *Camp America* (37 Queensgate, London SW7 5HR; tel. 01-589 3223), who find jobs for students, teachers, youth workers, social workers and anyone who has a good background of arts and crafts work (not necessarily qualified teachers, but who know enough to be able to teach it). Recruitment closes in April, and anyone aged from eighteen to about thirty-five (sometimes a bit older) with suitable qualifications can apply for a job as a camp counsellor. You go for eleven weeks, spending nine weeks working in one of the camps (very healthy outdoor life)

and you get two weeks' free time at the end for a holiday before returning home. Your return flight is paid for, you get free board and accommodation, mostly in camp cabins, during the nine weeks at camp and a small amount of pocket money which ranges from $100 for the season for under-twenty-ones who are first-time counsellors and $150 for over twenty-ones. You get *much* more the second time – up to about $200 for a repeat counsellor over twenty-one. You pay Camp America a deposit of £28, half of it when you apply and the other half when they get your camp job fixed up. This is returned to you when you are paid your earnings at the camp.

Most of the 300 camps are on the East Coast and in the mid-West, but there are also a few in California. Write to Camp America for their brochure and application form.

You can also find out about summer camp work and other jobs in all parts of the United States in the *Summer Employment Directory of the United States*, which is in the reference section of some public libraries. Or get it direct from the distributors, Vacation Work, 9 Park End Street, Oxford (tel. Oxford [0865] 41978), price £4. The directory, which is published each January, gives information about jobs for anyone over eighteen, in camps, national parks, nature reserves and restaurants.

PAID JOBS IN BRITAIN

There are two kinds of working holidays: those which are voluntary (unpaid) and those that pay you. *Voluntary work* in the holidays means a definite commitment to children, old people, the disabled, or to conservation schemes, so such work shouldn't be undertaken lightly. Usually board and lodging are free, though you may sometimes pay a nominal charge, perhaps £5. Occasionally, voluntary workers receive pocket money.

Holidays in Britain where they pay you

Short-term *paid work* is fairly difficult to find for those under eighteen, though some individual jobs may be found at home and abroad, through organizations like Vacation Work and the Central Bureau for Educational Visits and Exchanges (see addresses on pp. 374–5). There's plenty of work available in the children's camps I've recommended, but it's rock-bottom pay. The most lucrative work seems to be fruit-picking, often back-breaking work, often seven days a week for twelve hours a day.

You may find something suitable in the *Directory of Summer Jobs in Britain* (published by Vacation Work of Oxford, about £2.25 from W. H. Smith). Otherwise consider:

H. J. Highwood Ltd (Swigs Hole, Horsmonden, Tonbridge, Kent): Hop-pickers work a five-and-a-half-day week, for a minimum of three weeks from the beginning of September. Wages are, as I write, around £40 per week. Applicants must be eighteen or over.

Kent Land Corps (Employment Service Agency, 58 High Street, Maidstone, Kent ME14 1SY): Recruits casual labour for local farmers and growers around Maidstone and Chatham. Fruit-picking work is available from the end of July and applicants should bring their own tent. Hop-picking is available from the beginning of September, twelve hours a day, salary paid by the hour plus overtime.

Cantbaybruich, L. Fraser (Culloden Moor, Inverness, Scotland): Raspberry-pickers are needed in July and August to work seven days a week; wages are piecework, per pound picked. Camp site available.

Anglian Students International Centre (PO Box 2, Wisbech, Cambridgeshire): Fruit-pickers needed from June to October. Registration fee, which covers travel to and from London, is about £7. Minimal charge for board and lodging. Pay varies from year to year. Minimum age is seventeen.

Concordia (*Youth Service Volunteers*) *Ltd* (11A Albemarle Street, London W1X 4BE) needs fruit-pickers and agricultural workers for hop-picking and market gardening. It's a five-and-a-half-day week for wages. Comparatively large registration fee plus minimal weekly sum for board and lodging. Minimum age is sixteen.

Children's holiday camps: Some children's holidays camps employ young people to help run the camps, organize activities, cook food, and so on. Write to the following organizations, which run holidays for children on their own. Minimum age is generally sixteen or seventeen.

Colony Holidays (Linden Manor, Upper Colwall, Malvern, Hereford and Worcester WR13 6PP): Monitors are required, minimum age seventeen, to help run the colonies for children aged eight to fifteen (see p. 371). A great deal of enthusiasm and commitment is involved, and monitors must do a week's training beforehand. But they can then attend a number of colonies if they wish, each year at summer, Easter and New Year. Money had certainly better not be the prime object here. Basic pay plus board, lodging and travel.

Country-wide Holidays Association (The Domestic Staffing Officer, Birch Heys, Cromwell Range, Manchester M14 6HU): Need domestic staff at twenty holiday centres in Britain. Pay plus bonus, board and lodging provided.

Pontins Holiday Centre (Personnel Dept, Pine Grange, Bath Road, Bournemouth BH1 2NT): Catering and bar staff, cleaners and camp staff needed at twenty holiday camps. Free board and lodging and access to all camp facilities, as well as wages.

Butlin's Ltd (Divisonal Personnel Officer, Bognor Regis, Sussex PO21 1JJ): Need catering staff and staff for shops and bars throughout the summer.

Many other paid job opportunities for older teenagers can be found in *Working Holidays* (85p plus 15p postage) from the Central Bureau for Educational Visits and Exchanges.

VOLUNTARY WORK IN BRITAIN

Conservation work

Voluntary, stimulating and a healthy change from a desk. A number of work camps and general voluntary agencies carry out conservation work, but some organizations specialise in this field and need young people to help in the holidays. They include:

The National Conservation Corps (Zoological Gardens, Regent's Park, London NW1 4RY) need over 1000 volunteers to help on nature reserves and other sites throughout Britain, for one to three weeks at a time. Minimum age sixteen years. Volunteers pay a very small membership fee plus a small daily donation to the trust. Accommodation is provided, sometimes in tents. Physical fitness is essential.

The National Trust, Junior Division (The Old Grape House, Cliveden, Taplow, Maidenhead, Berkshire S1L 0HZ) organizes Acorn Camps in spring and summer throughout England and Wales. Fairly tough, mainly outdoor projects in woodlands, footpaths, coastline, moorland, etc. Volunteers pay a minimal sum towards costs of board and lodging; accommodation is sometimes spartan, minimum age is sixteen and a half and minimum duration of stay is one week.

The Waterways Recovery Group (37 Teignmouth Road, London NW2 4EB) needs volunteers to help restore canals, from July to September. Accommodation is provided in local halls, and low-cost food is available. Minimum age is sixteen.

Most local authorities run their own conservation schemes. For further details of voluntary opportunities in your area, consult the *Voluntary Service Opportunities Register*, free from the National Youth Bureau (17–23 Albion Street, Leicester LE1 6GD).

Summer work camps

Cardiff Student Community Action (Joint Students Union) (Park Place, Cardiff): Volunteers are needed to run projects including gypsy teaching, adult literacy, housing action and work with children, during both vacation and term periods.

Friends Service Council (Quaker Work Camps, Friends House, Euston Road, London NW1 2BJ): Volunteers are needed for two to three weeks to help with manual work and social schemes for adults and children, including the mentally handicapped. A contribution to food costs is welcome; take your own sleeping bag. Minimum age is eighteen.

Concordia Ltd (8 Brunswick Place, Hove, East Sussex) runs *International Agricultural Work Camps* in Britain and in Europe. Volunteers should be eighteen, medically fit, and carry a medical certificate to camp. Write to the Recruitment Secretary.

British Council of Churches (Youth Unit, 10 Eaton Gate, London SW1W

9BL): Four weeks of service at a time; volunteers contribute to camp costs but have free time for individual pursuits. Minimum age is eighteen.

Summer play schemes and children's camps

Write to your local education authority or community relations council for details of play schemes and camps which need help in your area or consult one of the following organizations:

North Devon Volunteers (7 Bontpart Street, Barnstaple, Devon): They help with children aged five to twelve in North Devon. Food, accommodation, travelling expenses and pocket money paid. Minimum age is sixteen, minimum stay two weeks.

Children's Country Holiday Fund (1 York Street, London W1H 1PZ): Camping holidays for underprivileged children, aged nine to thirteen. Holidays last two weeks each during July and August. Free board and lodging, travelling expenses and pocket money usually paid. Vacancies for male and female supervisors, minimum age of eighteen.

Birmingham Young Volunteers (Children's Adventure Camps, Birmingham Young Volunteers, 161 Corporation Street, Birmingham B46PT): Camps are run in Hereford and Worcester and Dyfed. Food, lodging and travelling expenses if you travel with the children. Minimum age is seventeen and minimum time is one week.

General voluntary work with children and old people

This is painting old people's flats, building adventure playgrounds, etc. Write to the following organizations:

TOCH (1 Forest Close, Wendover, Aylesbury, Buckinghamshire HP22 6BT) run play schemes and entertain old people. There's work throughout the UK. Volunteers pay a very small registration fee – but get free food and lodging. Minimum age sixteen.

Concordia (*Youth Service Volunteers*) *Ltd* (11A Albemarle Street, London W1X 4BE): Work includes running holiday camps for children and old people, and in homes for the physically handicapped. Volunteers pay a small registration fee and must work for two weeks. Minimum age for volunteers is eighteen.

International Voluntary Service (91 High Street, Harlesden, London NW 10 4NU): Volunteers pay the usual small registration fee, but food and lodging are free. There's work in hospitals; in running play schemes for children from the docks and mining areas; in rebuilding roads; in forestry; in house repairs; looking after multi-racial communities in forty international work-camps all over Britain from late June to mid September. Minimum age is sixteen.

Learn-something Holidays
for Them and You

You can combine a family holiday in the country with a little light learning. Holidays where you and your children study something interesting may be a week long, or may just provide a short weekend or mid-week break. There are courses which the whole family can enjoy – or you and the children can pursue separate interests. You might study bridge, millinery, pottery, painting, music, theatre, literature, a foreign language, politics, history of art, medieval music or even spiders. You don't all have to study millinery or spiders *together*: you each choose your own course. Study holidays are best enjoyed with children of twelve and over – in fact, many courses stipulate a minimum age of fourteen.

ACTIVITY HOLIDAYS

Some organizations which run family activity holidays are:

Loughborough University Summer Programme (Centre for Extension Studies, University of Technology, Loughborough, Leicestershire LE11 3TU): This famous annual programme has activities and courses for everyone from the under-fives to the most brilliant technologist. Adults can choose from highly scientific or technological courses or from a variety of creative and general studies courses. There's a crèche/playgroup for under-fives, activities and outings for five- to thirteen-year-olds and a thirteen-plus group.

Rees Holidays Ltd (Borehamgate House, Sudbury, Suffolk CO10 6ED) offers excellent self-catering accommodation at universities and polytechnics at many centres throughout the community for two to twelve people. Choose a four-bedroomed flat from £92.88 inclusive of VAT.

The Country-wide Holidays Association (Birch Heys, Cromwell Range,

Manchester M14 6HU) runs family holiday centres in the Lake District, by the sea and in Europe. Excursions are arranged and there may be walking programmes for families. Cots and other children's facilities are usually available, and there are good reductions for children.

The Holiday Fellowship Ltd (142 Great North Way, London NW4 1EG) run similar good-value family centres in Britain and abroad, and also arrange excellent activity holidays. They specialize in painting, archaeology, bowls, bridge, geology, golf, music, almost anything you like, at centres all over the country.

STUDY HOLIDAYS

Other organizations which offer study holidays and are not nearly as dreary as their names imply are:

English Folk Dance and Song Society (Cecil Sharp House, 2 Regent's Park Road, London NW1 7AY).

Field Studies Council (Preston Montford, Montford Bridge, Shrewsbury SY4 1HW; tel. Montford Bridge 674).

Council for British Archaeology (112 Kennington Road, London SE11 6RE, tel. 01-582 0494).

National Park Study Centres: One of their short family courses is in the Peak District National Park, where your family can learn about the flora and fauna in the middle of it all. Write to the Principal, Losehill Hall Study Centre, Castleton, Derbyshire S30 2WB.

To discover the wide range of study holidays available in this country write for *Study Holidays* (85p plus 15p postage) from the Central Bureau for Educational Visits and Exchanges, 43 Dorset Street, London W1H 3FN. You might also write to the National Institute of Adult Education for its six-monthly calendar of short residential courses, price 50p (19B De Montfort Street, Leicester LE1 7GH).

ADVENTURE HOLIDAYS FOR THE WHOLE FAMILY

There are many family adventure holidays, both in Britain and abroad. Some are heavily organized, others provide a programme which you needn't follow if you don't feel like it. Most provide a range of activities to suit parents and children of all ages, though sometimes they recommend that children under twelve should not attend, especially if the holiday includes fairly arduous activities.

You can often choose to follow one or several sports or interests. In general, prices include all tuition and hire of necessary equipment. Food and accommodation may be in dormitories, but is occasionally in family suites and sometimes in chalets or tents.

Action Holidays (Glenisla, near Alyth, Tayside, Scotland) organize holidays where the family can learn to glide, water-ski, orienteer or canoe, go hill-walking or do archery. Children can join one course, parents another.

Accommodation could be in a caravan (currently £100 for four people including tuition) or in a near-by farm, inn or hotel. They also run winter skiing holidays in Scotland. Write for further information.

The Reivers of Tarset Ltd (The Comb, Greenhaugh, Tarset, North Tyne Valley, Northumberland) offer superb outdoor holidays in conjunction with the Forestry Commission. Children are always welcome, but there are also special family weeks. At the Reivers of Tarset you can stalk with gun or camera, observe wildlife, including deer and badgers, rock climb, canoe or fish. Rooms are centrally heated and there is an à la carte menu including game dishes. Children over ten only. Costs (including activities) from £60 per week for an adult.

The Aviemore Centre (Aviemore, Highland, Scotland) is the famous scene for many family action holidays and includes packages where you can try several sports in a week. Self-catering accommodation is available at the centre, and there are near-by sites for camping and caravans, as well as hotels at the centre which offer family rooms. Excellent sporting facilities, including dry ski slope and ice rink. Free literature on request.

Camping and caravanning

Camping or caravanning can be a bargain and not necessarily uncivilized. A friend, who had never been in a caravan before, recently hired a six-berth van with a bath(!) for under £30 per week in the low season.

WORD OF WARNING: A caravan holiday in the mid season can be non-stop swab work (that's the activity, of course) and a wet holiday in a tent is more than most relationships can stand.

Cost of camping and caravanning: You can hire tents, caravans and all kinds of camping equipment from shops and organizations all over the country. A four-berth caravan will cost you from £33 a week in the low season (October/April), more like £50 in mid summer. Tents cost from £20 per week to hire for a family size (five- or six-person) tent. Overnight charges at camp-sites can be from as little as £1 for a tent or caravan, but many sites charge more. If you want to visit the bright lights from a camp near London, look for sites at Chigwell, Waltham Cross, Hackney or Harlow.

Addresses or organizations which can help with information and free advice include the Camping Club of Great Britain and Ireland (11 Lower Grosvenor Place, London sw1w 0ey) and the Caravan Club (East Grinstead House, East Grinstead, West Sussex). Also try the Caravan Advice Bureau (Link House, Dingwall Avenue, Croydon cr9 2ta) for free advice and the National Caravan Council Ltd (43 High Street, Weybridge, Surrey kt13 8bt) for a list of sites. The British Tourist Authority's booklet *Camping and Caravan Sites* details sites all over Britain (including the Channel Islands and Northern Ireland) and gives details about where and how to hire tents and caravans.

Pony-trekking

This can be enjoyed even by complete beginners. Children over twelve can go on their own or the whole family can ride together in rough moorland or mountain country. Most treks take from one to five days and are at a walking pace, though more experienced riders get the chance to trot and canter.

When you book a trekking holiday, give everybody's correct weight and say how much riding experience (if any) you've all had so that suitable ponies are found for you and the children. Wear jeans with thick tights underneath, or corduroy or whipcord trousers plus a warm anorak and stout boots or shoes with a thick heel.

Ponies of Britain (Brookside Farm, Ascot, Berkshire) organizes pony-trekking in England and will give information on all the centres of which it approves, including details of their social activities. Special pony-trekking holidays for the whole family are also listed in *England – Holidays '79*, from the English Tourist Board, and in *Wales 1979*, from the Wales Tourist Board; for pony-trekking and other activity holidays in Scotland, apply for the free list, *Adventure and Special Interest Holidays in Scotland*, from the Scottish Tourist Board (addresses on p. 385).

For *riding holidays* in Spain, France, Austria, Greece, Italy, Norway and Portugal, contact Erna Low, 21 Old Brompton Road, London s w 7.

Also, for pony-trekking abroad as well as in Britain, contact *P G L Adventure Holidays* (327 Station Street, Ross-on-Wye, Hereford and Worcester; tel. Ross-on-Wye [0989] 4211). They also offer cruising, camping, caving, sailing and snorkelling holidays for the family.

For more experienced riders the *British Horse Society* (National Equestrian Centre, Kenilworth, Warwickshire c v 8 2 l r) and the *Association of British Riding Schools* (Chesham House, Green End Road, Sawtry, Huntingdon, Cambridgeshire) will give details of riding schools throughout the country, and those which offer riding holidays and trekking holidays.

Tourist Information Centres in Britain

Information centres have been established by local authorities in co-operation with the national tourist boards in most large towns. They will provide information, tours and assistance in finding accommodation. (Telephone the local council offices for details.)

British Tourist Authority, Queen's House, 64 St James's Street, London SW 1 A 1 NF (tel. 01-499 9325).

England

English Tourist Board, 4 Grosvenor Gardens, London SW 1 0DU (tel. 01-730 3400).

Publications include a *free* colour brochure, *England – Holidays '79*; *Let's Go* (a *free* guide to short holidays from autumn to spring); *Special Interest and Hobby Holidays in England* and *Outdoor Activity and Sport Holidays in England*, which give information on outdoor holidays, cultural pursuits and caravan and camping sites; *Where to Stay in England*, divided into twelve regional parts, in-

cludes details of all accommodation registered under the official registration scheme.

There is also a handbook of information centres in England.

Scotland

Scottish Tourist Board, 23 Ravelston Terrace, Edinburgh EH 4 3EU (tel. 031-332 2433).

Send s.a.e. for their publications list.

Wales

Wales Tourist Board, Brunel House, 2 Fitzalan Road, Cardiff, CF 1 2UY (tel. 0222 499909).

Wales has an excellent range of publications: send a stamped addressed envelope to the above address for a list of them.

Regional Tourism Councils

There are regional boards for the following tourist areas. Their job is to tell you pretty well whatever you want to know and advise you how to get the best out of your precious holiday.

Cumbria: Ellerthwaite, Windermere LA23 2AQ (tel. Windermere [09662] 4444)

East Anglia: 14 Museum Street, Ipswich IP1 1HU (tel. Ipswich [0473] 214211)

East Midlands: Bailgate, Lincoln LN1 3AR (tel. Lincoln [0522] 31521)

Heart of England: PO Box 15, Worcester WR1 2JT (tel. Worcester [0905] 29511)

London: 26 Grosvenor Gardens, London SW1 0DU (tel. 01-730 3450)

Isle of Man: 13 Victoria Street, Douglas, I.O.M. (tel. Douglas [0624] 4323)

Isle of Wight: 21 High Street, Newport, I.O.W. PO30 1JS (tel. Newport [098 381] 4343)

Northumbria: Prudential Building, 140–150 Pilgrim Street, Newcastle upon Tyne NE1 6TQ (tel. Newcastle upon Tyne [0632] 28795)

North-west England: Last Drop Village, Bromley Cross, Bolton, Lancashire BL7 9PZ (tel. Bolton [0204] 591511)

South-east England: Cheviot House, 4 Monson Road, Tunbridge Wells, Kent TN1 1NH (tel. Tunbridge Wells [0892] 33066)

Thames and Chilterns: 8 The Market Place, Abingdon, Oxfordshire OX14 3HG (Abingdon [0235] 22711)

West Country: Trinity Court, Southernhay East, Exeter EX1 1QS (tel. Exeter [0392] 76351)

Yorkshire and Humberside: 312 Tadcaster Road, York YO2 2HF (tel. York [0904] 707961)

North Wales: North Wales Tourism Council, Glan-y-Don Hall, Civic Centre, Colwyn Bay, Clwyd (tel. Colwyn Bay [0492] 56881)

Mid Wales: Mid Wales Tourism Council, Glyndwr Centre, Maengwyn Street, Machynlleth, Powys (tel. Machynlleth [0654] 2401)

South Wales: South Wales Tourism Council, Darkgate, Carmarthen, Dyfed (tel. Carmarthen [0267] 7557)

Northern Ireland: River House, 48 High Street, Belfast BT1 2DS (tel. Belfast [0232] 46609)

Eire: Bord Failte Eireann, Baggot Street Bridge, Dublin, Eire (tel. Dublin 765871)

Superwoman Plays Away

Even though times are hard it is a great morale booster to take a holiday at home or abroad. To save money you can travel less expensively on package holidays by rail or coach instead of air. You can cut hotel bills by camping or hiring a caravan. If you don't mind roughing it a bit you can get a package holiday and stay in hostels or dormitories, which is no real hardship on a warm Greek island. You can take a package self-catering holiday in a hotel apartment, or swop your home for someone else's – and it really can be a chalet in St Moritz, a villa in Spain or a beach-house in Barbados.

CUTTING COSTS

If you want to cut your package holiday costs you have to *choose with care*. Nothing is what it seems in the travel business, which might be compared to a cross between an impenetrable jungle and an Arab street market. Travel agents like to say that you get what you pay for, but it ain't

necessarily so. Far from it. You can have two identical holidays (same time, same place, same plane or train, same hotel) but they may be two widely differing prices from two different tour operators, so don't automatically leave your choice to your travel agent: *check him out* with the information that follows. Take advice from him, of course, but don't take the first holiday you're offered. Get *all* the brochures and choose your holiday. Then, armed with your pocket computer, a large writing pad, a shopping bag for more brochures and a big dose of tenacity, go shopping for the cheapest version of it, just as you would when buying a refrigerator or potatoes.

Check the small print: one of the reasons that it is small, dreary and grey is because they don't want you to read it. Check the grammatical points: 'from £40' means that this price is the *starting* price: extras and surcharges are how the tour operators make money. By the time you've added on those necessary 'extras', what seems a cheap starting price can often end up costing you more than an expensive starting price.

To be fair, it's almost impossible for one travel agent to keep right up to date on world travel developments. But if your travel agent looks at you blankly or points out aggressively that *he's* the expert after thirty years in the business – don't wilt. Check direct with the travel firm, airline or whatever – and ask the travel agent for their telephone numbers.

Keep your mind switched on while you check. Cosmos, one of Britain's biggest package tour firms, has suggested that 'nine out of ten discounts are not true discounts at all'. They are either cynical gimmicks (something that is *already* available for free) or panic reductions in a tight-money period as the holiday season draws close and operators contemplate empty aeroplane seats. So if you risk late booking (or can't avoid it) always try to press for a discount. Look them straight in the eye, say it's more than you can afford and have they got anything else that's the same, only £10 cheaper (or whatever).

For instance, one firm may start charging high season rates four weeks before another, or there are surprisingly large differences in reductions for children (and definitions of a 'child' differ from company to company).

Discounts are a science in themselves, like trigonometry, and very few travel agents *seem* to know all about them. You will *probably* be entitled to a discount if you are young, old, married or a member of a family.

Apart from this, there are the normal bewildering cut-price commercial offers and often, as the season approaches, underbooked travel companies will desperately lower the price of perfectly good holidays in order to get rid of their surplus stock, just like greengrocers with post-weekend watercress.

Air discounts

Package holidays apart, *only novices pay the full price for air fares* – anywhere – except in an emergency. The price depends on where you book, the day you leave, date, time, place, and how long you're going to stay there, to mention but a few considerations. So try to keep an open mind about your arrival and departure planning.

There are almost as many different discounts for the same air flight as there are airlines. These reductions are called 'promotional fares' and individual airlines all have their poetic names for them – 'Earlybird', 'Pound Stretcher', 'Freewheeler'. They're all basically the same and don't be conned to the contrary. No national or international airline is *allowed* to have its own special offers because they have to stick to the regulations fixed by the international cartel (or price-rigging club) to which they all *must* belong.

The *cheapest way to travel* is to get some member of your immediate family to work for an airline (even if it's behind a desk in the booking office). Relatives get reductions on scheduled air fares to almost anywhere. Any member of the family can pay *only 10 per cent* of the cost of the ticket, although the discount is not so high during the first year of employment.

Young and old

If you are a hard-working, hard-up parent, it's depressing to see how many student discounts there are. Students should always check what's available with the travel office of their university or college. There are always special foreign travel discounts; for instance, *anyone* under the age of twenty-four can get up to 46 per cent discount on a trip to America.

A Student Rail Card, for anyone in full-time education aged over fourteen, costs £7 and lasts for the full academic year; with it you can buy half-price long-distance rail fares in Britain and also on the Sealink ferry to the Channel Islands and Ireland. Get an application form from your nearest station (two passport photos needed).

There are also a lot of discounts for the young who aren't necessarily students (up to twenty-six). After that I'm afraid there's a big, depressing gap until you get your old age pension. Senior Citizens should check with their local council (at the town hall) to find out whether there is a scheme for issuing *free* bus passes. British Rail has two schemes for OAP cheap travel. For £7 you can buy a *rail card* (from your nearest railway station) which entitles you to half-price travel anywhere, anytime – including first-class travel, and Sealink ferry to Channel Islands and Ireland.

There's a cheap OAP scheme for day trips. You pay £3.50 for an *Awayday or Day Return Senior Citizens' Rail Card*, which entitles you to pay half price on *any* day return ticket (already cheaper by about 45 per cent than an ordinary return).

The moral is – there's nearly always a way of getting there cheaper than the first price you were told. Now read on ...

Cheapest by Bus

The cheapest way to travel is by bus or coach, whether you're going a short or long distance at home or abroad, so if you want to go *anywhere*, to save money investigate the bus or coach services first. (See p. 397 for bus and coach information centres, or check with your local bus station.) For long distances choose a coach, which is generally more comfortable (with reclining seats), stops infrequently and travels long distances; and you can book in advance through the coach company or your travel agent. There are scheduled services (like trains) with such names as 'Express Service' or 'National Express': it just means coach.

Bus or coach

On the outskirts of London and in the surrounding rural areas is the London Country Bus Service, known to us all as the Green Line. Bus timetables and maps are available from the Green Line Enquiry Offices, Eccleston Bridge, London sw1, and 237–9 Oxford Street, London w1, or from London Transport Travel Offices situated in major Underground stations. For travel inquiries, telephone 01-834 6563 or 01-730 0202 or 01-222 1234 or Reigate [073 72] 42411. A *Golden Rover Ticket* gives you a day's unlimited travel (after 9 a.m. Monday –Friday, anytime Saturdays, Sundays and Bank Holidays) on Green Line buses (terminal, Victoria Coach Station) and you can buy it for around £1.60 (at the time of writing) from the driver or conductor, with half price for children. There are other similar schemes run by bus services in other parts of the country. Check with your local bus company for what's available.

A similar *Red Rover Ticket* allows you to go anywhere on London Transport buses for a day. You also get an even *cheaper* ticket for about £5.50 for a seven-day stay and you don't have to be a visitor: residents can buy them. Alternatively, you can go anywhere, anytime, on any red bus on a monthly *Red Bus Pass* from London Transport, and at weekends you can take a friend with you anywhere for only a few pence.

Outside London also most bus services run similar discount schemes with such names as 'Faresavers', 'Rover Cards' and 'Freedom Tickets'. Ask your local bus company what is available. A good money-saver is the National Bus Company's *Wanderbus* ticket, which gives unlimited travel for £2.40 a day. Some buses are run by local authorities and some are run by the giant National Bus Company (England and Wales) or the Scottish Bus Group (North of the Border), which have bought up lots of famous small companies such as the Bristol Omnibus, the Midland Red and Highland Omnibuses. The national bus network in Northern Ireland is called the Ulster Bus Company. In the Republic of Eire the national bus network is run by the CIE, who also operate day tours and all-in trips and do inclusive holidays with Aer Lingus or Sealink.

You can book any coach ticket tour excursion or holiday or any train ticket from any travel agent.

There are so many alternative coach routes that a map of National Express routes in Britain, with masses of wiggly red lines, looks like the brain in a headache advertisement, and the services are being *increased*, unlike British Rail services.

There are great bargains in day excursion trips. *Specialist day tours and excursions* leave daily from almost every city in Britain and you'll probably be surprised where you can get to-and-from in a day. For instance,

from Glasgow you can visit Edinburgh, Arbroath, Tay Bridge, Oban, Braymar, Balmoral, Glencoe, Glamis Castle, the Sir Walter Scott country, Loch Lomond, Blackpool and Morecambe. Details from the Travel Centre, Buchanan Bus Station, Killermont Street, Glasgow G2 3NP (tel. 01-332 0025).

From London you can whip out to visit (among other places) Bath, Bognor Regis, Brighton, Bristol, Cambridge, Canterbury, Cheltenham, Chichester, Malvern, Newmarket, Nottingham, Sheffield, Stratford-on-Avon and Winchester. Details from National Travel, Victoria Coach Station, Buckingham Palace Road, London SW1W 9TP (tel. 01-730 0202).

There are also many *guided tours* of cities and historical places. Try the local bus company or their deadly rival Wallace Arnold, and don't forget to compare prices. (Wallace Arnold often wins.) Thomas Cook also do a lot of good tours, but although good value they are not always cheap.

If you're going abroad ask the national travel office of the country you are going to whether there are any special schemes for concessionary fares for visitors on their buses or trains. Often you can't get them once you're there – you have to buy them beforehand. For instance, the best way to see the United States on a shoestring is to buy a Greyhound Bus ticket *here* for a month of unlimited travel *there* for £135 (Greyhound Bus Lines have an office in London at 199 Regent Street, London W1; tel. 01-439 1811).

For travelling long distances in Britain you can whizz along motorways in white coaches at high speed on the National Express (in England and Wales) or the Scottish Bus Group, in Scotland. Check details with local offices. (See rest of this section for addresses.) Incidentally, while double-checking the telephone numbers I found unfailingly fast, informed and courteous service on the other end of *all* of them – most unusual.

Long-distance coach travelling abroad isn't all that expensive. Check fares and time with National Transcontinental Express (see the map on p. 393): overnight stopovers and meals are often included in the price. You can get off and get on again two days later when the next bus comes along and you can do the same on the return journey. You can get as far as Istanbul, Athens, Brindisi, Madrid or Alicante in this way, and departure points are all over the UK.

I once travelled by bus from London to Saint-Tropez while pregnant and even then I found it a most comfortable trip and preferable to a car. Contact your travel agent (who may perhaps try to persuade you to go some more expensive way), local coach station or Victoria Coach Station passenger inquiries (tel. 01-730 0202).

Short package holidays by coach in Britain are extraordinarily good value.

For longer stays in Britain you can take a package *centred holiday*, which means you go to one hotel and take daily free excursions from it (or not, if you prefer to stay near the hotel).

Ask your travel agent for details of them in Scotland, the West Country, Wales, the Lake District and Southern Ireland.

For really good value, cut-price holidays in Britain and Western Europe, you should try *National Travel*. It's the National Bus Company with a different hat on and they have an excellent budget range of no-frills packages called *Ensign Holidays*. You go by scheduled express coach (the ordinary one that runs every day) and have full- or half-board with accommodation in small hotels and guest-houses with local excursions and privileged admission to local sights thrown in.

Packaged coach holidays abroad can also be relatively cheap: a camping holiday, with equipment included, in the South of France costing from about £99 for fifteen days through *National Travel linked with Camping Club Mediterranean*, 152A Holland Park Avenue, London W11 (tel. 01-602 0951).

SEE THE WORLD IN COMFORT
(as opposed to flying over it)

Coach travel

Short of hitch-hiking, coach travel is almost certainly the cheapest way to go on a sightseeing tour. In some ways it can also be the most luxurious way to tour. You're travelling by road but with more room than in a car, plus air conditioning, reclining seats

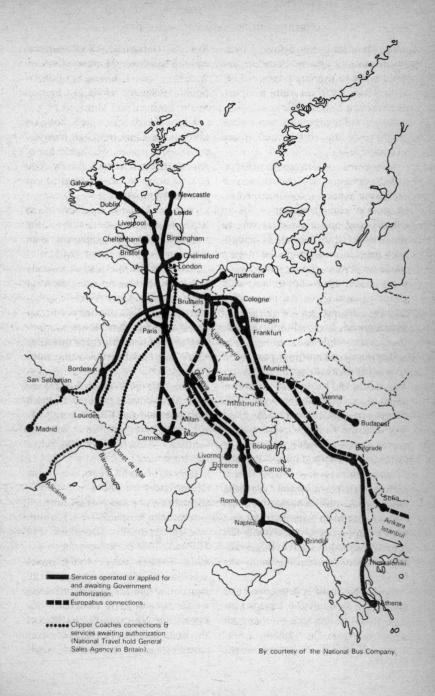

Galway
Dublin
Newcastle
Leeds
Liverpool
Birmingham
Cheltenham
Bristol
Chelmsford
London
Amsterdam
Cologne
Brussels
Remagen
Paris
Frankfurt
Luxembourg
Munich
Bordeaux
Basle
Vienna
San Sebastian
Geneva
Innsbruck
Lourdes
Milan
Budapest
Madrid
Cannes
Nice
Bologna
Belgrade
Livorno
Lloret de Mar
Florence
Cattolica
Barcelona
Rome
Sofia
Alicante
Naples
Ankara
Istanbul
Brindisi
Thessaloniki

Athens

━━━━ Services operated or applied for
and awaiting Government
authorization.
▬▬▬ Europabus connections.

•••••• Clipper Coaches connections &
services awaiting authorization
(National Travel hold General
Sales Agency in Britain).

By courtesy of the National Bus Company.

and far better springing. You're treated like the Queen or an idiot, and both attitudes are very relaxing. They *expect* you to forget your passport, they assume that you can't recognize your own luggage and are always going to be late, so you are nannied everywhere.

Thomas Cook say they've found coach travel is a very friendly way of travelling, especially for older people. A sense of companionship builds up on the road and it's a great way to make new friends as well as being a very good idea for people holidaying alone or anyone who feels they are in a rut. In fact, the cost of running such tours is getting so expensive that there's a distinct possibility that the lower-priced ones will shortly fade away. So go while you can.

The most exhausting part of a coach trip is reading the brochures and sorting out the twee brand names given to perfectly ordinary journeys. The worst offender is our nationalized National Bus Company who operate services under the following titles, to name just a few: Capitals Rapide, Channel Rapide, Eurobus, National Getaways, Coach Master, National Travel, National Holidays, National Ensign, Bee-Line National. This is a pity because I, for one, would feel more protected if I knew that I was travelling under the National umbrella.

But it's worth persevering and ploughing through the extravagant free brochures because you can get good value package holidays and tours in Romania, Bulgaria, Norway, Sweden, Denmark, USSR, Greece, Italy, Yugoslavia, Hungary, Czechoslovakia, Poland, Germany, Luxembourg, Belgium, Holland, France, Spain, Portugal and Morocco.

For cheap package holidays abroad, travelling by coach plus sea, try *Wallace Arnold*, who specialize in Austria, Spain, Greece and Italy. You go by overnight coach (called, of course, Nightrider).

National Holidays specialize in the Rhine Valley, the Austrian Tyrol, the Italian Riviera and the Spanish Costa Brava.

Thomas Cook offer a more leisurely holiday with the nauseating name of Tour-A-While, Stay-A-While (whoever thought that one up needs two years back in English classes) specializing in the Great Alps, Italy and the Tyrol. You spend a whole week in one place.

Blue Cars have good, special interest short holiday trips to the Dutch bulbfields and the Belgian beer festivals. They also specialize in Belgium, Germany, Austria, the Costa Brava and Italy.

Cosmos Coach Tours do some Grand Tours on a shoestring. There's an amazingly Grand North European tour through Russia, Poland, Finland, Sweden, Germany, Denmark and Holland (1979 price: seventeen days, £298). Their Grand Tour of Italy also takes in Brussels and Switzerland (fifteen days, from £173). A French tour, which includes Paris, Chartres, Normandy and the exquisite châteaux of the Loire Valley, costs £93 for seven days – just to put your car and family

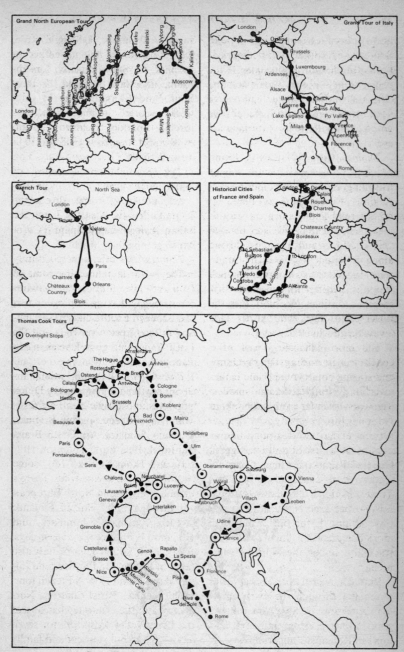

Some European coach tours by Cosmos and Thomas Cook

(return) on a cross-channel ferry can cost that. Another good historical cities tour in Europe includes Paris, Amsterdam, Brussels, Bonn and the cities of the Rhineland (eight days from £106 with all meals included). Or you can tour Paris for five days for £66.

Thomson offer good-value coach holidays – seven days in Venice from £135 or twelve days in Paris and eight other countries from £195.

For really Ritzy coach travel, the unrivalled expert people are *Thomas Cook*. Their Grand Tour of Europe, which is based on the sort of tour that young scions of noble families took in the eighteenth and nineteenth centuries, crosses six countries in twenty-eight days, and visits such famous cities as Paris and Vienna, Monte Carlo and Rome, as well as the French Riviera and the Alps. You stay at first-class hotels with private baths, have really good food and guided tours of the cities (1979 price from £855).

Cook's also do tempting grand tours of the United States. The biggest and the best is the Great Coast to Coast Adventure, 6000 miles from New York on the Atlantic across the Rockies to San Francisco on the Pacific and then back via the Deep South and Florida. (Two or three weeks escorted air and coach, from leaving London, Heathrow. Many other US tours from £802 to £1047, around £500).

The *French Travel Service* also do really *terrific* grand tours by motor-coach. You can go to the Auvergne or Brittany. You can also do a rail and Mediterranean cruise holiday. Well worth getting their brochure.

The prices are those operating in 1979 and, like all prices, are volatile. Similarly, by the time you plan one of these tours the routes may have varied and different ports may be used. The prices and details given here are useful as an indication of what to expect, but it is vital to check the up-to-date facts about anything that interests you. For good value package coach tours see your travel agent or contact direct: Cosmos, Wallace Arnold, Bee-Line National, Blue Cars, Thomson Holidays and Thomas Cook.

COACH TRAVEL
ADDRESS BOOK

National Travel

Passenger Inquiry addresses for England and Wales will answer inquiries from anyone about anything to do with coach travel in this country. They will also advise you about holidays and tours at home and abroad. The *main headquarters* address is: Victoria Coach Station, 164 Buckingham Palace Road, London SW1W 9TP (tel. 01-730 0202)

Regional offices:

London (for London, South-east England, Home Counties, East Anglia and Isle of Wight): National Travel (South East Ltd), Victoria Coach Station, 164 Buckingham Palace Road, London SW1W 9TP (tel. 01-730 0202)

Cheltenham (for South-west England, South Wales and South Midlands): National Travel (South West) Ltd, Coach Station, St Margaret's Road, Cheltenham GL50 4DX (tel. Cheltenham [0242] 38331)

Manchester (for North-west England, West Midlands and North Wales): National Travel (West) Ltd, Canada House, Chepstow Street, Manchester M1 5FU (tel. 061-228 6622)

Liversedge (for North-east England, Yorkshire and East Midlands): National Travel (East) Ltd, Frost Hill, Liversedge, West Yorkshire WF15 6AU (tel. Liversedge [0924] 408171)

National Holidays
(for coach holidays at home and abroad)

Head office: Charlotte Road, Sheffield S2 3HD (tel. Sheffield [0742] 7881) or inquire at National Travel at Victoria Station, London (tel. 01-730 0202)

Bee-Line National
(for coach holidays at home and abroad)

Area offices:

London (for Southern England, Midlands, South Wales and Scotland): Bee-Line Roadways International Ltd, 20–26 Nunhead Lane, London SE15 3OA (tel. 01-639 5261)

Leeds (for Yorkshire and Lancashire): Bee-Line Roadways Continental Ltd, 264A Roundhay Road, Leeds 9 (tel. Leeds [0532] 625121)

Middlesbrough (for North-east England): Bee-Line Roadways Ltd, 463 Linthorpe Road, Middlesbrough (tel. Middlesbrough [0642] 822950)

Whitchurch, Salop (for Salop, Cheshire, the Potteries and North Wales): Salopia Coaches Ltd, Green End, Whitchurch, Salop (tel. Whitchurch [0948] 2361)

Some major independent coach companies:

Wallace Arnold

Head office: 53 Corn Exchange, Leeds 1 (tel. Leeds [0532] 30691)

Main offices:

Bradford: 48/50 Morley Street (tel. Bradford [0274] 27371)

Castleford: 56A Carlton Street (tel. Castleford [0977] 552778)

Dundee: 45 Reform Street (tel. Dundee [0382] 22322/4)

Edinburgh: 10 Queensferry Street, Edinburgh 2 (tel. 031-225 1402)

Glasgow: 345 Sauchiehall Street, Glasgow C2 (tel. 041-332 5462/5662)

Hull: 13 Story Street (tel. Hull [0482] 20355)

London: 8 Park Lane, Croydon CR9 1DN (tel. 01-462 7733)

Paignton: Wallace Arnold Tours (Devon) Ltd, 16 Torbay Road (tel. Paignton [0803] 521441)

Scarborough: North Garage, Columbus Ravine (tel. Scarborough [0723] 75522)

Sheffield: 16 Arundel Gate (tel. Sheffield [0742] 731651)

Blue Cars (Southbound) Ltd

London Road, East Grinstead, Sussex RH19 1HU (tel. East Grinstead [0342] 27181)

Clipper Coaches

(good for Spain) Continental House, Royal Parade Chislehurst, Kent (tel. 01-467 0106)

Consort

(good for Spain) 12 New Burlington Street, London W1 (tel. 01-734 7492)

Cosmos *Coach Tours Ltd*

Cosmos House, 1 Bromley Common, Bromley, Kent BR2 9LXO (tel. 01-464 3477)

Thomas Cook

PO Box 36, Peterborough, and 45 Berkeley Street, London W1A 1EB (tel. 01-499 4000)

Thomson Holidays

Greater London House, Hampstead Road, London NW1 7SD (tel. 01-387 9321)

REGIONAL BUS COMPANIES
(National Bus)

In England and Wales

Bristol Omnibus Co. Ltd, Berkeley House, Lawrence Hill, Bristol BS5 0DZ (tel. Bristol [0272] 558211)

City of Oxford Motor Services Ltd, 395 Cowley Road, Oxford OX4 2DJ (tel. Oxford [0865] 774611)

Crossville Motor Services Ltd, Crane Wharf, Chester CH1 3SQ (tel. Chester [0244] 315400)

Cumberland Motor Services Ltd, PO Box 17, Tangier Street, Whitehaven, Cumbria CA28 7XF (tel. Whitehaven [0946] 3781)

Eastern Counties Omnibus Co. Ltd, PO Box 10, 79 Thorpe Road, Norwich NR1 1UB (tel. Norwich [0603] 60421)

Eastern National Omnibus Co. Ltd, New Writtle Street, Chelmsford, Essex CM2 0SD (tel. Chelmsford [0245] 56151)

East Kent Road Car Co. Ltd, Station Road West, Canterbury, Kent CT2 8AL (tel. Canterbury [0227] 66151)

East Midlands Motor Services Ltd, New Street, Chesterfield, Derbyshire S40 1LQ (tel. Chesterfield [0246] 77451)

East Yorkshire Motor Services Ltd, 252 Anlaby Road, Hull HU3 2RS (tel. Hull [0482] 27142)

Gosport & Fareham Omnibus Co., Gosport Road, Fareham, Hampshire (tel. Fareham [03292] 2208)

Hants and Dorset Motor Services Ltd, The Square, Bournemouth, Hampshire BG2 5AB (tel. Bournemouth [0202] 23371)

Lincolnshire Road Car Co. Ltd, PO Box 15, St Mark Street, Lincoln LN5 7BB (tel. Lincoln [0522] 22255)

London Country Bus Services Ltd, Bell Street, Reigate, Surrey RH2 7LE (tel. Reigate [073 72] 42411)

Maidstone & District Motor Services Ltd, Knightrider House, Knightrider Street, Maidstone, Kent ME15 6LR (tel. Maidstone [0622] 52211)

Midland Red Omnibus Co. Ltd, Midland House, 1 Vernon Road, Edgbaston, Birmingham B16 9SJ (tel. 021-454 4808)

Northern General Transport Co. Ltd, 117 Queen Street, Gateshead NE8 2UA (tel. Gateshead [0632] 605144)

Potteries Motor Traction Co. Ltd, Woodhouse Street, Stoke-on-Trent ST4 1EQ (tel. Stoke-on-Trent [0782] 48811)

Ribble Motor Services Ltd, Frenchwood Avenue, Preston, Lancashire PR1 4LU (tel. Preston [0772] 54754)

Southdown Motor Services Ltd, Southdown House, Freshfield Road, Brighton BN2 2BW (tel. Brighton [0273] 66711)

South Wales Transport Co. Ltd, 31 Russell Street, Swansea SA1 4HP (tel. Swansea [0792] 50751)

Southern Vectis Omnibus Co. Ltd, Nelson Road, Newport, Isle of Wight PO30 1RD (tel. Newport [098 381] 2456)

Thames Valley and Aldershot Omnibus Ltd, 3 Thorn Walk, Reading, RG1 7AX (tel. Reading [0734] 54046)

Trent Motor Traction Co. Ltd. Uttoxeter New Road, Derby DE3 3NJ (tel. Derby [0332] 43201)

United Automobile Services Ltd, United House, Grange Road, Darlington, Durham DL1 5NL (tel. Darlington [0325] 65252)

United Counties Omnibus Co. Ltd, Bedford Road, Northampton NN1 5NN (tel. Northampton [0604] 35661)

West Riding Automobile Co. Ltd, Barnsley Road, Wakefield WF1 5JX (tel. Wakefield [0924] 75521)

West Yorkshire Road Car Co. Ltd, East Parade, Harrogate, Yorkshire HG1 5LS (tel. Harrogate [0423] 66061)

Western National Omnibus Co. Ltd, National House, Queen Street, Exeter EX4 3TF (tel. Exeter [0392] 74191)

Western Welsh Omnibus Co. Ltd, 253 Cowbridge Road West, Ely, Cardiff, South Glamorgan CF5 5XX (tel. Cardiff [0222] 591371)

Yorkshire Traction Co. Ltd, Upper Sheffield Road, Barnsley, South Yorkshire S70 4PP (tel. Barnsley [0226] 82476)

Yorkshire Woollen District Transport Co. Ltd, Barnsley Road, Wakefield WF1 5JX (tel. Wakefield [0924] 75521)

In Scotland

For all inquiries from the south of England to Scotland:

Scottish Coach Travel Centre, 298 Regent Street, London W1R 6LE (tel. 01-636 9373)

For all inquiries from Scotland to south of the border:

Scottish Omnibus Ltd, New Street, Edinburgh, (tel. 031-556 2515)

The following companies in the Scottish Transport Group operate *both bus and coach* services:

W. Alexander & Sons (Northern) Ltd, The Bus Station, Guild Street, Aberdeen AB9 2DR (tel. Aberdeen [0224] 51381)

W. Alexander & Sons (Midland) Ltd, Brown Street, Camelon, Falkirk FK1 4PY (tel. Falkirk [0324] 23901)

W. Alexander & Sons (Fife) Ltd, Esplanade, Kirkcaldy, Fife (tel. Kirkcaldy [0592] 61461)

Central SMT Co. Ltd, Traction House, Hamilton Road, Motherwell ML1 3DS (tel. Motherwell [0698] 63575)

Highland Omnibuses Ltd, The Bus Station, Seafield Road, Inverness IV1 1LT (tel. Inverness [0463] 37575)

Scottish Omnibuses Ltd, New Street, Edinburgh (tel. 031-556 2515)

Western SMT Co. Ltd, Nursery Avenue, Kilmarnock (tel. Kilmarnock [0563] 22551)

In Northern Ireland

Ulster Bus Co. Headquarters, Milewater Road, Belfast 3 (tel. Belfast [0232] 44791)

In Republic of Ireland

CIE, Heuston Station, Dublin 8 (tel. Dublin [0001] 77187)

SOME OF THE BIG CITY BUS COMPANIES

Greater Glasgow Public Transport Executive (PTE), Buchanan St, Glasgow (tel. 041-332 6811)

Greater Manchester PTE (this includes Lancashire United Transport Ltd, Godfrey Abbott Group Ltd, Dial-A-Ride Ltd, Selnec Parcel Express Co. Ltd), Portland Street, Manchester (tel. 061-273 3322)

London Transport Executive, 55 Broadway, London sw1 (tel. 01-222 1234)

Merseyside PTE, 24 Hatton Gardens, Liverpool (tel. 051-236 7411)

South Yorkshire PTE, Exchange Street, Sheffield (tel. Sheffield [0742] 78688)

Tyne and Wear PTE, Cuthbert House, All Saints, Newcastle upon Tyne (tel. Newcastle [0632] 610431)

West Midlands PTE, 16 Summer Lane, Birmingham (tel. 021-622 5151)

West Yorkshire, Swinegate, Leeds (tel. Leeds [0532] 451601)

Many local authorities run their own bus services; for information contact the local Town Hall.

Cheap Rail Travel

You may *still* be able to afford train fares, provided you know what discounts are available and when they apply and are able to forge your way through the lunatic names they think up for their complicated schemes.

BRITISH RAIL AT HOME

What *is* the point of British Rail offering discounts – supposedly to entice us into keeping the railways running at full steam – when only about 2 per cent of their travelling public can understand them?

The *Economy Return* book-ahead bargain ticket for mid-week travel can save you 5 per cent. Booking at least one week in advance you get a return journey for the single fare. The minimum fare is £6, and you can book by telephone *with your local travel agent* if you wish. The catch is that you have to stay away for five or nine days.

Awayday Return is a day return ticket (generally second class) that gives discounts of up to 45 per cent on

the standard fare. On weekdays you can travel only after the rush hour ends at 9.30 a.m. and must return the same day.

Weekend Return (a very handy ticket). The Friday to Monday ticket that saves you up to 30 per cent on the standard return fare. First- and second-class tickets are available for most journeys over seventy-five miles, so if you're going anywhere at the weekend *never* pay the ordinary fare. You don't have to go on Friday or return on Monday; you can travel any time in between, except that you can't return on Friday.

The *Monthly Return* is the long-stay deal that saves you up to 25 per cent on the standard fare. First and second-class tickets are available on any day for most journeys over seventy-five miles. Valid for one month. The catch is that if you travel on a weekday you can't return before the following Saturday.

Economy Returns, Awayday, Weekend and Monthly Returns cannot be used on some trains, particularly during

*rush hours and at peak holiday times,
so check before booking.*

Anyone can get unlimited travel tickets called *Rail Rovers*, which give seven days of rail travel within different areas of the country. The price depends on the area, but if you intend to do much travelling they are marvellous money-savers. There is an even greater saving for one and a half people (or more) who remember to ask for a *Family Rail Rover*. Children are half price and nobody asks if they are *your* children, or whether the two of you are married or anything like that.

British Rail also do little package tour holidays in Britain called *Mini Maxi Holidays* and *Weekends*. They organize these with decent hotels (with no supplement for single rooms or private bath) in many of the major cities and seaside resorts. You can spend a weekend away from London in Canterbury or Chichester or Dover or Oxford at a very reduced rate. Children are half price (free if they're under three) provided that they share the parents' room.

Prices often include being met at the station, full English breakfast, V A T and service and sometimes dinner.

Other British Rail home discounts depend on your age. Children under three years of age travel *free*. Children over three and under fourteen travel for *half price*.

There are other British Rail concessions for students and old age pensioners (see p. 389).

Rail discounts are available for young people who travel abroad. *Transalpinó* specialize in them for under twenty-six-year-olds and run a number of schemes. One (in conjunction with Sealink) offers up to 50 per cent discount off standard rail fares anywhere in Europe. Details from Transalpino, 71 Buckingham Palace Road, London sw1 (tel. 01-834 9656).

For anyone under twenty-three there is the *Inter Rail Card* which buys a month's unlimited travel in nineteen foreign countries, and half-price fares in the country of origin and on Sealink. Currently it costs £83 and enables you to travel anywhere from the Arctic Circle to Marrakesh as well as Eastern Europe, or anywhere in between. The card also gets you reduced prices on many foreign shipping services. Get an application form from principal British Rail offices or travel agents and apply with passport or identity card at least five days in advance.

To plan your rail journeys, buy that travellers' Bible, the *Thomas Cook International Train Timetable*, which gives details of all principal rail routes in Europe, Eastern Europe, North Africa and the Near East. It's updated monthly and costs £2.50 from W. H. Smith.

France has a wonderful rail service, as one would expect in the cradle of modern civilization. You can get beautiful scenery: châteaux, rivers, good climate, the best food and wine in the world. If you want to go to Paris, my favourite way is by rail overnight, on the famous night ferry sleeper. You get on at Victoria, have a glass of champagne if you feel like it, and wake up at 8.30 a.m. in the middle of Paris, then trot off to the Ritz for breakfast. (Starve for the rest of the day, it's worth it.)

RAIL TRAVEL ABROAD

The *French Travel Service* is part of French Railways and offers very good package rail holidays – with accommodation not only in hotels but in flats, holiday villages, villas and camps. You can go to all the best places, including the Riviera, Brittany or the Pyrenees. Wherever you go on their packages (except Boulogne), travel from *any* mainland British Rail station in England, Scotland and Wales is included, so the inhabitants of Inverness or Penzance get a real bargain. Ten days camping in Brittany (La Boule, which has lovely beaches and pine forests) costs from £79 or around £110 in a hotel. A millionaire holiday in Cannes or Nice on the Riviera costs from £134 with half board, service included. Ten days full board in Menton costs from £144 (service included).

These are indicative prices for 1979; write for a mouth-watering *free* brochure to French Travel Services, Eastern Section Offices, Hudson Place, Victoria Station, London sw1v 1jx (tel. 01-834 9214).

There are also good inclusive rail package holidays to Belgium, the Netherlands and Germany via *British Rail Sealink*. Many foreign national rail services also offer all-in holidays or special tourist discount tickets, so it's well worth inquiring at the appropriate national tourist offices (see p. 459), your travel agent or British Rail stations, or Sealink Travel Ltd, Inclusive Tours Section, Victoria Station, London sw1v 1jx (tel. 01-928 5151, ext. 7493).

WHICH LONDON STATION?

Which London stations serve which areas of the country?

Paddington	for:	Cornwall and the West, Wales (Oxford, Reading, Worcester, Gloucester, Cardiff, Bristol, Bath, Plymouth, Exeter)
Waterloo	for:	South and South West (Southampton, Portsmouth, Salisbury, Exeter)
Charing Cross	for:	Kent (Folkestone, Dover) and the Continent
Victoria	for:	Brighton line and the Continent
Euston	for:	Scotland (via the West), Midlands (Coventry, Birmingham, Wolverhampton, Manchester, Liverpool, Carlisle, Glasgow, Inverness)
St Pancras	for:	Midlands (Sheffield, Derby, Nottingham, Leicester)

INTER-CITY TRAIN SERVICE

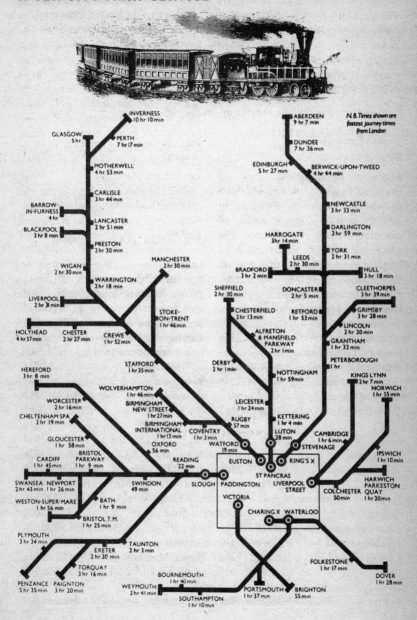

N.B. Times shown are fastest journey times from London

INVERNESS 10 hr 10 min
GLASGOW 5hr
PERTH 7 hr 17 min
MOTHERWELL 4 hr 53 min
CARLISLE 3 hr 44 min
BARROW-IN-FURNESS 4 hr
BLACKPOOL 3 hr 8 min
LANCASTER 2 hr 51 min
PRESTON 2 hr 30 min
WIGAN 2 hr 30 min
MANCHESTER 2 hr 30 min
WARRINGTON 2 hr 18 min
LIVERPOOL 2 hr 31 min
STOKE-ON-TRENT 1 hr 46 min
HOLYHEAD 4 hr 37 min
CHESTER 2 hr 27 min
CREWE 1 hr 52 min

ABERDEEN 9 hr 7 min
DUNDEE 7 hr 36 min
EDINBURGH 5 hr 27 min
BERWICK-UPON-TWEED 4 hr 44 min
NEWCASTLE 3 hr 33 min
DARLINGTON 2 hr 59 min
HARROGATE 3 hr 14 min
YORK 2 hr 31 min
LEEDS 2 hr 30 min
BRADFORD 3 hr 2 min
HULL 3 hr 18 min
SHEFFIELD 2 hr 30 min
DONCASTER 2 hr 5 min
CLEETHORPES 3 hr 39 min
CHESTERFIELD 2 hr 13 min
RETFORD 1 hr 53 min
GRIMSBY 3 hr 28 min
LINCOLN 2 hr 20 min
ALFRETON & MANSFIELD PARKWAY 2 hr 1 min
GRANTHAM 1 hr 32 min
PETERBOROUGH 1 hr
DERBY 2 hr 1 min
NOTTINGHAM 1 hr 59 min
KINGS LYNN 2 hr 7 min
NORWICH 1 hr 55 min

HEREFORD 3 hr 8 min
STAFFORD 1 hr 35 min
WOLVERHAMPTON 1 hr 46 min
WORCESTER 2 hr 16 min
BIRMINGHAM NEW STREET 1 hr 27 min
LEICESTER 1 hr 24 min
CHELTENHAM SPA 2 hr 19 min
BIRMINGHAM INTERNATIONAL 1 hr 13 min
RUGBY 57 min
KETTERING 1 hr 4 min
CAMBRIDGE 1 hr 6 min
GLOUCESTER 1 hr 58 min
COVENTRY 1 hr 3 min
LUTON 28 min
IPSWICH 1 hr 10 min
CARDIFF 1 hr 45 min
BRISTOL PARKWAY 1 hr 9 min
OXFORD 56 min
WATFORD 19 min
STEVENAGE
READING 22 min
EUSTON
KING'S X
SWANSEA 2 hr 43 min
NEWPORT 1 hr 26 min
SWINDON 49 min
SLOUGH
PADDINGTON
ST PANCRAS
LIVERPOOL STREET
HARWICH PARKESTON QUAY 1 hr 20 min
WESTON-SUPER-MARE 1 hr 56 min
BATH 1 hr 9 min
VICTORIA
COLCHESTER 50 min
BRISTOL T.M. 1 hr 25 min
CHARING X
WATERLOO
PLYMOUTH 3 hr 34 min
TAUNTON 2 hr 3 min
EXETER 2 hr 30 min
FOLKESTONE 1 hr 17 min
TORQUAY 3 hr 16 min
BOURNEMOUTH 1 hr 40 min
DOVER 1 hr 28 min
PENZANCE 5 hr 35 min
PAIGNTON 3 hr 20 min
WEYMOUTH 2 hr 41 min
PORTSMOUTH 1 hr 37 min
BRIGHTON 55 min
SOUTHAMPTON 1 hr 10 min

King's Cross   for: The North (via the East Midlands) (Doncaster, York,
                          Leeds, Newcastle, Edinburgh, Aberdeen, Grimsby)
Liverpool   for: The Continent, East Anglia (Cambridge, Norwich,
Street   Ipswich, Harwich, Colchester)

RAILWAY STATION TELEPHONE NUMBERS

It's easy to ring them, but whether or not they answer is another matter.

**London terminals and
telephone numbers**

Inter-city information:

Charing Cross	01-928 5100
Euston	01-387 7070
King's Cross	01-837 3355
Liverpool Street	01-283 7171
Paddington	01-262 6767
Victoria	01-928 5100
Waterloo	01-928 5100

Continental information:
Sealink Services

via Harwich	01-834 2345
via Folkestone and Dover	01-834 2345
via Newhaven	01-834 2345
Seaspeed Services	
via Dover	01-606 3681

Channel Islands information:
Sealink services

via Weymouth	01-834 2345

Irish services information:
Sealink services

via Fishguard	01-262 6767
via Holyhead	01-387 7070
via Stranraer	01-387 7070

Sleeper reservations:
Euston   01-387 9400, ext. 3901

King's Cross	01-837 3677
Paddington	01-723 7000, ext. 2608

Motorail information:

Kensington Olympia	01-603 4555

Other station telephone numbers

Station	Telephone
Aberdeen	[0224] 53511
Barrow-in-Furness	[0229] 20805
Bath Spa	[0225] 63075
Berwick upon Tweed	[0289] 6711
Birmingham International (for exhibition centre)	[021-643] 2711
Birmingham New Street	[021-643] 2711
Blackpool North	[0253] 20061
Bournemouth	[0202] 28216
Bradford Exchange	[0274] 33994
Brighton	[0273] 25476
Bristol Parkway	[0272] 294255
Bristol Temple Meads	[0272] 294255
Cambridge	[0223] 59711
Cardiff Central	[022] 28000
Carlisle	[0228] 25146
Carmarthen	[0267] 7483
Cheltenham Spa	[0452] 29501
Chester	[0244] 26511
Chesterfield	[0246] 74371
Cleethorpes	[0472] 61144

MAP OF LONDON UNDERGROUND

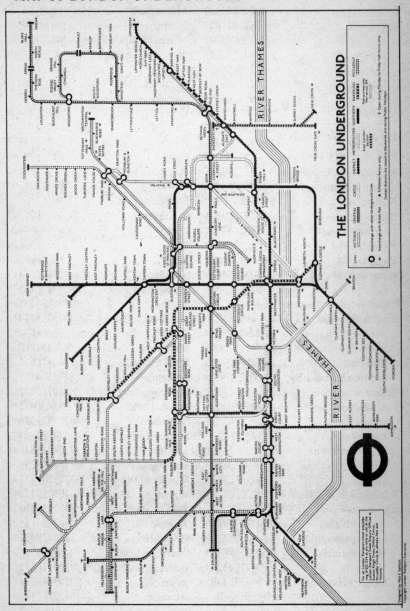

THE LONDON UNDERGROUND

Designed by Paul E. Garbutt
Copyright London Transport Executive

Station	Telephone	Station	Telephone
Coventry	[0203] 23131	Motherwell	[0698] 66122
Crewe	[0782] 411411	Neath	[0639] 56388
Darlington	[0325] 55111	Newcastle upon Tyne	[0632] 26262
Derby	[0332] 32051	Newport, Gwent	[0633] 57502
Doncaster	[0302] 20191	Norwich	[0603] 20255
Dover Priory	[0227] 65151	Nottingham	[0602] 46151
Dumfries	[0387] 5115	Nuneaton	[0682] 5600
Dundee	[0382] 26844	Oxford	[0865] 41744
Durham	[0385] 3737	Paris Nord	[010-331-326] 77-28
Edinburgh	[031-556] 2541	Penzance	[0736] 5831
Exeter St David's	[0392] 33551	Perth	[0738] 23366
Folkestone Central	[0227] 65151	Peterborough	[0733] 68181
Fort William	[0397] 3791	Plymouth	[0752] 21300
Glasgow Central	[041-221] 3223	Portsmouth and	
Gloucester	[0452] 29501	Southsea	[0705] 25771
Grimsby Town	[0472] 53556	Port Talbot	[063984] 4424
Halifax	[0422] 54207	Preston	[0772] 59439
Harrogate	[0423] 66421/2	Rugby	[0788] 6363
Hartlepool	[0429] 4039	Sheffield	[0742] 26411
Hereford	[0432] 66534	Shrewsbury	[0743] 51571
Holyhead	[0407] 2304	Southampton	[0703] 29393
Huddersfield	[0484] 31226	Stafford	[0782] 411411
Hull	[0482] 21633/4	Stirling	[0786] 3812
Inverness	[0463] 32651	Stockport	[061-832] 8353
Ipswich	[0473] 57373	Stockton	[0642] 67524
Kettering for Corby	[0536] 3416	Stoke-on-Trent	[0782] 411411
Kilmarnock	[0563] 23651	Stranraer Harbour	[0776] 2262
King's Lynn	[0553] 2021	Sunderland	[0783] 41218
Kirkcaldy	[0592] 65511	Swansea	[0792] 50317
Lancaster	[0524] 2333	Swindon	[0793] 6804
Leamington Spa	[0926] 23101	Taunton	[0823] 83444
Leeds	[0532] 36163	Torquay	[0803] 25911
Leicester	[0533] 29811	Wakefield Westgate	[0924] 71777
Lincoln St Mark's	[0522] 27234	Warrington Bank Quay	[0925] 32245
Liverpool		Weston-super-Mare	[0934] 21131
Lime Street	[051-709] 9696	Weymouth	[03057] 5501
Loughborough	[05093] 2201	Wigan North Western	[0942] 42231
Manchester Piccadilly	[061-832] 8353	Wolverhampton	[0902] 20995
Middlesbrough	[0642] 43208	Worcester Shrub Hill	[0905] 27211
Milford Haven	[0437] 4361	York	[0904] 25671

Your Flying Lesson

This section is intended to give a snapshot view of the sort of schemes and offers available at one particular time; it must be stressed that they are changing all the time, so the details given here cannot be regarded as definitive or constant.

The air is as full of initials as it is of planes and to find your way round the bureaucracy of the air it is wise to know what the initials stand for and what they are up to.

A LIST OF USEFUL INITIALS

CAA

Civil Aviation Authority, one of the two British government organizations which regulate airlines in Britain. The Department of Trade and Industry regulates foreign airlines that do business in Britain.

AUC

Airline Users' Committee (the ones you complain to in the last resort), which was set up by the CAA to represent the customers. The AUC is the flying *consumer's* watchdog organization. It looks into individual complaints if you haven't been able to get a complaint dealt with by the airline that did you wrong.

BAA

British Airports Authority. The state organization that operates some of the biggest airports (Heathrow, Gatwick, Stansted (Essex), Glasgow, Edinburgh, Prestwick and Aberdeen). The Scottish Highlands and Islands airports are owned by the CAA, and the rest of the public airports are owned by local authorities.

ABTA

Association of British Travel Agents and Tour Operators. This very powerful organization is the first one you complain to if something goes wrong on your holiday (flying or otherwise) *provided* you booked through one of their members. It runs a compensation scheme against members' bankruptcy, and enforces a code of conduct. Beware of operators and agents who don't belong to ABTA.

ATOL

Air Travel Organizer's Licence. Issued by the CAA to tour operators or ABC operators (see below) whose financial standing and fitness are approved by the CAA. But note that it refers only to air travel (coach holidays are excluded for example), and not to *all* air holidays (flying to the Channel Islands isn't covered for instance). Check that your travel operator is licensed. All licensed tour organizers must quote their ATOL number in advertisements and brochures. There are four types of ATOL and the type is indicated by a letter against the licence number:

A = advance booking charter flights (ABCs);

B = inclusive tour flights (ITs), e.g. as part of a package holiday;

C = seats on certain other flights, such as flights carrying a group of people to attend a special event;

D = the licence holder is a broker.

Example: ATOL 9999AB shows that the holder is authorized to advertise, offer and sell seats on ABC and IT flights. You can check directly with the CAA at: Civil Aviation Authority, CAA House, 45–59 Kingsway, London WC2B 6TE (tel. 01-379 7311, ext. 2680).

IATA

International Air Transport Association. The price-fixing club to which most of the national airlines belong.

IATA regulations and rulings are the key to nearly all the exasperating and illogical idiocies of air travel. It also runs a sort of financial clearing house, based in Geneva, where it efficiently settles all members' debts to each other, e.g. through switching of flights by passengers. However, ticket refunds to the public often take a long time (up to a year) because they are routed through Geneva.

Scheduled flights are the regular services which the major airlines contract to run, and must run according to their issued schedules. They are mainly for business travellers and passengers who are making their own independent travel arrangements, but this is beginning to change as some airlines (British Caledonian, for instance) introduce a third cabin for people using the really low fares. There are bargain buys on scheduled flights, known as 'promotional' fares (e.g. the British Airways 'Poundstretcher'), a general name to cover IATA-approved discount fares. There may easily be cheaper ways of getting where you want, so shop around.

APEX

Advance Purchase Excursion. These are for scheduled airline flights only. *Always* check the APEX fare, which, apart from the USA, is likely to be your cheapest bet on a scheduled flight; it might cut the cost by half. An APEX ticket must be bought at a specified time before the flight, from three weeks to three months, and insure against the possibility of your not catching the plane because cancellation charges can go up to 100 per cent. APEX destinations include Canada, United States, Bermuda, Caribbean, Mexico, Malta, South Africa, Pakistan, Sri Lanka, Bangkok, Kuala Lumpur, Singapore, Hong Kong, Italy, Greece, Yugoslavia, Turkey, Ireland, Manchester, Glasgow, Cyprus, Gibraltar, Scandinavia and Australia. More European destinations are gradually being introduced.

ABC

Advance Booking Charter is the charter equivalent of APEX, and can be cheaper, but do compare prices, especially for children. It only operates, at time of writing, to Canada, USA, and Caribbean. With ABCs you buy air travel twenty-one to forty-five days in advance. If you cancel a reservation or miss a plane the organizer is not required to return any of your money, so insure properly. The other fly in the ointment is that ABC prices can only be offered with full or near full loads and if a flight does not sell well it may be cancelled or consolidated with another flight, which may operate at a different time, on a different day, or from a different place – none of which might suit you. Get the CAA's free leaflet *Flight Plan* from CAA Printing & Publication Services, PO Box 41, Cheltenham, Gloucestershire, (tel. 0242-35151), or your travel agent.

On ABC or APEX you always have to book in advance and generally have to stay away for at least seven days. You cannot change departure and return dates once booked and paid for.

IPEX

Instant Purchase Excursions, for gamblers going to Europe, which can save up to 40 per cent of the normal return. This is a cut-price, last-minute specific booking with non-refundable fare for a *scheduled* airline. Fares mainly apply to short hops, when they can be very cheap indeed; destinations include Paris, Le Touquet, Amsterdam, Rotterdam, Brussels and Ostend. The ticket usually has to be booked after 2 p.m. on the day before you travel, at the earliest. IPEX tickets are for travel on a specific flight out and a specific flight back. Reservations cannot be changed and if you miss the outward flight you have to buy a new ticket for a later flight at the normal fare.

HOW TO SAVE MONEY ON AIRFARES

You can easily, safely and legally save *up to two thirds on airfares.* You should never have to pay the full, scheduled airfare for a return journey except in emergency, when you can't plan ahead, or if you are going to be away for less than four days.

It is easy but risky to be beguiled by the cut-price small ads in the personal columns of *The Times* or *Time Out*. But be careful. If it's a charter flight, or a package holiday, make sure that the tour operator has an ATOL licence in the right category (see p. 410), or you may never get your ticket, you may never arrive or if you do you may find yourself without a return flight.

The alternative is careful buying through a specialist agent who's got the time and the knowledge and can be bothered to take the trouble. But understanding the devious and complicated IATA fares and regulations is a specialist job which few agents understand. Much of the time the member airlines *themselves* don't know what fares they should be charging. In fact, the Airline Users' Committee say that the typical European fare structure is so irrational and complex that passengers cannot possibly know what fare they should be paying ...: 'There are plenty of opportunities for evasion, cheating and mistakes ...'

In my experience this applies worldwide, not just to Europe. You can lift the phone three times within an hour to the same airline and be quoted three different prices for the same trip. It is not surprising: there are at least forty different air fares between London and Paris (a flying time

of only forty minutes) and more than 100 different fares to New York. So, as with building and decorating estimates, it's worth getting at least two and preferably three quotes before buying your ticket. If you suspect your travel agent isn't quoting you the cheapest airfare available, contact the Tariff Section of the Civil Aviation Authority to check (tel. 01-379 7311, ext. 2347).

. There are guides to help you through the airfare jungle. One is a fascinating *free* leaflet, *A Plain Man's Guide to Air Fares*, intended for business travellers and published twice yearly (because winter and summer schedules are different). Get it from the Wakefield Fortune Group, either at one of their local travel agencies throughout Britain or from their head office at 97 Southampton Row, London WC1B 4BQ (tel. 01-580 8225). The guide is planned like a game of snakes and ladders; it takes only a minute to see what reductions might suit your arrangements in order to travel to a whole range of business destinations on *scheduled* flights (see Air Fares Chart, on facing page).

Thomas Cook also operate a special 'Air Fare Saving Guide' for people who travel a lot.

For the frequent and serious air traveller there is an excellent bimonthly magazine, *Business Traveller*, which charts the up-to-date and cheapest way to travel to different parts of the world. A yearly subscription costs £6. *Business Traveller*, Export Times Publishing Ltd, 60 Fleet Street, London EC4 (tel. 01-353 7582).

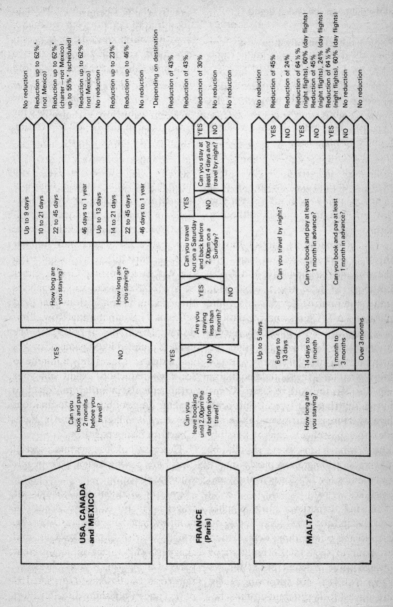

USA, CANADA and MEXICO

Can you book and pay 2 months before you travel?

- **YES** → How long are you staying?
  - Up to 9 days → No reduction
  - 10 to 21 days → Reduction up to 62%.* (not Mexico)
  - 22 to 45 days → Reduction up to 62%.* (charter—not Mexico) up to 55%.* (scheduled)
- **NO** → How long are you staying?
  - 46 days to 1 year → Reduction up to 62%.* (not Mexico)
  - Up to 13 days → No reduction
  - 14 to 21 days → Reduction up to 23%.*
  - 22 to 45 days → Reduction up to 46%.*
  - 46 days to 1 year → No reduction

*Depending on destination

FRANCE (Paris)

Can you leave booking until 2.00pm the day before you travel?

- **YES** → Reduction of 43%
- **NO** → Are you staying less than 1 month?
  - **YES** → Can you travel out on a Saturday and back before 2.00pm on a Sunday?
    - **YES** → Reduction of 43%
    - **NO** → Can you stay at least 4 days and travel by night?
      - **YES** → Reduction of 30%
      - **NO** → No reduction
  - **NO** → No reduction

MALTA

How long are you staying?

- Up to 5 days → Can you travel by night?
  - **YES** → No reduction
  - **NO** → Reduction of 45%
- 6 days to 13 days → Can you travel by night?
  - **YES** → Reduction of 24%
  - **NO** → Reduction of 64½% (night flights), 60% (day flights)
- 14 days to 1 month → Can you book and pay at least 1 month in advance?
  - **YES** → Reduction of 45%
  - **NO** → Reduction of 64½% (night flights), 60% (day flights)
- 1 month to 3 months → Can you book and pay at least 1 month in advance?
  - **YES** → No reduction
  - **NO** → No reduction
- Over 3 months

Discounts on scheduled flights

Some reductions are known as 'concessionary' or 'promotional' fares. For instance, in the UK it would cost you less to travel outside the peak hours to Belfast, Edinburgh and Glasgow from Gatwick, rather than from Heathrow.

Night flights are always cheaper than day flights and you can get reductions on particular days of the week. In Europe you can often get cheaper flights over the weekend because businessmen don't want to travel then.

Spouse Fares: These are available to husbands and wives travelling out and home together to any point in Europe, Algeria or Morocco for not longer than five days. *Reduction:* First passenger nil, spouse 50 per cent.

Youth Fares to Europe and North America: For passengers under twenty-two. *Reduction:* 25 per cent. Youth discounts are available on all European excursion fares (see p. 415). except APEX and those to Spain, the Group Three fares to Portugal, and the 'instant' fares to Belgium, France and Holland. Up to 44 per cent reduction (depending on destination) to USA, Canada and Mexico for passengers under the age of twenty-four who delay booking until five days (seven days for Mexico) before departure date in both directions.

Family Fares to the Middle East: These are available to husbands, wives and children between twelve and twenty-one inclusive, travelling outwards together (return travel may be undertaken independently). The fares do not apply to Tel Aviv. Everybody travelling gets 50 per cent reduction, except the head of the family.

Child Reductions: Infants pay only 10 per cent of the fare. *Children* two to twelve years old can get a 50 per cent reduction, except on IPEX. It can sometimes be cheaper to book this than a 'promotional' scheme such as 'Poundsaver', which doesn't offer such big reductions. The saving may even be greater than on a cheap package tour. On ABC fares reductions for children between two and twelve range from 10 to 25 per cent depending on season and provided that there is one adult travelling with each child. APEX fares normally give a 25 per cent reduction. Schoolchildren in groups of ten can get up to 65 per cent off economy fares.

Group Three Fares (Portugal): For a minimum of three people, spending multiples of from one to seven weeks away: the group could be three children, or two children and an adult (children aged between two and twelve years old). Group Three fares are available on regular scheduled services. Reductions can be over 60 per cent and you must book at least two weeks before you go and children *still* get their *full* 50 per cent reduction on the fare. By contract on a package tour holiday, a child may only get a discount of 10 per cent (opportunities here for Hire-a-Child). These tickets can be cancelled without losing money.

Group Two Fares (Spain): Exactly the same as Group Three, except that just two people (one can be a child) qualify.

Excursion fares: These fares are *not* APEX or ABC. They cost more, but you can travel on scheduled flights with no advance booking. It sounds crazy, but how long you can stay depends on where you go. For instance, Europe is generally a minimum six days, maximum thirty days, North America fourteen days to forty-five days (which is maddening if you want to go for a shorter business trip, but if that's your situation, see below). In theory Australia is twenty-one to 270 days, but by using a 'One Way Excursion' fare *both ways*, you can stay for a longer or shorter period than this. Fifty per cent reductions for children under twelve.

Where concessionary fares apply on British scheduled services:

Children: UK, Europe and beyond

School parties: UK and Europe, except Eire

Young persons: UK, Europe, North America and Middle East

Students: UK, Europe and beyond

Spouses: Europe, Algeria and Morocco

Blind passengers and attendants (accompanied): UK (not on holiday)

Members of HM Forces: UK, Europe, (Cyprus, Gibraltar, Federal Republic of Germany, Malta and Berlin) and Hong Kong

Ships' crews: Europe and beyond

Common interest groups: Europe

Groups of three passengers travelling together (this can be two adults and a child): Europe (Spain and Portugal)

There are various *businessmen's cut-price package deals*, schemes run by such firms as American Express, Thomas Cook and Wakefield Fortune, aimed at businessmen but available to everybody. I rather like Lunn Poly's example for travel to North and South America, Australia, Africa and the Far East. There are regular departures (for instance, every week to New York, every fortnight to Tokyo) and you needn't book weeks ahead, but around sixteen days in advance. You have to stay at least seven to fourteen days. You travel by normal scheduled flight – but the flight *plus* first-class accommodation (in the category of that country) can cost less than the normal scheduled excursion flights alone. It's called Fare Deal and claims to save up to 50 per cent on normal prices. Get further information from Lunn Poly Ltd, Special Business Tours, 232 Vauxhall Bridge Road, London, sw 1 v 1 ds (tel. 01-828 0505).

Throw-away accommodation schemes are the keenest cuts of all, run by independent tour operators, *not* scheduled flights. Basically it's a cunning legal idea to bring down the price of air travel.

The international regulations allow charter companies to undercut scheduled air flights if they provide accommodation as part of a package holiday. There is no need for the passenger to use the accommodation. So the charter companies do one of two things:

1 They provide minimal accommodation, possibly in dormitories (called Cheapies, Thrifties, Wanderer, etc.; see 'Bargain basement holidays', p. 435).

2 They don't bother to provide anything but charge you £1 to hire from you the accommodation that you have already arranged. They then immediately hire it back to you at no extra charge. That's the theory. There's no check as to where you stay and what you do. Schemes such as these are run by Laker and Thomson.

WHO PACKS THE PACKAGE?

A package tour usually consists of the return airfare, plus hotel accommodation and food at the other end. It can also include car hire, villa holidays, sea cruises and camping trips instead of hotel accommodation.

The tour operator is the person who packs and ties the package. He keeps prices down in a number of ways. The IATA regulations allow him to cut airfares only if he throws in the extras that make up a package. Freed from the restrictions of IATA scheduled flights (and their fancy prices) he can charge something like the real cost price of a flight. One travel agent estimated that charter company flights can run at one third of the cost of a scheduled airline, largely because they run only the flights they can fill. They don't use clapped-out planes.

The days are over when charter flights were made on wobbly turbo-props pensioned off from the national airlines. Most big tour operators use the same planes as the big airlines, although a tour operator will generally put more seats in.

If tour operators have empty seats on their planes they often cut prices to make sure they fill them. That's why odd-length holidays (eleven days from Tuesday to eight days from Wednesday) and out-of-season trips are cheaper. You can often get a very good discount package if you have the nerve to wait until the last moment when many big companies will knock a few pounds off the brochure prices.

The other area in which tour operators save money is in accommodation, largely through long-term block bookings of hotel rooms.

In general the *best bets* are holidays run by a major tour operator which has its own airline. Laker, Thomson and Cosmos operate their own jet airline and other companies are setting them up. British Airways have package holiday subsidiaries, called Enterprise and Sovereign. Enterprise fly charter flights by British Airways and specialize in family packages at a fairly low price. They cost about 20 per cent less than Sovereign holidays and usually pick cheaper hotels in more popular areas (Benidorm rather than Mombasa, for instance). Sovereign flies holidaymakers out on scheduled flights. They often go to the more expensive places (Kenya, for instance) and they stay in more expensive hotels.

SOME OF THE BEST AND CHEAPEST AIR PACKAGES

Specialists in certain areas are worth investigating, because they may be more experienced and are on the spot; they have already made their first mistakes and are therefore the most likely to offer the best deal, which may not always be the cheapest.

Before you go to your travel agent, do some preliminary research through the national tourist offices of the countries you want to visit (see pp. 459–61 for addresses) and then ask your travel agent to give you brochures.

Here is a list of the most popular holiday resorts and the firms that specialize in them:

Spanish mainland

Britain's number one choice for sunny budget holidays.

Leisure Holidays, Thomson, Cosmos, Intasun, Global, Sovereign, Blue Sky, Laker, Wings.

Many operators offer free holidays for children out of season but you must inquire early in the year. Thomson lay on special extras for children in many resorts, including *free baby-sitting service.* Try Intasun for really low prices, but don't expect little extras.

Balearic Islands

Minorca: A lovely island for children – beautiful beaches and safe bathing, *but* transport is needed and public transport is difficult. There are some wonderful secluded beaches waiting to be found by the explorer who hires a car and goes looking for them.

See Spanish mainland (above) for operators.

Majorca: Still has something for everyone; Palma with its cathedral, excellent shopping, bull-ring and innumerable bars (including the inevitable British pub). Some beautiful spots, especially on the north-east and north-west coasts. Formentor on the extreme north of the island is also well worth a visit.

See Spanish mainland for operators.

Ibiza: Traditionally the anything goes resort for hippies and flower children, it's carefree, cheaper, sunny.

Canary Islands

Most popular as winter and early spring resorts. Not very suitable for children. Good, cheap cigars.

Tenerife: Adult-orientated. Except in the South and East, most beaches are black volcanic sand and not very safe for swimming.

Gran Canaria: Some good beaches; not as mountainous as Tenerife.

Lanzarote: Good beaches and swimming, less commercialized than the other two islands; quite barren in places with large moon-like craters.

Laker, Wings, Enterprise, Sovereign, Intasun, Global, Leisure Holidays, Cosmos (most offer the same good hotels, so check prices; Cosmos also feature self-catering hotel apartments, with excellent studio apartments, but the attached restaurants not always very inspiring).

Tunisia

A wonderful bargain. The food isn't special, but Tunisia offers miles of clean sea, miles of safe, golden beaches, tranquillity and gaiety. Everyone gathers round the huge hotel swimming pools, and there are lovely, cheap, jolly nightclubs, wonderful gardens awash with delphiniums, marigolds, daisies, wallflowers – and you are waited on hand, foot and everything else. After dusk, the night has a thousand hands and the waiters hide rosebuds in your table napkin. No need to diet because this is the land of the larger lady: the more there is, the more she is admired. Very restful.

You can ride camels into the Sahara desert, you can visit the Roman remains at Carthage and stand in the Colosseum and imagine that you are a Christian waiting for a lion (or vice versa). Avoid *Tunis*, but anywhere else is wonderful. *Hammamet* is one big lemon-tree-filled garden by the sea, *Sousse* is less resort-conscious, or you can fly to *Jerba* for a really restful island holiday.

Thomson, Cosmos, Enterprise.

Portugal

All the advantages of Spain without being so full of tourists.
Thomson, Enterprise, Sun Tours, Wings, Laker, Sovereign. Laker is good value and so are Wings and Sovereign (more expensive).

Malta

Not too many beaches – poor bathing. Some nightlife in hotel casinos. Be prepared for a quiet life. Added advantage – it is in the sterling area.

Intasun, Enterprise, Cosmos, Leisure Holidays, Thomson (their own hotel 'Mellieha Bay' is good for children, but a little isolated).

For more sophisticated holidays, try Exchange, Cadogan, Medallion, Malta Tours, Sovereign, Laker. (Exchange and Cadogan are perhaps the most expensive.)

Greek mainland

Athens: It's all been said and it's as good as you've heard. Of the main resorts, try Sounion with its beautiful sunsets. *Glyfada:* The Athens beach resort, very noisy; right in line of Athens Airport approach, and an American Airforce base is situated behind the resort. *Vouliagmeni:* Between Glyfada and Sounion.

Cosmos, Enterprise, Intasun, Thomson, Pontinental. Pontinental have three clubs which are very popular.

For *a really cheap holiday*, try Olympic Holidays 'Poundsavers', which provide air ticket and vouchers for basic accommodation in private homes and dormitories. No meals. Also try organized all-in packages, camping, cycling and youth hostelling holidays. This is probably the cheapest way of holidaying in Greece and the islands, and in a way (in season) it's one of the best.

Greek Islands

Not really cheap but exquisitely romantic. Ruined temples, wonderful bathing, dramatic views and some really remote islands where you can forget civilization.

Corfu: Thomson, Enterprise, Global OSL, Cosmos, Laker, Wings. Although not exactly inexpensive, these are about the best value for money. The more expensive operators are Olympic (except for their 'Poundsaver' deals), Sovereign, Allsun, Cooks.

Crete: As Corfu, with the exception of Global who do not deal in Crete:

Rhodes: As Corfu, with the exception of Global.

Yugoslavia

Still unspoilt, unexploited, beautiful, full of contrasts. Friendly people, good clean hotels, edible food, and choice of (usually stony) beaches, islands, lakes and mountains. Because of this variety contact the Yugoslavian Tourist Office rather than a travel agent to choose the sort of holiday you want. Address: 143 Regent Street, London w1 (tel. 01-734 8714 or 439 0399).

Yugotours (all resorts), Pilgrim (all resorts), Thomson (coast, mountains), Cosmos (coast, mountains), Laker (coast, cities), Sovereign (coast, cities), Enterprise (coast, cities), Blue Sky (coast, mountains and cities).

Romania

Also very cheap, with good beaches, soaring mountains, wonderful lakes and forests. Balkan, Sovereign, Sunquest, Blue Sky.

Italian Adriatic

There's nowhere as beautiful as Italy and the good news is that we can now afford to go there again because the Italian economy is in a worse state than ours, making the exchange to our advantage.

Blue Sky, CIT (which is owned by Italian State Railways, so it knows what it's doing; but it can be very expensive, so watch out), Cosmos, Cooks, Global, Thomson, Enterprise.

Sardinia

Charming island with plenty of local colour and history and the Aga Khan and all those jet-set people on the Costa Smeralda. Very friendly natives (and still a few bandits – so if you're driving out to the hills, stick to main routes and let someone know where you are going: seriously).

Magic of Sardinia, Thomson, Cooks or CIT for Forte Village, where there's masses to do for every age group and type; a really fun place – but not cheap (belongs to Trust House Forte, so a reliable standard).

Sicily

For romance, sunshine, wonderful scenery and the occasional vendetta. Again take bandits seriously: this is Godfather country.

Thomson, Cosmos, CIT, Wings.

France

Packaged air holidays aren't cheap. Contact the French Tourist Office for what's available and check with the French Travel Service for rail holidays (see p. 404). Inghams Discovery Tours do good-value tours of châteaux and have tours (with free tasting) in Burgundy and the Bordeaux district. Good package deals to Paris, notably the famous 'Time Off' hand-tailored, flexible, superbly comfortable tours in several price ranges. Also try Paris Travel Service, Stallards, Pegasus, Travelscene.

USA and Canada

Until ten years ago the average Briton didn't have as much hope of holidaying in North America as did Columbus. But then came charters ... and Fairy Godfather Freddie Laker. North American hospitality is amazingly warm, spontaneous and understanding; you're sure of a wonderful welcome. All the following operators offer many destinations. Camper holidays, which allow greater freedom, are increasingly popular.

Laker Airways do mini-packages with vouchers for hotels which you book when you arrive. (Food not usually included at hotels.) Laker fly about half a million people across the Atlantic each year. Otherwise try: American Express, Thomas Cook (USA only), TWA Getaway, Americana (USA only), Pan Am's World, Sovereign, Speedbird, Jetsave Vacations, Wembley Travel Centre (which flies by TWA and runs tours all over the USA and Canada, also holidays in Mexico).

If it is just the flight you want, then these are the options (the USA must now have more fare variations than any other destination; not all fares are available to all USA cities so you'll have some careful comparison to do):

ABC:* Advanced Booking Charters operated by Laker, Jetsave and British Airways Charter Travel. Fares vary according to season and destination but are some of the cheapest available. Advance booking twenty-one days. Period of stay must be between seven days and one year. For certain periods over sixty days there is an additional 'long stay' reduction.

APEX:* Not quite as cheap as charter (although good child reductions) but travel on guaranteed scheduled flights to a bigger choice of cities. Advance booking conditions the same as for charters. Period of stay seven to sixty days.

Budget (scheduled flights): Can be cheaper than ABCs to some destinations especially at high season. You must register for travel three weeks before the intended week of departure – the airline will then decide which day in that week you can travel so your arrangements must be flexible. A firm date is given at least ten days before date of travel.

---

* For Canada, the advance booking period on ABCs is thirty days, and the stay is typically two to six weeks with some operators offering longer periods; for APEX the advance booking period is thirty days and the period of stay fourteen to forty-five days.

Standby (scheduled flights): For those that are prepared to turn up at the airport on the chance that a seat will be available; the reduction is much the same as for Budget. Try the less heavily booked airlines such as Iran Air and Air India for a better chance of success.

Skytrain: Laker's famous pioneer cut-price from-Gatwick-to-New-York service. The principle is the same as stand-by except of course the whole aircraft is filled on the same basis, so you should have a better chance of a place.

Price comparable with A B Cs, Budget and Stand-by. Check in from 0400 hours at the Skytrain desk at Platform 2, Victoria Station, or at Gatwick; call 01-828 7766 for up-to-date availability, 01-828 4300 for general information.

Kenya

It's not cheap, but it's amazing value for a most luxurious holiday. Formerly possible only for Hemingway and sporting Royalty. All-in about £400 for a fortnight.

Sovereign, Rankin Kuhn, Wings and Speedbird offer a choice of beach or (more expensive) beach plus safari holidays.

Ireland

Cara Ireland Tours, for inclusive holidays with sea travel from Britain and thatched cottages to order: 52 Poland Street, London, w 1 v 4 A A (tel. 01-439 3987).

WINTER SPORTS

For wonderfully healthy winter holidays, Spain is definitely cheapest, followed by Austria and Italy, then France and finally Switzerland, which is undoubtedly the most expensive. You can even ski in the States now. Inghams are offering Lake Tahoe and Aspen.

If you want to stay in a chalet, contact Supertravel (22 Hans Place, London s w 1; (tel. 01-584 5060) either to join a party or form your own; discounts on a sliding scale for parties of six or more. You might apply to them for a job as a chalet girl (cook-housekeeper) for four or five months. You don't get paid very much (about £15 a week) but everything is thrown in including food and wine, fare out and free ski pass. Best to apply around June.

Spain

Easily the best skiing is at Solynieve, with ski-lifts and après-ski life (cheaper than in Austria or France, based on beer and *la bumba* – a half-pint mug of brandy and hot chocolate). Spain is good for beginners, second- and third-year skiers but the runs aren't long enough for experts, although there are good opportunities for off-piste skiing (fifteen-day air package around £90).

Thomson Holidays (who seem to have the run of Spain) for everywhere including Formigal, Cerlest and Panticosa; also Erna Low for Solynieve, Horizon Midlands for La Molina and Massela.

Austria

Inghams are the specialists for everywhere in Austria. Best bets are Kitzbuhel (magnificent skiing and exuberant nightlife) and St Anton. Both are internationally famous with very good facilities and those famous ski schools for advanced skiers as well as beginners (especially the renowned one at St Anton). Austria is especially cheerful and friendly, with all the cuckoo-clock-and-sleigh-bells atmosphere of Switzerland at far lower prices.

Specialists are:

For St Anton: Inghams; Global; Hards Ski-Plan. For Kitzbuhel: Inghams; Thomson. For Lech: Inghams, Erna Low. For Zurst: Erna Low. There are Supertravel chalets at St Anton and Lech.

Italy

Cortina is the most famous resort, then Cervinia and Sestriere. The Italian off-piste life has possibly more style and glamour than the Austrian, but it's just as cheerful and full of beans.

Inghams, Hards Ski-Plan, Swan, and John Morgan and Supertravel for chalets. Erna Low for Sestriere.

France

France has the best food, the best wine, the best nightlife, the best ski fashion and the toughest ski instructors (vicious little old gnomes, not big handsome blond beasts, as in Austria or Switzerland).

There are two sorts of resort, the old and the new. Of the well-established resorts, try Val d'Isère (I'd rather ski there than anywhere else in the world), Chamonix and Meribel. Specialists are Inghams, Thomson, Erna Low and Supertravel.

The new, modern Haute Savoie resorts are all huge concrete blocks that house almost the entire population. They're very compact so there's hardly any walking; you step straight out of your hotel on to the slopes. Very popular with families.

For Les Arcs: Thomson. For Avoriaz: John Morgan (chalets). For Flaine: Global Tours.

They all teach *ski evolutif* (short ski) so you learn quickly. The Ski Club of Great Britain, which takes complete beginners, finds that, if they learn with this method, beginners can take the most difficult runs within their first week, *and they generally get their bronze medal in two weeks.*

It's a good idea to join the SCGB before you go. The club has cheap charter flight schemes, cheap Saturday flights to Zurich and Geneva, cheap insurance and all the necessary ski know-how. Annual membership from £4 junior outside London to £12 for family country membership. Details from Ski Club of Great Britain, 118 Eaton Square, London sw1 (tel. 01-235 4711).

SOME BRITISH AIRLINES OPERATING SCHEDULED AND CHARTER SERVICES
(with area of operation of scheduled services)

Scheduled services

Air Anglia
UK, mainly eastern, Holland and Norway.
Norwich Airport, Fifers Lane, Norwich (tel. Norwich [0603] 44244).

Aurigny Air Services
UK – Channel Islands and Southampton – and France.

Weybridge, St Helier, Jersey, Channel Islands (tel. Jersey [0534] 35733).

British Air Ferries (not for cars any more)
Belgium, France, Holland and Switzerland.
Municipal Airport, Southend-on-Sea, Essex (tel. Southend-on-Sea [0702] 48601).

424

British Airways (Domestic, European, International)
London departure: Cromwell Road, London sw7 (Domestic and European without check-in facility).
London departure: Victoria Terminal, Buckingham Palace Road, London sw1w 9sr (Intercontinental with check-in facility).
All reservations: tel. 01-370 5411.
Departures and arrivals: tel. 01-759 3131

British Airways Helicopters
UK – Cornwall, Isles of Scilly.
The Heliport, Eastern Green, Penzance, Cornwall (tel. Penzance [0736] 4296).

British Caledonian Airways
UK, Belgium, France, Holland, Italy, Portugal, South America, Central Africa, West Africa and North Africa.
193 Piccadilly, London w1v 0ad (tel. 01-434 1676; reservations 01-668 4222).

British Island Airways
UK, France and Ireland.
Berkeley House, 51 High Street, Redhill rh1 1rx (tel. 01-668 7161).

British Midland Airways
UK, Belgium, Federal Republic of Germany, France and Holland.
East Midlands Airport, Castle Donington, nr Derby (tel. Derby [0332] 810741).

Brymon Aviation
UK – West Country and Scilly Isles

direct from Heathrow London and France.
Plymouth Airport, Plymouth, Devon, (tel. Plymouth [0752] 778002).

Dan-Air Services
UK, France, Holland, Norway and Switzerland.
Bilbao House, 36 New Broad Street, London, ec2m 1nh (tel. 01-638 4080).

Intra Airways
UK – Channel Islands, West Country and Cambridge – Belgium and France.
States Airport, Jersey (tel. Jersey [0534] 44171).

Charter services

British Airtours (part of British Airways)
Gatwick Airport, Horley, Sussex (tel. Crawley [0293] 36321.

British Caledonian
Far East, Europe, Africa, South America.
Gatwick Airport, Horley, Sussex (tel. Crawley [0293] 30211).

Britannia (affiliated to Thomson Holidays)
Mainly Europe.
Luton Airport, Bedfordshire (tel. Luton [0582] 21461).

Dan-Air
Europe, North America.

Gatwick Airport, Horley, Sussex (tel. Crawley [0293] 28822).

Laker Airways

North America, Spain, Balearics, Canaries, Italy and Greece.

9 Grosvenor Street, London w1 (tel. 01-493 5601; passenger inquiries 01-668 9363); and Gatwick Airport, Horley, Sussex (tel. Crawley [0293] 31222).

AIRPORT TELEPHONE NUMBERS

Aberdeen (Dyce) Dyce [0224] 722331
Alderney, Channel Isles
　　　　　　　　Alderney [048-182] 2711
Belfast (Aldergrove)
　　　　　　　　Belfast [0232] 29271
Benbecula, South Uist [0870] 2051
Birmingham　　　　　[021] 743 4272
Bournemouth (Hurn), Christchurch, Dorset Christchurch [020-15] 6311
Bristol (Lulsgate)
　　　　　　　　Lulsgate [027 587] 4441
Cardiff　　　　Rhoose [0446] 710296
Carlisle　　　　Carlisle [0228] 73641
Cork　　　　　　　　Cork 25341
Coventry　　Coventry [0203] 301717
Dublin　　　Dublin [0001] 379900
East Midlands (Castle Donington)
　　　　　　　　Derby [0332] 810621
Edinburgh [031] 333 1000
Exeter　　　　Exeter [0392] 67433
Glasgow　　041-887 1111, ext. 504/5
Guernsey (St Peter Port)
　　　　　　　　Guernsey [0481] 37766
Inverness (Dalcross) Inverness [0463] 32471

Isle of Islay (Islay)
　　　　　　　　Port Ellen [0496] 23 61
Isle of Man (Ronaldsway)
　　　　　　　　Castletown [0624-82] 3311
Jersey (St Helier)　　　[0534] 41272
Leeds and Bradford (Yeadon)
　　　　　　　　Leeds [0532] 503431
Liverpool　　　　051-427 4101
London (Gatwick)
　　　　　　　　Crawley [0293] 31299
London (Heathrow)　01-759 4321
Luton, Beds.　　Luton [0582] 36061
Lydd, Kent　　Lydd [0679] 20401
Manchester, Wythenshawe
　　　　　　　　061-437 5233
Newcastle upon Tyne
　　　　　　　　Newcastle [0632] 860966
Newquay　　Newquay [06374] 270
Norwich　　Norwich [0603] 411923
Orkney (Kirkwall)
　　　　　　　　Kirkwall [0856] 2421
Plymouth　Plymouth [0752] 772753
Prestwick　　Prestwick [0292] 79822
Scilly Isles (St Mary's)　Scillonia 677
Shannon, Eire　　Shannon 61444
Shetland, Sumburgh　Sumburgh 345
Southampton (East Leigh)
　　　　　　　　East Leigh [0703] 612341
Southend-on-Sea
　　　　　　　　Southend [0702] 40201
Stansted
　　Bishops Stortford [0279] 502380
Stornoway, Isle of Lewis
　　　　　　　　Stornoway [0851] 2256
Tiree, Isle of Tiree
　　　　　　　　Tiree [08792] 456
Tees-side, nr Darlington
　　　　　　　　Olnsdale [0325 73] 2811
Wick, Caithness　　Wick [0955] 2215

FOREIGN AIRLINES

Aer Lingus – Irish:
52 Poland Street, London w1 (tel. 01-734 1212)

Aeroflot – USSR:
69 Piccadilly, London w1 (tel. 01-493 7436)

Air Canada:
140 Regent Street, London w1 (tel. 01-759 2636)

Air France:
158 New Bond Street, London w1y 0ay
Reservations: (tel. 01-499-9511)
Other inquiries: (tel. 01-499-8611)

Air India:
17 New Bond Street, London w1y 0ba (tel. 01-491-7979)

Alitalia – Italy:
251 Regent Street, London w1r 8aq (tel. 01-734-4040)

El Al-Israel:
185 Regent Street, London w1r 8bs (tel. 01-437 9255)

Loftleidir – Iceland:
73 Grosvenor Street, London, w1x 9dd (tel. 01-499 9971)

Iberia (Airlines of Spain):
169 Regent Street, London w1r 8be (tel. 01-437-9822)

Japan Air Lines:
8 Hanover Street, London w1r 0dr (tel. 01-408 1000)

KLM (Royal Dutch Airlines):
Time & Life Building, New Bond Street, London w1 (tel. 01-568-9144)

Lufthansa – Germany:
28 Piccadilly, London w1v 0ej (tel. 01-437-9797)

Olympic Airways – Greece:
141 New Bond Street, London w1y 0bd (tel. 01-499-8712)

Pakistan International Airlines Corporation:
45 Piccadilly, London w1v 0ld (tel. 01-734-5544)

Pan American World Airways Inc.:
193 Piccadilly, London, w1v 0ad (tel. 01-734 7731)

Qantas – Australia:
49 Old Bond Street, London w1x 4aq (tel. 01-995-1344)

SAS – Scandinavian Airlines:
52 Conduit Street, London w1r 0ay (tel. 01-734-4020)

Sabena – Belgium:
36 Piccadilly, London w1v 0ad (tel. 01-437-6950)

South African Airways:
251 Regent Street, London w1r 7ad (tel. 01-734-9841)

Swissair:
3 New Coventry Street, London w1v 4bj (tel. 01-439-4144)

Trans World Airlines Inc. (TWA) – America:
200 Piccadilly, London w1v 0ad (tel. 01-636-4090)

TIPS FROM A TRAVEL AGENT

The travel business is a volatile, competitive, cut-throat business. Don't be lured by glossy promises – check the facts and the grey print and know how to translate the hieroglyphics.

Before you sign the booking form or hand over the deposit you should know how to avoid trouble: you should also know your rights and how to get them. You should know how to complain for maximum compensation if things go wrong. There was an avalanche of travel scandals in the early seventies, when some big airlines and tour operators, as well as small ones, went bankrupt overnight, leaving people stranded abroad or with useless tickets for non-existent journeys and holidays. Coach and train package holidays have a *very* good record, but because of the trouble with air package holidays, the British government set up the Air Travel Reserve Fund. This Disaster Piggy Bank is intended to provide some financial protection for holidaymakers on air packages or travelling on the cheap Advance Booking Charter (ABC) flights.

When you're buying an ABC or air package holiday, ask for the tour operator's ATOL number (Air Travel Organizer's Licence), which shows that he has contributed money to the Disaster Piggy Bank and therefore *by law* his customers are entitled to compensation if anything goes wrong, whether the travel agent goes bankrupt or the tour operator goes bankrupt. *Customers of an unlicensed company will get no refunds from the Air Travel Reserve Fund.*

Tour operators have not only a licence number, but a letter or letters as well. This shows the services they are licensed to give. *If you're buying an inclusive air package holiday make sure that the tour operator holds a B number and if you're buying an ABC*

flight make sure that he holds an A number (see p. 410).

Here, out of the mouths of travel agents, is your checklist.

The insider's guide to having a wonderful time:

1 Check the ATOL number of the tour or ABC operator or organizer selling your holiday or charter flight. Is it in the correct category?

2 Make sure that your travel agent and tour operator are members of ABTA – (Association of British Travel Agents). They contribute to a central ABTA fund to compensate customers if an ABTA member goes out of business. The ABTA sign should be displayed.

3 There are many, many different prices for the same trip. Make sure you investigate and compare what's available. Do a bit of comparative shopping.

4 Make sure you know what you are buying – and what you are not. *Before you hand over your money for the ticket* check the following points:

5 *Conditions:* Check that the conditions are *not* on the back of the booking form which you're about to hand back to your travel agent. If they are, get them to give you another copy (perhaps there's one in the brochure), and take it with you on holiday.

ABTA members' brochures must *not* contain clauses saying they take no responsibility for:

(a) their staff or agents who make misleading statements about holidays; or

(b) negligence on the part of their staff in arranging your holiday; nor should they say that complaints will be considered only if they are made within a period of twenty-eight days.

6 *Cancellations:* What are the cancellation clauses if *you* cancel or if *they* cancel?

(a) *If you are forced to cancel* (jury service, trouble 't' mill) you could be liable to pay almost the full price of the holiday for nothing. The holiday brochure must explain the cancellation conditions and how much money you may have to forfeit. If you're going on a charter flight and many scheduled flights, you can't cancel without forfeiting your money.

(b) *If they are forced to cancel* after the date when you are due to pay the full balance of the cost (usually eight to ten weeks before you go), a tour operator can cancel your holiday only for reasons beyond his control – things such as fight-

ing or political unrest, or an outbreak of disease. If this happens, you should get prompt and full refund of your money (less his reasonable expenses) or the offer of an alternative similar holiday.

7 *Alterations:* If a tour operator or travel agent wants to alter your holiday in a significant way, he must tell you immediately and give you the choice of either accepting the change (which must *not* lower the standard of your holiday) or of having your money promptly refunded. He can't *insist* on your having a different holiday.

8 *Children:* It's worth saying twice that families should always carefully check rates for children. Discounts vary from 15 per cent to 50 per cent but may be less in high season. Quite often your total family bill may be lower if you go with expensive tour operators – because they offer bigger and better discounts for children.

9 *Surcharges:* Watch the surcharges or you may get stung for extras. The brochure should explain what sort of surcharges could crop up, and why. No ABTA member may now impose currency surcharges less than thirty days before your holiday, provided you have booked and paid in full. Other surcharges such as fuel could be asked for nearer the date of departure, but they must be imposed for reasons beyond the tour operator's control. Some tour operators offer even *more* protection by saying, for example, that you can cancel your holiday if

surcharges increase the price by more than a certain percentage or that no surcharges will be made after you have paid the final invoice, or by guaranteeing the maximum amount of the surcharge.

10 *Overbooking:* ABTA members cannot guarantee that some foreign hotels will not be overbooked by the hotel management.

If they find out this has happened before you go, they must offer you the choice of another holiday of at least the same standard, or a prompt refund of your money. If overbooking is discovered after you leave *the tour operator must find you somewhere else to stay, and pay you 'disturbance' compensation if the hotel facilities and location are of a lower standard than booked.* (Better take this book on holiday with you.)

11 When picking your hotel, be wary of hotel star ratings. Different countries have different standards. 'A 2-star hotel in Spain will be the equivalent of a hostel in Scandinavia. In Austria the plainest boarding house will be " terrific",' one travel agent explained. So before you make a final booking get an unbiased assessment of your chosen hotel by asking your travel agent to look it up in the insider's intelligence guide, *The Agent's Hotel Gazetteer.* Or you can look it up yourself in the reference section of a public library. (Ask the librarian to help you.) The Gazetteer, which is like a *Which?* report on hotels, is in two volumes, one for resorts and one for tourist cities in Europe and Scandinavia. Independent inspectors have visited the hotels and reported on *what they saw.* Descriptions are factual and not the fantasies of a desk-bound brochure writer. Some typical comments are: 'at the back of town – inconvenient' ... 'overlooking wasteground and bus terminal' ... 'on the edge of town where many apartment blocks have already been built so almost only view from the terraces and garden is – apartment blocks' ... 'close to a thoroughly repulsive beach' ...

Both Gazetteers are produced and published by C.H.G. Travel Publications, 30 Grove Road, Beaconsfield, Buckinghamshire (tel. Beaconsfield [04946] 4040).

CHEAP PACKAGE HOLIDAYS CHECK – ABROAD

To calculate the *total* prices of the holidays you're being offered here's *your checklist:*

1 Basic quoted brochure price
2 Surcharge conditions
3 Currency surcharge
4 Supplements (what they mean is extras)
5 Airport charges
6 Children's reductions
7 How inclusive is it?
8 Possibility of date juggling (will it be a lot cheaper if you travel midweek or the week before you had intended?)
9 Special bargains (e.g. recently devalued country)

10 Special bargain offers
11 Special reductions (e.g. if your companion is blind)

You think it's unnecessary? The surcharge alone can *easily* add as much as £100 on a family holiday for four and the basic price of your holiday can increase by more than 60 per cent. Here's an example of how it all adds up.

BASIC COST of a holiday for one in Sweden: £100 (for two weeks)

1 Basic quoted brochure price, £100 per person   £100
2 Fuel surcharge, £5 per person   £5
3 Currency surcharge, £10 (10 per cent) per person   £10
4 Supplements: single room, bathroom, balcony – £30   £30
5 Airport charges, £2   £2
6 Not applicable
7 No midday meal. Allow £15 extra   £15
8 No possibility of changing the date
9 Currency unfortunately stable
10 No bargain situation
11 No special reductions

                                   £162

Actual total cost is £162, or 62 per cent more than the basic cost of £100.

Why do package prices differ?

The costs depend on:

Where you go: Distance alone doesn't affect all prices. Italy, for example, is still cheaper than France because its hotel rates are lower.

Travel to more distant lands is getting relatively cheaper and often the costs when you arrive are very low. For instance, on a quiet two weeks' package in Kenya, my spending money for a fortnight was under £20. I spent far more on a two weeks' package in the Canary Islands.

State of the country's exchange rate: The few countries with a weaker currency than ours, or any place that has just devalued its currency, are best bets. Just as the rich Europeans flock to shop in Britain – we can get (more modest) bargains in countries such as Italy and Portugal. Germany, Scandinavia and Switzerland are expensive for Britons. If you're uncertain, check with a bank or the financial pages of a serious Sunday newspaper.

Where you stay: Quiet sleepy villages are often more pricey than busy resorts. A grand hotel in a package may cost less than a more modest place you book yourself in the same resort. *Package camping holidays* in the sun are getting more organized and popular.

When you book: Some firms offer discounts for early booking. Some offer discounts for late booking (it's their clearance sale-price to shift unsold seats).

Some guarantee no surcharges of any kind if you book early (check with your travel agent) and so they all should because you're losing the bank interest on your money and *they* are earning interest on it.

Many operators offer good budget deals, especially off-peak. You can often bargain for last-minute holidays (ask them to take 15 per cent less, say you can't afford more). Some travel operators have monthly clearance sales (like bargain basements) with a best-buy-of-the-month which can be 15 per cent cheaper. (Try Thomsons, Blue Sky and Swans.)

When you go: Prices zoom up during school holidays, especially during the summer: August is peak season. Everywhere costs more over Easter, Christmas and the New Year. Don't forget that if you take an 'off' peak season holiday (i.e. the cheapest), there is probably 'some very good climatic reason why no one wants to go there at that time – humidity, rain, wind, no snow, the monsoon period.

Date juggling: Apart from seasonal differences, different tour operators have different high, low and middle seasons. Many might be low priced from one operator and medium priced from another. Particularly watch July dates: some high-season rates start 1 July, others don't start until the 21st. The same applies to Easter. The best bargains are usually in April, May, September, October, but check whether it's the local monsoon period. *Don't* believe your travel agent; ask the appropriate national tourist office in London (see 'Useful addresses', p. 459).

How long you go for: Short holidays, at all-in prices, to European cities like Paris or Amsterdam still give good bargains abroad without breaking the budget. Also a stay of an unusual length – four, five, eleven or seventeen days – can mean a dis-

count, because the operator wants to fill left-over plane seats, so doesn't mind selling them off at below brochure prices. Thomsons do a lot of this between their summer and winter seasons.

The surcharge situation changes constantly and is currently the most volatile part of the travel scene. It's the most important point to watch, in order to avoid last-minute holiday shocks (it can be as much as £100 for a family of four) with obvious opportunities for genteel blackmail. Read those guarantees and *check* what they are *guaranteeing.*

Check list:

What period does the guarantee cover?
Does it apply to when you go or when you book?

The best guarantee is for no surcharge at all, or as second best, one limited to (say) £5 per person per week (try Thomsons, Enterprise, Cosmos).

Child fares: There is no standardized child fare. Discounts vary from around 10 per cent to 75 per cent of the adult fare, depending on time of travel and number of adults in the party. Some operators will take one child *free* on some holidays (try Intasun) and some travel operators give one child discount per travelling adult (important with a one-parent family). Others only allow one child discount for two adults. Intasun are particularly good for child-value: check not only the price reduction but whether the children sleep in a separate room and whether day travel is possible so you don't arrive at 3.00 in the morning. Some discounts apply to children under seven, others to children under twelve or fourteen and occasionally under eighteen (try the Travel Club of Upminster).

Children under two can nearly always travel free so long as they don't occupy a seat in the plane and sleep in their parent's room.

How you travel: Bus/coach/train/ your own car with ferry/charter flight/ scheduled flight/boat. Prices vary from low to high in that order. But like everything in travel it all depends ... Never assume *anything*.

Travelling by bus or coach abroad is cheap (look for Euroways to Spain, Italy, Greece and Russia) unless you're doing a Grand Tour, which can be a marvellous bargain if you want to see a lot in a short time, in comfort if not luxury. Wallace Arnold and Cosmos run holidays to resorts in Spain, Austria and Germany, plus hundreds of different tours of the UK and Europe. You can do a complete coach package to take you to your holiday place or you can tour in a coach or you can combine coach with air travel in one package. There are similar train package holidays run by different national railways. Contact national tourist offices in London.

Who you book with: Once you decide where you want to go, get a clutch of brochures and compare what the different tour operators have to offer. A good *travel agent* who belongs to ABTA can still be your best holiday guide. (*Cooks* is always professional and efficient.)

You can of course book your holiday direct but you don't save anything because with most firms, rather unfairly, you don't get the travel agent's commission. However, Scandinavian operators like Tjaereborg and Vingresor, who specialize in low-cost holidays sold direct to the public, now have big air holiday programmes from the UK and are worth trying (Tjaereborg: 7 Conduit Street, London, W1R 9TG; tel. 01-499 8676).

If you want to find out more about a certain country, its climate and what's available in it, contact the appropriate national tourist and travel office in London, which will provide information, off-beat local advice, suggestions, and any current special offers or concessions for tourists. Best to write (see addresses on p. 459).

They can't *sell* you anything or book anything for you but *they know who the best agents are, all right*, and will recommend a selection. They can also tell you the *difference* between resorts ('that's fine for children but there aren't any discos if you want night life'). They'll also know of any upcoming local festivals or carnivals (which you might want to miss).

Bargain Basement
Holidays

A cheap holiday abroad is more than travelling cheaply: it's also staying cheaply when you get there.

CAMPING IT UP IS ONE WAY

Camping abroad isn't like it was in the Guides, the Scouts or the Army. It can be very luxurious and today there are camping packages to beautifully landscaped sites or farmland with modern lavatories, free showers, hot and cold water, electricity, on-site village shops, bars and even restaurants. The Association of Camping Tour Operators are trying to set standards.

You can have an all-in-cost package holiday. This includes your fare to the resort and payment of your camp site charges. Your caravan or tent is set up and waiting for you.

You can travel by air-conditioned coaches to the South of France where all the equipment awaits you on site – tent, beds, sleeping bags, table, chairs and crockery. Operators are Mediterranean Camping Holidays, Sunsaver Holidays (Hemel Hempstead).

Car ferries also offer well-organized camping holidays with an all-in price covering sea crossing, insurance, camp fees, camping equipment and list of sites. Try British Rail Sealink or the superbly organized Townsend Thoresen Line and Canvas Holidays (Bull Plain 70, Hertford; tel. Hertford [0992] 59933), which go to France, Switzerland and Austria by sea ferry, with motorail where applicable. They offer insurance and camp fees, as well as fully-equipped tents.

One of the most rewarding is probably Olympic Holidays' 'Poundsavers'. You get a return flight, first-night hotel accommodation, vouchers for camping site and the gear. In air package camping holidays there are

434   BOOK 3: SUPERWOMAN TAKES OFF!

the inevitable lunatic bureaucratic air regulations – and ways of getting round them. If you're going on a cheap charter, the British Civil Aviation Authority requires that all tour operators who arrange inclusive holidays by air for campers must supply tents as well as booking sites. If you prefer to take your own tent, you can borrow one, the travel operator will hire it from you – and then hire it back to you at the same charge. Many major operators do this.

Alternatively, you can make your own travel arrangements and hire all the gear before you go, or take your own camping equipment, travel on a cheapie air flight which includes accommodation and not use it. You can buy or rent camping equipment from Benjamin Edgington (29 Queen Elizabeth Street, London SE1; tel. 01-407 3734): anything from groundsheets and roofracks to baggage trailers, children's cots and insulated ice-boxes.

You can also hire superb equipment from Blacks of Greenock, who have branches all over the country (sometimes operating under different trading names). Write for *free* brochure and local details to 53 Rathbone Place, London W1P 1AN (tel. 01-636 6645). A smaller camp hire firm which gives personal service and is interested in helping to organize family expeditions is Rentatent, Third Way, Off Southway, Wembley Trading Estate, Middlesex HA9 0TE (tel. 01-903 3473), or Twitch Hill, Horbury, Wakefield WF4 6LZ (tel. Wakefield [0924] 275131), or 40 Ducie Street, Man-

chester M1 2JN (tel. 061-273 3623).

It's worth joining the Youth Hostel Association which has recently started a new scheme called 'Supertramps'. This offers package deals, including flight and vouchers for any youth hostel in Austria, Germany, Greece, Norway, Italy, Switzerland and Yugoslavia. For international membership (there's no age limit, you just have to be young in spirit) and a list of their information booklets write to the Youth Hostels Association, 14 Southampton Street, London WC2 (tel. 01-836 854).

Two good literary investments are *Hitchhiker's Guide to Europe* by Ken Welsh (Pan, 95p) and *The Traveller's Survival Kit to Europe* (Vacation Work, 9 Park End Street, Oxford, £1.95 plus 25p postage).

SELF-CATERING
HOLIDAYS

Another way to cut holiday costs – especially for a family. Most tour operators have a selection. OSL, Cosmos and Thomsons have the widest range. They are not necessarily plushy villas, but the idea is that you can cook as much or as little as you want, in Apartotels, which are studios with small fitted kitchens. This saves you the cost of highly priced cups of tea, kid's cokes and drinks in the bar. You can stock up on wine, liquor, soft drinks, tea and coffee from the local supermarket and eat your main meal in local restaurants.

THE CHEAPEST AIR PACKAGE HOLIDAYS

An interesting growth area in the travel business is the Bargain Basement Holiday, sold under various brand names such as Wanderer (Thomson), Cheapies (Cosmos), Easy-Rider (Intasun), and Pound-savers (Olympic). There are two advantages to these deals:

1 These are the cheapest inclusive packages possible. Accommodation is in three- or four-bedded rooms, without H&C, and with minimum service: no meals, no extras. Prices, as I write, start at around £27 for seven days in Spain (Intasun Easy Rider).
2 They are so cheap that many business people or visitors who intend to stay with friends use them just for the air journey and throw away the accommodation vouchers. This is a legal way of getting round the national airlines' price-fixing club, IATA, which rules that you can cut plane fares only if accommodation is included for the visit.

If you actually want to use the accommodation, it varies from basic hostels to private homes or rough and ready pension conditions. You can't expect more than the minimum of somewhere to lay your head down in a dormitory (probably a single-sex one). Very good for students on a shoe-string – with prices from £30 for a fortnight in Spain.

SOME BARGAIN BASEMENT PACKAGE HOLIDAYS

Thomson Wanderer Holidays for Morocco, Portugal, Spain (including Majorca), France, Switzerland and Austria.

Cosmos Cheapies to Spain, Majorca, Ibiza, Minorca, Italy, Yugoslavia, Greece, Canaries, Tunisia, Malta, Madeira.

Intasun Easy-Riders for Spain, Portugal, Canaries, Malta.

Olympic Holidays Poundsavers for Greece on the cheap. Athens on the mainland and the islands of Corfu, Crete, Rhodes, Lesbos, Mykonos and Skiathos. Price includes return boat fare from Athens to the islands.

Chancery Travel Budget Tours for Switzerland, Greece, Spain, Corsica, Italy, Portugal.

A sophisticated development of the European cheapie is the idea already mentioned, pioneered by Thomson (Airfares), Laker (Budget) and Thomas Cook (Fare Shares), to give rockbottom airfares to people who make their own accommodation arrangements to stay in a hotel or with friends or swap a home. To get round the IATA charter regulations, you offer your already arranged accommodation to the tour operator for £1 to lease to 'a suitable tenant'. You then both decide that the 'suitable tenant' will be you. *All you have to do* is give some address at the other end to your travel agent (no one will even check whether it exists). The great advantage is that you get cheap travel *without booking months in advance*. You need not book more than one day ahead of your flight, but you must stay away for seven days or more. You can't go just anywhere but there's plenty of choice to the major holiday resorts.

People who own villas abroad can also get cheap flights to and from them using this principle. They hire their villa to the tour operator *only* for *their* holiday period, whereupon he immediately rents it back to them. Two such holiday villa agencies are Owners Services Ltd, Broxbourne House, Broxbourne, Hertfordshire (tel. 01-804 8191) and Owners Abroad Ltd, Guild House, Upper St Martin's Lane, London w c 2 (tel. 01-836 8685).

HOME SWAPPING

One way of avoiding hotel bills and holiday extras is *home swapping*. This is increasingly popular all over the world, which means that *homes are available all over the world*. There are three ways to do it:

1 Through friends or friends of friends.
2 By advertising in the local press in the place you want to visit or through the classified advertisements or personal columns in *The Times*, the *Telegraph*, the *New Statesman* or *Time Out* (for basic pads).
3 By going to a specialist agency, which is easiest and will probably give you the most choice.

Swapping your home is just about the most economical way a family can have a holiday abroad – especially in the more faraway places. As well as free accommodation, there are all the extras, like saving money on eating out and having a washing machine to hand for laundry. It's often possible to swap all sorts of extra home comforts such as car, bicycles, and, if you're lucky, a boat, and domestic help and baby-sitters. Some families have even exchanged their membership in the local golf club.

I have house-swapped with a dear friend whose farmhouse in the South of France fell apart as soon as we arrived – in the worst rain for fifty years. We had to mend the road with pickaxes before we could drive down the mountain to get help. I have also swapped with a stranger for a flat in New York which was bliss. As my absent hostess had worried about my comfort, rose-sprinkled Christian Dior sheets, lemon silk cushions and dozens more wine glasses kept mysteriously arriving, unsolicited by me, from Fifth Avenue stores. There's a certain amount of risk, but then there always is in life and if you're swapping with another home-owner, they generally feel more responsible for your property because they're used to looking after their own – and they hope that you are looking after theirs in the same way.

How to have a trouble-free exchange

Avoid misunderstandings later by being precise in the beginning. Tell the others how many children will be with you and their ages, as well as the size of your home and rooms. Make sure you both agree in writing on the exact dates and times of arrival and departure. Don't vaguely agree on a time like 'the end of August' – there can be several days' difference between what you each think that means.

'You must be explicit about everything: you'd be surprised how casual people can be,' I was told by a house-swapping agent. So once you have lined up a suitable exchange, be businesslike about it. Don't think you needn't bother about nasty little legal details – because the other family sound so nice and friendly, and you don't want to spoil the relationship by being too fussy.

Make sure you both exchange references, more than one, preferably from a bank and an employer. 'Some people are rather shy about asking for references, but they should be exchanged as a matter of course,' says Sara Holden, of Homes Directory. 'And if you know people living nearby it is worth asking them to call on your exchange family and look at the house. You should take the same precautions as you would if you were letting your flat or house.'

Otherwise, there are three main points to watch: theft, damage and the service bills (telephone, electricity, gas). Both sides should pay a *sizeable* deposit to a lawyer to hold against possible claims, and the service bills can be dealt with from your end by sending *recorded delivery* letters to the companies concerned asking for your electricity and/or gas meter to be read the day before you leave. Some agencies say there is no point in getting electricity and gas meters read before you go, as your guest family will be supplying you with utilities as part of the exchange. At the mere thought of all this warning bells sound in the back of my head. I would prefer each family to pay for what it consumes but whatever you decide to do – get it signed, in writing, in advance.

Your telephone bill can also be made up to that date. The Post Office will take a verbal instruction over the telephone, *provided that you immediately confirm it in writing, by recorded delivery*.

Phone bills are the biggest potential problem, so decide in advance how you are each going to pay for the phone bills. *Don't ever consider* doing a *quid pro quo*. It's a good idea to get your exchange family to pay a separate deposit in advance to cover the telephone bill because they may not realize how expensive the British telephone system is, or how muddling the billing system.

In many countries telephone subscribers get their local calls free and they don't realize how quickly British phone bills can rocket with local calls alone. And there is always the likelihood that they'll be phoning their friends and relatives 5000 miles away – just to keep in touch.

Insurance: You *must* tell your insurance company (recorded delivery) that you are going to have another family living in your home, otherwise if your house is burgled while they are there you might not get *any* insurance money at all. The insurance company will want to see photostats of the references of your exchange family, so make sure you get them in plenty of time. If your insurance company is happy with them, it will probably agree to continue your insurance cover without any problems. *But the company must know and agree* before you make the exchange, so send everything recorded delivery.

You should also make sure that your exchange family have covered their insurance. Ask for a copy of the letter of agreement from their insurance agent, and send them a copy of yours. If you're swapping cars, make sure that both cars are appropriately insured.

Both exchangers should agree in advance what responsibility each will take for loss or damage to each other's property. Even so *put away* anything of value or which is treasured and which you wouldn't want lost or smashed.

Compensation: In spite of precautions you can't guarantee that all will go as arranged, If your swap family suddenly has to cancel because of illness or some other unexpected crisis, you might find that it's too late to find another swap and you have to abandon the whole holiday. Some people work out and agree a compensation for such an unlikely occurrence.

Home Interchange has an annual membership of around 4000. It specializes in North America and Canada, but also arranges home swaps in Western Europe, the Middle East, Scandinavia, Hong Kong, Singapore, Japan and Australia. Contact Mrs Suzanne Barnard, PO Box 84, London NW8 7PR (tel. 01-262 3822).

Home exchange companies merely publish lists of interested parties for a fee of around £8, which you pay annually. This buys you an entry in their directory or supplement and you get a copy of the directory or supplement from which to make your choice. You are expected to list details about your own home, what you want in exchange and the dates on which you want to swap. Once you are in the list you are on your own: *you* write after the homes you want, *you* make your own negotiations and *you* take your own precautions. Directory companies do not claim to be letting agencies. They will not accept responsibility for inaccurate statements, for making any arrangements, or for anything that goes wrong.

Hotel Booking Services

There's nothing that kills holiday anticipation faster than wasting time by ringing round (especially if long distance) to find or book a room. However, there are now some reliable *free* or minimal charge booking services that will do the work for you, whether you want a bed *immediately* or you're planning a ten-day tour in a month's time.

BRITAIN OR ABROAD

You can book for Britain or abroad *from* Britain or abroad. Some booking services are run by specific hotel chains who will help you to find a bed in a little corner of their empire. Try: *Trust Houses Forte*, Reservation Centre, 71 Uxbridge Road, London W5 (tel. 01-567 3444); *British Transport Hotels*, Central Reservations, St Pancras Chambers, Euston Road, London NW1 (tel. 01-278 4211); *Holiday Inns*, Hotel Reservations (who will book you internationally and at home), 10–12 New College Parade, Finchley Road, London NW3 5EP (tel. 01-722 7755).

Some booking services are run by reasonably impartial advisers such as the London Tourist Board, Paddington Chambers of Commerce and British Airways. The trade organization is the Association of Hotel Booking Agents, which checks the standards of its members (the firms starred in the list): it's wise to stick to the members and the organizations mentioned here because there's a very high casualty rate.

For immediate bookings

The London Tourist Board Information Centre books accommodation in all price categories and has very strict standards. It is at Victoria Station, opposite Platform 15, and at Heathrow Underground station, is open daily and will make immediate reservations. A £2 deposit (or 50p fee for budget accommodation) is charged. You can't telephone.

For advance bookings

Four weeks' notice is necessary. Apply to *Accommodation Services*, London Tourist Board, 4 Grosvenor Gardens, sw1 0du (tel. 01-730 0791).

Only 50p fee is charged for *budget accommodation* in hostels, dormitories and pensions. Central locations are more expensive than those in the suburbs. Apply at Victoria Station on the day, or advance-book by writing six weeks in advance.

* *Hotac Hotel Accommodation Services Ltd* welcome the general public (instead of just beaming at businessmen). They will book you anywhere in the world. No charge is made for reservations in Great Britain, £2 for foreign bookings. For all bookings apply to Globegate House, Pound Lane, Willesden, London nw10 2lb (tel. 01-451 2311) Telex 8814032.

* *Expotel* (*Hotel Reservations*) *Ltd* deal only with business firms, but don't charge. Strand House, Great West Road, Brentford, Middlesex (tel. 01-568 8765).

* *Hotel Bookings International Ltd*, Globegate House, Pound Lane, Willesden, London nw10 2lb (tel. 01-459 1212).

* *Hotel Booking Services Ltd* mostly deal with business organizations but they will book the general public provided there is a deposit (returnable) on the first night's accommodation. Goldsmith House, 137 Regent Street, London w1r 8eb (tel. 01-437 5052 for London 01-437 3212; for UK outside London).

* *Hotel Guide*, Faraday House, 8–10 Charing Cross Road, London wc2h 0hg (tel. 01-240 3288).

Before Taking Your Car Abroad

Don't assume that your normal car insurance policy will automatically cover you abroad.

Don't assume that if you've got a green card you are fully protected. Few drivers realize that the insurance agreement signed by the Green Card Bureau provides only the *minimum* legal cover.

In fact, never assume *anything*. Telephone your insurance agent and tell him where you're going and with whom and in what and for how long. He will then arrange additional insurance for that specific trip. It will cost you a lot extra, especially if you're thinking of taking a car to some place like Spain, where, if you have an accident, they may impound the car and throw you into prison until the authorities decide what to do about it.

GETTING YOU HOME

It's a good idea to take out an additional get-you-home policy for you *and* your passengers *and* the car, or to pay for car hire so that you can continue your holiday.

The A A and the R A C can arrange excellent insurance for their members for about £10; if you run into trouble they will get the car back home for you. The insurance package can include vehicle, towing and personal security, comprehensive cover, spare parts and recovery service, and immediate credit facilities for over £400. Both organizations will also give you vouchers to pay for repairs abroad. You repay them when you return. A A membership is £11.50 a year for existing members, plus £2.75 when joining for the first time. R A C, £11, plus £2.50 for new members – this covers husband and wife.

A A Head Office: Fanum House, Basingstoke, Hampshire (tel. Basingstoke [0256] 20123).

R A C Head Office: Lansdowne

Road, East Croydon CR9 2JA (tel. 01-839 7050).

Get your car thoroughly serviced if a service is due. Don't leave it until the last minute. Book an appointment for a couple of weeks before you go so that you can take it back to the garage if you have any complaints.

Pack a folding emergency windscreen and a spare fanbelt.

Pack a heavy red warning triangle (not a flimsy one). You can buy them from the AA or on the ferry. If you break down on the Continent it's illegal to stop without one.

Carry a bottle of water and a sponge to wipe the windscreen.

Ferries are cheaper at midweek. Weekends are more expensive; July and August even more so. If you Hover across it's quickest and best for an early start but you're not *absolutely* certain that you'll get there on time. Services are cancelled if the weather is very bad.

It's always worth asking what the special concessions and special offers are, because the information probably won't be offered to you. You can, for instance, save 50 per cent if you travel mid-week to Ireland from somewhere such as Birmingham or by Sealink economy return.

If you're speeding towards your trendy ruin in the Dordogne or around Bordeaux or South West France, your choice of ferry is very important. If you travel to a northern port (such as Calais) it can add an extra day's drive to your journey, all that petrol and an expensive overnight stop at an hotel. So aim for Le Havre, or sail on Brittany Ferries to Saint-Malo.

If you're driving farther south, easily the most luxurious way to travel is by putting your car on the train. You can pick up the French Motorail from Boulogne to Biarritz, Narbonne, Avignon, Saint-Raphael (handy for Monte Carlo or Italy) or Milan. Details from French Railways, 179 Piccadilly, London W1V 0BA.

If you travel on an overnight ferry, don't economize and sleep in chairs. The bunks are well worth the money for a good sleep (and cheaper than fancy foreign hotels), and you get up fresh for an early morning start.

Fill up with petrol before you board the ferry in Britain – petrol is even more expensive abroad. Calculate sixty miles an hour on the autoroutes, forty miles per hour everywhere else. Country roads are not always *that* much slower and they're nicer. Buy your picnic from the supermarkets, where all prices are marked. Pack a box of tissues, paper plates, yoghurt spoons, knives, thick, cheap tumblers, tea towels, corkscrew and bottle opener. Remember that Continental shops close from 12.30 to 2.30 p.m. and if you're late you won't be able to buy your lunch.

When stopping overnight, stop an hour earlier than you intended, check the price of the hotel room and *always ask to see it*. Then ask if they have anything cheaper.

Bergen

Fred Olsen Bergen Line

Stavanger

Kristiansand

Gothenberg
— *Torline*

Esbjerg
DFDS

Hamburg — *Prins Ferries*

Bremer-Haven — *Prins Ferries*

Scheveningen — *Norfolk Line*
Rotterdam — *North Sea Ferries*
Hook of Holland — *Sealink*
Flushing — *Olau Line*
Ostend — *Sealink*   Zeebrugge — *Townsend Thoresen·North Sea Ferries*
Dunkirk — *Sealink*
Calais — *Sealink ·Townsend Thoresen·Hoverlloyd·
Seaspeed Hovercraft*
Boulogne — *Sealink·Seaspeed·Normandy Ferries*
Dieppe — *Sealink*
Le Havre — *Townsend Thoresen·Normandy Ferries*
Cherbourg — *Townsend Thoresen·Sealink*
St Malo — *Brittany Ferries*
Roscoff — *Brittany Ferries*

0   100   200
Kilometres
0   75   150
Miles

CROSS-CHANNEL FERRIES

WHICH CAR FERRIES GO WHERE

Here's a list of the ferry services (summer only; winter sailings are less frequent) for different countries. Car ferries also take people *without* cars: a popular way for students to hop over, then hitch.

Belgium

Felixstowe–Zeebrugge: Townsend Thoresen have up to three sailings a day, depending on season; 5 hours for day crossing.

Dover–Zeebrugge: Townsend Thoresen, up to 6 departures daily; 4 hours.

Hull–Zeebrugge: North Sea Ferries, daily; 15 hours.

Dover/Folkestone–Ostend: Sealink have up to 13 sailings a day; $3\frac{1}{2}$–$4\frac{1}{2}$ hours.

Channel Islands

Portsmouth Guernsey/Jersey: Sealink, daily; 7–$9\frac{1}{2}$ hours.

Weymouth–Guernsey/Jersey: Sealink, twice daily. Average time Guernsey $4\frac{1}{2}$ hours, Jersey 7 hours.

Denmark

Harwich–Esbjerg: DFDS daily; 19 hours.

Newcastle–Esbjerg: DFDS 3 weekly; 18 hours.

France

Dover–Dunkirk: Sealink, 4 times daily; $2\frac{1}{2}$ hours.

Dover–Calais: Both Townsend Thoresen and Sealink provide up to 12 crossings a day; $1\frac{1}{2}$ hours.

Dover–Boulogne: Normandy Ferries, up to 4 times a day; 1 hour 45 minutes. Also Sealink up to 7 sailings a day, depending on season; 1 hour 45 minutes.

Folkestone–Calais/Boulogne: Sealink up to 5 times a day; 1 hour 45 minutes.

Dover–Calais/Boulogne: The Seaspeed Hovercraft have 7–10 crossings a day; 35 minutes.

Ramsgate–Calais: Hoverlloyd hovercraft have up to 14 crossings per day, depending on season; 45 minutes.

Newhaven–Dieppe: Sealink sail up to 6 times a day; 4 hours.

Southampton–Cherbourg/Le Havre: Townsend Thoresen twice daily; 7–8½ hours; 5–10 hours.

Southampton–Le Havre: Normandy Ferries, 2 to 3 sailings daily; 7–8½ hours.

Portsmouth–Cherbourg/Le Havre: Townsend Thoresen, twice daily; 4–6½ hours.

Weymouth–Cherbourg/Le Havre: Townsend Thoresen, twice daily; 4–5½ hours.

Weymouth–Cherbourg: Sealink, twice daily; 4 hours.

Portsmouth–St Malo: Brittany Ferries, daily; 10 hours.

Plymouth–Roscoff/St Malo: Brittany Ferries; twice daily/one weekly; 7/9 hours.

Germany

Harwich–Hamburg: Prins Ferries, every 2 days; 20 hours.

Harwich–Bremerhaven: Prins Ferries, every 2 days; 16½ hours.

Holland

Great Yarmouth–Scheveningen: Norfolk Line sail up to 3 times daily; 8–9 hours.

Harwich–Hook of Holland: Sealink sail up to 3 times a day, depending on season; night 8 hours, day 6 hours.

Hull–Rotterdam: North Sea Ferries daily; 14 hours.

Sheerness–Flushing: Olau Line, twice a day; 7 hours.

Felixstowe–Rotterdam: Townsend Thoresen, daily; 8 hours.

Irish Republic

Liverpool–Dublin: B + I Line sail twice daily; 7 hours.

Holyhead–Dun Laoghaire: Sealink sail up to 4 times daily; 3½ hours.

Fishguard–Rosslare/Dun Laoghaire: Sealink, up to 4 times daily; 3¾ hours.

Swansea–Cork: B + I Line daily; 10 hours.

Isle of Man

Liverpool–Douglas/Fleetwood–Douglas/Ardrossan–Douglas: Isle of Man Steam Packet. Frequent crossings; 4/2¾/6 hours.

Northern Ireland

Cairnryan–Larne: Townsend Thoresen sail up to 4 times a day; 2½ hours.

Stranraer–Larne: Sealink, up to 6 times daily; 2¼ hours.

Liverpool–Belfast: P & O Ferries (Irish Sea Services) have a daily crossing; 10 hours.

Norway

Newcastle–Stavanger/Bergen: Fred Olsen/Bergen Line have up to 3 sailings per week; 17½–23½ hours.

Newcastle–Kristiansand: Fred Olsen/Bergen Line, weekly; 19 hours.

Harwich–Kristiansand: Fred Olsen/

Bergen line, once weekly; 22 hours.

Harwich–Oslo: Fred Olsen/Bergen Line, once a week; 31 hours.

Shetland and Orkney

Aberdeen–Lerwick: P&O Ferries (Orkney and Shetland Services) sail 3 times weekly; 14 hours.

Scrabster–Stromness: P&O Ferries (Orkney and Shetland Services) sail up to 6 times daily; 2 hours.

Sweden

Newcastle–Gothenburg: Danish Seaways sail twice a week; 21–25 hours.

Felixstowe–Gothenburg: Tor Line, 3 times a week; 23 hours.

CAR FERRY ADDRESS BOOK

Aznar Line, 26–28 Tower Place, London EC3 (tel. 01-493 8774 or 629 1995)

B + I Line, 155 Regent Street, London W1 (tel. 01-734 4681); 16 Westmorland Street, Dublin (tel. Dublin 778271)

British Rail (see Sealink and Seaspeed)

Brittany Ferries, Millbay Docks, Plymouth PL1 3EF (tel. Plymouth [0752] 27941)

DFDS, Mariner House, Pepys Street, London EC3N 4BX (tel. 01-481 3211)

Hoverlloyd, International Hoverport, Pegwell Bay, Ramsgate, Kent (tel. 01-499 9481 or Thanet [0843] 54761)

Isle of Man Steam Packet (Liverpool). India Buildings, 40 Brunswick Street, Liverpool (tel. 051-236 3214)

Normandy Ferries, Arundel Towers, Portland Terrace, Southampton (tel. Southampton [0703] 32131)

North Sea Ferries, King George Dock, Hull (tel. Hull [0482] 795141)

Norfolk Lines, Atland House, Southgates Road, Great Yarmouth (tel. Great Yarmouth [0493] 795141)

Olau Line, Sheerness Docks, Sheerness, Kent (tel. Sheerness [07956] 3355)

Fred Olsen/Bergen Lines, 229 Regent Street, London W1 (tel. 01-437 9888)

P & O Ferries (Orkney and Shetland Services), PO Box 5, Jamiesons Quay, Aberdeen (tel. Aberdeen [0224] 29111)

Prins Ferries, 67 Grosvenor Street, London W1 (tel. 01-629 7961)

Sealink, Car Ferry Centre, 52 Grosvenor Gardens, London SW1 (tel. 01-730 3440)

Seaspeed (British Rail Hovercraft Ltd), The Hoverport, Eastern Docks, Dover (tel. Dover [0304] 202266 or 01-606 3681)

Swedish Lloyd, 8 Berkeley Square, London W1 (tel. 01-289 2151)

Townsend Thoresen, 127 Regent Street, London W1 (tel. 01-734 4431 or 437 7800);

Car Ferry House, Canute Road, Southampton SO9 5GP (tel. Southampton [0703] 34444);

The Ferry Centre, The Docks, Felixstowe IP11 8TA (tel. Felixstowe [039 42] 78711);

The Harbour, Larne, County Antrim, N. Ireland (tel. Larne [0574] 4321); and Cairnryan, nr Stranraer, Dumfries and Galloway (tel. Cairnryan [05812] 276)

Tor Line, West Gate, Immingham Docks, Grimsby, South Humberside (tel. Immingham [0469] 73131); and 34 Panton Street, London s w 1 (tel. 01-930 0881)

Those Tedious Travelling Chores

PASSPORT

Make sure you have a valid passport. Look at the date when you book your ticket. Apply for a new one or for a renewal of your passport well in advance of travel. The application form (obtainable from passport offices, travel agents and post offices) explains how to apply. If your passport is out of date they will allow you out of Britain, but they might not allow you back. However, don't get upset if this is threatened. They'll have to let you back *sometime*. Concentrate on sounding contrite and terribly humble to the nice officer.

A full passport now costs £11 and lasts for ten years. Normally it's not worth getting the cheaper British Visitor's Passport because it lasts only a year, but you can get it immediately from any post office. It applies mainly to Europe.

There are passport offices at:

1st Floor, Empire House, 131 West Nile Street, Glasgow G1 2RY (tel. 041-332 0271)

5th Floor, India Buildings, Water Street, Liverpool L2 0QZ (tel. 051-227 3461)

Clive House, 70 Petty France, London SW1 9HD (tel. 01-222 8010)

Olympia House, Upper Dock Street, Newport, Gwent NPT 1XA (tel. Newport [0633] 52431)

55 Westfield Road, Peterborough PE3 6TG (tel. Peterborough [0733] 263636)

Foreign and Commonwealth Office Passport Agency, 1st Floor, Marlborough House, 30 Victoria Street, Belfast BT1 3LY (tel. Belfast [0232] 32371)

You will need

1 Two identical passport pictures 5 × 5 cm (2 × 2 inches), signed on the back by an MP, JP, doctor, accountant, vicar, bank manager or anyone they can look up in a reference book, to confirm that this is indeed you.

You can get a *quick photograph* from a booth in Woolworths or a railway station.

2 A copy of your birth certificate.

3 A copy of your marriage certificate, if any (only if you're a woman, Grrrr).

4 Your naturalization certificate or registration document if you weren't born in Britain.

5 Your old passport, if any.

6 Your filled-in application, which also has to be witnessed by the authoritative person who signed your passport picture.

You can get documents photocopied at libraries or some office suppliers.

You can get a copy of your birth certificate from the Office of Population Censuses and Surveys, St Catherine's House, 10 Kingsway, London WC2 (tel. 01-242 0262), or New Register House, Edinburgh (tel. 031-556 3952). You should allow at least four weeks for the application to be processed by the passport office. Add to this at least a further two weeks if you find you require a visa (see more below).

Urgency

You can normally get a passport within twenty-four hours if you collect all these documents and go along to the office prepared to sit there all day while being processed by different departments. If you need an emergency passport go to your nearest passport office personally and *let them know immediately*, don't wait in line. As soon as you step foot in the place explain your need for urgency. *In dire emergency* you can get a passport in two hours, but it has to be a proveable case of national interest, urgent business or emergency personal matters.

Emergency

If your passport runs out while you're abroad and you don't want to risk trouble when you get back, go to the nearest British consulate (look it up in the local phone book) and ask to have your passport extended.

If you want urgently to contact the nearest powerful Briton, to get you out of trouble, then the telegraphic address of British embassies is 'PRODROME'; of high commissions, 'UK REP'; and of all British consulates, 'BRITAIN', followed by the name of the town.

You should also make a note in your diary, or in your suitcase, of the number of your passport, the date and place of issue, just in case it gets lost or stolen. And they do, they do. Don't take your health insurance policy with you but carry the relevant details, such as policy number, name of insurer and broker, in your passport. This is necessary in case some harsh foreign hospital demands payment *before* attending to your broken leg or fluttering heart. And they do, they do.

VISAS

Allow at least two weeks to get a visa. (Visas for Russia and some East European countries can take at least one month. however.) If your travel is part of a package trip, the tour organizer (not the travel agent) will normally get a visa for you, but check that this is done. Ask your travel agent if you need a visa or telephone the London tourist office of the country you intend to visit, or the embassy or consulate or high commission. Tell them how long you intend to stay and why and ask them to allow extra time to cover any emergencies. They will send you an application form, which you must fill in and return with your passport. It's not a bad idea, once you've filled in your application form, to phone them and check that you've filled it in correctly. I always do.

Getting a visa is a serious business and it is not automatically granted or automatically extended and over-running your visa time is generally taken very seriously by the country which issues it. North America is particularly tough about visas if they suspect, for instance, that you don't intend to return to Britain but want to take a job in America. If a country suspects your travel motives, your visa may be delayed or refused.

If you have an APEX ticket on scheduled services or are travelling on an ABC flight, it is your responsibility to get your visa (as well as passport) and if you haven't got one they may refuse to let you aboard, and *you won't get your ticket money refunded.*

If you apply for a passport by post any passport office will automatically give you a booklet which tells you at a glance what countries need what visas and where to apply for them. Write for a *free* booklet called *Essential Information for Holders of UK Passports Who Intend to Travel Overseas* (pithy title).

HEALTH

In order to enjoy a carefree holiday there are three things to consider before going abroad:

1 Whether any vaccinations or malaria preventatives are needed.
2 What you will do if anyone is ill.
3 Whether you need any extra insurance to cover the possibility that you or one of your party may need expensive medical or hospital treatment. Even if you're not the casualty, you may have to stay

abroad expensively while someone else's appendix is being taken out. Incidentally, if death's wing brushes your trip, it can cost well over £500 to get the body back.

You may need a course of injections, so check as soon as you know where you're travelling. It won't involve more than a couple of visits to doctor or nurse.

Smallpox, cholera and typhoid injections are compulsory for many countries outside Europe. Get an International Certificate of Vaccination and take it with you. Protection against hepatitis is strongly advised. Also check tetanus injections (very important if you're camping) and drops for polio. Injections can sometimes make you feel very groggy for a few days so have them well in advance, two months beforehand if possible. You can get these injections on the National Health.

Few people realize that you don't have to go to the tropics to get malaria. It can also be contracted in the Mediterranean, North Africa and the Middle East. If you're visiting these areas – even for a plane stop – you must take malaria preventatives. (Get ICI's Paludrine – you only have to take one a day but you must continue for at least two weeks after you return.) Also take Panadol or aspirins, a box of Actal for indigestion and Diacalm for the inevitable diarrhoea.

You can find out the latest health controls by phoning the Department of Health (01-407 5522) and asking for Health Inquiries or by sending for the free leaflet *Notice to Travellers – Health Protection*, which lists vaccination requirements. This is obtainable from the Department of Health and Social Security, International Relations Division, Alexander Fleming House, Elephant and Castle, London SE1 6BY. You can also ask the immunization centres run by the international airlines or a tropical diseases hospital or ask your doctor (though he probably won't know offhand).

INSURANCE

Don't assume you're covered by your general insurance policies and certainly don't rely on the NHS's reciprocal health agreements: just reading about how to qualify for them gives me all the symptoms of advanced phormofillia (blurred vision, migraine, knotted stomach, panic, tears, despair, hysterical laughter, rage). You can either spend two days learning about it or you can insure against illness, but don't do neither.

Most of the tour operators provide health insurance policies as an optional extra (and invoice them automatically) or you can buy a policy direct from one of the big insurance firms. Plan on spending not less than £15 total premium for a small family for a fortnight in Europe. Premiums depend on how long you're going for and where, etc. But check what you're getting. Any decent holiday policy should cover at least £1000 hospital expenses and pay for getting you home.

Insure for more than you think. In Britain we are cushioned against the real cost of medical treatment, which is terrifyingly high. In the United States a toothache can cost you £50; a mild heart attack (and I knew a man who had one on his honeymoon) can cost £10,000. An ambulance will not pick you up or a hospital treat you unless you or your companions can prove that you have *enough* money or *enough* medical insurance. Make sure the policy you choose is for a sufficiently long period and that the cover is adequate, which is at least twice what you think you need.

Apart from health, check whether you are covered for holiday cancellations; medical expenses; loss of baggage, personal effects, money; personal liability, and a range of benefits for personal accident or loss of bits of you. There seem to be endless permutations of what you pay in order to show a profit on one eye plus one limb lost. Oddly enough, the one form of cover you don't really need is cover against air crashes. The risk is lower than of being knocked down in the street and anyway the airlines all have their own compensation schemes which cover you. You're more likely to catch measles than get blown up in mid-air.

Companies that specialise in holiday insurance packages are Norwich Union, Commercial Union, Home and Overseas or J. Perry & Co. (Holiday Insurances), who are under-

written at Lloyds. Before insuring, *check* that you aren't already covered by private medical schemes (PPP or BUPA) or on the all-risks section of your home or personal effects policy. If so, ask for a deduction on your holiday insurance policy package.

If you are ill abroad, British Consular offices can't pay your hospital bills or medical expenses, although they may be able to help you get back home. If they have to lend you money to get home you will travel steerage and they'll keep your passport until the money has been repaid and I shouldn't make a habit of it. They can also inform your next of kin if something serious happens to you. It is a very good idea to put in your passport the name and address of any relative, friend or solicitor who should be informed in an emergency.

If it's a genuine case of illness while on holiday and medical proof is given, a charter passenger is allowed not to travel as planned but can be treated as an 'emergency case' and put on the first plane back when she or he recovers.

The National Health Service stops at Calais. However, you can get *limited emergency medical treatment* in some countries, but *not* in Australia, Canada, Greece, Portugal, Spain, Switzerland, USA. In certain countries you merely have to produce your passport to get free emergency treatment (although not necessarily medicine or dental work). They are: Austria, Bulgaria, Czechoslovakia, Gibraltar, New Zealand, Norway, Poland, Romania, Sweden, USSR and Yugoslavia. Yet another strong reason for holidaying in beautiful, inexpensive Yugoslavia. An explanatory leaflet (SA 30) gives details of the benefits available and the documents you must have in your possession to prove you're entitled to treatment. Get a copy from the local office of the Department of Health and Social Security.

Britain has special health agreements with countries in the EEC but they are very complicated and you must organize it weeks before you go and you are generally not covered if you're self-employed or non-employed. First, check with your local social security office to find out if you're eligible. Get leaflet SA 28 'Medical Treatment for Visitors to EEC Countries'. Fill in form CM 17 (it's on the back of SA 28) in order to receive Form E 111, which is your Certificate of Entitlement. The whole system will break down if you don't take E 111 abroad with you. If you forget it, you are not normally covered by EEC arrangements.

In a way, it would be maddening to do all that and *not* be ill, but even if you trot through the necessary procedure you may still only get a percentage of your medical costs refunded and *only* if you see the right doctor, dentist or hospital and fill in the right foreign forms. You might not remember to check all these details if you have a high fever or a broken leg and are trying to communicate in sign language with a Spanish midwife (they seem to handle injections as well as babies).

In all countries not mentioned above you have to pay for medical treatment, and the price might easily give you *another* coronary.

Holiday insurance check list

Medical (see p. 451)
Car (see p. 441)
Holiday Home Swaps (see p. 437)
Luggage (see below)

You may be already covered for luggage under a personal policy or extended household policy, so check before you shell out another fiver simply because it's on the tourist operator's ticket booking form.

If you use the tour operator's scheme, check if medical expenses and accident compensation are covered for people on sports holidays, pregnant women, people over seventy or those known to be suffering from a disease or disability.

Should you have to claim, on no account admit or claim that the contents of your baggage was higher than the amount you insured for, because the insurance assessor will simply say that you were underinsured by say 50 per cent, so they will not pay you 50 per cent of your claim.

DUTY-FREE ALLOWANCE

Avoid buying at the duty-free shops or on board boat or plane. Buy cigarettes and drink at a supermarket before you leave for home. It will be cheaper (you certainly won't get cheap plonk in a duty-free shop) and you will also be able to bring back more.

Can you bring back more duty-free goods from the Common Market countries? You are entitled to the extra allowance from EEC countries only if you buy the goods from a shop rather than the duty-free airport, boat or plane.

If you are over seventeen you may bring in 300 cigarettes or 400 g of tobacco, 3 litres of wine, $1\frac{1}{2}$ litres of spirit, $\frac{3}{8}$ litre of toilet water, 75 g of perfume and up to £50 of other goods – *provided you purchased them in a non-duty-free shop.*

From a duty-free shop or a non-EEC country, the allowance is only 200 cigarettes or 250 g of tobacco, 2 litres of wine, a litre of spirits, $\frac{1}{4}$ litre of toilet water, 50 g of perfume and up to £10 of other goods.

List any other purchase in your diary if you want to confess to customs.

BAG WITH BAGGAGE

Perfect Packing starts with buying sensible suitcases. Cheap suitcases (unless they are tough canvas) are a waste of money, because they collapse fast. Choose light strong ones, but not in a light colour – it gets filthy so fast. Try to stick to one colour, if you care about looking pulled together.

Not until you open your case and see someone else's underpants do you realize how easy it is to walk away from the airport with someone else's suitcase, so always *stick two* labels on each suitcase and knot a piece of wide red ribbon, or something else distinctive, around the handles.

Since I was stranded in Paris in a porters' strike with four suitcases and a pair of skis I've never travelled with more than I can carry. However long my stay, my luggage is one light 60-cm (24-inch) suitcase for clothes, another for heavy stuff and a large tote bag into which I can slip a small handbag along with a pair of flat pumps and the rest of my tat. You might look like an Arab street seller, but if you're properly balanced you are less likely to tire or slip a disc.

If you have one large suitcase packed in trad manner, with heavy stuff on the bottom and light gear on top, it invariably travels upside down and upon arrival you find that all your finery has been crushed by rubber flippers. One day I'm going to stick a 'This way up' notice on the wrong way up and see if I can outwit the fiends.

The packing theory of relativity is that, even if you buy nothing and lose quite a bit on your trip, you will nevertheless have more to repack than when you started. So the first thing to pack is an empty collapsible suitcase. If your luggage is overweight, pack the heaviest items, such as ski boots, in an ordinary plastic supermarket-type carrier bag. I've never yet been outweighed at an airport.

When deciding what to take, always aim for the minimum. Lay it all out on the bed or the floor and sort it into two piles, like the soft/hard method.

Then put 50 per cent back in your wardrobe. Then make a list of what's left and do not pack the list. Put it in your handbag.

If I'm going way for a weekend I make a list of clothes, then stick to that list for all weekends away until the weather changes or the clothes wear out. All my family have their own lists (written and kept by me or they'd never get written) and I carry them on holiday with me. I tick off every item as it is put out to be packed and also when repacking. This means that you are more likely to remember to look for the nightgown that got kicked under the bed.

I work on the empirical theory that unless every item of your clothing is creaseproof your clothes are bound to get creased, however you pack them. So, like a valet, I do up as few buttons as possible on all the garments, then fold them into the suitcase, rather than folding them on the bed and transferring them to the suitcase. I pack clothes on dry-cleaners' wire hangers and just pick them up and hang them up the other end, reversing the procedure before going home. I roll everything else up into balls and stuff them in the corners. If you don't do this, take hangers, because hotels never provide enough.

Grand stores sell organdie packing bags to rich travellers. You can file your underwear and stockings in plastic sandwich bags measuring about 30×35 cm (12×14 inches). When packing, I sub-file as much as possible into even more plastic bags and keep the clothes in the bags upon arrival at destination. This simplifies unpacking and repacking to a five-minute operation. Take a dozen extra *empty* large plastic bags to accommodate sandy seashells, damp bathing suits, dirty drip-dries and wet toothbrushes.

Carry your make-up with you, for when you lose your luggage. You can stay in the same travel outfit until it starts to move of its own accord, but a naked face makes a woman feel vulnerable.

Sooner or later in life a bottle in your suitcase is bound to break or leak and ruin the other contents, so don't put bottles in your suitcase but in your hand baggage, and first put them in a plastic bag. If your bottles do leak you are more likely to notice the drips if you're carrying them and you're less likely than the average porter to stand the whole lot upside down.

If you're flying do *not* pack the following in the suitcase, in case it never arrives:

list of contents of suitcase
passport
money
travellers' cheques
chequebook
credit cards
keys
make-up and toothbrush
jewellery
expensive cameras
business documents
medicines and spectacles
any other item which is valuable, fragile or irreplaceable.

If you're travelling by air your total free baggage allowance (which is supposed to include hand baggage) is 20 kg (44 lb). Weigh the suitcase on the bathroom scales. Some charter flights don't allow you to take more than your baggage allowance whether or not you are prepared to pay extra for it.

Hand baggage allowance that you are allowed to carry into the aircraft:

overcoat, wrap or blanket
umbrella or walking stick
lady's handbag
infant's food for consumption in flight
infant's carrying basket
small camera
portable typewriter
small bag or case for overnight requisites
pair of binoculars
reasonable amount of reading material for the flight
wheelchair, crutches or other device on which the passenger is dependent.

Draped with this lot, you may be able to stagger along like a walking Christmas tree, but remember that you may have a long walk at your destination airport and a lot of hand baggage can exhaust you. Another point is that although the personal items can supposedly be carried free, the authorities might grab you and weigh your hand baggage (which they generally don't) to see if your total baggage is more than your free allowance, which of course it is. They may ask you to pay extra.

There are other ways to avoid paying the excess baggage charge. If two passengers are travelling together, they can 'pool' their baggage. So strike up a relationship with anyone at the counter check queue who looks empty-handed. The alternative is to ship your overweight baggage *as cargo*, which is less expensive. Flying intercontinental from Heathrow, for example, overweight baggage can often travel as cargo in the same aircraft as the passenger – at about half the excess baggage rate.

If you're going for only a short air trip and you can manage to pack the minimum into a bag or small cabin suitcase – do so, because you can then carry it with you and avoid all that hanging around at the other end.

If your baggage is lost, report it *immediately* and make the most terrific fuss about it. After all, it hasn't disappeared off the face of the earth, it has merely flown on to Johannesburg, or maybe it is *still* in the aircraft and you can get them to look for it before the plane takes off again.

If it's not found on the aircraft see that the airline completes a report before you leave the airport and *read this report* yourself. After describing my missing suitcase to an airline menial, I insisted on reading his report and found that my navy blue, red-piped missing suitcase had been described as 'green tartan with blue handle'.

Do not hand over your baggage check until you have been safely reunited with the baggage. Don't hand over your list of suitcase contents:

let them copy it. Also immediately report if you find that your checked baggage has been damaged. Airlines will usually compensate for damage, except if you are responsible by packing bags too full, or by packing breakables.

HOW TO BE A FRAGILE TRAVELLER

If you're convalescing and/or traveling out of season . . .

1 Remember that out of season means out of season, and that generally means 'instead of sun'.

2 Tell your travel agent that you're looking for sun and make sure he knows what he's talking about: get him to prove it with temperature charts. Then check with the appropriate tourist office. Ask for copies of his letters to airline and hotel manager or whoever was supposed to arrange that bathchair that isn't waiting for you at the airport.

3 Spend your money on distance. It's no use going to a grand hotel with unlimited outdoor tourist attractions if there's no sun and you're sneezing too hard to enjoy them. Put your convalescence money on sun, not sightseeing.

The cheapest place for guaranteed sun between November and April is Kenya. Otherwise British invalids should go to N. Africa and avoid the Atlantic. There are extremely good inexpensive package tours to Tunisia, which is also a great place for an out of season holiday with a young family in, say, April or May.

4 Although there are plenty of coloured pictures of white sandy beaches, out of season the seaside is not always the best place for the sun, and waving palms can mean lots of wind: the reason that the white sandy beach in the brochure is empty may be because you have to be over 14 stone to stand upright in that sort of gale, and if you lie down, you risk dying of exposure.

5 Don't be stubborn, especially if you're convalescing. Don't insist on lying on the beach or swimming just because you expected to be able to do so; that way *double* pneumonia lies. If the weather is bad, do not assume that it is going to change.

6 It is expensive if, in order to survive, you have to buy a heavy overcoat because you left yours at home; so take as warm a coat as possible.

7 Take a warm bedjacket and woollen bedsocks, if not a hotwater bottle. Pack scarves, sweaters and covered shoes as well as swimsuits. They don't take up much room and you may not have to use them.

8 Insure against illness in case you get iller.

9 Take a transistor radio; you can generally find a friendly noise on it.

10 As well as the suntan oil that you so optimistically packed, take

aspirin, gargle, cough mixture, nasal spray and any other treatments for your minor winter illnesses.

11 Take indoor entertainment – playing cards, books, a travelling bridge set or a companion who can talk well; words sometimes speak more than actions, especially if you've both been huddling under the same eiderdown for the past fortnight.

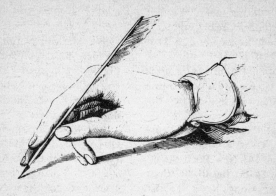

Useful Addresses

This section includes the London addresses of national tourist offices, foreign embassies, Commonwealth high commissions, and other official offices.

NATIONAL TOURIST OFFICES IN LONDON

Australia: Australian Tourist Commission, 49 Old Bond Street, London w1 (tel. 01-499 2247)

Austria: Austrian National Tourist Office, 30 St George Street, London w1r 9fa (tel. 01-629 0461)

Bahamas: Bahama Islands Tourist Office, 23 Old Bond Street, London w1 (tel. 01-629 5238)

Belgium: Belgian National Tourist Office, 66 Haymarket, London sw1y 4rb (tel. 01-930 9618)

Bermuda: Bermuda Department of Tourism, 84 Baker Street, London w1m 1dl (tel. 01-487 4391)

Canada: Canadian Office of Tourism, Canadian High Commission, Canada House, Trafalgar Square, London sw1 (tel. 01-930 9741)

Czechoslovakia: Czechoslovak Travel Bureau (Cedok), 17/18 Bond Street, London w1x 3da (tel. 01-629 6058)

Denmark: Danish Tourist Board, Sceptre House, 169–173 Regent Street, London w1r 8py (tel. 01-734 2637)

Finland: Finnish Tourist Board, UK Office, Finland House, 53–54 Haymarket, London sw1y 4rn (tel. 01-839 4048)

France: French Government Tourist Office, 178 Piccadilly, London w1v 0al (tel. 01-493 3717)

Germany (Federal Republic): German National Tourist Office, 61 Conduit

Street, W 1 R 0EN (tel. 01-734 2600)

Gibraltar: Government Tourist Office, Arundel Great Court, 179 The Strand, London WC2R 1GH (tel. 01-836 0777)

Greece: National Tourist Organization of Greece, 195–197 Regent Street, London W 1 Y 0AQ (tel. 01-734 5997)

Holland: Netherlands National Tourist Office, Savory & Moore House, 2nd Floor, 143 New Bond Street, London W 1 Y 0AQ (tel. 01-499 9367)

Hong Kong: Hong Kong Tourist Association, 14 Cockspur Street, London SW1Y 5DP (tel. 01-930 4775)

India: Indian Government Tourist Office, 21 New Bond Street, London w 1 (tel. 01-493 0769)

Ireland: Irish Tourist Board, 150 New Bond Street, London W 1 Y 0AQ (tel. 01-493 3201). Also offices in Birmingham, Bristol, Edinburgh, Glasgow, Manchester.

Italy: Italian State Tourist Office (ENIT), 201 Regent Street, London W 1 R 8AY (tel. 01-439 2311)

Jamaica: Jamaica Tourist Board, 6 Bruton Street, London w 1 (tel. 01-493 3647)

Kenya: Kenya Tourist Office, 13 New Burlington Street, London w 1 (tel. 01-734 6296)

Luxembourg: Luxembourg National Trade and Tourist Office, 66 Haymarket, London SW1 4RF (tel. 01-930 8906)

Malaysia: Malaysia Tourist Development Office, 17 Curzon Street, London w 1 (tel. 01-499 7388)

Malta: Malta Government Tourist Office, Malta House, 24 Haymarket, London SW1 (tel. 01-930 9851)

Mexico: Mexican National Tourist Council, 52 Grosvenor Gardens, London SW1 (tel. 01-730 0128)

Morocco: Moroccan National Tourist Office, 174 Regent Street, London W 1 Y 0AQ (tel. 01-734 6509)

Norway: Norwegian National Tourist Office, 20 Pall Mall, London SW1Y 5NE (tel. 01-839 6255)

Portugal: Portuguese National Tourist Office, 1–5 New Bond Street, London W 1 (tel. 01-493 3873)

Romania: Romanian National Tourist Office, 98 Jermyn Street, London SW1 (tel. 01-930 0812)

Spain: Spanish National Tourist Office, 57 St James's Street, London SW1 (tel. 01-499 0901)

Sweden: Swedish National Tourist Office, 3 Cork Street, London W 1 (tel. 01-437 5816)

Switzerland: Swiss National Tourist Office, Swiss Centre, New Coventry Street, London W 1 v 3HG (tel. 01-734 1921)

Tunisia: Tunisian National Tourist Office, 7A Stafford Street, London W 1 Y 0AQ (tel. 01-493 2952)

Turkey: Turkish Tourism Information Office, 49 Conduit Street, London W 1 R 0EP (tel. 01-734 8681)

USA: The United States Travel and Information Service won't deal direct with the public but there are about 200 British travel agents at United States Travel Planning Centres to advise on travel to and in America. The American Embassy is at 24 Grosvenor Square, London w1 (tel. 01-499 9000)

USSR: Intourist, 292 Regent Street, London W1R 7PO (tel. 01-580 4974)

SOME FOREIGN EMBASSIES

Argentina: 9 Wilton Crescent, London SW1X 8RP (tel. 01-235 3717)

Austria: 18 Belgrave Square, London SW1X 8HU (tel. 01-235 3731)

Belgium: 103 Eaton Square, London SW1W 9AB (tel. 01-235 5422)

Brazil: 32 Green Street, London W1Y 4AT (tel. 01-629 0155)

China: 31 Portland Place, London W1N 3AG (tel. 01-636 5726)

Czechoslovakia: 25 Kensington Palace Gardens, London W8 4QY (tel. 01-229 1255)

Denmark: 55 Sloane Street, London SW1 (tel. 01-235 1255)

Egypt: 26 South Street, London W1Y 6DD (tel. 01-499 2401)

Finland: 38 Chesham Place, London SW1 (tel. 01-235 9531)

France: 58 Knightsbridge, London SW1X 7JT (tel. 01-235 8080)

Germany (Democratic Republic): 34 Belgrave Square, London SW1X 8QB (tel. 01-235 9941)

Germany (Federal Republic): 23 Belgrave Square, London SW1X 8PZ (tel. 01-235 5033)

Greece: 1A Holland Park, London W11 3TP (tel. 01-727 8040)

Hungary: 35 Eaton Place, London SW1X 8BY (tel. 01-235 7191)

Iran: 16 Prince's Gate, London SW7 1PX (tel. 01-584 8101)

Ireland, Republic of: 17 Grosvenor Place, London SW1X 7HR (tel. 01-235 2171)

Israel: 2 Palace Green, London W8 4QB (tel. 01-937 8050)

Italy: 14 Three Kings Yard, Davies Street, London W1Y 2EH (tel. 01-629 8200)

Japan: 43–46 Grosvenor Street, London W1X 0BA (tel. 01-493 6030)

Luxembourg: 27 Wilton Crescent, London SW1X 8SD (tel. 01-235 6961)

Mexico: 8 Halkin Street, London SW1X 7DW (tel. 01-235 6393)

Netherlands: 38 Hyde Park Gate, London SW7 5DP (tel. 01-584 5040)

Norway: 25 Belgrave Square, London SW1X 8QD (tel. 01-235 7151)

Pakistan: 35 Lowndes Square, London SW1X 9JN (tel. 01-235 2044)

Poland: 47 Portland Place, London W1N 3AG (tel. 01-580 4324)

Portugal: 11 Belgrave Square, London SW1X 8PP (tel. 01-235 5331)

Saudi Arabia: 30 Belgrave Square, London SW1 (tel. 01-235 0831)

South Africa: South Africa House, Trafalgar Square, London WC2N 5DP (tel. 01-930 4488)

Spain: 24 Belgrave Square, London SW1X 8QA (tel. 01-235 5555)

Sweden: 23 North Row, London W1R 2DN (tel. 01-499 9500)

Switzerland: 16–18 Montagu Place, London W1H 2BQ (tel. 01-723 0701)

Turkey: 43 Belgrave Square, London SW1X 8PA (tel. 01-235 5252)

USA: 24 Grosvenor Square, London W1A 1AE (tel. 01-499 9000)

USSR: 13 Kensington Palace Gardens, London w8 4qx (tel. 01-229 3628)

Yugoslavia: 5 Lexham Gardens, London w8 5jj (tel. 01-370 6105)

COMMONWEALTH HIGH COMMISSIONS
(the Commonwealth equivalent of embassies) and
LONDON OFFICIAL OFFICES

Australia: Office of the High Commissioner, Australia House, Strand, London wc2b 4la (tel. 01-438 8000)

Bahamas: Office of the High Commissioner, 39 Pall Mall, London sw1y 5jg (tel. 01-930 6967)

Bangladesh: Office of the High Commissioner, 28 Queen's Gate, London sw7 5ja (tel. 01-584 0081 or 589 4842)

Barbados: Office of the High Commissioner, 6 Upper Belgrave Street, London sw1x 8az (tel. 01-253 8686)

Bermuda: Bermuda Government Tourist Office, 1st Floor, 9–10 Savile Row, London w1 (tel. 01-734 8813)

Botswana: Office of the High Commissioner, 162 Buckingham Palace Road, London sw1w 9tj (tel. 01-730 5216)

Canada: Office of the High Commissioner, Macdonald House, 1 Grosvenor Square, London w1 (tel. 01-629 9492)

Ceylon: See Sri Lanka

Cyprus: Office of the High Commis-

sioner, 93 Park Street, London w1y 4et (tel. 01-499 8272)

Eastern Caribbean Commission (Antigua, Dominica, Grenada, Montserrat, St Christopher–Nevis–Anguilla, St Lucia, St Vincent): King's House, 10 Haymarket, London sw1y 4da (tel. 01-930 7902)

Fiji: Office of the High Commissioner, 34 Hyde Park Gate, London sw7 5dn (tel. 01-584 3661)

Gambia: Office of the High Commissioner, 60 Ennismore Gardens, London sw7 1nh (tel. 01-584 1242)

Ghana: Office of the High Commissioner (Passport Section), 38 Queen's Gate, London sw7 5ht (tel. 01-584 6311)

Gibraltar: Government Tourist Office, Arundel Great Court, 179 The Strand, London wc2r 1gh (tel. 01-836 0777)

Grenada: Office of the High Commissioner, King's House, 10 Haymarket, London sw1y 4da (tel. 01-930 7902)

Guyana: Office of the High Commissioner (Passport Section), 3 Palace Court, Bayswater, London w2 4lp (tel. 01-229 7684)

Hong Kong: Hong Kong Government Office, 6 Grafton Street, London w1x 3lb (tel. 01-499 9821)

India: Office of the High Commissioner, Consular Department, India House, Aldwych, London wc2b 4na (tel. 01-836 8484)

Jamaica: Office of the High Commissioner (Passport Section), 50 St James's Street, London w1 (tel. 01-499 8600)

Kenya: Office of the High Commissioner, Kenya House, 45 Portland Place, London W1N 4AS (tel. 01-636 2371)

Lesotho: Office of the High Commissioner, 16A St James's Street (1st Floor), London SW1A 1EU (tel. 01-839 1154)

Malawi: Office of the High Commissioner, 33 Grosvenor Street, London W1 (tel. 01-491 4172/7)

Malaysia: Office of the High Commissioner, 45 Belgrave Square, London SW1X 8QT (tel. 01-245 9221)

Malta: Office of the High Commissioner, 24 Haymarket, London SW1Y 4DJ (tel. 01-930 9851)

Mauritius: Office of the High Commissioner, 32 Elvaston Place, London SW7 5NW (tel. 01-581 0294)

New Zealand: Office of the High Commissioner, New Zealand House, Haymarket, London SW1Y 4TQ (tel. 01-930 8422)

Nigeria: Office of the High Commissioner (Passport and Visa Section), 56 Fleet Street, London EC4 (passport: tel. 01-353 3776; visa: tel. 01-353 4139)

Seychelles: Office of the High Commissioner, 2 Mill Street, London W1 (tel. 01-499 9951)

Sierra Leone: Office of the High Commissioner, 33 Portland Place, London W1N 3AG (tel. 01-636 6483)

Singapore: Office of the High Commissioner, 2 Wilton Crescent, London SW1 (tel. 01-235 8315)

Sri Lanka (Ceylon): Office of the High Commissioner, 13 Hyde Park Gardens, London W2 2LX (tel. 01-262 1841)

Swaziland: Office of the High Commissioner, 58 Pont Street, London SW1X 0AE (tel. 01-589 5447/8)

Tanzania: Office of the High Commissioner, 43 Hertford Street, London W1Y 8DB (tel. 01-499 8951)

Tonga: Office of the High Commissioner, 17th Floor, New Zealand House, Haymarket, London SW1Y 4TE (tel. 01-839 3287)

Trinidad and Tobago: Office of the High Commissioner, 42 Belgrave Square, London SW1X 8NT (tel. 01-245 9351)

Zambia: Office of the High Commissioner, 7 Cavendish Place, London W1M 0HB (tel. 01-580 0691)

World Time Abroad and GMT

Country	City	Hours fast or slow on GMT
Argentina	Buenos Aires	− 3
Australia	Sydney	+10
Austria	Vienna	+ 1
Bangladesh	Dacca	+ 6
Belgium	Brussels	+ 1
Brazil	Rio de Janeiro	− 3
Canada	Toronto	− 5
Czecho-slovakia	Prague	+ 1
Denmark	Copenhagen	+ 1
Egypt	Cairo	+ 2
Finland	Helsinki	+ 2
France	Paris	+ 1
Germany (Federal Republic)	Bonn	+ 1
Greece	Athens	+ 2
Hungary	Budapest	+ 1
India	Delhi	+ 5½
Iran	Tehran	+ 4
Ireland, Republic of	Dublin	GMT
Israel	Jerusalem	+ 2
Italy	Rome	+ 1
Japan	Tokyo	+ 9
Malaysia	Kuala Lumpur	+ 7½
Mexico	Mexico City	− 6
Netherlands	Amsterdam	+ 1
New Zealand	Wellington	+12
Nigeria	Lagos	+ 1
Norway	Oslo	+ 1
Pakistan	Islamabad	+ 5
Poland	Warsaw	+ 1
Portugal	Lisbon	GMT
South Africa	Pretoria	+ 2
Spain	Madrid	+ 1
Sweden	Stockholm	+ 1
Switzerland	Berne	+ 1
Turkey	Ankara	+ 2
UK	London	GMT*
USA	Washington	− 5
USSR	Moscow	+ 3
Yugoslavia	Belgrade	+ 1

* In summer we go on British Summer Time, which is an hour ahead of GMT. We go on it in March (which means one hour less sleep and turn clock forward). In October we go back to GMT, which means turning the clock back at night, and one hour more sleep.

Mnemonic is: *Spring Forward, Fall Back.*

Other countries also put their clocks forward and back, but not all of them.

The Simple Life and Do You Want It?

This book is about doing more and getting more out of life. But you may think that you'll get more out of life if you do *less*. Running a home, running a job, or just running around – your problem may easily be emptying your spare time, not filling it. On the other hand, you may want to adopt leisurely simplicity as a way of life and spend *all* your time doing it.

It's often when the monthly bills drop in that you think wistfully of dropping out, selling out and heading for a commune in Gloucestershire, or spending your savings on a smallholding made for two, where you can grow your own goat and weave your own rush matting. But I suspect that the only people who live the self-sufficient life in comfort are those who write expensive books about it in order to finance it.

A long time ago, I used to worry about the Bomb. Not if it got me, of course, but if I survived and had to lead the simple life. My problem would then be how would I get to the mountains in order to start procreating with the other few survivors? So I went out and bought myself a pair of stout walking shoes for ladies at an explorers' shop. These were every bit as flattering to the ankle as they sound and I realized that I would have to take them off fast if I was ever to get anyone to procreate with me.

I also bought a book on self-sufficiency, which, with my shoes, added up to the Complete Survival Kit. It told a sheltered girl like me, brought up on fish fingers and television, just the sort of thing I might find expected of me when I eventually arrived in the mountains, late as usual.

Survival book in hand, I would know how to slit the throat of an ox, gaff salmon and what to do if a cow had diarrhoea.

Wise words would drip from my lips. ('When you have got the cow there is no more care about manure' – William Cobbett.) The exercise would make me lean and agile and the sun would bleach my hair. I would cultivate popularity, when not slitting throats, by making delicious butter, cream, honey, jams, jellies, pickles, cheese, bread, beer and wine . . .

I would produce pickled herrings and my own smoked salmon. If the children were good I might let them tend my fish farm. While hoeing my vegetable garden I would plan my orchard and keep beehives humming underneath the fruit trees. I would pickle the peaches, walnuts and watermelon, eat only asparagus tips (my own) and trap pheasants when I got bored. I would have the most mouthwatering larder, full of smoked hams, bunches of fragrant herbs, shelves of apples and rows of bottled preserves.

Frankly, between feeding the pigs, hoeing the garden, and running the fish farm I couldn't see when I would find the time to procreate.

Of course, that was fantasy . . . In fact, the simple life can be very complicated and you can't lead it if you can't afford it.

'It's got to make financial sense; you're not going to be happy ever after just by raising a few cows,' I was told by a one-time trendy girl-about-Chelsea now running a six-field farm and two babies.

'Farming is a business and I don't think anyone can make a lot of money from it ' You get a very poor return on your capital, unless you're a big, mechanized combine.

'If you want to lead the self-sufficient life you have to be self-sufficient in the head. After money, what's most important is organization and common sense, because every day's problem is as different as the weather and you must think things out rationally in your head before doing them.

'You also need the proper knowledge. Learning by experience is too expensive and too slow. I did a year's day release course at Isle of Wight technical college.

'It's no hardship to give up the glamorous life, because in the country it seems so pointless. I found it no sacrifice to give up trendy clothes or hair-dos because they became irrelevant. You have to get used to being uncomfortable, damp, smelly and dirty. You can't be proud or houseproud or care about what people think. It's hard work, non-stop, seven days a week, whether the sun is shining or not. And you have to be physically strong.'

Some people like to lead a part-time simple life and head for a cottage in the country on weekends and holidays. Two city friends of mine with three daughters under fourteen bought a derelict shepherd's cottage in the Welsh hills. It is a quarter of a mile from the road, four miles from the nearest shop and has no running water or electricity.

'Discomfort and dirt are basic facts of life. You don't wash and it doesn't occur to you to think that you're dirty. You have to accept the cold and the wet as part of the pleasure. All your standards just slither. Food and alcohol become very important, because they are comforts. Life is completely physical. We always take books but are too tired to read. You work, eat, sleep and that's all.

'The amount of organization it involves is fantastic. It takes a complete day to pack, a complete day to unpack, and a week to get the mud off the clothes afterwards. That's one reason we don't go just for weekends any more. But overall it's a financial saving and we couldn't afford to go away for a holiday otherwise. You have to remember that if you're doing something like this as a family it won't give equal pleasure to everyone. We all like it, but let's say that some of us like it less than others.'

The part-time simple life can be very pleasant if you don't have children and a job outside the home. With these and with no one else to help, I found that running a weekend idyllic retreat was beyond my stamina and powers of organization.

But there's always the possibility that, instead of escaping into a fantasy life, you can improve reality. It can be easier to simplify the life you already have. It should be life (yours) and style (yours), not some souped-up form of living beyond your means that may be dictated to you by other people. Whose standards are you living up to? Why not try living down

to mine? Consider this checklist for ways to simplify and uncomplicate your life-style and strip it down to basics before improving it.

Try scribbling a few personal additions to this list, just to give yourself something to argue about. (I've marked with a dot my own crossed-off items.)

THE SIMPLIFY-LIFE CHECKLIST

Before you buy anything (or before you give anything to Oxfam) try asking yourself: Do I want it? Do I need it? Can I live without it?

Will discarding it save me Space/Money/Time/Worry/Upkeep/Insurance?

· Jewellery
· Parties (going to or giving)
· Dinner parties (going to or giving)
· Theatres
· Cinemas
· Concerts
· Excess furniture
· Excess rooms
  Transport (if in town)
· Inessential home equipment (there's always one machine not working and in need of attention)
  Houseplants
· Pets
· Snacks
  Three meals a day, with different dishes on offer
  More clothes than are necessary
  A second home
  A second anything (or anyone)

However, the things that weigh you

down so heavily that you don't have enough free time may not be material possessions but excessive demands on your emotional strength. Perhaps *you* happily submit to these demands? If so, learn to say no (with no qualifying clauses) and then learn not to feel guilty about it.

Paradoxically, you are more likely to achieve the simple life (and it *is* an achievement) in your own home, because in our highly complicated civilization, it is the only life which we have been trained to lead. And life can be as simple as you care to make it.

Index

Meynell Valves Ltd (showers), 267
Midwifery, how to enter, 113
Miele (kitchen units), 263
Ministry of Overseas Development, 128
Mirrors, for bedrooms, 176
Mothercare-by-Post, 202
Mothers:
achieving time for 'self', 20–23
how to cope with children while working, 25–9
profile of working, 16–18
Museums, location and description of, 340–42
Buckinghamshire, Hughenden Manor, 340
Cambridgeshire, Cromwell Museum, 340
Cumbria, Dove Cottage and Wordsworth
Museum, 340; Hill Top, 340
Dorset, Cloud's Hill, 340
Hampshire, Jane Austen's House, 341
Kent, Downe House, 341; Ellen Terry
Memorial, Smallhythe Place, 341; Chart-
well, 341
North Yorkshire, Bronte Parsonage Museum,
341
Oxfordshire, Kelmscott Manor, 341
Roxburgh, Abbotsford House, 342
Strathclyde, Burns Cottage and Museum, 342;
David Livingstone Memorial, 342
Suffolk, Gainsborough's House, 342
Museums, unusual (location and description of):
Avon, SS Great Britain, 343
Bedfordshire, Shuttleworth Collection, 343
Berkshire, Stanley Spencer Gallery, 343
Cambridgeshire, a number of museums, 343–4
Cheshire, Lady Lever Art Gallery, 344
Cumbria, Carlisle Museum, 344
Derbyshire, Donnington Collection, 344;
Tramway Museum, 344
Durham, Bowes Museum, 344; Beamish Open
Air Museum, 344
Fife, Museum of Fishing, 345
Gloucestershire, Cotswold Farm Park, 345
Gwynedd, Portmeirion Village, 345
Hampshire, Museum of Ancient Farming, 345;
Royal Naval Museum and HMS Victory,
345
Hereford and Worcester, Avoncroft Museum,
345
London and surrounding area, a number of
museums, 345–7
Lothian, a number of museums, 347
Norfolk, Bressingham Steam Museum, 347
Northamptonshire, Waterways Museum, 347

Oxfordshire, a number of museums, 348
Salop, Coalbrookdale and Blist's Hill, 348
Somerset, a number of museums, 348–9
South Glamorgan, Welsh Folk Museum, 349
Staffordshire, Wedgwood Museum, 349;
Stoke-on-Trent Museum, 349; Gladstone
Pottery, 349
Sussex, Toy Museum, 349
Warwickshire, Royal Shakespeare Memorial
Gallery, 350
West Midlands, Museum of Science and In-
dustry, 350
West Sussex, Fishbourne, 350
Yorkshire, Castle Museum, 350; National
Railway Museum, 350
Museum work, training and qualifications for,
113
Music, courses on, 10

Nairn Coated Products (wallcovering), 269
Nairn Floors Ltd (flooring), 259
National Advisory Centre on Careers for Women
(NACCW), 47
National Association of Plumbing, Heating and
Mechanical Services Contracts, 227, 231
National Campaign for Nursery Education, 30
National Caravan Council Ltd, 383–4
National Conservation Corps, voluntary work,
378
National Council for Home Economics
Education, 105
National Council for the Training of Journalists,
107
National Farmers' Union, 98
National Federation of Building Trades Em-
ployees (NFBTE), 218, 227
National Federation of Roofing Contractors,
227
National Inspection Council for Electrical Instal-
lation Contracting, 227
National Institute of Adult Education, 84
National Park Study Centres, study holidays, 382
National tourist offices in London, addresses of,
459–61
National Trust, Junior Division, voluntary work,
378
National Union of Students, 83
Nature trails, location and description of:
Avon, Ebbor Gorge Nature Trails, 356
Berkshire, Snelsmore Common, 357
Essex, Hatfield Forest, 357

Women, *cont.*
    what sort of women work, 19
    what to do with the children, 25–9
Women's Engineering Society, 103–4
Women's Farm and Garden Association, 98
Woodcraft Folk, 371
Woodwork, painting, 278, 279, 282–3
Woodworm, in furniture, 164
Wool carpet, 185
F. W. Woolworth (paints), 267
Workers' Educations Association (WEA), 85
    see also Evening classes
Working from home, 70–81

    see also Freelance work
Working heights in your kitchen, 168–9
Working Holidays (booklet), 378
World time abroad, 464
Wrighton (kitchen units), 263

Yale Security Products Division:
    doors, 255
    window fittings, 270
Youghal Carpets, 252
Youth and community service, training in, 89
Youth Hostels Association, 369, 434
Youth work, opportunities and training in, 126–7

NOTES

NOTES